CW01655676

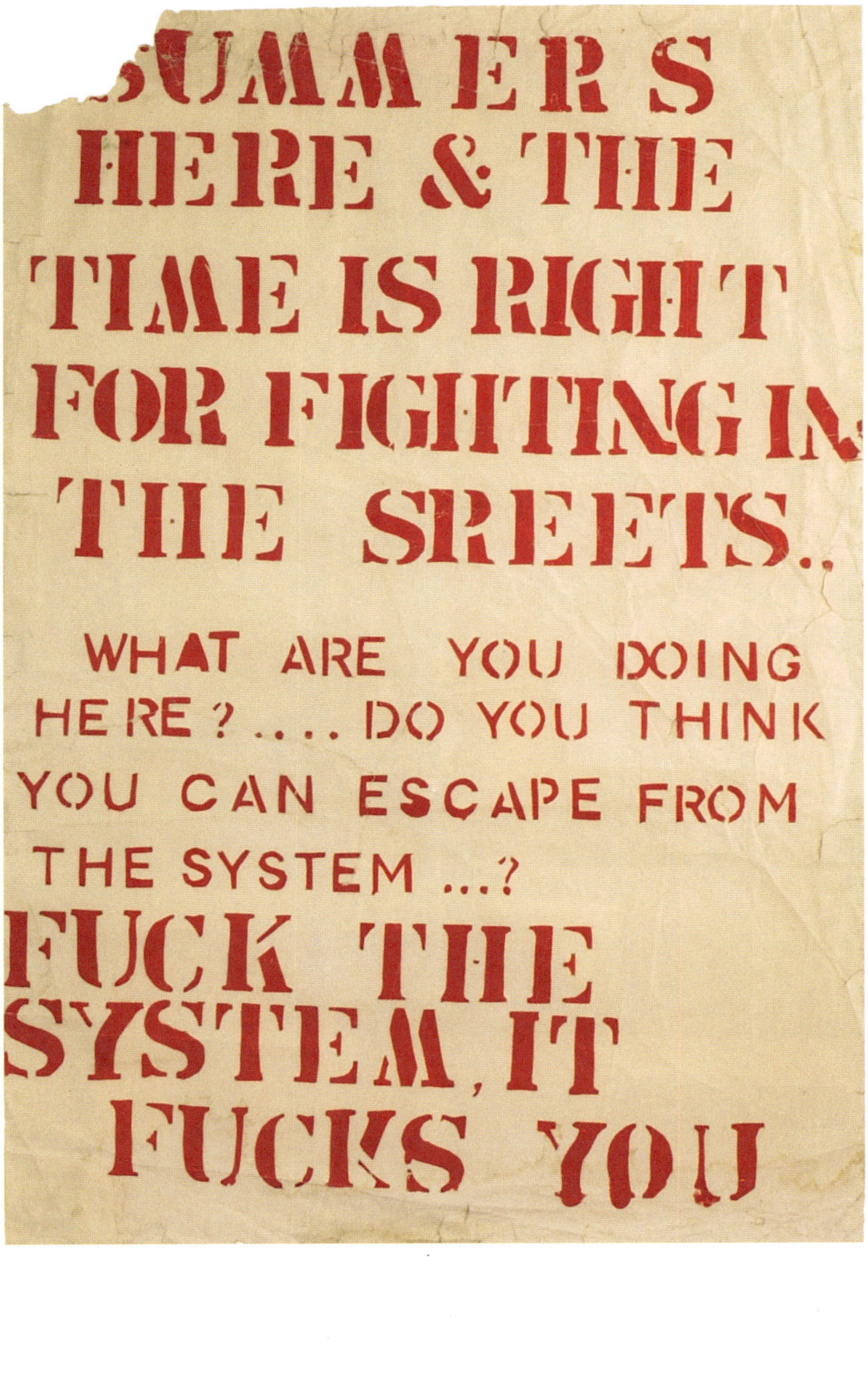
SUMMERS
HERE & THE
TIME IS RIGHT
FOR FIGHTING IN
THE SREETS..
WHAT ARE YOU DOING
HERE?.... DO YOU THINK
YOU CAN ESCAPE FROM
THE SYSTEM ...?
FUCK THE
SYSTEM, IT
FUCKS YOU

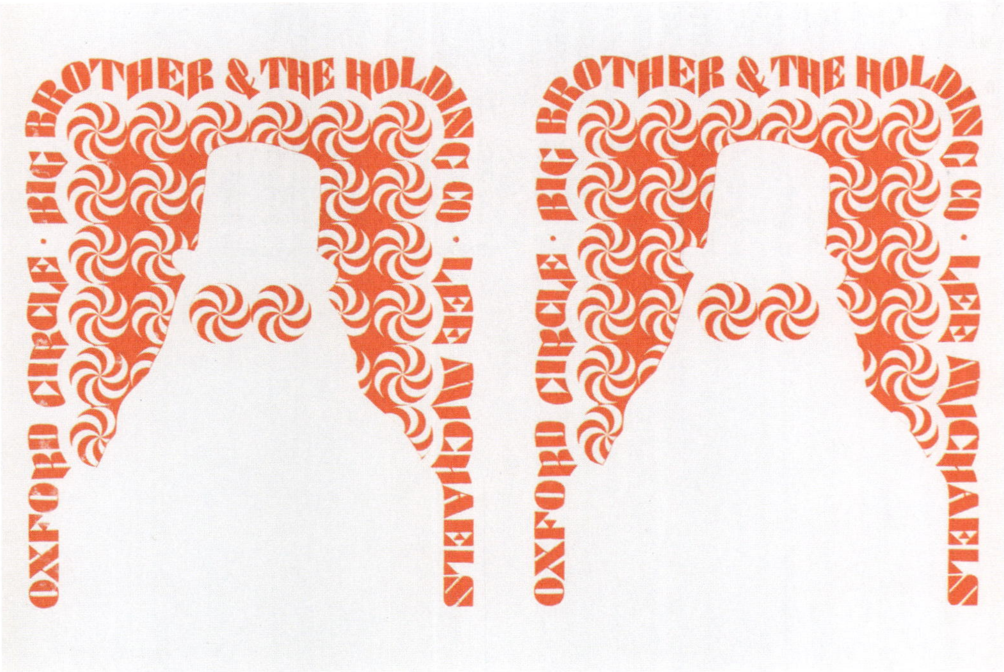

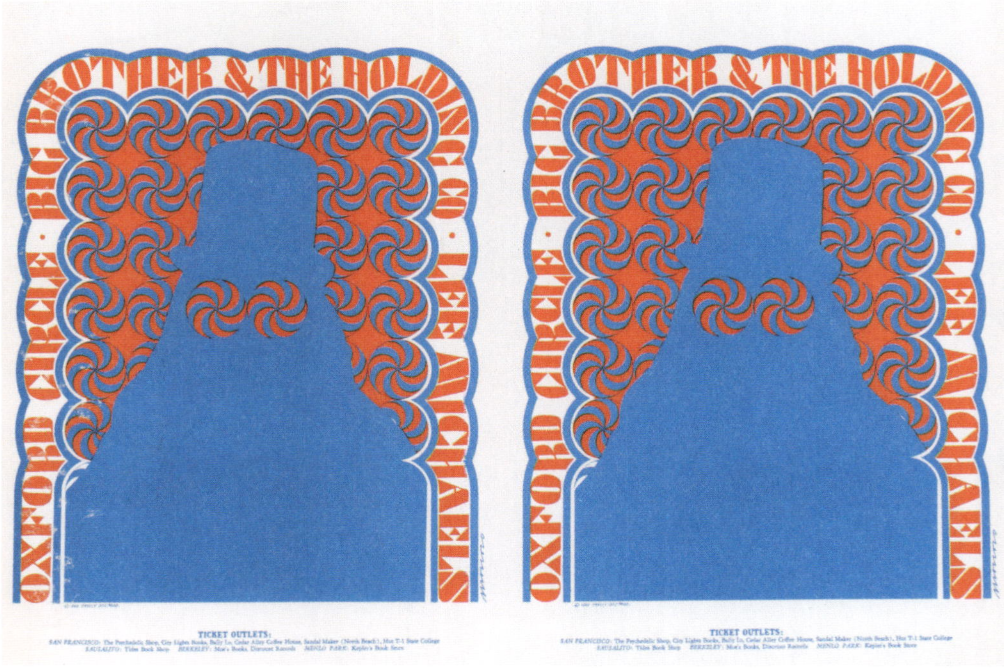

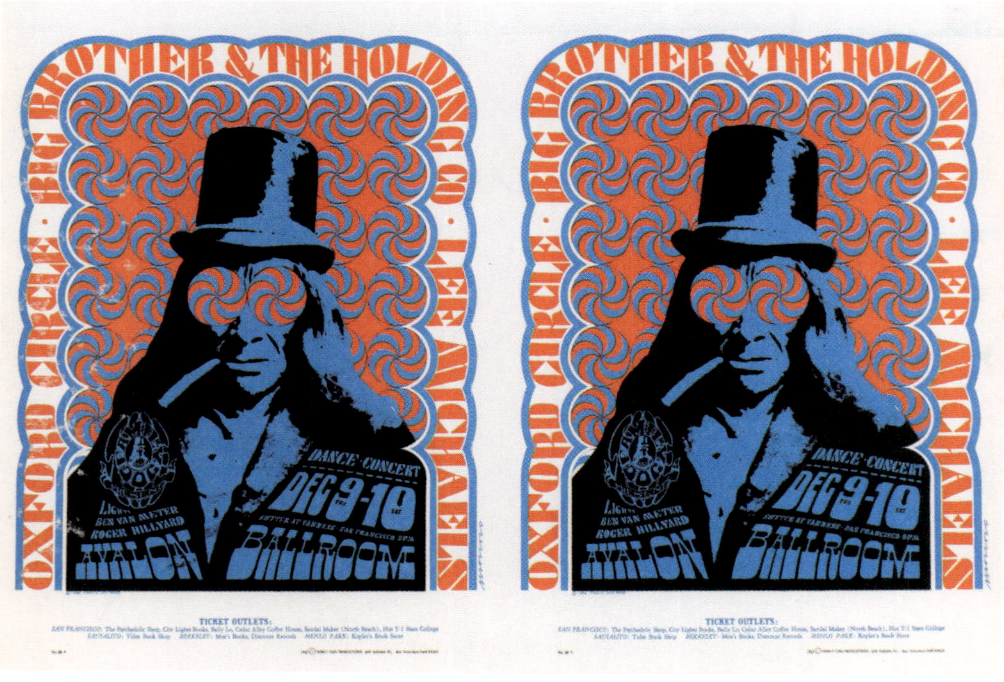

→ Previous page: a hand-stencilled poster by an unknown artist from the Legalise Pot Rally in Hyde Park, London, July 16, 1967. → This page: a poster for a Big Brother and the Holding Company concert at San Francisco's Avalon Ballroom in December 1966. The artist is Victor Moscoso, for Family Dog Productions. The central image of a behatted Native American was the Family Dog logo and appeared on posters for events organized by the company. → Pages 4–5: two brooding posters by Paul Kagan. The artist's erotic black-and-white photographs, coupled with blocks of glaring color, are in marked contrast to the more playful styles adopted by most West Coast designers. East Coast proto-punks The Velvet Underground made an unlikely appearance at the Avalon Ballroom in July 1968, in a concert headlined by Tim Buckley (left). The poster was doubled up with another Kagan design at the printer, this time for The Steve Miller Band, from earlier in July 1968 (right). → Pages 6–7: color separations and the finished full-color 'Skeleton and Roses' design by Stanley Mouse and Alton Kelley for Grateful Dead handbills and tickets. → Pages 8–9: in 1985, artist Rick Griffin created a series of images referencing the minutemen of the American Revolutionary War to feature on promotional material for the 'Grateful Dead: 20 Years So Far' anniversary celebrations. The image of the minuteman with guitar on p. 9 was used on a banner that hung behind the band as they played. It also appeared on a handbill, the rear of which featured a poem by Dead lyricist Robert Hunter entitled 'Twentieth Anniversary Rag.' → Pages 10–11: two British bands played at this modestly sized club in Greenwich Village in 1968. The Yardbirds' appearance was to be their farewell New York concert. → Pages 12–13: Dennis Larkins's Stonehenge-themed stage set for the 1977 Day on the Green festival. This annual music event was overseen by legendary promoter Bill Graham from 1973 until his death in 1991. Although it was not known at the time, Led Zeppelin's 1977 appearance was to be the band's final US show.

ROCK GRAPHIC ORIGINALS
REVOLUTIONS IN SONIC ART
FROM PLATE TO PRINT
'55–'88

PETER GOLDING
WITH BARRY MILES

WITH 738 ILLUSTRATIONS

Thames & Hudson

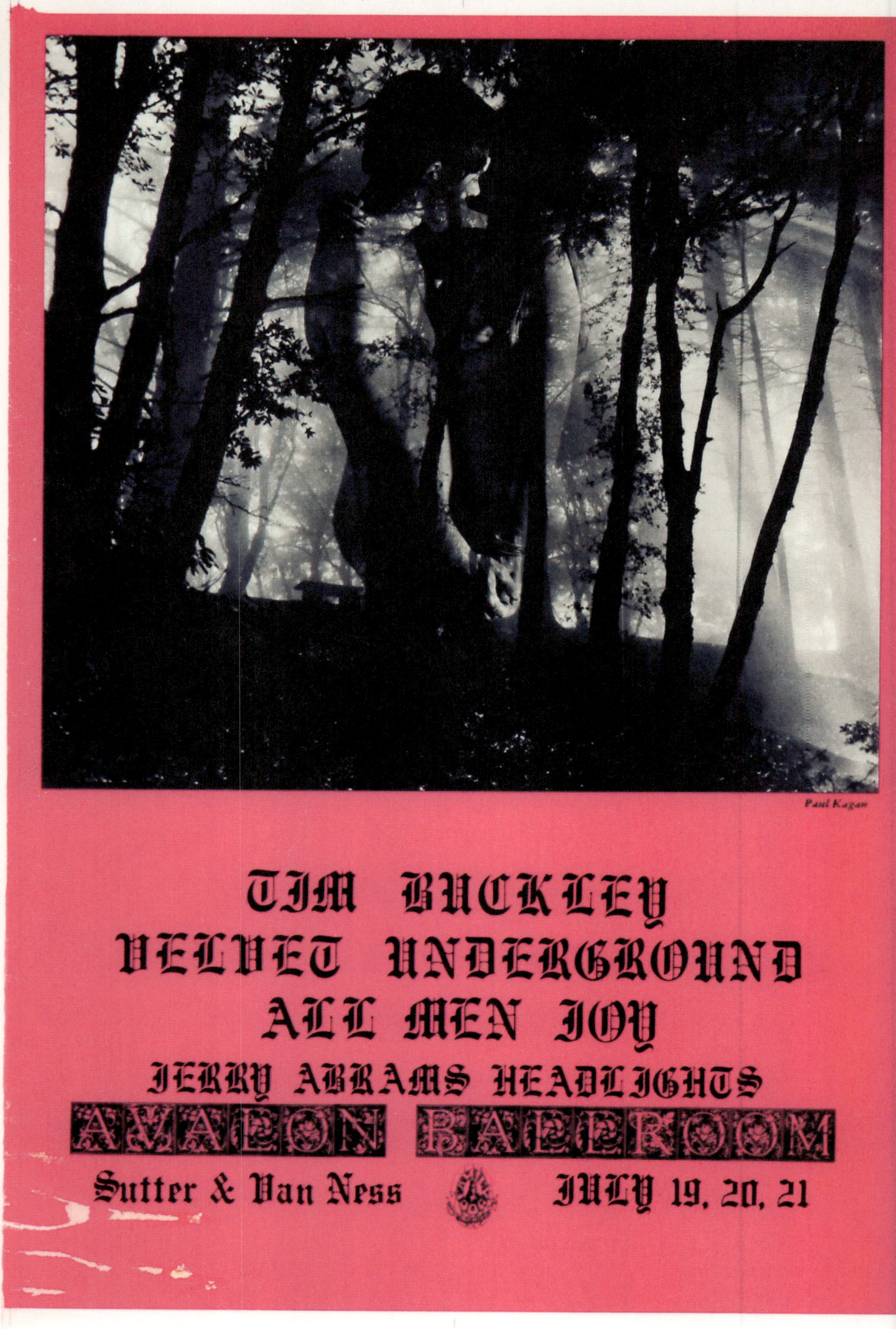
Paul Kagan
TIM BUCKLEY
VELVET UNDERGROUND
ALL MEN JOY
JERRY ABRAMS HEADLIGHTS
AVALON BALLROOM
Sutter & Van Ness
JULY 19, 20, 21

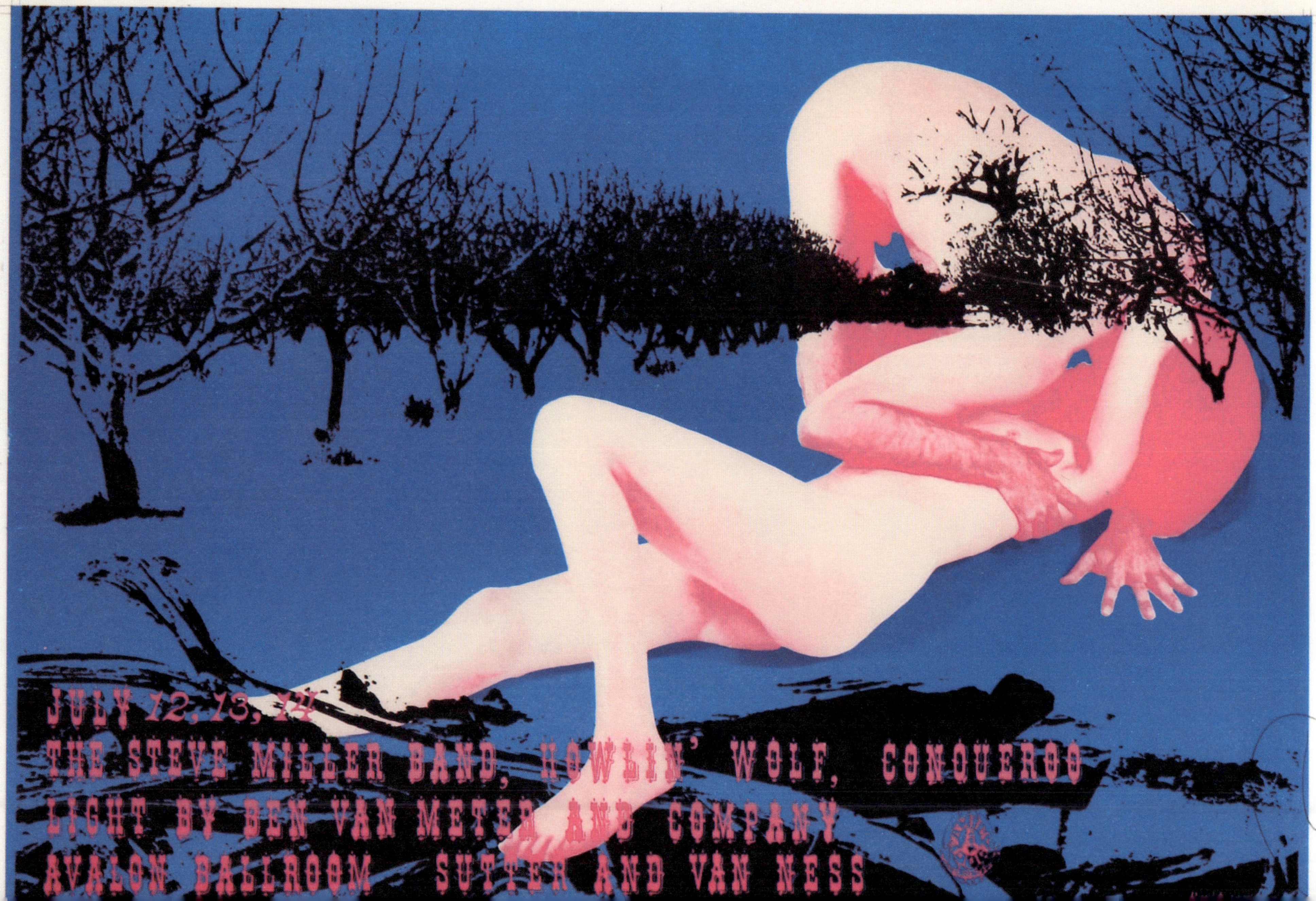
JULY 12, 13, 14
THE STEVE MILLER BAND, HOWLIN' WOLF, CONQUEROO
LIGHT BY BEN VAN METER AND COMPANY
AVALON BALLROOM SUTTER AND VAN NESS

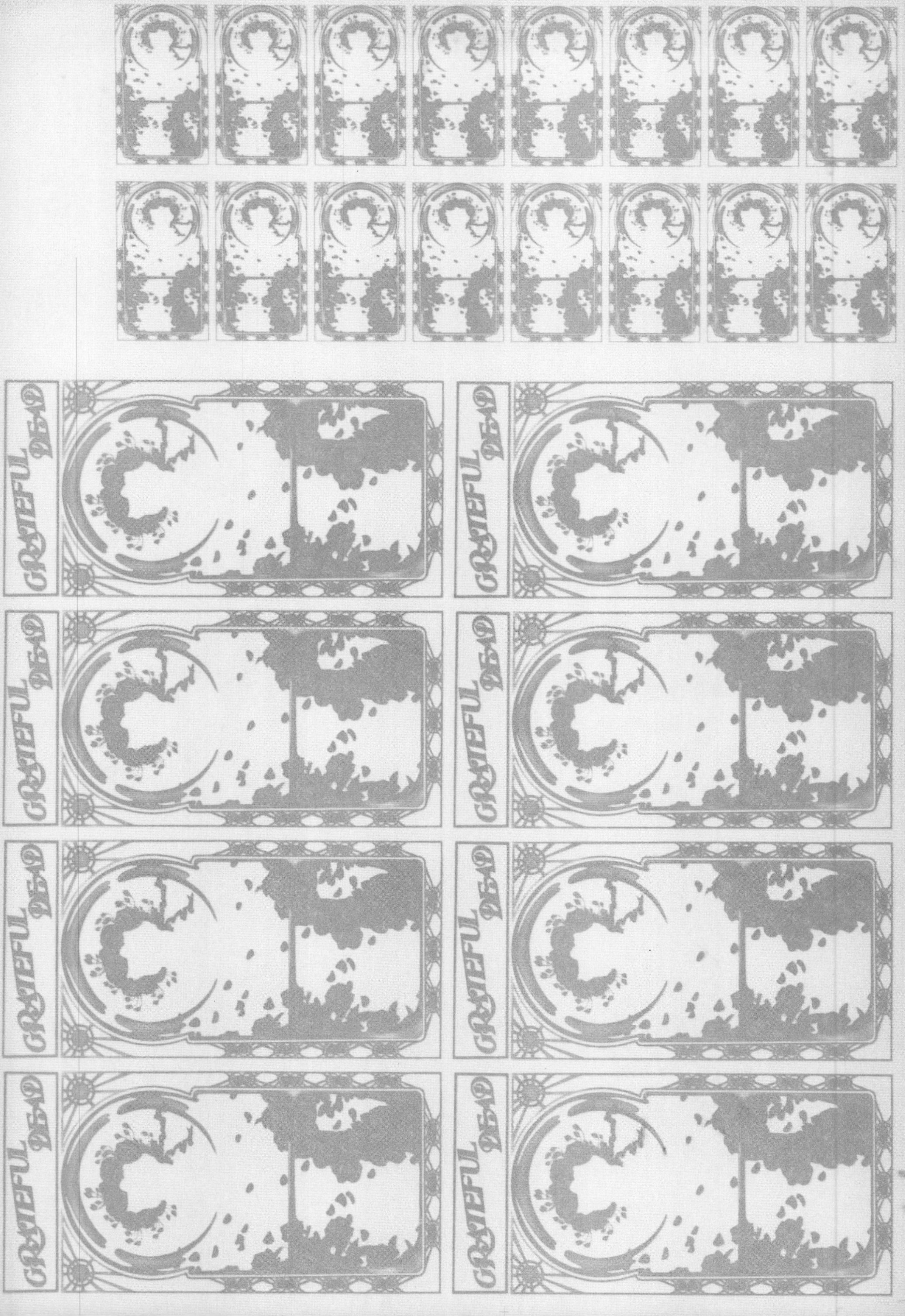
GRATEFUL DEAD
GRATEFUL DEAD
GRATEFUL DEAD
GRATEFUL DEAD
GRATEFUL DEAD
GRATEFUL DEAD
GRATEFUL DEAD
GRATEFUL DEAD

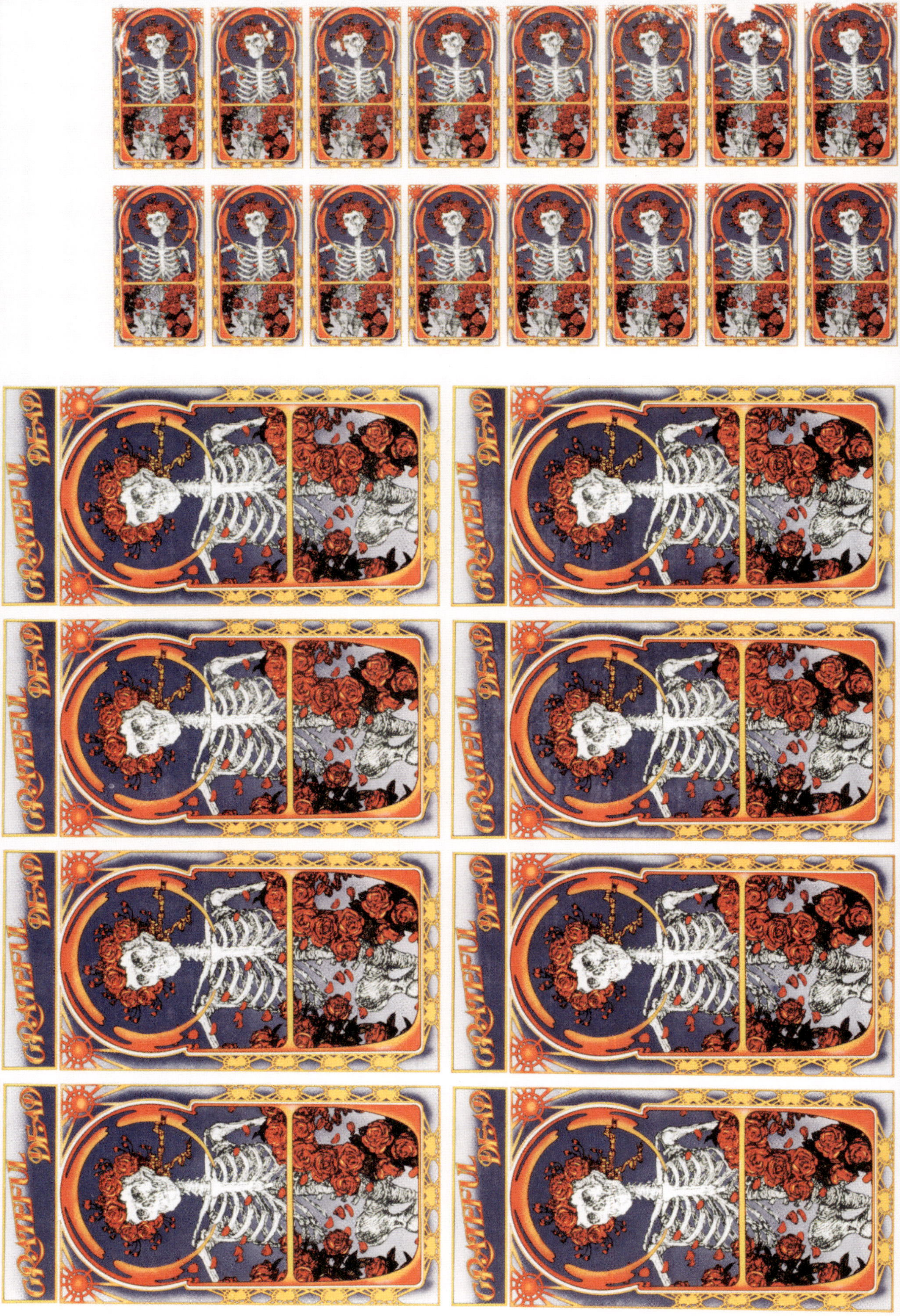
GRATEFUL DEAD

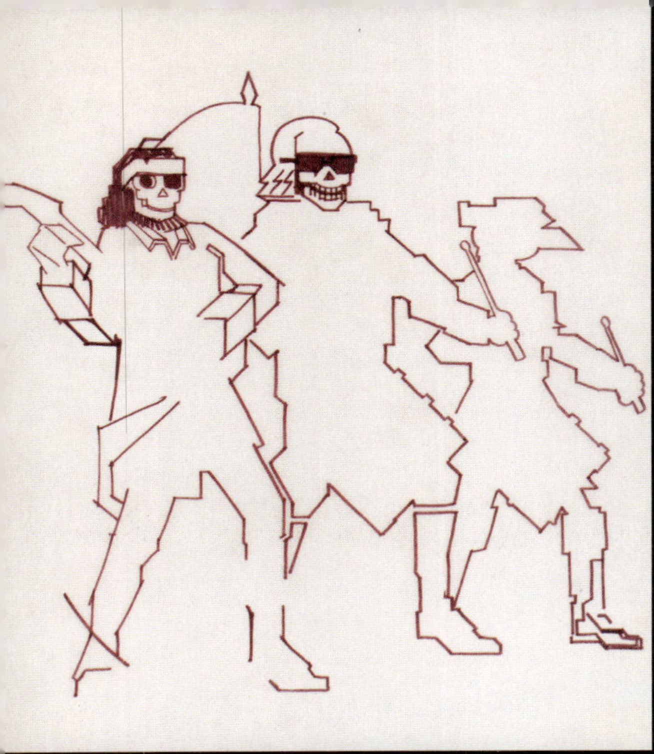

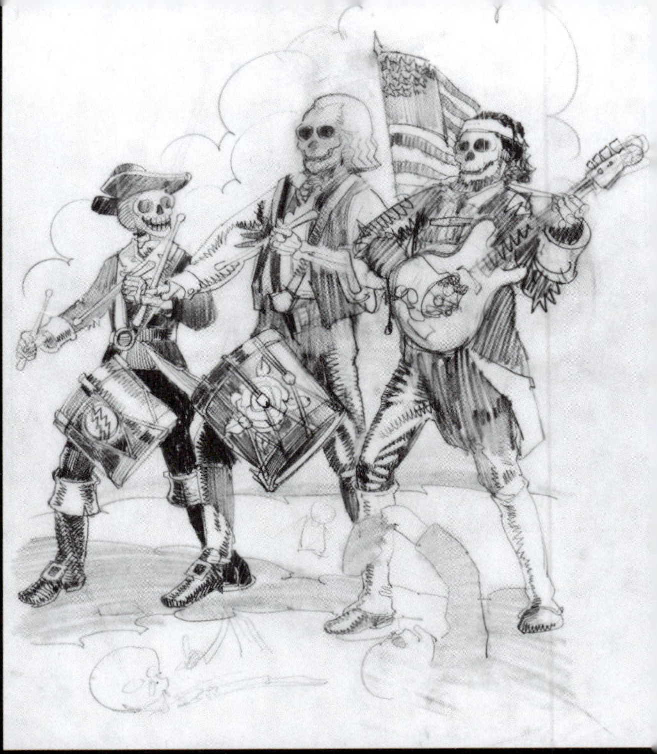

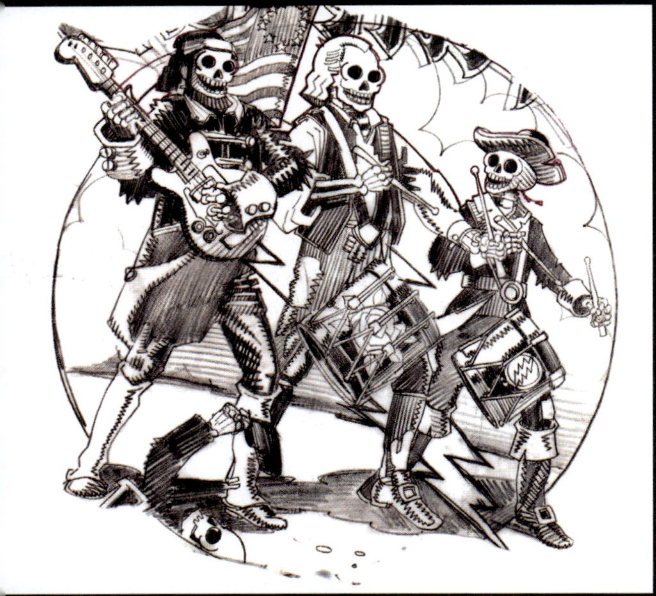

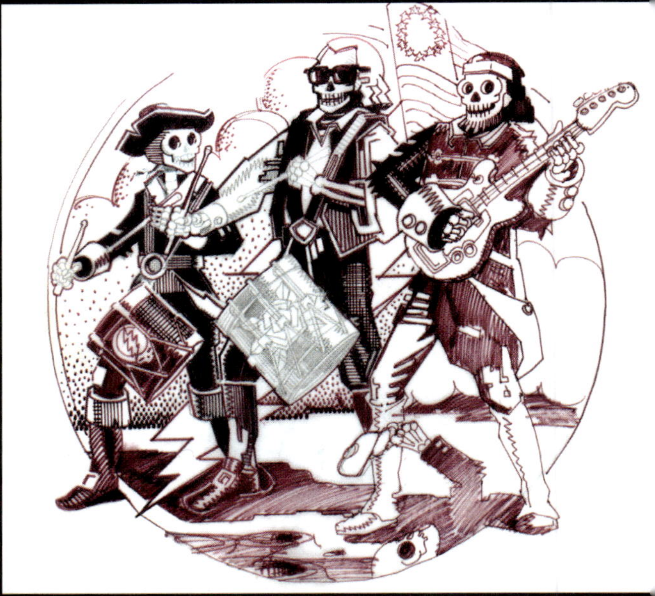

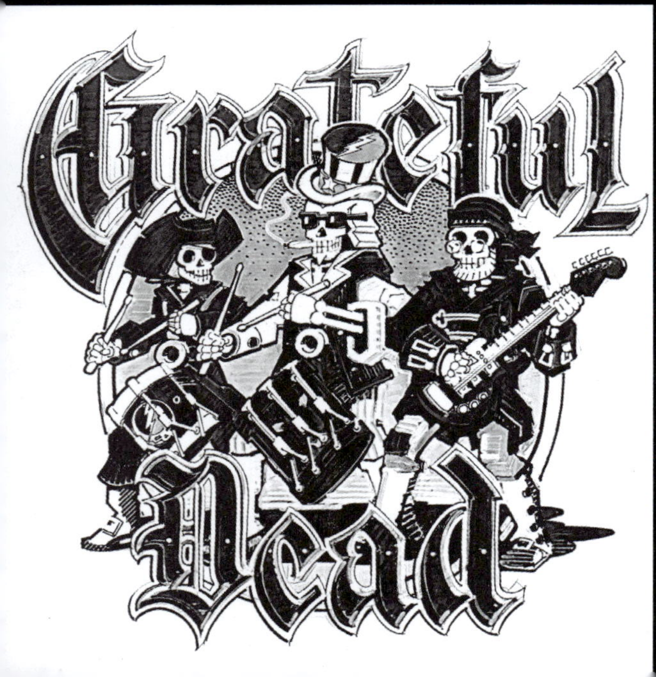
Grateful
Dead

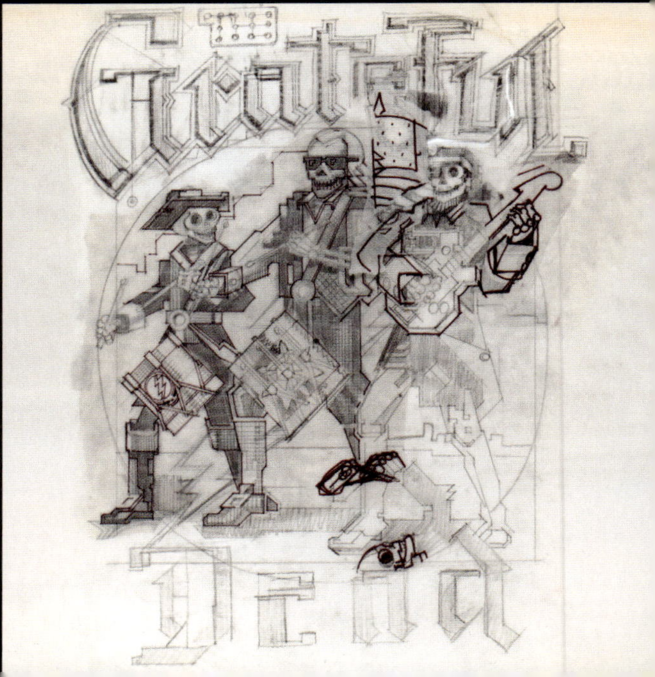

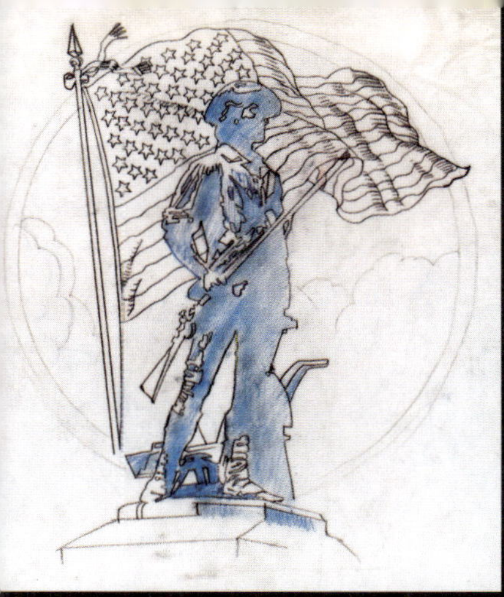

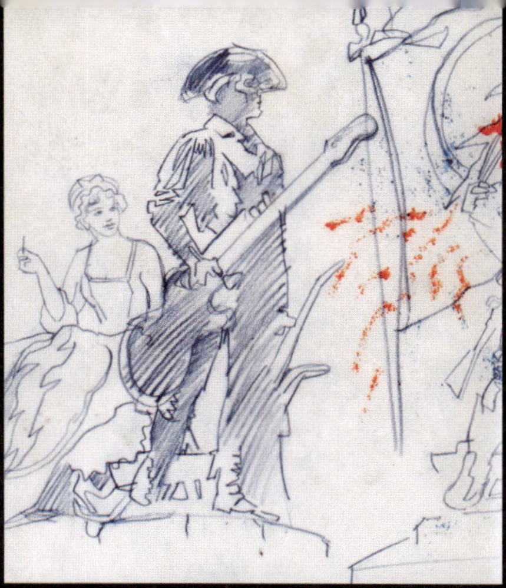

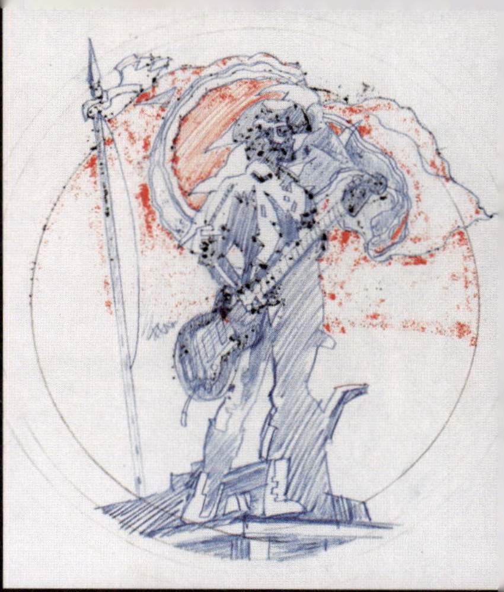

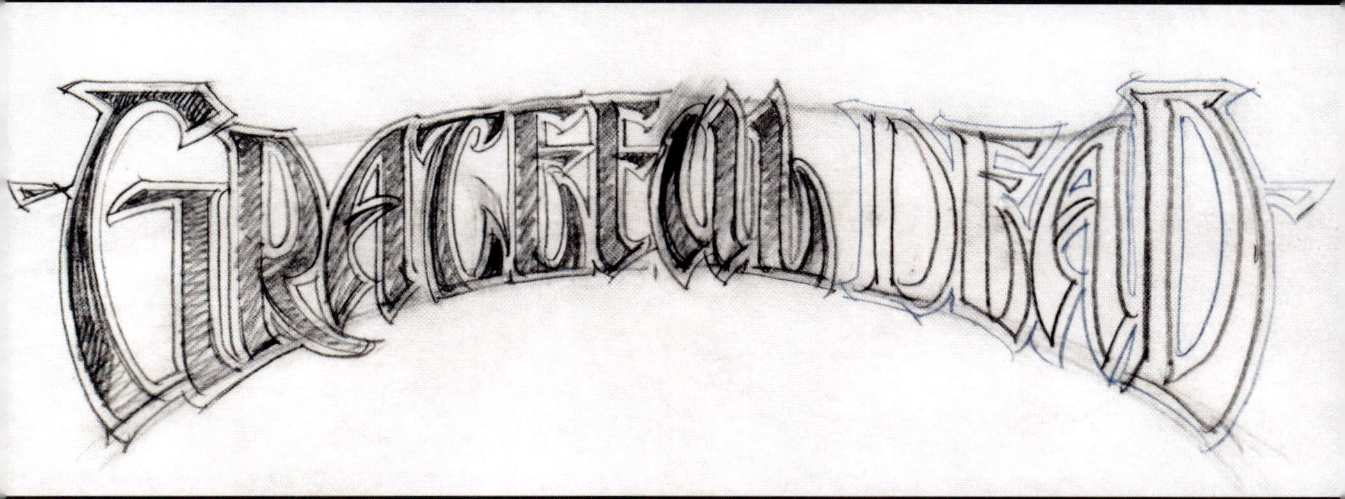
GRATEFUL DEAD

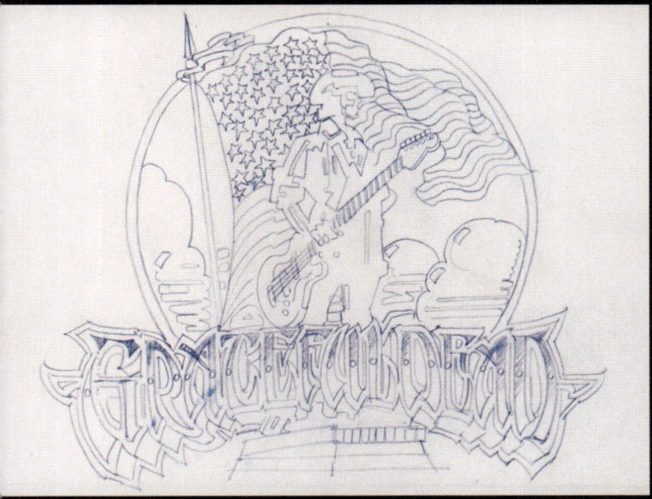
GRATEFUL DEAD

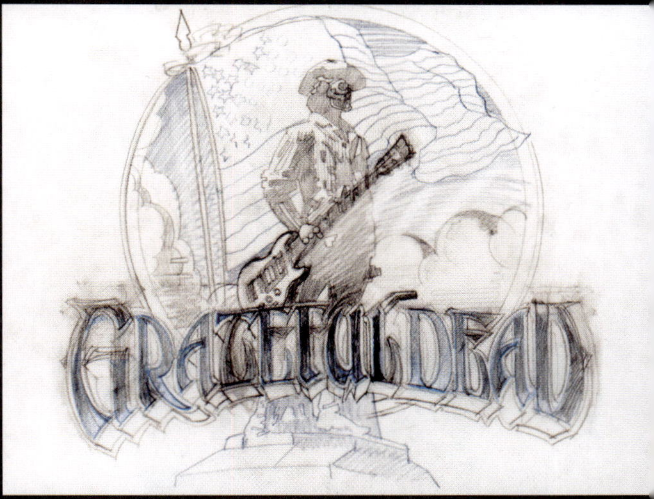
GRATEFUL DEAD

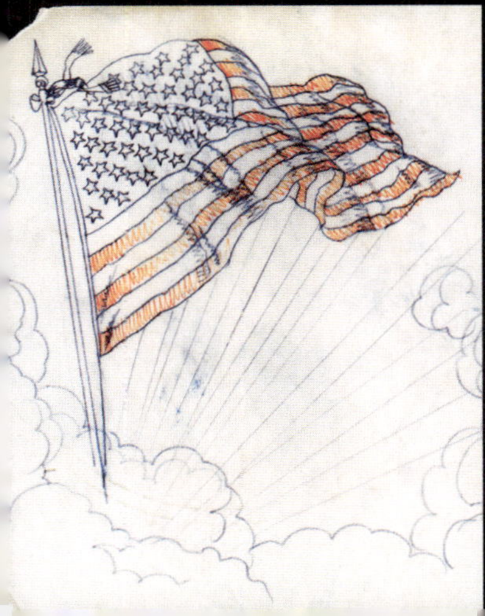

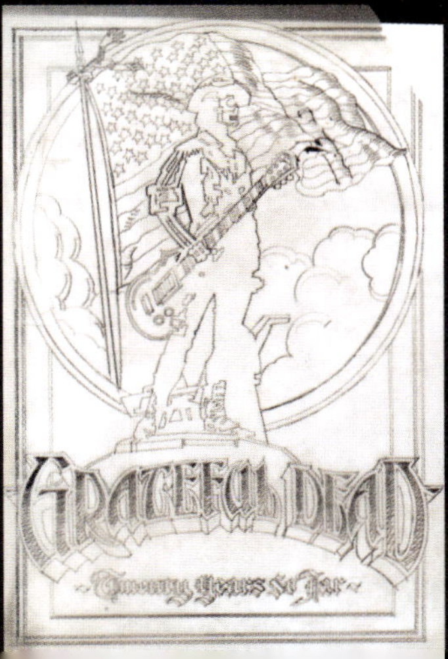
GRATEFUL DEAD
Twenty Years So Far

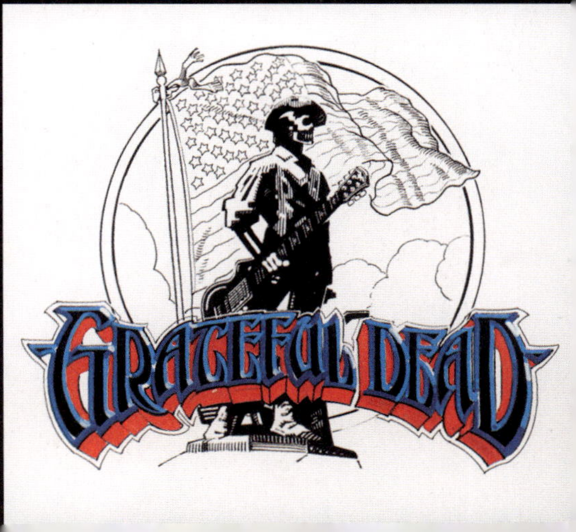
GRATEFUL DEAD

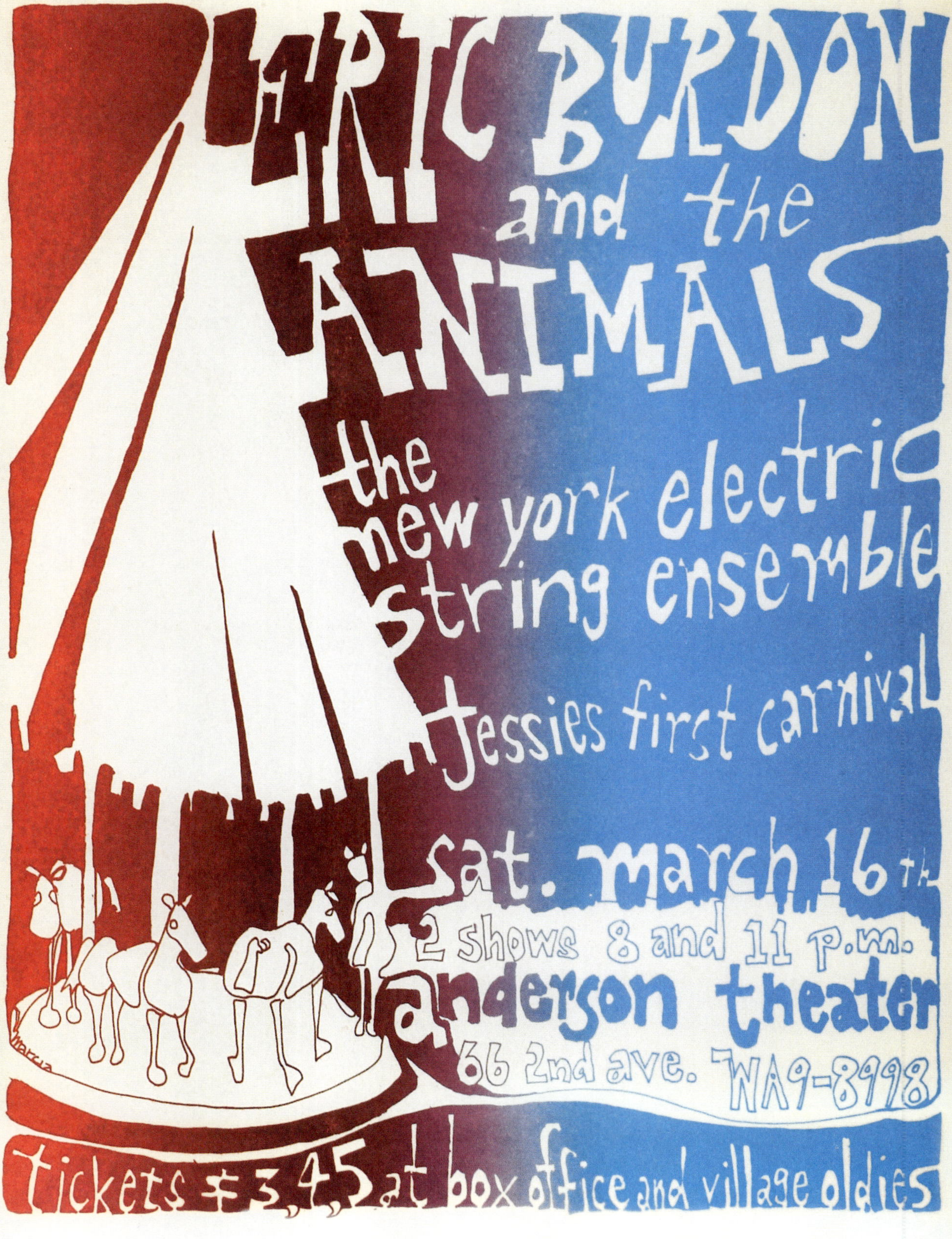
Eric Burdon
and the
Animals
the
new york electric
string ensemble
jessies first carnival
sat. march 16th
2 shows 8 and 11 p.m.
anderson theater
66 2nd ave. WA9-8998
tickets $3,4,5 at box office and village oldies
marcia

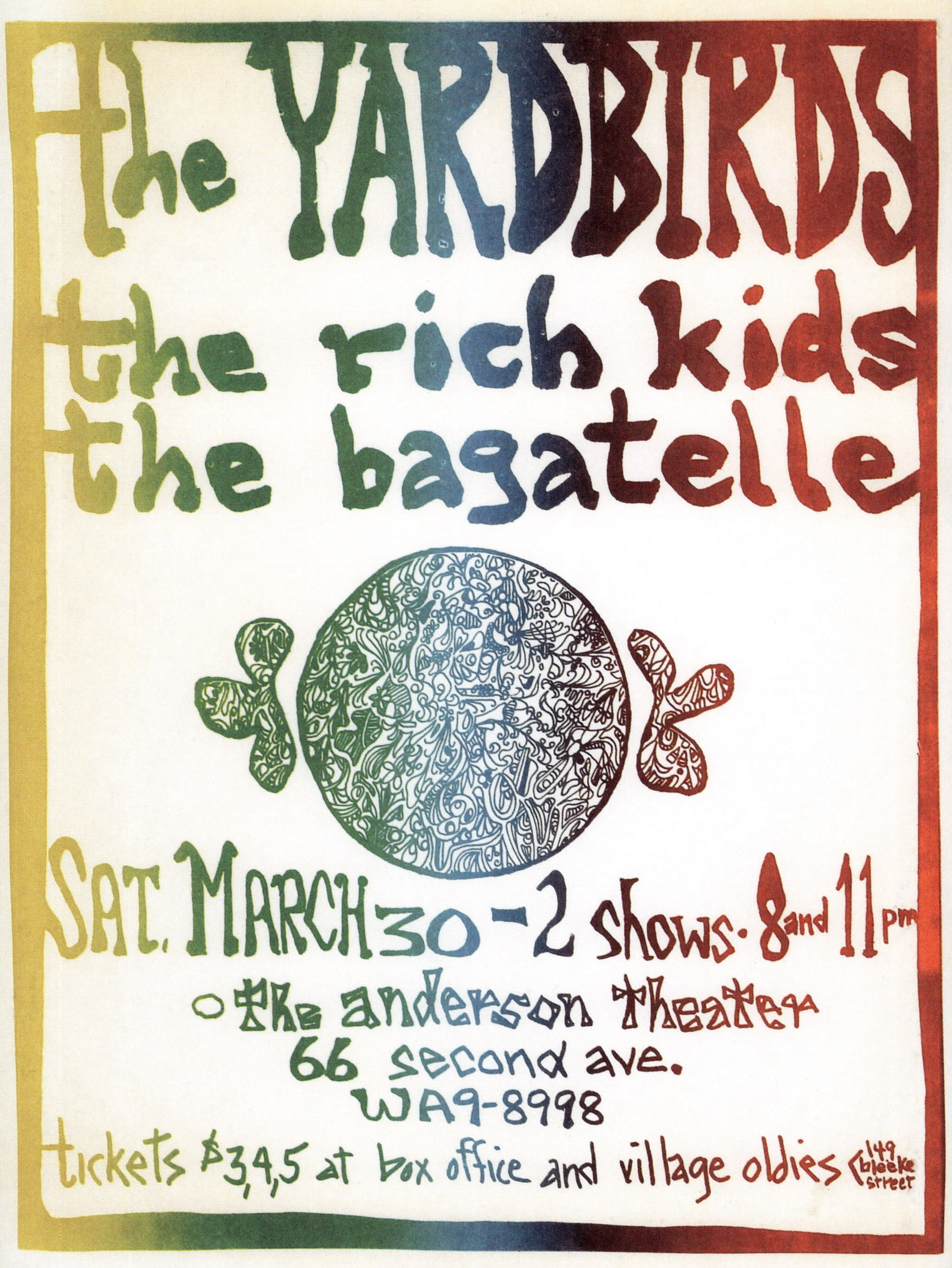
the YARDBIRDS
the rich kids
the bagatelle
SAT. MARCH 30 - 2 shows · 8 and 11 pm
the anderson theater
66 second ave.
WA9-8998
tickets $3,4,5 at box office and village oldies
149 bleeke street

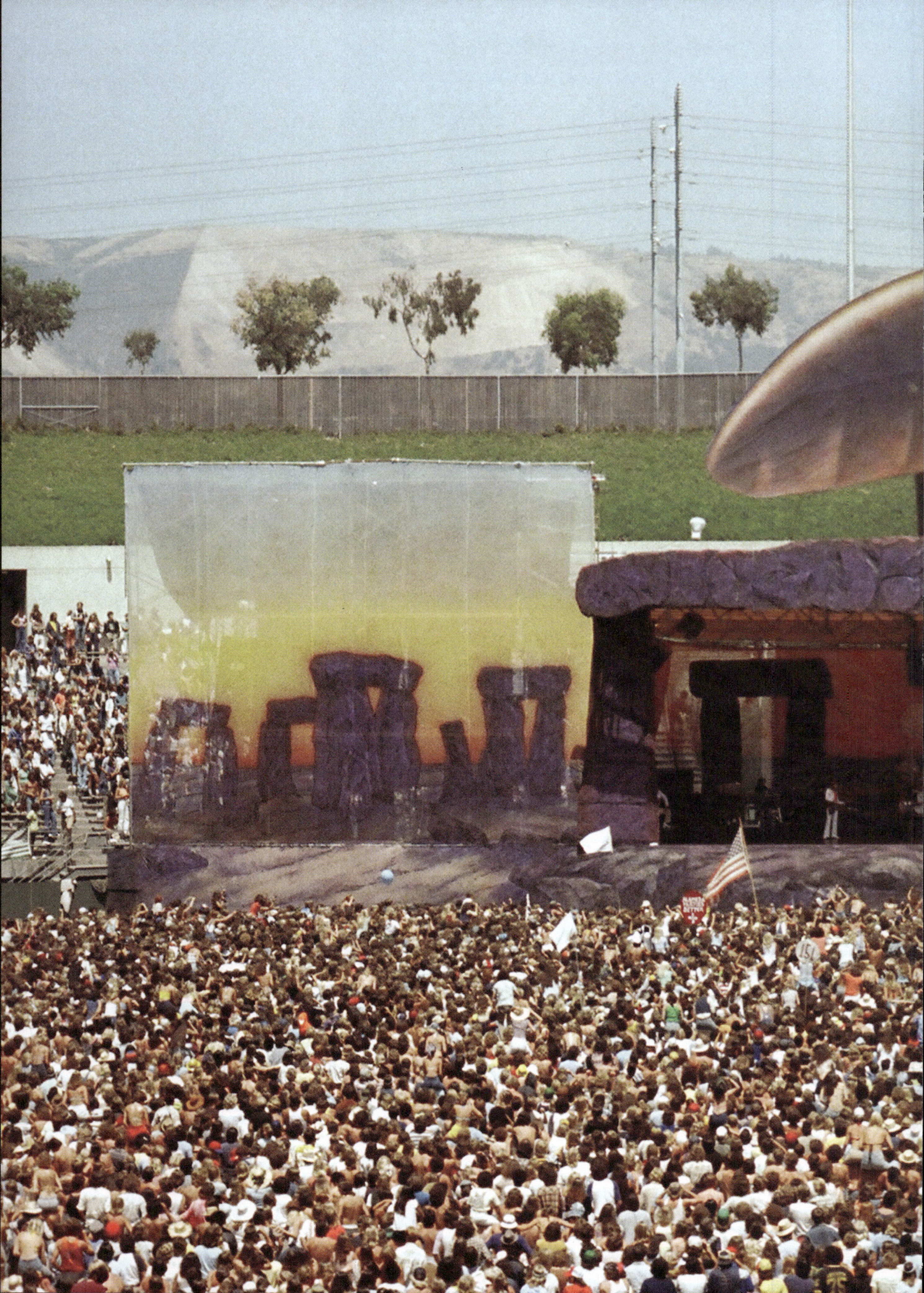

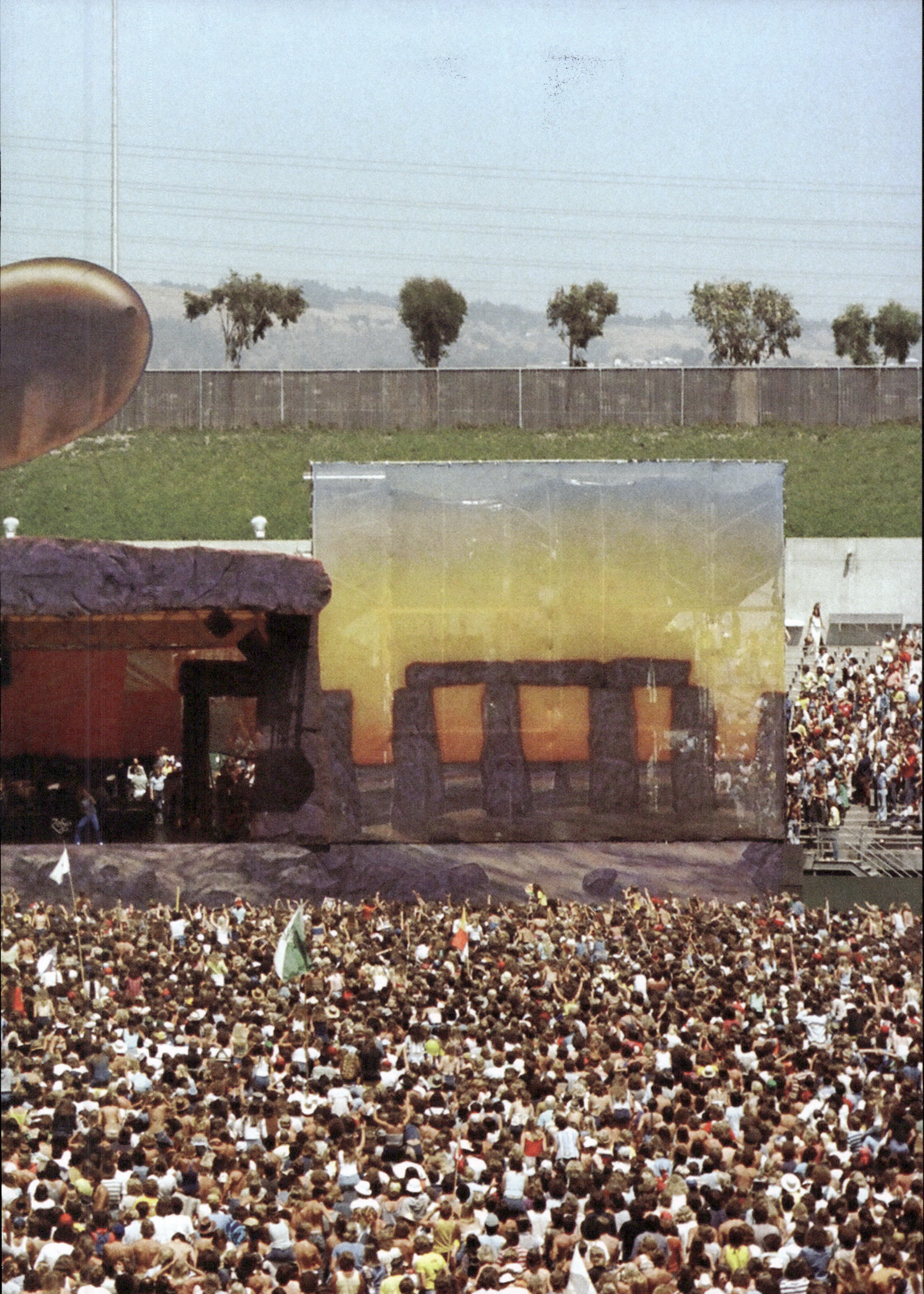

TUNE IN.

INTRO.
YOU'RE EITHER ON THE BUS OR OFF THE BUS 016

—

1. HAIGHT-ASHBURY TO ALTAMONT '66 TO '69 038
2. COUNTER-CULTURE TAKES CENTER STAGE '70 TO '77 148
3. MONSTERS OF ROCK '78 TO '88 184

—

BIOS OF THE DUDES 214 ENDNOTES AND FURTHER READING 218
SOURCES OF ILLUSTRATIONS 218 INDEX 220
ACKNOWLEDGMENTS 224

INTRO.

YOU'RE
EITHER
ON
THE BUS
OR
OFF
THE BUS

1954

Aldous Huxley publishes *The Doors of Perception*, which describes his experience of taking LSD.

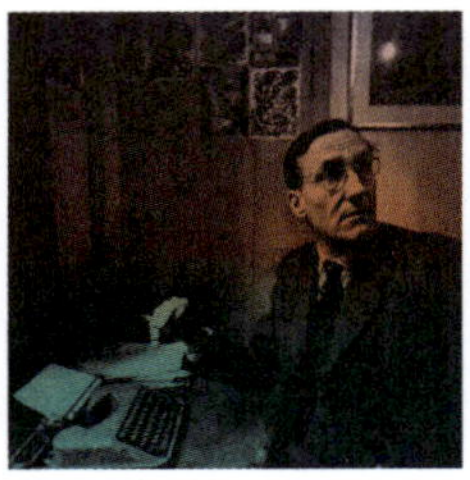

1957

Allen Ginsberg and Peter Orlovsky stay at The Beat Hotel in Paris's Latin Quarter. The same year, William S. Burroughs completes *The Naked Lunch* here.

1957

On the Road is published. Jack Kerouac's stream-of-consciousness account of a US road trip is hugely influential, not least on Bob Dylan.

1960

After a dramatic court case, Penguin Books wins the right to publish D. H. Lawrence's sexually-explicit *Lady Chatterley's Lover*. The print run of 200,000 sells out at once.

1965

The USA steps up its deployment of combat in Vietnam, in response to the increasing success of communist North Vietnam military forces.

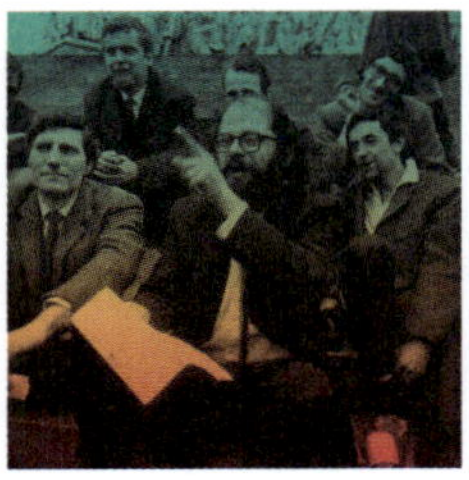

1965

US and UK beat poets (including Allen Ginsberg, Michael Horovitz, and Adrian Mitchell) take part in the International Poetry Incarnation at London's Royal Albert Hall.

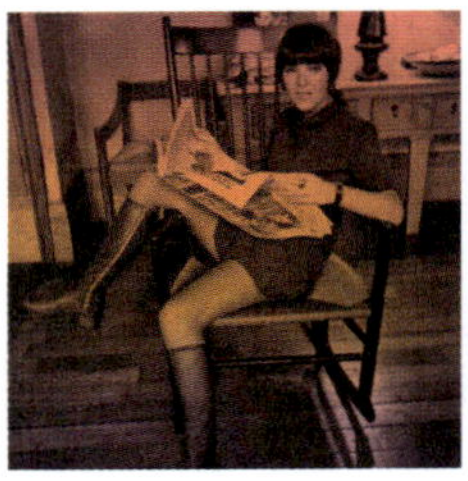

1965

Jean Shrimpton turns heads by wearing a miniskirt to the Melbourne Cup Carnival. Several designers have popularized the skirt, including Mary Quant (left).

1966

Ken Kesey and his group of 'Merry Pranksters' step up their Acid Tests in California. Audience members are invited to try LSD (still legal in the state until October 6).

1966

The Black Panthers are founded in Oakland, California. They embody a militant demand for civil rights, in areas from education to housing and employment.

1967

The Beatles' psychedelic masterpiece *Sgt. Pepper's Lonely Hearts Club Band* is released and becomes a worldwide best-seller.

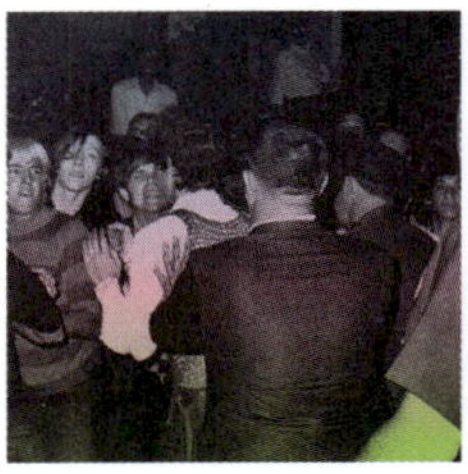

1969

Members of the gay community engage in a violent stand-off against New York police after a raid on Greenwich Village club the Stonewall Inn, in a pivotal moment for gay rights.

1969

The sweet vibes turn sour at another free Rolling Stones concert, this time at Altamont in California. Amid escalating violence, a fan is killed by Hells Angels.

1969

In a milestone for the hippie era, Woodstock Festival sees rock icons (including Jimi Hendrix and The Who) perform to around 400,000 people in New York state.

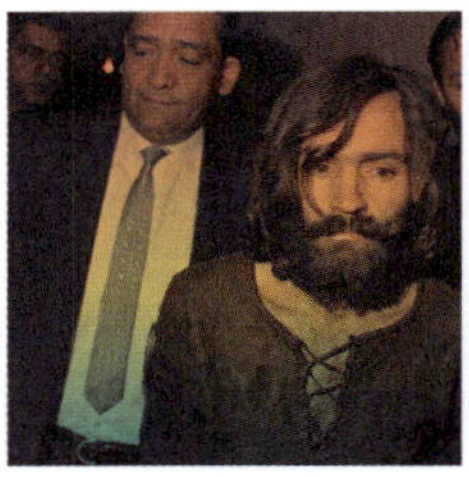

1969

Charles Manson is arrested as ringleader of 'The Family,' a cult whose members had gone on a murder spree, killing pregnant film star Sharon Tate, among others.

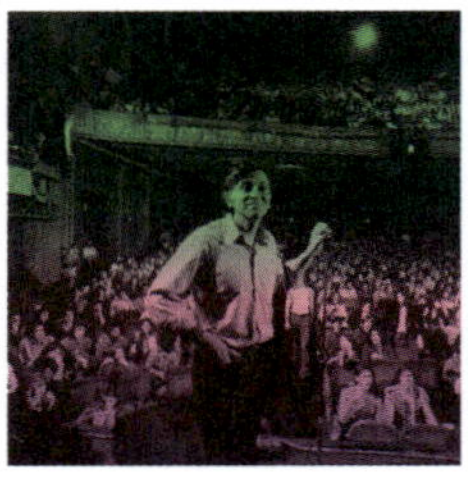

1971

Bill Graham closes his Fillmore West venue with five nights of shows by artists such as the Grateful Dead and Santana. The Fillmore East shuts the same year.

1989

The leader of the East German Communist Party declares free passage to the West. Jubilant crowds swarm to the Berlin Wall and start to dismantle it.

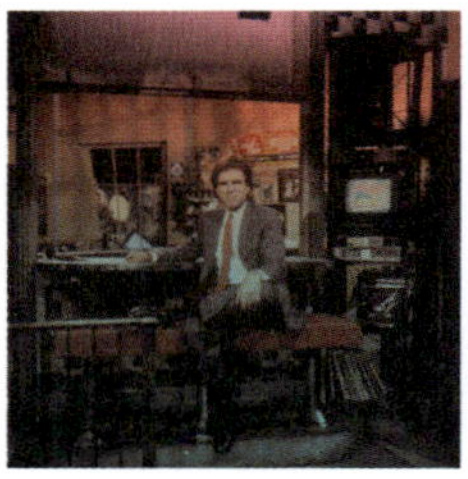

1981

MTV is founded as a round-the-clock music platform. It helps propel the rise of music videos, but is criticized at first for inadequate coverage of non-white artists.

1977

Punk classic *Never Mind the Bollocks, Here's the Sex Pistols* enters the UK album charts at No.1. The title prompts its own obscenity trial, which the Pistols win.

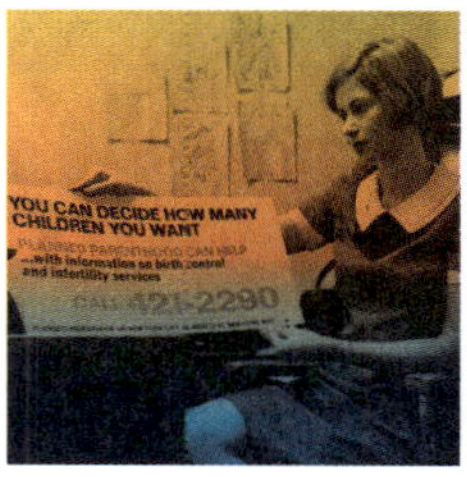

1960

The US Food and Drug Administration (FDA) approves the use of the birth-control pill, enabling greater sexual freedom for women and a more sexually liberal society.

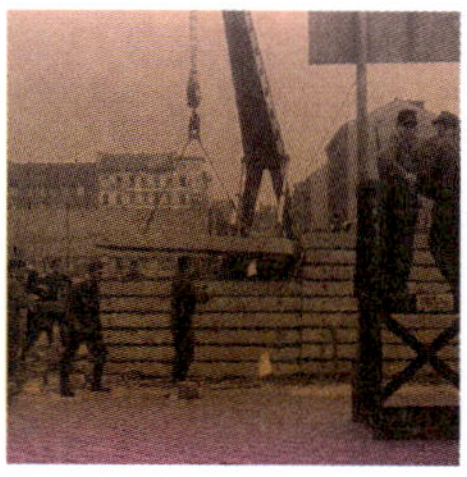

1961

Construction begins on the Berlin Wall. The move is an attempt by Soviet and East German authorities to prevent the migration of citizens to the West.

1961

Yuri Gagarin becomes the first man in space. He only completes one orbit of Earth before re-entry, but it marks an important victory in the USSR's space race with the USA.

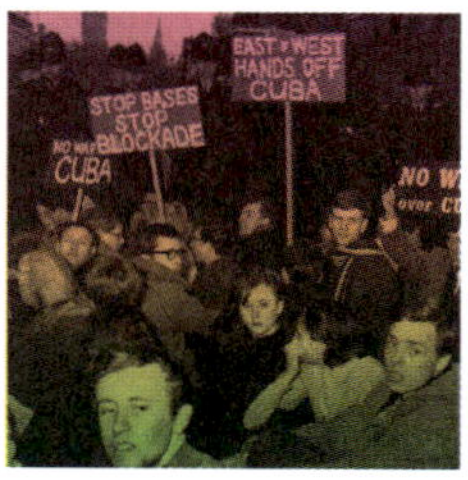

1962

Soviet Russia places nuclear missiles on the communist island of Cuba, escalating the Cold War with the USA. After a tense thirteen-day stand-off, they are withdrawn.

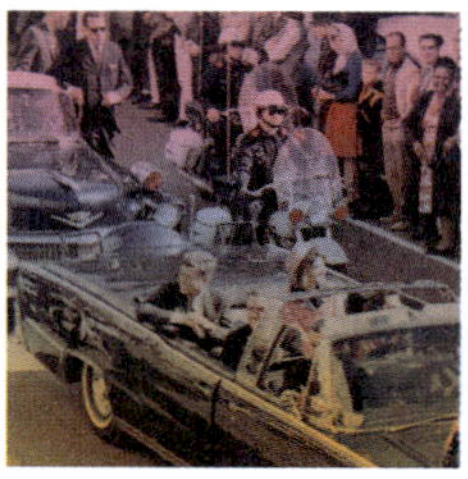

1963

US president John F. Kennedy is assassinated in an open-top car on a visit to Dallas, Texas. His presumed assailant, Lee Harvey Oswald, is himself shot dead soon after.

1967

400,000 people march from New York's Central Park to the UN in protest against the Vietnam War. Speeches are given by Martin Luther King and Stokely Carmichael.

1967

Rolling Stone rock magazine is founded by Jann Wenner and Ralph J. Gleason. It promotes a liberal, hippie-oriented ideology.

1967

Counter-cultural landmark the Human Be-In sees thousands gather in San Francisco's Golden Gate Park for rock music, poetry readings, and other events.

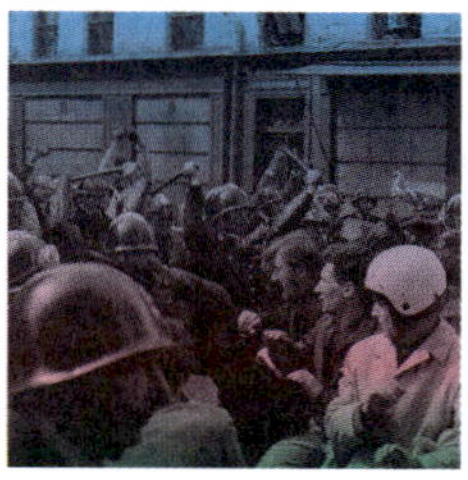

1968

Anti-establishment student protests in Paris erupt into battles with police. When workers' unions strike in sympathy, the French economy struggles to cope.

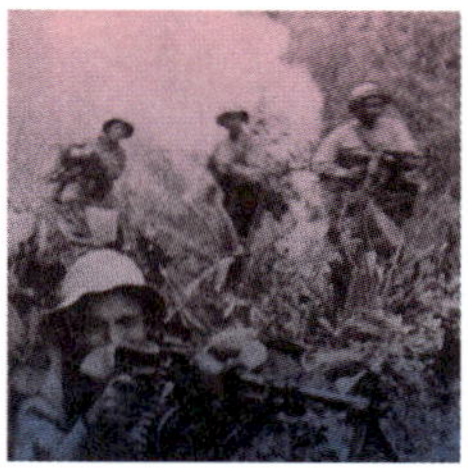

1968

The Tet Offensive sees North Vietnamese attacks in more than a hundred locations in South Vietnam. US public confidence is shaken and anti-war sentiment rises.

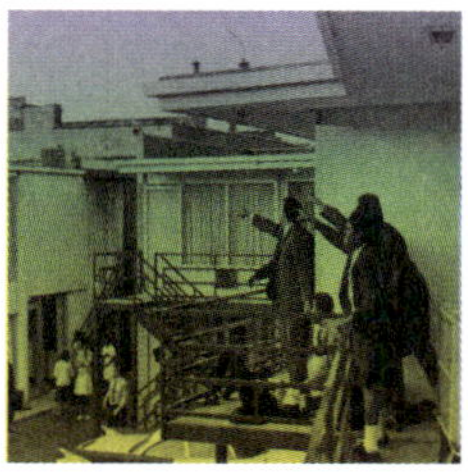

1968

Civil-rights leader Martin Luther King, Jr. is assassinated in Memphis, Tennessee, prompting a national outpouring of grief and a series of riots in US cities.

1969

The Rolling Stones play a free concert for around half a million people in Hyde Park. It includes a tribute to ex-member Brian Jones, who had died two days earlier.

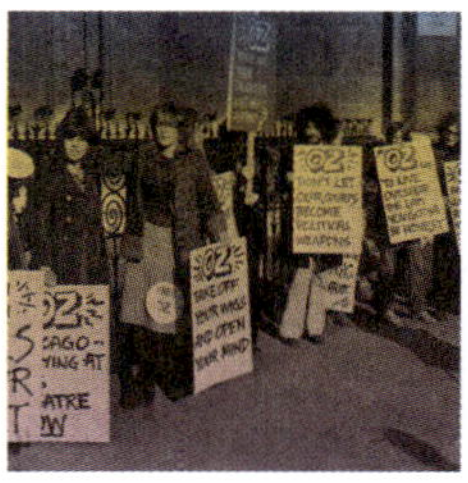

1971

Editors of *Oz* magazine are charged with obscenity over the 'Schoolkids Oz' issue. The sentences are quashed, but not before their long hair has been shorn in jail.

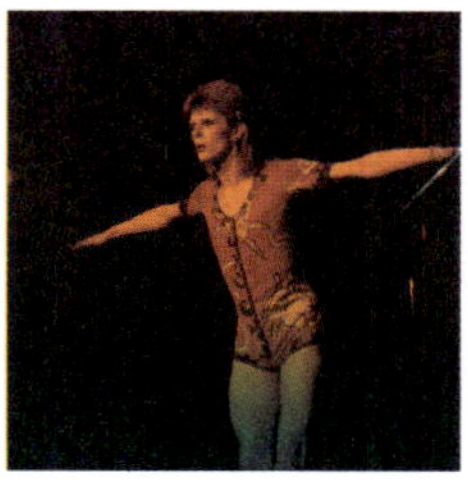

1973

David Bowie plays his last concert as Ziggy Stardust. However, when he cryptically announces this at the Hammersmith Apollo, many believe that Bowie himself is retiring.

1973

Nasty Tales—which republishes underground US comix by the likes of Robert Crumb—faces trial on obscenity charges. Despite the not-guilty verdict, it folds soon after.

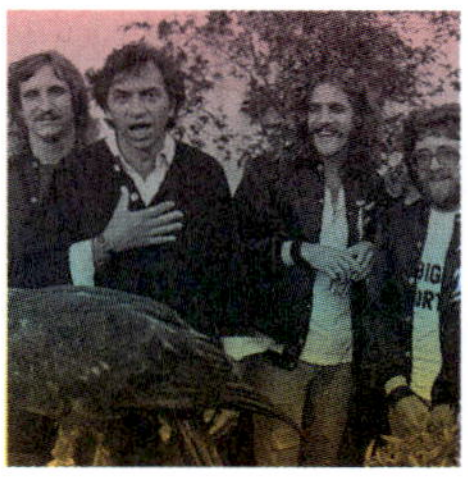

1973

The first Day on the Green festival sees Leon Russell, Loggins and Messina, Elvin Bishop, and Alvin Lee appear in Oakland, California. Bill Graham is the promoter.

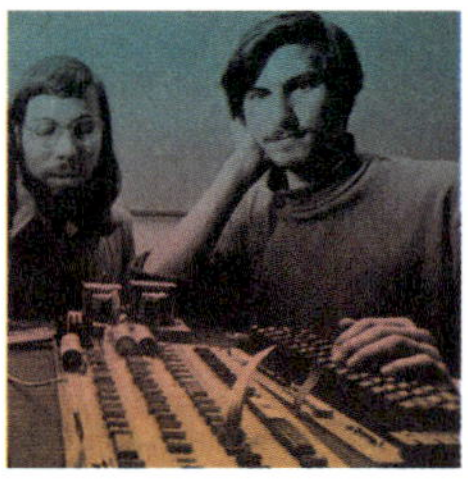

1976

Apple is co-founded by Steve Jobs, Ronald Wayne and Steve Wozniak, initially to produce the latter's Apple I computer.

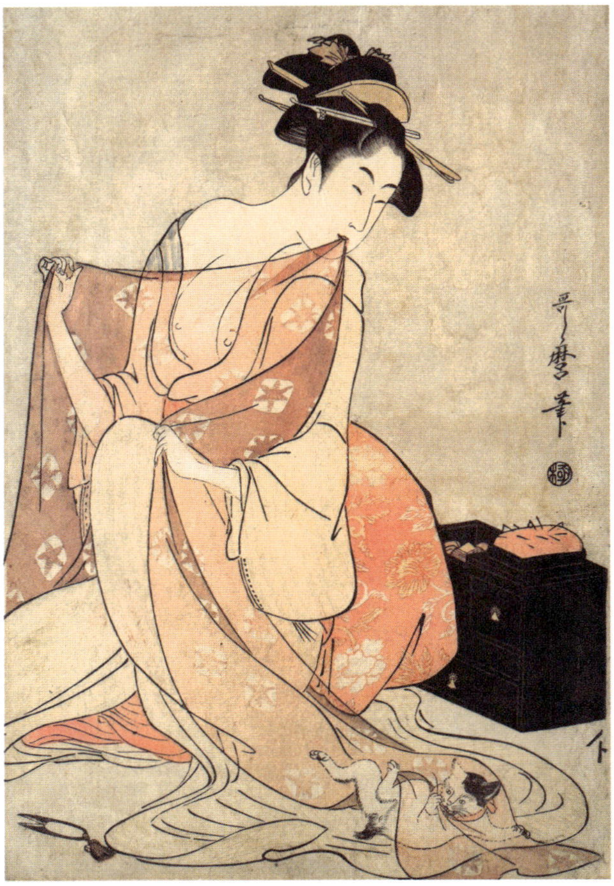

A Woman and a Cat (c. 1793–94), by Kitagawa Utamaro, ink and color on paper. This is one sheet of a triptych of polychrome wood-block prints.

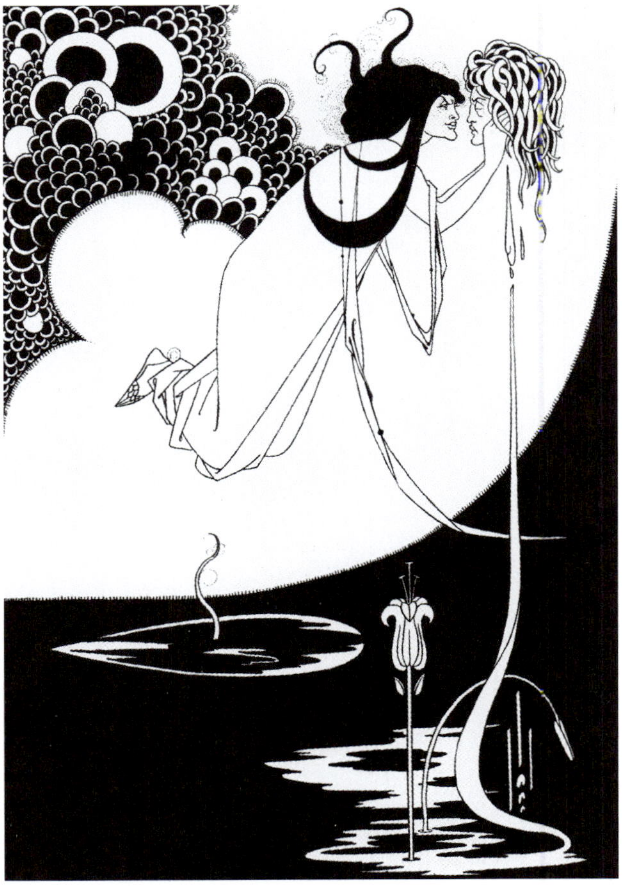

The Climax (1894), by Aubrey Beardsley. The illustration shows a scene from Oscar Wilde's play *Salome*, in which the eponymous character holds the head of John the Baptist.

The illustrated poster as we know it begins in the 1860s. One of the first was the celebrated 'Les Chats' (1868) by Édouard Manet (1832–83) for an illustrated book about cats, the first publication by J. Rothschild, Editeur. A central drawing of cats was surrounded by text. This new form of advertising was quickly taken up by the theater—tall, narrow bills, suitable for the advertising kiosks of Paris—and the circus, which developed multi-sheet posters to cover entire walls.

Posters are distinguished from artists' prints by two characteristics: the combination of image and words, and the need to be suitable for mass reproduction. Psychedelic posters were later to challenge both of these features, with greater or lesser success. Clear antecedents of the psychedelic art of the mid-sixties began to appear in the last quarter of the 19th century. One forerunner was Jules Chéret (1836–1932), who began drawing his theater posters directly onto lithographic stone, combining the words and illustration so that, to quote Max Gallo, 'The words announce the content and the illustration describes it in minute detail.'[1] The most recognizable practitioner of this method was, of course, Henri de Toulouse-Lautrec (1864–1901), whose influences included Vincent van Gogh, Paul Gauguin, and Japanese wood engraving. His figures were not generic, like those of Chéret, but of specific individuals, and he balanced the words and illustration to give a combined narrative message. By the end of the century, the wordy messages had been pared down to the most basic information, as exemplified in Lautrec's 'Jane Avril' series of the 1890s.

By this time, the Art Nouveau style (also known as Stile Liberty and Jugendstil) had emerged in Europe, producing a variety of celebrated poster artists who are still influential today: Aubrey Beardsley (1872–98), Charles Rennie Mackintosh (1868–1928), Alphonse Mucha (1860–1939), and Gustav Klimt (1862–1918) among many others. The work of this group of artists entered the canon and became part of the received knowledge of mid-sixties poster-makers.

The latter grew up with the straightforward 'boxing-style' posters that dominated in the fifties and early sixties. These were created by the printers and had their origins in posters for circuses, minstrel shows, carnivals, and boxing matches. They featured large wood-block display fonts, sometimes hand carved for a specific event, and often used eye-catching, primary-colored backgrounds. The same style was in use in both the USA and the UK, although American posters employed more color. Black-and-white photographs of the acts were frequently incorporated into the image, which was often a set-piece design; its top quarter could be given over to the names of different venues.

In locations such as San Francisco's Bay Area, poster design was inevitably also influenced by the beat generation, whose books and magazines had more advanced designs than mainstream equivalents. Youth culture was in transition from the beat generation, through beatniks and folk singers, to hippies and hard rockers.

It is generally agreed that the San Francisco psychedelic scene began not in that city but at the Red Dog Saloon in the old silver-mining town of Virginia City, Nevada, 40 miles (64 km) south of Reno. The building—a three-story hotel, The Comstock House, at 76 North C Street—was bought by Mark Unobski's father, who was delighted that his son had finally found himself a project. Mark wanted to restore the building to its 1860s Victorian heyday and provide food and live music in a relaxed, laid-back setting. He gathered together like-minded staff, including: Chandler Loughlin (who had experience of running folk-music coffee houses); Don and Roz Works, former house painters already living in Nevada; chef Jenna

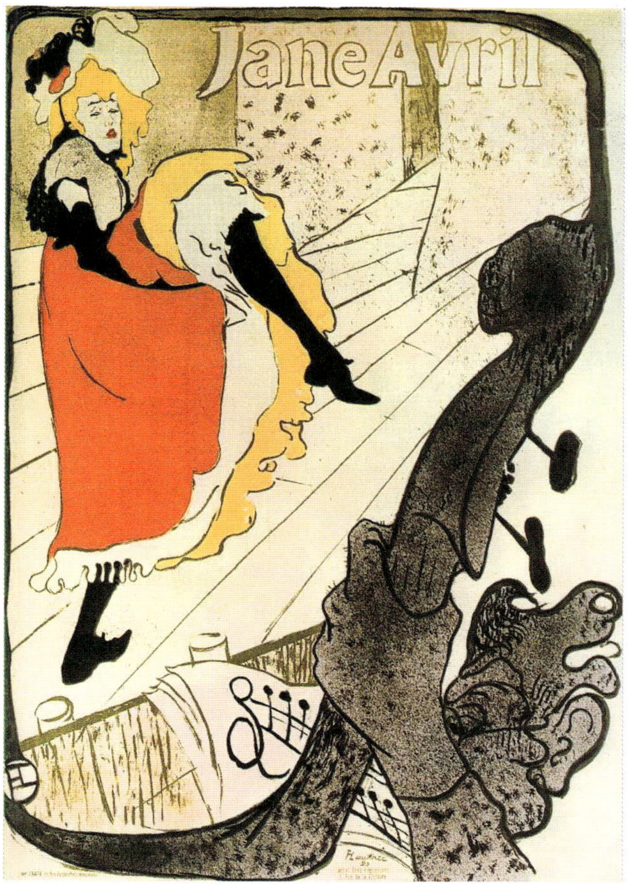

➸ *Jane Avril* (1893), by Henri de Toulouse-Lautrec. The artist's loose, sketchy posters were influenced by the asymmetric compositions and areas of flat color characteristic of Japanese prints.

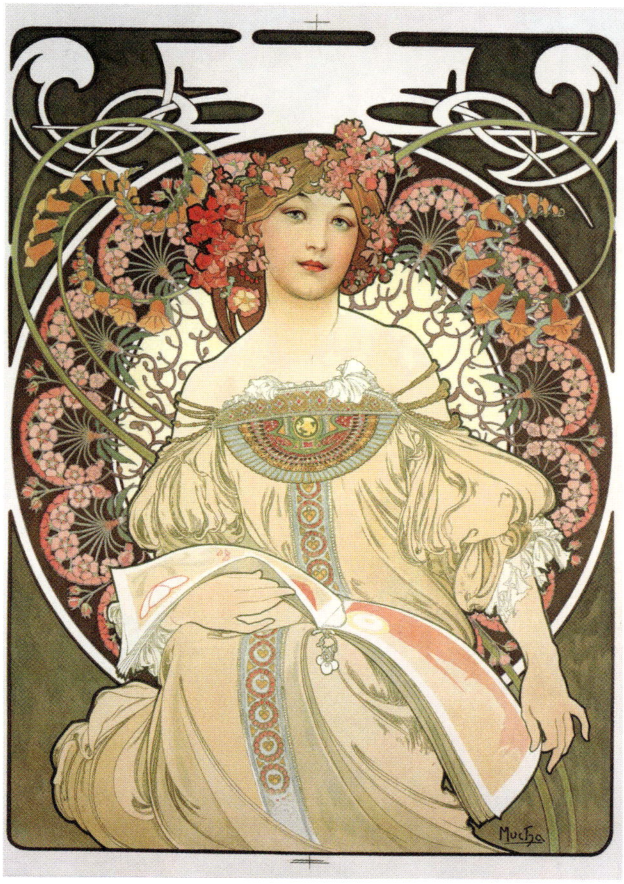

➸ *Dreaming* (aka *Reverie*, 1897), by Alphonse Mucha, lithograph. Mucha's sensual line typified the arts and architecture of the Art Nouveau era.

Worden; Seattle folk singer Lynne Hughes, who served as the mistress of ceremonies; a giant Washoe Indian bouncer, Mike Jones; and political activist Luria Castell's Family Dog Collective—consisting of her friends Ellen Harmon, Jack Towle, and Alton Kelley—who worked on restoring the building. Pretty soon, they had all taken to wearing old-fashioned Edwardian outfits, with the women in long gowns. The music was provided by The Charlatans, a folk-rock band who had been rehearsing in San Francisco but had never performed live before.

It is the poster from their residency that concerns us here: known as *The Seed*, it is regarded as the first psychedelic poster. Charlatans keyboard player Mike Ferguson designed everything except the distinctive lettering of the band's name, which was created by the group's leader, George Hunter. It was small—just 10 × 14 inches (25 × 36 cm)—but collectors still regard it as a poster rather than a handbill. It contains virtually all the elements that characterize San Franciscan psychedelic art: cartoony drawings, blobby lettering, decorative borders, dingbats, and other references to old-time Western advertising. The ultra-rare first printing was made in blue ink and gave the dates of the band's residency as June 1–15, 1965. But the venue was not yet ready, and a second printing, in black ink, revised this to 'Opening June 21.' In fact, The Charlatans ended up playing a six-week run. Although the Red Dog was a bar, the customers were mostly friends and their drugs of choice were pot and acid. This, combined with The Charlatans' extended, improvisational sets, and a rudimentary light show provided by Bill Ham and Bob Cohen that threw blobs of color across the walls and tripped-out customers, inspired a new, loose style of communal dancing. It was a world removed from jerky dances for three-minute pop songs. By the end of the summer, the Red Dog Saloon had created free-form acid music, the psychedelic light show, and the psychedelic poster.

The Family Dog Collective returned to San Francisco, settling at the Dog House, 1836 Pine Street, across town from the Haight. A rooming house managed by Bill Ham, the building owed its name to the fact that the dozen or so residents all owned dogs. Energized by their experience that summer, Luria, Ellen, Jack, and Alton started a company, The Family Dog, with the slogan 'May The Baby Jesus Shut Your Mouth And Open Your Mind.' Intent on recreating the Virginia City scene in San Francisco, they soon found that while they had been away, things had already begun to happen. Chet Helms, who began staging civil-rights benefits in Texas before he even went to college, had been organizing dance concerts at fifty cents a head with local musicians in the large basement of a boarding-house at 1090 Page Street. Deciding to combine forces and put on a large event together, Helms and The Family Dog rented Longshoremen's Hall on Fisherman's Wharf for a Saturday night 'Rock 'n' Roll Dance And Concert' on October 16, 1965. Called 'The Family Dog Presents A Tribute To Dr Strange,' the evening, which ran from 9:00 p.m. until 2:00 a.m., featured The Charlatans, Jefferson Airplane, The Marbles, The Great Society, and another new band—the Grateful Dead—who lived communally a few doors down from The Charlatans at 710 Ashbury. The poster was designed by Family Dog member Alton Kelley, a motorcycle mechanic who had been doing a lot of collages, with some help from Amy Magill. The 'Dr Strange' reference came from Family Dog member Ellen Harmon, who had a huge collection of Marvel Comics. Alton Kelley told Paul Grushkin: 'We printed up a couple hundred handbills for the first dance, just as we did for the next two dances. I remember finishing the art right on top of the counter down at the printer, Joe Buchwald's Rapid Repro Shop. There were also a few special silk-screen posters done, not many at all, which would go up at places like The Committee Theatre.'[2]

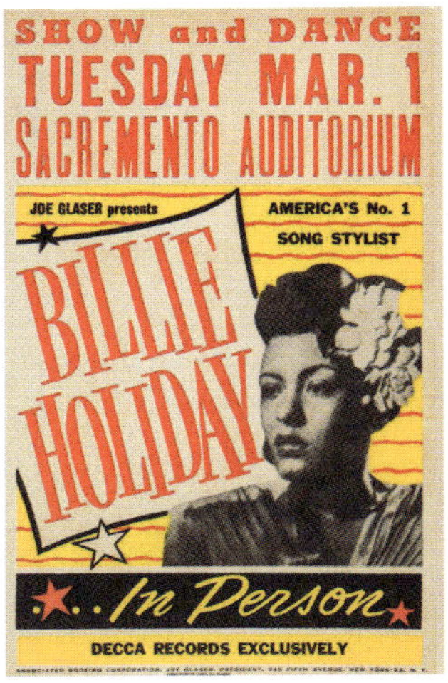

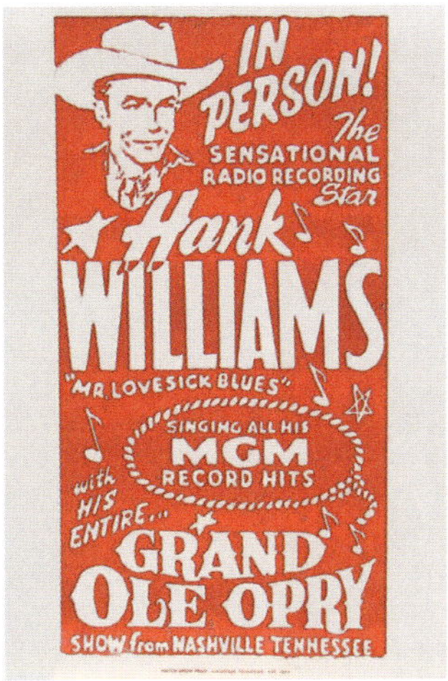

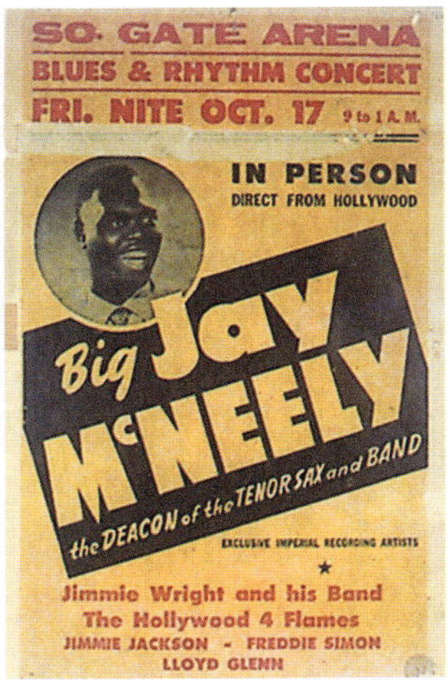

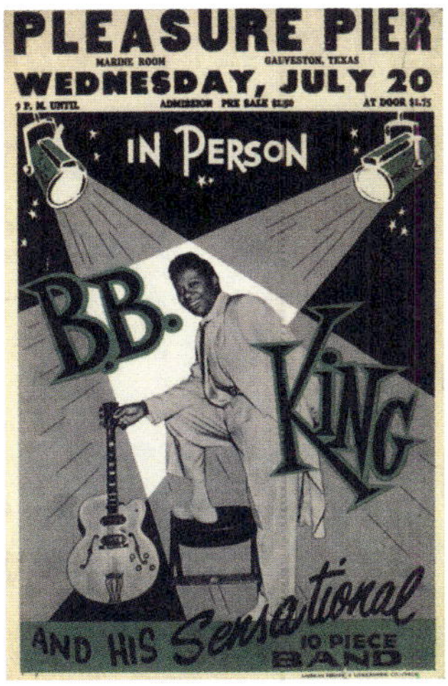

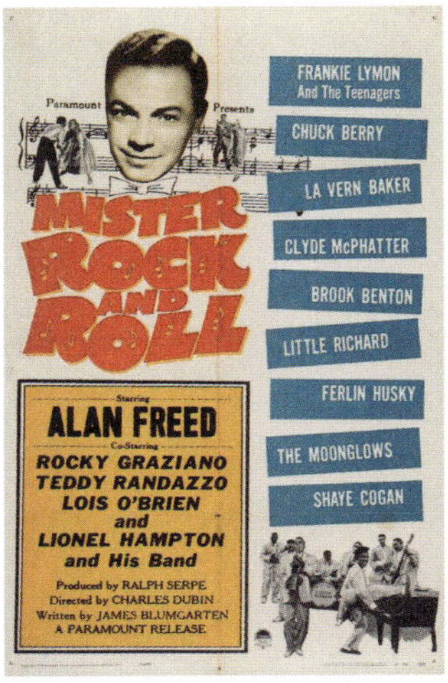

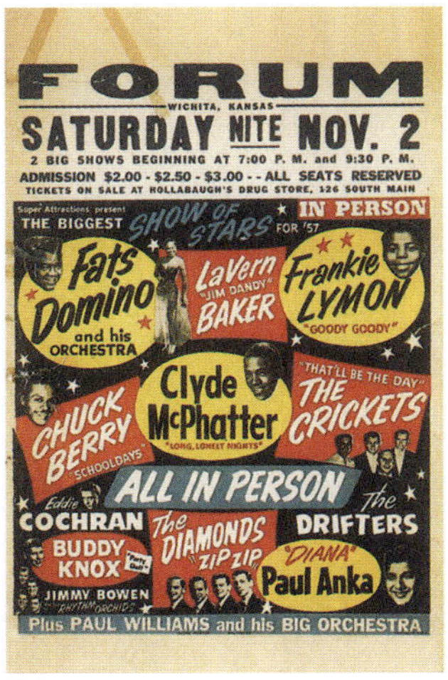

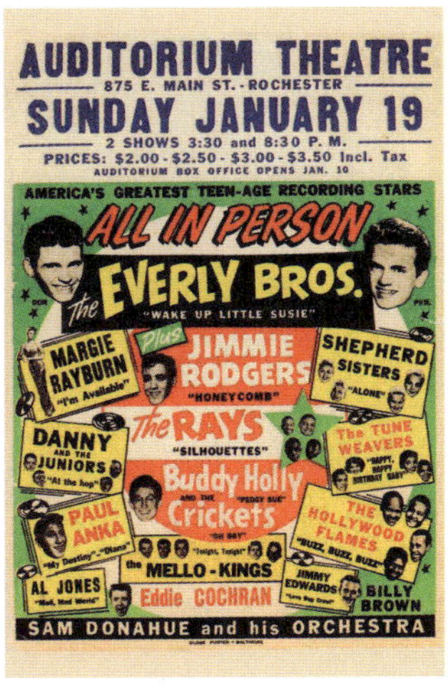

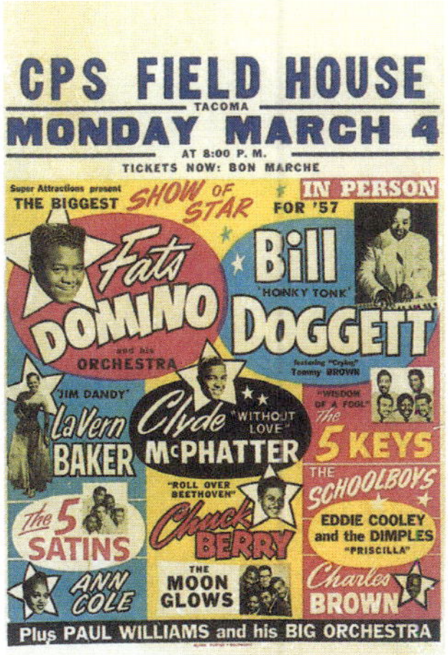

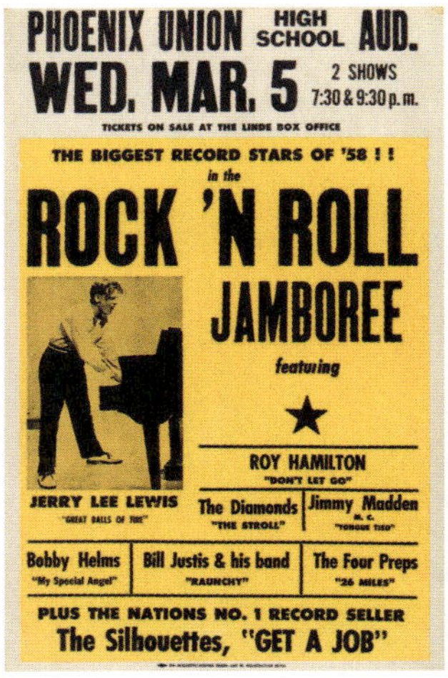

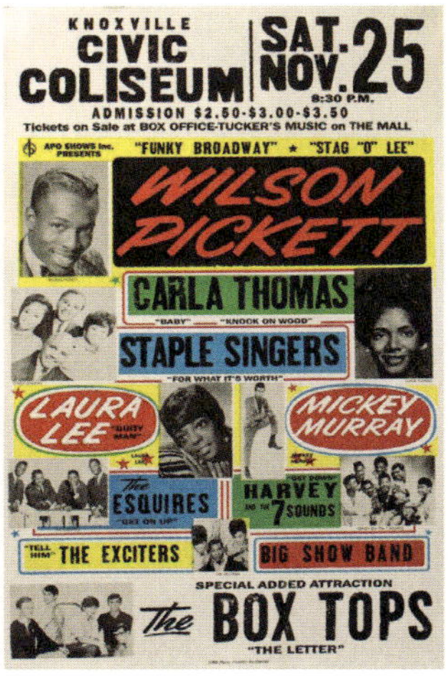

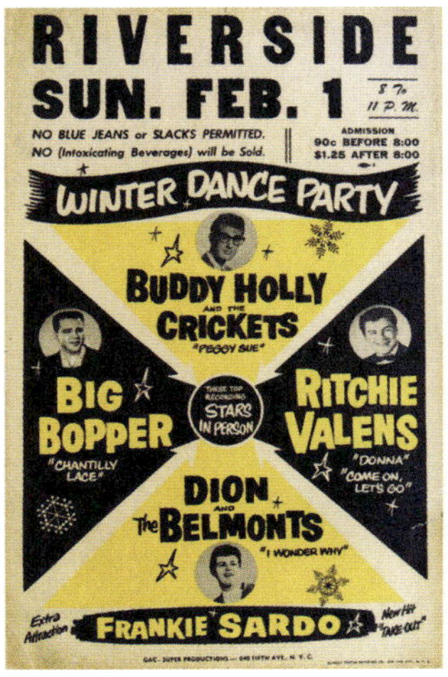

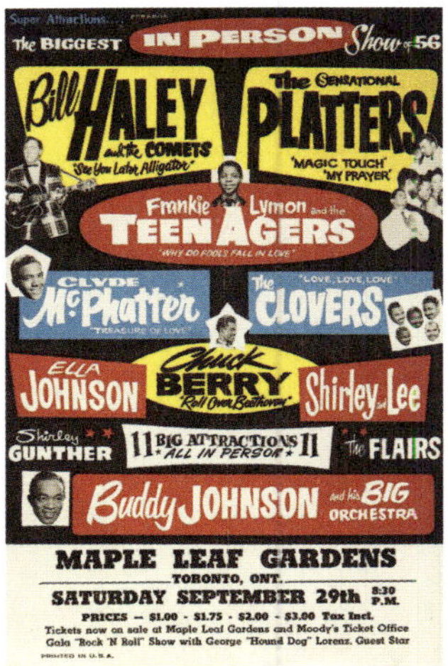

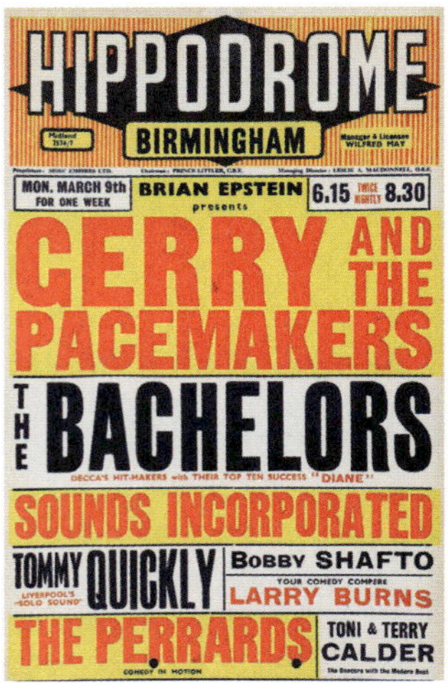

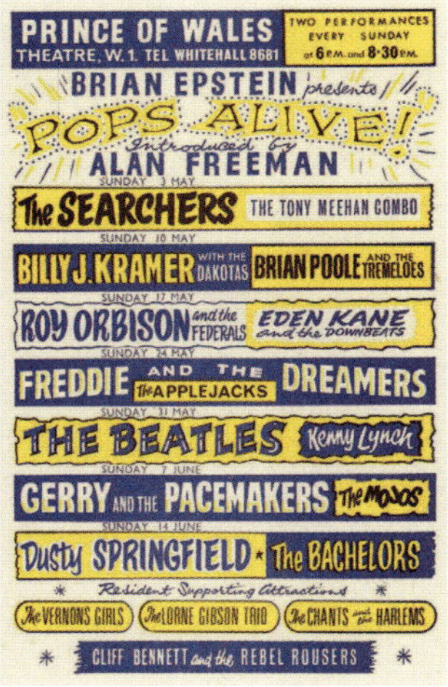

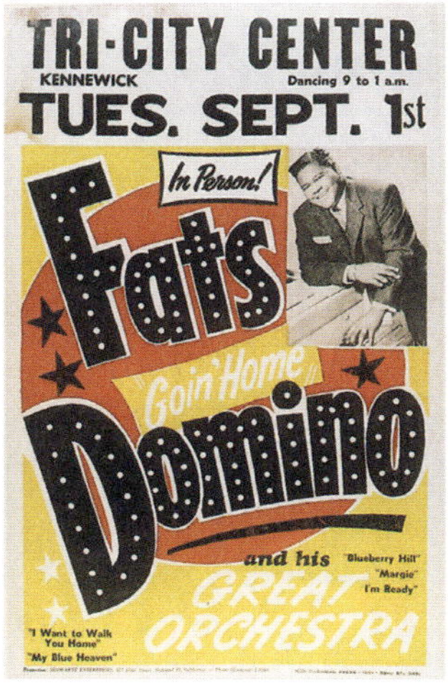

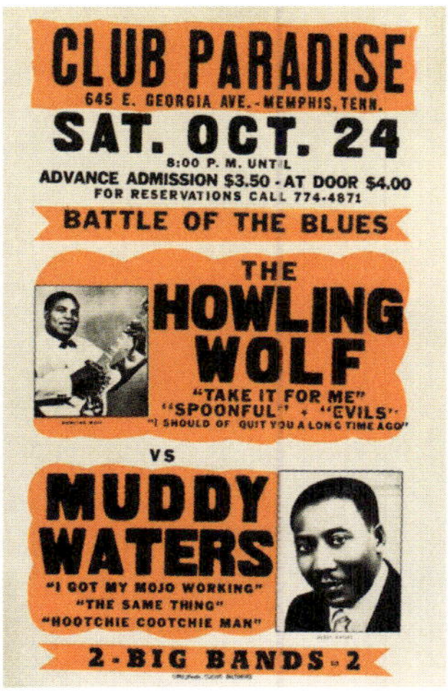

From jazz, to country & western, blues, and rock 'n' roll, early concert posters were never intended to be beautiful, or to reflect a lifestyle (although some jazz posters were more self-consciously 'arty'). Rather, they were functional, designed by the printers at the request of booking agents and promoters. In format, they drew upon similar posters that were being produced for dance events, circuses, and, in the past, minstrel shows. Their design remit

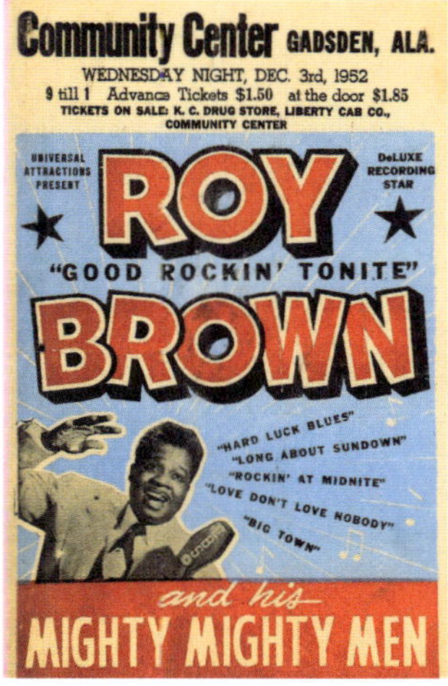

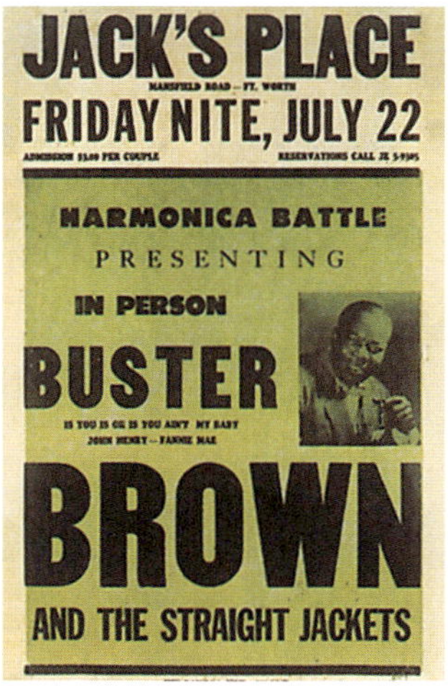

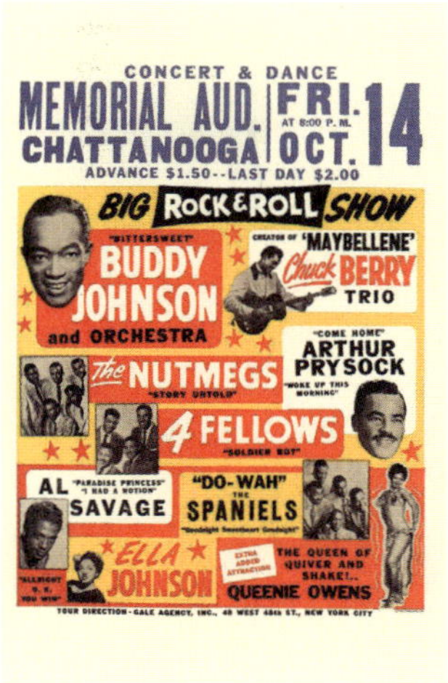

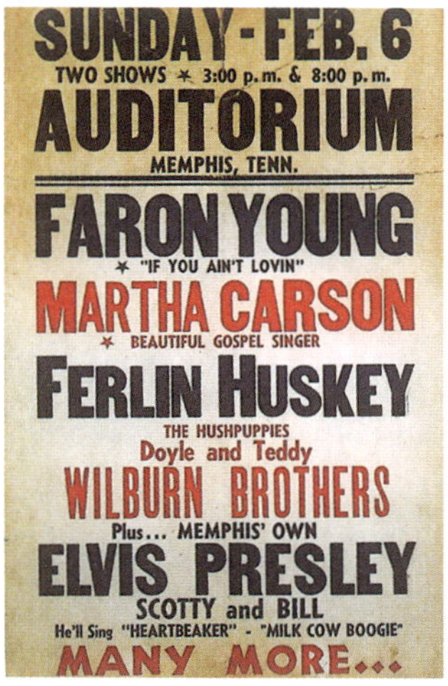

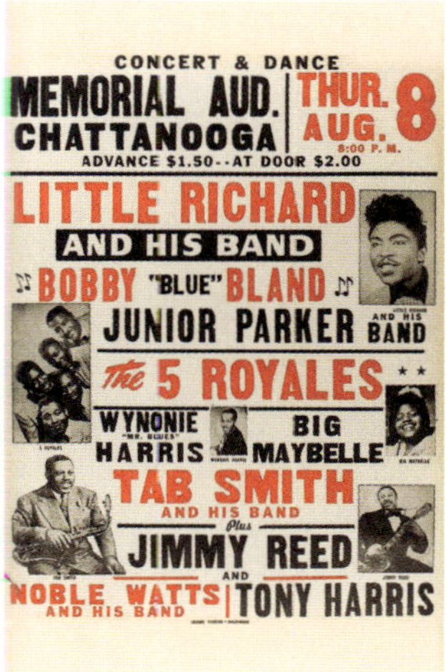

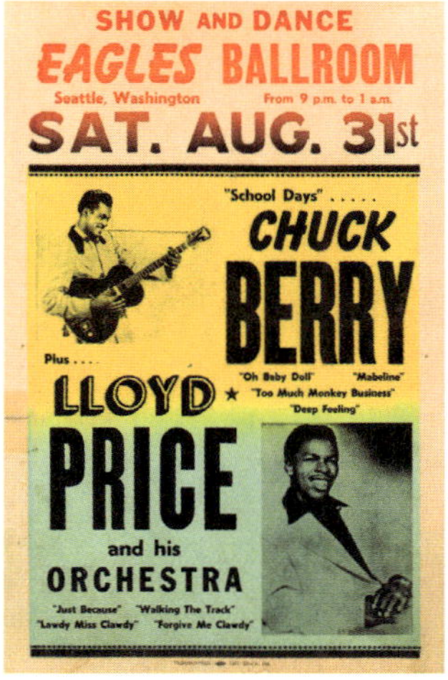

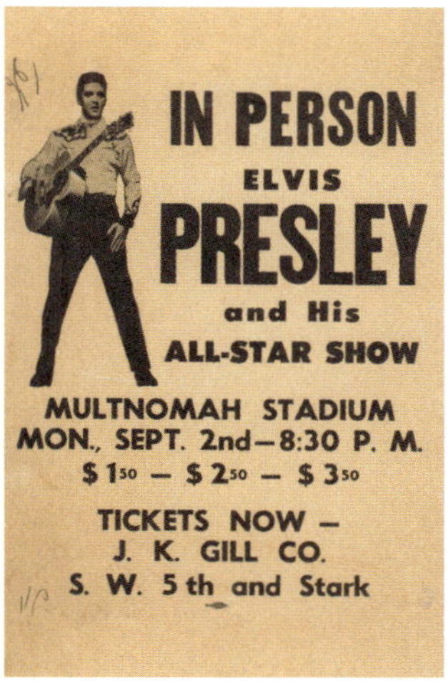

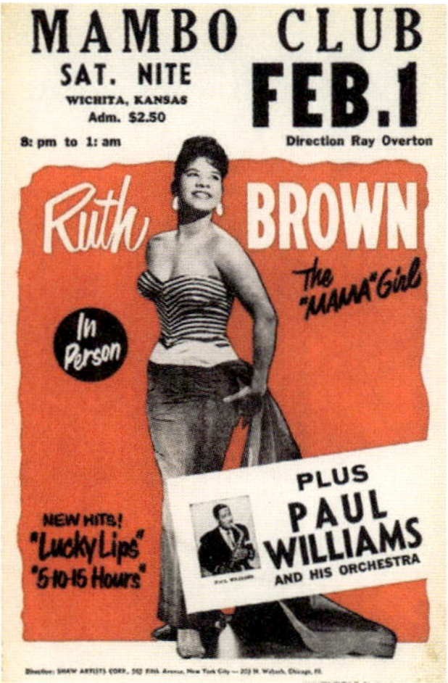

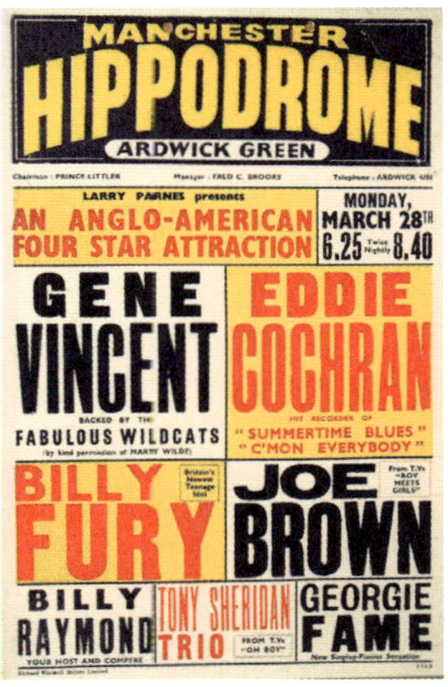

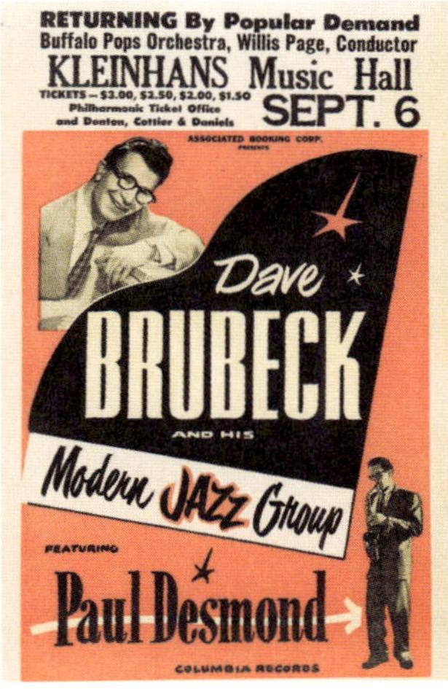

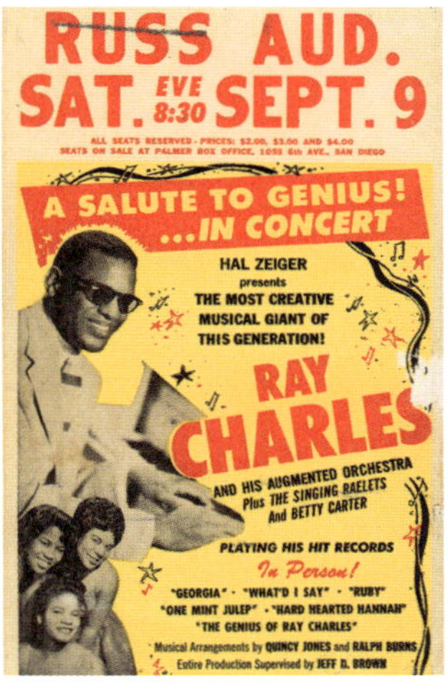

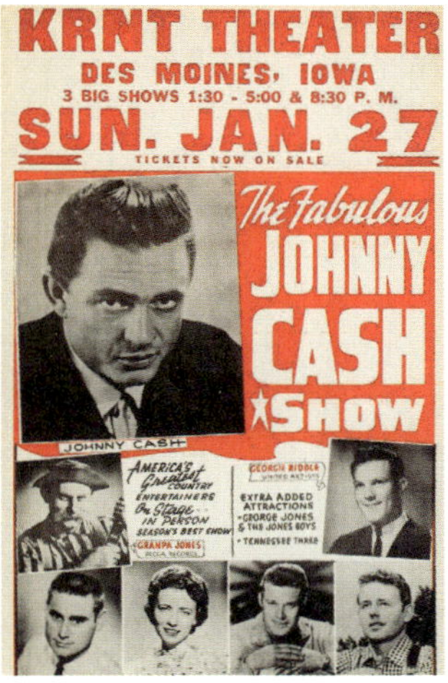

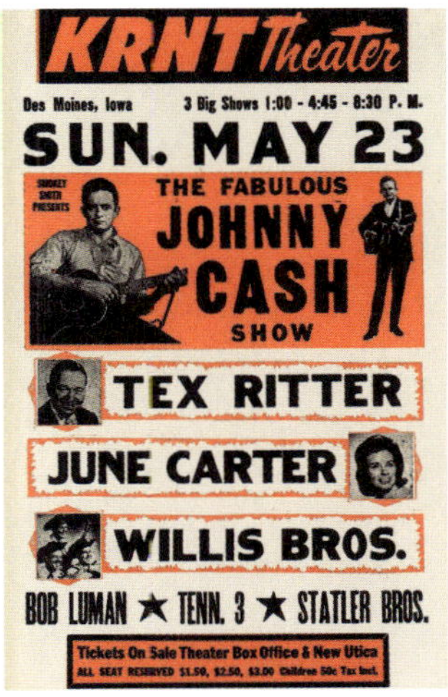

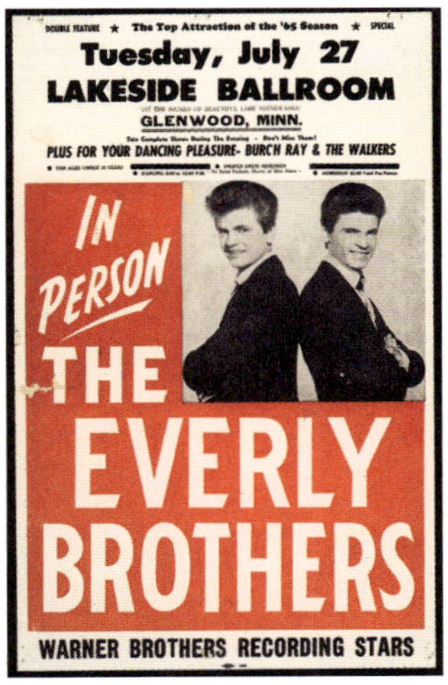

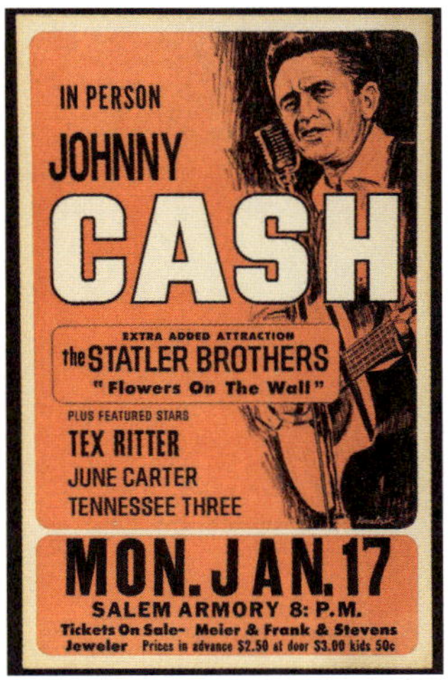

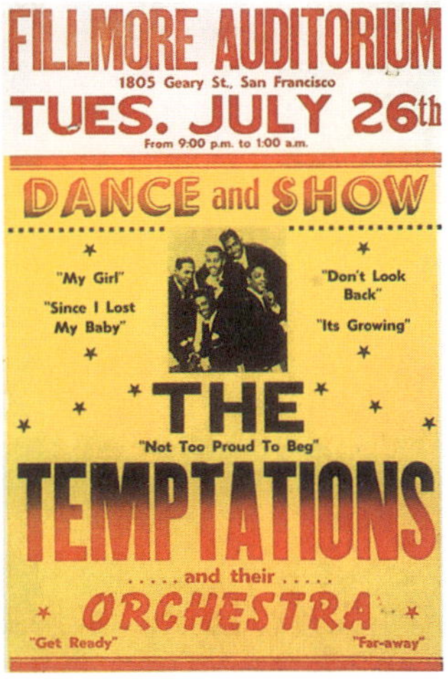

was simply to be eye-catching. To that end, these posters comprised bright, often clashing colors—note the vibrant red and yellows in the examples here, taken from the forties to the sixties—and maximized the most famous names.

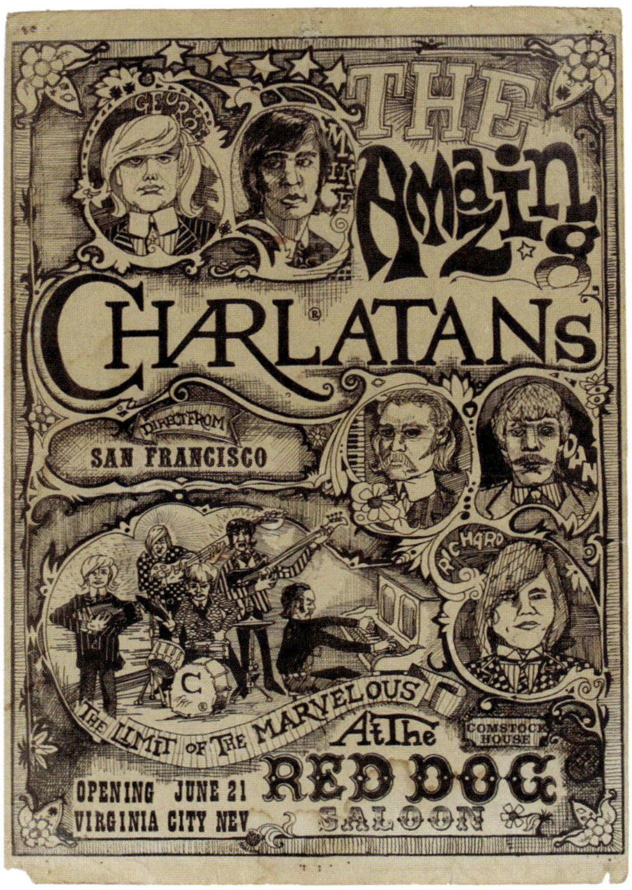

The Seed, by Charlatans George Hunter (logo) and Michael Ferguson (cartoons and borders). The hand-drawn, packed design, recalling medicine shows from the distant past, broke new ground.

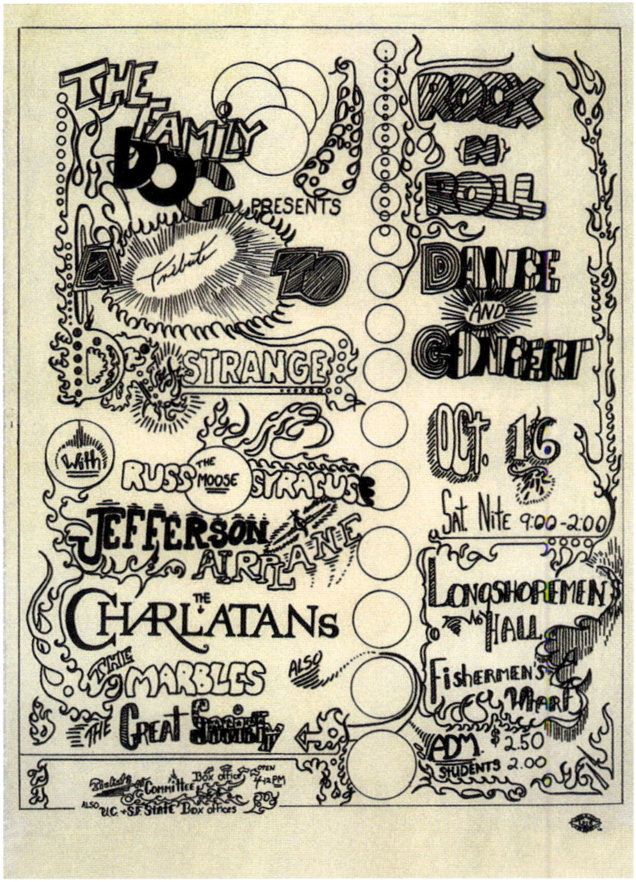

A handbill for the first Family Dog concert at Longshoremen's Hall. The Dr Strange reference was inspired by keen Marvel Comics fan (and Family Dog member) Ellen Harmon.

The silk-screen posters were not much bigger than the handbills. The first two were made either by Amy Magill, according to Luria, or by Jefferson Airplane's Marty Balin, who may have collaborated with her. The final posters (there may only have been three) were hand-finished in color. Alton Kelley: 'About four hundred or five hundred people showed up—it was *such* a revelation. Everybody was walking around with their mouths open, going, "Where did all these freaks come from? I thought my friends were the only guys around!"'[3]

Of the two other dances at Longshoremen's Hall, the first took place on October 24, 1965. Called 'The Family Dog Presents A Tribute To Sparkle Plenty,' it featured The Lovin' Spoonful—whom Luria Castell had met in Los Angeles and invited up to San Francisco—supported by The Charlatans. The second was held on November 6, 1965 and titled 'The Family Dog Presents A Tribute To Ming The Merciless'; it featured The Mothers of Invention and The Charlatans. The handbill for this event was designed by Amy Magill. She also designed some posters, but all were hand-drawn, not printed. The Family Dog had borrowed funds from Chet Helms to put on the shows, but they had still lost money. No one at the Dog wanted to stage concerts anymore, so Luria moved out and did a couple more under the Family Dog moniker at California Hall with The Charlatans, helped by Danny Rifkin and Rock Scully, the Grateful Dead's 'managers.' Luria told Paul Grushkin: 'It was after this final concert, the fifth produced under the name Family Dog, that I decided to split the scene.'[4]

The Family Dog borrowed more cash from Chet Helms, leaving him some antiques as collateral, to head off to Mexico. The idea was that he could either sell the antiques or they would pay him back on their return. It was understood that Helms would be the Family Dog caretaker and put on dances while they took a break. However, once in Mexico, they split up. Luria's daughter, Moanna, told *Shindig!* magazine, 'By the time my parents got back my brother was on the way.... They kick-started something into a different direction and then got the hell out of the way. It was never about Luria, or Ellen, or Jack or Alton and it wasn't about Chet. Her disillusionment was that the masses got "it" but let it go. The movement was co-opted into a hierarchical business venture in which coliseums are packed with assigned seating, fame supersedes interaction and, once again, you can't dance.'[5]

Soon after The Family Dog returned to San Francisco, Stanley Mouse went to visit them and met Alton Kelley for the first time. Mouse recalled: 'He was in this empty room on Pine Street sitting on a pile of trash telling funny stories to a room full of people sitting on the floor. An AM radio full of static was blasting away in the corner.... Kelley was great at telling odd funny stories. The people were listening so intensely. I wondered who was this guy. It was Kelley, he always had great ideas.'[6] It was not long before Mouse and Kelley began working together. They made their posters at 715 Ashbury, in the heart of the Haight-Ashbury scene; Janis Joplin was down the block, often calling out to friends from her window, and the Grateful Dead lived across the street.

They spent hours in the San Francisco Public Library, absorbing images in art books and catalogs—everything from photographs of American Indian braves, twenties Hollywood movie stars such as Gloria Swanson or Carole Lombard, and cartoon characters from their childhood, to stylized Art Deco and Art Nouveau compositions. The latter are the most obvious influence on all San Francisco psychedelic graphics.

The most recognizable appropriations by Mouse and Kelley were 'The Girl With Green Hair' and 'Zig-Zag Man.' In the former, Alphonse Mucha's 1897 poster for 'JOB' cigarette papers was used as the illustration for a dance at the Avalon Ballroom on the weekend of October 7 and 8, 1966, featuring Big Brother and the Holding Company and the Jim Kweskin

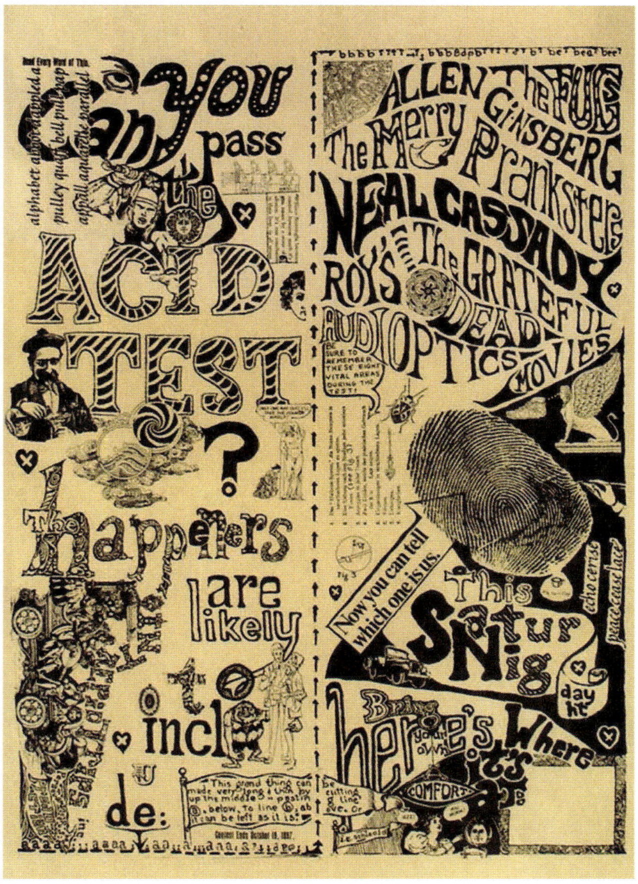

➳ Misattributed for many years to Norman Hartweg, in 2016 this handbill—the first design for Ken Kesey's Acid Tests, in 1965—was revealed to be by Paul Foster.

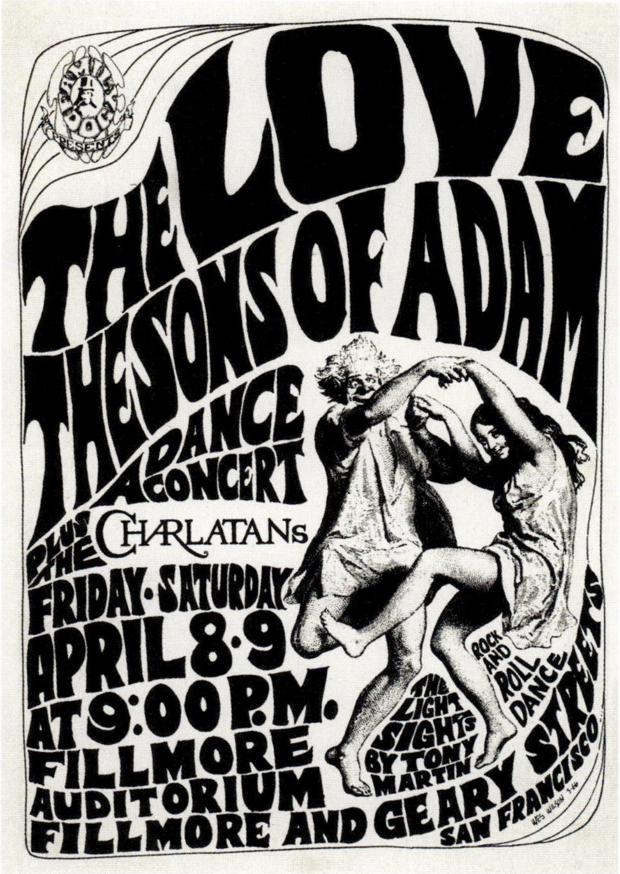

➳ A poster by Wes Wilson and Chet Helms for a 1966 show at the Fillmore Auditorium. This very early Family Dog concert took place before they moved to the Avalon Ballroom, leaving the Fillmore Auditorium to Bill Graham.

Jug Band. For 'Zig-Zag Man,' they adopted a trademark picture of a Zouave soldier belonging to the French North African Regiment, from packaging for French cigarette paper manufacturers Zig-Zag. They used him as a stylized image of a dope smoker for a Family Dog poster advertising a Big Brother and the Holding Company gig on June 24–25, 1966.

'Because the poster artwork was so trippy, crowds of people would gather around them to collectively decipher the message,' Kelley reflected. 'What a great feeling it was to work on a poster in black-and-white ink and then see it plastered all over San Francisco, transformed into blazing colors by the printing press.'[7] 'You'd see crowds standing there, grooving on them,' he told Sheila Weller.

The acid that people had been taking came mostly from the Grateful Dead's soundman and chemist, Owsley Stanley, who apparently produced around ten million doses between 1965 and 1967. (The drug was only made illegal in California on October 6, 1966.) The use of acid on the West Coast was popularized by Ken Kesey with his Acid Test parties, a series of weekly events at which LSD was available, alongside live music, improvisational theater, and movies. The first was held at his friend Ken Babb's house on November 27, 1965, in Soquel, California, about 75 miles (121 km) south of San Francisco. The next, held on December 4 was in San Jose, and featured the first performance by the Grateful Dead, who until that day had been known as The Warlocks. An Acid Test took place at Muir Beach on December 11, followed by another at Palo Alto on December 18, while another took place on Christmas Eve in Portland, Oregon. The first Test in San Francisco occurred on January 8, 1966, at the Fillmore Auditorium but the biggest, most memorable such gathering was the Trips Festival, held over a three-day period at the Longshoremen's Hall on January 21–23. It was staged by Kesey, Ramon Sender—who provided synthesizer music—and *Whole Earth Catalog* publisher Stewart Brand, who set up a tepee. This was the first time any of the three had met Bill Graham. Owsley Stanley provided the LSD, which was in the ice cream.

On Saturday, January 22, a crowd of 6,000 people arrived to dance to the Grateful Dead and Big Brother and the Holding Company, witness the first fully developed light show of the period, and drink the magic punch (also spiked with LSD). A thousand more people were turned away. A standard 'Can You Pass The Acid Test?' handbill advertised the events from the Palo Alto Test onwards, designed by Paul Foster (although it has been falsely attributed to Norman Hartweg) and with a space in the bottom right-hand corner for the name of the venue to be added in by hand. The handbills were printed in black on white, blue, or orange ('goldenrod') paper, but some were hand-colored with magic marker pens in fantastic psychedelic rainbow hues. The Trips Festival also used a black-and-white handbill designed by Wes Wilson, a Bridget Riley-style optical device in the center. This marked the start of a convention of making the handbills approximate the visual equivalent of an acid trip. From now on there would be a constant battle between the promoters—who wanted legibility—and the artists—who wanted people to have to study the artwork carefully in order to decipher the meaning.

The two main promoters of rock dances in the Bay Area were Chet Helms (with The Family Dog) and a newcomer —Bill Graham, the manager of the San Francisco Mime Troupe, a radical theater organization. Born into a Jewish family in Berlin during the rise of Nazism, Graham was transferred by his mother first to one of the city's orphanages, then sent to France and, in due course, the USA. He later earned a Bronze Star in the Korean War. Watching this new scene, says Carolyn Garcia, 'Graham decided that he could take everything he saw here and make a fortune.'[8] On February 2, he promoted a Jefferson Airplane concert at the Fillmore Auditorium, with a poster by Peter Bailey.

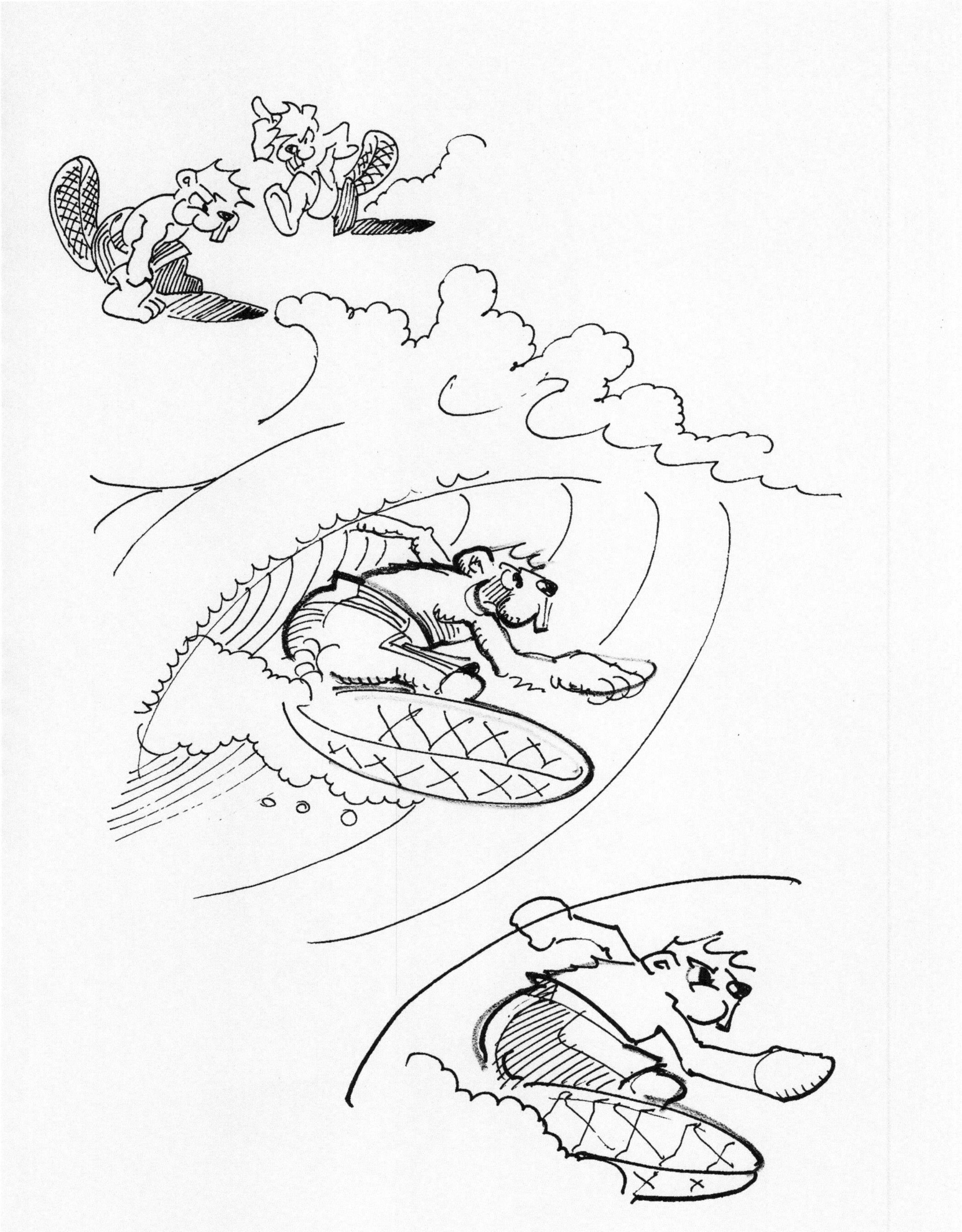

⋙→ This page: in the early sixties, surfing culture was evolving on the US West Coast. In contrast to the straighter 'boxing-style' format, something of its ethos did come through in its posters, usually in the form of cartoon surfing figures with whom surfers identified. Rick Griffin thrived during the craze, devising a much-loved character called Murphy for *Surfer* magazine. Above is a series of pen-and-ink cartoons of surfing chipmunks from his sketch book. ⋙→ Opposite: the artist drew 'The Adventures of Griffin and Stoner' for *Surfer*. Griffin draws himself with an eyepatch, a reference to a car accident that left him scarred; his signature is on a sombrero. Ron Stoner was a surf photographer.

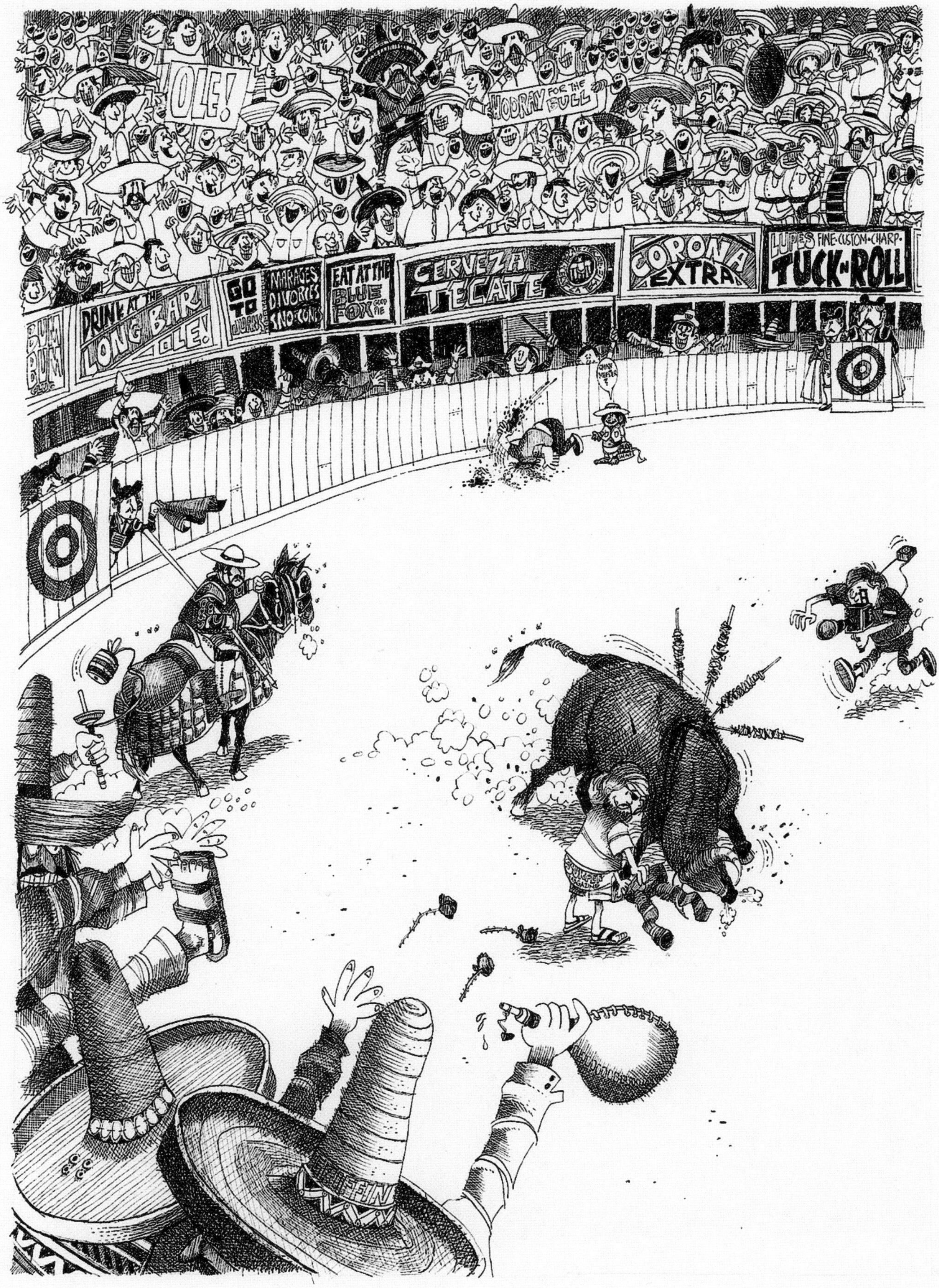
OLE!
HOORAY FOR THE BULL
DRINK AT THE LONG BAR OLE!
GO TO
MARAGES DIVORCES SNO-CONES
EAT AT THE BLUE FOX
CERVEZA TECATE
CORONA EXTRA
LUPE'S FINE-CUSTOM-CHARP-
TUCK-N-ROLL

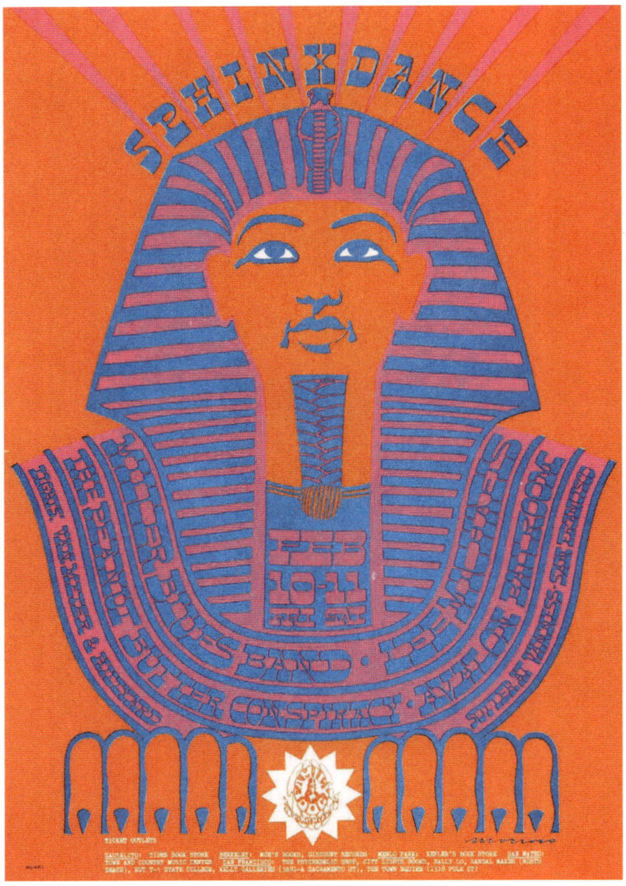

⋙→ Moscoso's Family Dog poster for a Steve Miller Blues Band gig at the Avalon Ballroom in February 1967.

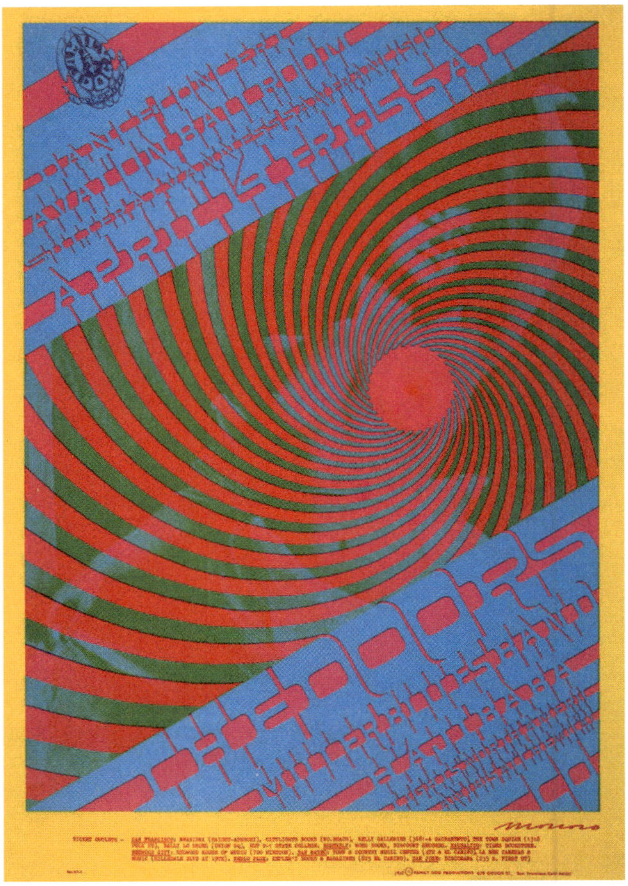

⋙→ Moscoso's poster for Moby Grape and the Jeff Beck Group at the Fillmore West in July 1968.

On February 19, 1966, Chet Helms and Family Dog Productions produced his first concert at the Fillmore Auditorium, featuring Jefferson Airplane with the band he managed, Big Brother and the Holding Company. The poster for the event was by Wes Wilson. The Summer of Love, which in San Francisco took place in 1966, was underway. With it came rivalry between the two big promoters: The Family Dog were attempting to build a new-age tribe and were not in it for the money; Bill Graham, on the other hand, saw the scene as a way of becoming a millionaire. Initially the two promoters alternated weekends at the Fillmore, resulting in inevitable conflicts over bookings. Then Helms organized the permits needed to hold events at the Avalon Ballroom, an old dancehall at 1268 Sutter Street at Van Ness. Big Brother and the Holding Company were the first group to play there, in June 1966.

Most bands had already experimented with pot, and by 1966 many of them had tried acid. Surf instrumental 'LSD-25,' the B-side of The Gamblers' debut single 'Moon Dawg' (1960), was the first record to reference the drug, although the first time acid was mentioned in a song lyric was when Ken Weaver sang about it on 'I Couldn't Get High' on The Fugs' first album in August 1965. By the end of that year, members of many bands—including the Beatles, the Rolling Stones, The Doors, The Byrds, Love, The 13th Floor Elevators, the Grateful Dead, The Great Society, and Big Brother and the Holding Company—as well as solo stars such as Donovan had not only taken it, but were alluding to it in their lyrics. Popular music was transforming itself from lightweight variety—'pop'—to a serious art form—'rock'—capable of spreading ideas and attitudes to society. The culture was becoming permeated by an LSD consciousness; it was a passage from innocence to experience. The style of the accompanying poster art was defined early on. Victor Moscoso remembers seeing the design for 'A Tribute To Ming The Merciless' (November 1965) by Kelley and Mouse. He muses, 'I thought, like Bob Dylan, "Something is happening, but you don't know what it is, do you, Mr Jones?"'[9] Moscoso did know, though. They *all* knew.

These were the days before paid radio slots or bought advertising space in the local press. Concerts were advertised by handbills and posters in coffee-shop windows, on lampposts, and on walls. With so many concerts, the need for poster designers increased and soon there was a group of artists who devoted their entire time to this task. They became known as the San Francisco Five: Stanley Mouse and Alton Kelley, Rick Griffin, Victor Moscoso, and Wes Wilson.

Wilson, responsible for many of the early Family Dog and Bill Graham posters, came across an exhibition catalog for the Viennese Secessionist painter Alfred Roller (1864–1935) and was struck by Roller's Art Deco typeface: thick, with heavy horizontals, lighter verticals, and rounded serif edges. Wilson filled every inch of his posters with the boxy typeface and sensuous illustrations. 'Wes freed us!' Moscoso enthuses. 'It clicked: *Reverse everything I have ever learned!* A poster should transmit its message quickly and simply? No! *Our* posters were taking as long as they could to be read, and were hanging up the viewer!'[10] Moscoso decided that he would gain more by running his own poster company than by signing away his rights to Family Dog and other promoters. From then on, most of his posters were for concerts at The Matrix, the small club on Fillmore where The Great Society, featuring Grace Slick, got their start. Rick Griffin's poster for four gigs featuring Jimi Hendrix, John Mayall, and Albert King on February 1–4, 1968 (issued as BG 105) has frequently been cited as the most perfect example of San Francisco psychedelic poster art, for its colors, imagery—Griffin's trademark flying eyeball—and characteristic blobby lettering.

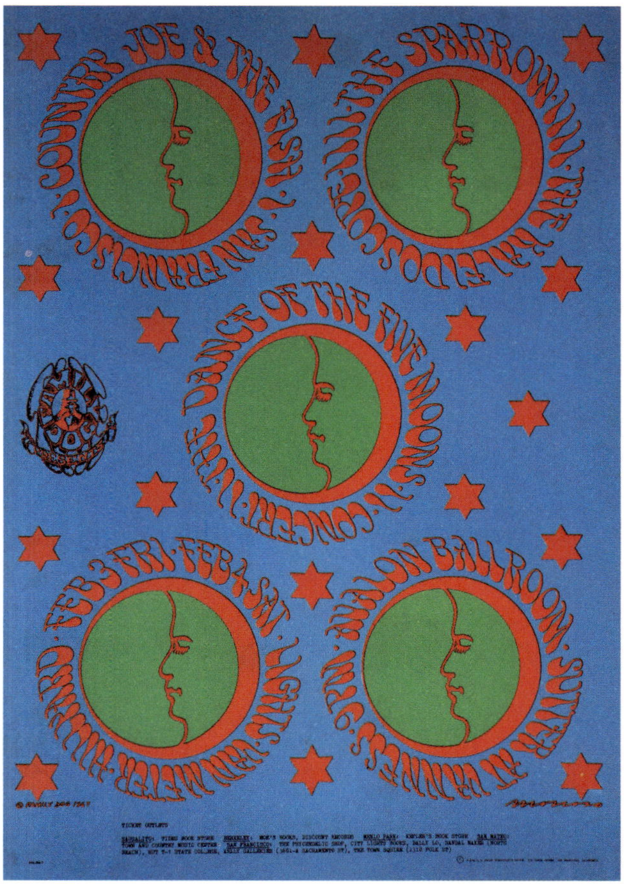

➾→ Moscoso's *Dance of the Five Moons* poster for a Country Joe and the Fish gig in early 1967.

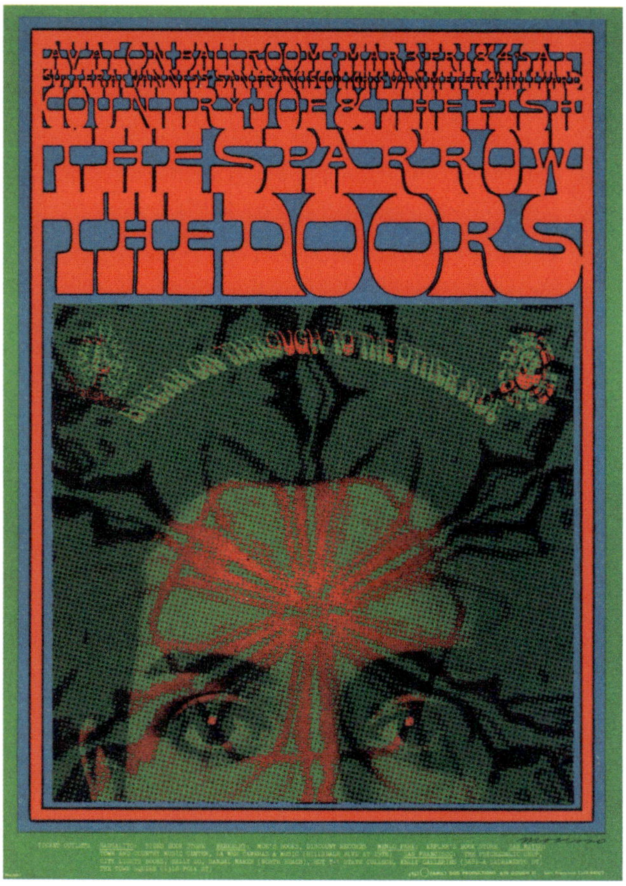

➾→ Moscoso's poster for The Doors' March 1967 appearance at the Avalon Ballroom.

A number of other significant poster artists were working in San Francisco in the late sixties, including Joe McHugh at East Totem West. Their posters were designed for people's walls, however, and not to advertise concerts and push psychedelic art to its limits. Their number included: Sätty, who also worked for East Totem West; Robert Fried; Greg Irons, who did a number of Bill Graham posters and one for Osiris in London; Bob Schnepf and Thomas Weir; Bonnie MacLean—married to Bill Graham, who thought it would be cheaper to keep it all in the family; and Nick Nickolds.

One prominent source of imagery, and an influence on the lifestyle of many artists, was Eastern mysticism. With the values of American consumer society increasingly being questioned, many people had discovered Zen Buddhism, Tibetan Buddhism, and most of all, Indian Hinduism. The Maharishi Mahesh Yogi's Transcendental Meditation practice was popularized by bands such as the Beatles and The Beach Boys, and many Indian holy men, gurus, lay teachers, and frauds moved to the States to set up study centers.

Meanwhile, almost seven thousand miles away, a similar scene was taking place. No one in Britain had heard psychedelic music from San Francisco (none had yet been released on record), nor had they seen any of the iconic posters. Like their American counterparts, British music posters used the 'boxing-style' format and, because so many venues in Britain were municipally owned and therefore notoriously conservative, they continued to do so up until the end of 1967—later, in some cases. As a way of gaining recognition on the cluttered posters, band names adopted logos: the drop-T in 'Beatles'; the raised 'o' in 'Pink Floyd'; and, perhaps best of all, the modern jazz lettering devised for The Yardbirds in 1965 by Hamish Grimes.

Unlike the USA, a very large percentage of British sixties rock 'n' roll bands went to art school and as soon as the bands were big enough to have a say in their own promotion, they added their input. The clean mod lines of The Who's record and gig posters—particularly the 1964 'Maximum R&B' poster by Brian Pike—influenced many other British bands. Then came something completely new.

Osiris Visions posters were originally produced by Joe Boyd to advertise the acts appearing at the UFO Club, the all-night dance concerts and multi-media shows held weekly from 10:30 p.m. until 6:00 a.m. at the Blarney Club, an Irish dance hall in Tottenham Court Road, London. It opened in December 1966. The first couple of posters were made by Michael English, who was joined thereafter by Nigel Waymouth; the two of them worked under the name of Hapshash and the Coloured Coat. English recalled: 'I was fascinated by the sinuous yet romantic shapes found in Mucha's posters and the work of Beardsley and [Arthur] Rackham. Meeting Nigel brought this to life; I responded to his romanticism. All the underground posters are packed with secret signs, prehistoric forms and flying saucers.'[11]

Nigel Waymouth told Mike Evans: 'Our concept was to plaster the streets of London with this very brightly colored and beautiful poster work at a time when most of the posters in the streets were rather drab and wordy [...] We were trying to push the boundaries of the visual aspect of pop. We felt that we were illustrating an ideal.'[12] When people began to tear the posters off the walls before the concerts even happened, Joe decided to reprint them and make them available for sale—initially at the club, then in a few boutiques and bookshops and eventually on a commercial basis.

The posters were silk-screened, which meant that if two screens were used, it was possible to spread a rainbow of color in each direction by feeding different colored inks into the reservoir and making one long sweep with the squeegee for each. Some posters used more than that. English and

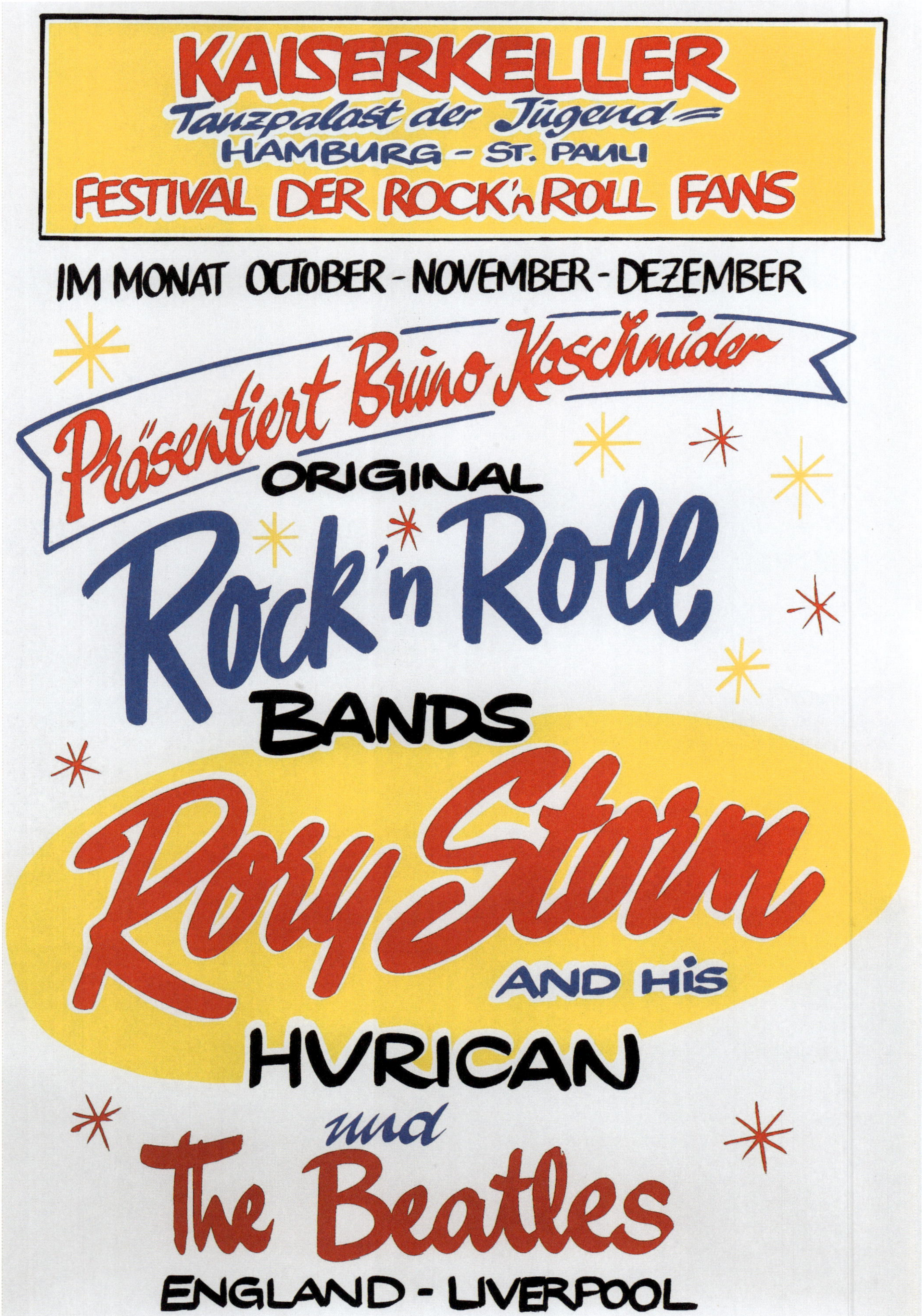

➳ Rock 'n' roll posters used the same design language around the world. ➳ This page: poster for early Beatles performances at the Kaiserkeller club in Hamburg, Germany. ➳ Opposite, top: two posters produced by Sheffield's Colin Duffield, who remains the city's most prolific poster designer. ➳ Bottom left: Brian Epstein's favorite designer, Tony Booth, used 'cartoon' or 'freestyle' lettering, popular in the early fifties. ➳ Bottom right: a hand-painted poster for the night the Beatles came to Mold, a small town in north Wales.

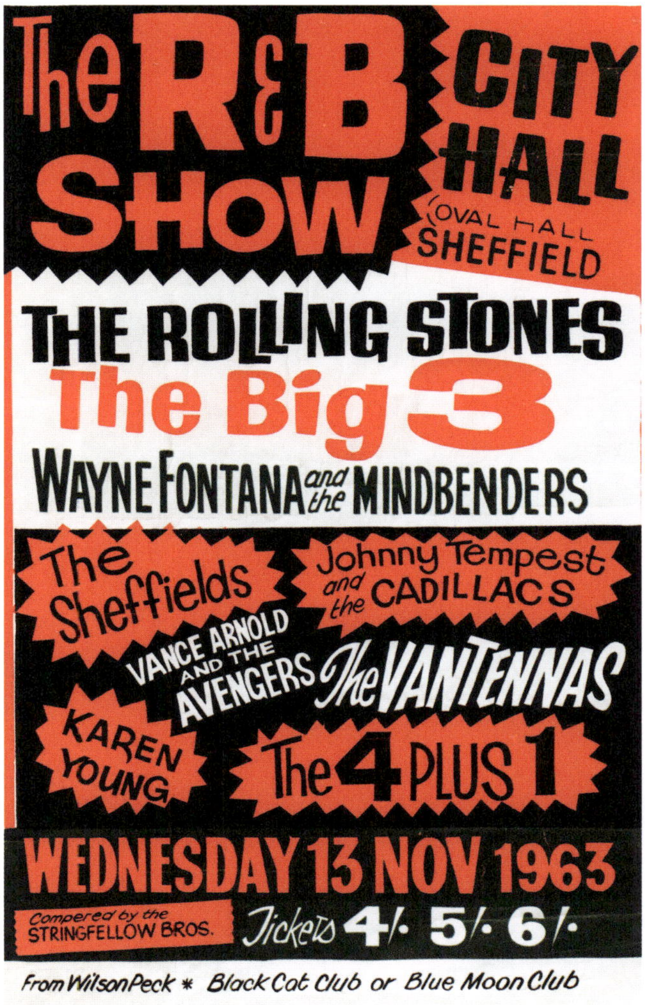
The R&B Show
CITY HALL
(OVAL HALL
SHEFFIELD
THE ROLLING STONES
The Big 3
WAYNE FONTANA and the MINDBENDERS
The Sheffields
Johnny Tempest and the CADILLACS
VANCE ARNOLD AND THE AVENGERS
The VANTENNAS
KAREN YOUNG
The 4 PLUS 1
WEDNESDAY 13 NOV 1963
Compered by the STRINGFELLOW BROS.
Tickets 4/- 5/- 6/-
From Wilson Peck * Black Cat Club or Blue Moon Club

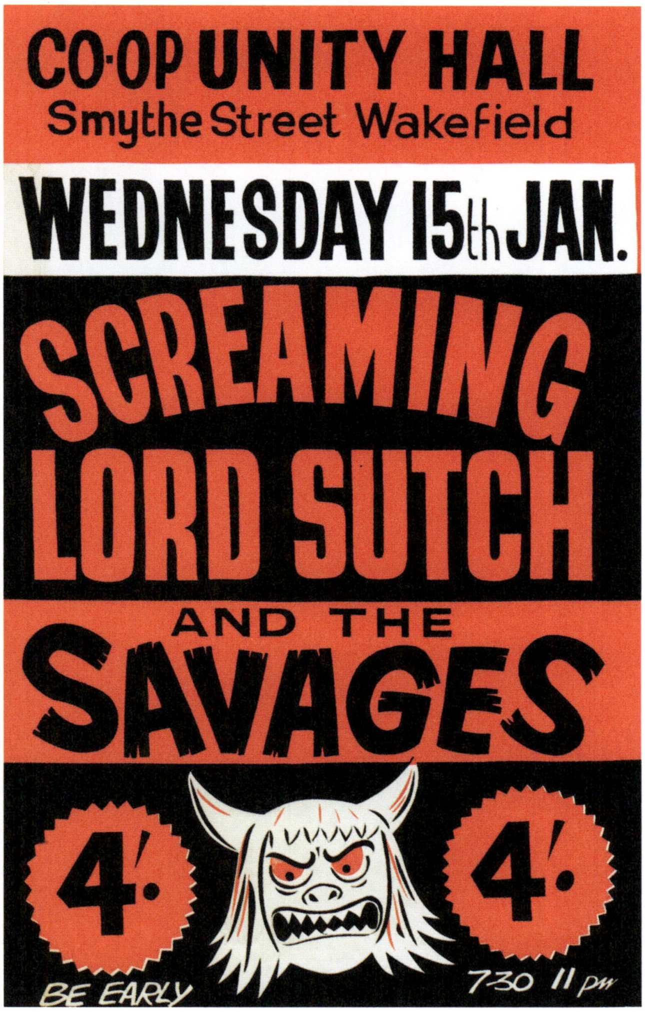
CO-OP UNITY HALL
Smythe Street Wakefield
WEDNESDAY 15th JAN.
SCREAMING LORD SUTCH
AND THE
SAVAGES
4/.
4/.
BE EARLY
7-30 11 pm

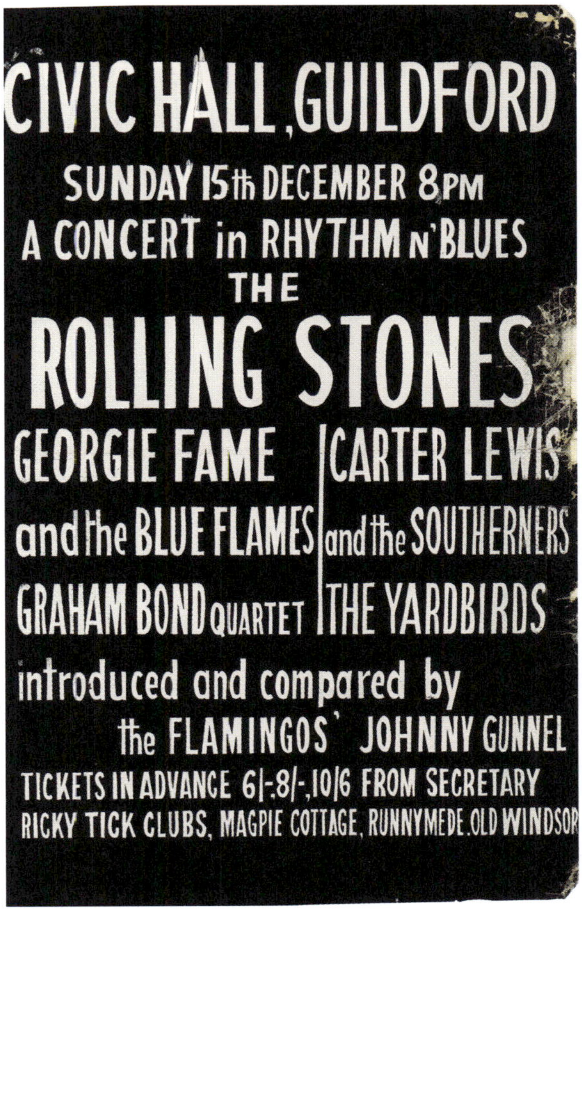
CIVIC HALL, GUILDFORD
SUNDAY 15th DECEMBER 8PM
A CONCERT in RHYTHM N' BLUES
THE
ROLLING STONES
GEORGIE FAME and the BLUE FLAMES
CARTER LEWIS and the SOUTHERNERS
GRAHAM BOND QUARTET
THE YARDBIRDS
introduced and compared by
the FLAMINGOS' JOHNNY GUNNEL
TICKETS IN ADVANCE 6/-,8/-,10/6 FROM SECRETARY
RICKY TICK CLUBS, MAGPIE COTTAGE, RUNNYMEDE, OLD WINDSOR

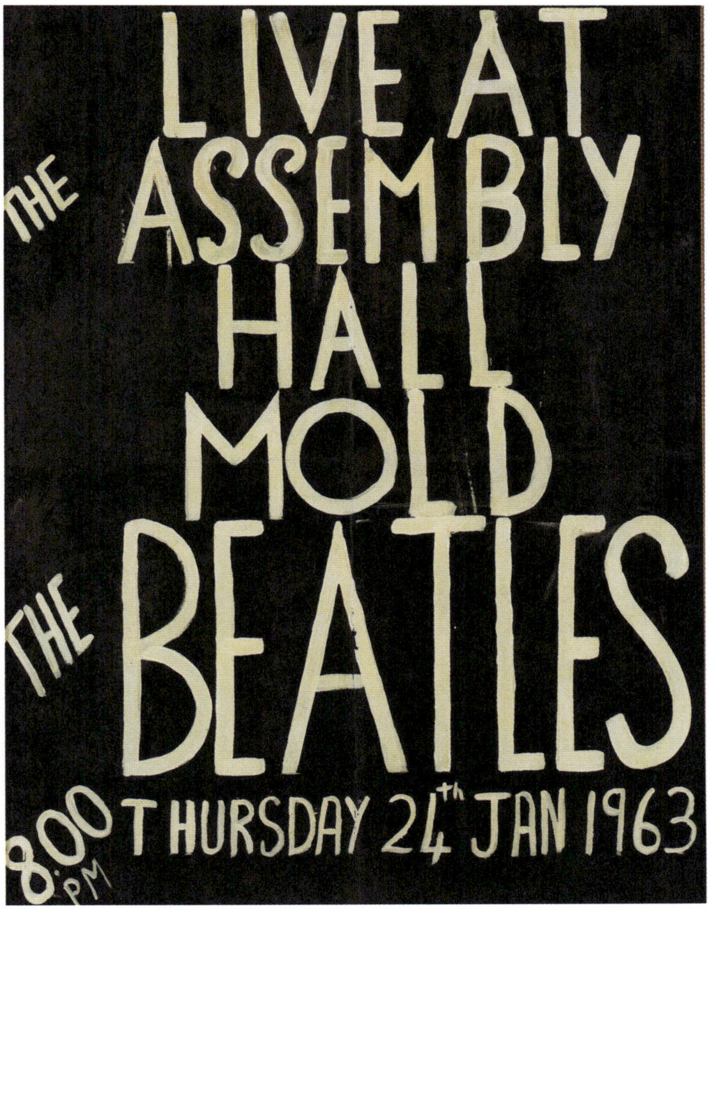
LIVE AT
THE ASSEMBLY HALL
MOLD
THE BEATLES
8.00 PM
THURSDAY 24th JAN 1963

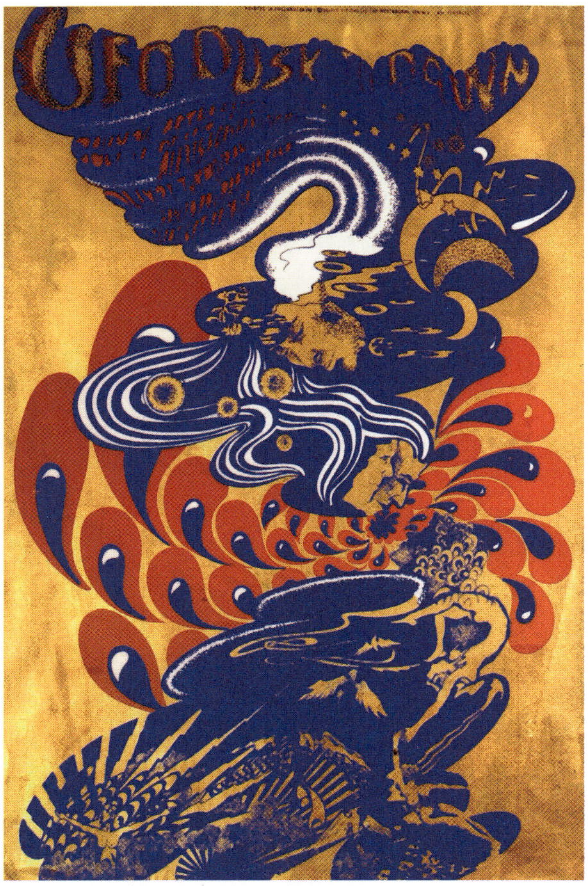

⋙→ A Mike McInnerney poster for several all-nighters in July 1967 at London's UFO Club. McInnerney had worked for the London Free School and was art director for *International Times* (*IT*) until March 1967.

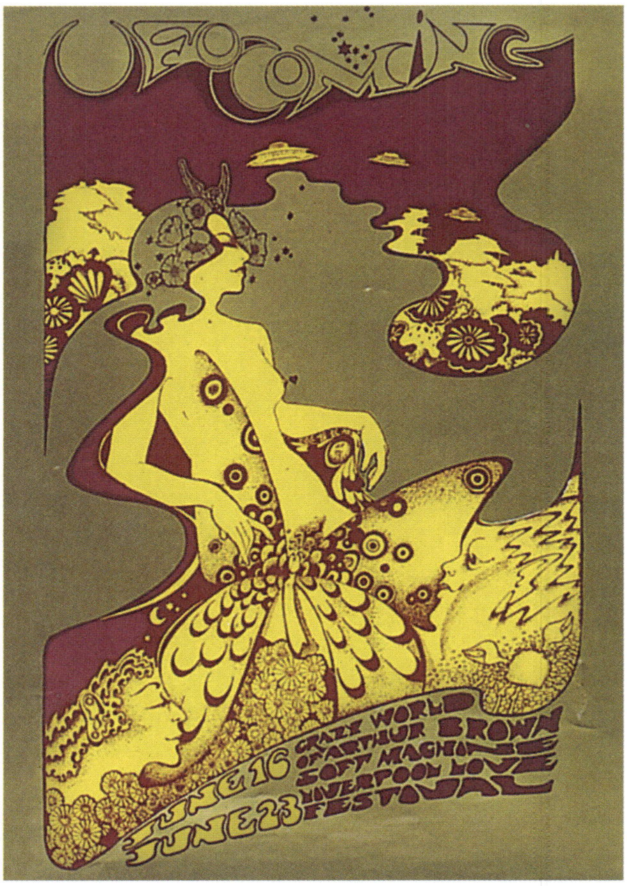

⋙→ This screen-printed Hapshash and the Coloured Coat image for forthcoming UFO attractions borrows from the sensual lines of late 19th-century illustrators such as Aubrey Beardsley.

Waymouth produced a number of the most distinctive and interesting posters this way, experimenting with Day-Glo and silver and gold inks, pushing the technique to its limit. When it was decided to manufacture copies for sale, the same method was used. It was very labor intensive; indeed, when a costing was finally done, the designers realized that the posters cost more to make than they were selling for. The price was upped from five shillings to seven shillings and sixpence. Osiris Visions fairly quickly changed from silk-screen printing to off-set lithography, bringing the cost down considerably.

English and Waymouth were central figures of the English underground scene and created most of the posters for the UFO Club. One of the functions of UFO was to employ the staff of *International Times* (*IT*), the local underground paper. *IT* often found itself short of funds. Contributors were never paid, but the printers had to be; sometimes there was not enough left to pay the staff. However, with the UFO Club running every week, staff were at least guaranteed enough to live on. The UFO Club had three house bands: Pink Floyd, Soft Machine, and The Crazy World of Arthur Brown. It only ran for six months, starting just before Christmas 1966, but was to have a long-lasting impact on the London club scene. English and Waymouth's work was so successful that Brian Epstein commissioned them to do four posters to advertise his Saville Theatre, using the same template (see p. 105).

In January 1967, a second underground publication appeared in London: *Oz*, run by recently arrived Australians Richard Neville and Martin Sharp, who had taken six months to reach Britain by the land route. Neville had previously published *Oz* in Sydney and continued the tradition upon reaching London. Sharp was the design director and quickly succumbed to the hedonistic psychedelic lifestyle offered by the King's Road in Chelsea. His designs became more and more mind-bending until he produced one entire issue of *Oz* in collage, with no texts or photographs except his own convoluted and remarkable artwork. His first posters were to announce issues of *Oz*. As with Osiris, Sharp found that they were in demand as decorative objects in their own right. Big O Posters, run by Peter Ledeboer, was essentially a poster-manufacturing spin-off of *Oz* magazine and in the early days strongly reflected its editorial policy. Sharp was a painter and his twin obsessions with Vincent van Gogh and Max Ernst are evident in his choice of subject matter. He later simplified his vision and experimented with back-lit posters and unusual printing methods. He was best known for his sleeves for two of Cream's albums; for the band's *Wheels of Fire* (1968), he used silver-coated paper, one of his signature techniques.

The fourth member of this London psychedelic school was Mike McInnerney, who also sometimes worked on the design team at *IT*. He is probably best known for his fold-out album sleeve for The Who's rock opera *Tommy*.

Associated with the group was Marijke Koger, whose *Love Dylan* was probably the first British psychedelic poster. She was a member of the Dutch graphic team The Fool, based in London, whose work ranged from painting pianos and fireplaces for the Beatles to album sleeves and dress design. Other London poster-makers included Adrian George, David Vaughan (who also worked as part of Binder, Edwards and Vaughan), Ivan Tyrrell, and Peter Broxton, but they all concentrated on posters intended for the walls of living rooms or teenage bedrooms, usually with no text. Broxton is best known for the celebrated *Ptooff!* album sleeve for The Deviants. In Brighton, the American poet Bill Butler published Unicorn Posters from his Unicorn Bookshop as an answer to Osiris and Big O, although his were less commercially successful. Again, they were designed entirely to be hung at home, not to advertise concerts—two posters for Breezes dress shop being the commercial exceptions.

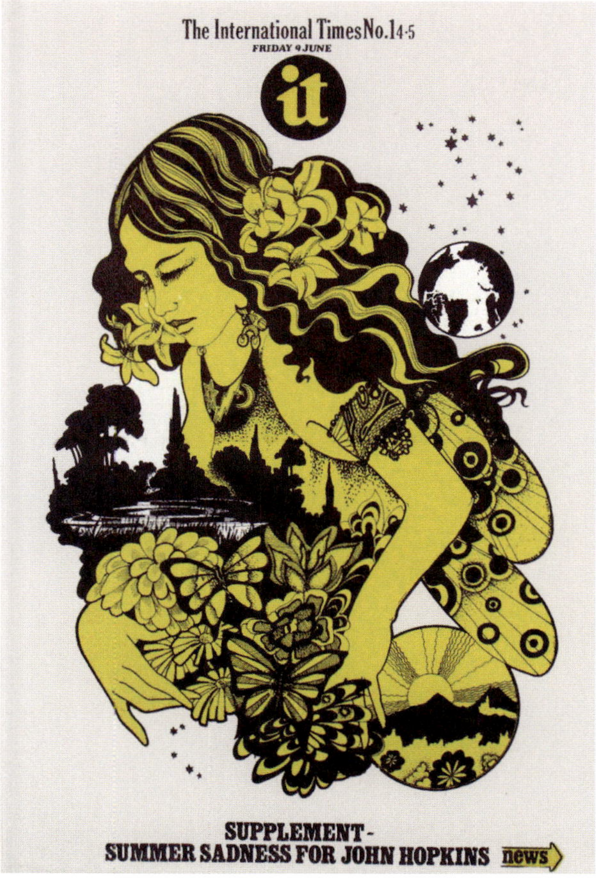

Hapshash and the Coloured Coat favored the butterflies and flowers redolent of the times for a 1967 *IT* supplement. Its news was less rosy: *IT* co-founder John Hopkins had been jailed for marijuana possession.

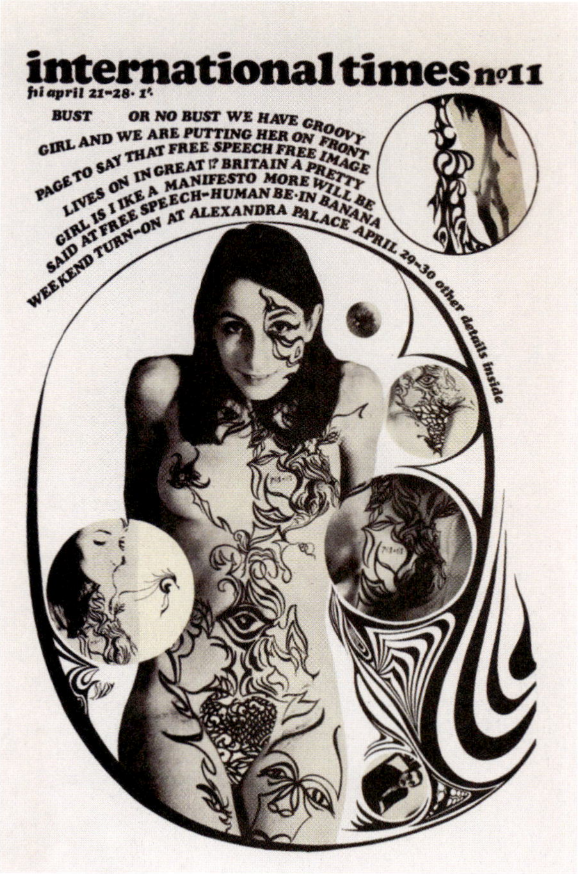

The front cover, designed by McInnerney, of *IT* issue #11, April 21–28, 1967—the first full issue released after *IT* was raided by the police in April 1967. It features Susie Gawler-Wright wearing only psychedelic body paint.

Having outgrown the Blarney Club, the UFO Club moved to the Roundhouse in Camden. It quickly became known as a venue both for one-off gigs and, following on from UFO, as the weekly venue for Middle Earth, which had moved there from 43 King Street in Covent Garden. Middle Earth was promoted by Jeff Dexter and featured John Peel as DJ until mid-1968. They produced only one psychedelic poster—by Hapshash—relying on adverts in the underground press to inform people who was playing. With weekly music papers—including *New Musical Express* and *Melody Maker*—to inform music fans, concert posters were not as necessary in London as they were in the USA, which had no weeklies.

There appears to have been little in the way of analysis of the poster art of the sixties except possibly in London, where George Melly, jazz singer and expert in Surrealism, was critical of the appropriation of images. He observed, 'When it comes to imagery there is no attempt to conceal a magpie approach to any artist past or present who seems to strike the right psychedelic note.'[13]

Egged on by Scott McKenzie's anthem 'San Francisco (Be Sure To Wear Flowers In Your Hair),' which remained at No.4 in the *Billboard* Hot 100 for four weeks in July 1967, an estimated 75,000 young people (according to police figures) from across the States descended upon the city that summer. The original counter-culture community there—numbering no more than a few thousand people—had largely dropped out from consumer society and shared beliefs in free love, expanding the consciousness with the aid of drugs (notably LSD), communal living, and non-violent opposition to war (particularly the conflict in Vietnam). Now they braced themselves for the onslaught and found their ideals of communal living pushed to the limit.

When school finished that summer, hordes of young people began to arrive. They were accompanied by scores of drug dealers, hippie clothing designers, sexual predators, reporters, and religious fanatics, all of whom descended on Haight-Ashbury, a scruffy quarter of San Francisco. One bus company even organized coach tours so that gawping Midwesterners could see the hippies. American capitalism, vigorous as ever, responded to this new market as one would expect. Dozens of psychedelic poster publishers sprang up to cash in on the phenomenon, producing wall posters: one company, San Francisco's Funky Features ('We're Really Funky!'), did a set of posters of the signs of the zodiac; Brown and Company in New York produced tarot cards as posters, and with the advent of the first head shops, companies made posters that glowed in the dark with ultraviolet light, or were printed on velvet. Berkeley Bonaparte published some of Rick Griffin's posters (he also worked for Funky Features, designing a blacklight poster, *Ascent to Olympus*, in 1970), but most of the cash-ins were amateurish or simply bad art.

New ways were found to make money out of this new community, usually by producing identification product that young people could take home and use to define their beliefs: posters, badges, T-shirts, and drug paraphernalia. The latter was sold exclusively through head shops. The first was the Psychedelic Shop on Haight Street, opened by Ron and Jay Thelin on January 3, 1966. It was followed in May 1966 by Jeff Glick's Head Shop on East Ninth Street in New York, and then by dozens of others, including the wonderfully named Psychedelicatessen in New York, at the corner of Avenue A and Tompkins Square in the Lower East Side, and Ye Olde Psychedelic Shoppe on Sunset Strip in Hollywood. They sold roach clips, hash pipes, rolling papers, rolling machines, posters, T-shirts—in fact, everything for the lifestyle except the drugs themselves.

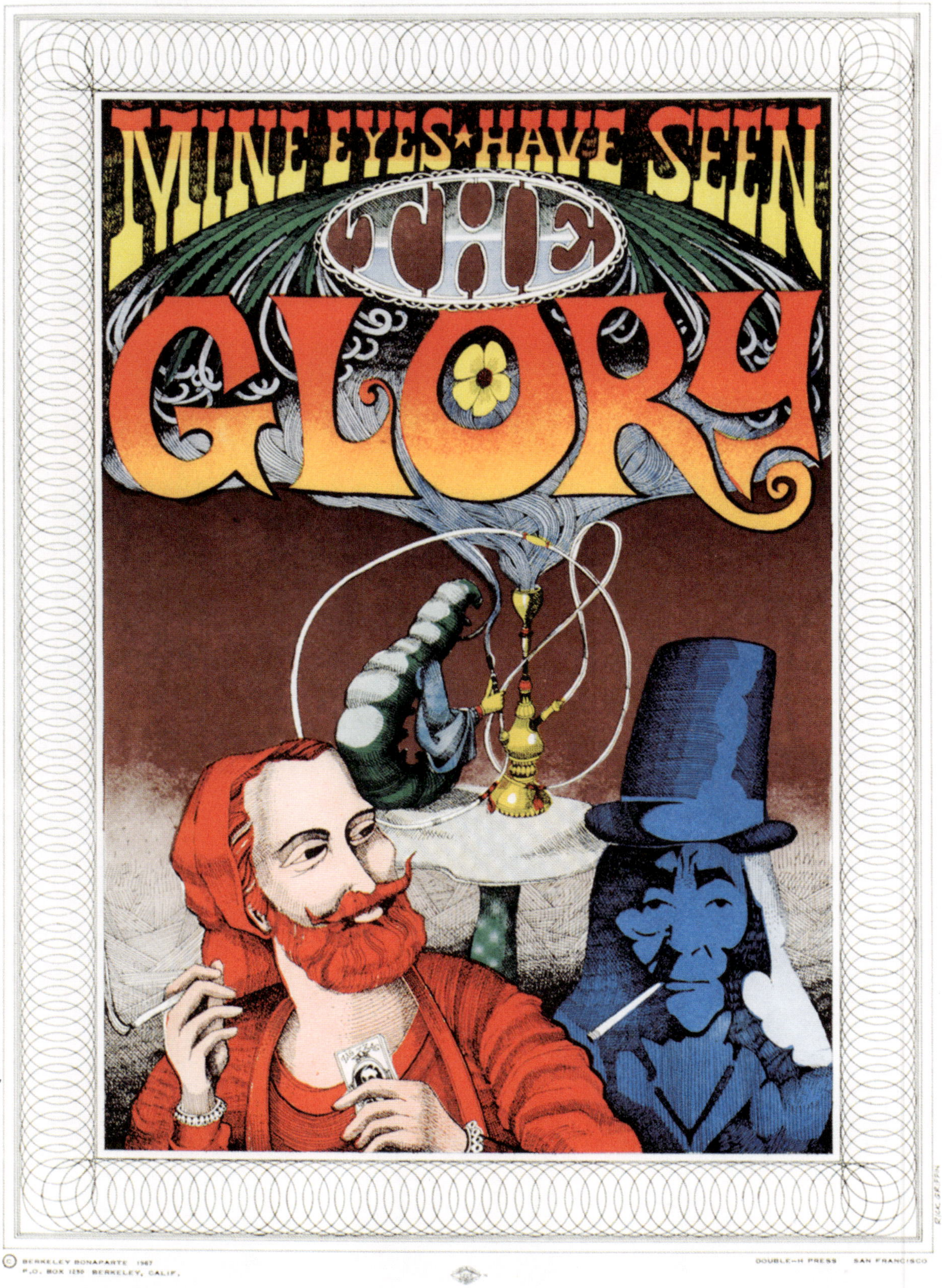

→ This page: a hookah-smoking caterpillar from *Alice in Wonderland* (and Jefferson Airplane's 'White Rabbit') features in this 1967 head-shop poster by Rick Griffin.

→ Opposite: 'In God We Trust,' a 1967 Rick Griffin head-shop poster for Berkeley Bonaparte, employs the 'Eye of Providence' motif from the reverse of the US dollar bill.

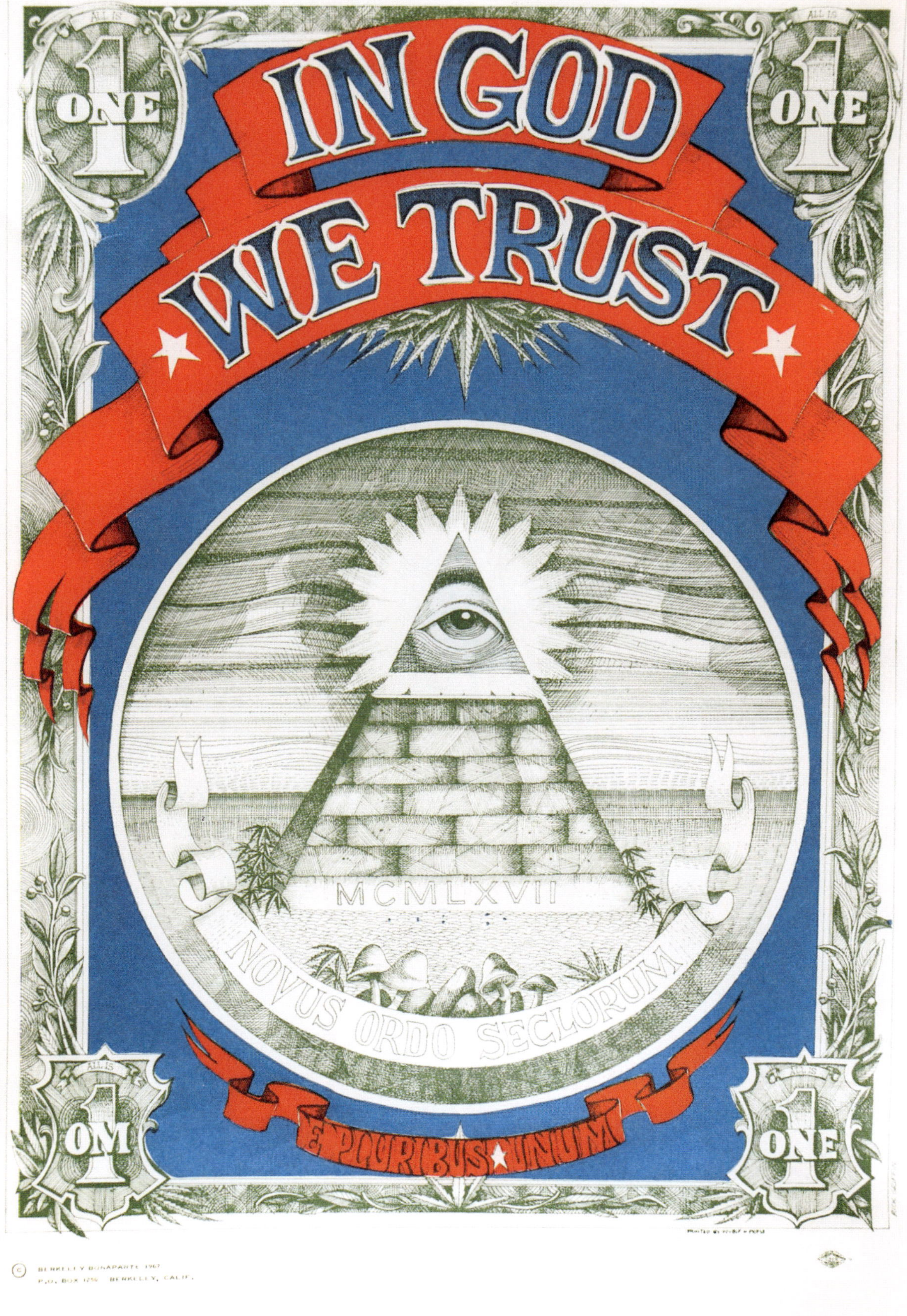
IN GOD
WE TRUST
ONE
ONE
OM
ONE
MCMLXVII
NOVUS ORDO SECLORUM
E PLURIBUS UNUM
© BERKELEY BONAPARTE 1967
BERKELEY, CALIF.

INTRO

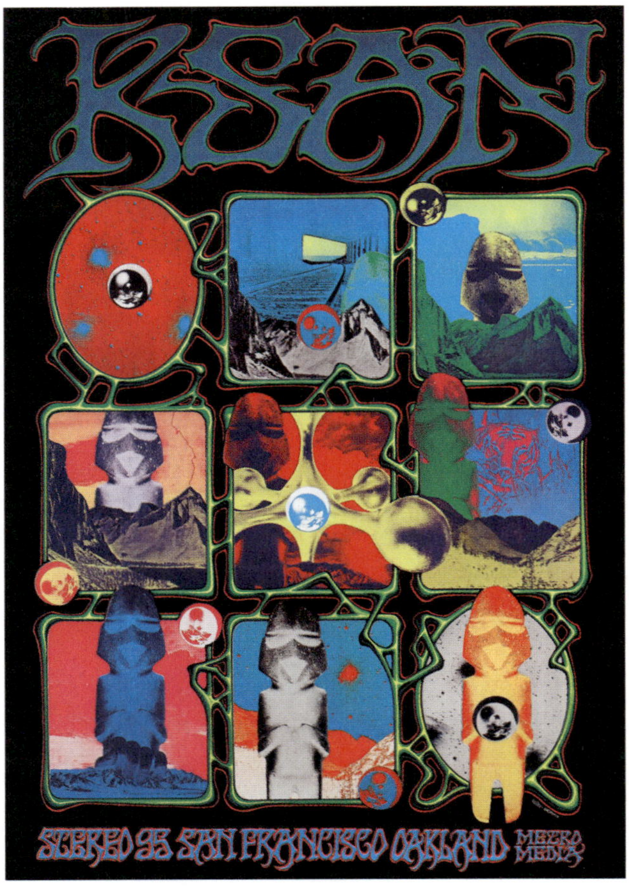

This poster by Rick Griffin and Alton Kelley, advertising KSAN radio station in the San Francisco Bay Area, suggests the shape-shifting fluidity of a light show.

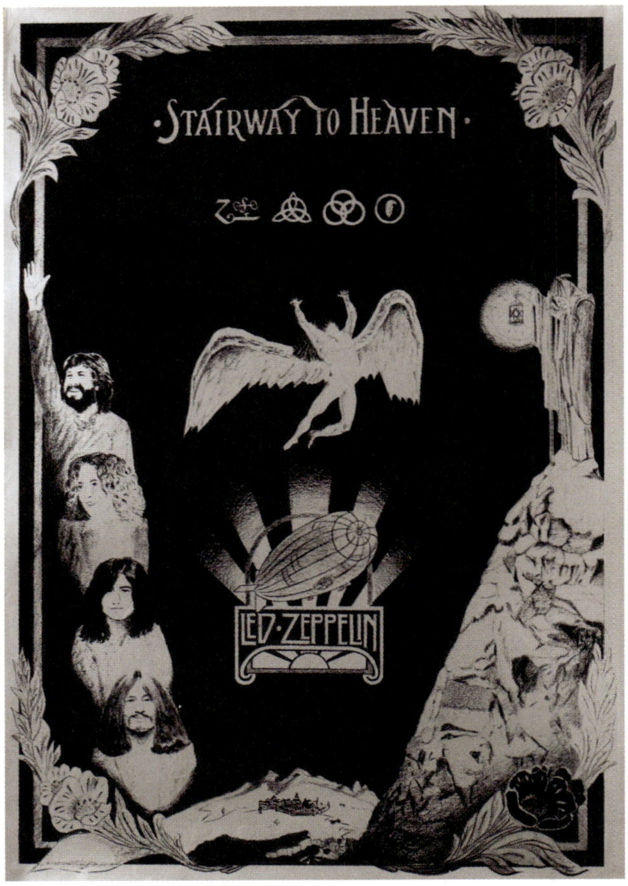

Poster for Led Zeppelin's 'Stairway to Heaven' (1971). The artwork relates to the band members, the song, and the group's fourth album.

Until then, few posters were sold as wall decorations, and these were usually Spanish bullfight scenes or art gallery images. Though posters were still made for music events, most were now for household display: posters of the peace symbol, posters referencing drugs, underground cartoon characters—particularly by Robert Crumb or Gilbert Shelton—and pictures of various heroes. The celebrity poster market was led by Personality Posters from New York, who produced scores of black-and-white images featuring a wide range of subjects, from John Lennon, Marlon Brando, and Andy Warhol to Black Power activists and American Indians.

A whole new market emerged in the form of pins (badges) carrying underground slogans. These were mostly produced in New York, where there was an entire shop on Eighth Street devoted to them. The illustrated T-shirt also comes from this period. One of the first was Crumb's 'Keep On Truckin',' but there were several dozen available by the summer of 1967 as other manufacturers caught on.

The counter-culture movement—whose followers were known as hippies in San Francisco, freaks in Los Angeles, and the underground in New York and London—can be said to have ended on October 6, 1967, when those original hippies who had not already fled Haight-Ashbury held a 'Death of Hippie' mock funeral procession to signal the end of the Summer of Love. It was organized by radical collective the Diggers to request the media to stop covering the Haight and to end the rabid commercialization of the hippie lifestyle and appropriation of their experiment in social and alternative living. The 'mourners' burned counter-culture newspapers, posters, and hippie apparel, then carried a coffin down Haight Street and conducted a 'kneel-in' at the corner of Haight and Ashbury.

Bill Graham continued at the Fillmore Auditorium until July 1968, when he switched to the Carousel Ballroom and renamed it The Fillmore West. Graham was a hard-nosed businessman and his manipulations often caused conflict between himself and Hells Angels, Diggers, or other Haight-Ashbury groups who felt that he should contribute more to the community. On the other hand, the bands all made good money playing at his venues (which later included the Fillmore East in New York) and were prepared to tolerate his screaming and tantrums because he was honest and provided good facilities. Groups such as Jefferson Airplane, the Grateful Dead, Quicksilver Messenger Service, and Big Brother and the Holding Company played an enormous number of free concerts and benefit concerts for the 'community' but needed to make some money to sustain themselves. In many ways, apart from the Diggers and drug dealers (who also made contributions to causes such as the free health clinics), they were the only source of money in the community. Graham went on to present most of the defining American acts of the sixties and early seventies.

The market for reprinted concert posters continued to expand. Bill Graham added new artist names to his roster, such as Randy Tuten, who designed thirty-four posters for him, beginning in January 1969 (the last was for a concert at MGM Grand in Las Vegas in August 1995). Tuten had already done one design for a Family Dog concert at Winterland on October 31, 1968. David Singer did even more, producing fifty for Graham between January 1969 and September 1970. Both artists drew heavily upon the work of the San Francisco Five. The final poster for Graham was BG 289, for the Rolling Stones at Winterland in 1972. The Family Dog retired from concert posters earlier, producing 147 posters from San Francisco (and a few from Denver) ending with a Quicksilver Messenger Service poster for November 28, 1968.

The psychedelic poster was a design solution to a specific problem. Los Angeles was too big for posters,

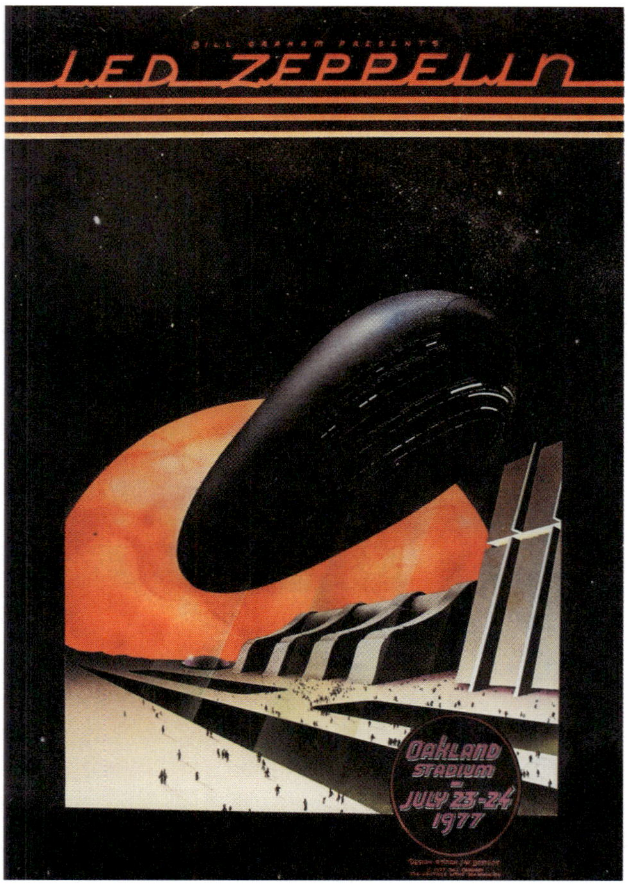

⋙→ A 1977 poster for Bill Graham Presents, by Randy Tuten and Bill Bostedt, touts Led Zeppelin's appearance at Oakland Stadium.

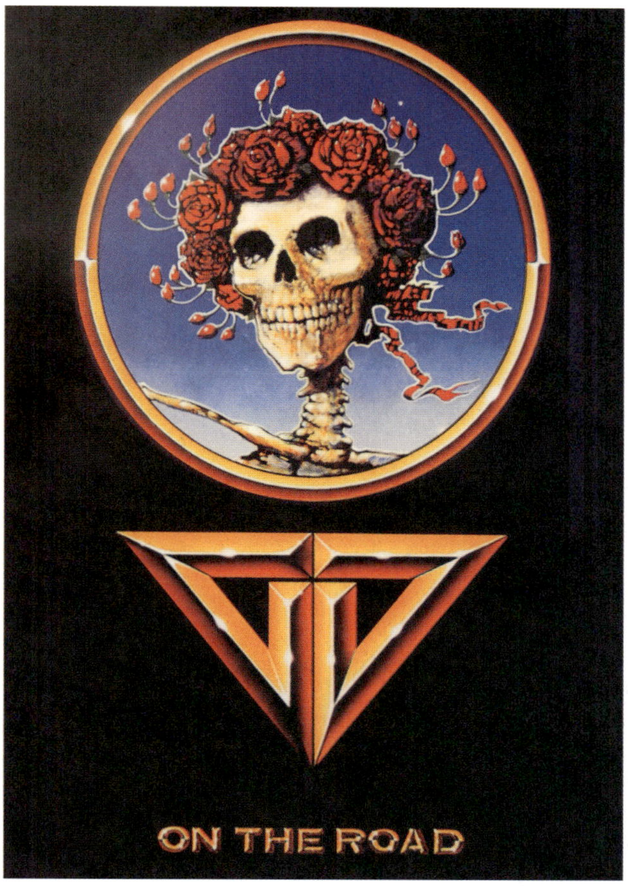

⋙→ The iconic 'Skull and Roses' emblem graces this Stanley Mouse and Alton Kelley poster for a 1978 Grateful Dead tour.

other than the giant billboards on the boulevards and beside the freeways. There were a few designers, like John Van Hamersveld, but he quickly moved on to album sleeves, murals, and photography. New York simply had nowhere to put full-sized posters, so shop flyers and radio advertising were used instead. NY artists Peter Max and Milton Glaser both did concert poster work, but quickly turned to more commercial projects: Peter Max famously designed the cover of the New York Yellow Pages. In London, Hipgnosis became leading album sleeve designers, known for their work with Pink Floyd. In Austin, Texas, the Vulcan Gas Company venue produced some outstanding posters —on a par with the San Francisco group—by artists such as Jim Franklin, and the Armadillo World Headquarters continued the tradition when it opened in 1970. One other remarkable psychedelic artist was Gary Grimshaw, who was central to the counter-cultural scene in Detroit, producing concert posters and album sleeves, and working closely with the MC5, John Sinclair, the Detroit Artists Workshop, Translove, and the underground press. He had lived briefly in the Haight and knew, and was strongly influenced by, Mouse, Griffin, and Moscoso.

As poster work dried up, or became a closed shop, many of the original poster artists moved on to album sleeves and underground comix, which provided more scope for their imagination and, if the title was successful, more money. The big four of the underground comix world were Robert Crumb, Gilbert Shelton, Spain Rodriguez, and S. Clay Wilson, who worked collectively for *Zap Comix* and individually for *Yellow Dog* and underground newspapers such as the *East Village Other*. By 1974, there were over 400 underground comix titles on the market—which collapsed shortly afterwards.

As Helms and Graham turned to younger, cheaper artists, the San Francisco Five—the original creators of psychedelic poster art—moved on to other areas. In 1968, Stanley Mouse settled in Toronto to run a waterbed company, but in 1971 he returned to California to collaborate with Alton Kelley on album sleeves and to work with the Grateful Dead, turning their original 1966 skeleton-with-roses poster into a brand image for the group. He worked with Kelley until 1980 before focusing on fine art and other media. In his later years, Kelley continued to paint, concentrating on his first love of hot rods and custom cars. He died in 2008 after a lengthy illness.

Rick Griffin moved on from posters to underground comix, becoming a regular contributor to publications including *Zap Comix* and *Yellow Dog*. In November 1970, he became a born-again Christian and from then on focused on religious art. He died in a motorcycle accident in 1991. Victor Moscoso also moved into underground comix, working for *Zap Comix*, but continued to design posters, album sleeves and, later, T-shirts, billboards, and animation for commercials.

After an acrimonious break with Bill Graham, Wes Wilson went on to produce posters for Chet Helms and others until 1976, when he moved to a cattle ranch in the Missouri Ozarks. Since 1989, he has curated, and been featured in, many gallery shows but now devotes his time to fine art painting.

A new generation of artists followed, prominent among them stage designer Dennis Larkins, who painted the monumental backdrops for Bill Graham's Day on the Green concerts. As a commercial designer, Larkins has worked with everyone from Sega GameWorks to Walt Disney. In a long series of concert posters for the Grateful Dead, he placed their skeleton (minus the flowers) in imaginative situations, bringing the sixties' visual sensibility into the mainstream.

The psychedelic poster art of the sixties is now a part of the canon, used and referred to in the same way that the original sixties artists looked back to Mucha and Toulouse-Lautrec. It is a part of graphic history.

1

HAIGHT-ASHBURY

↓

ALTAMONT

'66

↓

'69

FROM SMALL BEGINNINGS
WEST-COAST PSYCHEDELIC
SEXUAL FREEDOM, COMMUNAL
EASTERN SPIRITUALITY.
DANCE CONCERTS,
JOLTING POSTERS. AS THE
PEACE SPREAD, THOUSANDS
TO SAN FRANCISCO. BUT
UNSCRUPULOUS DRUG
PREDATORS ERODED THEIR
IN A DISASTROUS

IN A DESERT SALOON, THE
SCENE GREW TO EMBRACE
LIVING, POT, LSD, AND
EACH WEEKEND SAW
ADVERTISED BY EYE-
MESSAGE OF LOVE AND
OF YOUNG PEOPLE FLOCKED
HIPPIE MERCHANTS,
DEALERS, AND SEXUAL
INNOCENCE, CLIMAXING
CONCERT AT ALTAMONT.

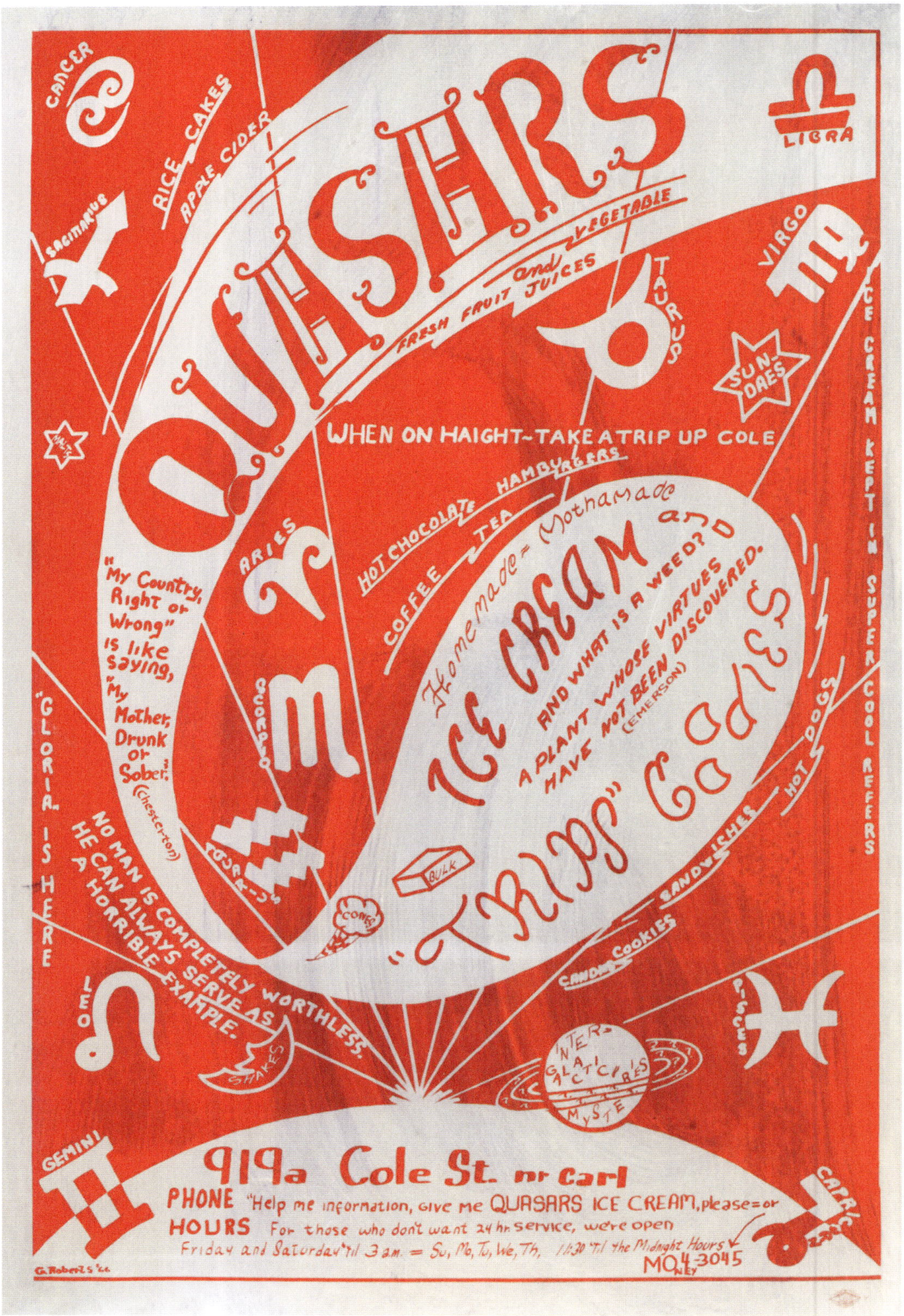

EARLY PSYCHEDELIC PRINTING PLATES

The majority of psychedelic posters created in the sixties were produced using a technique known as flat multicolor photo offset lithography. In this process, each layer of color is printed separately and applied to a sheet of paper using a pre-prepared aluminum plate. Each new color requires a separate plate. The individual plates shown here were prepared by exposing a negative of the poster design onto light-sensitized aluminum sheets under a strong ultraviolet light. The plate is then wrapped around a cylindrical roller in the printing press, ready to roll over each sheet of paper. The same piece of paper is run through the printing press again for every color in the design. In this way, the final poster, consisting of several layers of color, is built up. One of the advantages of this method is that it makes it possible to produce large quantities of posters at a relatively low cost. It also allows for a great deal of artistic experimentation.

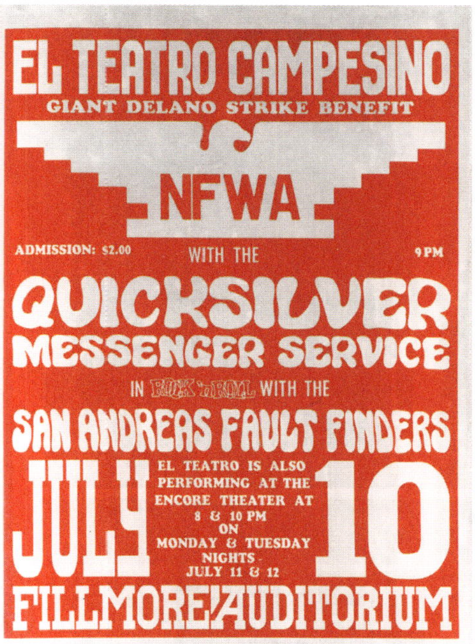

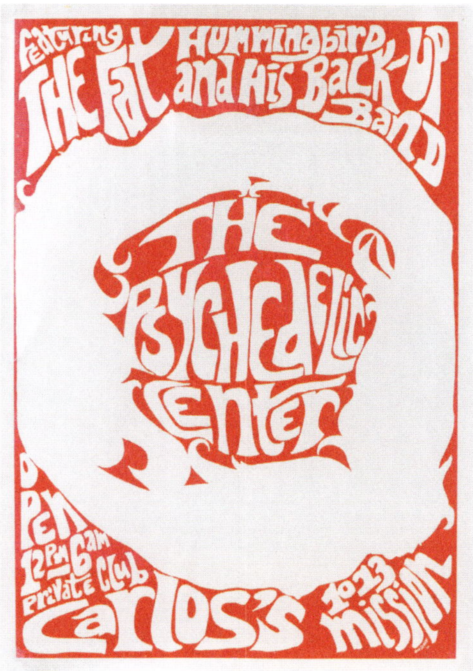

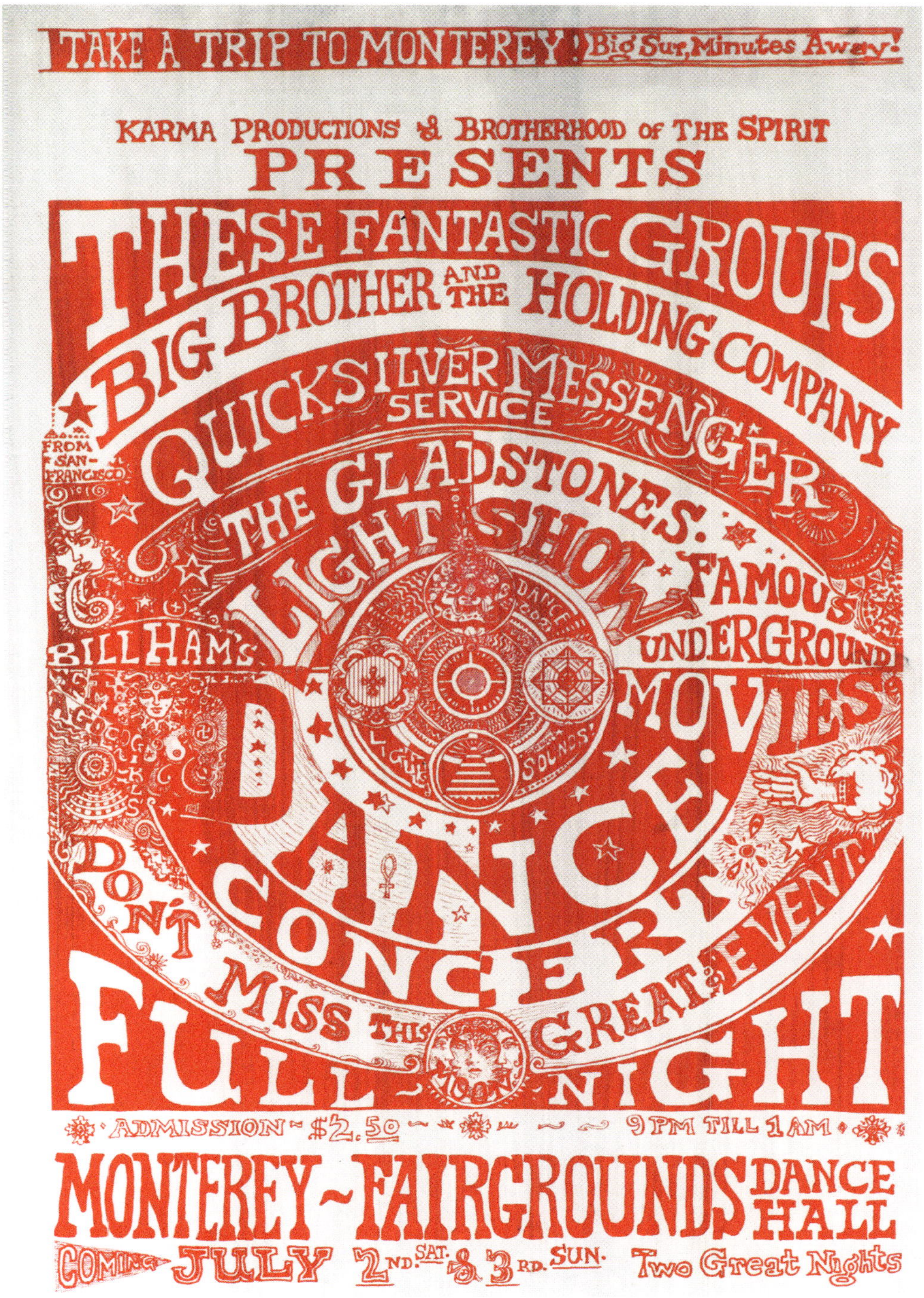

⇛→ Poster designs such as these were usually produced on relatively crude printing presses using single-color plates made from aluminum. The emphasis was on getting the message across as quickly as possible. Here, one-color printing plates are shown for four 1966 posters. ⇛→ Opposite: this advert for Quasar's ice cream store in San Francisco's Haight-Ashbury district is clearly targeted at the area's hippie crowd. ⇛→ This page: star acts include The Fat Hummingbird and His Backup Band, Quicksilver Messenger Service, and Big Brother and the Holding Company, playing at various Californian venues.

SKULL AND ROSES

The Grateful Dead and their management had early misgivings about Mouse and Kelley's appropriation of Edmund Joseph Sullivan's 'Skeleton and Roses' illustration from a 1913 edition of *The Rubaiyat of Omar Khayyam*. They were concerned about its 'negativity.' (The artists simply added color.) It was used as a literal interpretation of the band's name, but hardly represents the acid-rock music that they helped to pioneer. However, Mouse and Kelley turned it into a logo. The elements became so familiar that the single rose adorning the sleeve of the Dead's 1970 album *American Beauty* was enough to evoke the band.

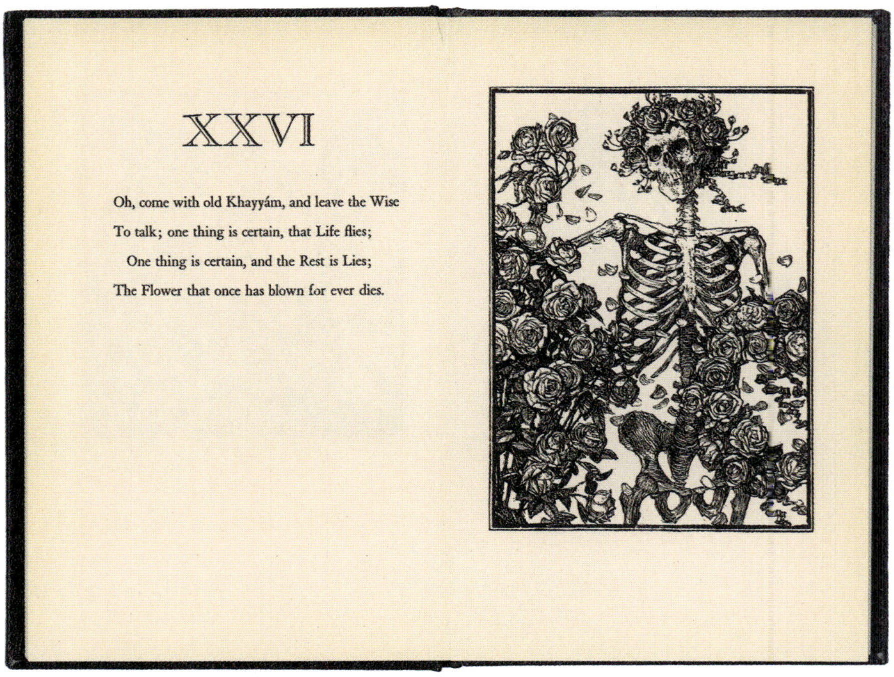

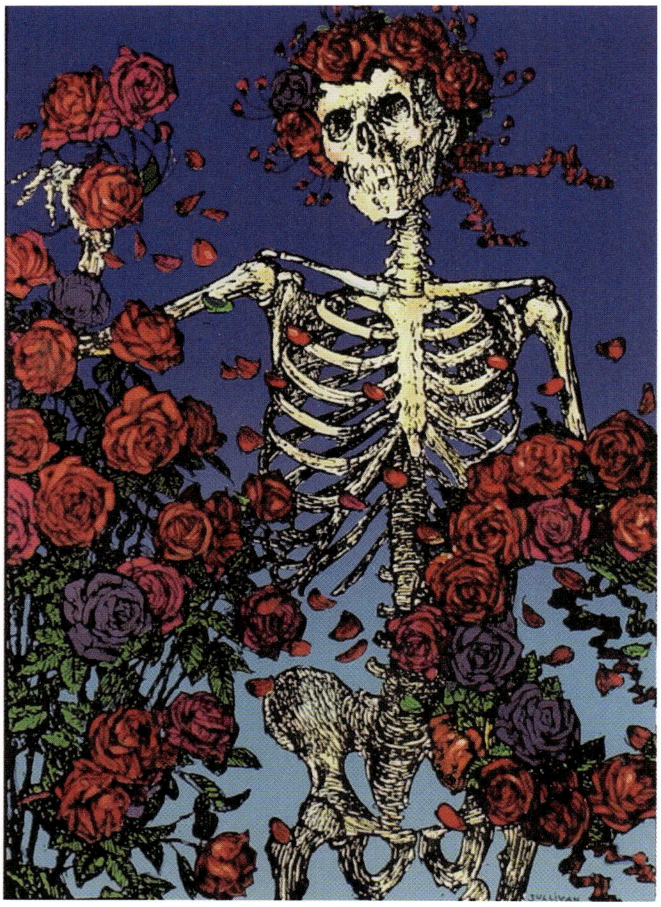

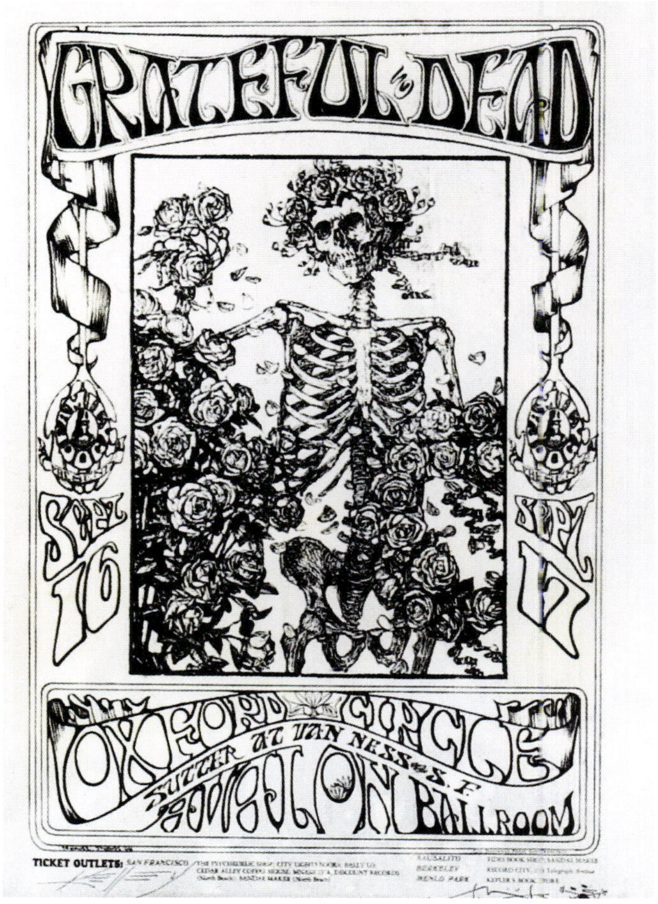

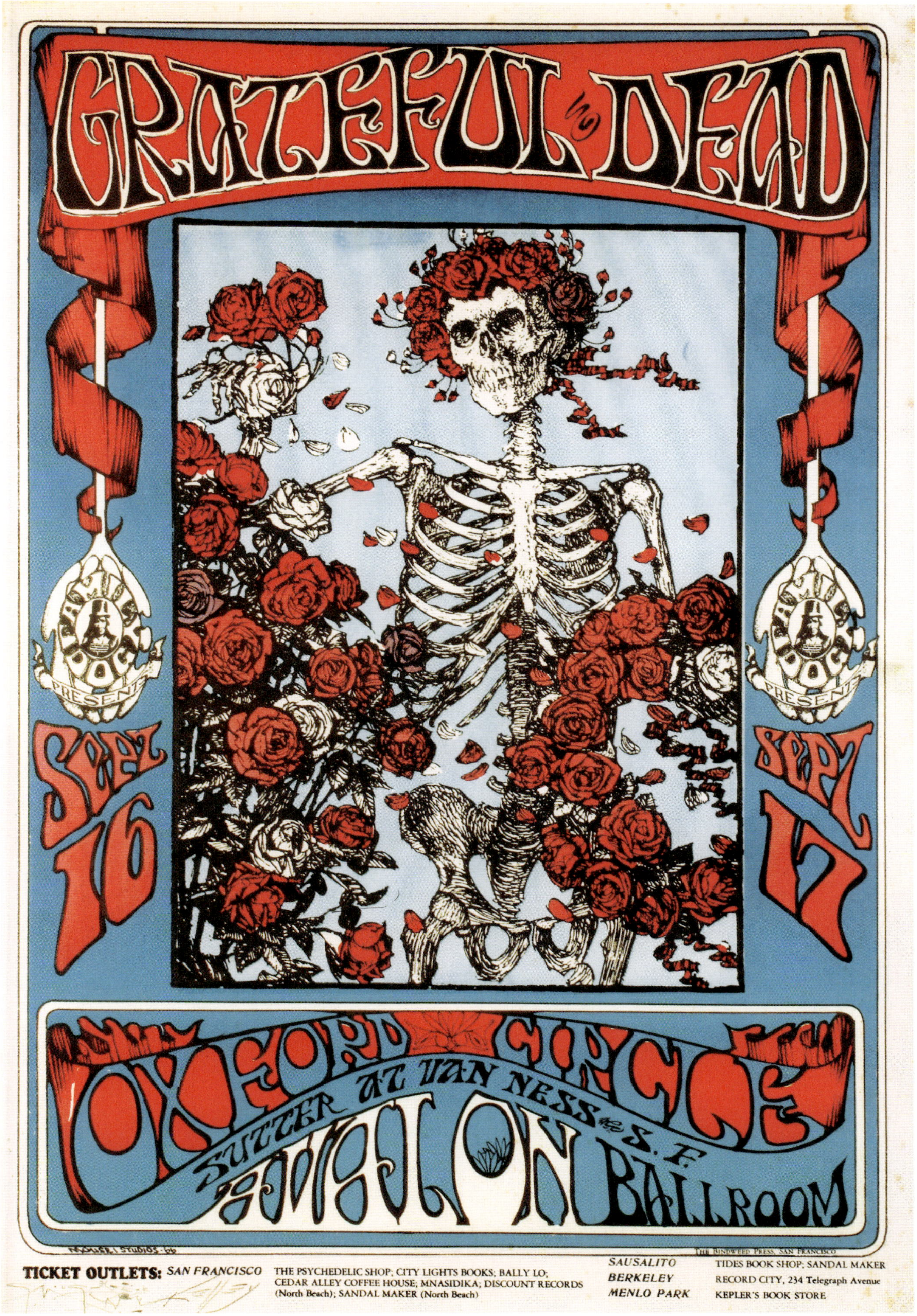

⋙→ Opposite, top: the original illustration by E. J. Sullivan that inspired Stanley Mouse and Alton Kelley's definitive Grateful Dead image. ⋙→ Bottom left: a painting of the 'Skull and Roses' design by Mouse and Kelley. ⋙→ Bottom right: a printing plate for a Grateful Dead show at San Francisco's Avalon Ballroom in September 1966, with 'Skull and Roses' at its heart. ⋙→ This page: the full-color design—probably the best-known poster made for The Family Dog.

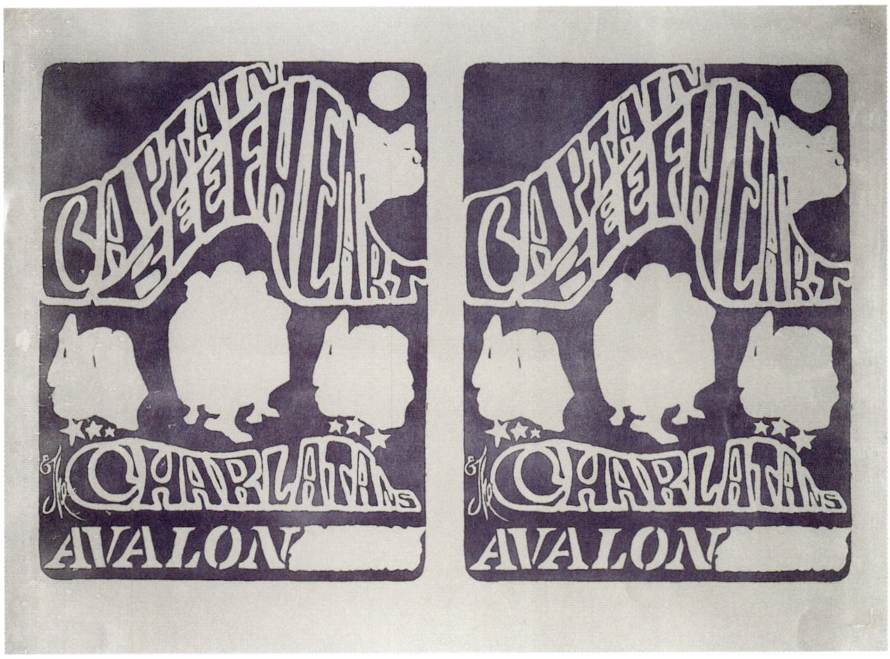

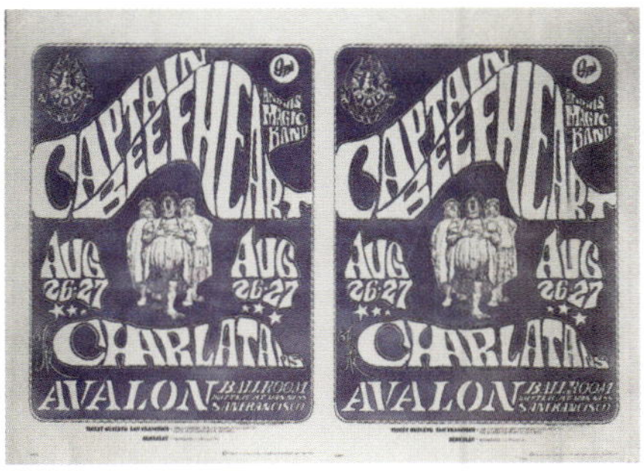

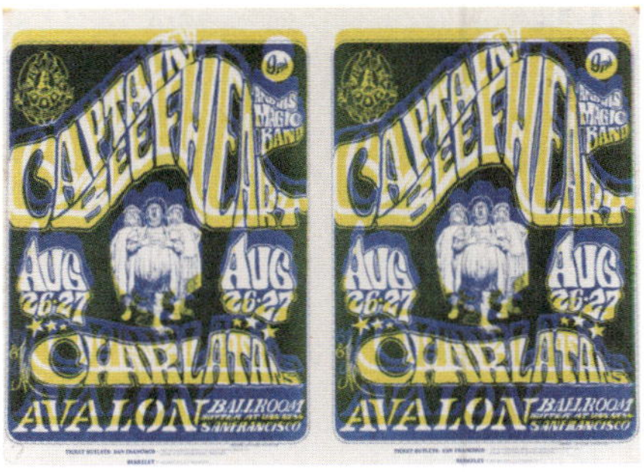

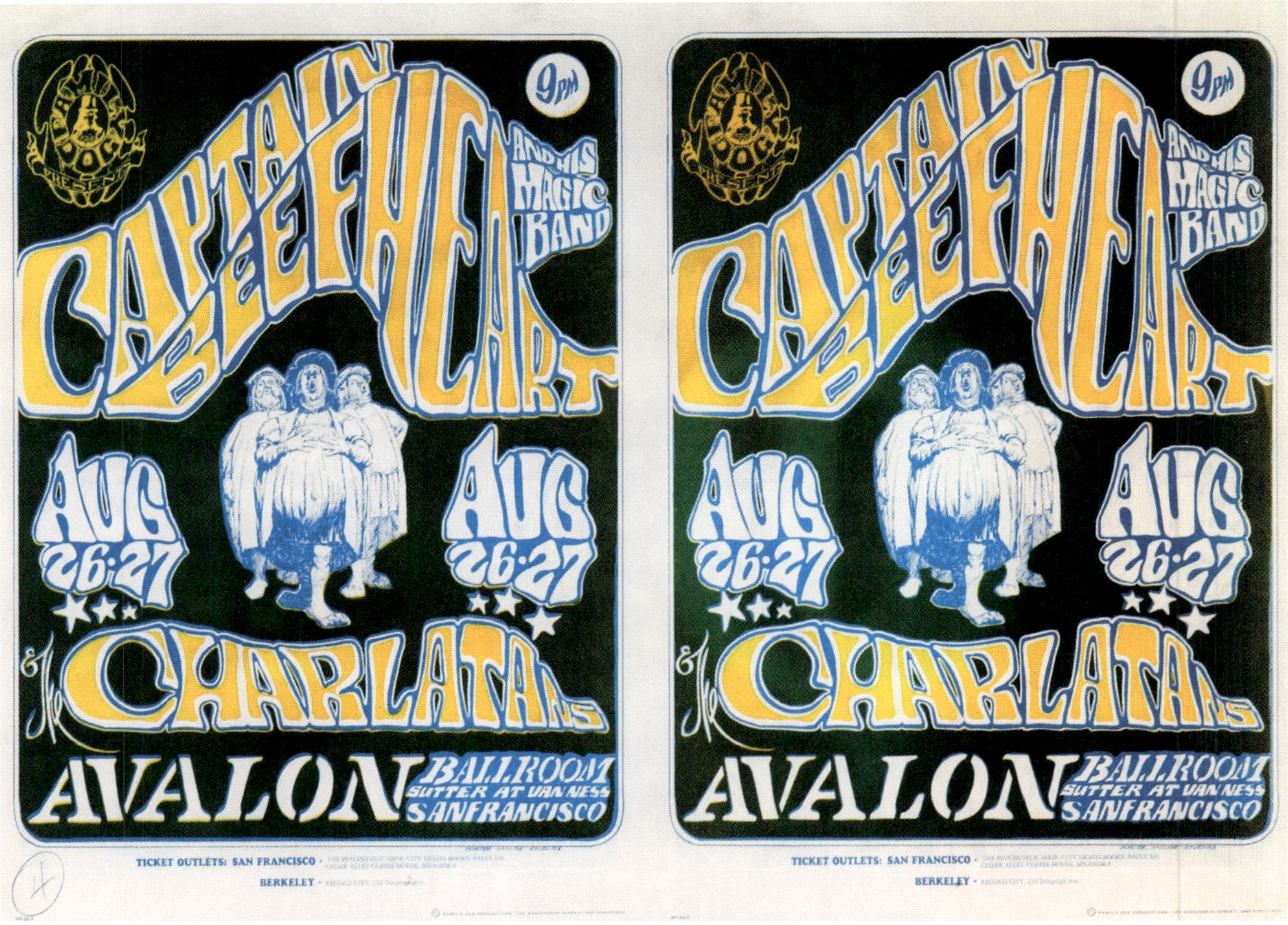

THE MOUSE-KELLEY PARTNERSHIP

Mouse and Kelley met in San Francisco in 1966. Their best work dates from that year, when they were central to the emerging psychedelic scene. The two made their name working on early poster designs for productions by The Family Dog. They worked together at the same easel, with right-handed Mouse on the left and left-handed Kelley on the right. Kelley said, 'When I used an image I didn't steal it. I made it my own. I did something with it. It was a tool. It was art. I felt I had a right to use it.' Joel Selvin remembered, 'While Kelley initially served as the idea man, and Mouse the draftsman, eventually the pair developed an interchangeable unity in their work.'

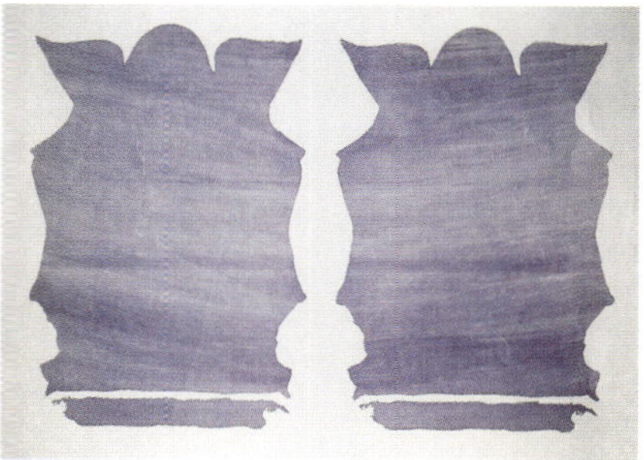

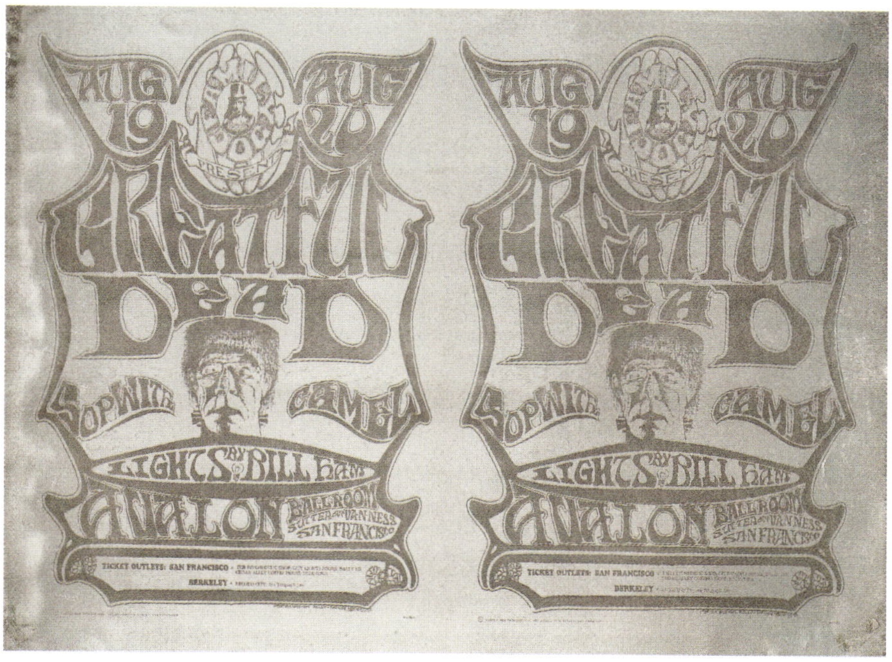

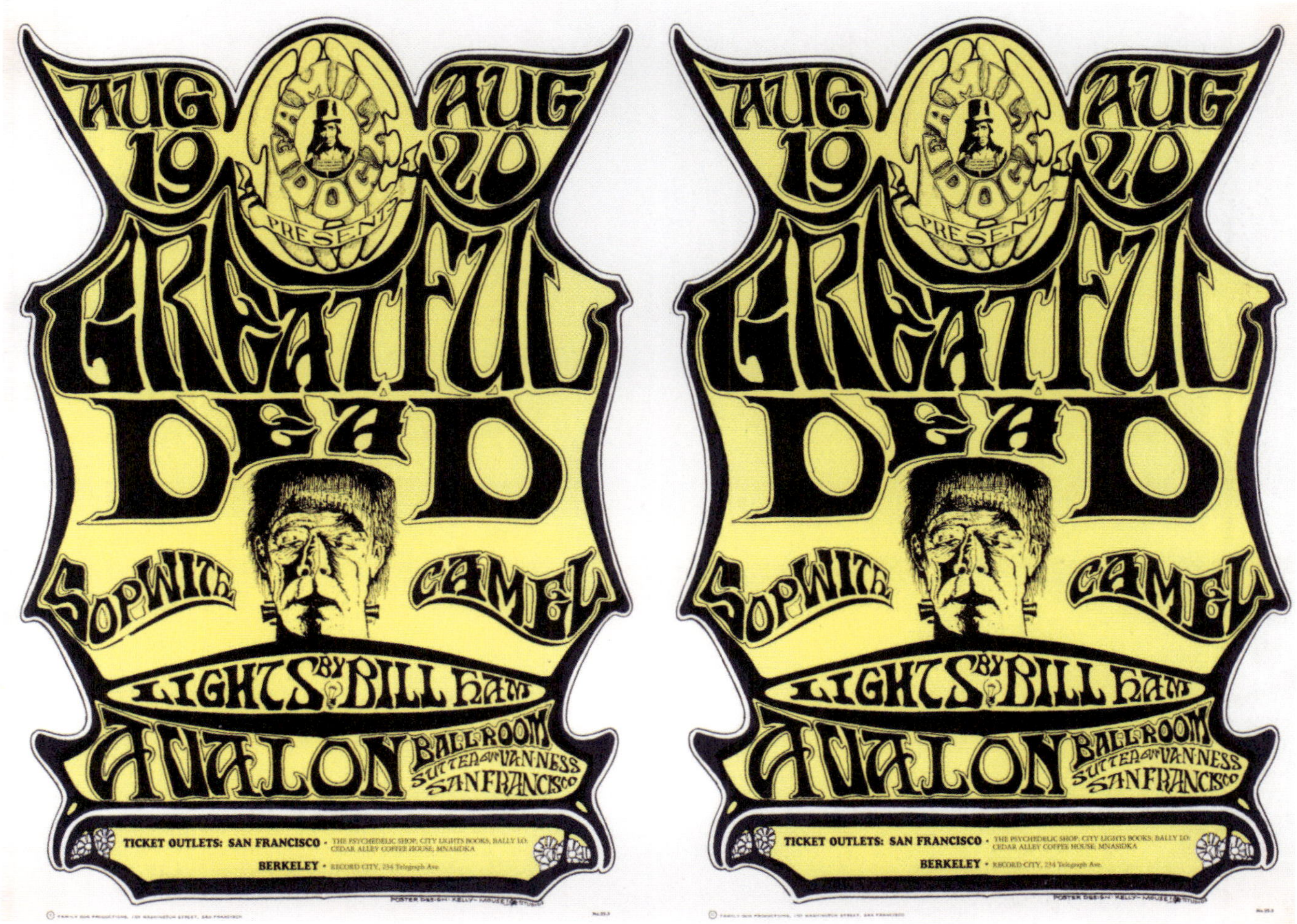

⋙→ Progressive plates and color separations of two examples of Mouse and Kelley's style, showing their mastery of offset lithography. ⋙→ Opposite: a poster for a 1966 Captain Beefheart concert. Posters were often printed twice on the same piece of paper and cut after drying to save time and money. ⋙→ This page: Frankenstein's monster adorns this two-color poster for a 1966 Grateful Dead show.

➳ A late 1966 poster design by Mouse and Kelley. It is based on a profile photograph of Bear Bull, a Native American from the Blackfoot Tribe. The original photograph was taken by Edward S. Curtis in 1926.

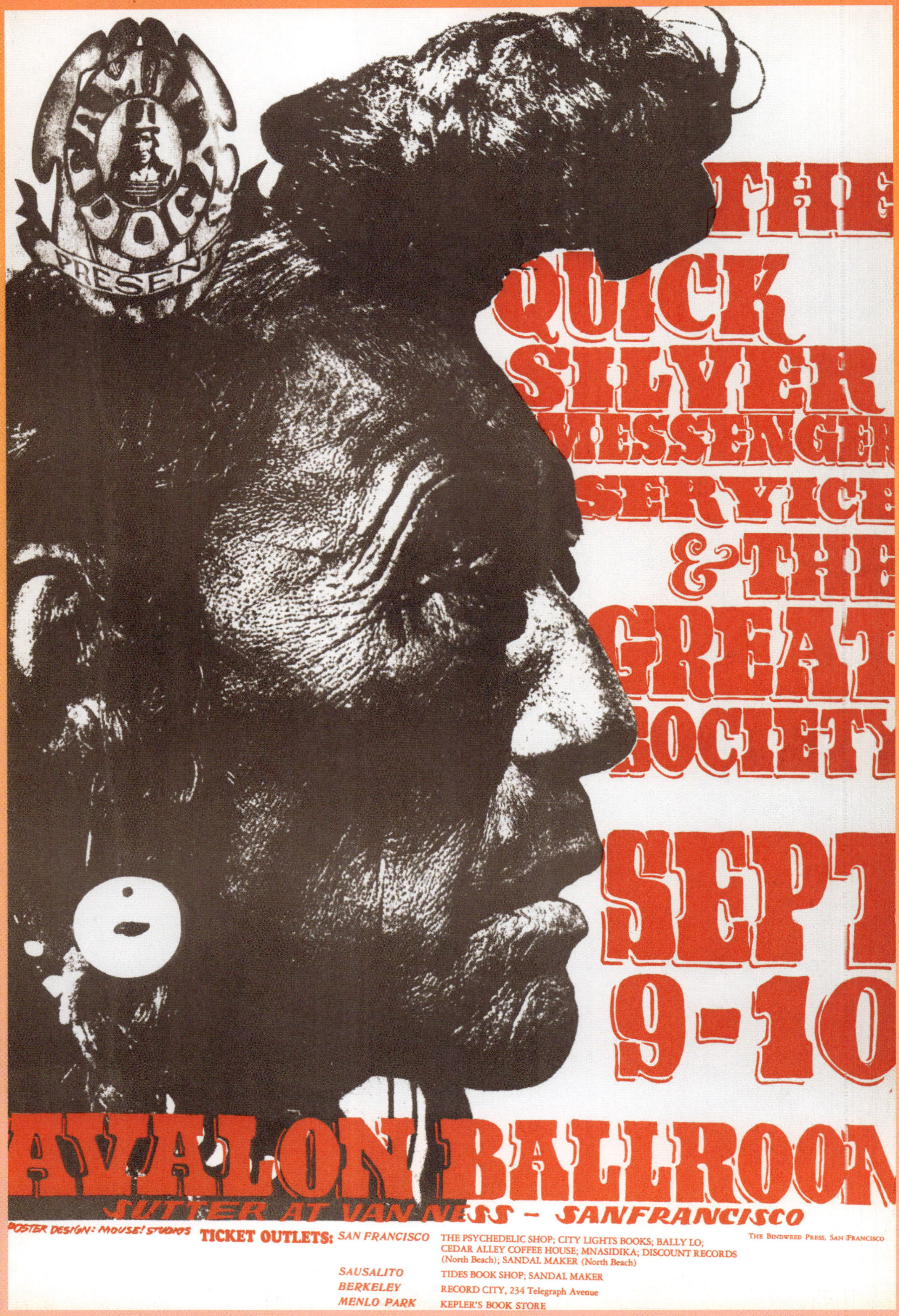

MOUSE AND KELLEY (STANLEY MOUSE, 1940–; ALTON KELLEY, 1940–2008)

BOTH STANLEY 'MOUSE' MILLER AND ALTON KELLEY HAD A PASSION FOR AUTOS IN THEIR YOUTH, AND MADE THEIR FIRST STEPS TOWARD AN ARTISTIC CAREER BY FLAMING AND PINSTRIPING HOT-RODS AND (IN KELLEY'S CASE) MOTORCYCLE TANKS. MOUSE WAS SOON AIRBRUSHING IMAGES OF HOT-RODS AND MONSTER CARS ONTO T-SHIRTS THAT HE COULD THEN SELL AT CUSTOM CAR SHOWS, WHICH DEVELOPED INTO AN EARLY BUSINESS VENTURE. ⟶ MOUSE DROPPED OUT FROM HIGH SCHOOL IN DETROIT (HIS FAMILY HAD MOVED THERE FROM CALIFORNIA) FOR SAN FRANCISCO, WHERE HE MET KELLEY. THE LATTER HAD BEEN PART OF FLEDGLING CONCERT PROMOTION OUTFIT THE FAMILY DOG, AND HAD ALREADY DESIGNED POSTERS FOR LOCAL CONCERTS. SOON AFTERWARD, THE TWO PRODUCED ONE OF THEIR EARLIEST AND MOST ENDURING IMAGES: THE 1966 'SKULL AND ROSES' POSTER FOR THE GRATEFUL DEAD. IT ESTABLISHED THEIR REPUTATION FOR CREATING SOMETHING ENTIRELY NEW FROM A TIME-WORN ARTWORK, AS SEEN ALSO IN THEIR CREATION OF THE 'ZIG-ZAG MAN.' BOTH WERE EXAMPLES OF THE DUO'S PRACTICE OF RAIDING THE GRAPHIC 'FLEA MARKET' FOR UNFAMILIAR IMAGES THAT THEY COULD THEN REINVENT. EARLY ON, MOUSE EMERGED AS AN ADEPT DRAFTSMAN AND PAINTER, WHILE KELLEY EXCELLED IN CONCEPTS AND COLLAGE. ⟶ BETWEEN 1966 AND 1969, MOUSE AND KELLEY CREATED AROUND 150 ARTWORKS TOGETHER, INCLUDING A NUMBER OF POSTERS FOR PROMOTER BILL GRAHAM'S SAN FRANCISCO VENUES, AND WORKED ON A STRING OF ALBUM COVERS FOR THE GRATEFUL DEAD. ⟶ BOTH CONTINUED TO WORK FOR THE GRATEFUL DEAD, MOUSE CREATING THEIR ICONIC 'JESTER,' BUT BOTH WERE COMMISSIONED BY OTHER BANDS TOO, NOTABLY JOURNEY, FOR WHOM THEY DEVISED DISTINCTIVE WINGS-AND-BEETLES GRAPHICS ON SEVERAL ALBUM COVERS. ⟶ KELLEY PASSED AWAY IN 2008, FOLLOWING A LENGTHY ILLNESS. MOUSE CONTINUES TO RUN THE SUCCESSFUL 'MOUSE STUDIOS.'

WES WILSON'S EARLY PSYCHEDELIC POSTERS

Wes Wilson produced the flyer for the 1966 Trips Festival at Longshoremen's Hall. He came away 'freshly psychedelicized,' as Jerry Garcia put it, and worked both for Chet Helms's Family Dog and for Bill Graham. In August 1966, he stopped working for Helms: 'Chet almost always had a theme already picked out, but with Bill you could do your own thing.' Influenced by Alfred Roller and the Vienna Secessionists, Wilson's morphed lettering made people stop and look hard.

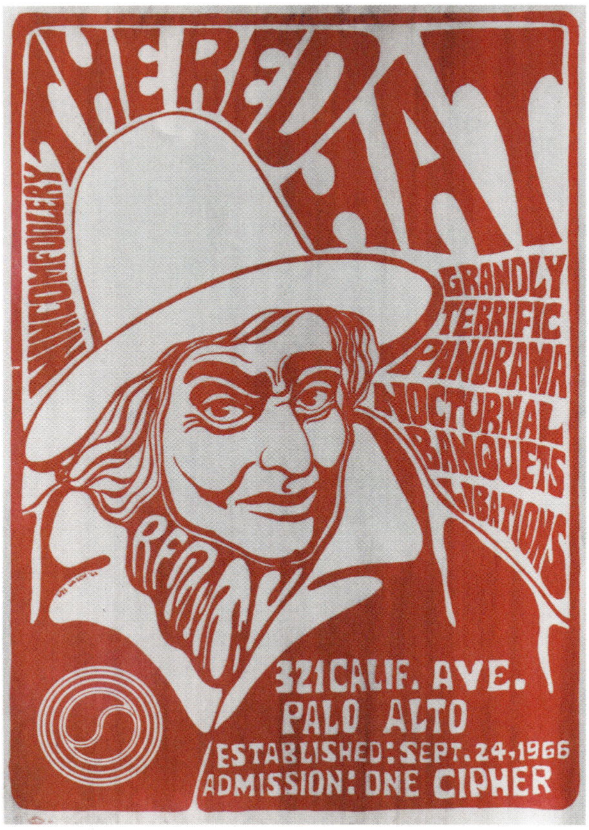

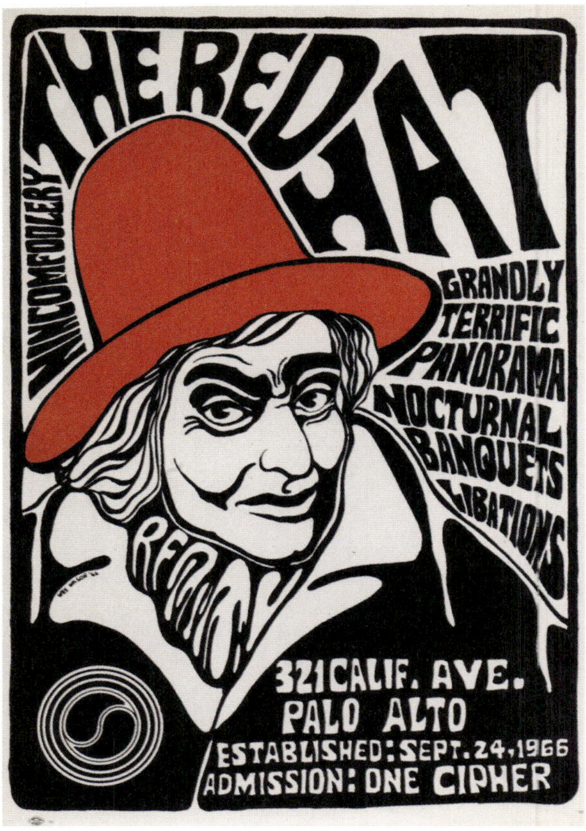

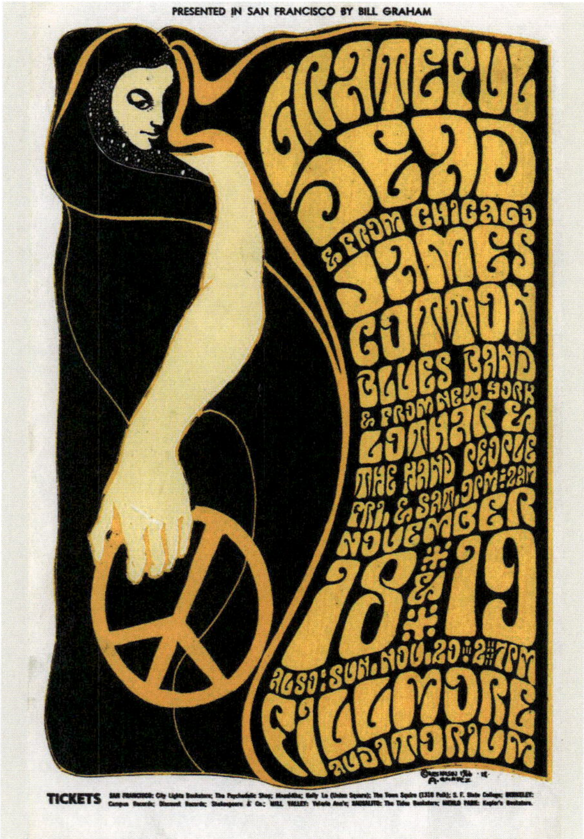

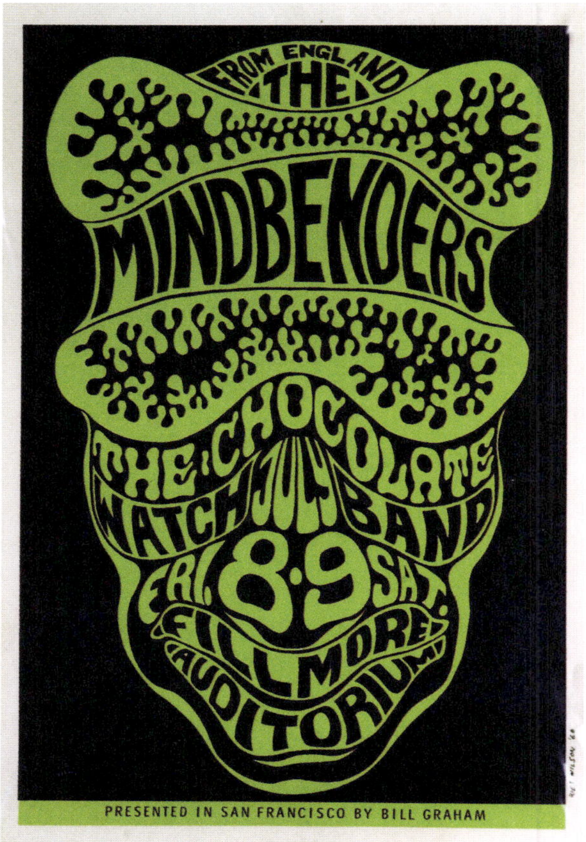

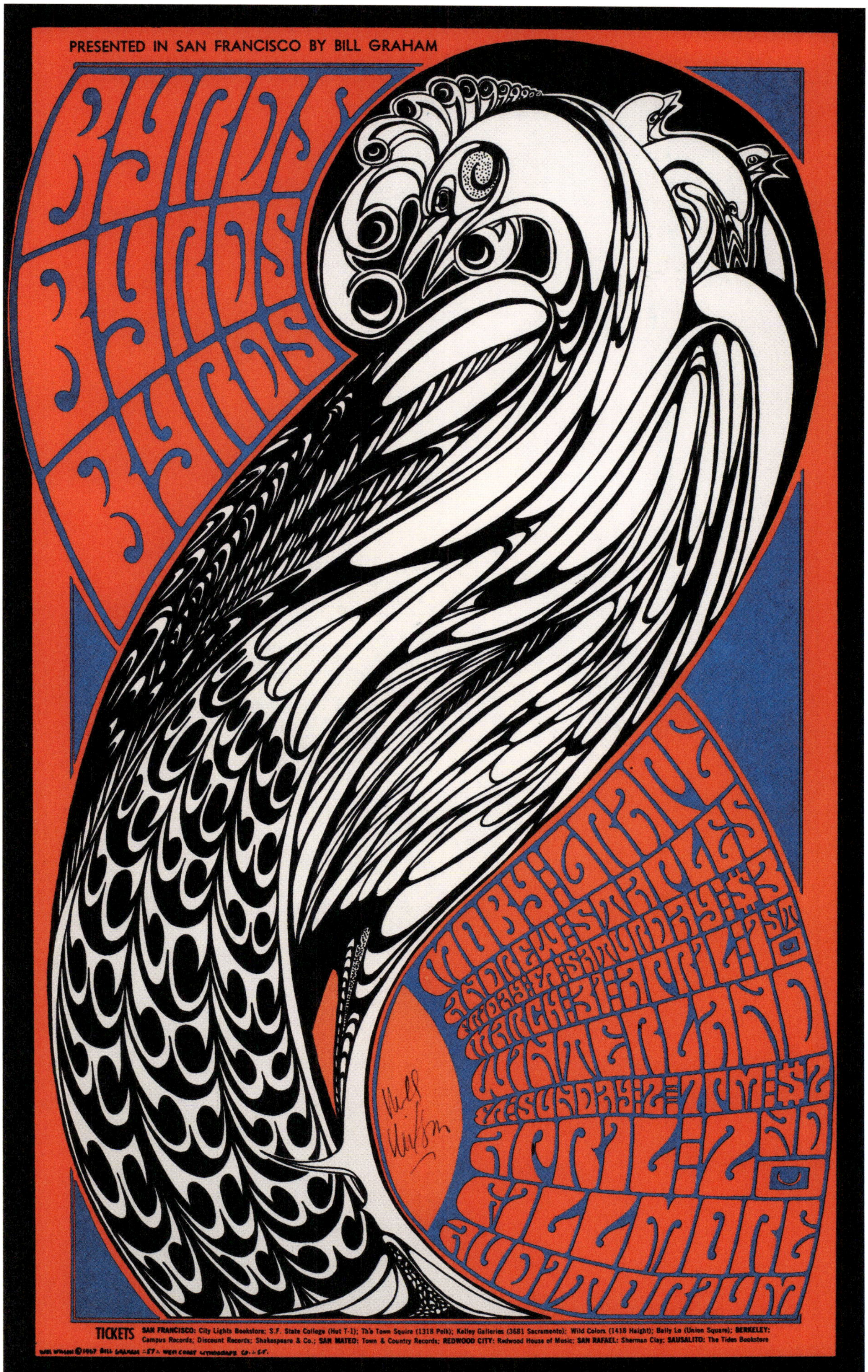

⋙→ Wilson's lettering style was partly inspired by a *Jugendstil and Expressionism* catalog he'd seen for an exhibition in California in late 1965. Bill Graham recalled: 'I would say to Wes, "Just watch people standing there, trying to read your poster!" Their bodies actually would be trying to follow the curvature of the words, the lettering.'

⋙→ Opposite, top left and right: a printing plate and poster by Wilson from 1966, for a restaurant. ⋙→ Bottom left and right: two 1966 posters by Wilson for Fillmore Auditorium shows. ⋙→ This page: a 1967 Winterland/Fillmore Auditorium poster by Wilson plays on the name of lead act The Byrds.

THE FAMILY DOG

Chet Helms decided that The Family Dog needed a logo to distinguish them from Bill Graham's promotions. He found the image of an Indian fur trader smoking a long-stemmed pipe and gave it to Wes Wilson, who told Paul Grushkin, 'I designed the logo on a little piece of paper and I said, "Well Chet, how about this?" And he went, "Wow, that's great. Looks sort of like a deputy sheriff's badge."' Wilson had turned the pipe into a long thin joint. They used it on all their posters, starting with catalog number FD-1 in February 1966.

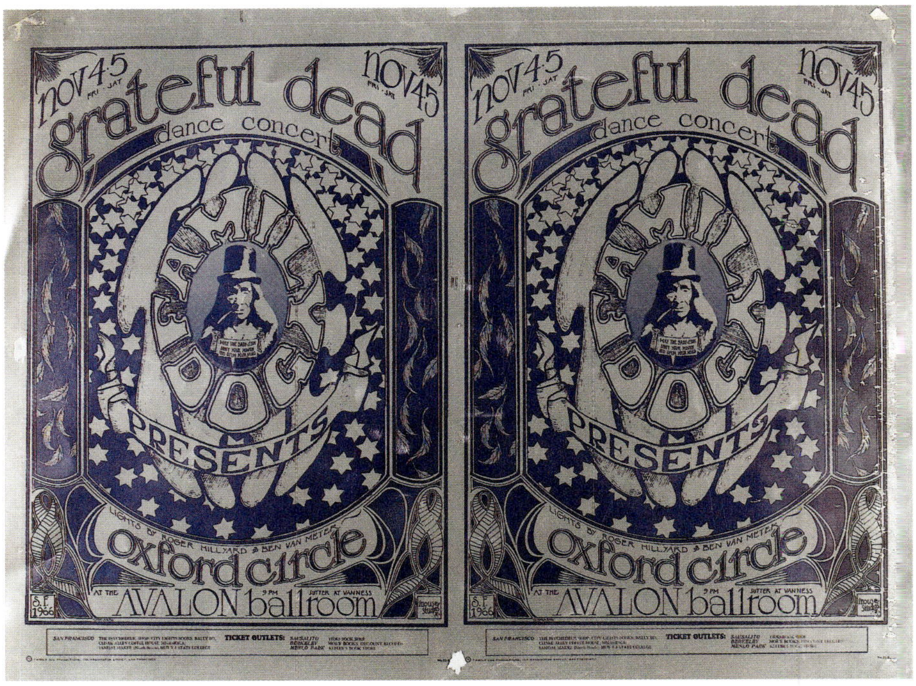

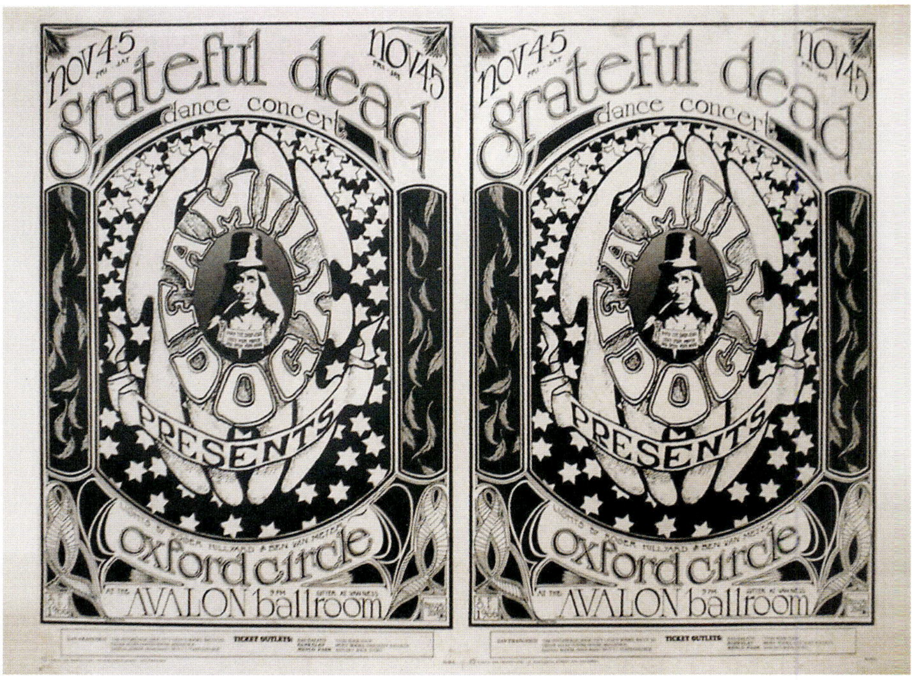

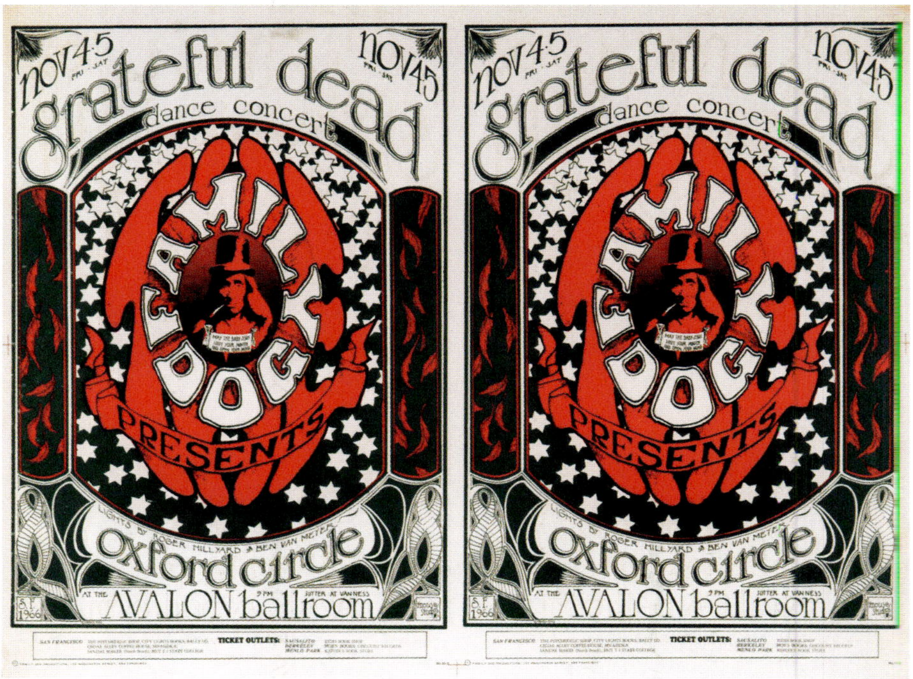

➳ This page: Wes Wilson's Indian fur trader logo appears at the center of this Family Dog poster by Mouse and Kelley, shown from printing plate to finished poster.
➳ Opposite: printing plate and finished poster of the *Dollar Bill*, a handbill for a 1966 show featuring the rock 'n' roll legend Bo Diddley and future stars Big Brother and the Holding Company, by Mouse and Kelley. The space in the center would be filled by the distinctive Family Dog logo.

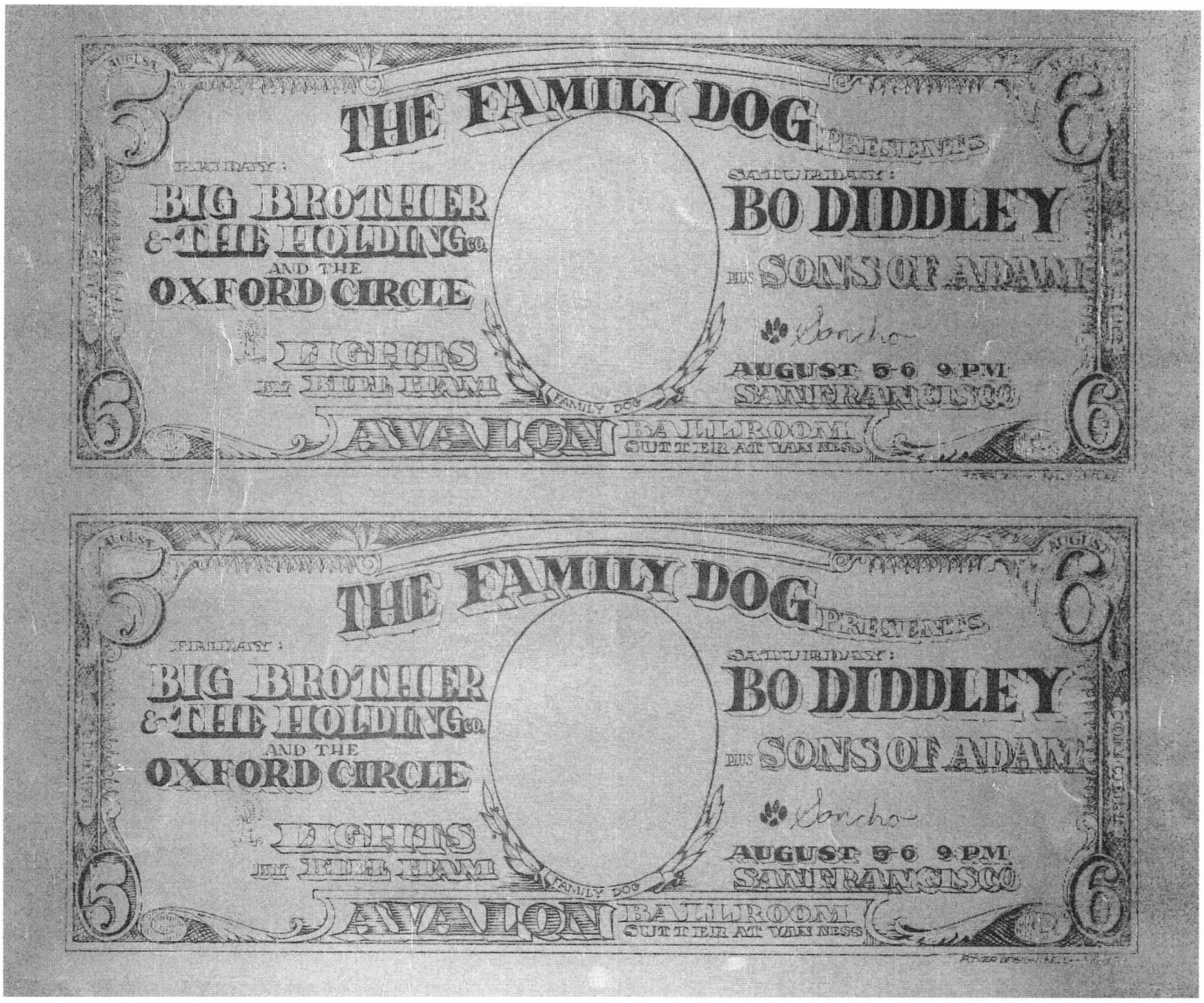
THE FAMILY DOG PRESENTS
FRIDAY:
BIG BROTHER
& THE HOLDING CO.
AND THE
OXFORD CIRCLE
LIGHTS
BY BILL HAM
FAMILY DOG
AVALON
BALLROOM
SUTTER AT VAN NESS
SATURDAY:
BO DIDDLEY
PLUS SONS OF ADAM
Sancho
AUGUST 5-6 9:PM
SAN FRANCISCO

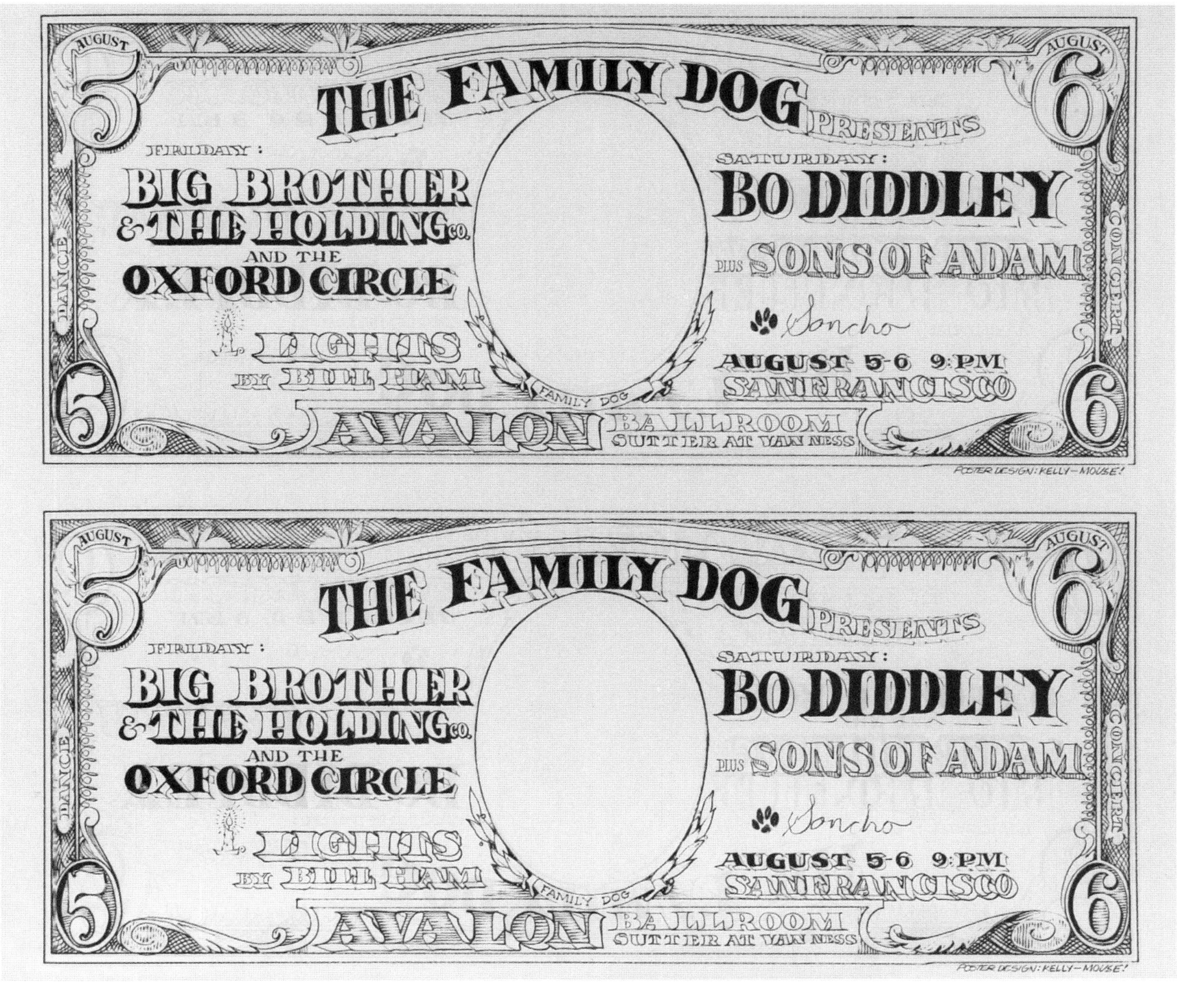
AUGUST
THE FAMILY DOG PRESENTS
FRIDAY:
BIG BROTHER
& THE HOLDING CO.
AND THE
OXFORD CIRCLE
LIGHTS
BY BILL HAM
FAMILY DOG
AVALON
BALLROOM
SUTTER AT VAN NESS
SATURDAY:
BO DIDDLEY
PLUS SONS OF ADAM
Sancho
AUGUST 5-6 9:PM
SAN FRANCISCO
DANCE
CONCERT
POSTER DESIGN: KELLY-MOUSE!

THE DIGGERS

This social collective issued a handbill in March 1967, explaining the origin of the term 'diggers': 'A small group of extreme radicals founded by [George] Winstanley, who began digging the common at St. George's Hill, Surrey (1649). Opposed to physical force, they were easily suppressed by the army leaders. They held that the political revolution must be based on a social revolution.'

During the influx of young people in 1967's Summer of Love, the Diggers organized free food stores, persuading many supermarkets and farmers to give up past-sell-by-date food or surplus produce for their store in Golden Gate Park. They leafleted much of the city, asking citizens to provide 'crash pads' for the newcomers, and distributed signs for willing hosts to place in their windows.

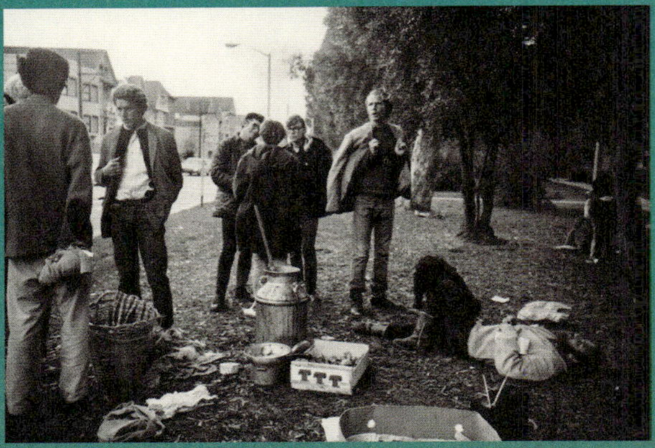

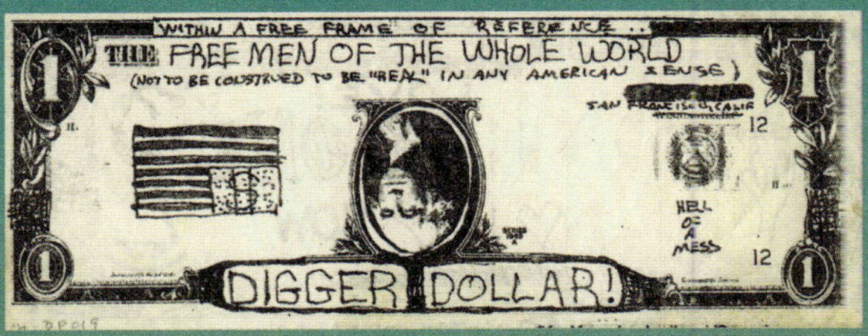

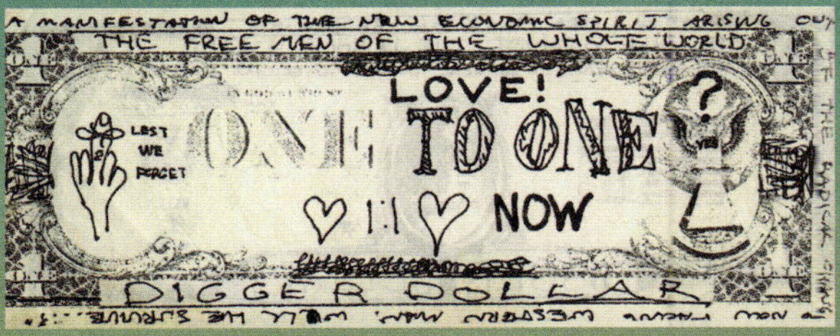

The Diggers ⋙→ The Diggers issued their own currency—the 'Digger Dollar'—which, naturally, was worthless, as everything in the Digger Store was free.

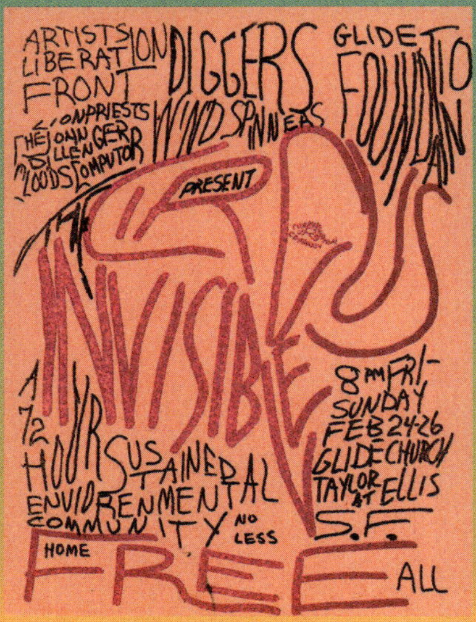

The Invisible Circus, Dave Hodges, 1967 ⋙→ The Circus was a seventy-two-hour 'community happening.' Dave Hodges created this handbill and the poster at the bottom of the opposite page.

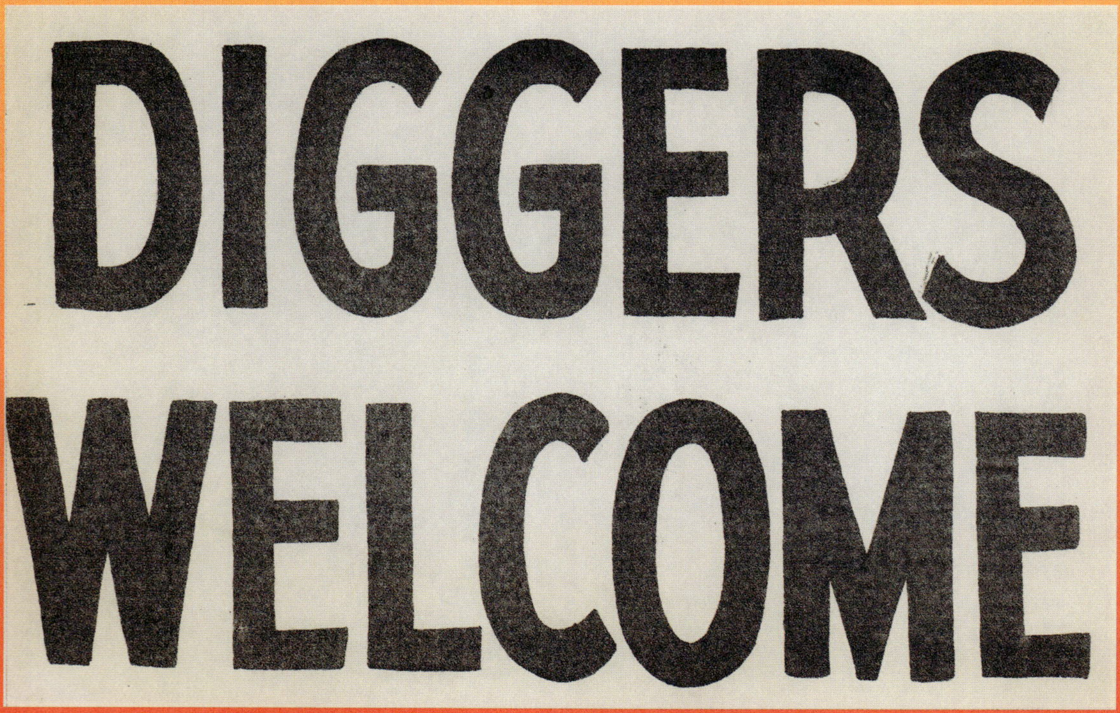

Diggers Welcome, flyer, 1967 ⋙→ The reverse side read: 'Place this sign in your window all through the summer whenever you have food, clothing or shelter for any of the young seekers.'

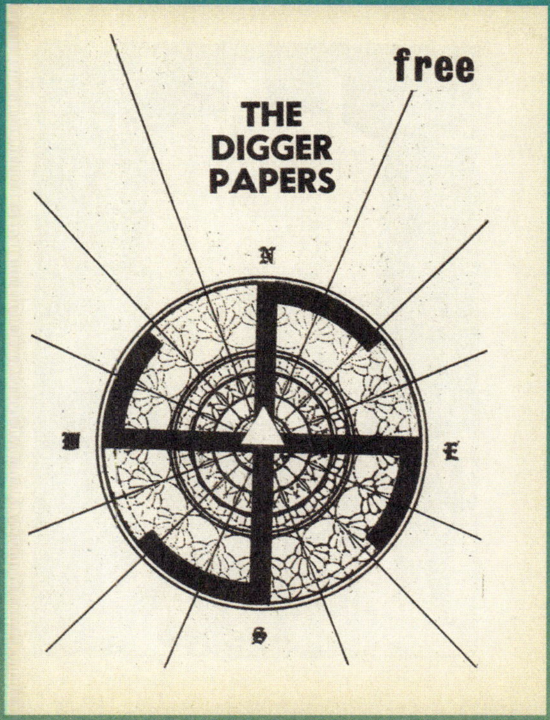

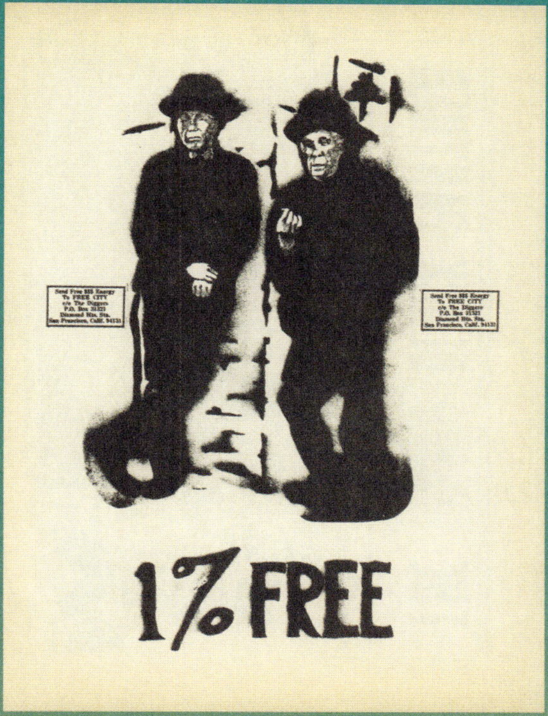

The Digger Papers, front cover and interior page, 1968 ⋙→ *The Digger Papers*—the group's free house magazine—began in the autumn of 1965 in San Francisco and ran until the summer of 1968. For their final issue, they agreed with Paul Krassner, editor/publisher of *The Realist*, that he could use the contents in issue #81 of his magazine in return for printing 40,000 extra copies with the name changed to *The Digger Papers*. These would be given away free on the streets and in stores. The twenty-four-page issue contained some new material as well as the best articles from the previous two years reprinted.

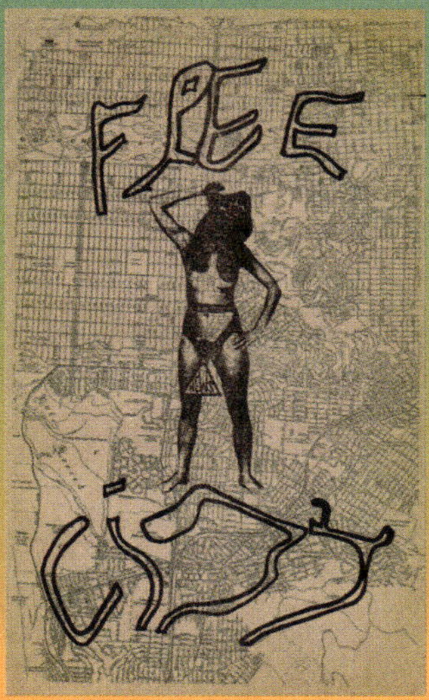

Free City, back page, 1967 ⋙→ In July 1967, the Diggers changed their name to the Free City Collective. They 'appropriated' the duplicator used by the Communications Company and moved it to their Trip Without a Ticket basement at 901 Cole Street, where they issued their own, often beautifully produced, flyers. 'So beautiful, in fact, that the research department of the Gestetner Corporation couldn't believe that their equipment could produce such technically fine and attractive color combination graphics' (Emmett Grogan, *Ringolevio*). Twelve individual flyers were bound together with a paperclip and given away as *Free City* in October 1967, using this as the back page.

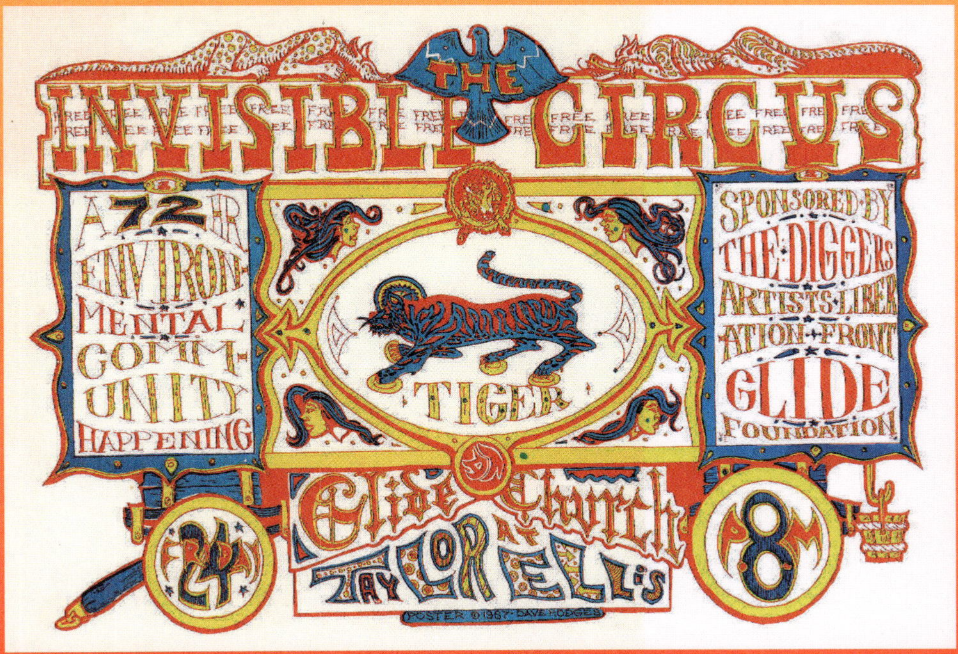

The Invisible Circus, Artists Liberation Front, Dave Hodges, 1967 ⋙→ The Diggers collaborated with The Artists Liberation Front and the Glide Foundation for The Invisible Circus. Hodges's poster utilized primary colors and embraced circus imagery. It was not unusual for two or three posters to be made for a community event such as this.

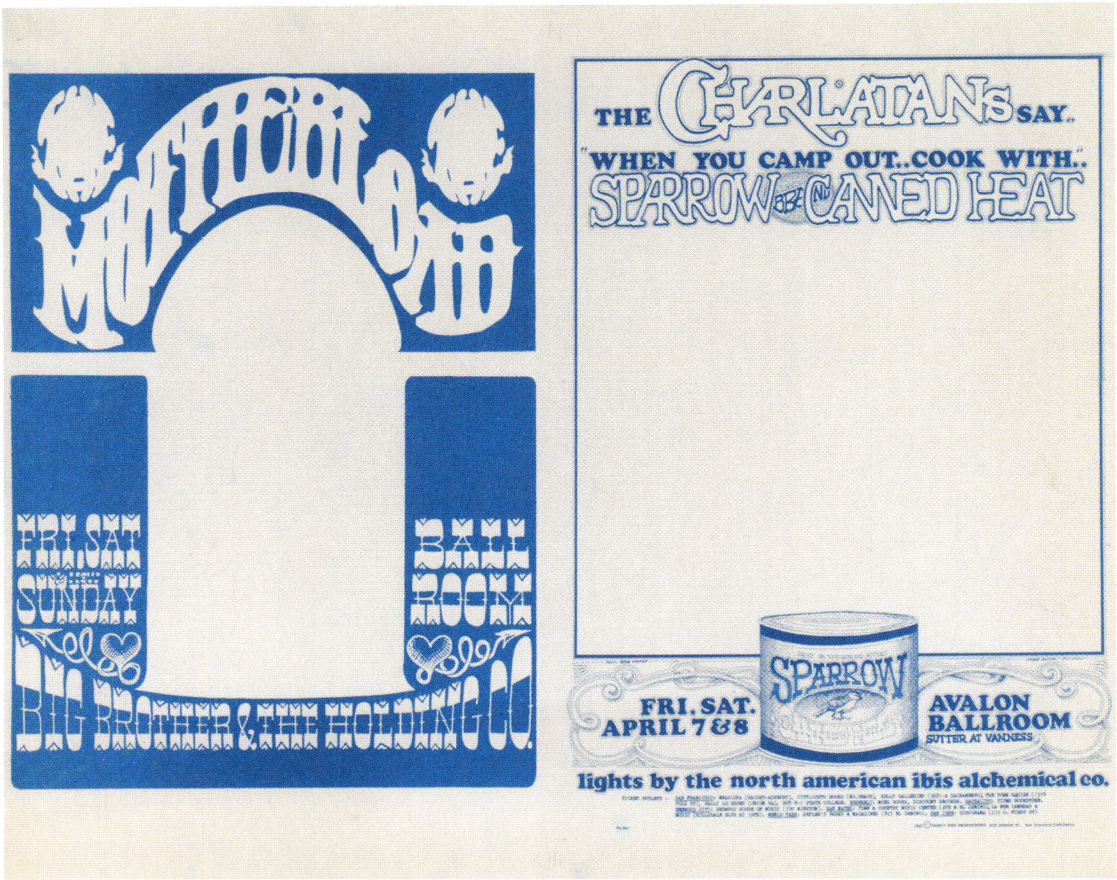

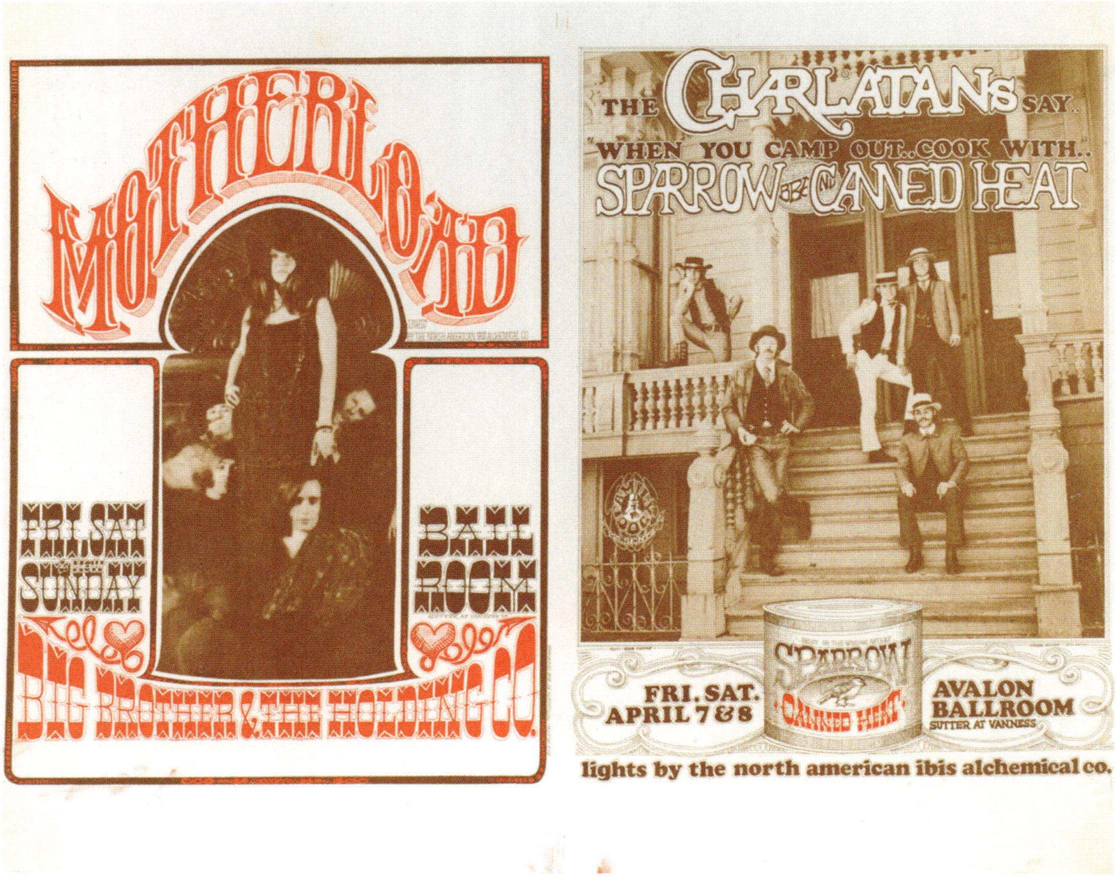

VICTORIANA

The Charlatans were hired to play the Red Dog Saloon largely because of their look. It was created by bandleader George Hunter, who assembled their outfits from San Francisco's thrift shops, right down to the celluloid collars, straw hats, cowboy hats, and guns. They all packed at least one weapon—including the ladies, who wore Derringers. The same attention to detail applied to their posters: Hunter designed the band's logo and many of the posters featured old-fashioned 'Wild West' fonts.

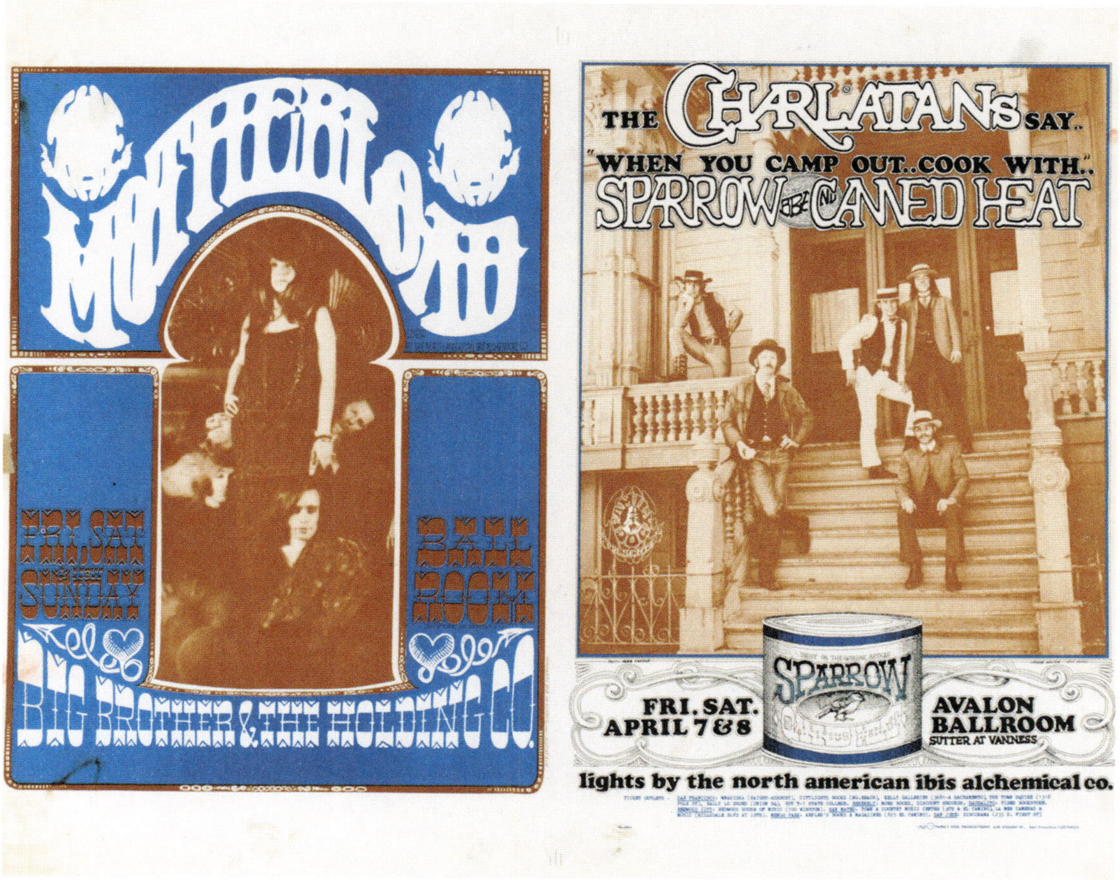

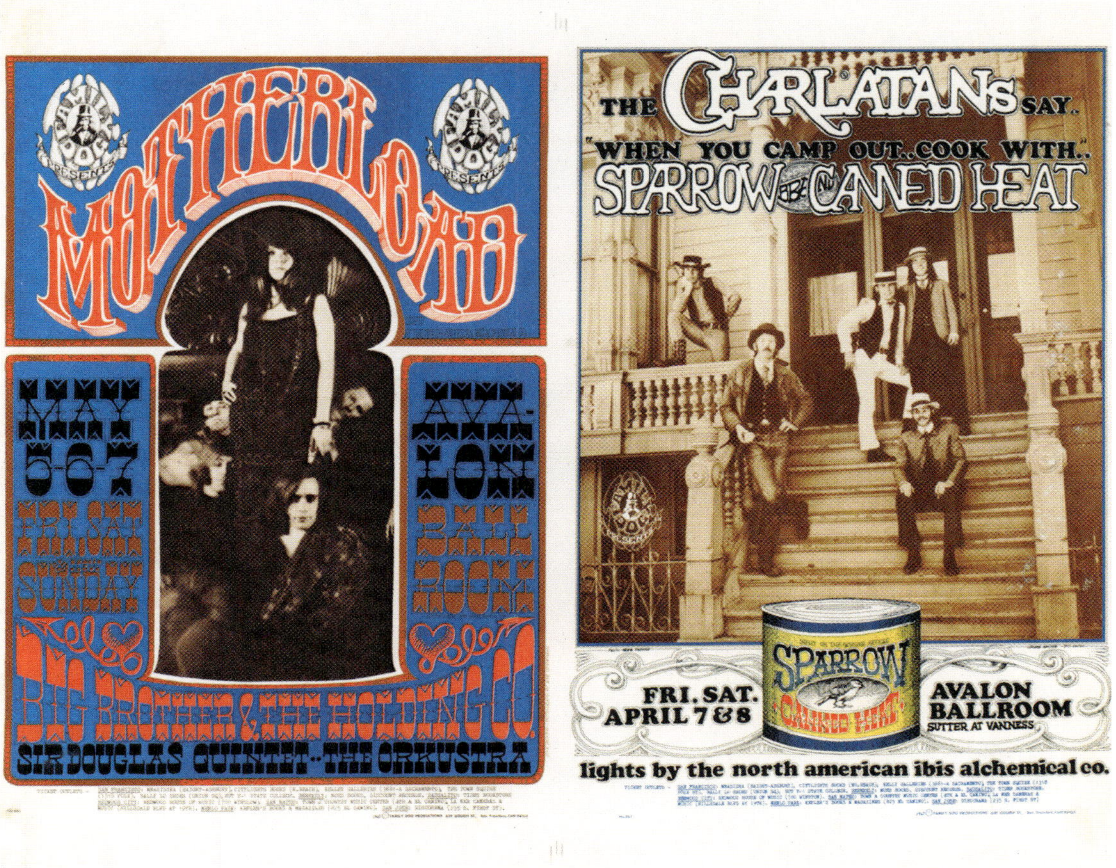

⟫→ Progressive proofs for posters advertising two gigs at the Avalon Ballroom. Both posters hark back to Western mythology, most clearly in the antiquated look of the photographs, and (in the 'Motherland' poster) the font—although its color treatment is pure psychedelic West Coast. Rick Griffin designed the poster for the 1966 show, utilizing a photograph by Bob Seidemann. The Charlatans poster dates from 1967 and again Griffin is the designer, although in collaboration with George Hunter. The sepia-toned photograph of the band was taken by Herb Greene.

Griffin hallmarks within this 1972 design include eye-challenging script and his signature staring eyeball, winged heart, and scarab beetle. The poster was created by Griffin to commemorate the appearance of Captain Beefheart and His Magic Band at Crawford Hall, University of California, in 1968.

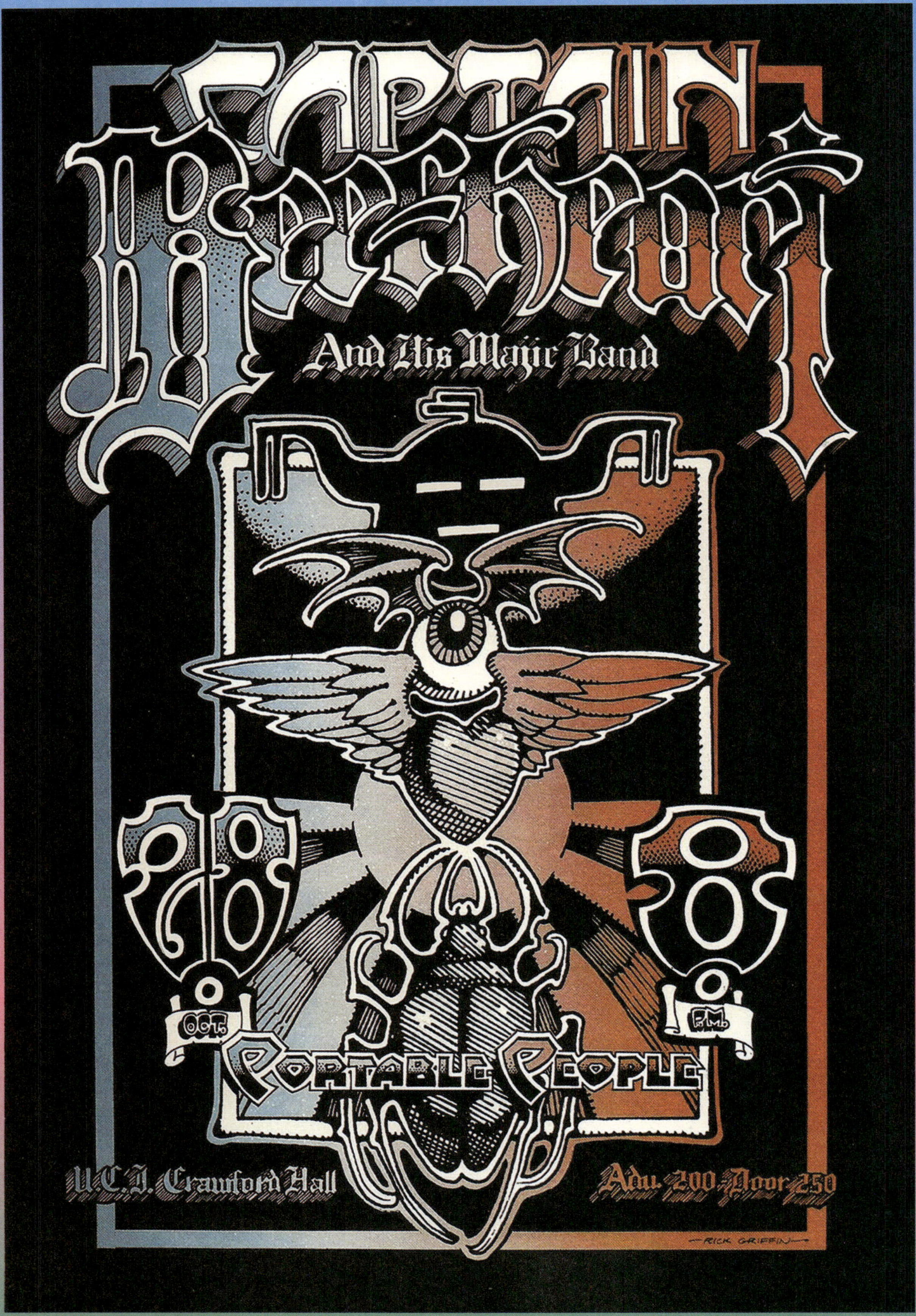

RICK GRIFFIN (1944–1991)

BY IDA GRIFFIN

RICK GRIFFIN'S BODY OF WORK WENT THROUGH EVOLUTIONARY LEAPS ACROSS HIS CAREER, BEGINNING AS A LOOSE AND SKETCHY CARTOONIST IN HIS YOUTH. LETTERING BECAME KEY TO HIS IMAGERY AND DESIGN WHEN MAKING POSTERS, WHICH HE APPROACHED FROM TOP TO BOTTOM IN A METHODICALLY DETAILED PROCESS. AS HE GREW INTO A PAINTER, HIS WORK WAS BOLDER, MORE PROFESSIONAL, AND REQUIRED MORE PRELIMINARY SKETCHING AND COMPOSITION LAYOUT. ⟶ HE FOUND INFLUENCE EVERYWHERE THROUGHOUT HIS LIFE: FROM FAMILY VACATIONS TO OLD GHOST TOWNS AND INDIAN RESERVATIONS; FROM THE MEXICAN CULTURE THAT SURROUNDED HIM AS A CHILD TRAVELING ACROSS THE SOUTHWEST; FROM COMIC BOOKS, CARTOONS, AND *MAD* MAGAZINE AND FROM HIS LIFELONG LOVE OF MUSIC. AS A YOUNG MAN, HE FOUND INSPIRATION IN THE METAPHYSICAL AND THE SPIRITUAL. AND OF COURSE, ALWAYS, SURFING. ⟶ THE ART SCHOOL RICK HAD ATTENDED FOCUSED ON MODERN ART, AND LEFT LITTLE TO NO ROOM FOR HIS INTEREST IN COMICS AND CARTOONS. IT WAS IN SAN FRANCISCO, IN THE COMPANY OF OTHER WORKING ARTISTS MAKING POSTERS, THAT HE WAS ABLE TO PUSH HIS CREATIVE BOUNDARIES AND FURTHER HIS ARTISTIC EDUCATION. POSTER WORK GAVE RICK COMPLETE ARTISTIC FREEDOM TO EXPRESS HIS OWN INNER VISION. HE BEGAN TO STUDY THE PROCESS OF LITHOGRAPHY, PRINT, AND COLOR SEPARATION, AND WAS OPENED UP TO A NEW WORLD OF EQUIPMENT AND POSSIBILITIES THAT LED TO MUCH OF THE WORK FOR WHICH HE WAS MOST RECOGNIZED. ⟶ WHILE HE MIGHT BE BEST REMEMBERED FOR A LEGACY OF SURF CARTOONS, PSYCHEDELIC CONCERT POSTERS, UNDERGROUND COMIX, GRATEFUL DEAD ALBUM COVERS, AND DEEPLY COMPLEX RELIGIOUS PAINTINGS, SUCCESS, TO RICK, MEANT HE COULD CONTINUE TO SURF, DRAW, LISTEN TO MUSIC, AND KEEP $100 IN HIS POCKET.

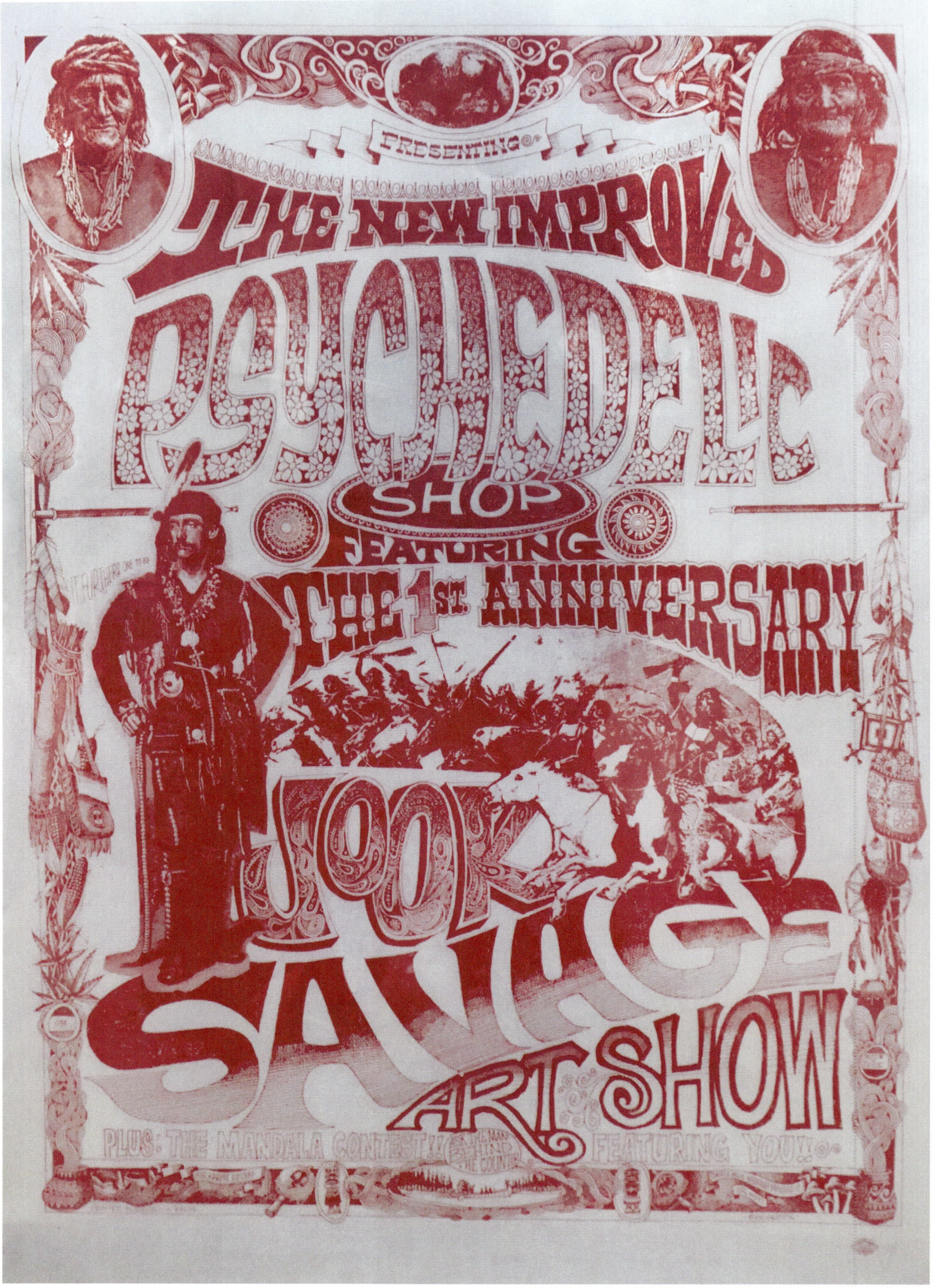

This page: the plate for Griffin's debut psychedelic poster, made in late 1966 for the first anniversary of the Psychedelic Shop, on the corner of Haight and Ashbury in San Francisco. Marijuana leaves, mushrooms, peyote buttons, and hippie paraphernalia line the border. En route to the printer, he met organizers of the Human Be-In, and wound up making a poster for that event.

Opposite: a black-and-white and split-fountain version of Griffin's debut psychedelic poster (above) with his poster based on the handbill for 1967's Human Be-In organized by Michael Bowen in black and white (signed by Timothy Leary) and in color (below). Griffin's design of the latter led Chet Helms to recruit him for the Avalon Ballroom.

RICK GRIFFIN'S EARLY PSYCHEDELIA

Fresh from high school, Rick Griffin joined *Surfer* magazine as a staff artist. He had been a part of a Los Angeles 'art gang/jugband group,' the Jook Savages, before moving to San Francisco at the end of 1966. His first poster was for a Jook Savage art show at the Psychedelic Shop; his second was for the Human Be-In in January 1967. He was also in the Be-In edition of *The Oracle*.

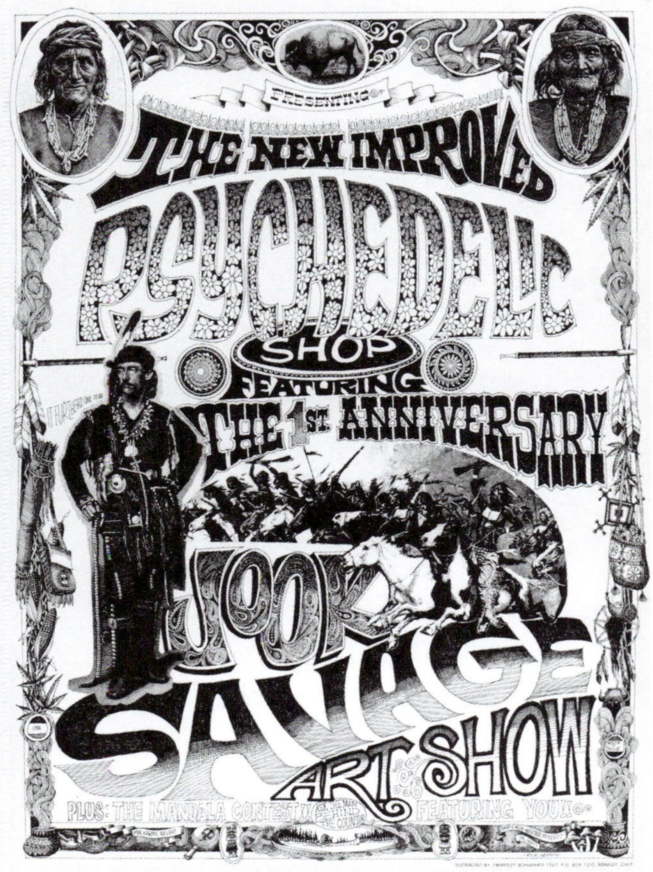

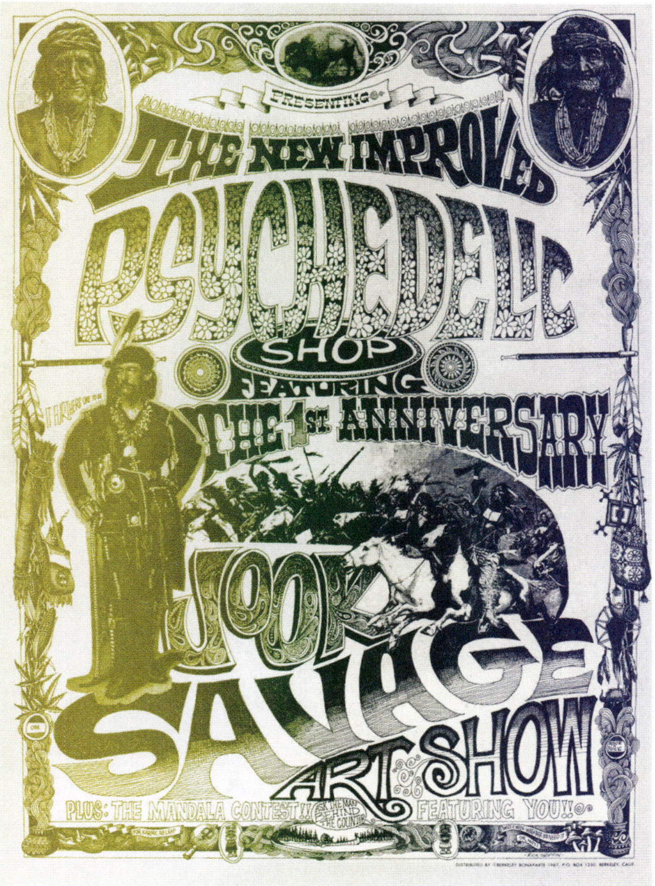

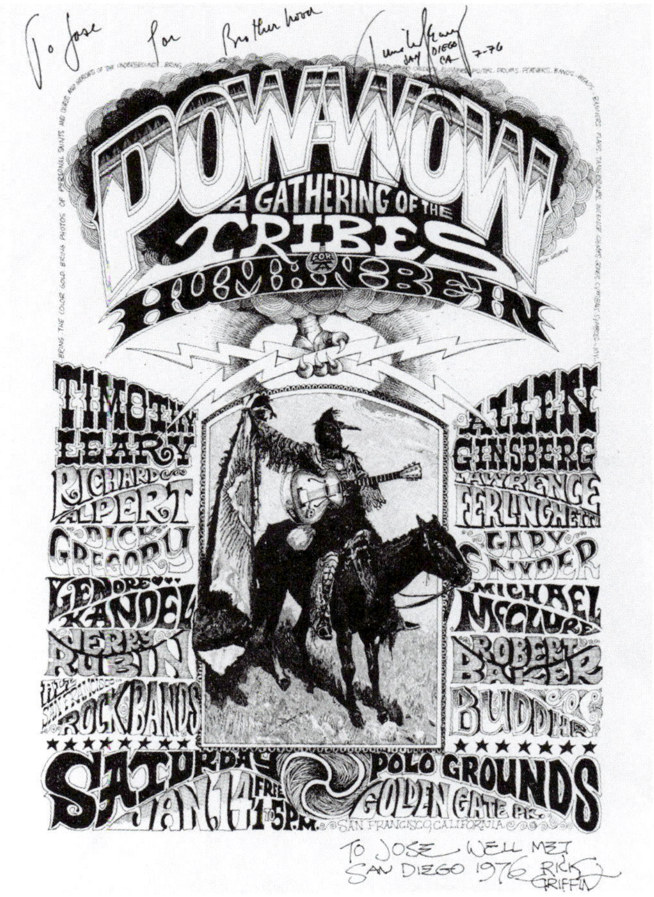

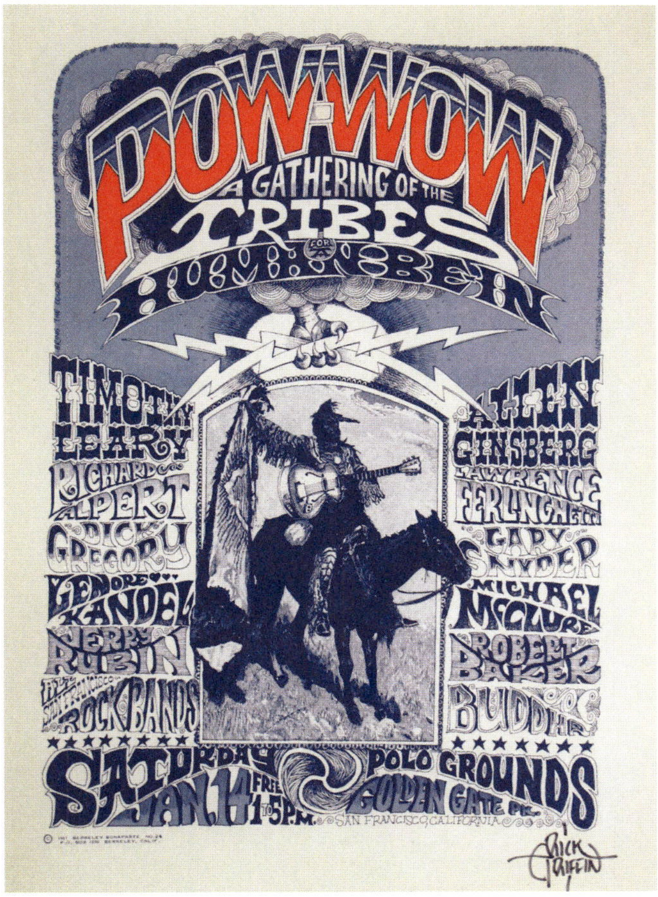

GRIFFIN TAKES OFF

Griffin's Be-In poster was well received, and both Chet Helms and Bill Graham asked him to work for them; his first Family Dog poster appeared in March 1967. Griffin may have made his name penning cartoons for *Surfer* magazine, but he experimented with a range of different styles throughout his career. He had visited the Red Dog Saloon in 1966 and bought into the Old West design aesthetic, but confined it largely to his fonts. His Family Dog work featured puns and humorous take-offs on images of everyday life. He raided well-known commercial labels and adverts as well as Michelangelo, Victorian engravings, share certificates and images that other artists had already borrowed, from Wes Wilson's Indian (for Family Dog Productions) to Mouse's 'Zig-Zag Man.' He took a particular interest in 19th-century photography and illustration, as well as Native American history and iconography, and experimented with boldly ambitious typefaces. He worked mainly for The Family Dog, although in 1967 he also set up the distribution agency Berkeley Bonaparte (with Stanley Mouse, Alton Kelley, Victor Moscoso, and Wes Wilson) to design and market psychedelic posters.

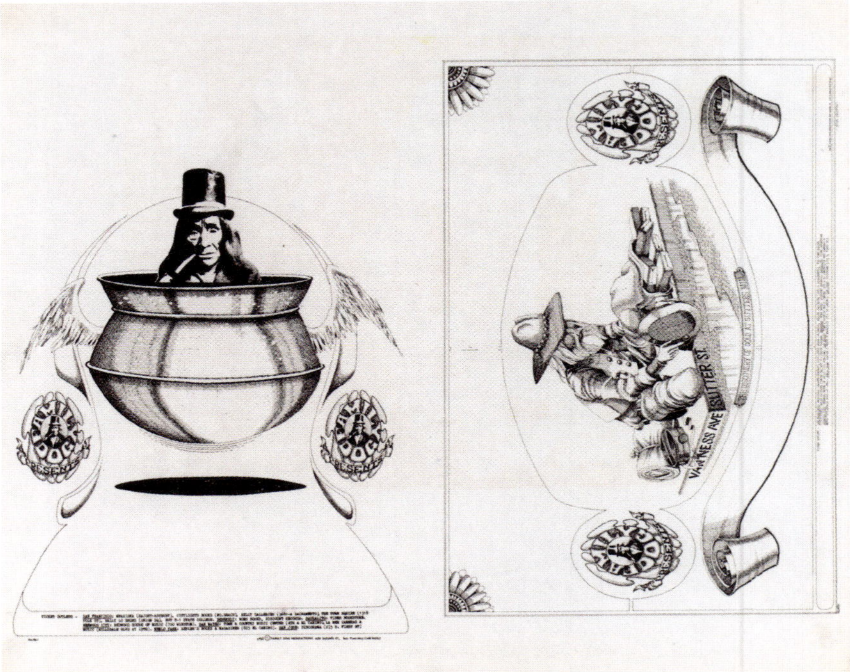

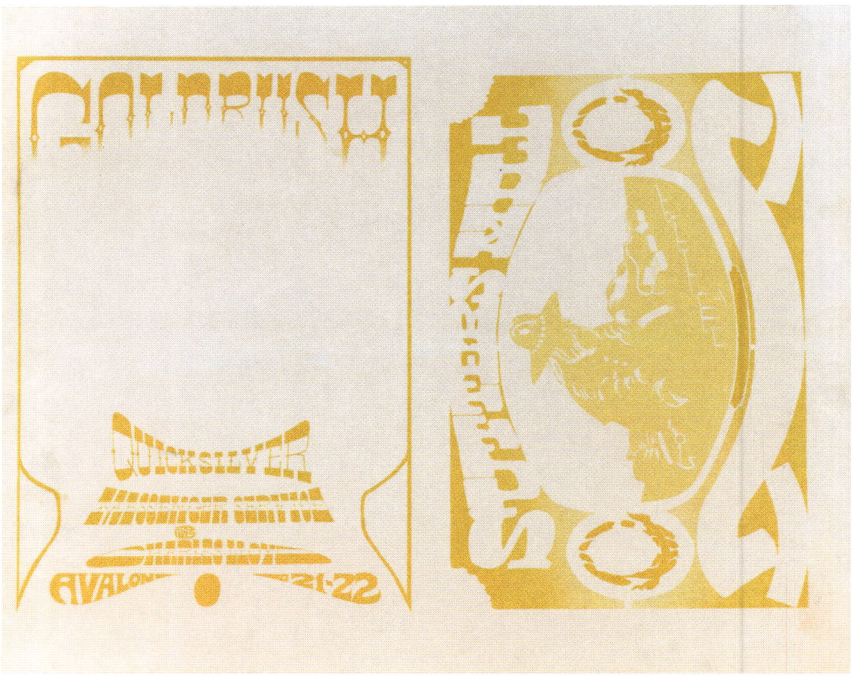

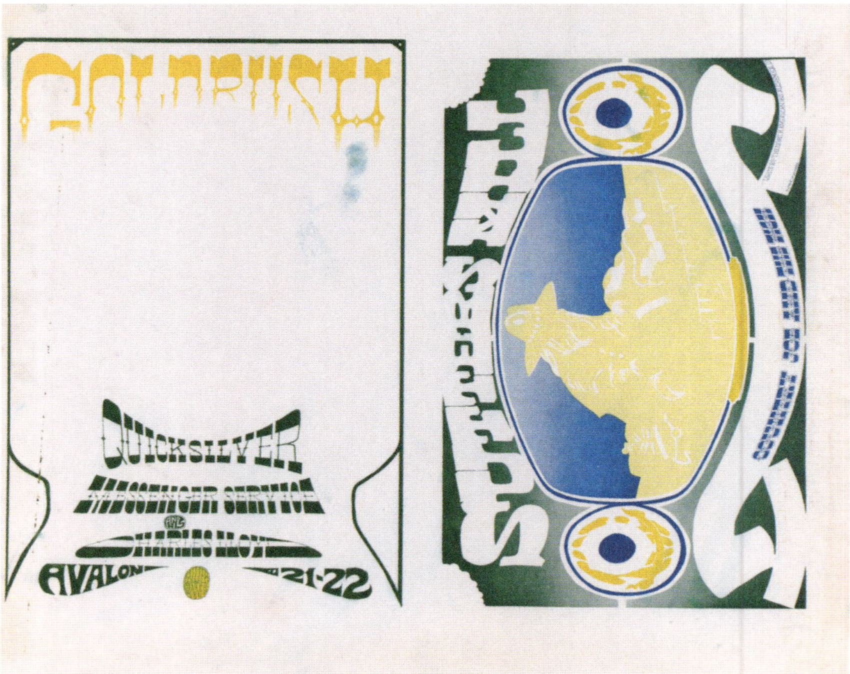

➳ Progressive color proofs and finished posters for two Rick Griffin posters advertising Avalon Ballroom concerts in April and May 1967. In both cases, the design and Family Dog Productions logo take precedence over the name of the headline act (in this case, Quicksilver Messenger Service).

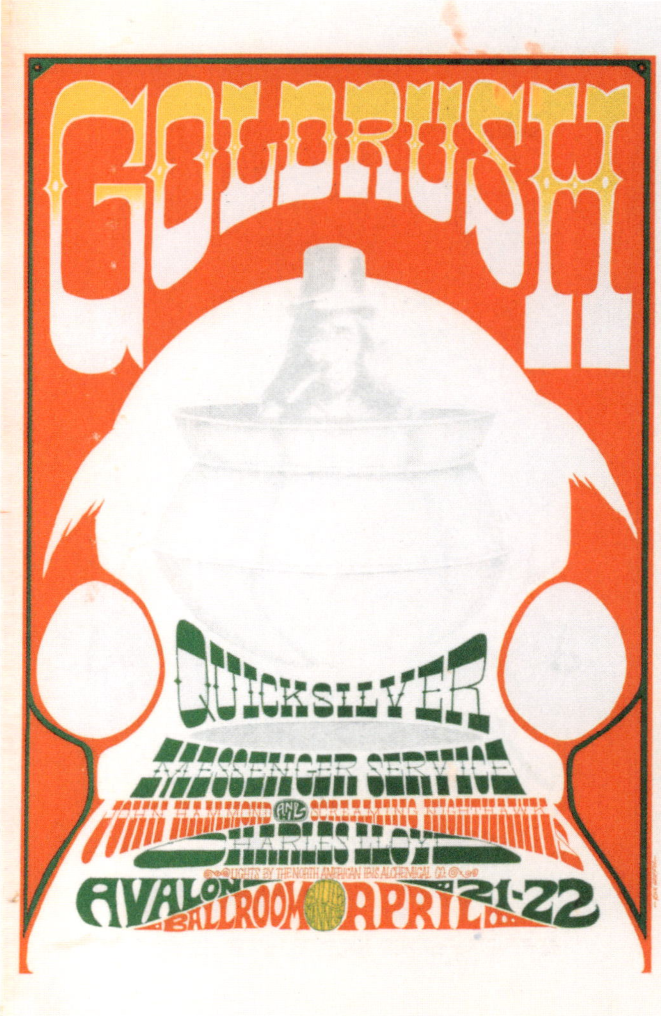
GOLDRUSH II
QUICKSILVER
MESSENGER SERVICE
JOHN HAMMOND AND SCREAMING NIGHTHAWKS
CHARLES LLOYD
LIGHTS BY THE NORTH AMERICAN IBIS ALCHEMICAL CO.
AVALON BALLROOM APRIL 21-22

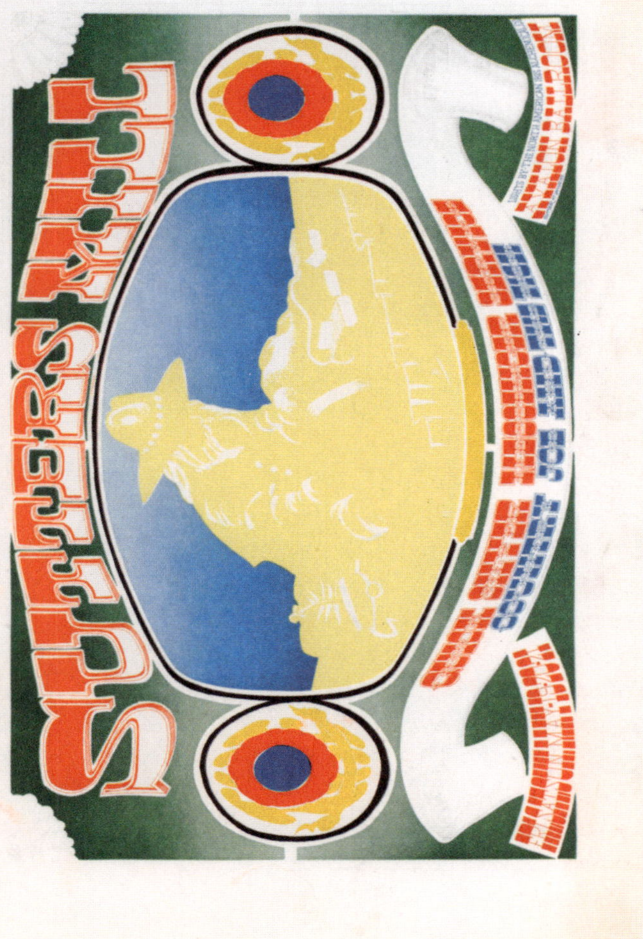
SUTTER'S MILL

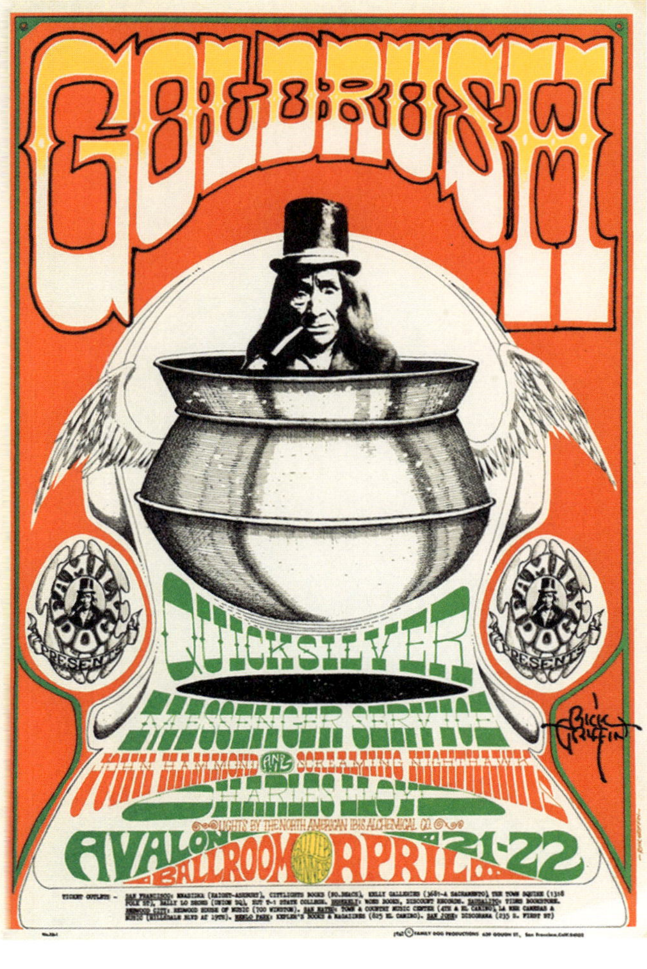
GOLDRUSH II
QUICKSILVER
MESSENGER SERVICE
JOHN HAMMOND AND SCREAMING NIGHTHAWKS
CHARLES LLOYD
LIGHTS BY THE NORTH AMERICAN IBIS ALCHEMICAL CO.
AVALON BALLROOM APRIL 21-22
RICK GRIFFIN

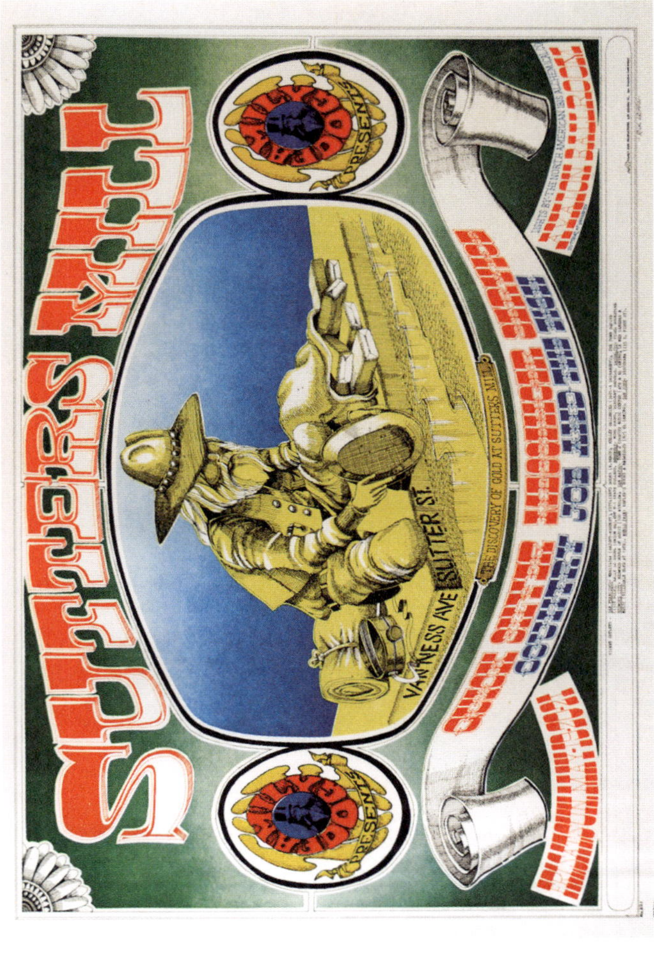
SUTTER'S MILL
THE DISCOVERY OF GOLD AT SUTTER'S MILL
VAN NESS AVE
SUTTER ST.

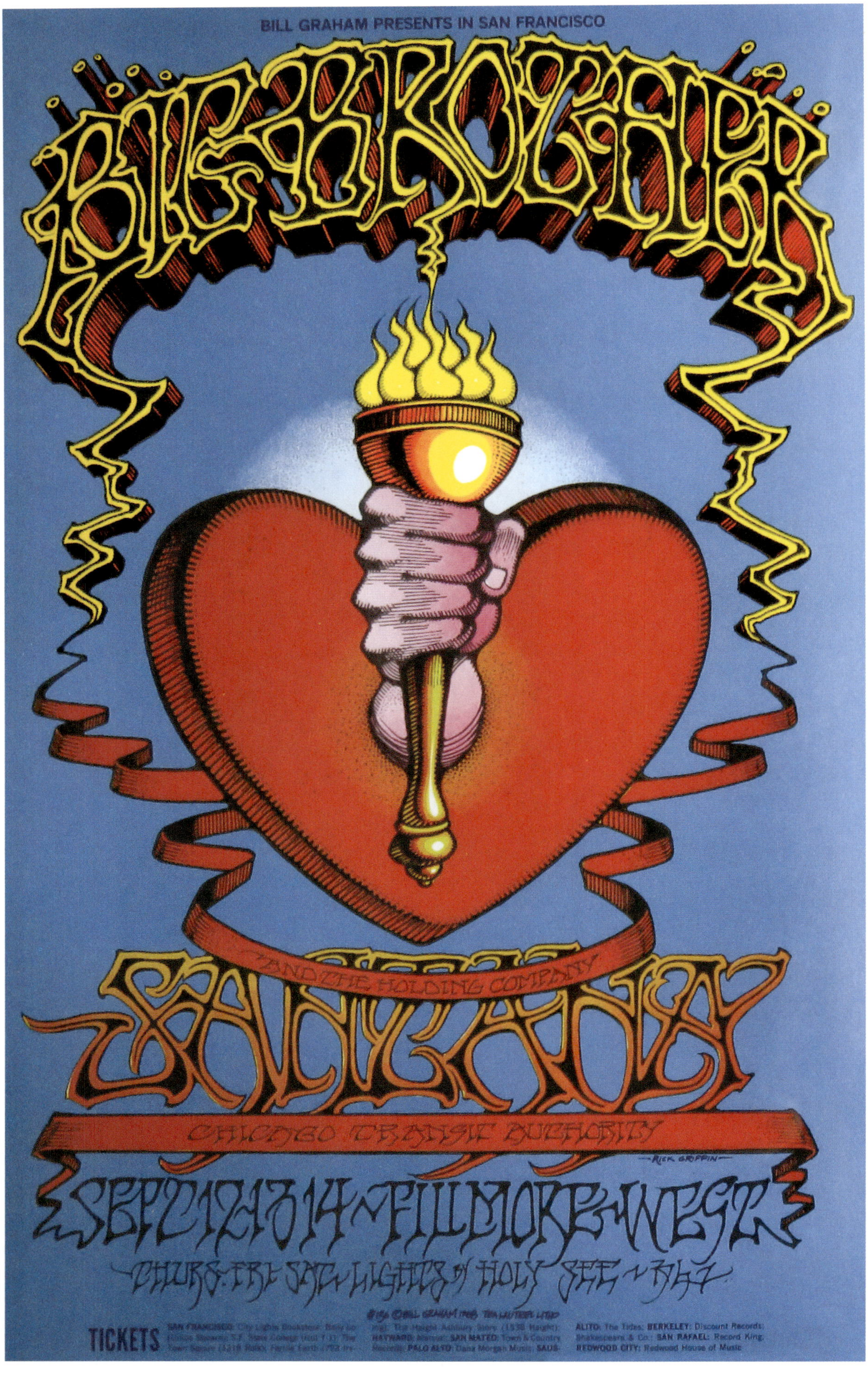

⟿ This page: the bold *Heart and Torch* from 1968 promotes a show headlined by Big Brother and the Holding Company and Santana. Janis Joplin was to leave Big Brother soon afterwards. ⟿ Opposite: Griffin's skill as a cartoonist is amply demonstrated in this comic-strip-style design—unprecedented for a rock poster—for Quicksilver Messenger Service at the Avalon Ballroom in October 1967. Three color stages and the full-color proof are shown here. It had unexpected repercussions: Victor Moscoso told Griffin he'd been planning a similar design, which led to the two of them working together. It also inspired cartoonist Robert Crumb (then working on *Zap Comix* No.1) to re-evaluate his own approach. Crumb invited Griffin to join him and S. Clay Wilson on the second issue; Griffin invited Moscoso along too.

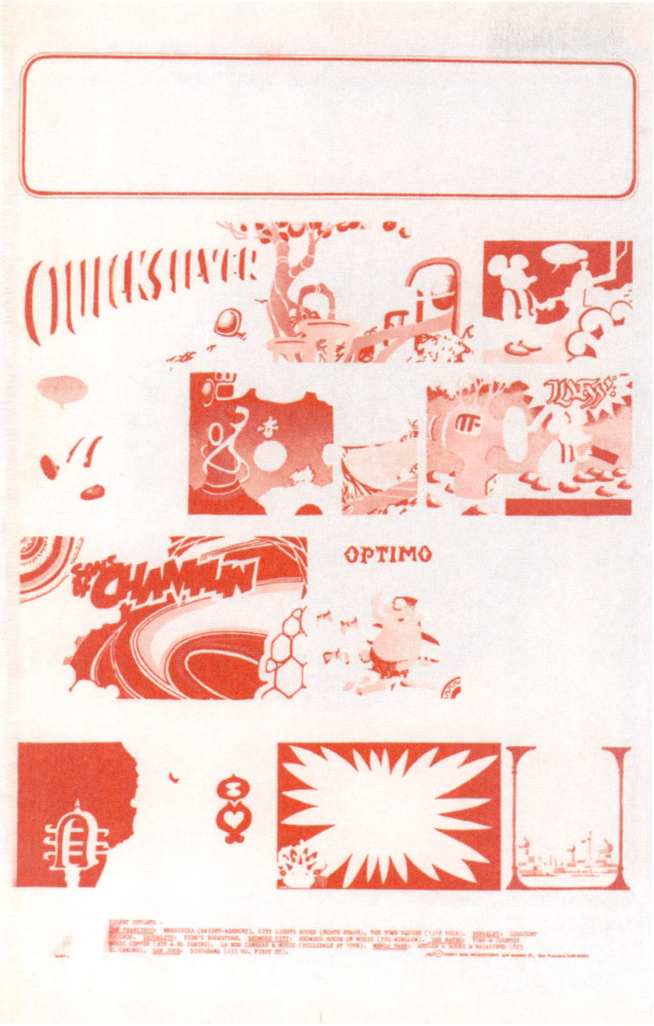
QUICKSILVER
OPTIMO

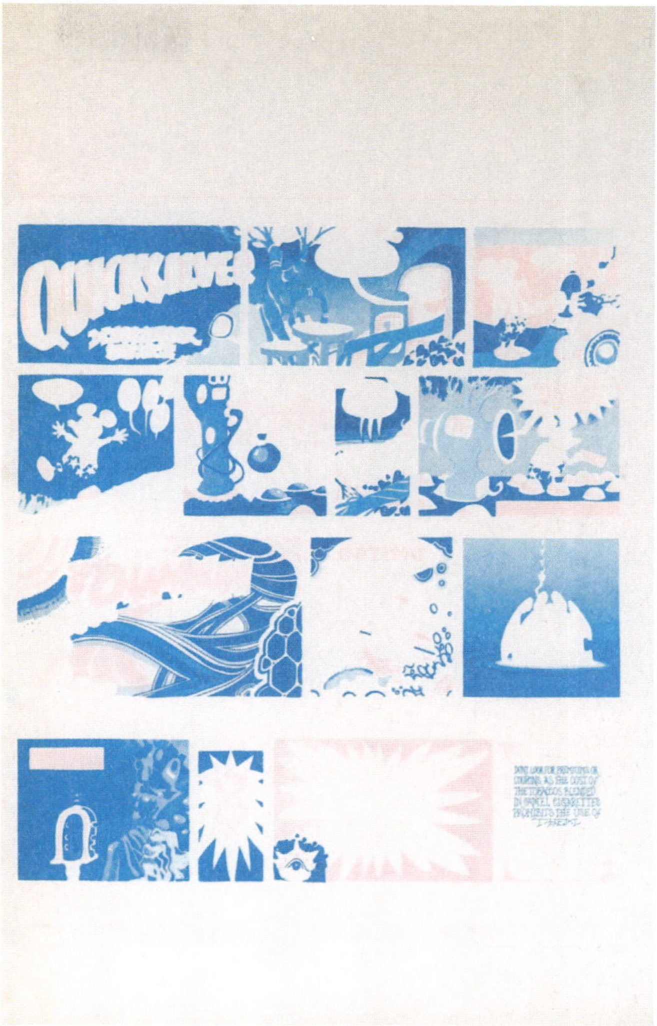
QUICKSILVER

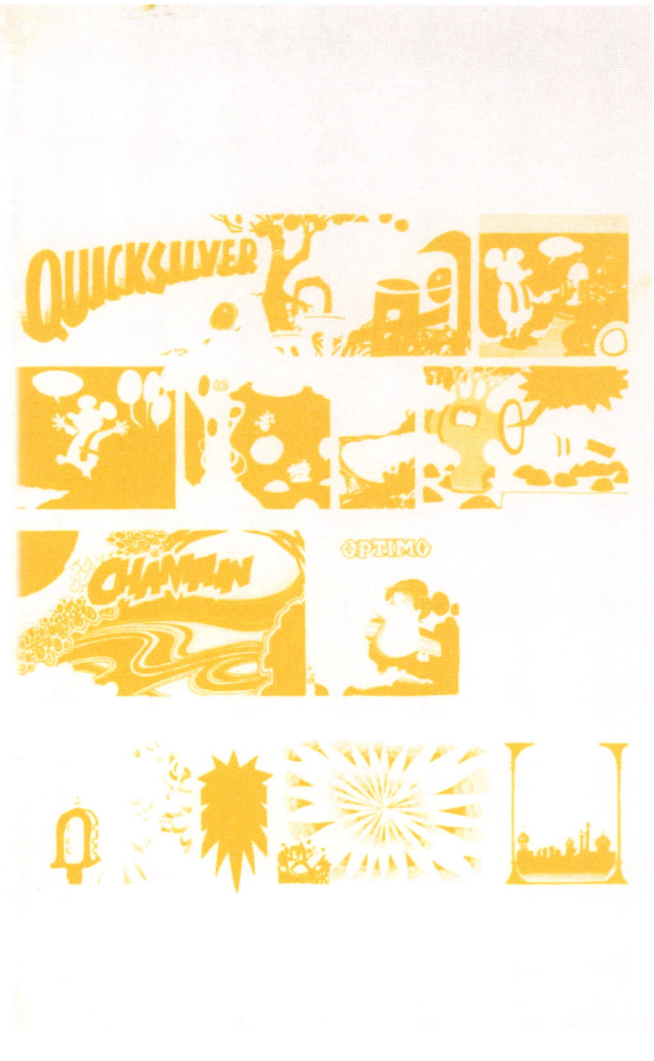
QUICKSILVER
OPTIMO

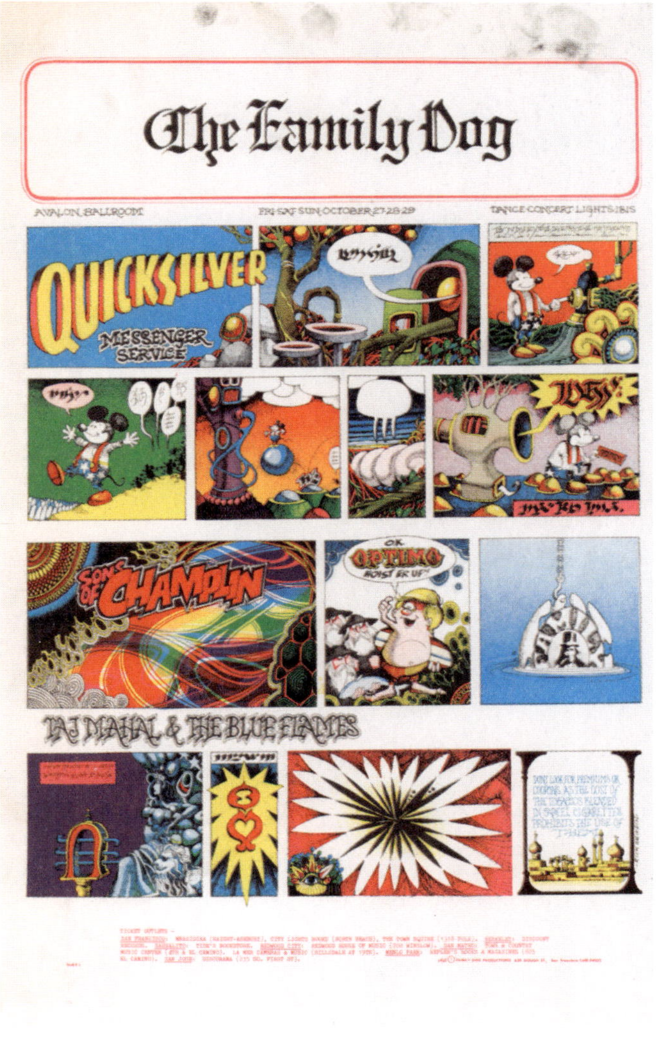
The Family Dog
AVALON BALLROOM
FRI-SAT-SUN OCTOBER 27-28-29
QUICKSILVER
MESSENGER SERVICE
SONS OF CHAMPLIN
OPTIMO
TAJ MAHAL & THE BLUE FLAMES

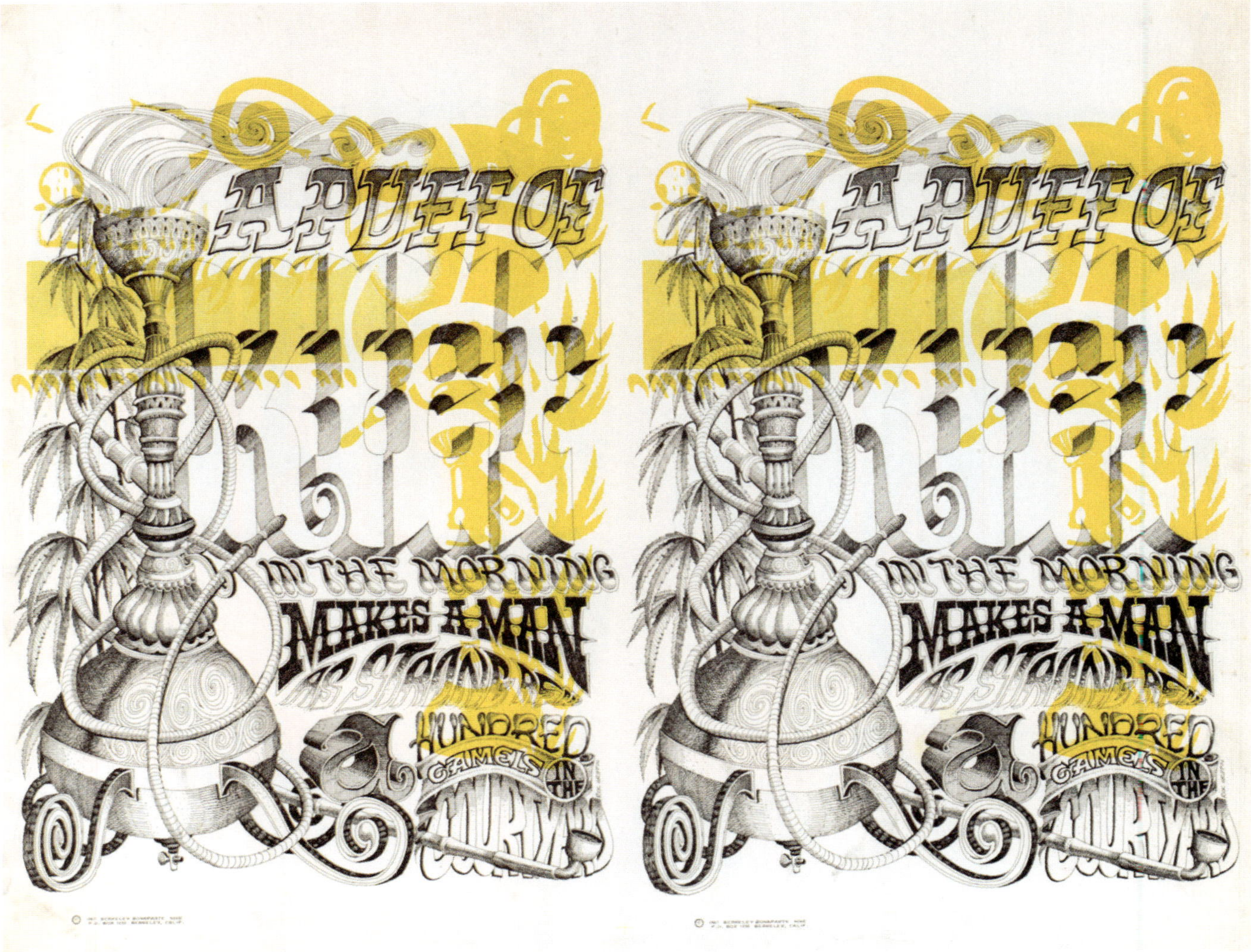

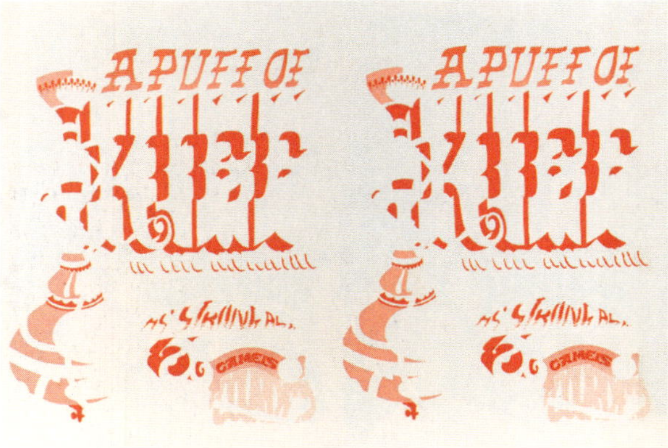

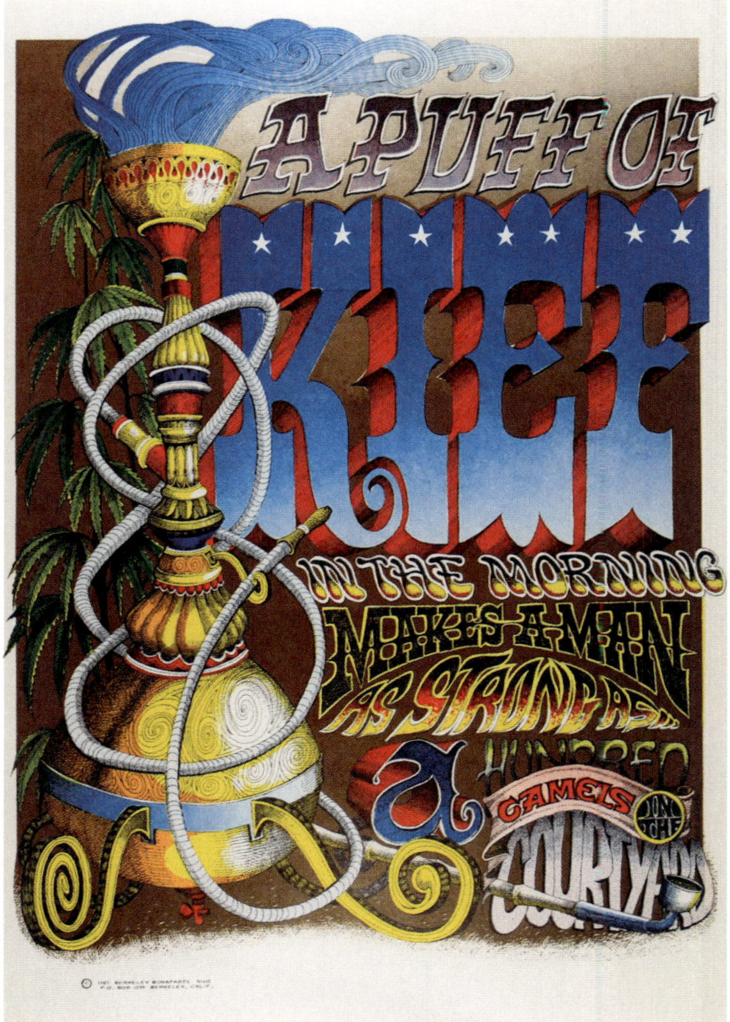

⟿ Printing plates, progressive proofs, and complete artwork for two Rick Griffin head-shop posters. Griffin's working methods involved hand color separation—producing a separate piece of artwork for the color plate for each color. Humorous (the 'can' in 'Can-a-blis' was a beatnik term for an ounce of marijuana) as well as deftly executed, both these designs date from *c.* 1967 and were made for Berkeley Bonaparte. They were two of a series of posters that were inspired by Griffin's collection of twenties tin and label designs.

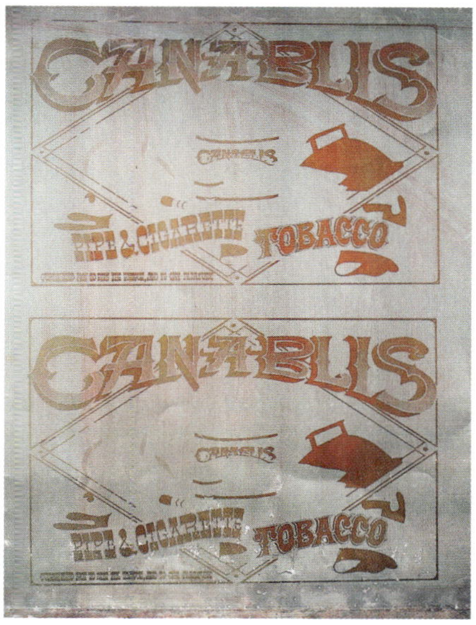
CAN-A-BLIS
PIPE & CIGARETTE
TOBACCO

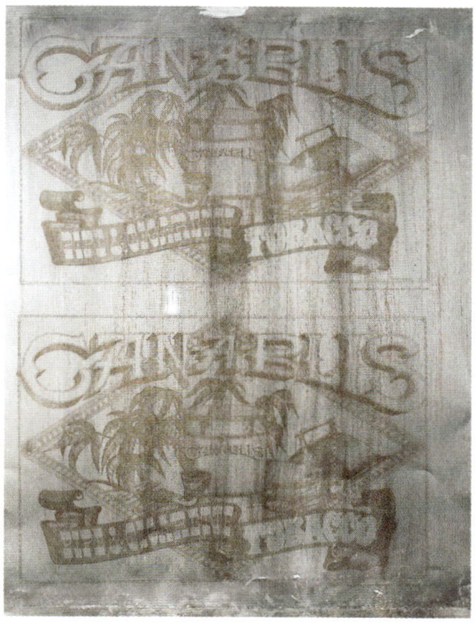
CAN-A-BLIS
TOBACCO

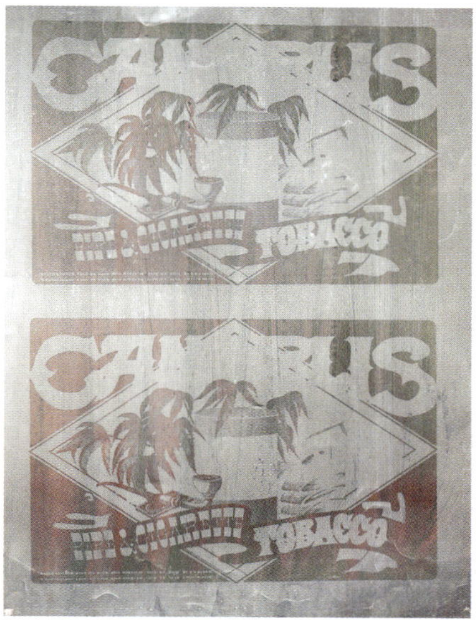
CAN-A-BLIS
TOBACCO

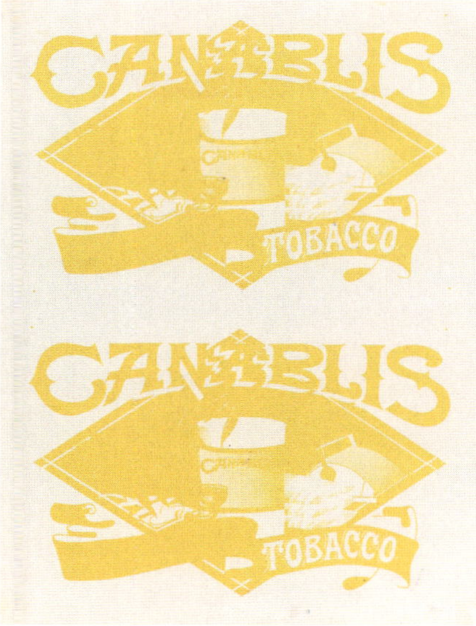
CAN-A-BLIS
TOBACCO

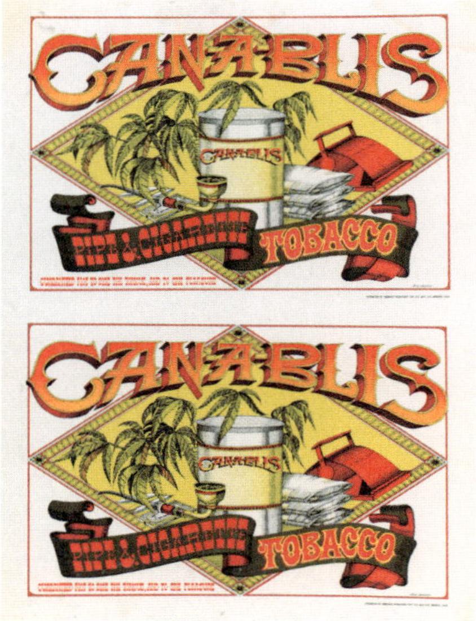
CAN-A-BLIS
PIPE & CIGARETTE
TOBACCO

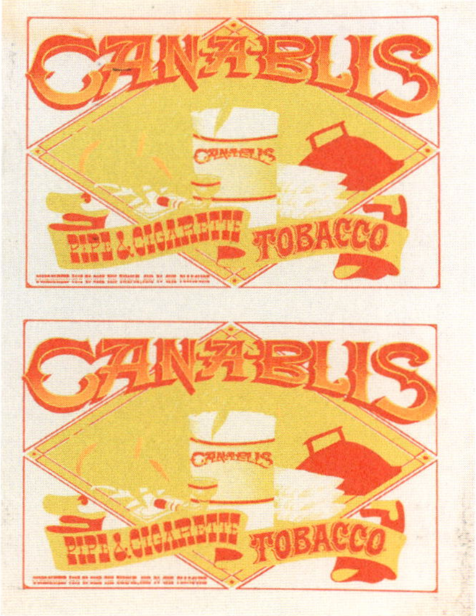
CAN-A-BLIS
PIPE & CIGARETTE
TOBACCO

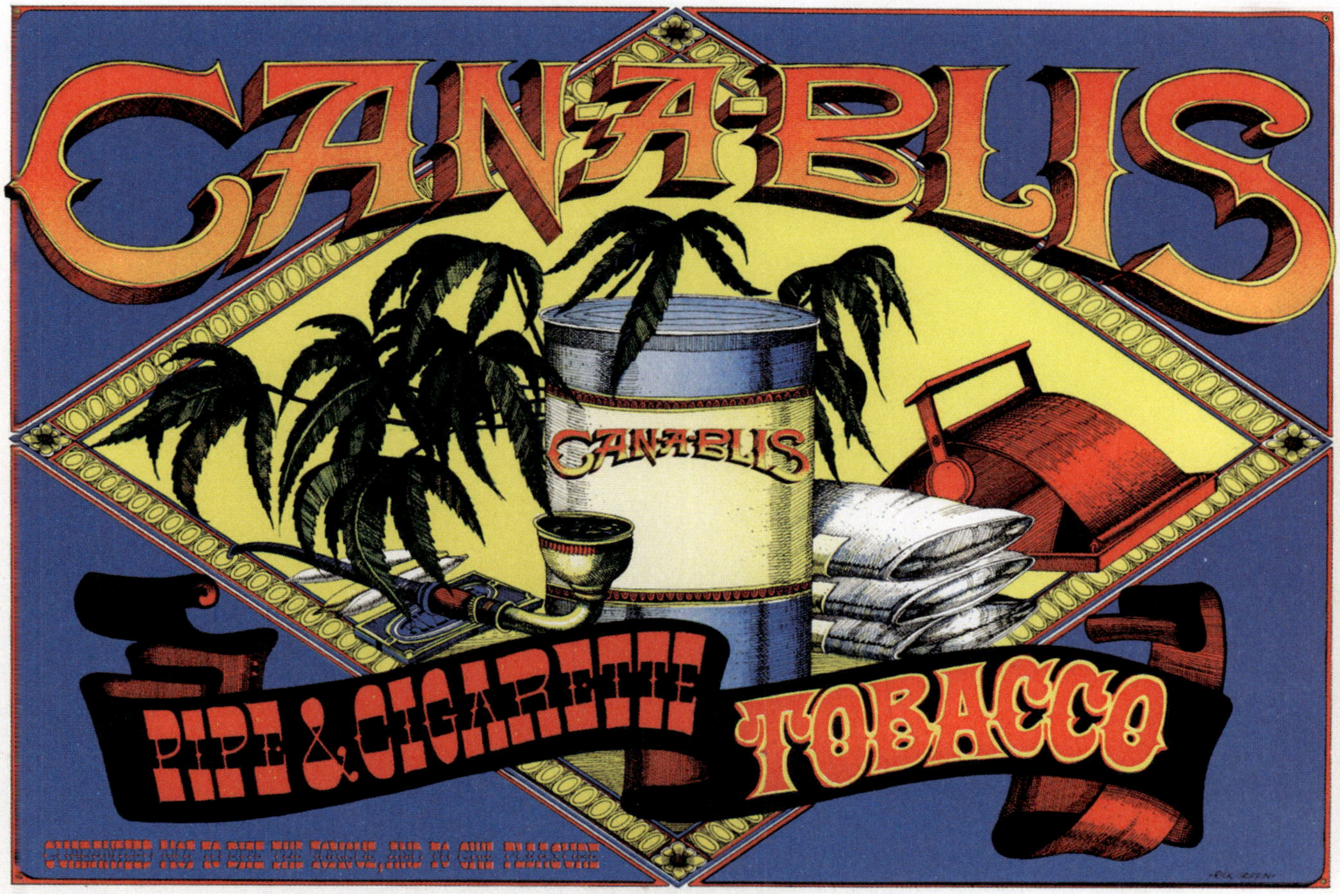
CAN-A-BLIS
CAN-A-BLIS
PIPE & CIGARETTE
TOBACCO

HAIGHT-ASHBURY

Haight-Ashbury took its name from a cross street in a rundown area of the city east of Golden Gate Park, south of the university, filled with old Victorian mansions that lent themselves to communal living, particularly for rock bands such as Jefferson Airplane and the Grateful Dead. It became the center for the new psychedelic community: musicians, artists, and underground newspaper publishers (*The Oracle* came from the area), poets and political activists. After the national publicity given to the Human Be-In, which was staged on January 14, 1967, it also became home to thousands of young people from across America, attracted to the hippie lifestyle, and to the inevitable drug dealers and other associated predators.

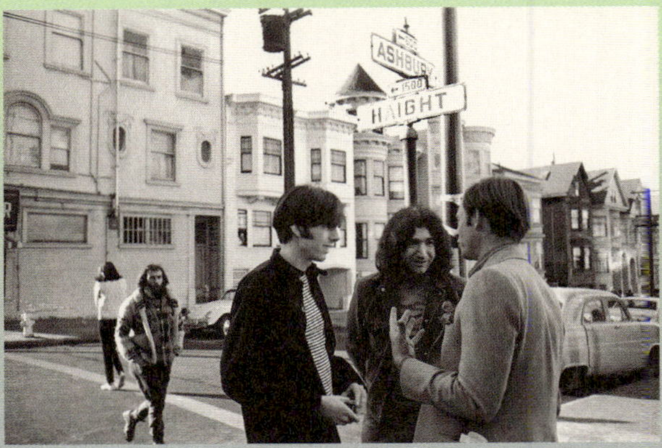

Dead on the street, October 1966 ⋙→ Writer Tom Wolfe (right) chats with Grateful Dead guitarist Jerry Garcia (center) and the band's manager, Rock Scully (left) in Haight-Ashbury. Wolfe's book *The Electric Kool-Aid Acid Test* (1968) documented the lifestyle of Ken Kesey and his Merry Pranksters.

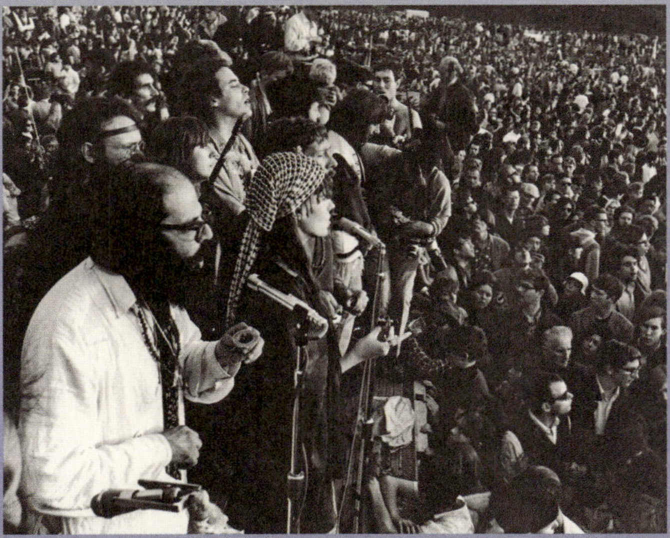

Poet Allen Ginsberg at the Human Be-In ⋙→ Ginsberg embodied a link between the writers of the beat generation and the new counter-culture on the West Coast. During the course of the day, he led mantra chants with fellow poet Gary Snyder.

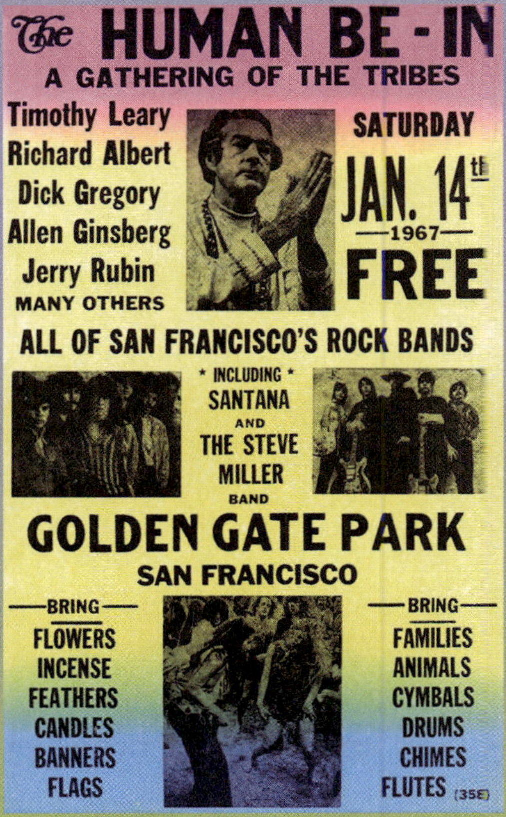

Human Be-In poster, 1967 ⋙→ A straight-forward piece of promotion for the day.

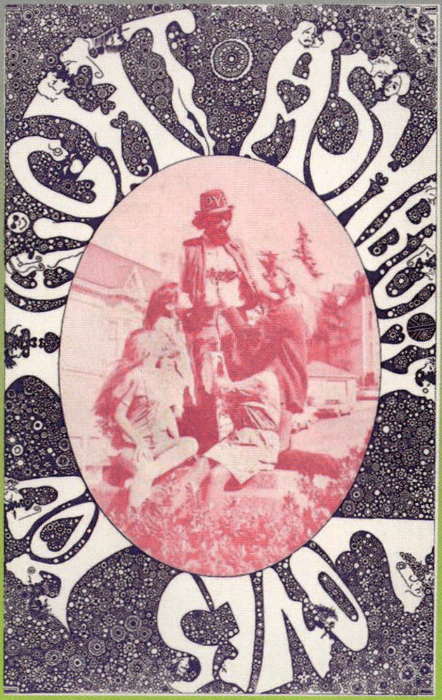

Head-shop poster, 1967 ⋙→ This Joe Gomez design incorporates playful lettering based on the contorted shapes of human figures.

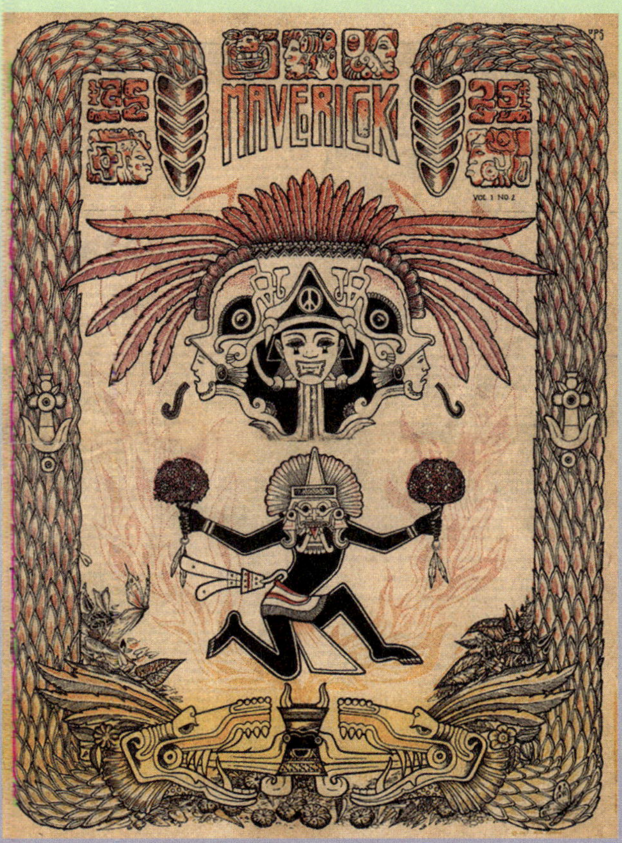

Volume 1, issue #2 of *The Haight Ashbury Maverick*, 1967 ⋙→ This underground magazine ran for just a year. This cover references symbols from ancient American civilizations.

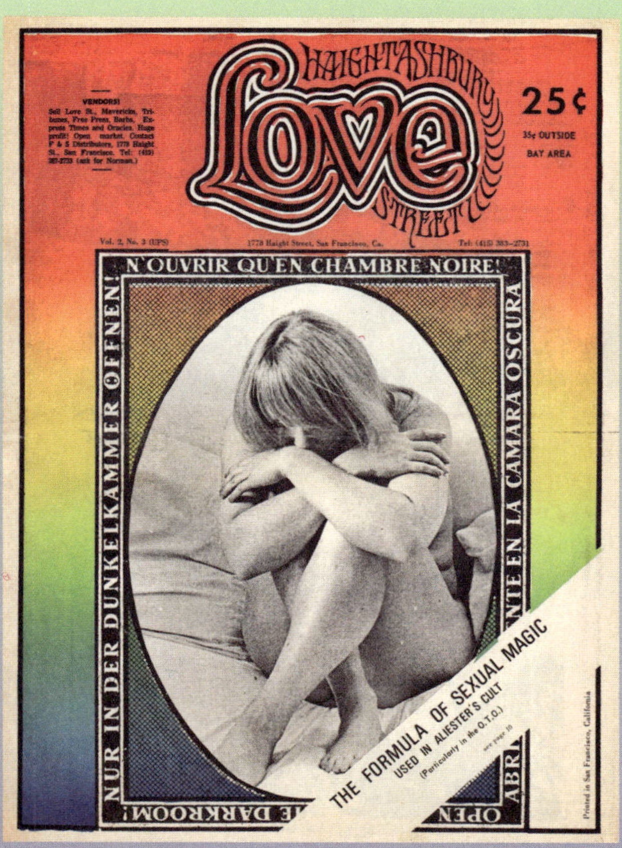

Haight Ashbury Love Street magazine ⋙→ A titillating cover that deliberately plays on the more open sexuality of the hippie era ('Only open in a dark room!' advise the multi-lingual taglines tantalizingly—if somewhat illogically).

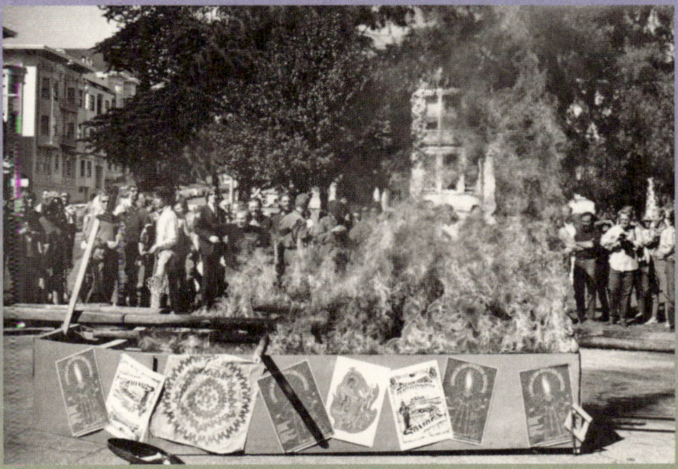

'Death of Hippie,' October 6, 1967 ⋙→ A symbolic coffin was burned at the close of a day's festivities to mark the end of the original hippie ideals and the commercialization of hippie culture.

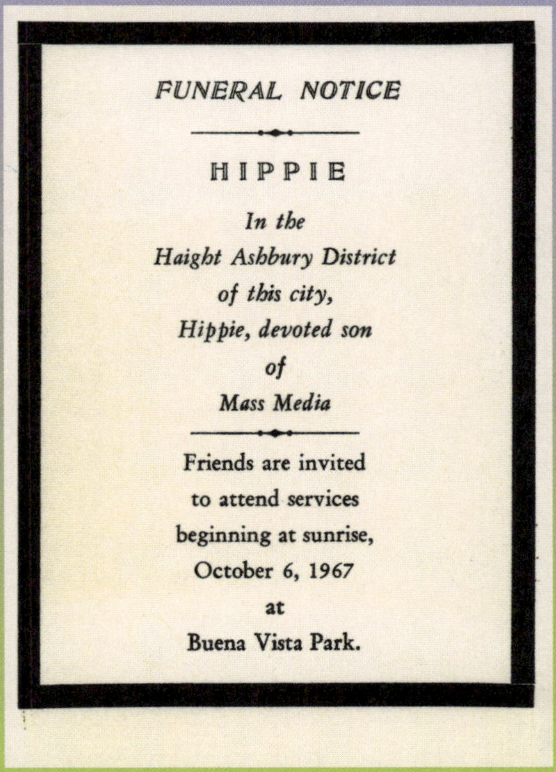

FUNERAL NOTICE

HIPPIE

In the
Haight Ashbury District
of this city,
Hippie, devoted son
of
Mass Media

Friends are invited
to attend services
beginning at sunrise,
October 6, 1967
at
Buena Vista Park.

Hippie funeral notice ⋙→ Commercialization and exploitation of the hippie dream was already well underway by late 1967. Reflecting this, the Diggers organized a mock 'Death of Hippie' service in San Francisco.

⋙→ 'Pink Panther,' a Moscoso poster created for a set of June 1967 Family Dog dance concerts at the Avalon Ballroom featuring The Miller Blues Band and The Doors. The design showcases Moscoso's trademark vibrating colors and mind-bending typography.

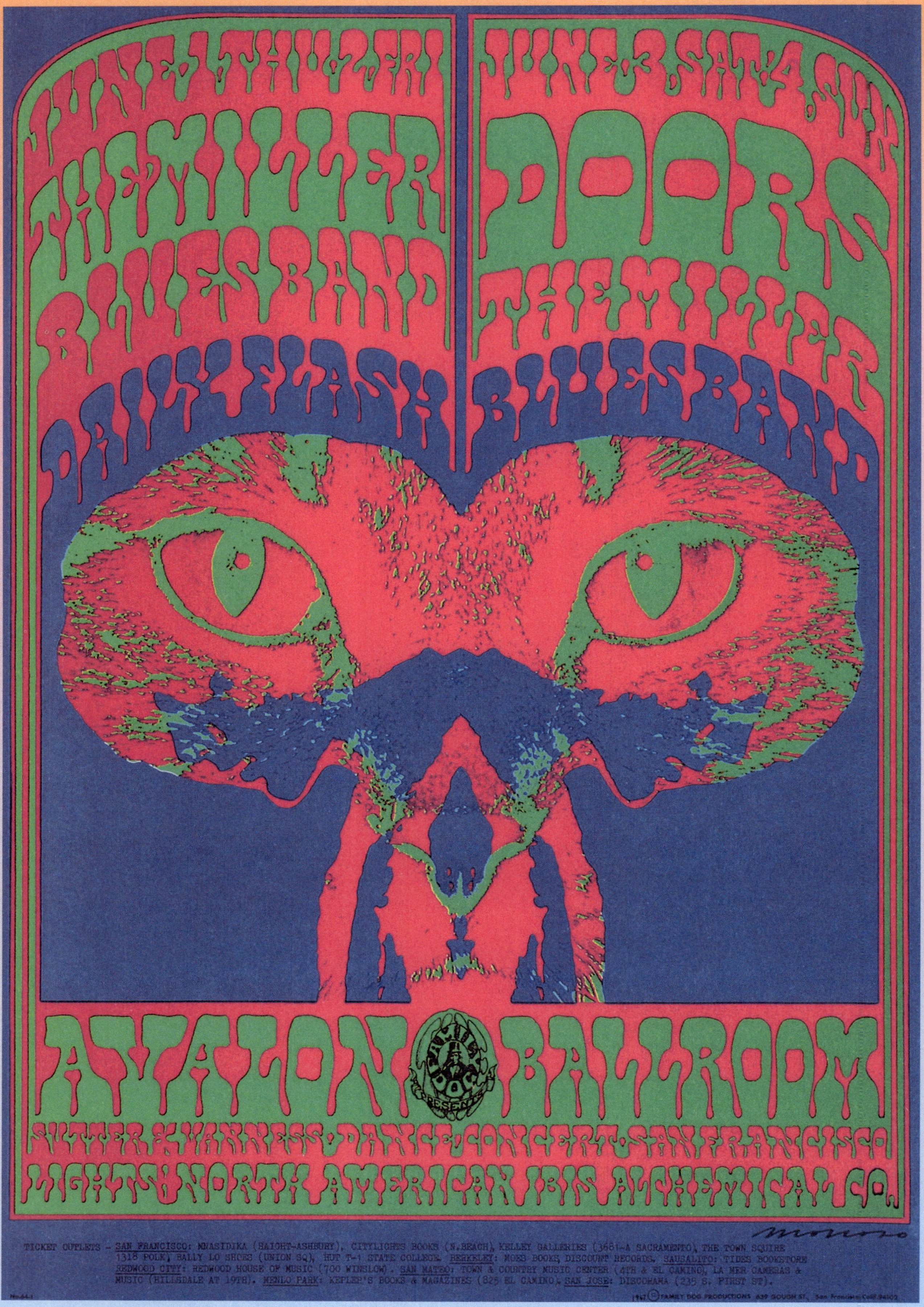

VICTOR MOSCOSO (1945–1973)

BORN IN SPAIN, VICTOR MOSCOSO WAS THE FIRST OF THE SIXTIES ROCK POSTER ARTISTS TO HAVE FORMAL ACADEMIC TRAINING AND EXPERIENCE. AFTER STUDYING ART AT COOPER UNION IN NEW YORK CITY AND AT YALE UNIVERSITY, HE MOVED TO SAN FRANCISCO IN 1959. THERE, HE ATTENDED THE SAN FRANCISCO ART INSTITUTE, WHERE HE EVENTUALLY BECAME AN INSTRUCTOR. → PROFESSIONAL LIGHTNING STRUCK FOR MOSCOSO IN THE FORM OF THE PSYCHEDELIC ROCK-AND-ROLL POSTERS CREATED FOR THE SAN FRANCISCO HIPPIE DANCE HALLS AND CLUBS. MOSCOSO'S POSTERS FOR THE FAMILY DOG DANCE CONCERTS AT THE AVALON BALLROOM AND HIS NEON ROSE POSTERS FOR THE MATRIX BROUGHT HIS WORK INTERNATIONAL ATTENTION DURING THE SUMMER OF LOVE IN 1967. → WITHIN A YEAR, LIGHTNING WOULD STRIKE AGAIN IN THE FORM OF UNDERGROUND COMIX. AS ONE OF THE *ZAP COMIX* ARTISTS, MOSCOSO AND HIS WORK ONCE AGAIN RECEIVED INTERNATIONAL ATTENTION. HE HAS CONTINUED TO PRODUCE COMIX AND POSTER WORK RIGHT UP UNTIL THE PRESENT DAY, INCLUDING ALBUM COVERS FOR MUSICIANS SUCH AS JERRY GARCIA, BOB WEIR, HERBIE HANCOCK, AND DAVID GRISMAN. MOSCOSO HAS ALSO CREATED ART FOR USE ON T-SHIRTS, BILLBOARDS, ANIMATED COMMERCIALS FOR RADIO STATIONS (FOR WHICH HE HAS RECEIVED TWO CLIO AWARDS), AND MORE. → MOSCOSO'S PIONEERING USE OF VIBRATING COLORS IN HIS POSTERS WAS INFLUENCED BY PAINTER JOSEF ALBERS, ONE OF HIS TEACHERS AT YALE. VIBRATING COLORS ARE CREATED BY JUXTAPOSING COLORS FROM OPPOSITE ENDS OF THE COLOR WHEEL THAT HAVE EQUAL VALUE (DARK TO LIGHT) AND INTENSITY (BRIGHTNESS), SO THAT THE VIEWER'S EYE DOES NOT KNOW WHICH ONE TO FOCUS ON AS THE COLORS 'COMPETE' ALONG THE EDGES WHERE THEY TOUCH. MOSCOSO WAS ALSO THE FIRST OF THE ROCK POSTER ARTISTS TO USE PHOTOGRAPHIC COLLAGE IN MANY OF HIS POSTERS.

MOSCOSO'S TYPOGRAPHIC STYLE

The Spanish-born Moscoso studied at Yale University Art School under Josef Albers and subsequently at the San Francisco Art Institute, where he went on to teach lithography. However, his breakthrough came when he decided to disregard the conventions of good design, employing violently clashing colors that seem to pulse before the eyes (e.g. the red and blue seen in the design on this page), and lettering that actively disguises its message, forcing the reader to spend time deciphering it. He characterized this as 'a world turned upside down.'

Moscoso's blobby lettering has its direct origin in the title typography on the Beatles' *Rubber Soul* album (1965), designed by Charles Front, which was to become a huge influence on the San Francisco psychedelic artists a couple of years later.

Moscoso was one of the 'San Francisco Five' and his work was central to the movement. He is best known for his use of blocks of lettering as the formal elements of the composition of his posters, designed with more than a nod toward Alphonse Mucha, Jan Toorop, Hans Christiansen, and the Vienna Secession.

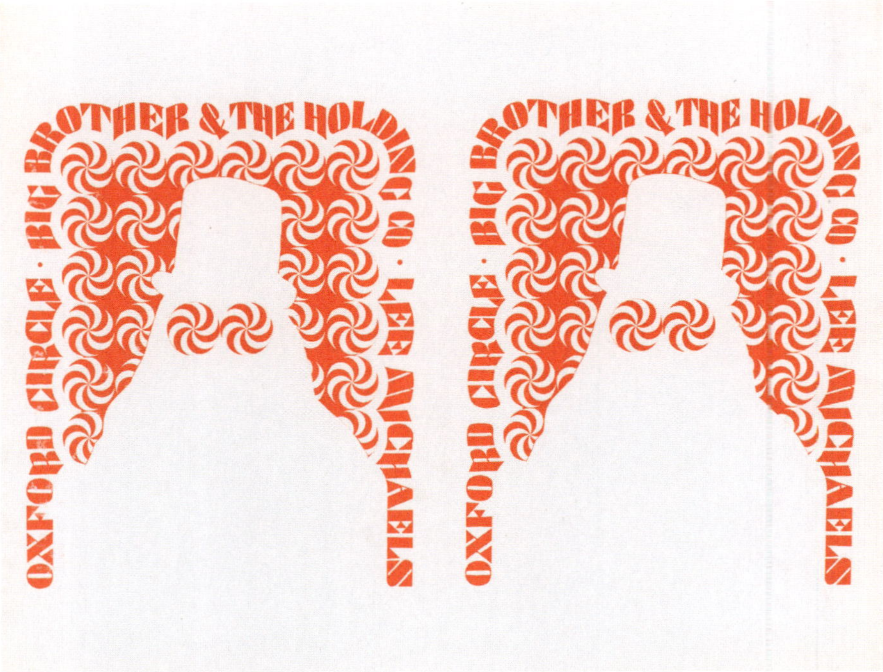

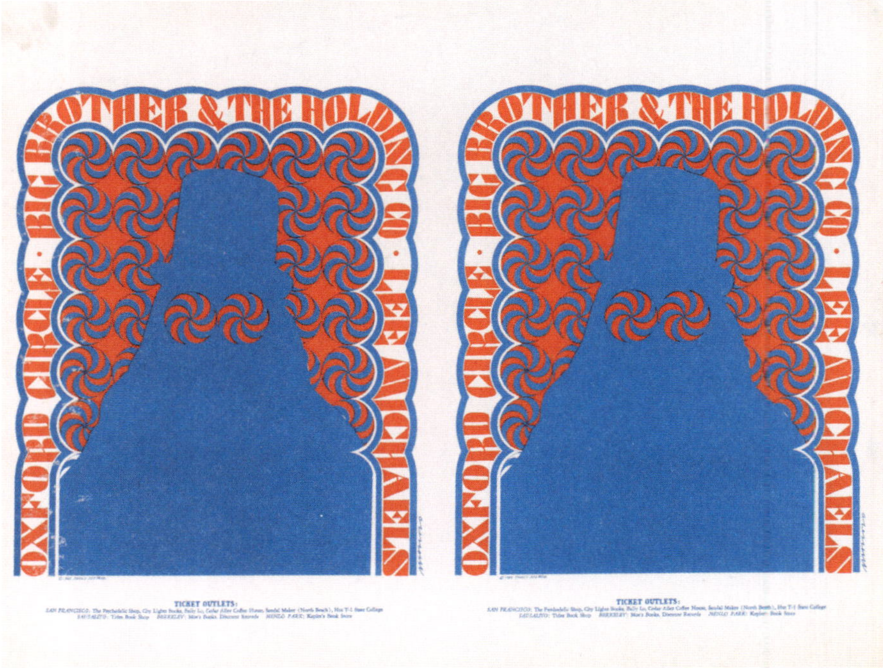

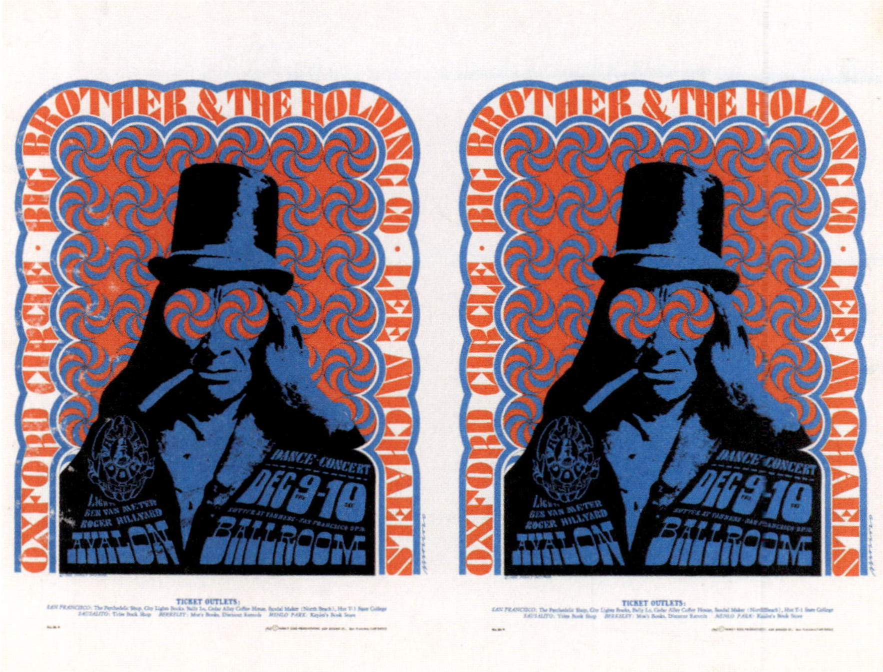

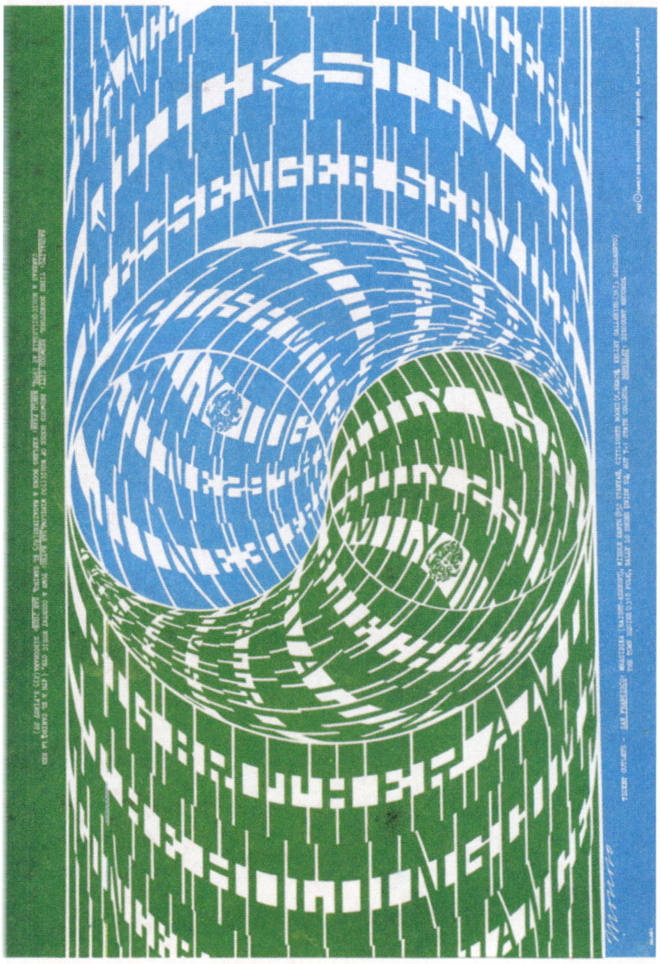
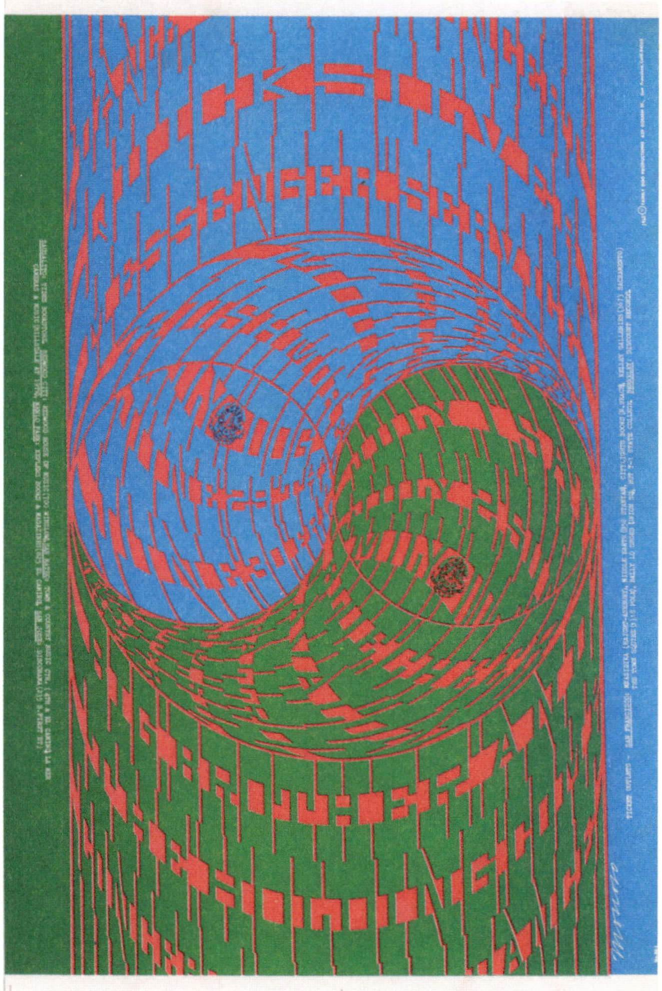

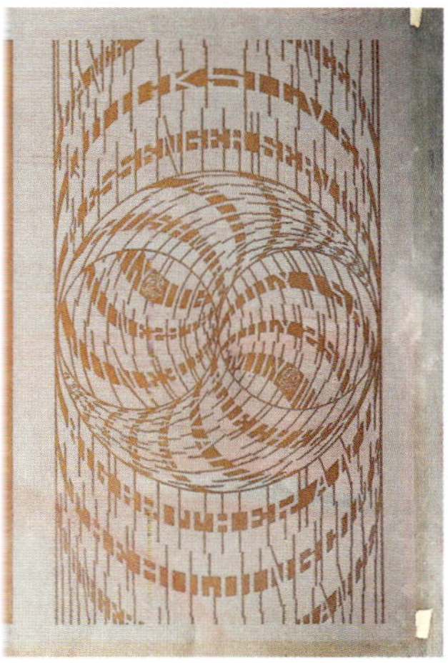
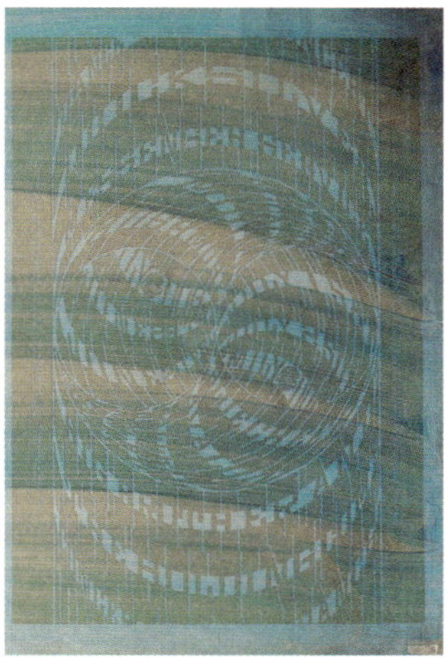
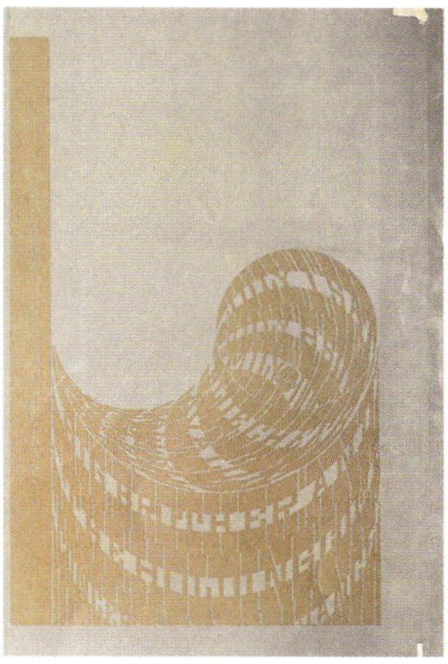
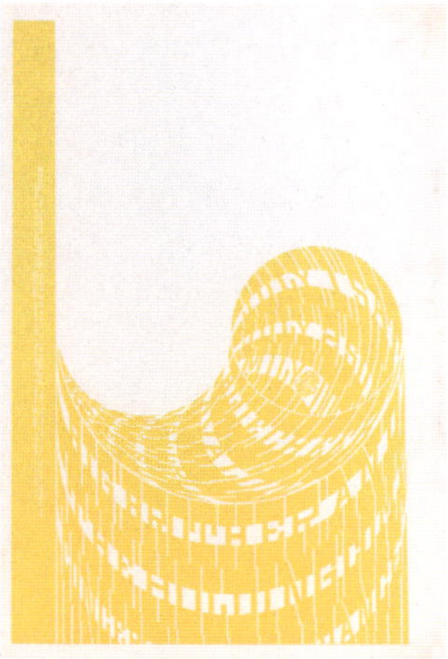

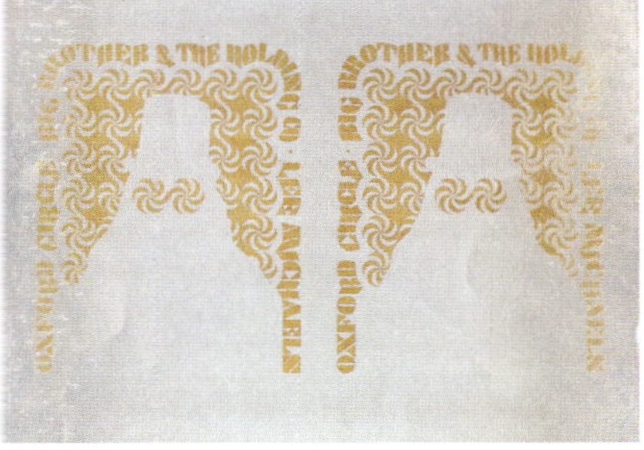
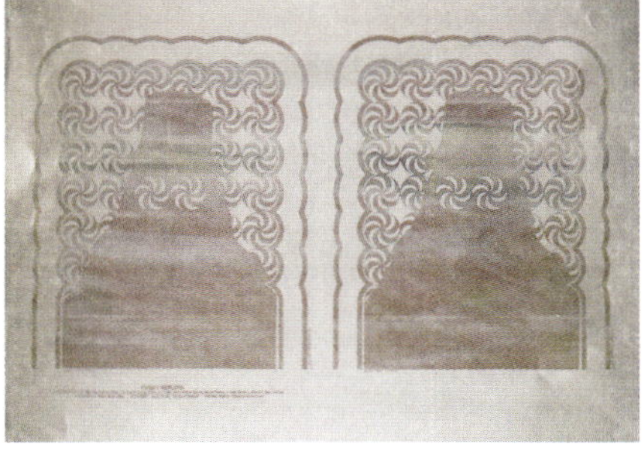
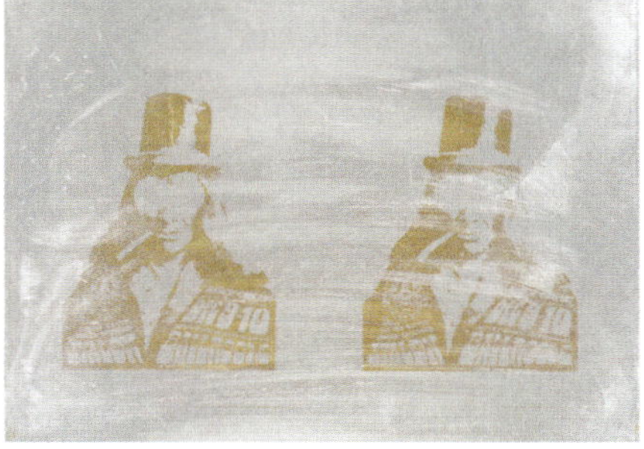

➳ Opposite: Moscoso psychedelicizes the Native American figure in the Family Dog logo on this poster for two Avalon Ballroom shows in December 1966. Progressive printer's proofs are shown here. ➳ This page, top and center: plates and progressive proofs for Moscoso's design promoting late June and early July concerts at the Avalon Ballroom featuring Quicksilver Messenger Service. ➳ Bottom: some of the printing plates for the December 1966 Family Dog poster (see opposite).

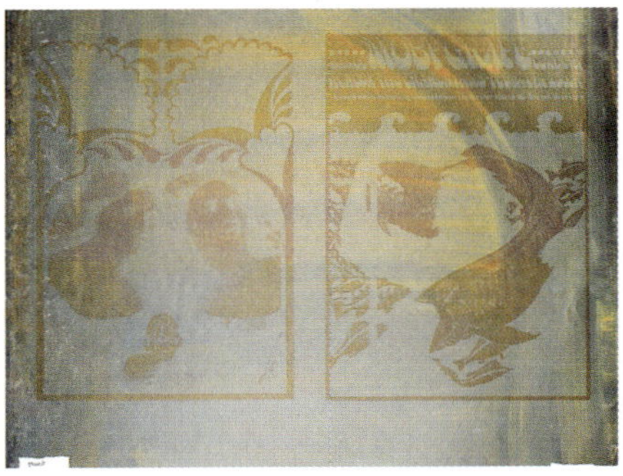
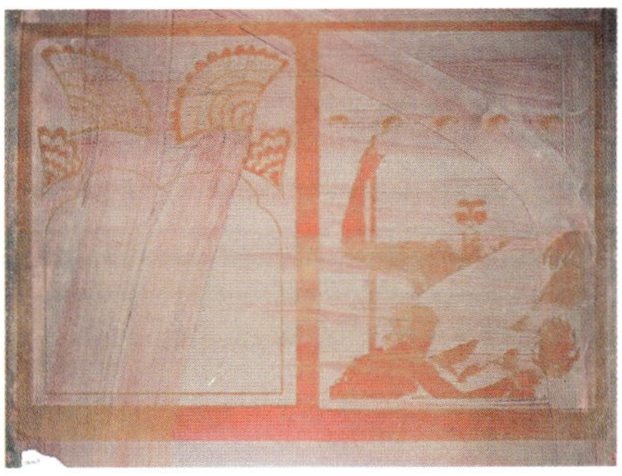
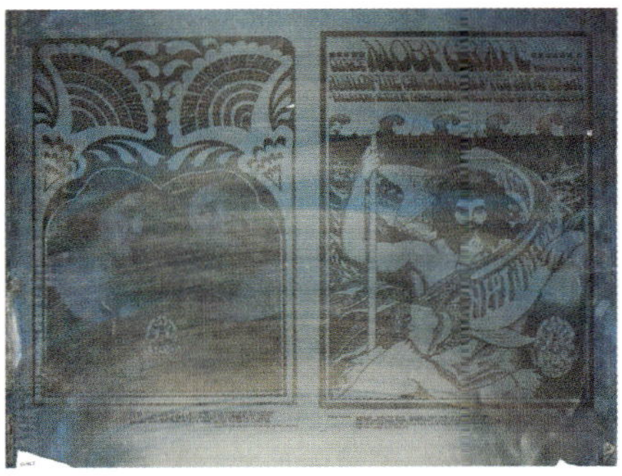
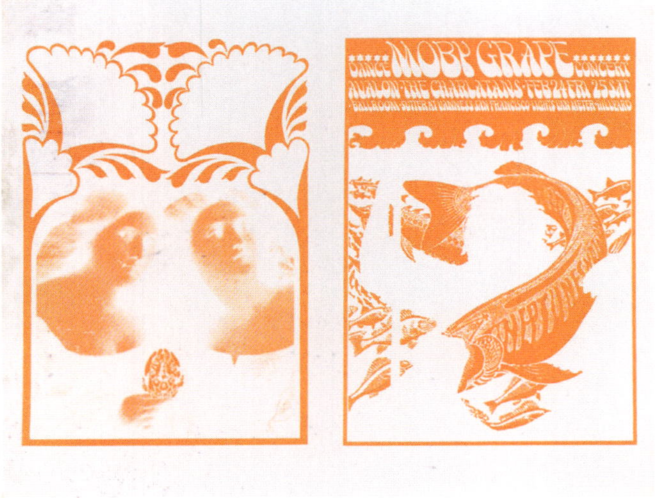
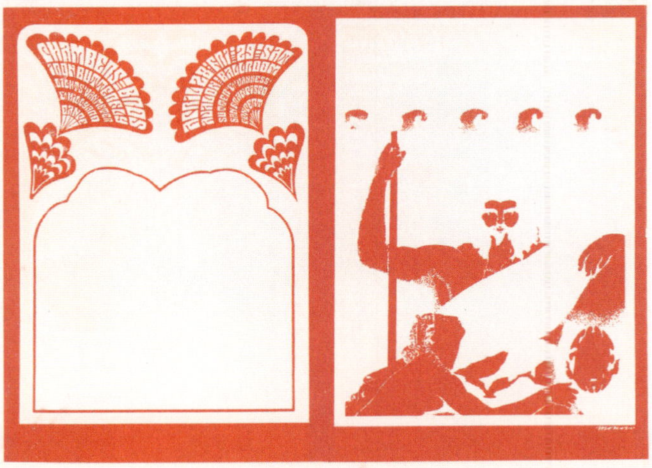
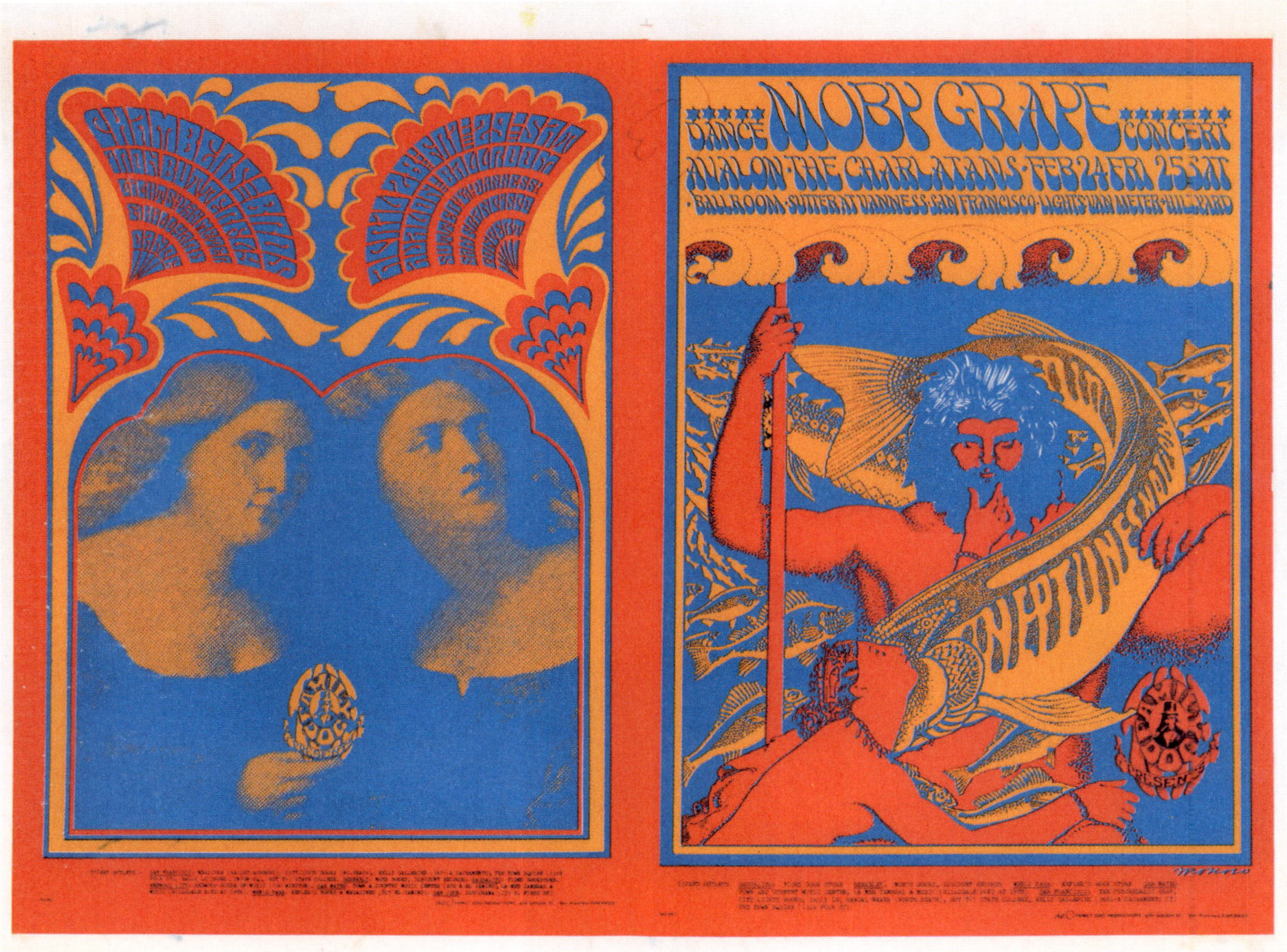

⋙→ This page, top and center: printing plates, single-color and full-color proofs of Moscoso designs, proofed together and sharing the same color palette. ⋙→ Bottom left: the *Bobbsey Twins* poster for The Chambers Brothers and Iron Butterfly in late April 1967. ⋙→ Bottom right: a design known as *Neptune's Notions* promotes two February 1967 gigs headlined by Moby Grape.

⋙→ Opposite: printing plates, progressive and final full-color proofs for the *Peacock Ball*, promoting Quicksilver Messenger Service and The Miller Blues Band in March 1967.

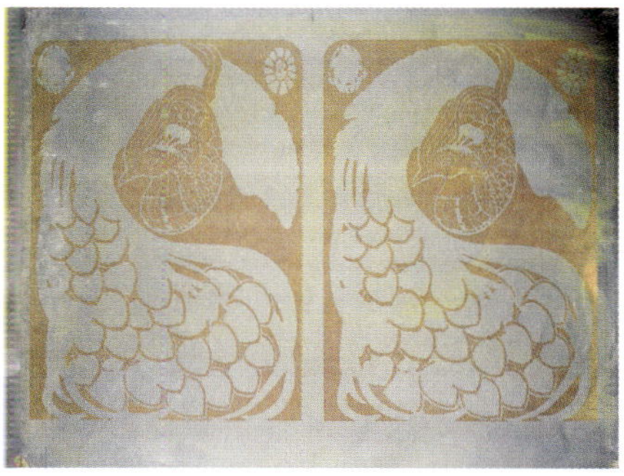

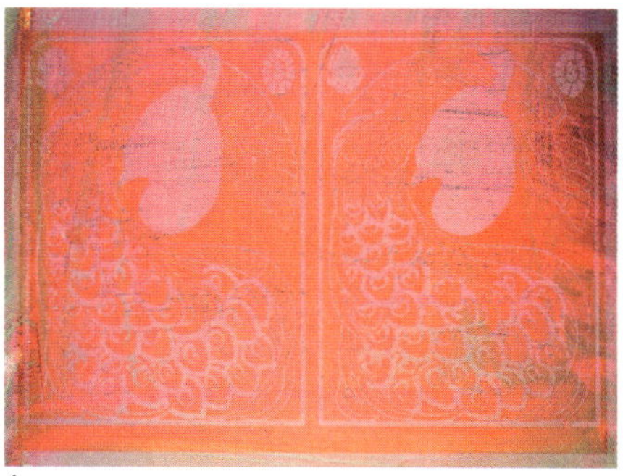

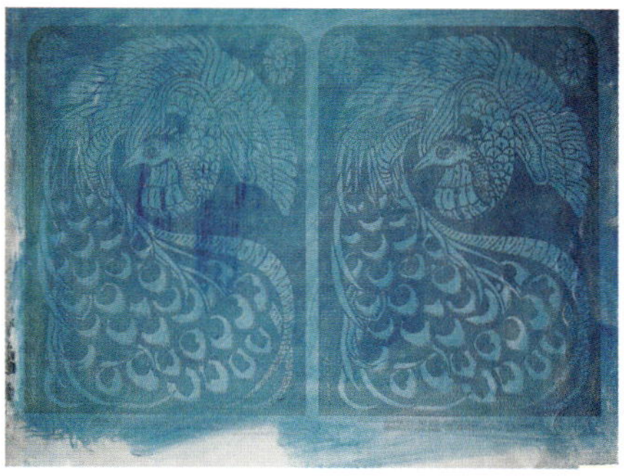

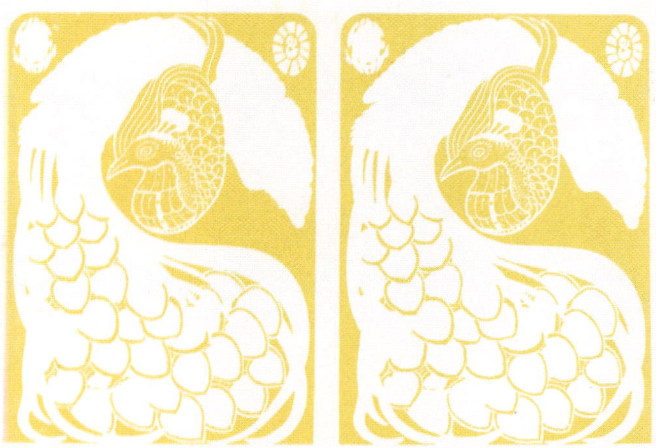

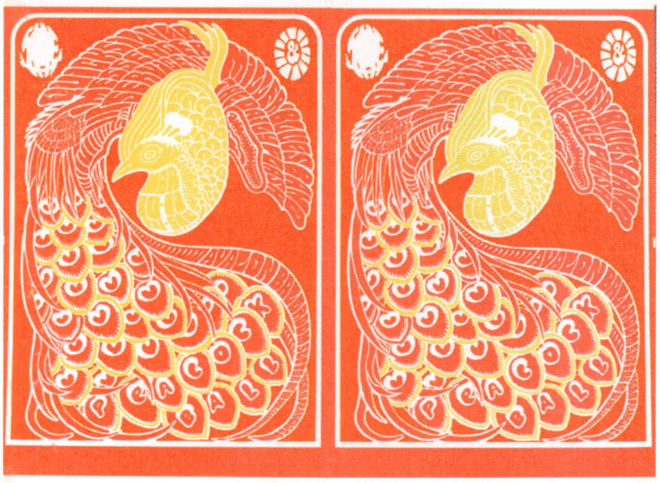

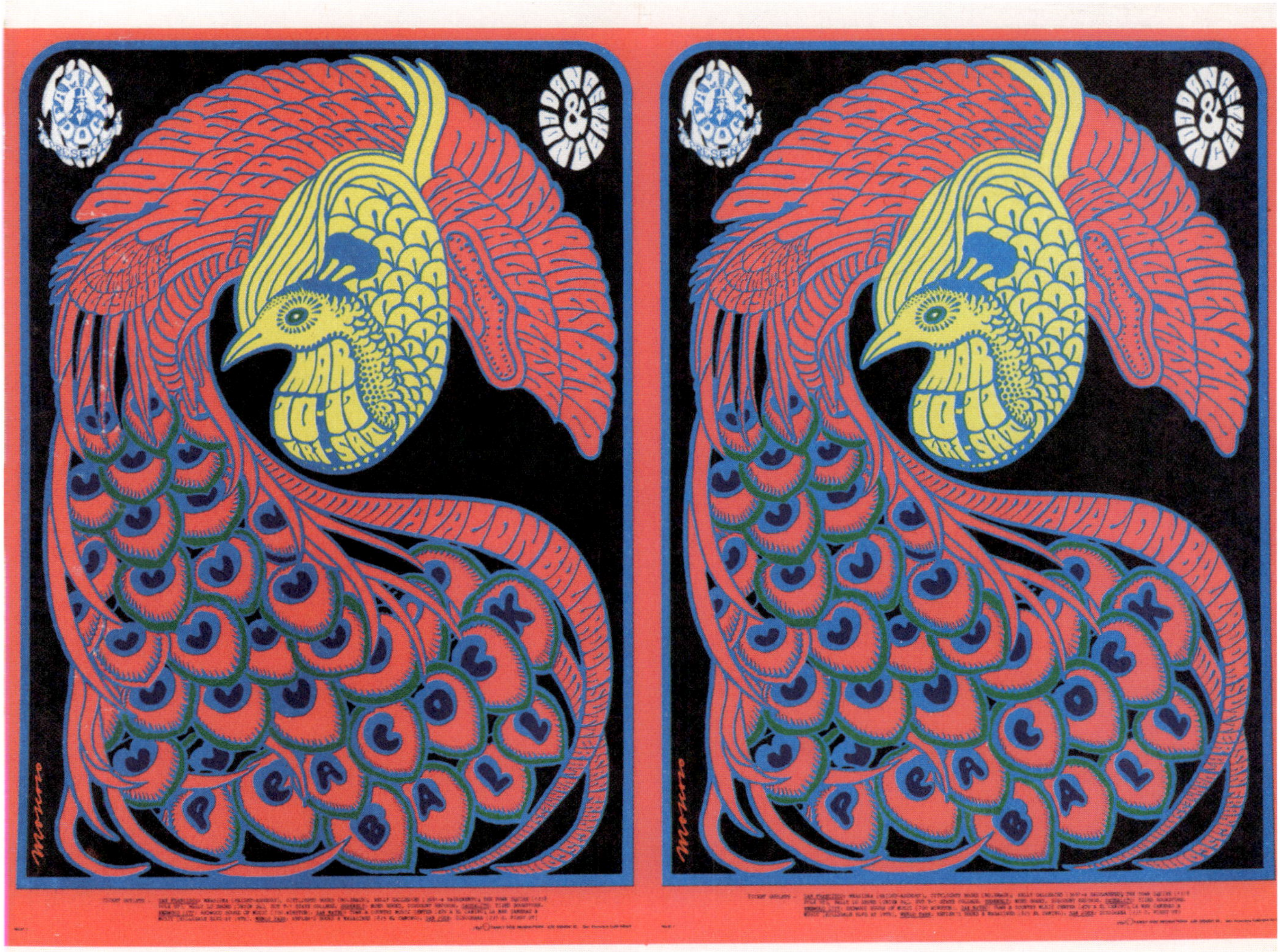

THE NEON ROSE SERIES

In 1966, Victor Moscoso decided that rather than signing away his rights to Family Dog or Bill Graham, he would gain more by running his own poster company. He called it Neon Rose. Most of the posters seen here were for concerts at The Matrix—the small club on San Francisco's Fillmore Street where The Great Society, featuring Grace Slick, got their start. The club was co-owned by Marty Balin of Jefferson Airplane, the band that Slick joined in late 1966.

Moscoso's distinctive use of color saturation comes from Josef Albers's 'squares'—a series of paintings, each featuring quadrate blocks in a range of different hues, that occupied him for nearly thirty years. Moscoso's fine-art training and knowledge of lithographic technique equipped him to take enormous risks, pairing triadic colors—such as orange and blue, or green and magenta—to produce a vibrating edge, while being able to anticipate how the printed result would look. This disregard for legibility meant that his posters only reached those capable of deciphering the vibrating letters—in other words, the target audience.

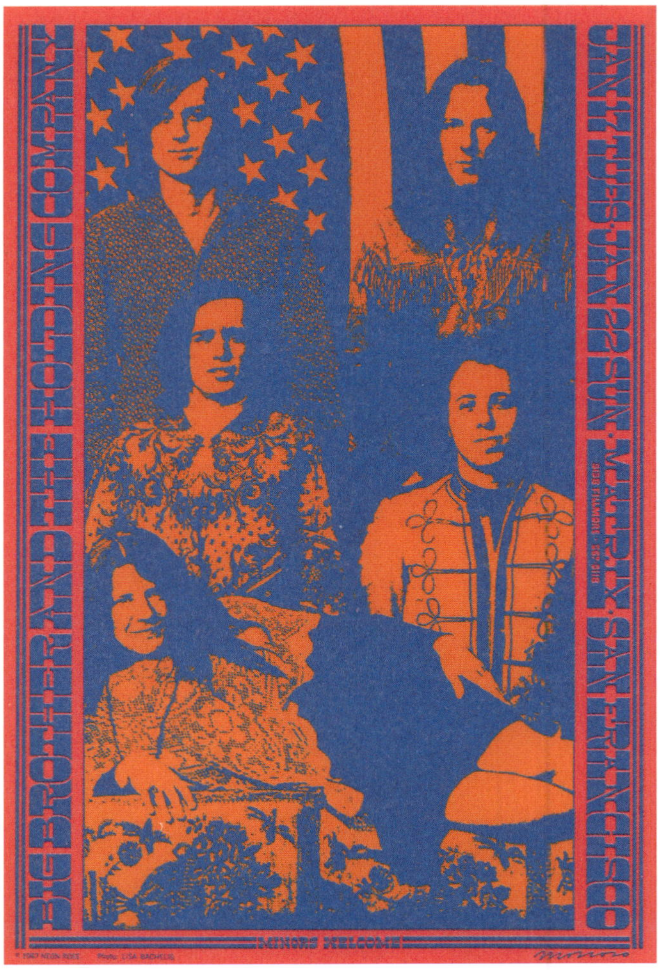

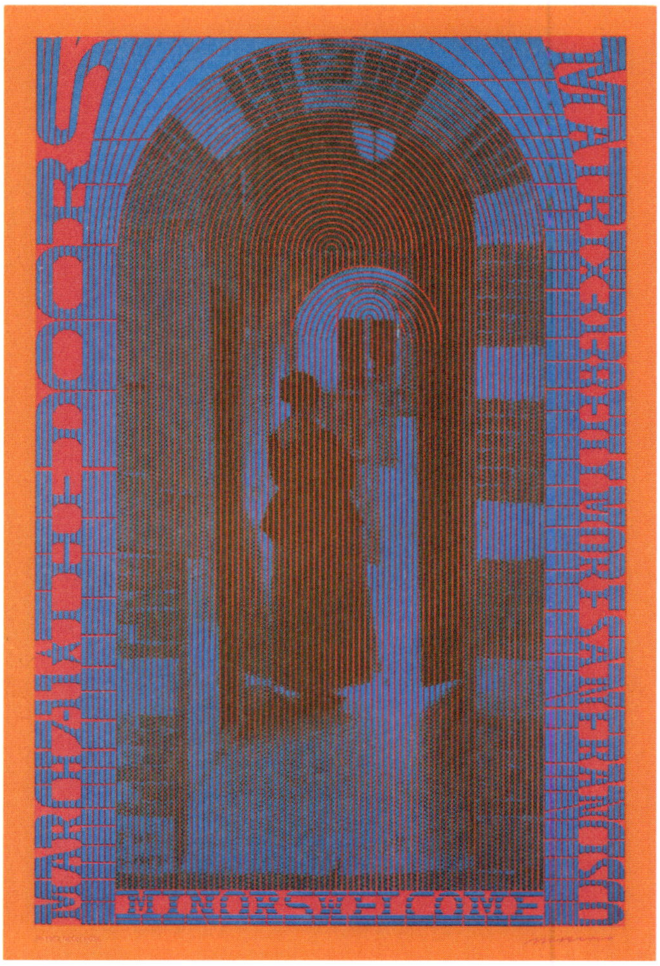

➳ This page, top: a Moscoso poster for a week of Big Brother and the Holding Company concerts at The Matrix in January 1967. The original band photograph was by Lisa Bachelis. At the time, Big Brother were living in an old hunting lodge in Marin County. ➳ This page, bottom: Moscoso described this image, for a gig in March 1967, as 'A trip through The Doors to a Dutch town, some time past.' ➳ Opposite, clockwise from top left: Wildflower, March 1967. ➳ The Chambers Brothers, March 1967—perhaps the single most famous design by Moscoso. ➳ The Cloud and The Plastic Explosion at Webb's in Stockton, April 1967. ➳ The Miller Blues Band, January 1967.

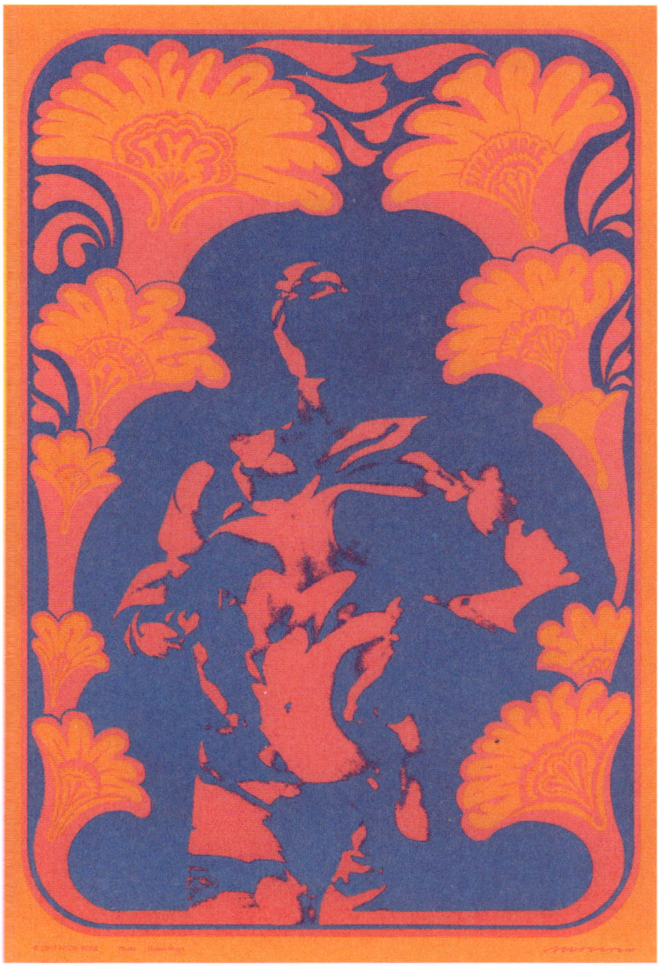

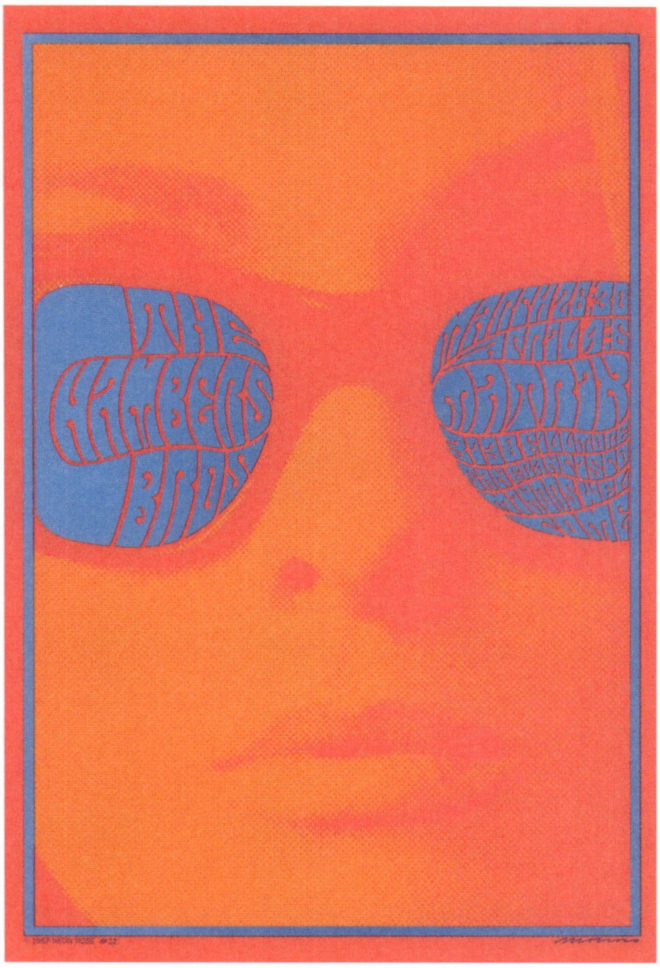

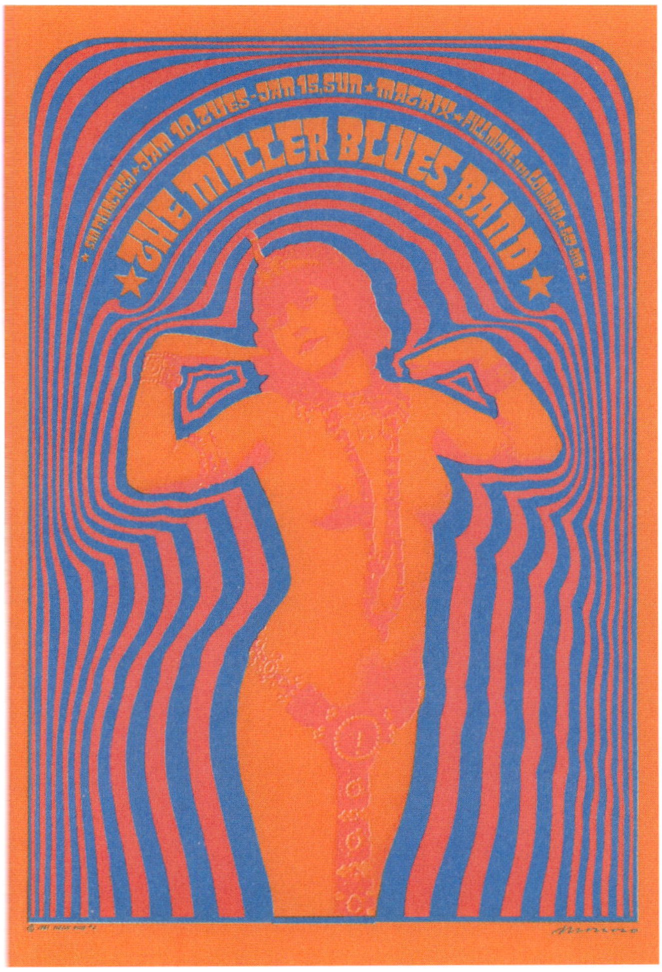
THE MILLER BLUES BAND

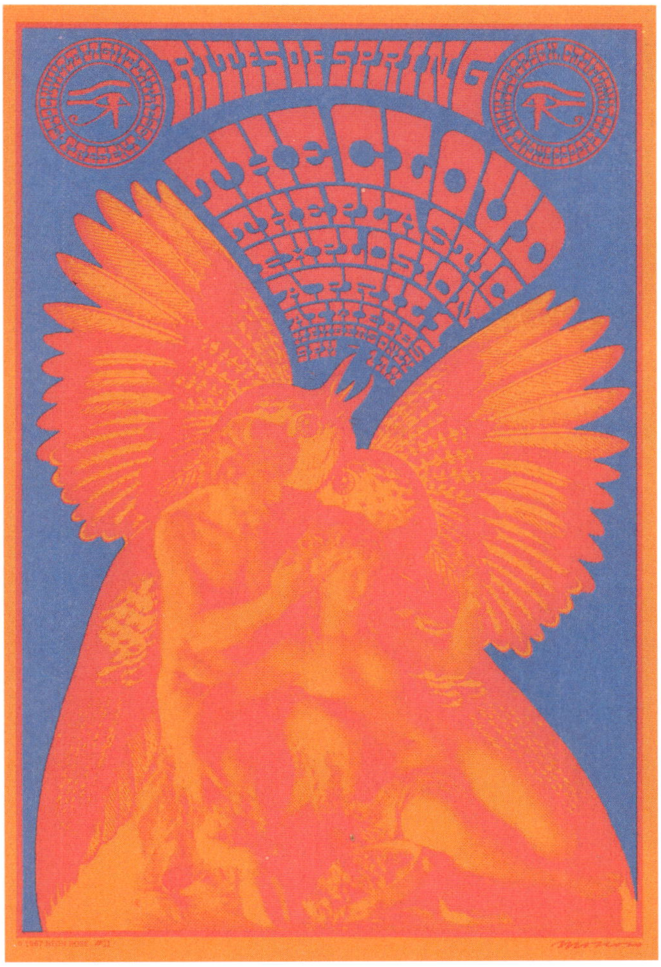
RITES OF SPRING

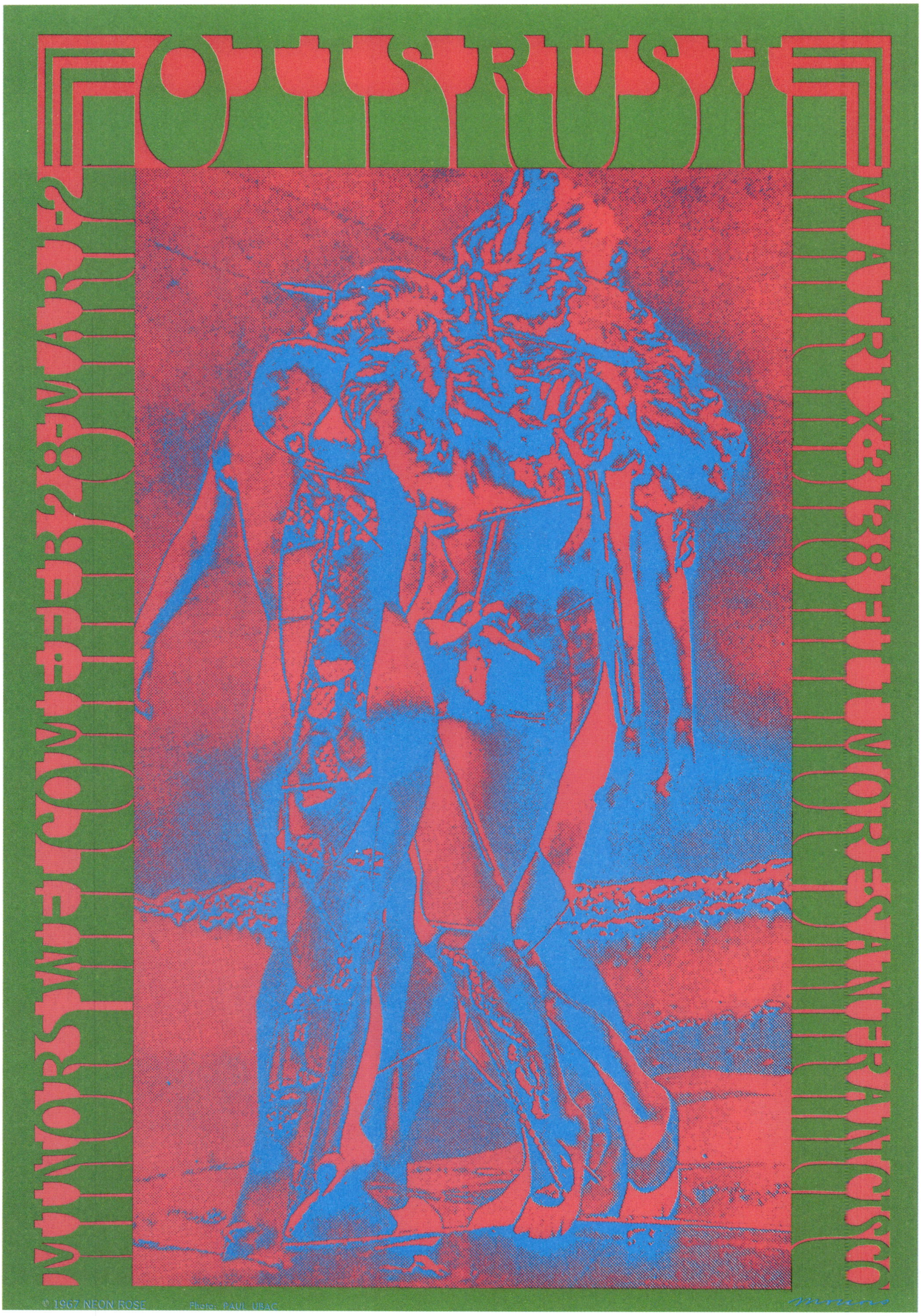

➳→ This page: a poster for shows by Otis Rush at The Matrix. Moscoso himself summarized it as: 'Photo by a surrealist and solarized with ideal use of vibrating colors.'

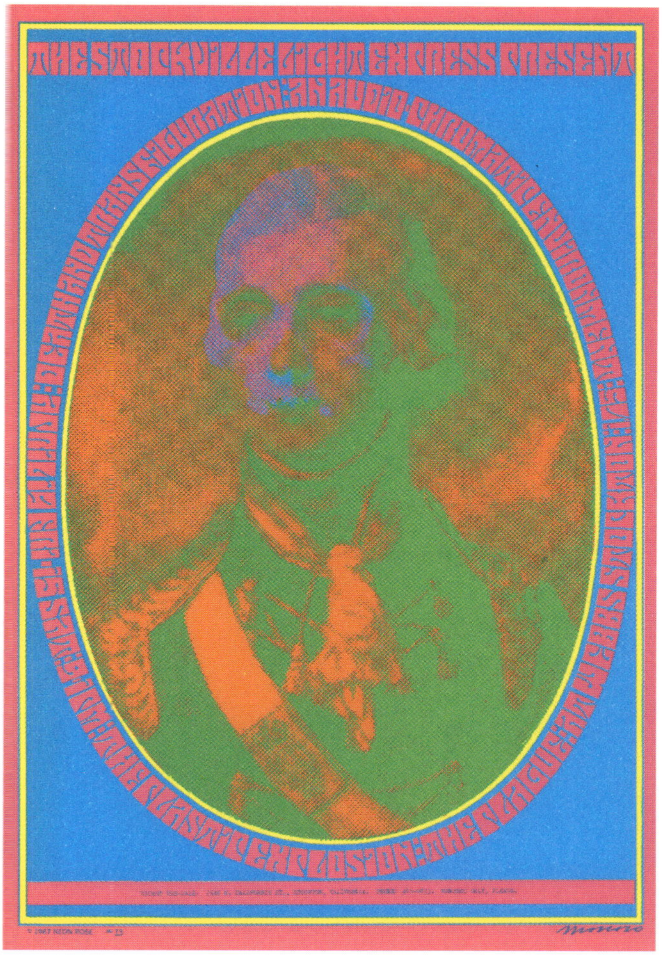

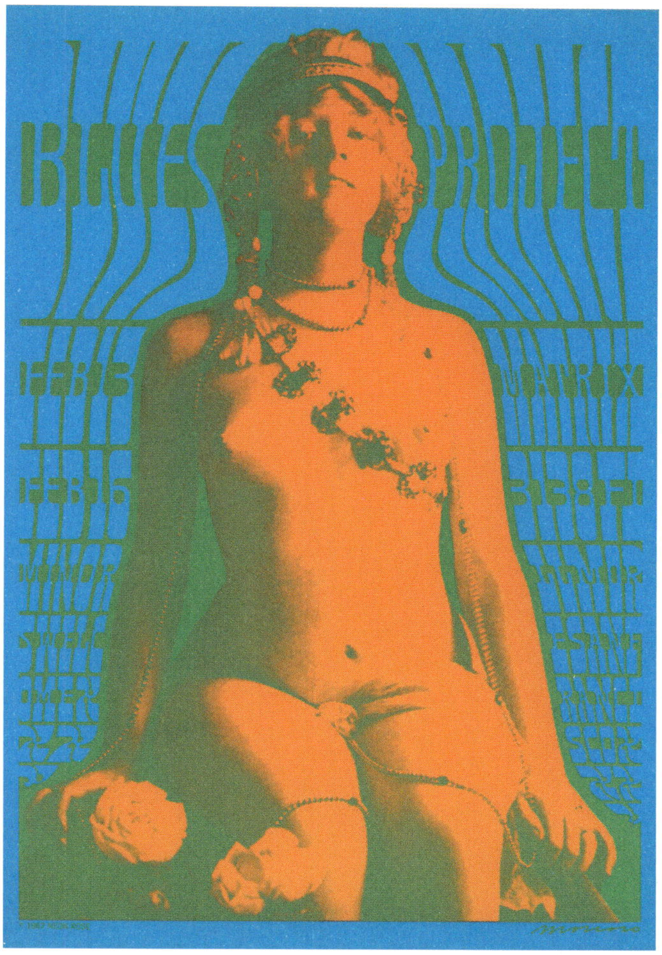

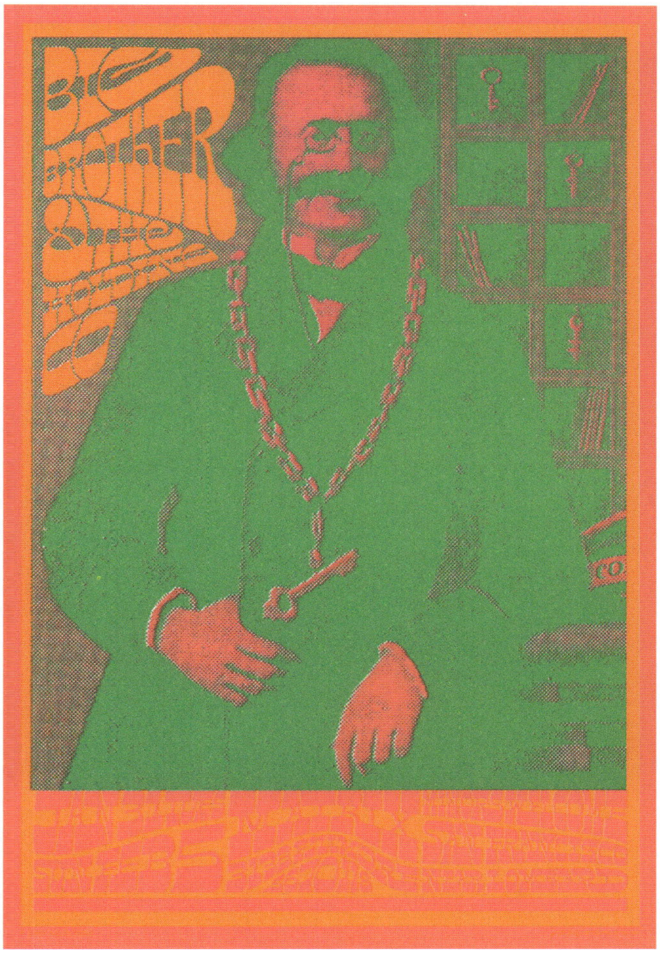

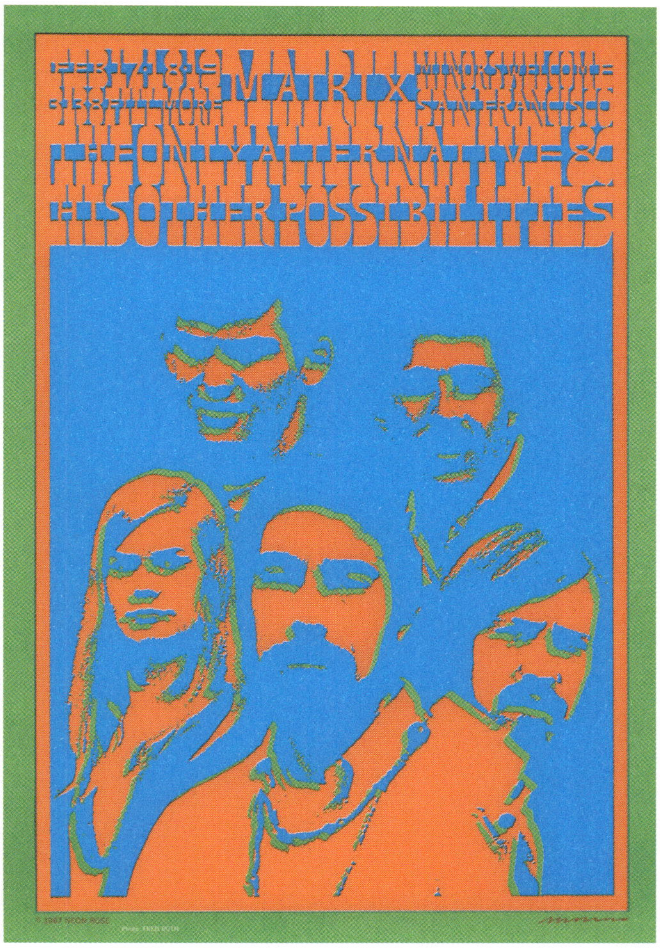

→ This page, clockwise from top left: a poster for Webb's in Stockton, California. Moscoso said: 'The Stockton light show wanted the title to read "Death and Transfiguration." Finding the skull, which prints in yellow, was the hardest part.' The image, which shows Lafayette, transforms into a skull when viewed under a black light. → Blues Project at The Matrix, based on a French photo from the 1890s. → A design for The Only Alternative and His Other Possibilities at The Matrix in February 1967. → Moscoso found the source picture for this poster in a small advert within an old magazine. He enlarged it and printed it both negative and positive so that the colors would vibrate.

THE ORACLE

Founded in 1966 by head-shop owners Ron and Jay Thelin, Allen Cohen (editor), and Michael Bowen (art director), *The City of San Francisco Oracle* used psychedelic graphics to communicate a counter-cultural message. Its much-copied use of split-fountain rainbow inking started with issue #6. Based at 1371 Haight Street, *The Oracle* was the main organizer of the Human Be-In.

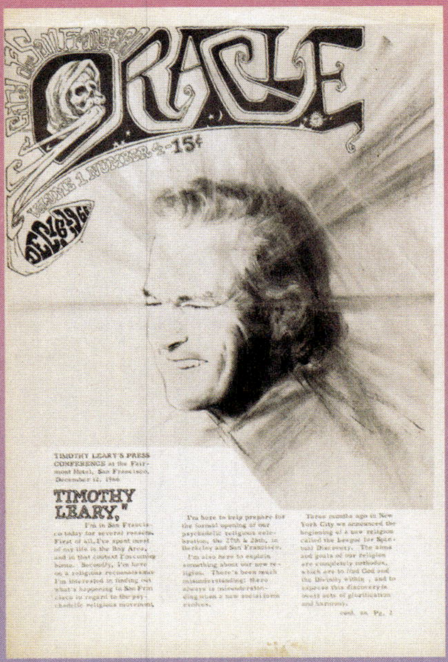

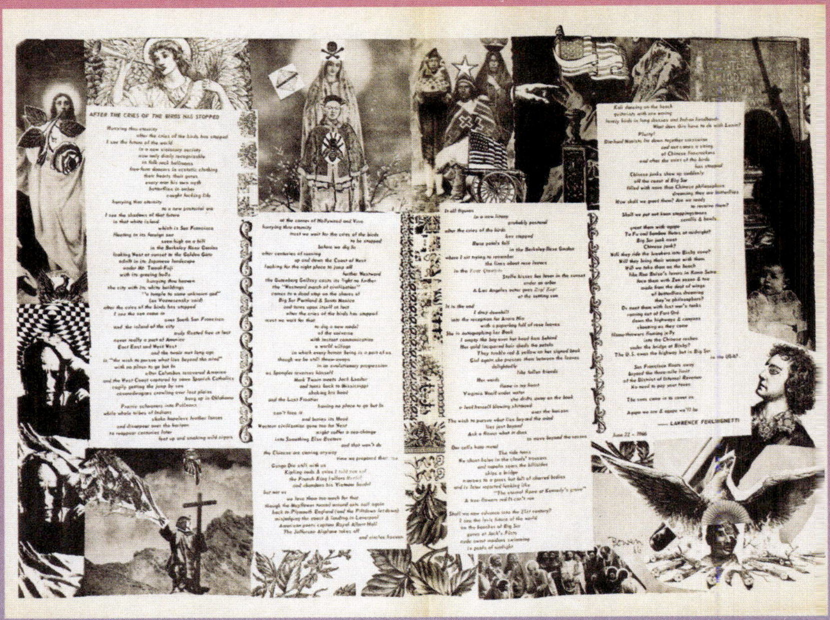

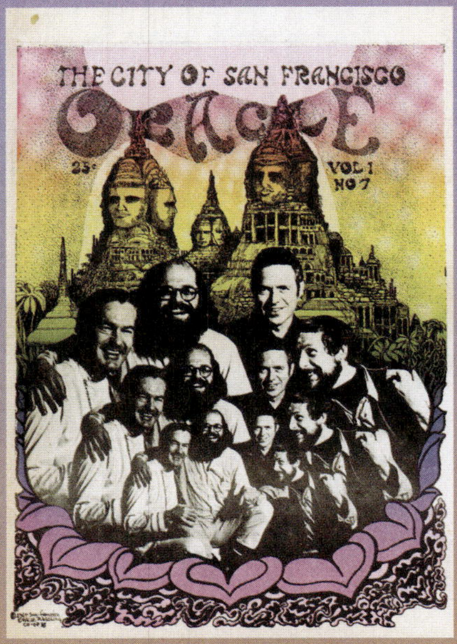

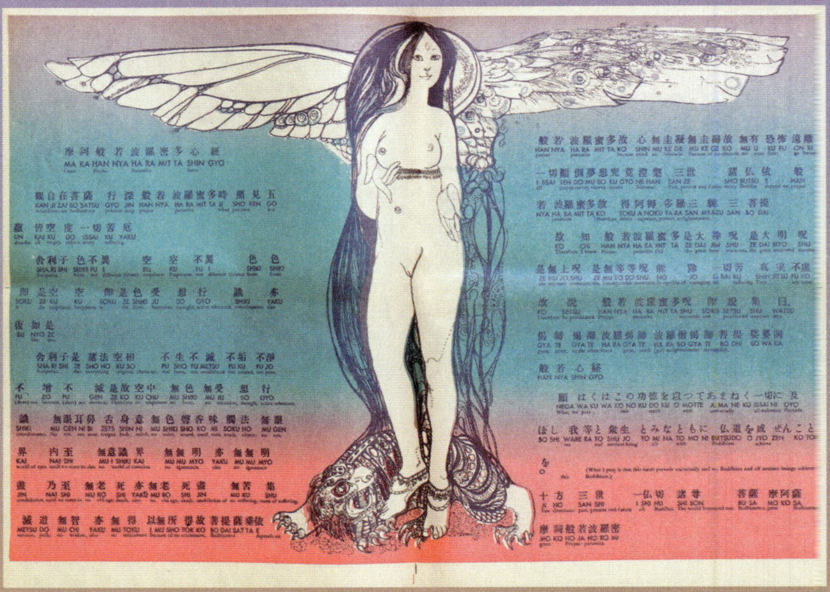

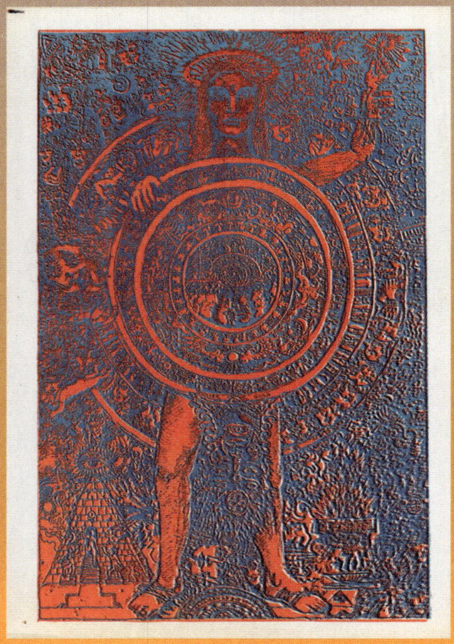

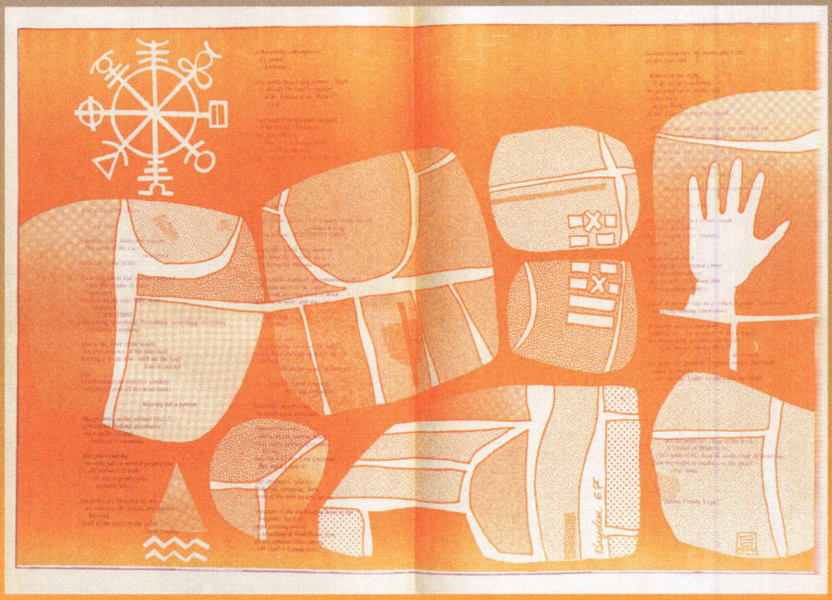

➳➝ Front covers and interiors from *The Oracle* ➳➝ Opposite: cover star Timothy Leary (#4, December 1966), the 'Houseboat Summit' issue uniting Leary, Allen Ginsberg, Alan Watts, and Gary Snyder (#7, March–April 1967), and the mandala cover for the 'Politics of Ecstasy' issue (#10, October 1967). ➳➝ This page: #5 (January 1967) announced the Human Be-In; the image was also used as a poster. The detailed 'Renaissance or Die' centerfold is by Rick Griffin. Also seen here are front covers and spreads from #9 ('Psychedelics, Flowers, and War') from August 1967—Bruce Conner created the mandalas for the cover—and #11, the 'City of God' issue, from December 1967. The latter included (bottom right) a spread seemingly inspired by The Revelation of St. John The Divine: chapter 21, verse 9–27. The work is signed 'Bryden '67.'

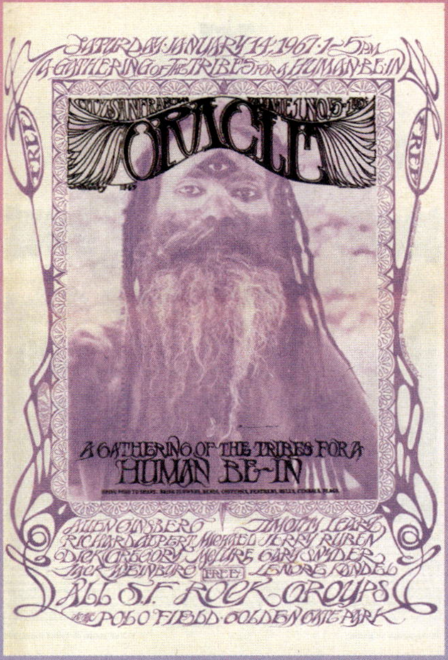

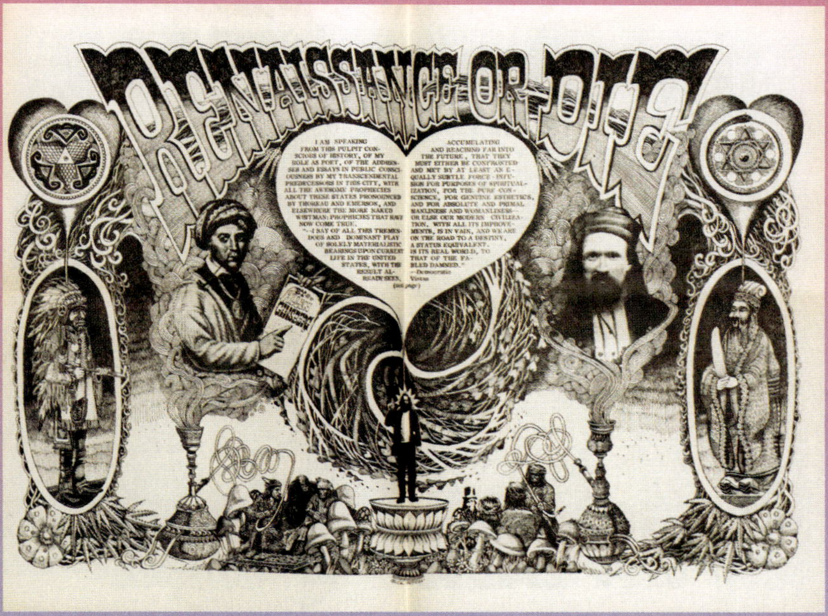

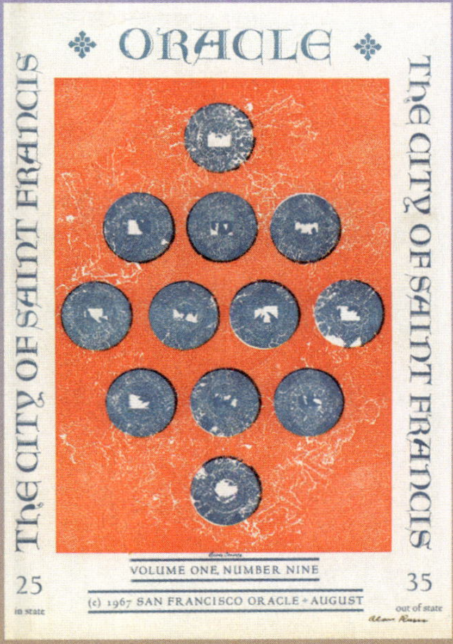

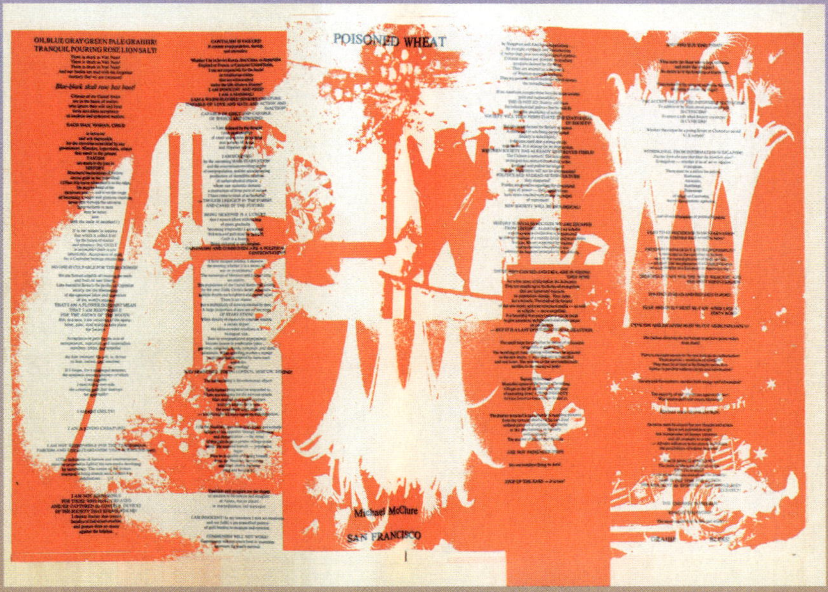

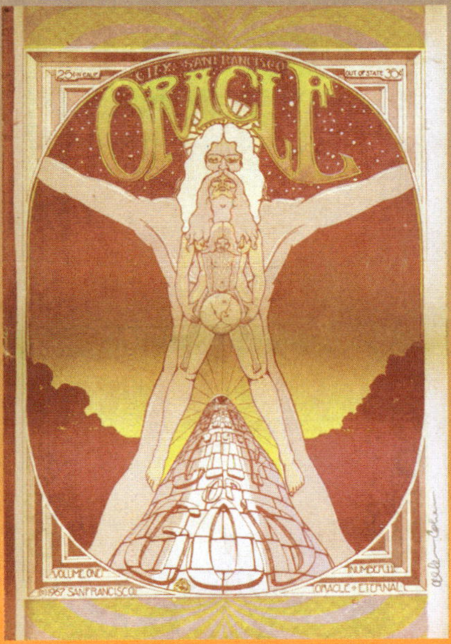

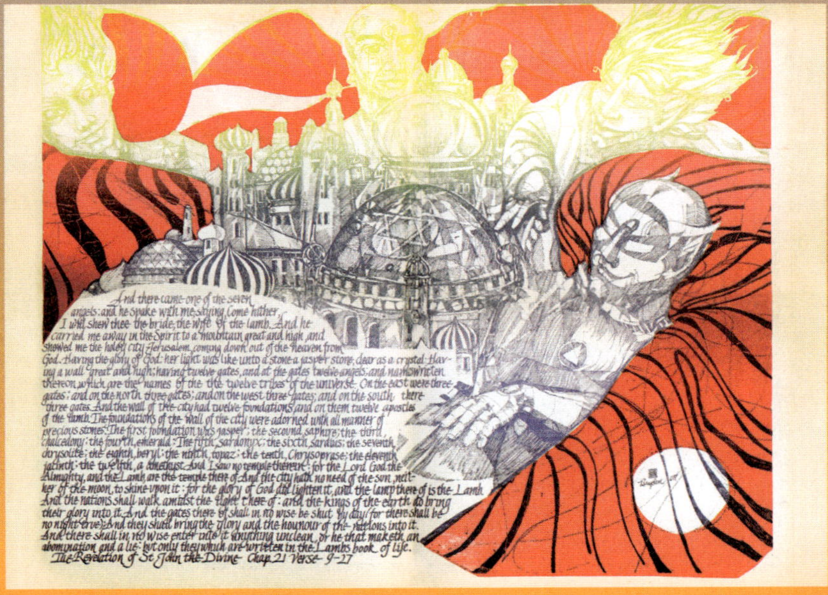

ART NOUVEAU

Most of the San Francisco psychedelic poster artists had little in the way of art training, but quickly searched out images from the past that they could use. Many used the traditional Western typefaces, enlarging the serifs and playing with the spaces between letters, but others discovered the lettering of the Belle Époque and the work of Alphonse Mucha, Cacao Vanhouten and Henri Privat-Livemont et al. They copied the lettering and simply appropriated the imagery; they were, for the most part, incapable of such a high standard of drawing.

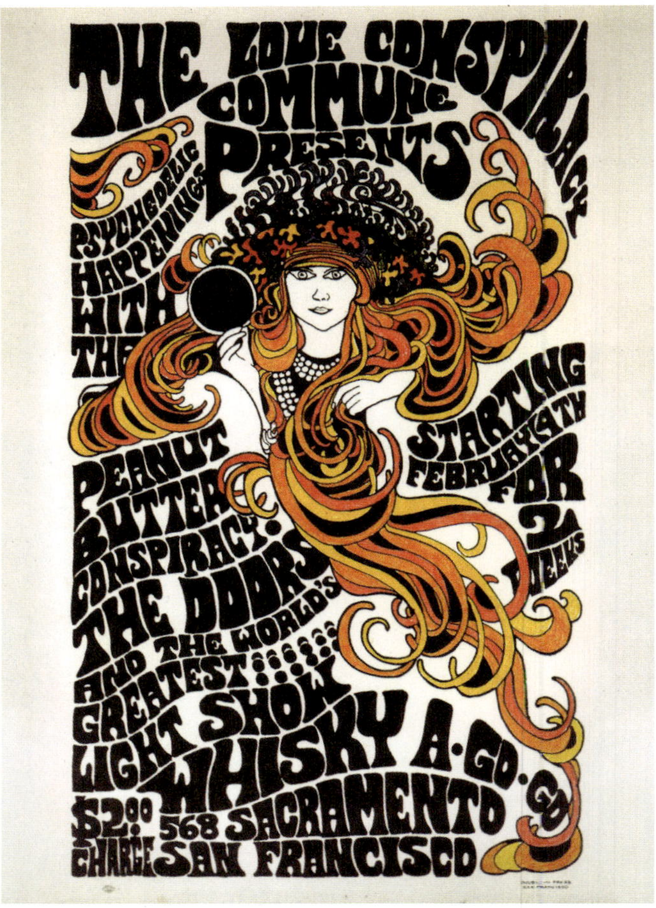

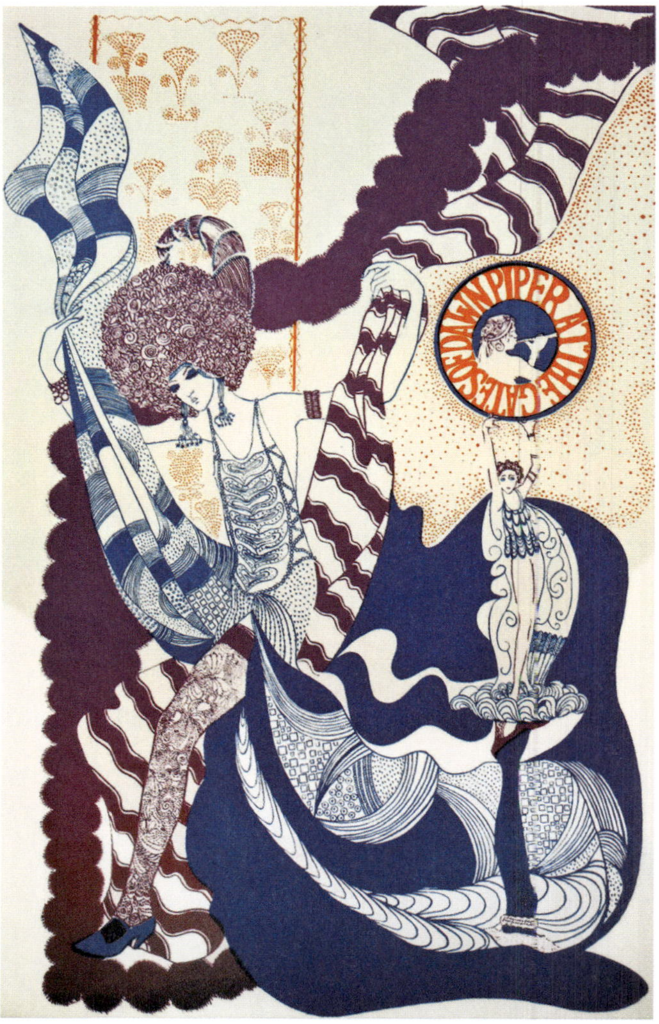

Top: Lee Conklin's poster for a two-week event at the Whisky A-Go-Go in early 1967. Bottom: poster by an unknown artist for the first Pink Floyd album *Piper at the Gates of Dawn* (1967).

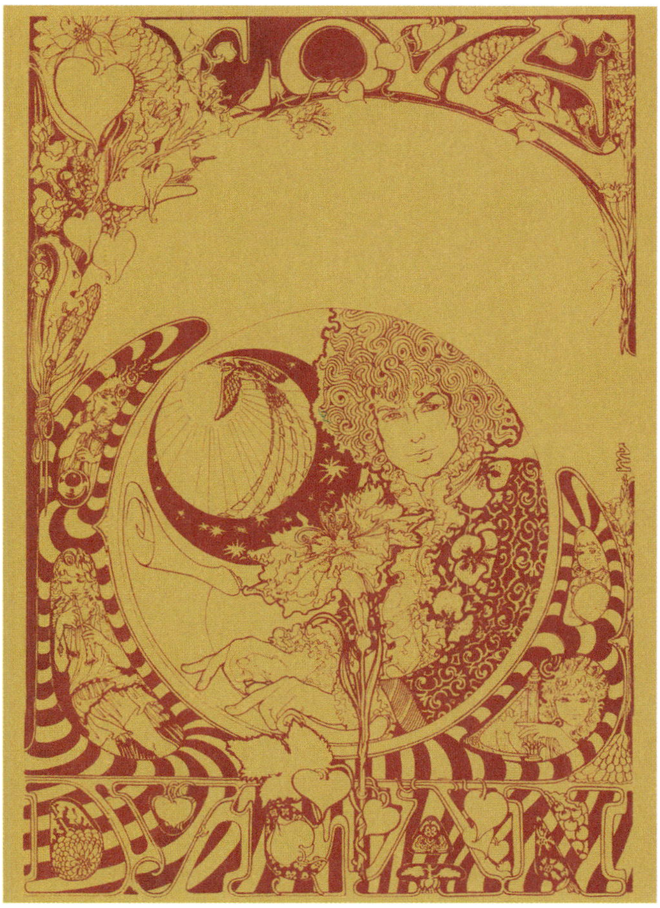

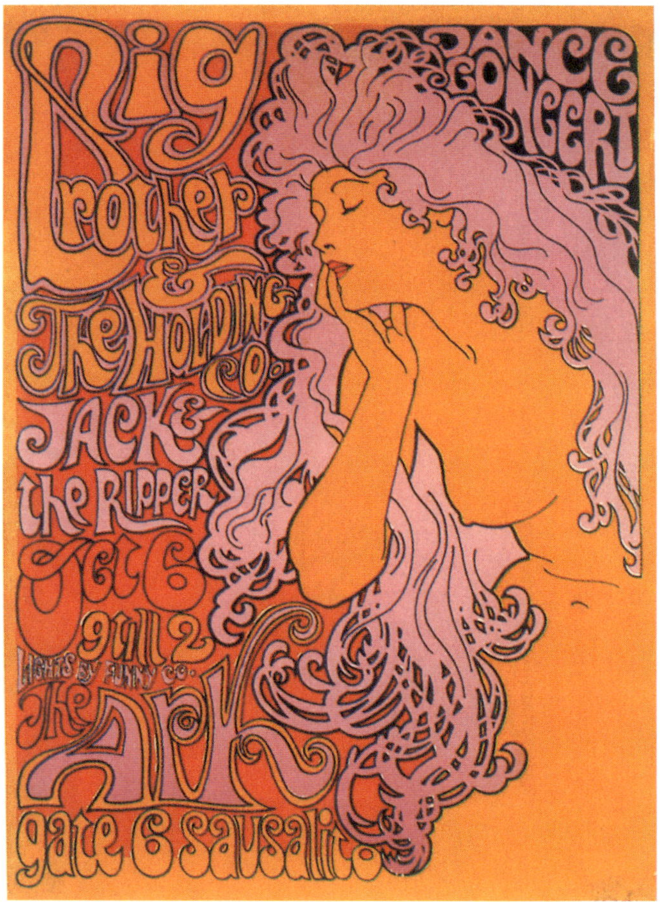

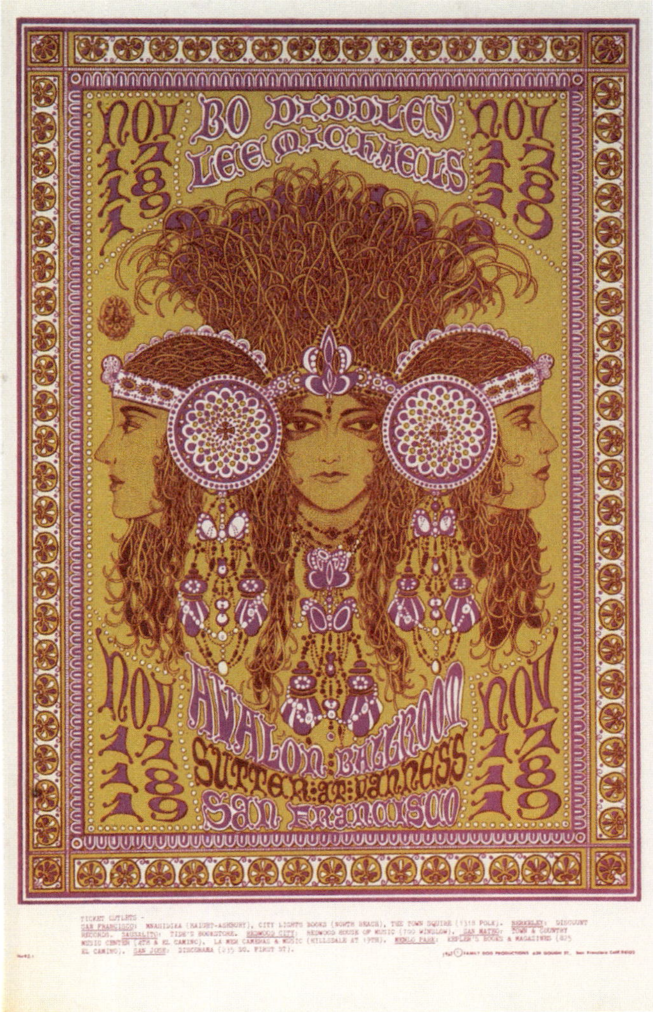

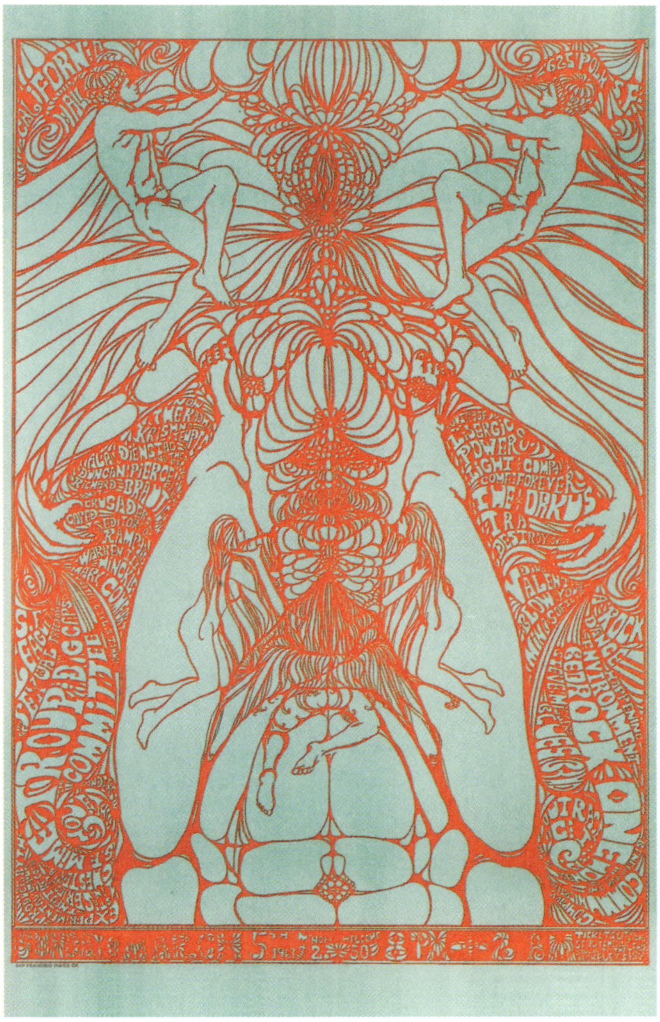

➳ Top: the 1966 *Love Dylan* poster by Marijke Koger of Dutch design group The Fool. ➳ Bottom: William Henry's poster for a 1967 Avalon Ballroom gig. It is known as the *Squiggly Trinity*.

➳ Top: poster for an October 1967 gig at The Ark in Sausalito, based on a work by Alphonse Mucha. ➳ Bottom: design for an early 1967 benefit for the publishers of the Diggers' newsletters.

PSYCHEDELIC SHOPS

The great communal interest in psychedelics and cannabis culture naturally gave rise to hippie merchants willing to sell the appurtenances and merchandise needed to use them—and, in some cases, to provide the substances themselves. Brightly-colored clothing, headbands, bells and beads, underground magazines, books, and records were all quickly made available. The shops commissioned the same artists whose concert posters they were selling to produce posters for the shops. In due course, the clothes boutiques and bookshops selling beat generation literature and counter-cultural publications began demanding posters. Soon, the entire scene had its own advertising industry.

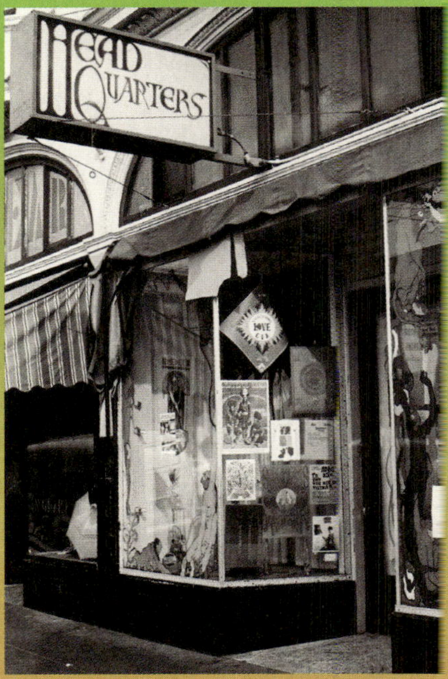

➳ A San Francisco head shop.

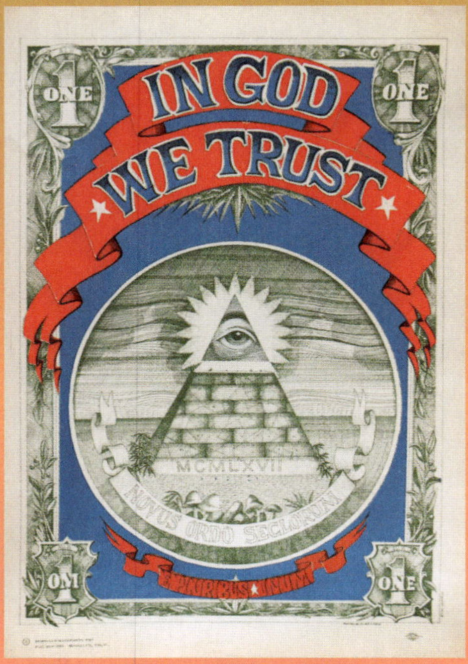

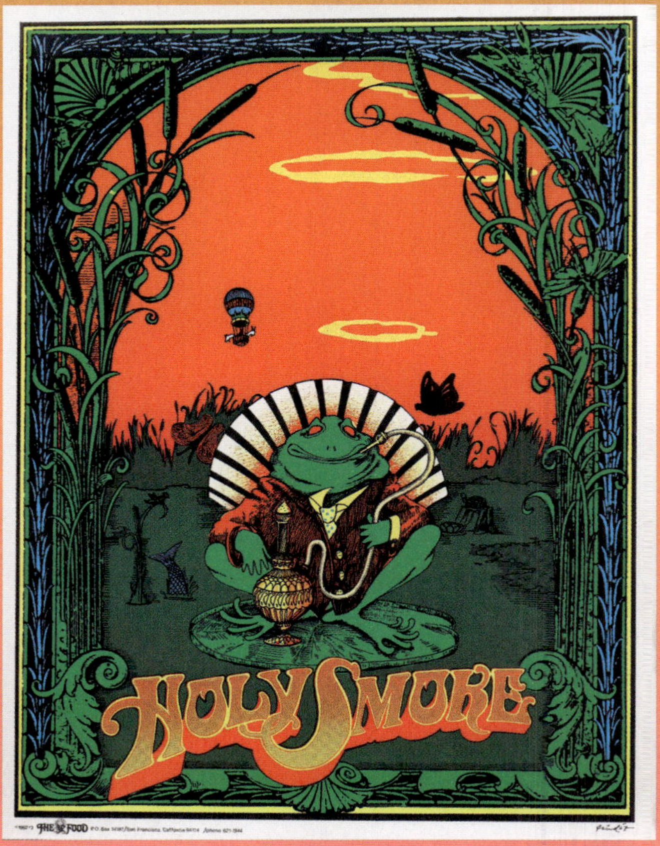

A San Francisco head-shop poster ➳ The artist is Robert Fried, who produced several memorable posters for local venues such as the Avalon Ballroom.

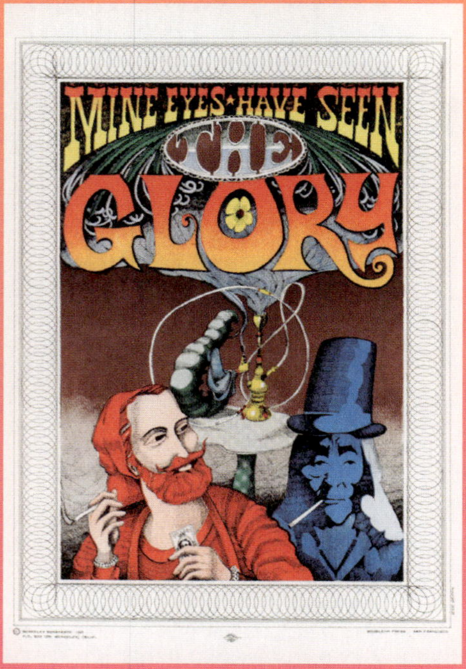

Two head-shop posters designed by Rick Griffin as part of Berkeley Bonaparte ➳ Berkeley Bonaparte was a company formed by the 'San Francisco Five.' This allowed them to create and sell posters outside the control of concert promoters. The marijuana references and imagery from sources such as the US dollar bill and *Alice in Wonderland* encouraged head-shop patrons to trip out on these designs.

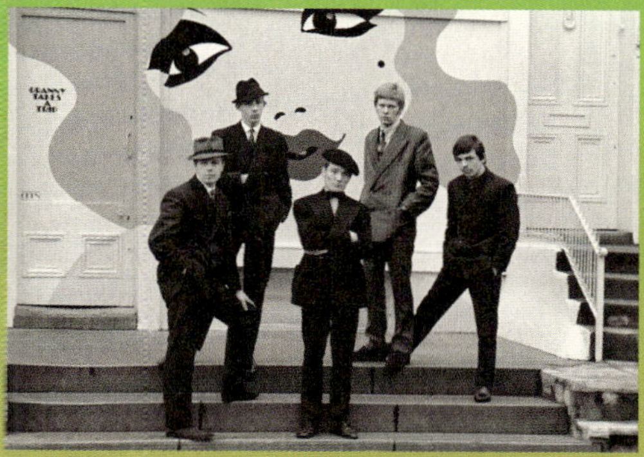

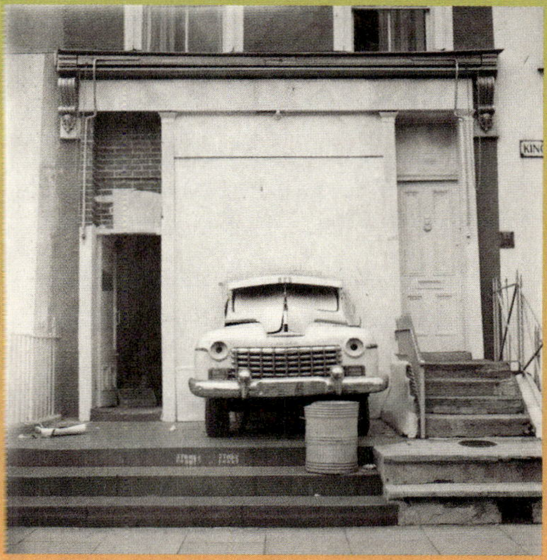

Granny Takes a Trip ⟿ This iconic clothing emporium, located at 488 King's Road in the then unfashionable end of Chelsea, opened in 1966. Nigel Waymouth was one of its owners, and took responsibility for regularly re-working the design of the shop's exterior. The top image features The Purple Gang in front of a painting of Jean Harlow. In the bottom picture, a 1948 Dodge saloon appears to be driving out of the shop front.

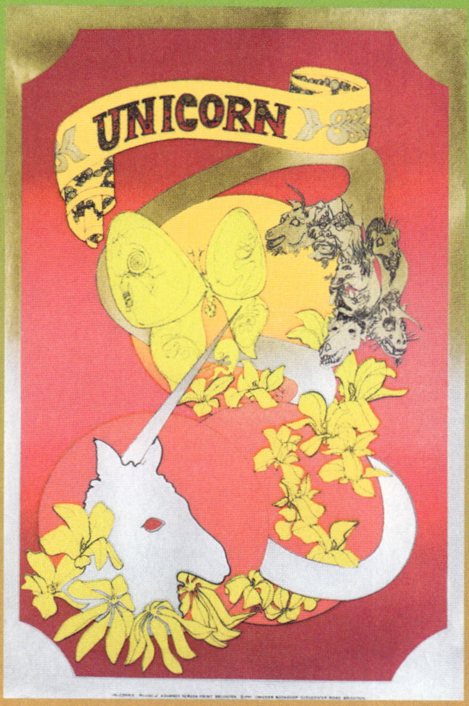

Unicorn Bookshop poster ⟿ Produced by an unknown artist, this 1967 design was for the Unicorn, a book store and counter-culture hub in Brighton, Sussex, run by Bill Butler.

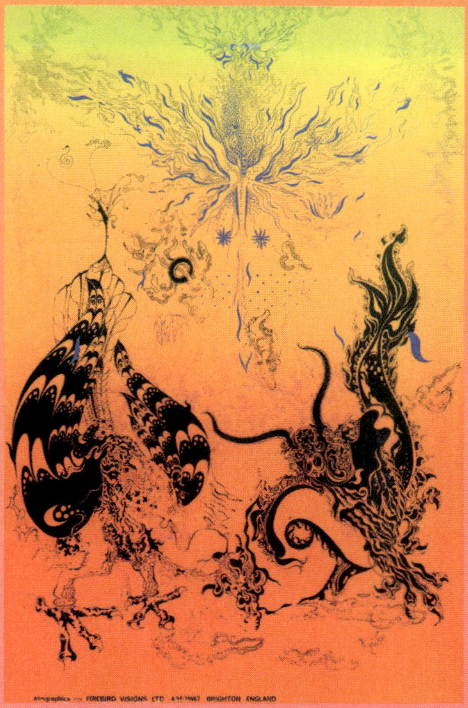

Poster for Unicorn Bookshop, Brighton ⟿ A fantasy image created by Ivan Tyrrell, inspired by a dream of fighting mythical creatures.

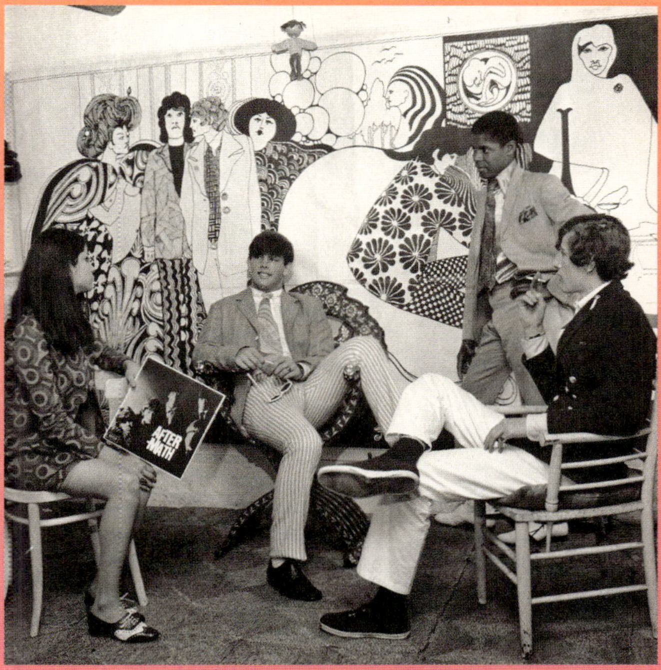

Hung on You boutique, UK ⟿ Designer Michael Rainey ran this boutique in Chelsea, London, catering mainly to men and favored by members of the Beatles, the Rolling Stones, and The Kinks, among others. The Beardsley-esque mural was created by Albert Little. The Stones' *Aftermath* album suggests that this photo was taken in 1966.

THE SAN FRANCISCO UNDERGROUND

There were many lesser-known but interesting artists making posters on the West Coast during the late sixties, usually for smaller concert venues such as The Ark in Sausalito—for which the Moby Grape poster below was produced—or the Whisky A-Go-Go (see Lee Conklin's 1967 artwork on p.82). Mark Kanen's *Acid Man* poster (opposite, bottom), takes psychedelic lettering to an almost unreadable extreme, as do many of the more obscure examples of poster art from San Francisco's underground scene. Unlike Mouse and Kelley (who produced a poster for the Sunday supplement of radical San Francisco magazine *Ramparts*—see below), many of the creators remain anonymous, despite the best efforts of sixties poster scholars.

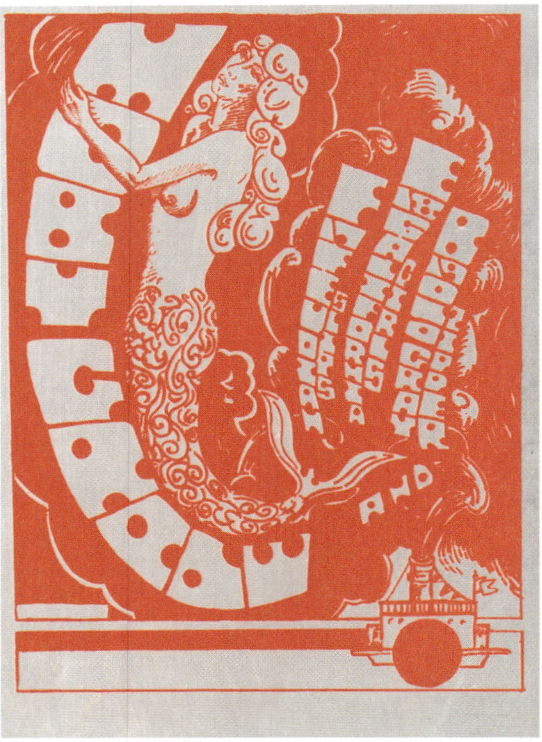

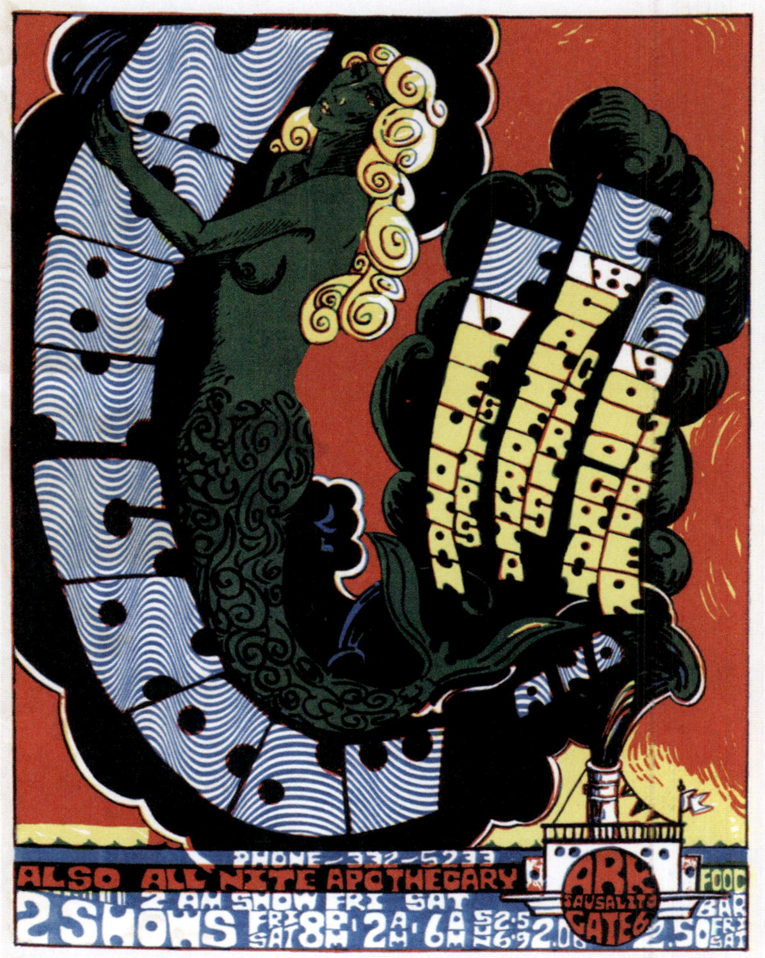

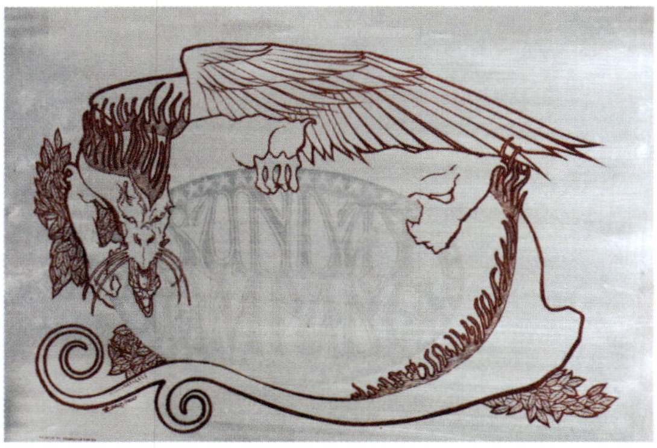

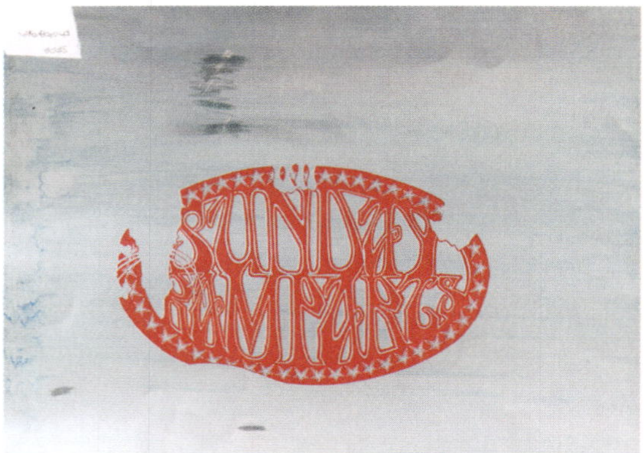

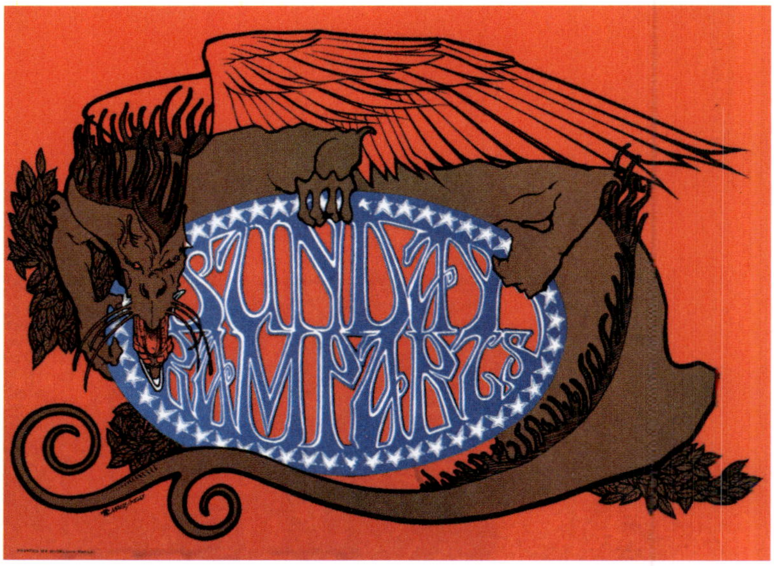

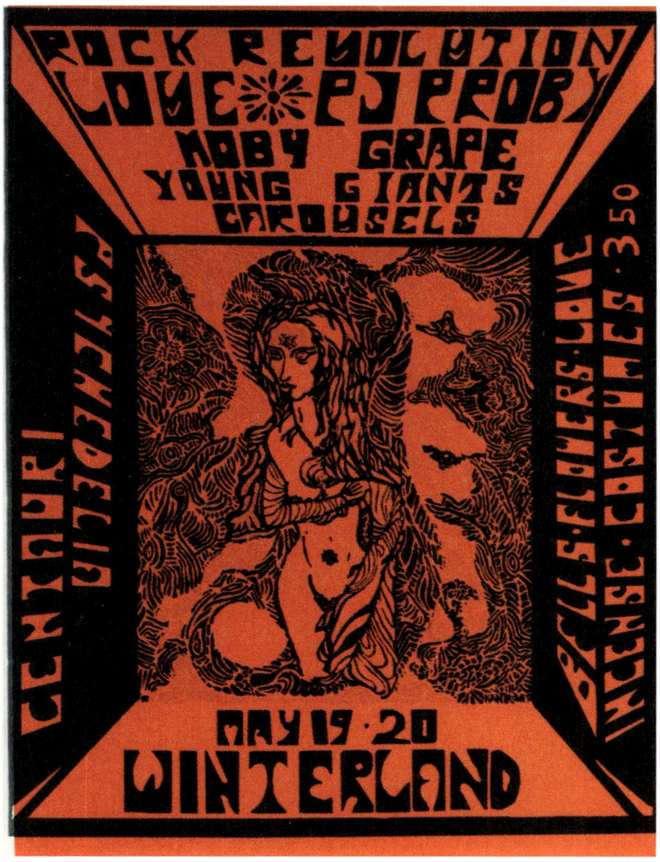

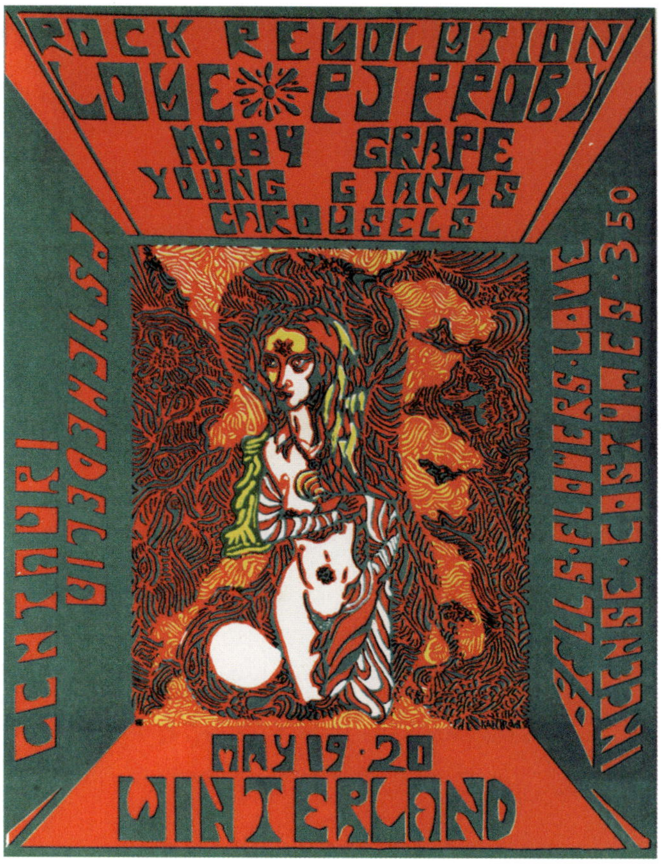

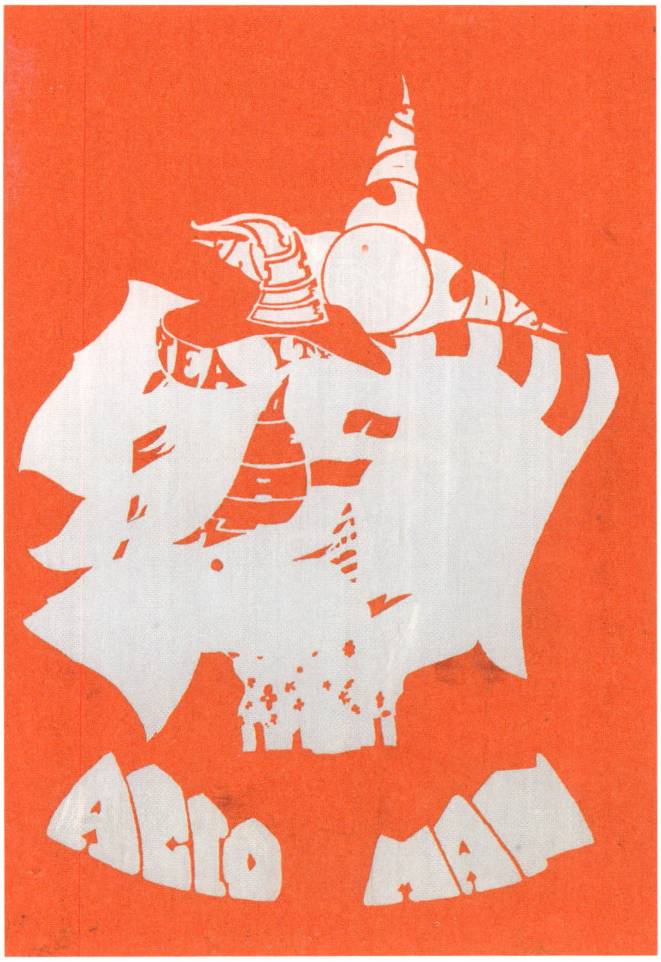

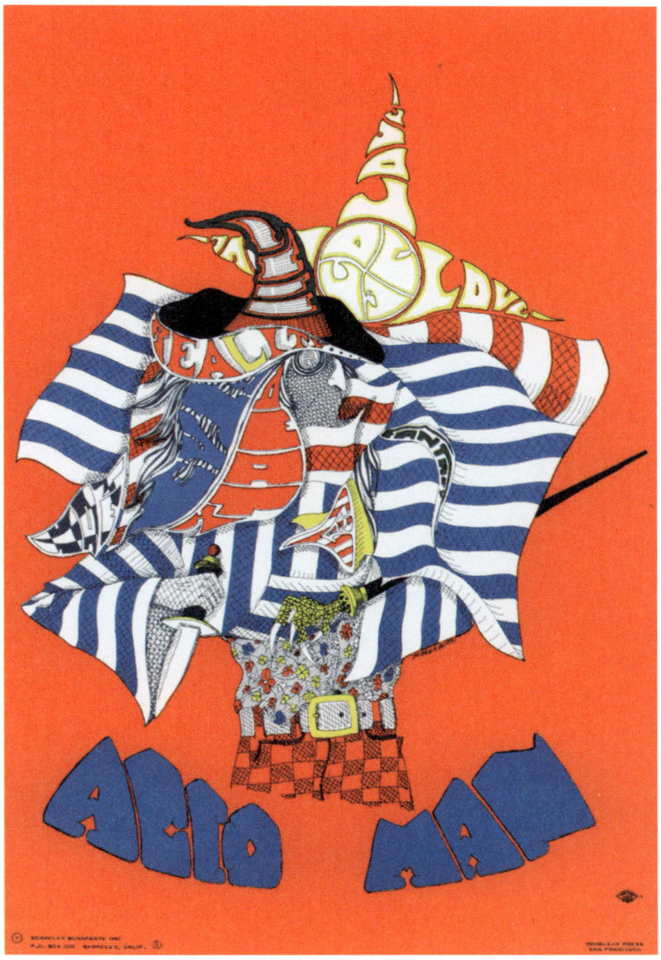

→ Opposite, top: an aluminum plate and final poster by an unknown artist advertising a 1967 concert by Moby Grape and The Freudian Slips at The Ark in Sausalito. The venue was in the remains of a wheelhouse boat, moored just across the bay from San Francisco. →Center left and bottom: printing plates and final poster by Mouse and Kelley advertising *Sunday Ramparts*, a supplement to the radical San Francisco magazine *Ramparts*.

→ This page, top: two color variations of a poster for the 1967 Rock Revolution tour held at Winterland in San Francisco featuring Love, Moby Grape and PJ Proby. →Bottom: plate and 1967 poster by Mark Kanen depicting Acid Man. Head-shop posters such as this one gave psychedelic artists additional freedom to create wildly fantastical designs—often evoking the trips experienced by their intended audience.

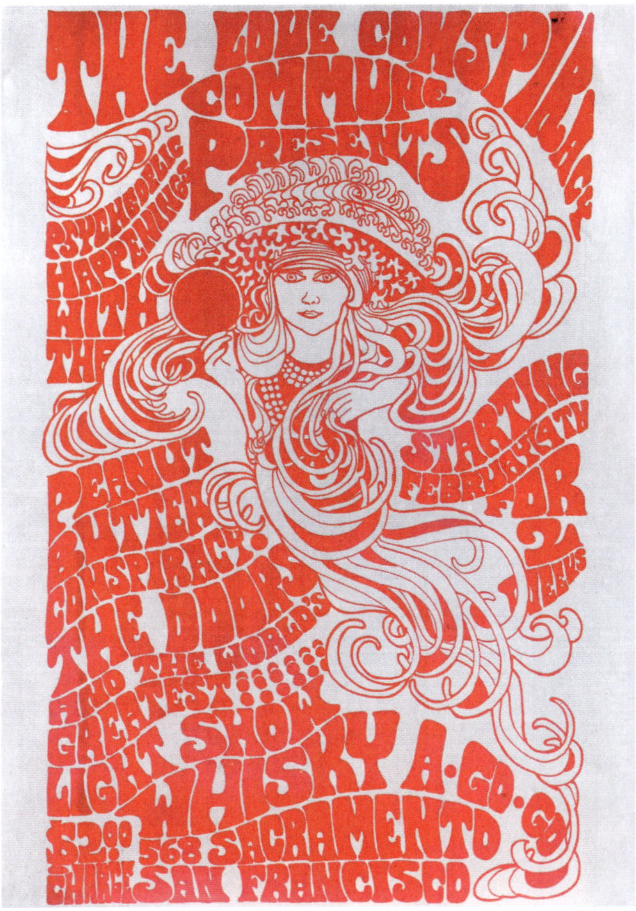

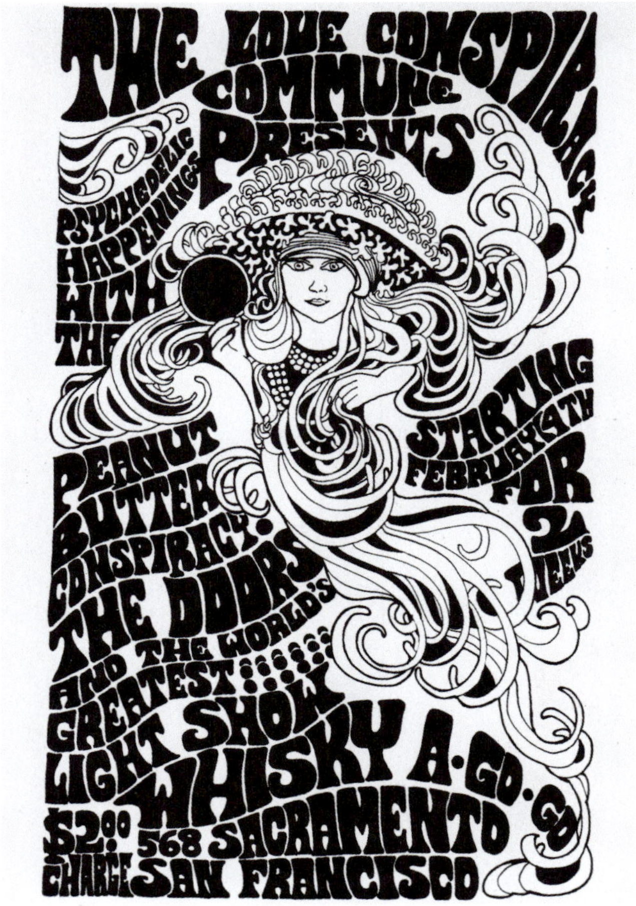

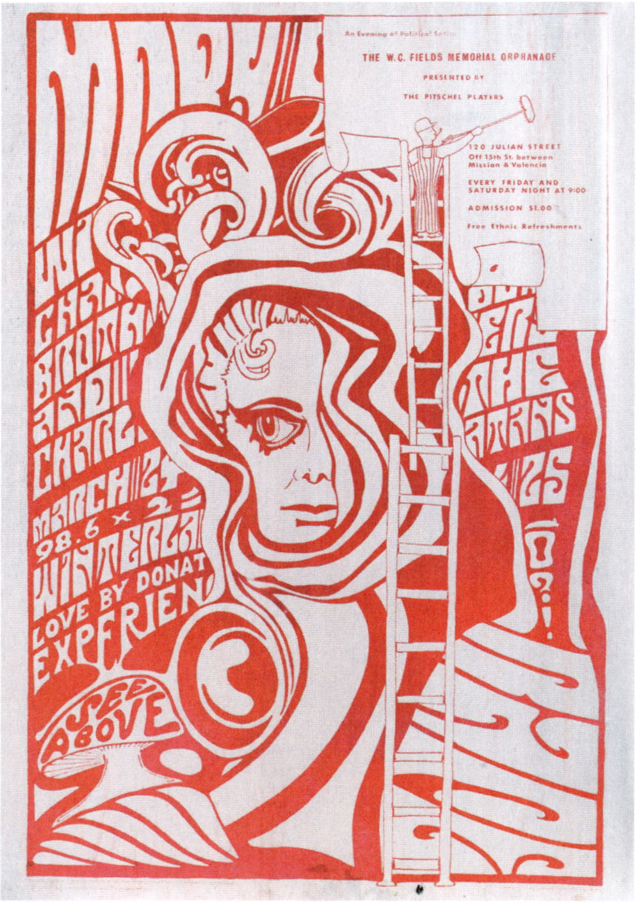

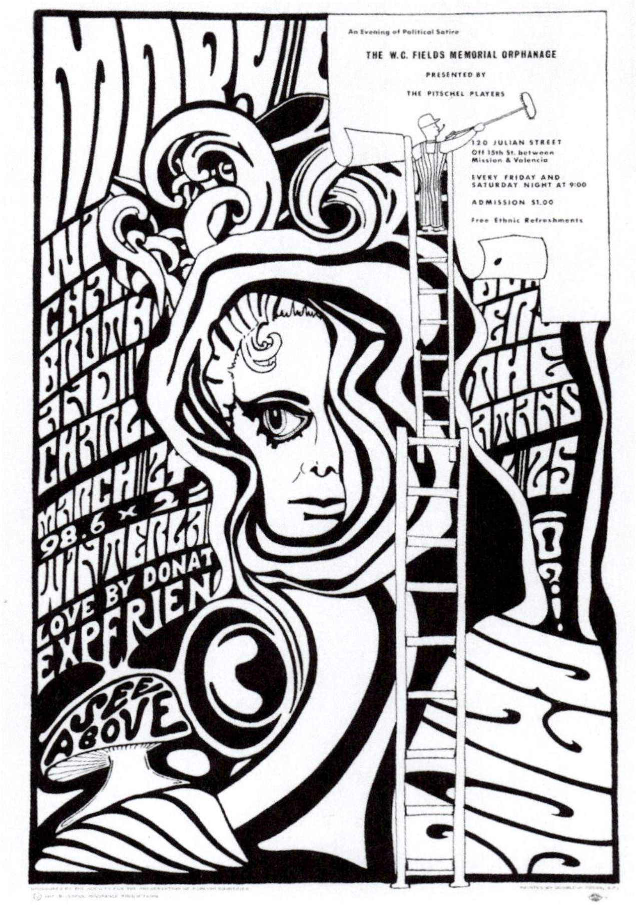

➳ One-color posters were the cheapest and easiest to make. Printing plates are shown to the left and posters to the right. ➳ This page: these 1967 designs were printed by Double-H Press in San Francisco, a popular print shop run by common-law husband and wife Jennie and Robert Hill. ➳ Top: design by Lee Conklin for an event by the Love Conspiracy Commune in early 1967 (see also p. 82). ➳ Bottom: unknown artist's 1966 design for Blissful Ignorance Productions, advertising the Pitschel Players theater group's appearance in 'The W.C. Fields Memorial Orphanage—An Evening of Political Satire.' The poster is an amusing take on one of Wes Wilson's Fillmore posters, seen here being 'papered over.'

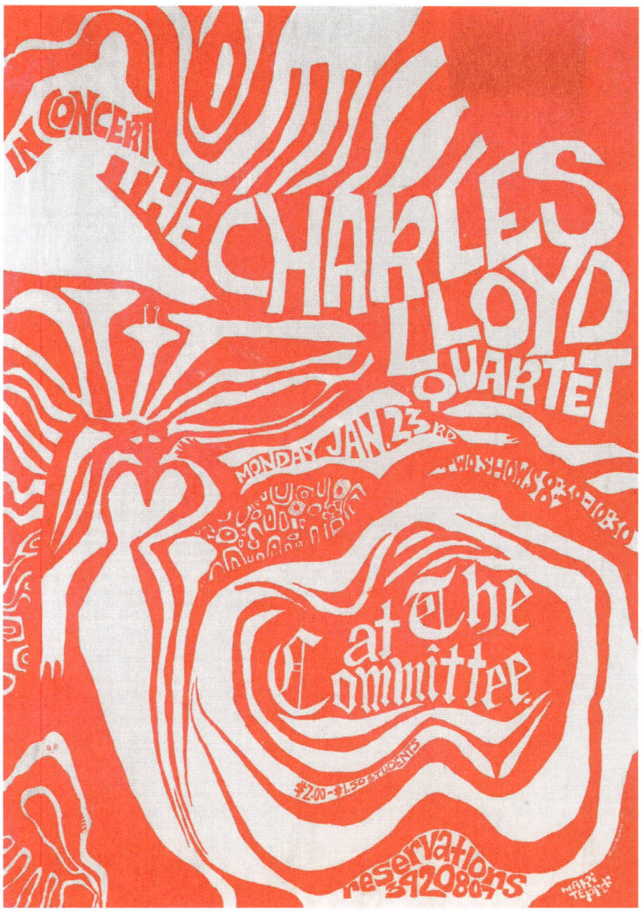

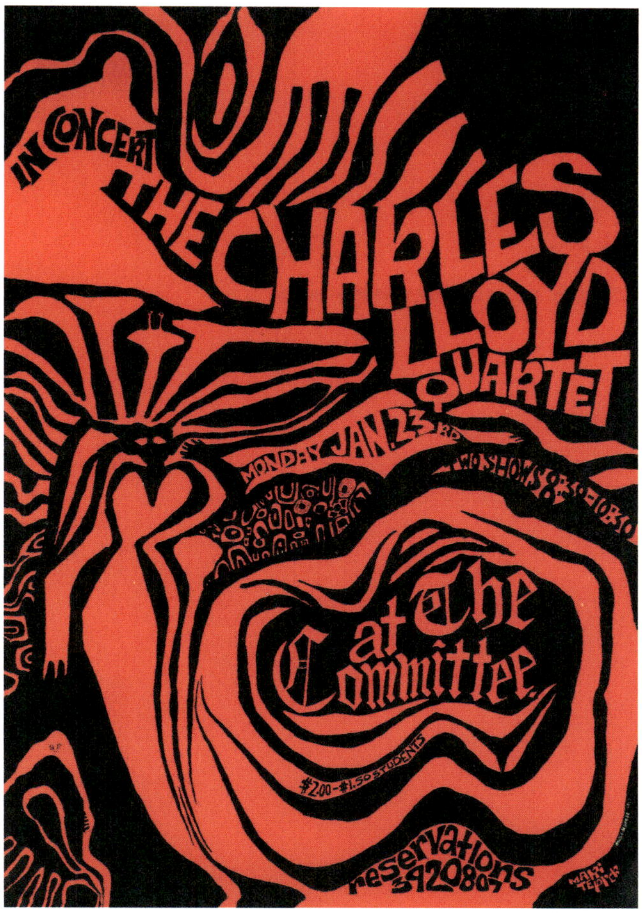

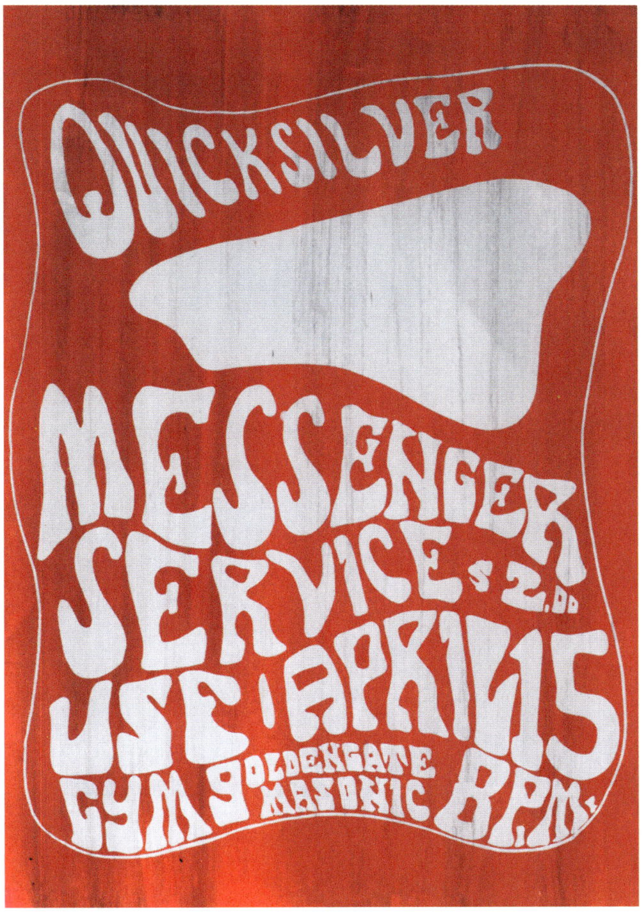

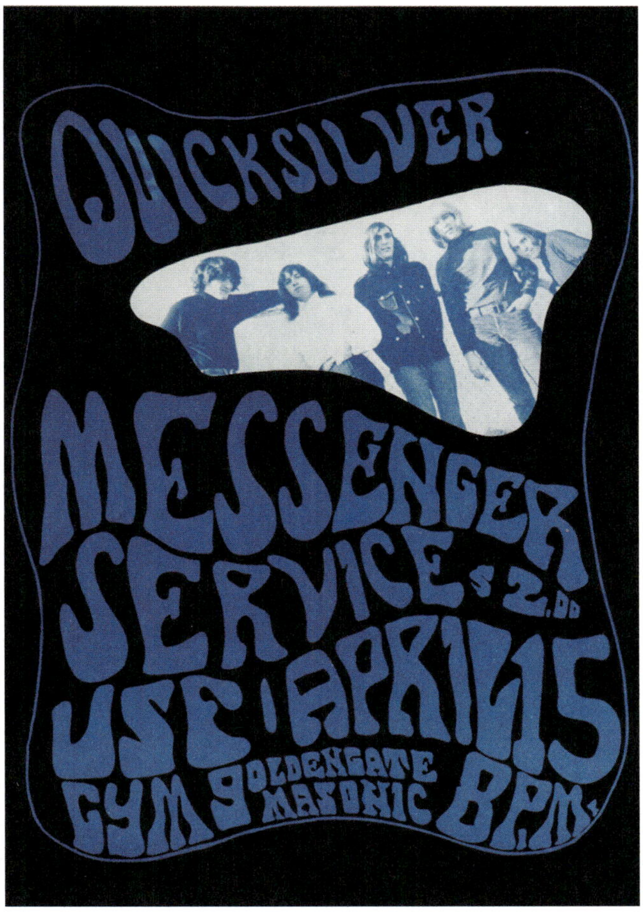

⟫→ Printing plates and corresponding posters. ⟫→ This page, top: 1967 design by Mari Tepper, one of a handful of female poster artists working at this time, for a Charles Lloyd Quartet show at the Committee Theatre. ⟫→ Bottom: design by an unknown artist for a 1967 Quicksilver Messenger Service gig at the University of San Francisco gymnasium.

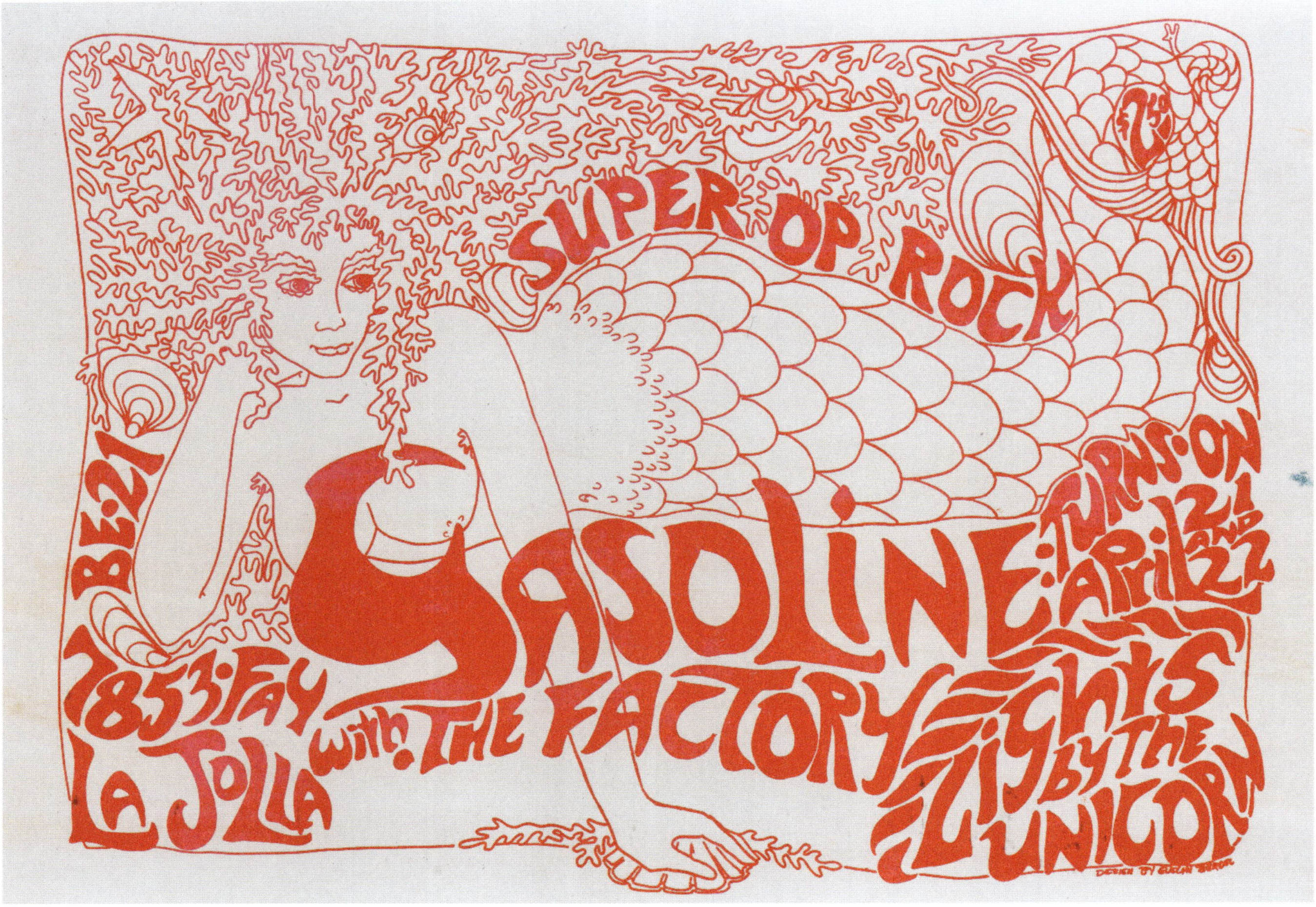

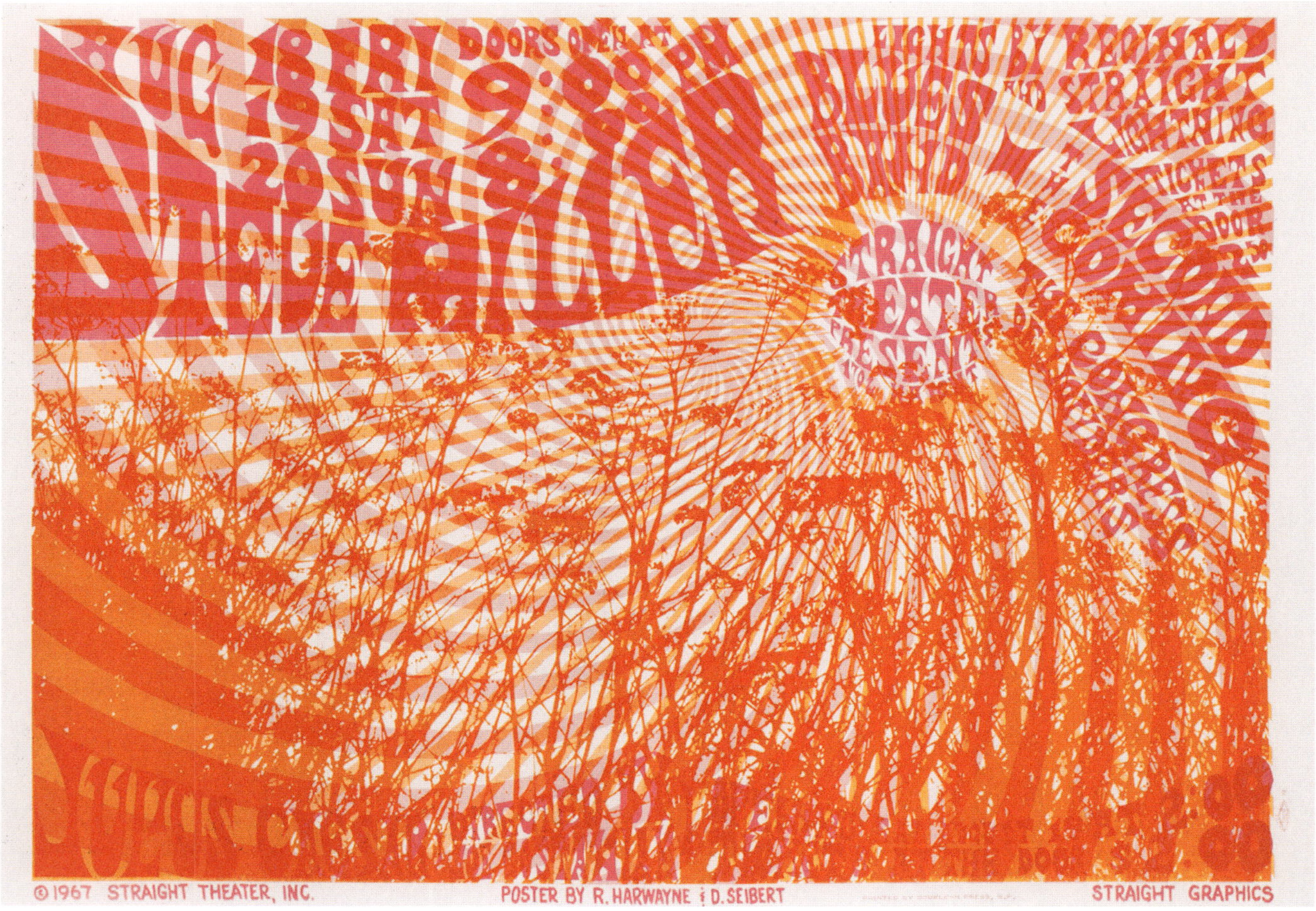

➳ This page, top: printing plate for a 1967 concert poster by Evelyn Berdel for 'Gasoline' in La Jolla, California, featuring the Factory, Lowell George's first band. George formed the band in 1966; he even appeared on the TV show *F Troop* with the band (as 'the Bedbugs') before forming Little Feat in late 1969. ➳ Bottom: a poster by R. Harwayne and D. Seibert for an August 1967 event headlined by The Steve Miller Blues Band at San Francisco's Straight Theater.

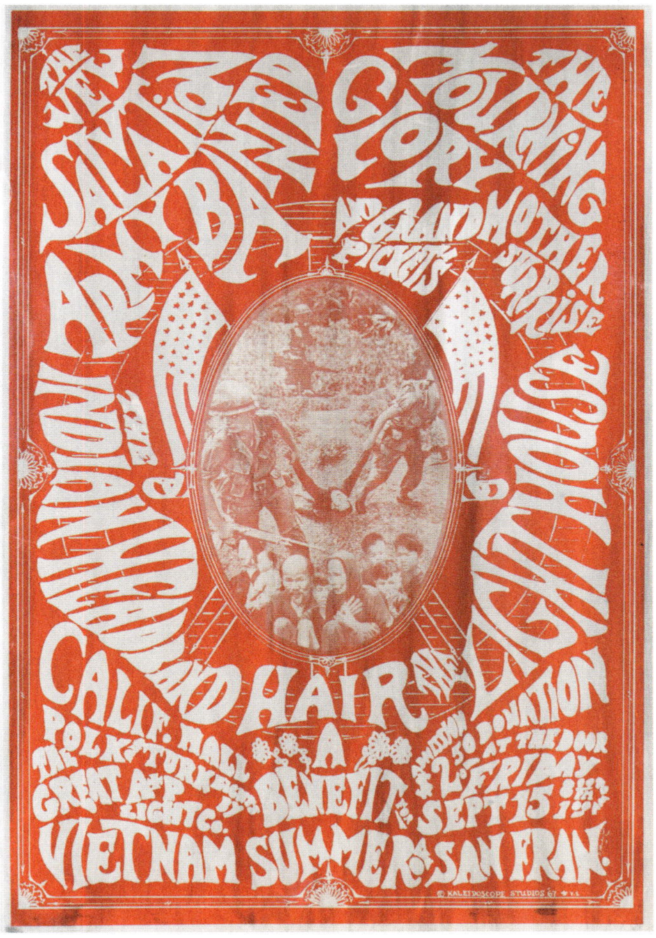

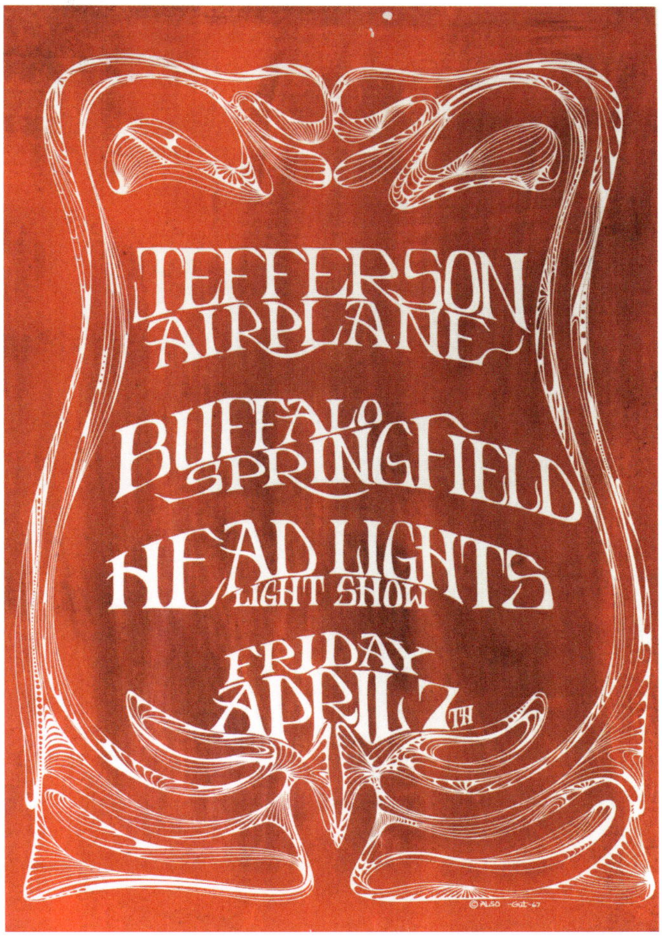

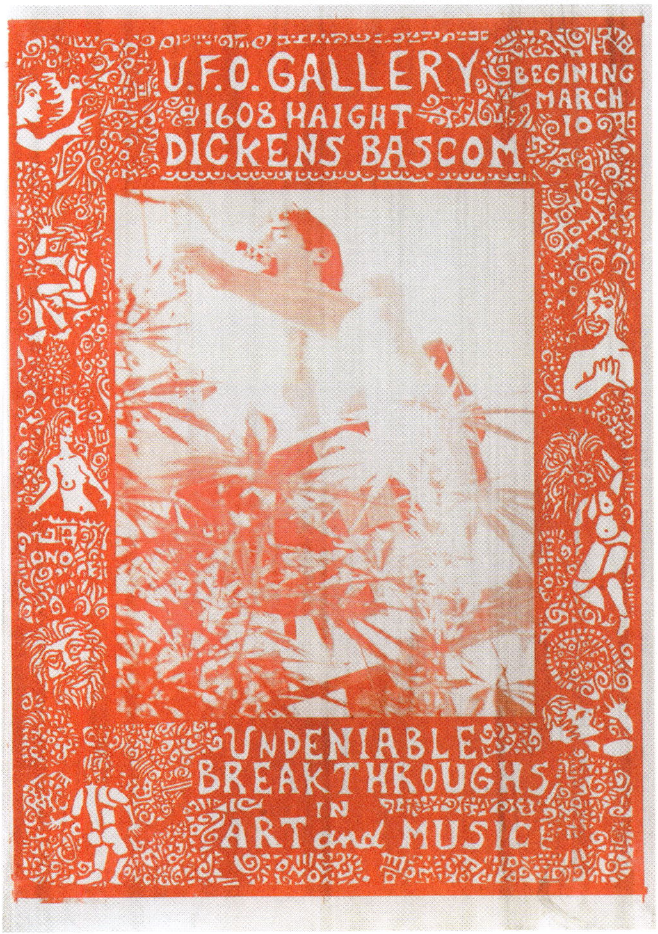

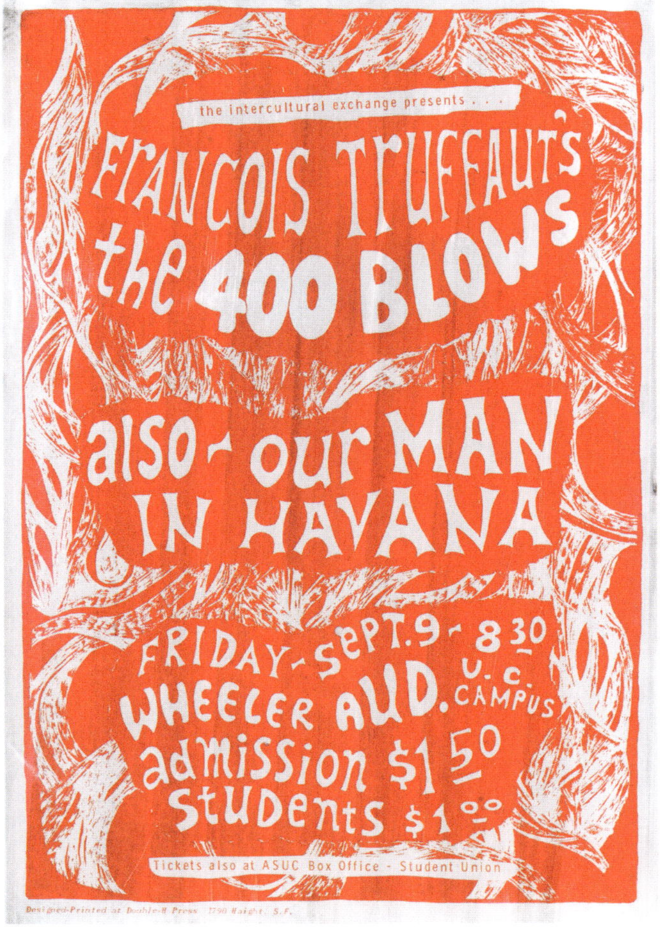

⋙→ This page: four one-color printing plates. One-color posters were often made by less well-known artists as they were cheaper to produce. ⋙→ Clockwise from top left: D. Pallavicini's design advertises a September 1967 anti-Vietnam War benefit event, with a photograph from the conflict at its heart. ⋙→ Hell's Angel and artist Allen 'Gut' Terk created this for a concert at the University of San Francisco gymnasium in April 1967. ⋙→ Poster by an unknown artist, printed by popular San Francisco shop Double-H Press, promotes a showing of François Truffaut's drama *The 400 Blows* at the University of California. ⋙→ Poster by an unknown artist for U.F.O. Gallery, an underground art gallery in San Francisco.

DENNIS NOLAN

In addition to sensitive portraits of Janis Joplin and the other group members, Dennis Nolan's delicate central pencil drawing of guitarist James Gurley of Big Brother and the Holding Company makes his work stand apart from the other artists. Best known for his poster promoting the Grateful Dead at the Denver Family Dog—incorporating a skull, of course—he proves that not all art from the Bay Area was psychedelic.

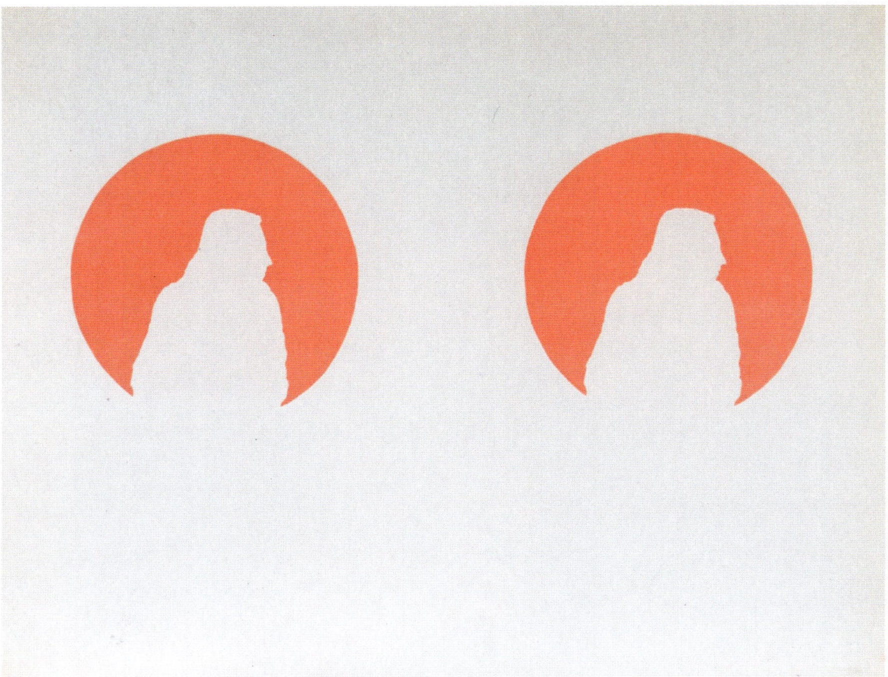

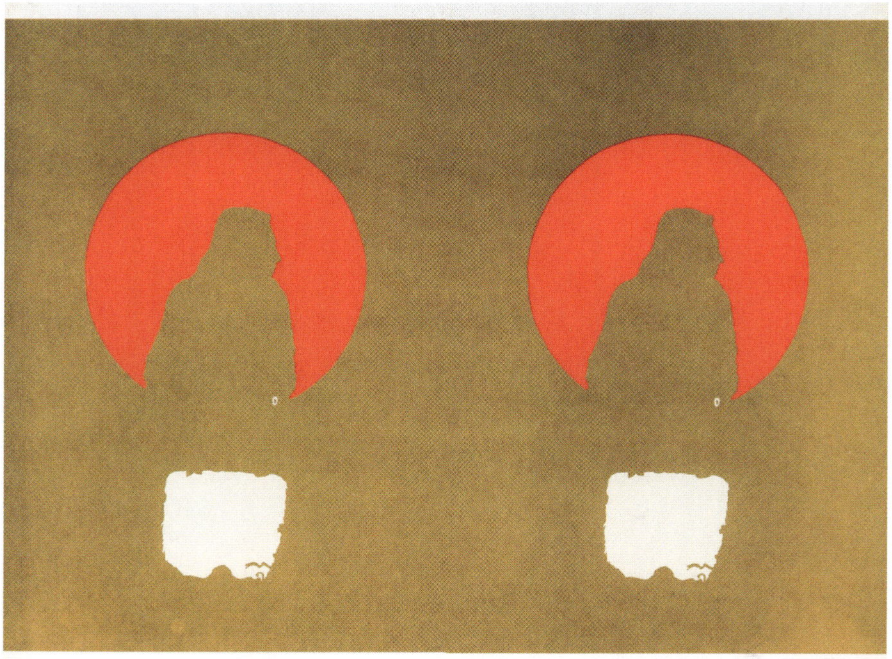

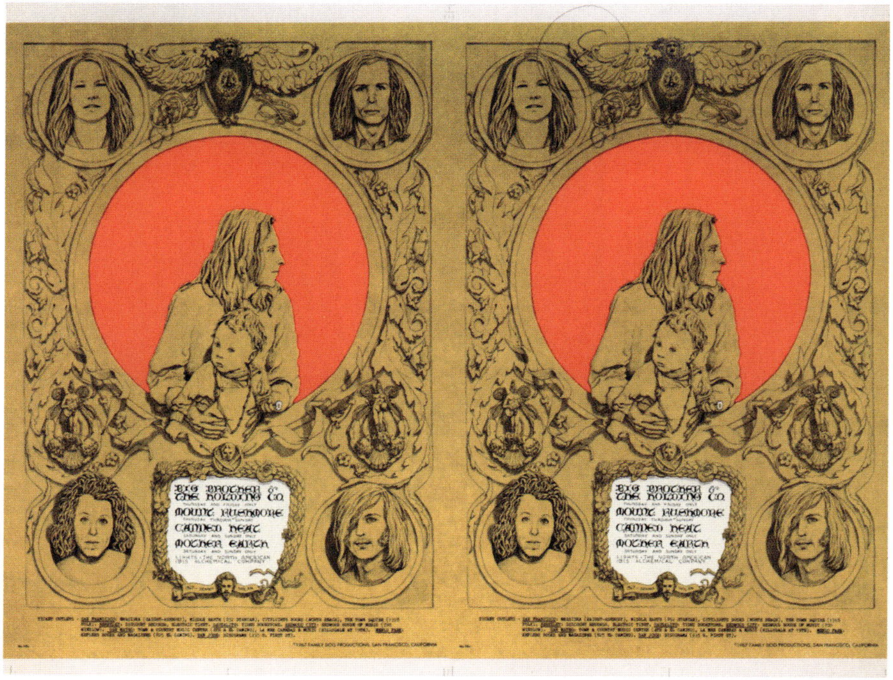

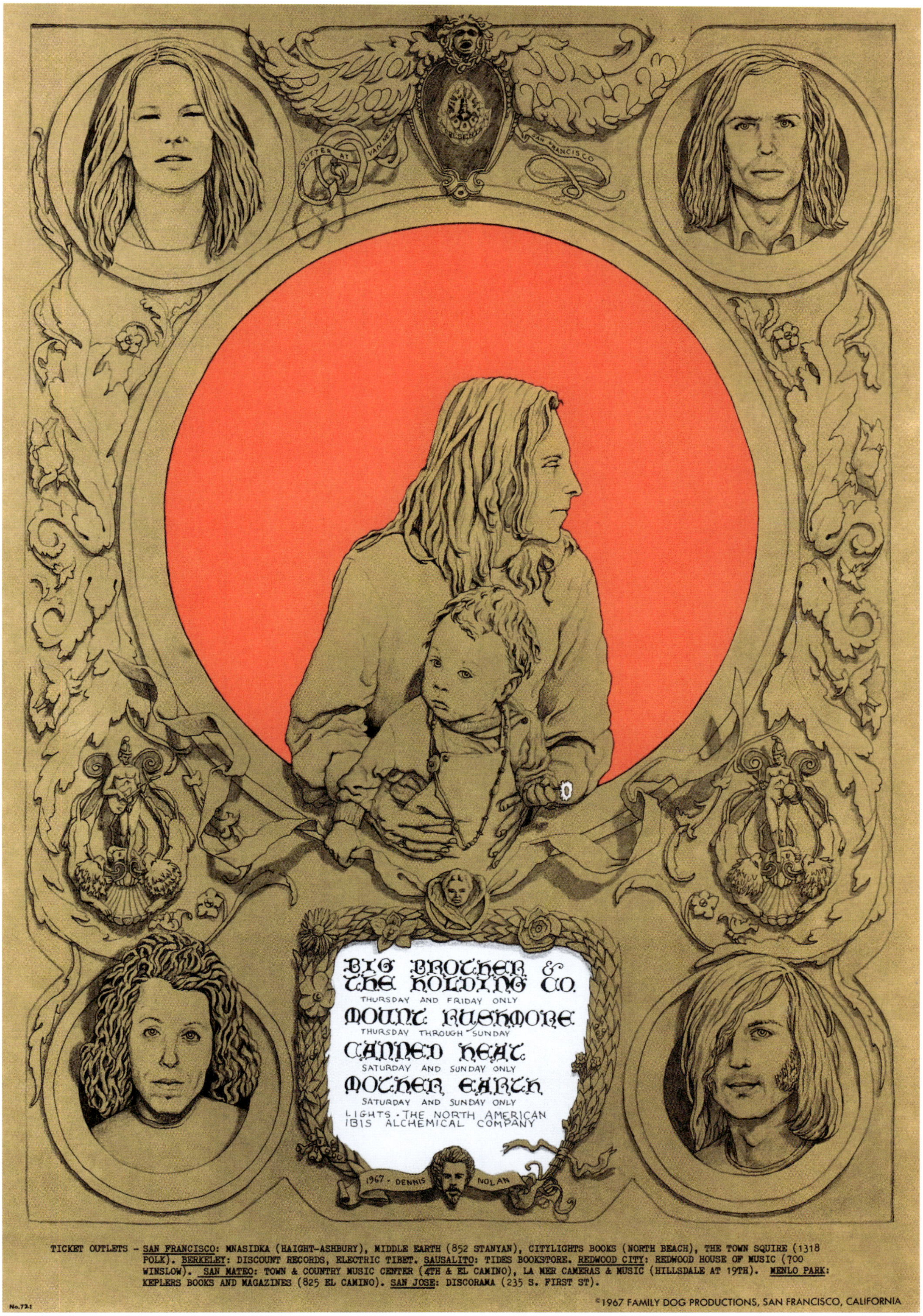

→ Progressive proofs and final poster (dubbed *Family Portrait*) for a July 1967 gig at the Avalon Ballroom headlined by Big Brother and the Holding Company.

INDIAN RELIGION AND EASTERN MYSTICISM

A widespread interest in Eastern mysticism and religion developed on both sides of the Atlantic as the sixties wore on, following on from the beat generation writers of the previous decade. For members of the counter-culture, this was complemented (and often initially inspired) by LSD use. Astrology, ley-lines, and flying saucers were embraced in Britain, while American Indian tribal ritual, Tibetan and Zen Buddhist meditation, and Transcendental Meditation were more common in the States. Needless to say, these were all superb subjects for posters and resulted in many striking designs.

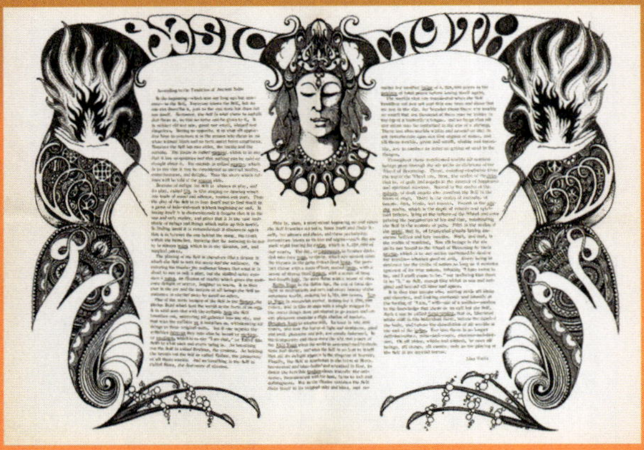

A spread from *The Oracle*'s 'Aquarian Age' issue (#6, February 1967) ⋙→ Readers are offered an introduction to non-Western myth.

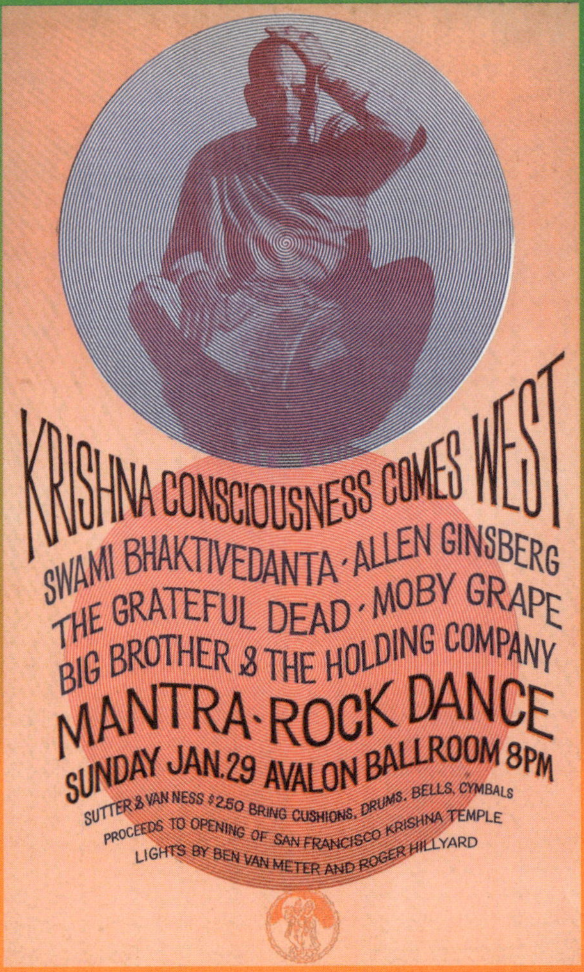

Avalon Ballroom poster for the Mantra-Rock Dance, 1967 ⋙→ As in the work of Victor Moscoso, this image by Harvey W. Cohen bedazzles the eye, although by means of intersecting concentric lines rather than clashing colors.

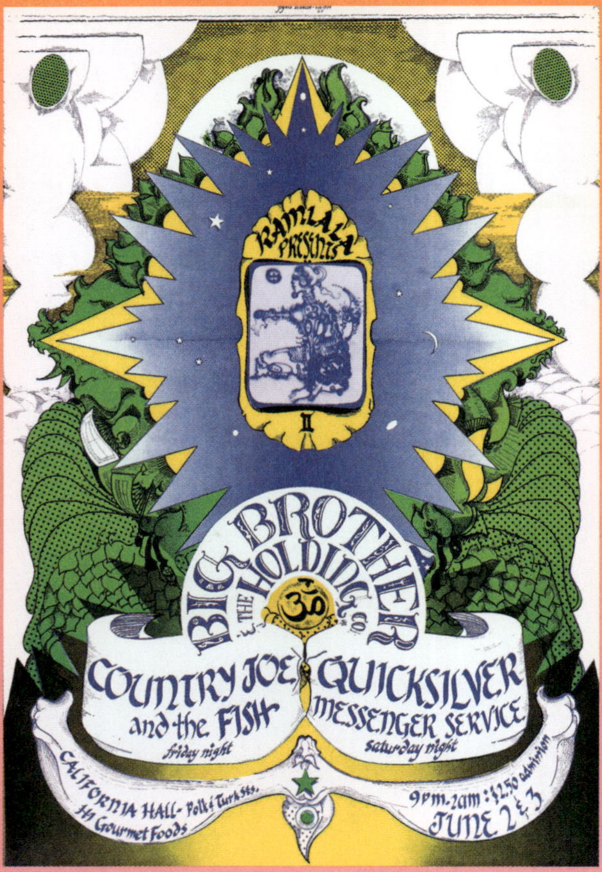

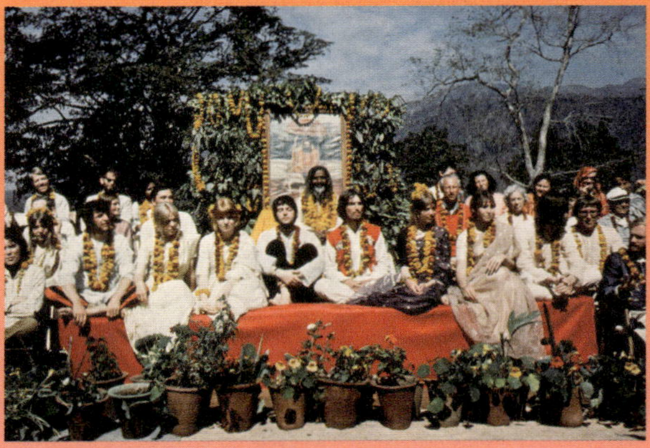

The Beatles with the Maharishi Mahesh Yogi in Rishikesh, India, 1968 ⋙→ The Fab Four embraced Transcendental Meditation, at least for a time, and were on a visit to the Maharishi's retreat along with their wives and partners Maureen Starkey, Jane Asher, Patti Boyd, and Cynthia Lennon.

Big Brother and the Holding Company at California Hall, June 1967 ⋙→ As this image by Michael Wood/Pyxis Studios shows, Eastern beliefs and practices were becoming more familiar to Western minds by mid-1967, partly through rock music.

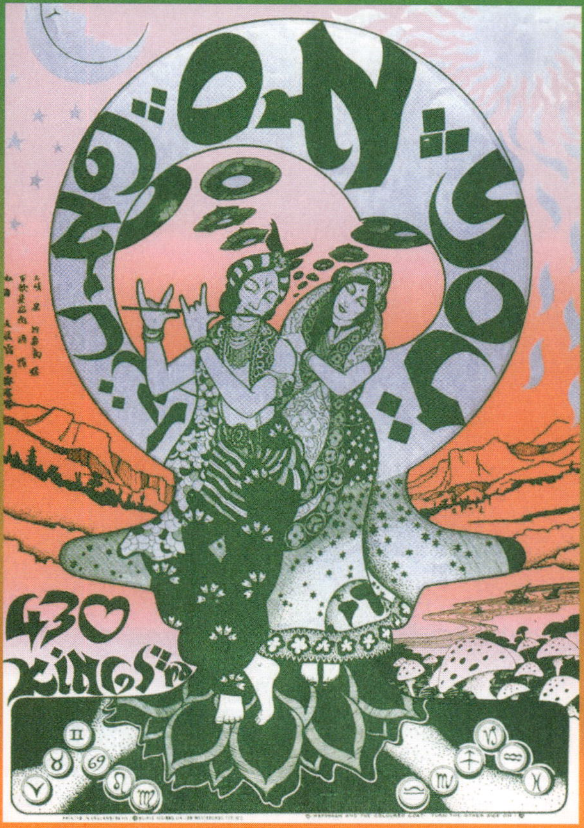

Hapshash and the Coloured Coat, Hung On You poster, 1967 ⟿ English and Waymouth added sylph-like Eastern girls to their familiar flying saucers and zodiac signs for this poster promoting clothes boutique Hung On You, which by now had moved within Chelsea, from Cale Street to the King's Road.

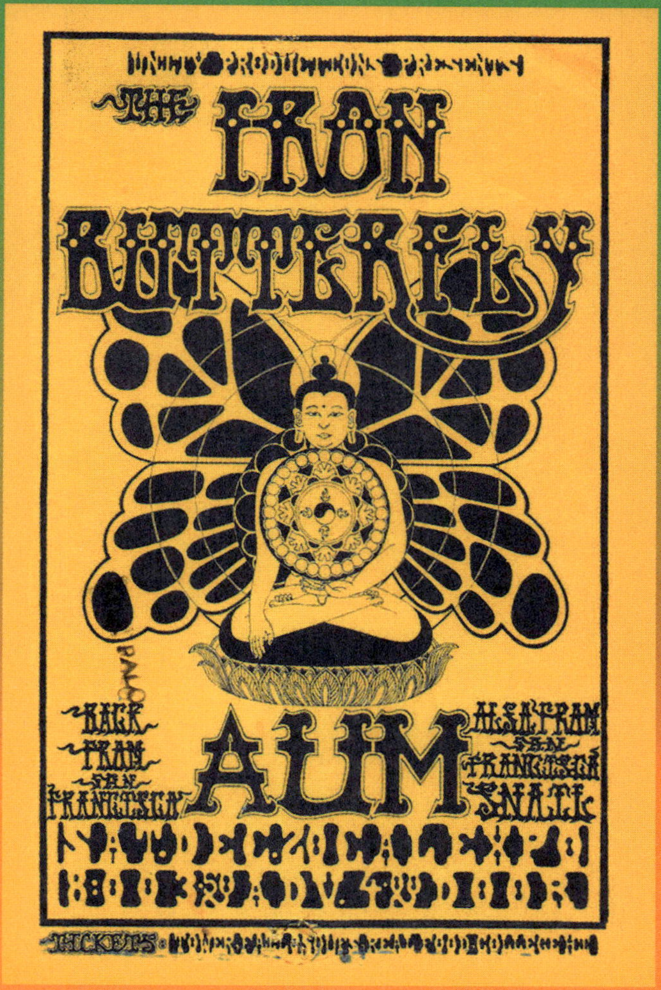

Iron Butterfly poster for a concert at the Cal Expo Events Building in Sacramento, 1969 ⟿ The central image of a Buddha with butterfly wings is accompanied by the sacred word 'aum.' Uttered as a mantra in various faiths, including Hinduism, Buddhism, and Sikhism, its shades of meaning encompass the divine, the whole of cosmic creation, and the essence of existence.

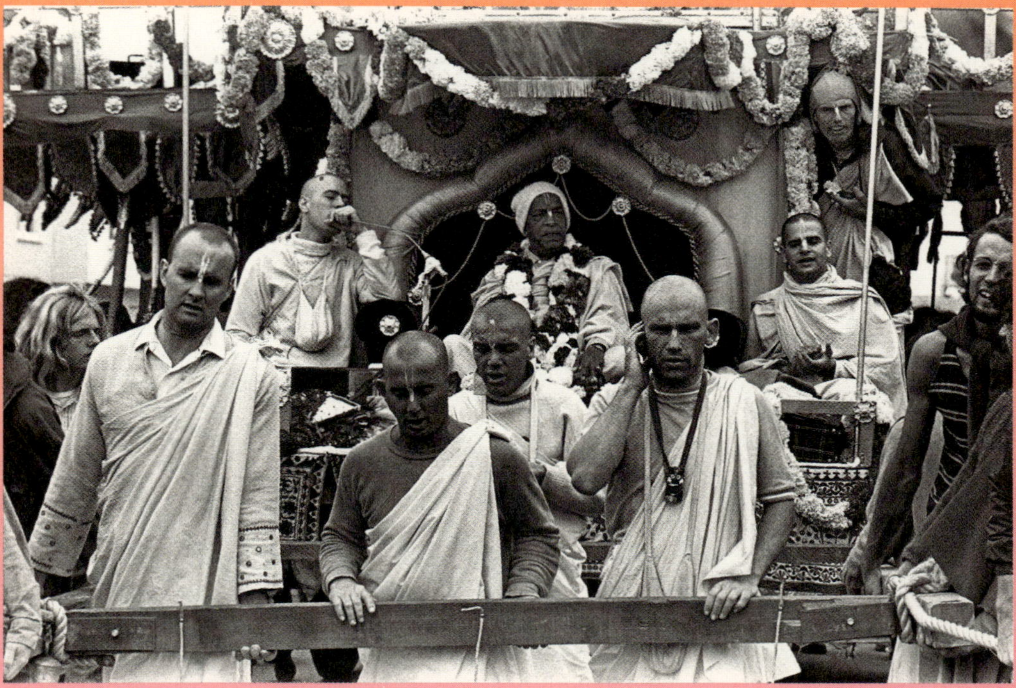

Hare Krishna devotees in San Francisco, 1969 ⟿ The picture was taken during the Ratha Yatra ('Chariot Festival'), held by the International Society for Krishna Consciousness in San Francisco on July 27, 1969. A three-ton car (the 'ratha') was taken from Haight-Ashbury to the ocean, mimicking an annual ritual that takes place at Puri in India.

CATS 'N' DOGS 'N' ROCK 'N' ROLL

Chet Helms's Family Dog expanded to include concerts in Denver, at 1601 West Evans. The run began in September 1967, with Janis Joplin, ending on December 31 with a performance by The Doors.

The one-color proofs of this poster, by Robert Fried, demonstrate the care taken by designers and print-makers when separating out the colors of the design. Each layer of color interlocks with the other, with space left for the color to come through, as in the orange lines emerging from the red background, or to blend with another—see how the blue and red create a purple hue in the full-color poster.

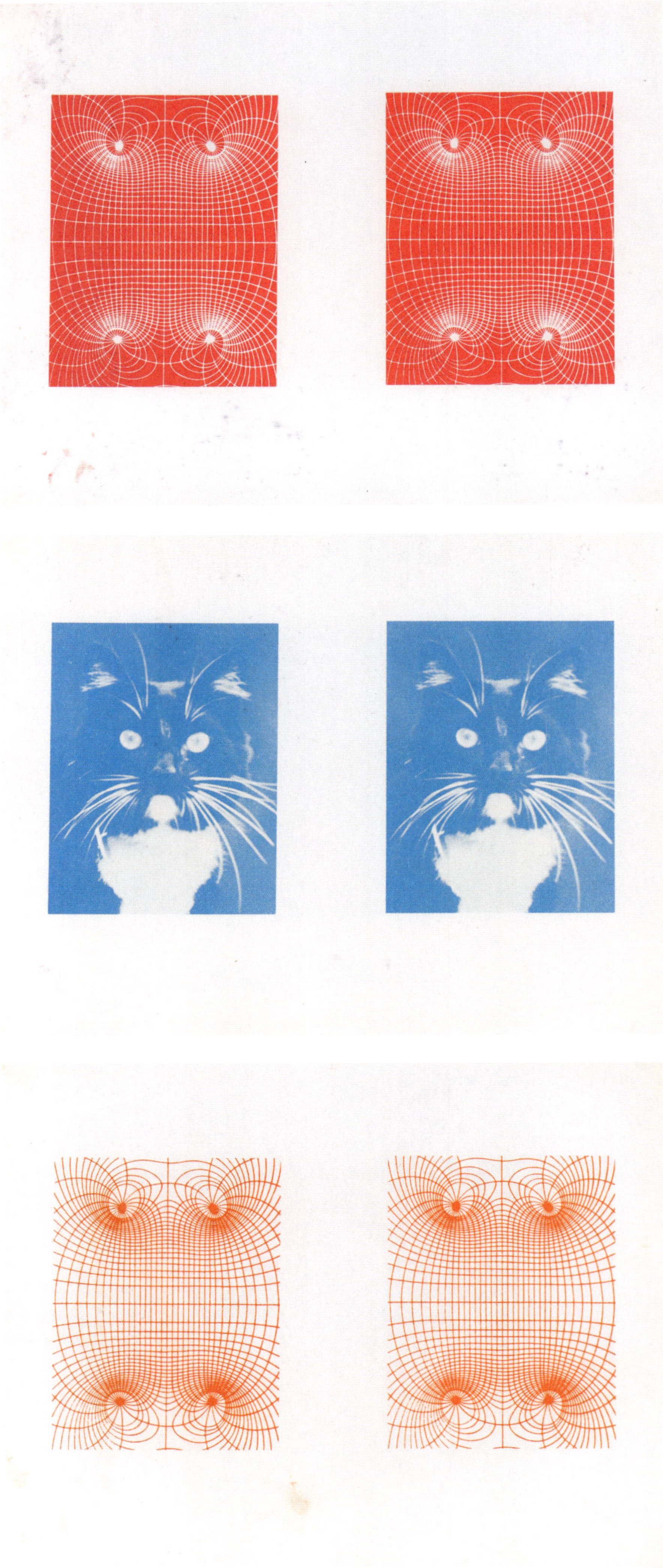

→ Printing plates, progressive prints, and the finished poster (known as *Kitty*) for a Buffalo Springfield concert at 1601 West Evans in Denver, Colorado, in October 1967.

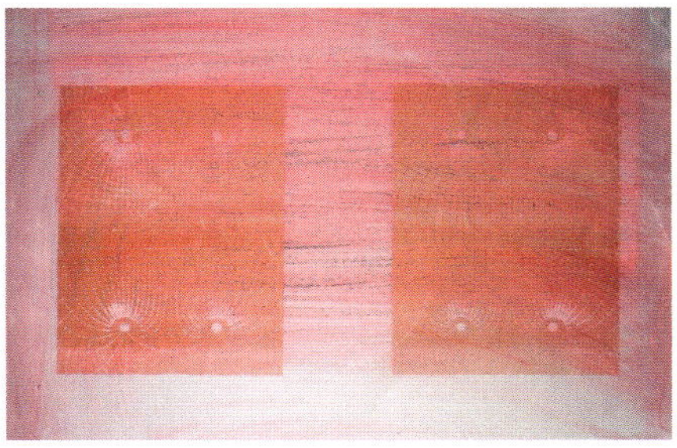

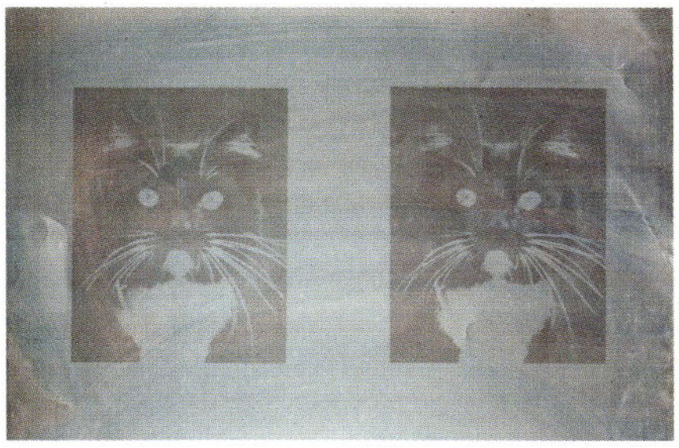

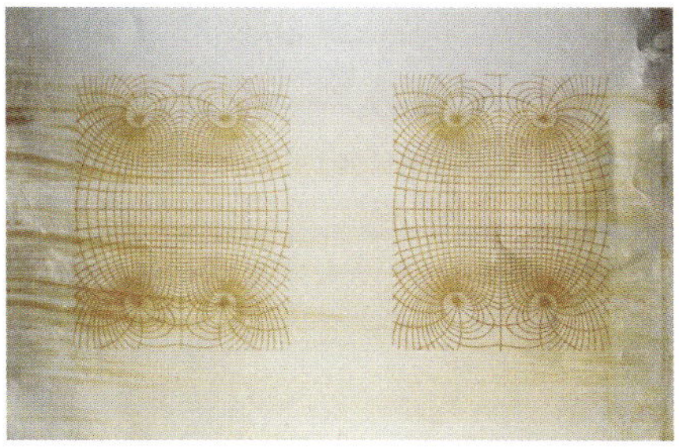

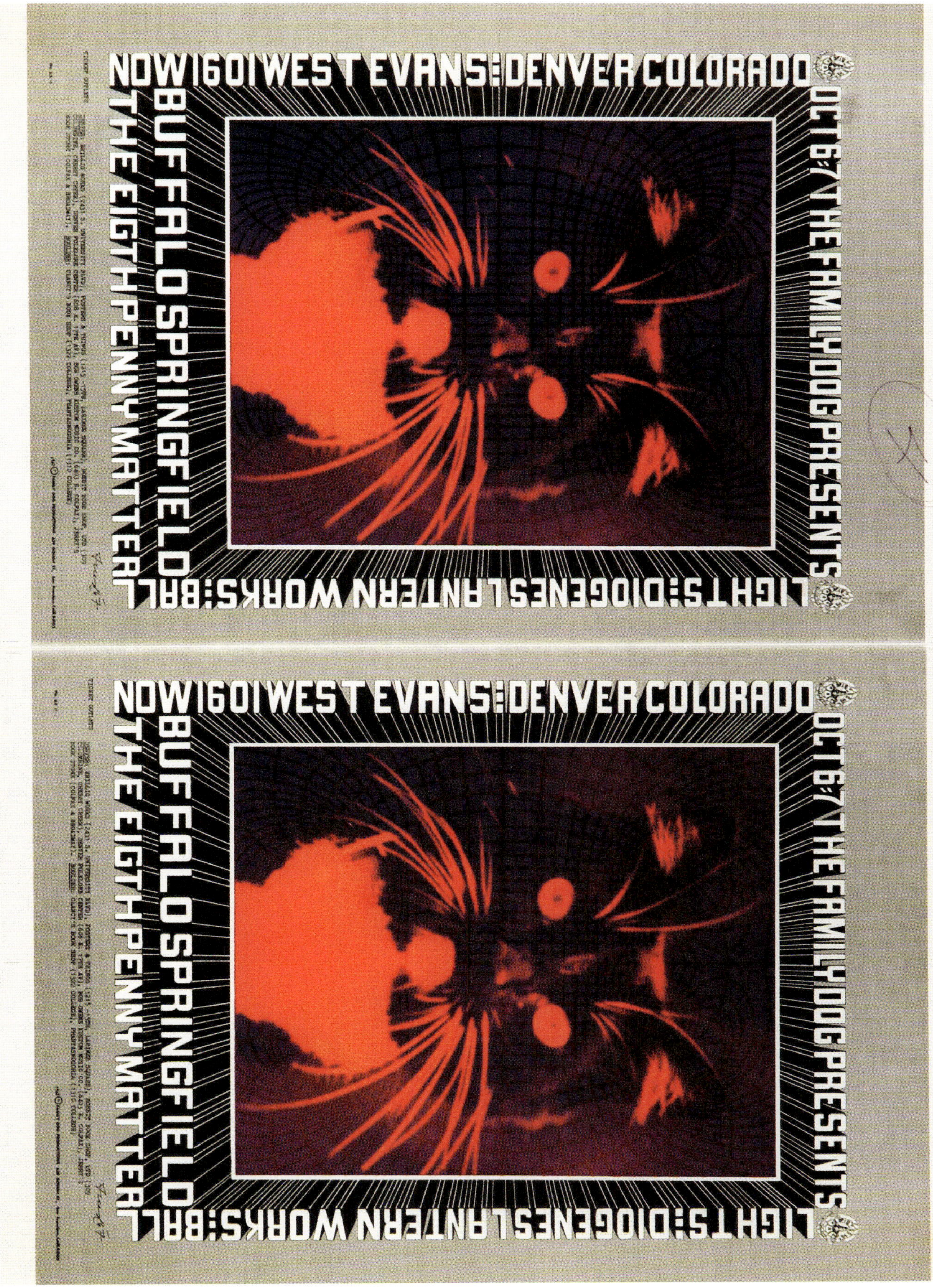
OCT 6 '67 THE FAMILY DOG PRESENTS
LIGHTS: DIOGENES LANTERN WORKS: BALL
NOW 1601 WEST EVANS: DENVER COLORADO
BUFFALO SPRINGFIELD
THE EIGTH PENNY MATTER
OCT 6 '67 THE FAMILY DOG PRESENTS
LIGHTS: DIOGENES LANTERN WORKS: BALL
NOW 1601 WEST EVANS: DENVER COLORADO
BUFFALO SPRINGFIELD
THE EIGTH PENNY MATTER

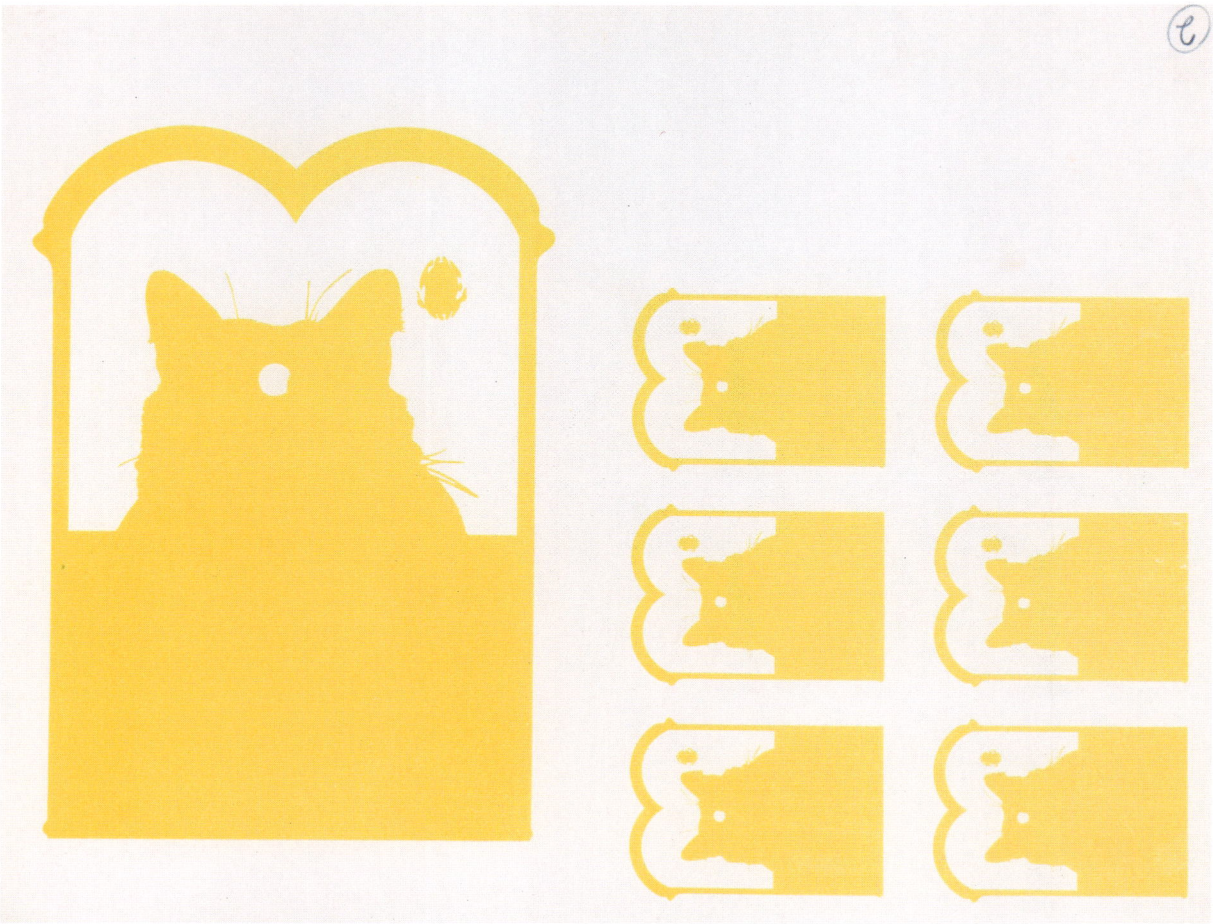

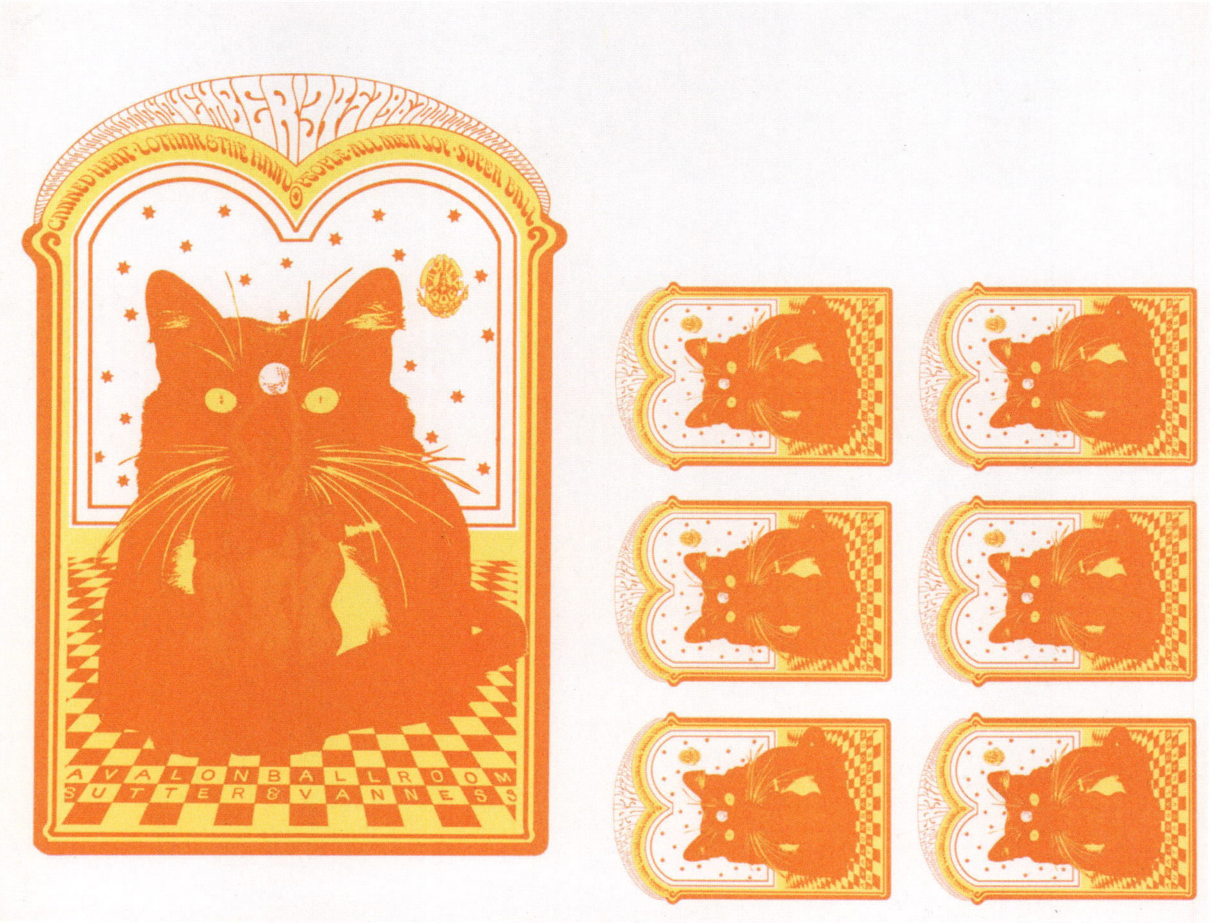

⟫→ Progressive proofs and variants of posters and handbills by Robert Fried for the 'Super Ball,' headlined by Canned Heat, at the Avalon Ballroom in November 1967.

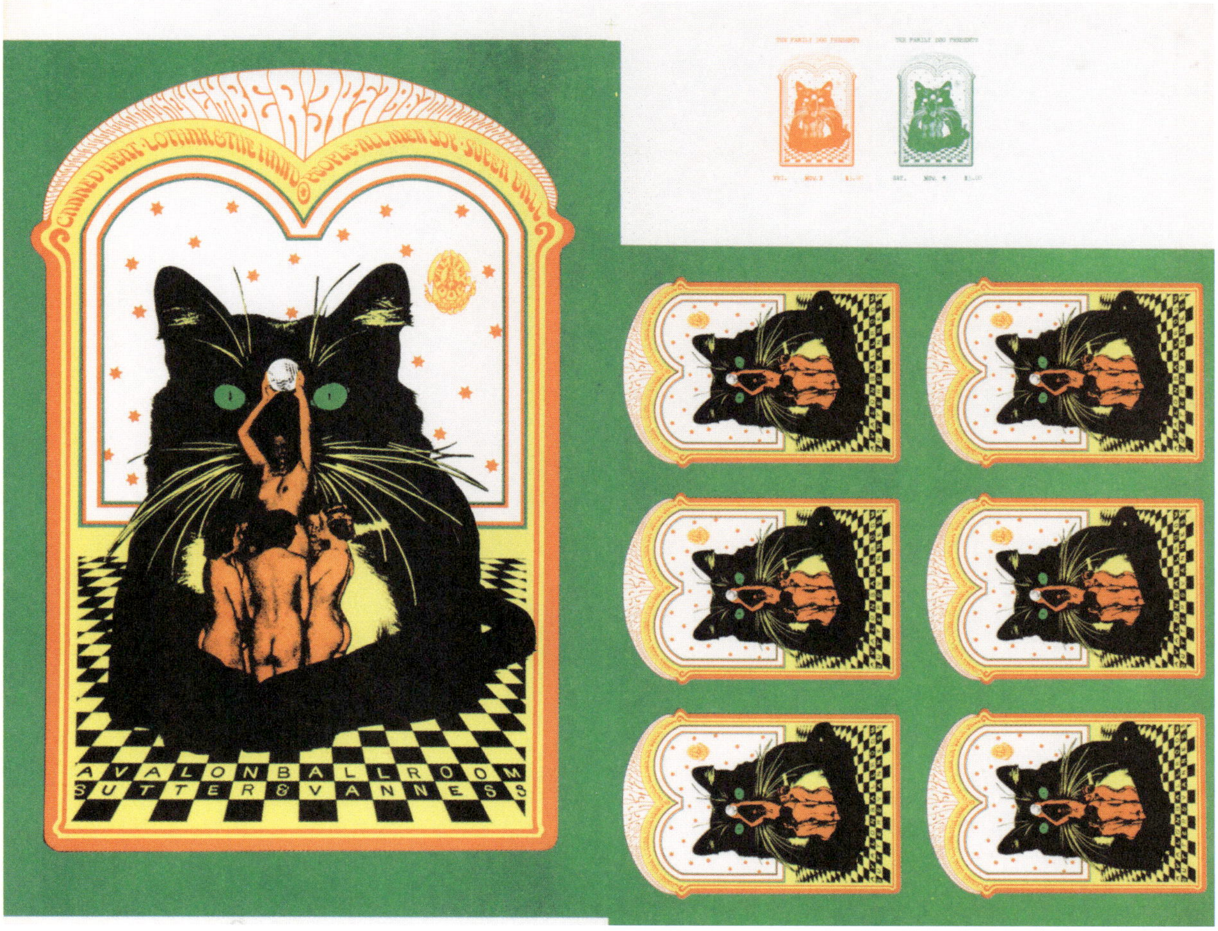
AVALONBALLROOM
SUTTER&VANNESS

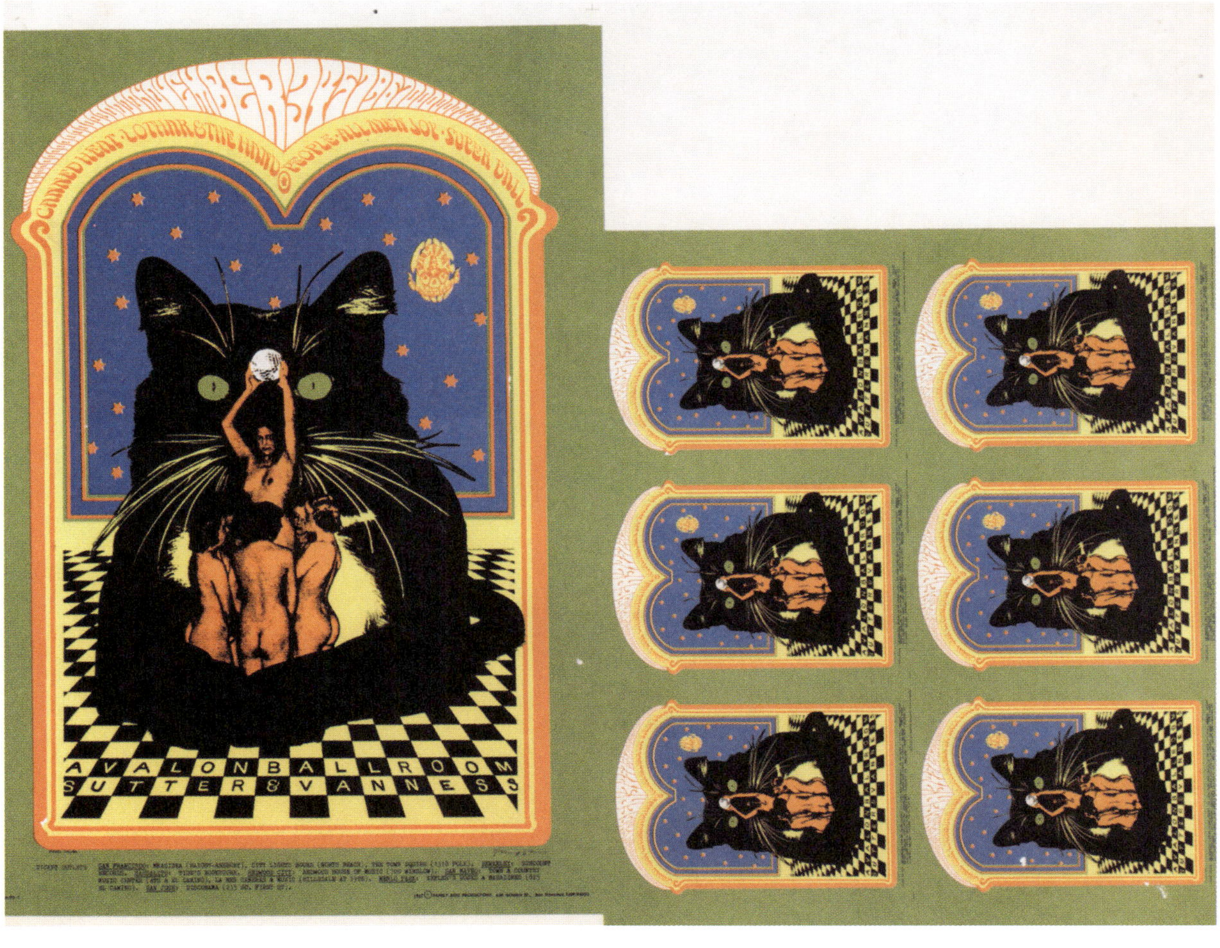
AVALONBALLROOM
SUTTER&VANNESS

INTERNATIONAL TIMES

When *International Times* (*IT*), Europe's first underground newspaper, began in October 1966, there were only eight offset litho printers in Britain, and none of them would touch such a publication. *IT* had to use hot metal, just like all the national and daily newspapers. Eventually, however, a printer was found who agreed to do it, and suddenly Britain had its first paper to feature color (although color photographs were still not a possibility). *IT* was the voice of the UK underground community, constantly subjected to police raids and provocation; it remained an important conduit via which counter-cultural ideas reached young people in Britain.

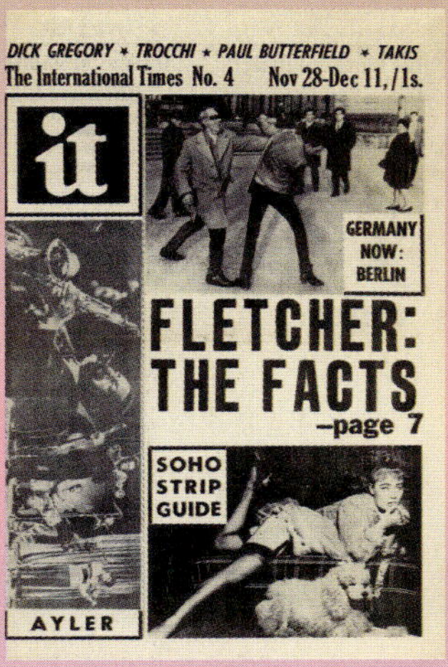

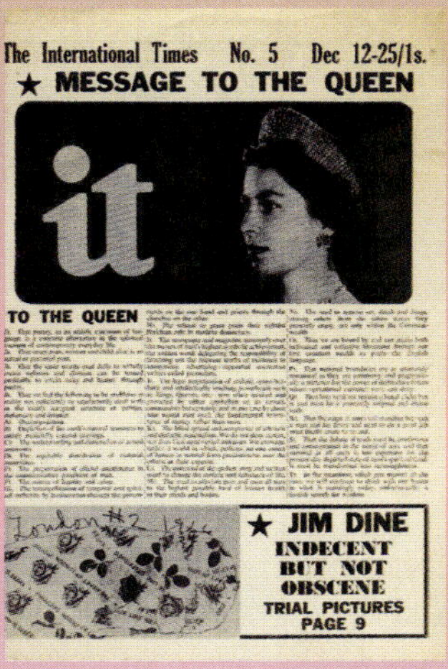

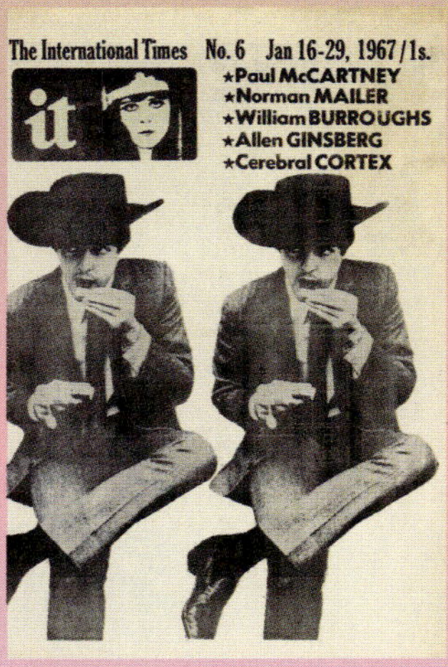

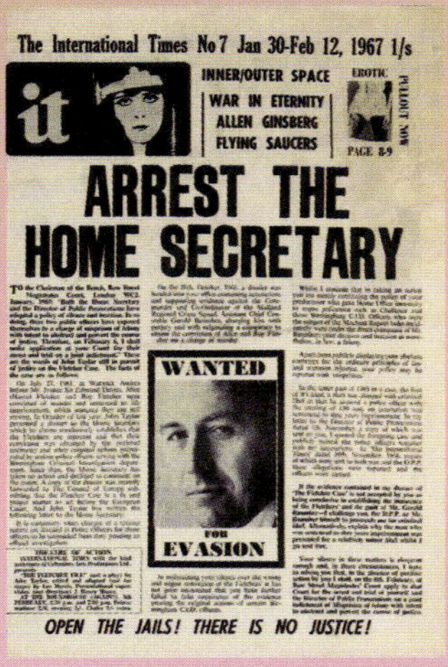

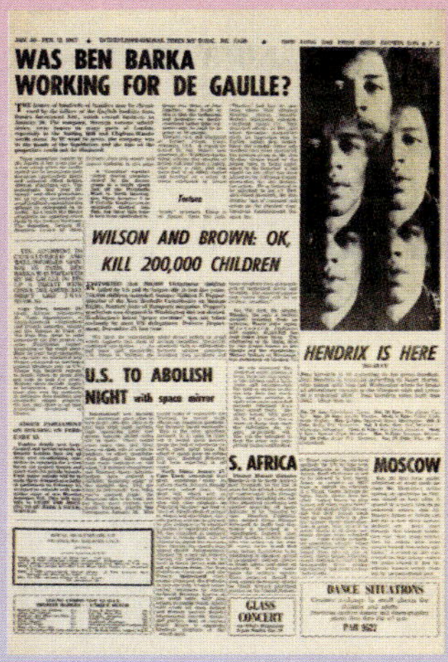

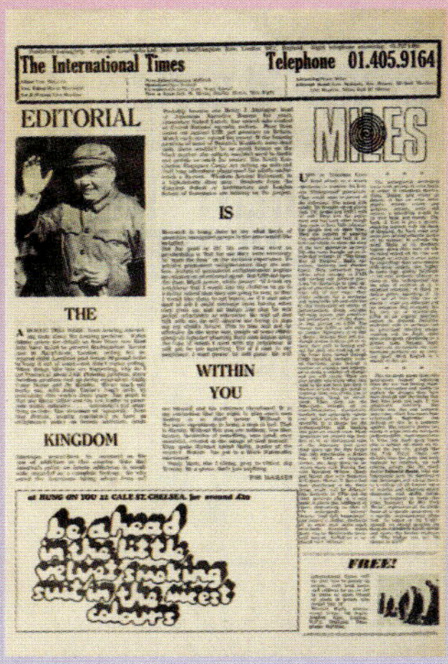

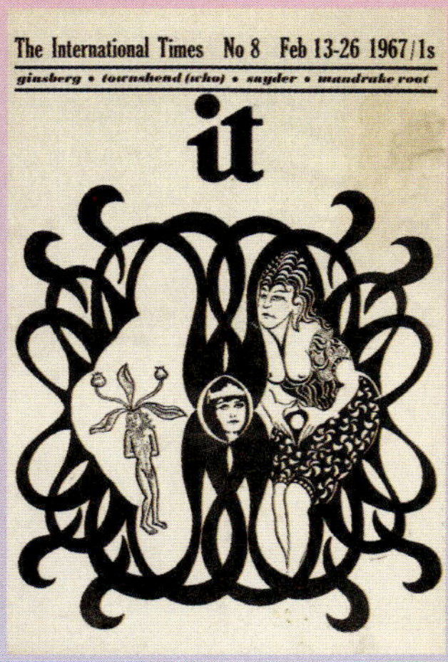

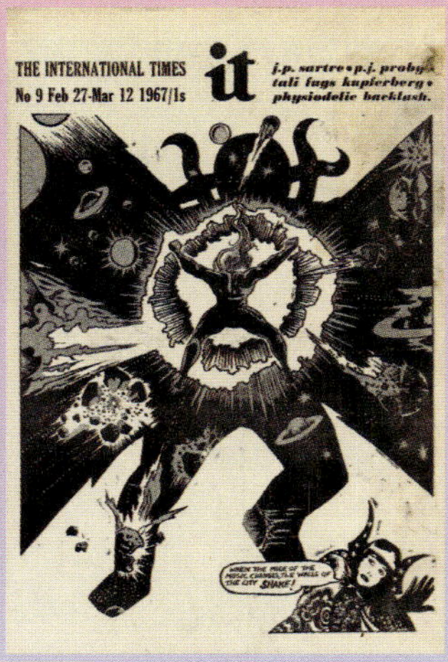

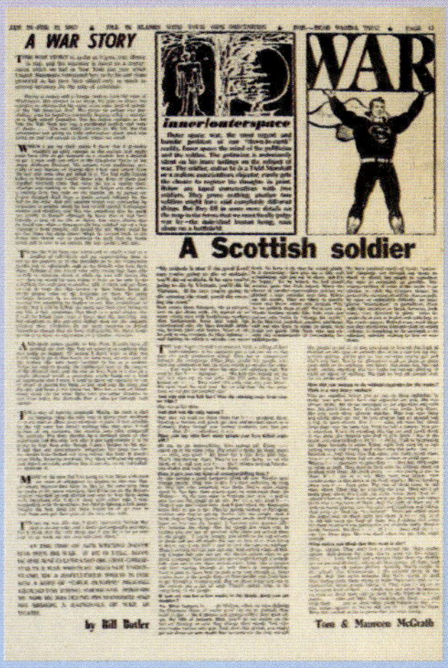

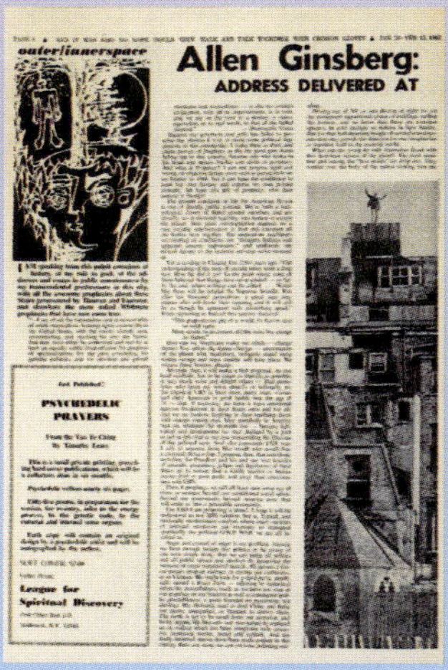

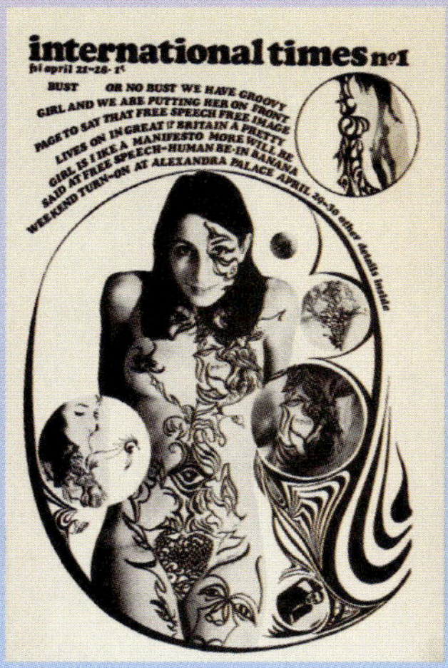

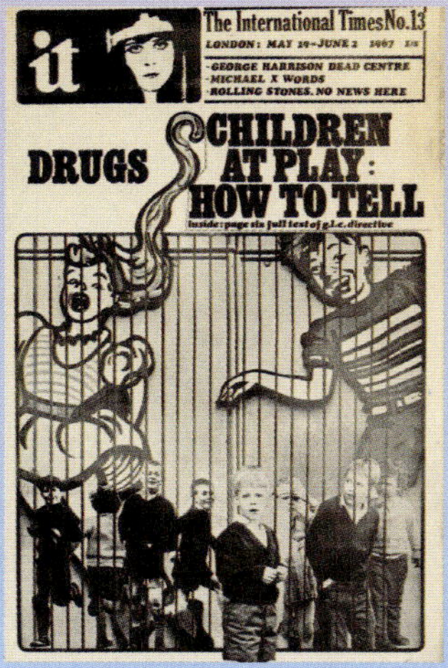

➳ *IT*'s graphic designers were aware that the cover was a poster for the paper and made sure that it reflected the editorial stance. Sex, drugs, and rock 'n' roll featured heavily. The covers from 1966 were closer to the format of traditional newspapers, although monochrome comic-book and Art Nouveau stylings appeared in early 1967. But the advent of color litho meant that anything could be used. When the International Situationists covered the front of the *IT* building with posters, the paper's designers carefully peeled one off and used it as the cover for #26, published in February 1968 (see opposite, top row, third from left).

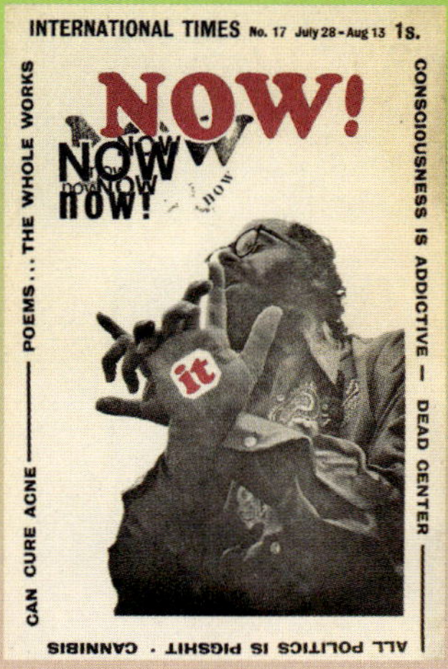

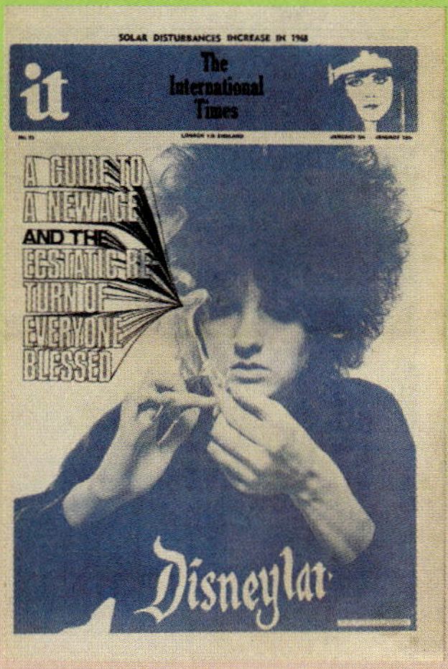

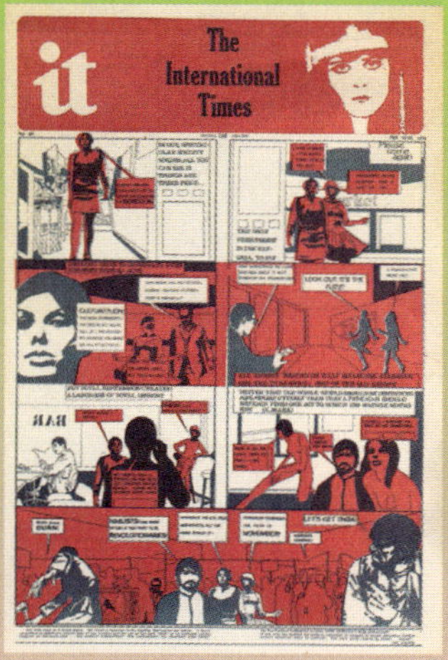

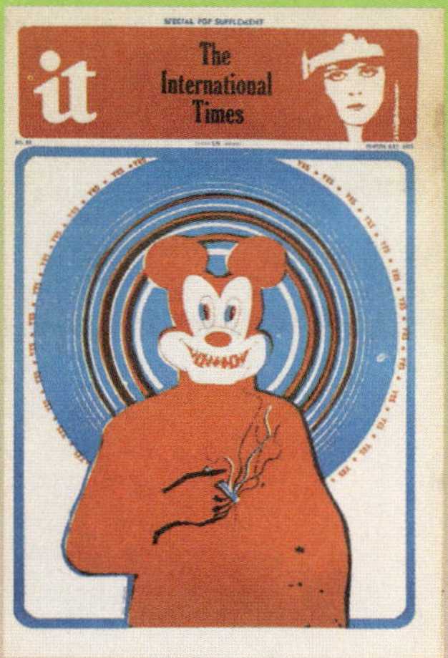

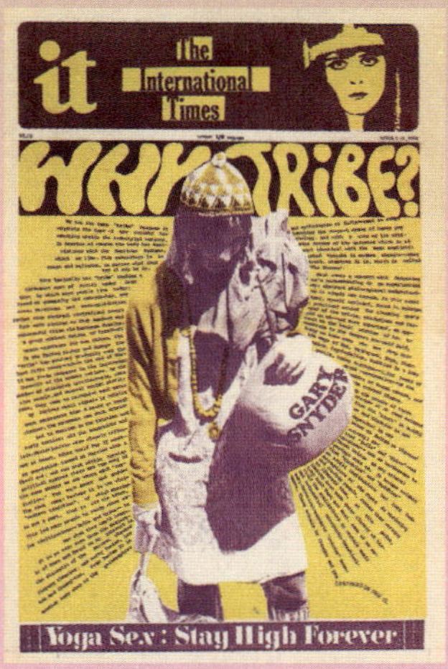

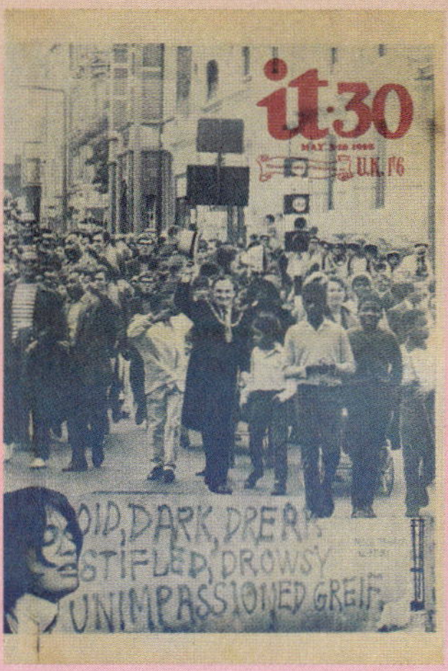

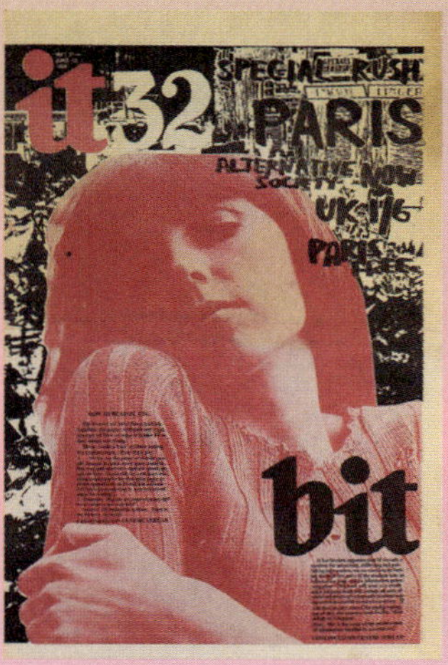

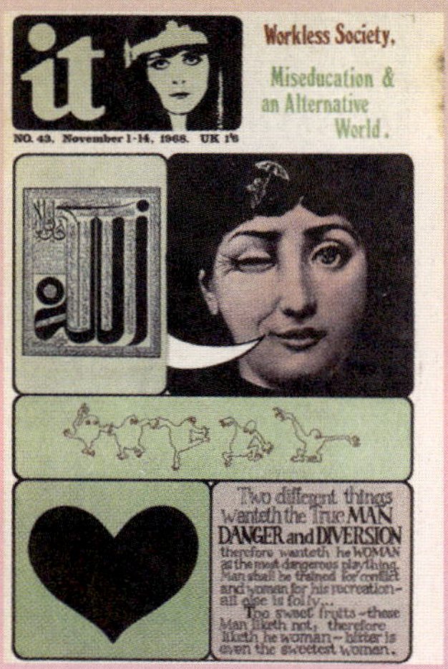

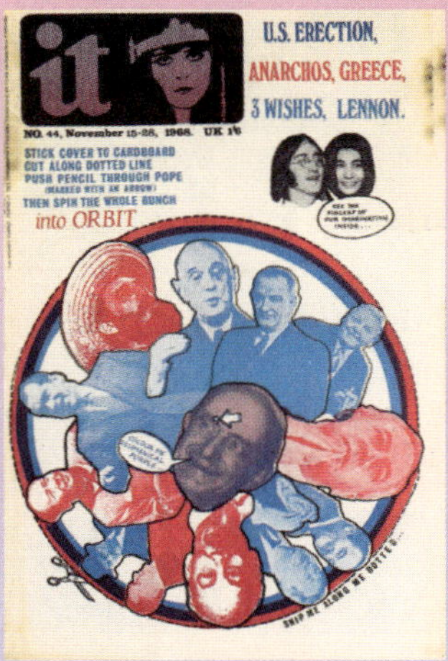

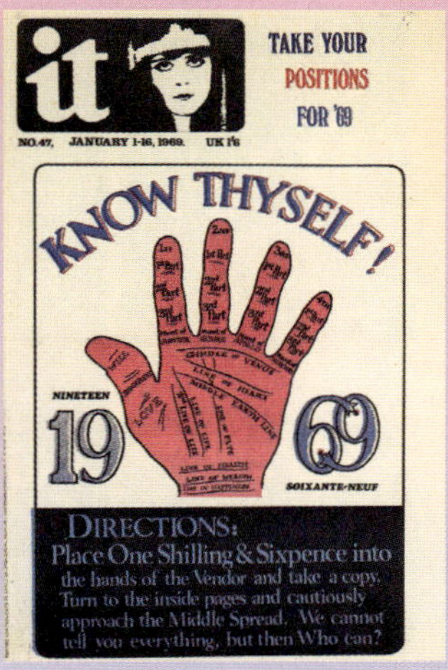

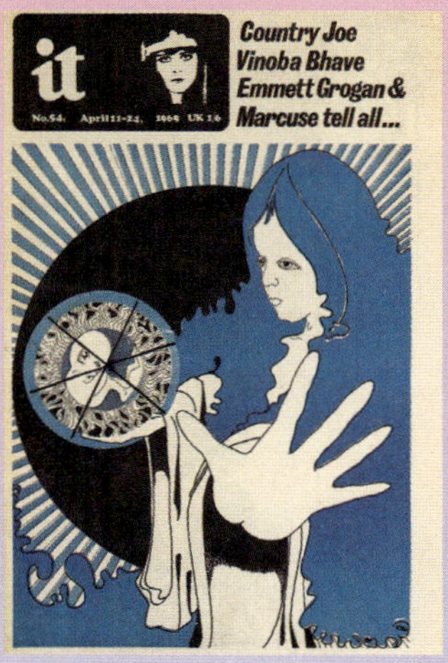

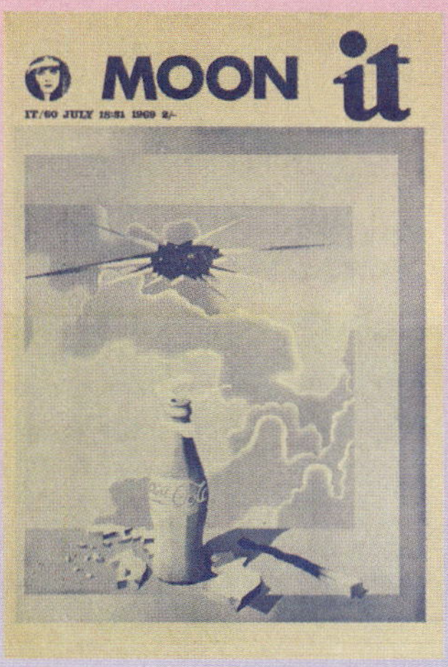

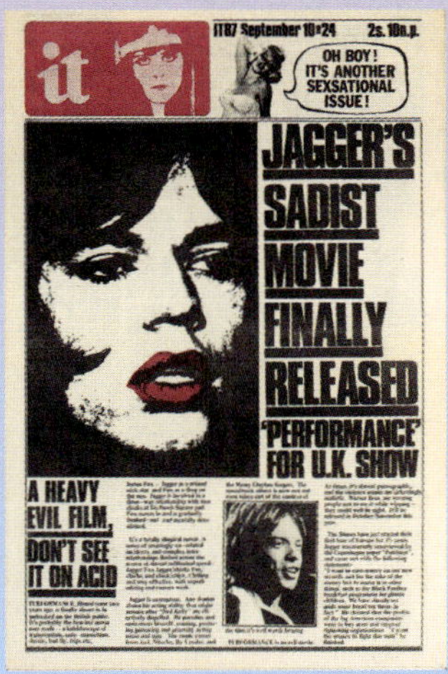

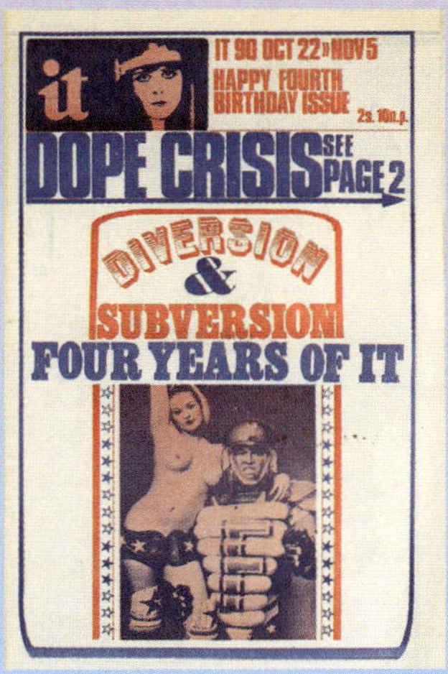

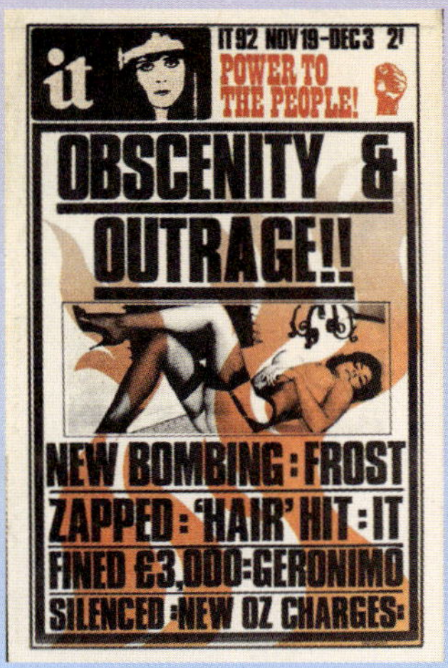

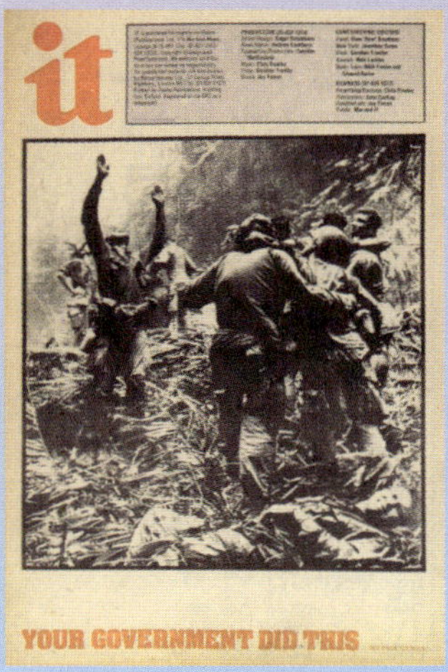

➽➝ For *IT* #30 (second row, second from left), from May 1968, Barry Miles created a collage across the back and front of the paper. Seen to its right here is #32, which reported on the May 1968 events in Paris. A new headline was scrawled on the artwork in felt-tip pen just as the paper was about to be printed. Meanwhile, #90 (bottom row, second from left) used the shortage of marijuana as a headline. Provocative and sensitive to the zeitgeist, *IT* wrote about everything from mystical New Age concerns to Hells Angels and police harassment. And *IT* still exists—you can find its latest incarnation online.

THE UFO CLUB

Beginning in December 1966, the UFO Club all-night dance concerts and multi-media shows were held in London weekly, from 10:30 p.m., as a way of paying the staff of *International Times*, Britain's underground paper. John Hopkins initially hired Michael English to design the posters, but co-founder Joe Boyd wanted Nigel Waymouth to be the graphic artist. They compromised by creating the partnership known as Hapshash and the Coloured Coat. The duo silk-screened their earlier posters using simple, powerful designs and Day-Glo ink. This was before anyone in Britain had seen any of the psychedelic posters made in San Francisco, and in fact pre-dates most of them. However, the sensibility was similar and there emerged a 'London Psychedelic School.' The UFO was influential both in its easygoing format—film shows, poetry readings, spontaneous theater, and performance as well as late-night jam sessions (Jimi Hendrix took part in one with the band Tomorrow)—and in terms of its posters, which established a unique, very British approach to promoting this type of event.

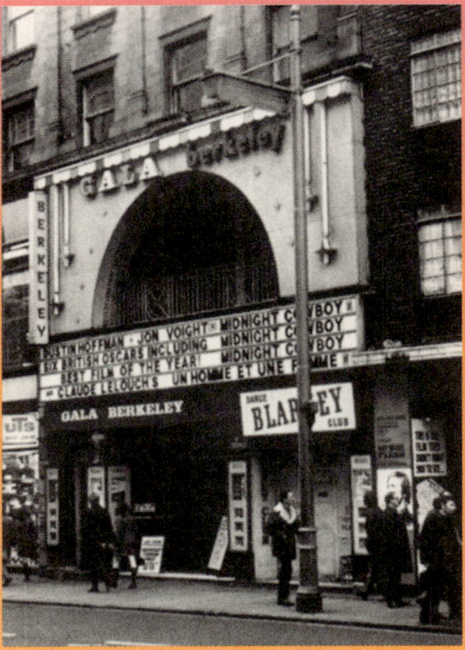

The Blarney Club, 31 Tottenham Court Road, London ⋙→ This Irish dance hall, located below the Gala Berkeley Cinema, became the venue for UFO.

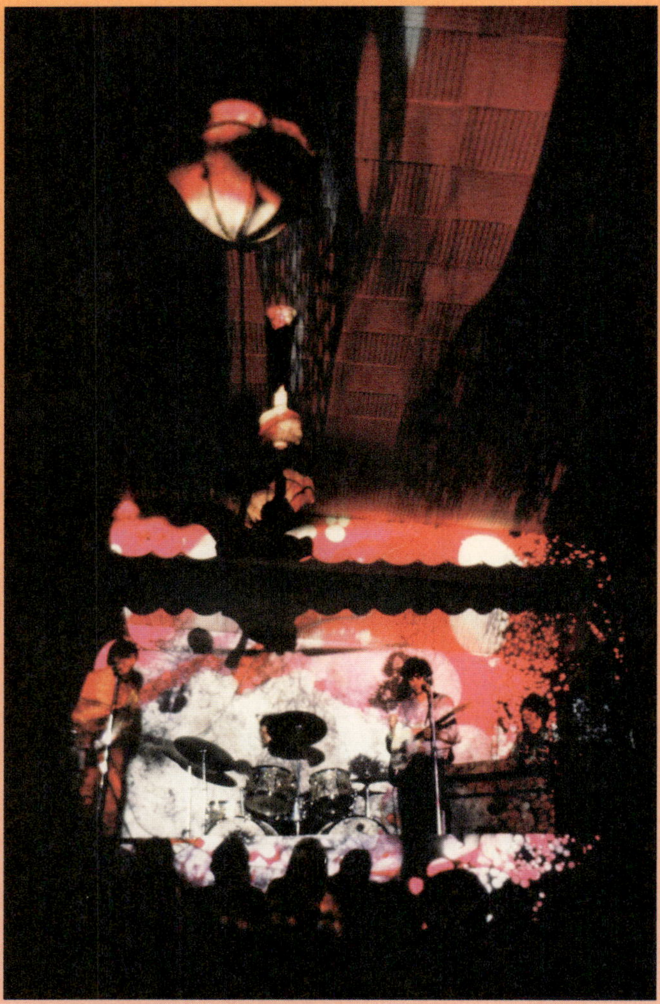

Pink Floyd on stage at the UFO, December 1966 ⋙→ The group pioneered oil-slide projections in their live shows.

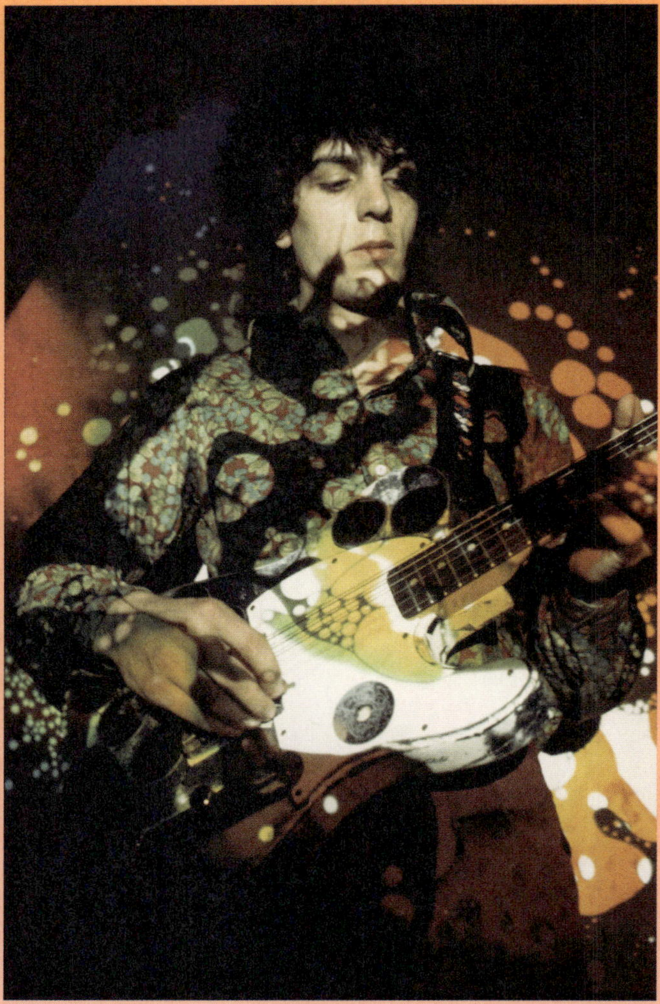

Syd Barrett on stage at the UFO, 1967 ⋙→ Pink Floyd's charismatic songwriter produced most of the material on the band's debut album *Piper at the Gates of Dawn* (1967). He struggled with the demands of fame, however, and this, coupled with the effects of LSD, saw him leave the band in early 1968, to be replaced by David Gilmour.

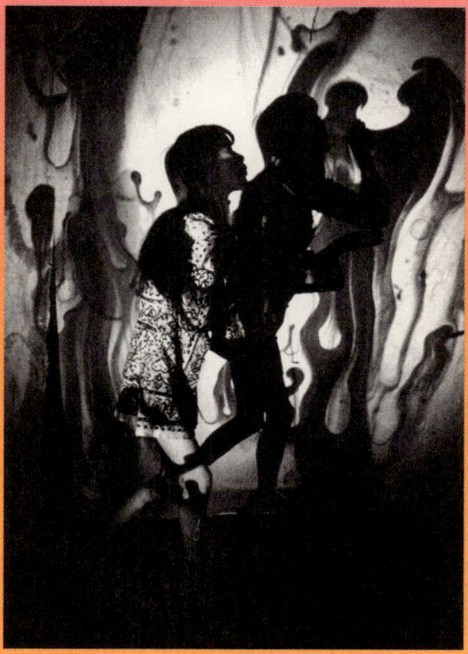

⋙→ A hippie girl dances amid slide projections at UFO, 1967.

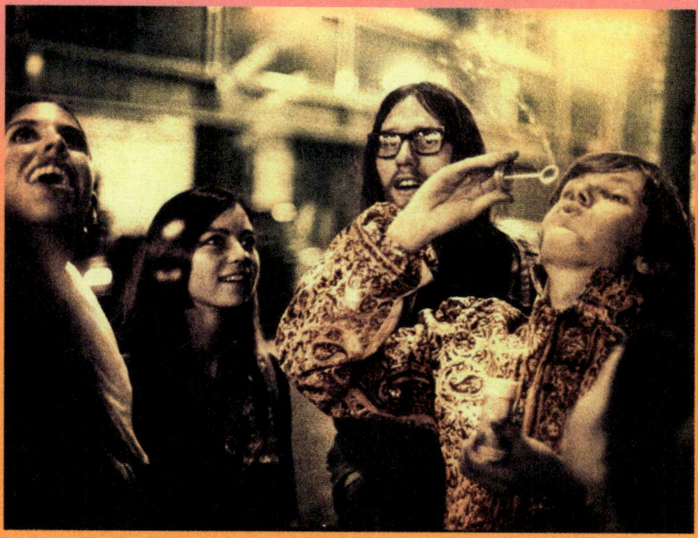

⋙→ Outside the UFO Club, 1967.

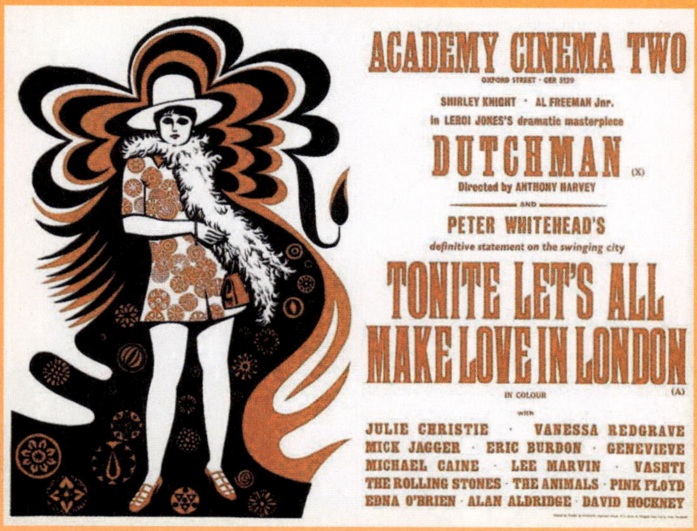

Tonite Let's All Make Love in London, documentary about the London club scene, 1967 ⋙→ Peter Whitehead's film included interviews with major cultural figures of the period, along with live footage of the Rolling Stones, and Pink Floyd playing their early signature piece 'Interstellar Overdrive.'

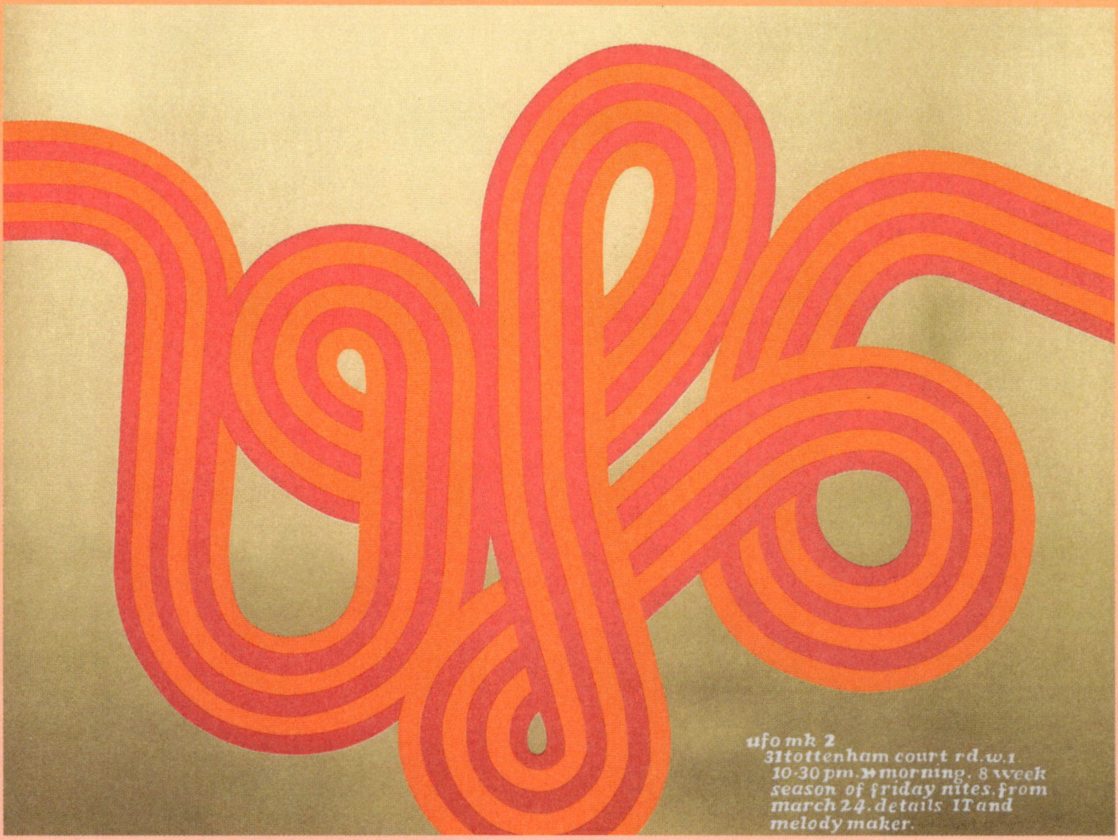

UFO poster by Hapshash and the Coloured Coat, 1967 ⋙→ This *UFO Mk 2* poster was created for a re-launch of the club after house band Pink Floyd became too big to play there for the same wage.

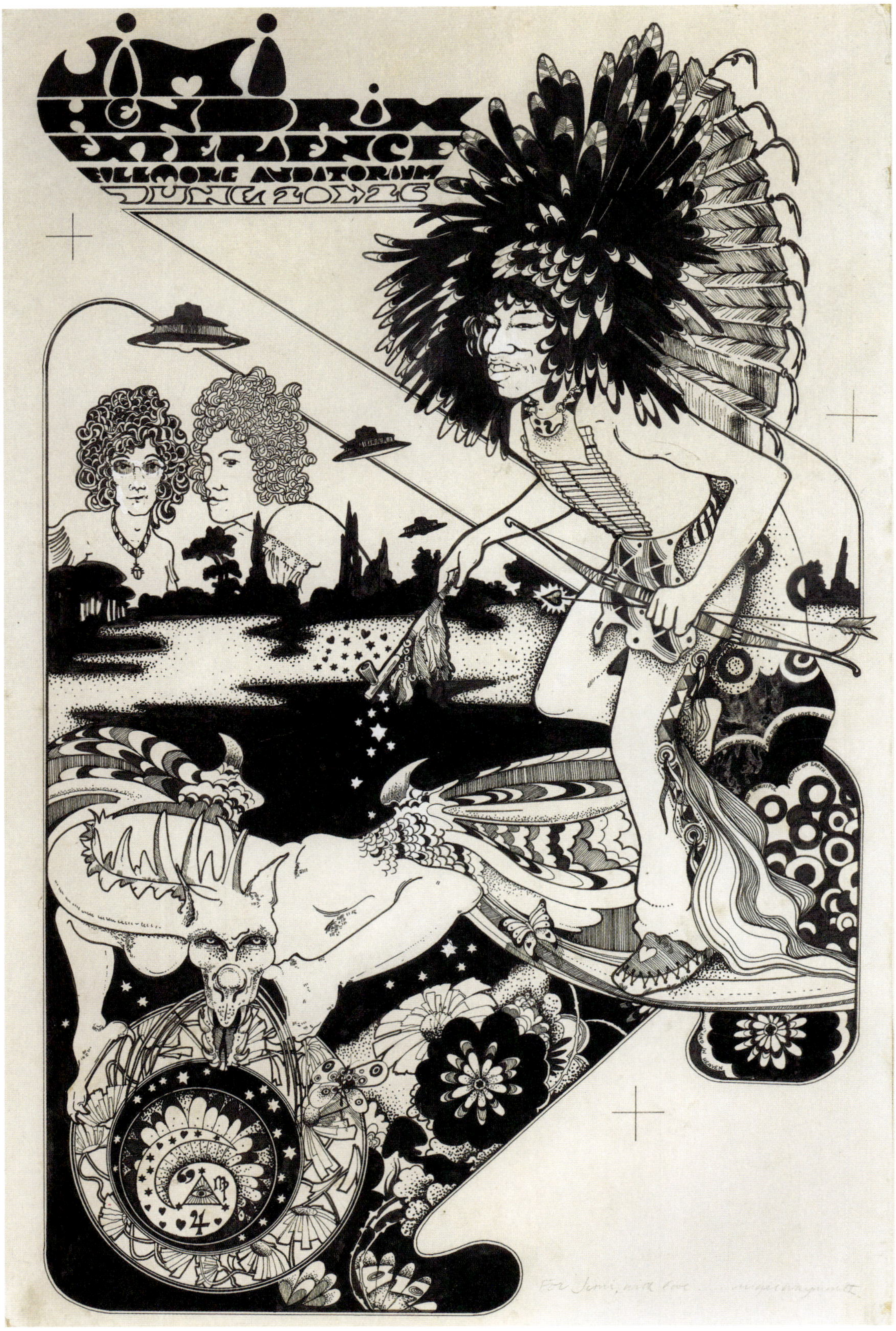

HAPSHASH AND THE COLOURED COAT

Unlike their American peers, Hapshash rarely appropriated images, preferring to create new ones themselves. Michael English: 'We believed and adopted anything that contradicted the rational world: our science was rooted in alchemy and black magic. Sexuality too was a strong force and there is a lot of that happening in the posters. Dragons and pubic hair!' Hapshash used borders as an integral part of the image, even when designing a frame for repeated use, such as the one for Brian Epstein's Saville Theatre posters.

⋙→ This page: design for a poster reportedly commissioned by Hendrix himself. Signed by Nigel Waymouth, it was never used, but the same design with altered lettering promoted Hendrix's first album, *Are You Experienced*. ⋙→ Opposite, top left: poster advertising The Who's single 'I Can See For Miles,' 1967. ⋙→ Top right: poster for Brian Epstein's concerts at the Saville Theatre, London, in early October 1967. ⋙→ Bottom left: poster for The Move at the UFO Club; May 26, 1967; credited to 'Jacob and the Coloured Coat.' ⋙→ Bottom right: a 1968 offset lithography poster advertising iconic boutique Granny Takes a Trip; Waymouth was a co-owner.

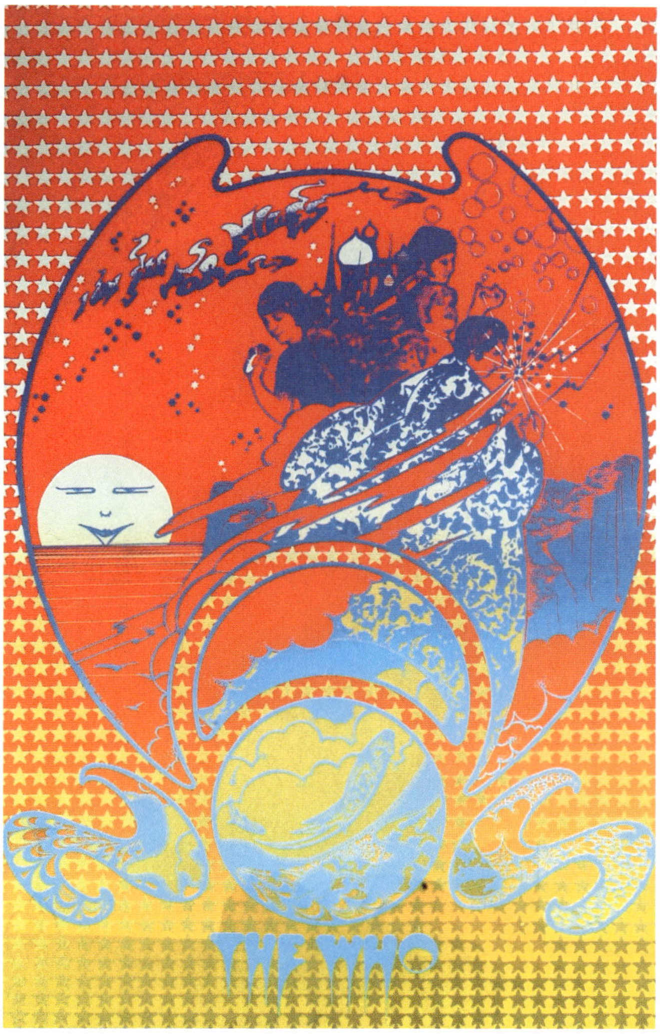
THE WHO

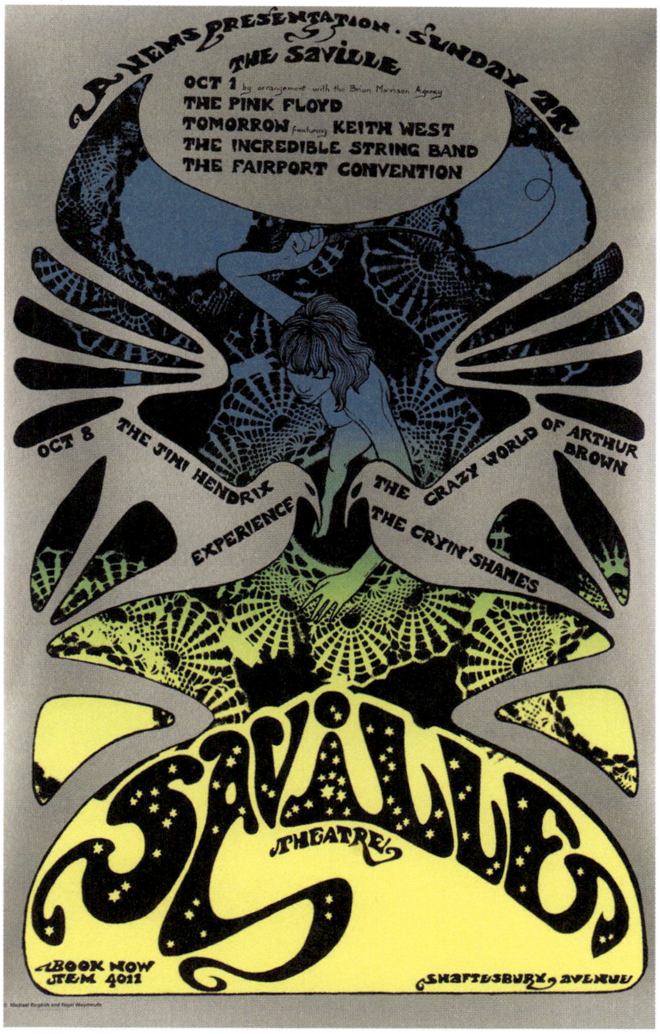
A NEMS PRESENTATION · SUNDAY AT
THE SAVILLE
OCT 1 by arrangement with the Brian Morrison Agency
THE PINK FLOYD
TOMORROW featuring KEITH WEST
THE INCREDIBLE STRING BAND
THE FAIRPORT CONVENTION
OCT 8 THE JIMI HENDRIX EXPERIENCE
THE CRAZY WORLD OF ARTHUR BROWN
THE CRYIN' SHAMES
SAVILLE
THEATRE
BOOK NOW TEM 4011
SHAFTESBURY AVENUE

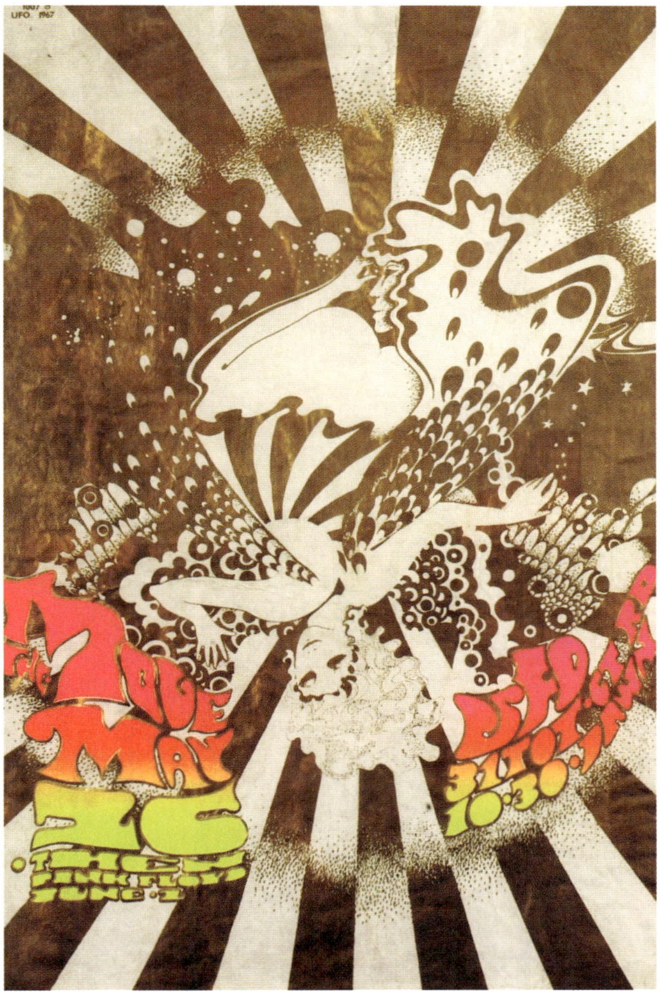
MAY
26
PINK FLOYD
JUNE 1
10·30

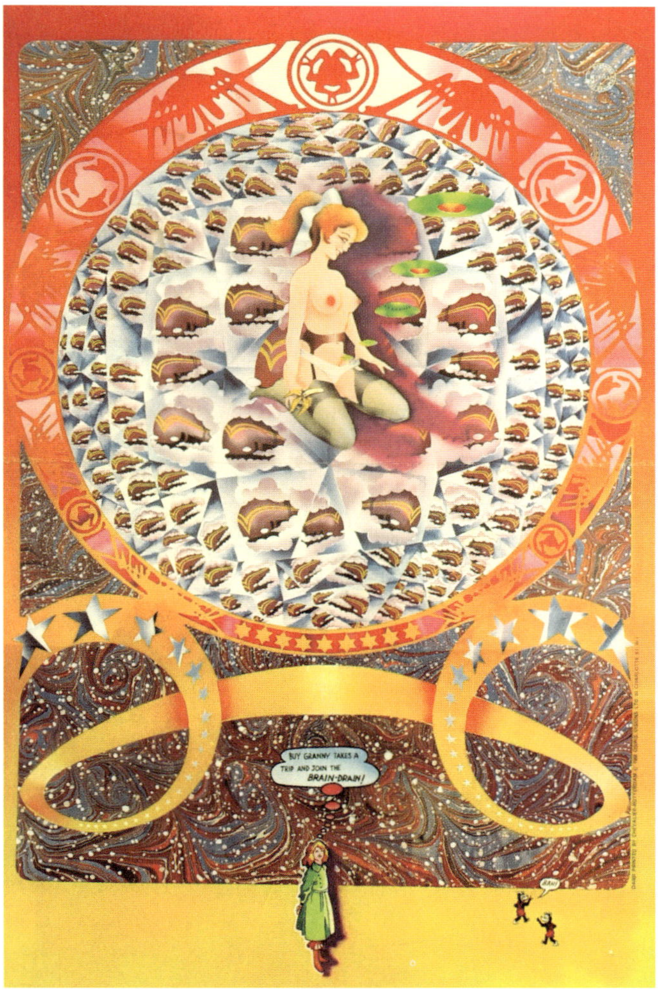
BUY GRANNY TAKES A TRIP AND JOIN THE BRAIN-DRAIN!

Poster for Pink Floyd's appearance at the UFO Club on July 28, 1967. Michael English and Nigel Waymouth came up with the 'CIA v UFO' concept to represent the conflict between the repressive forces of the establishment and the new counter-culture.

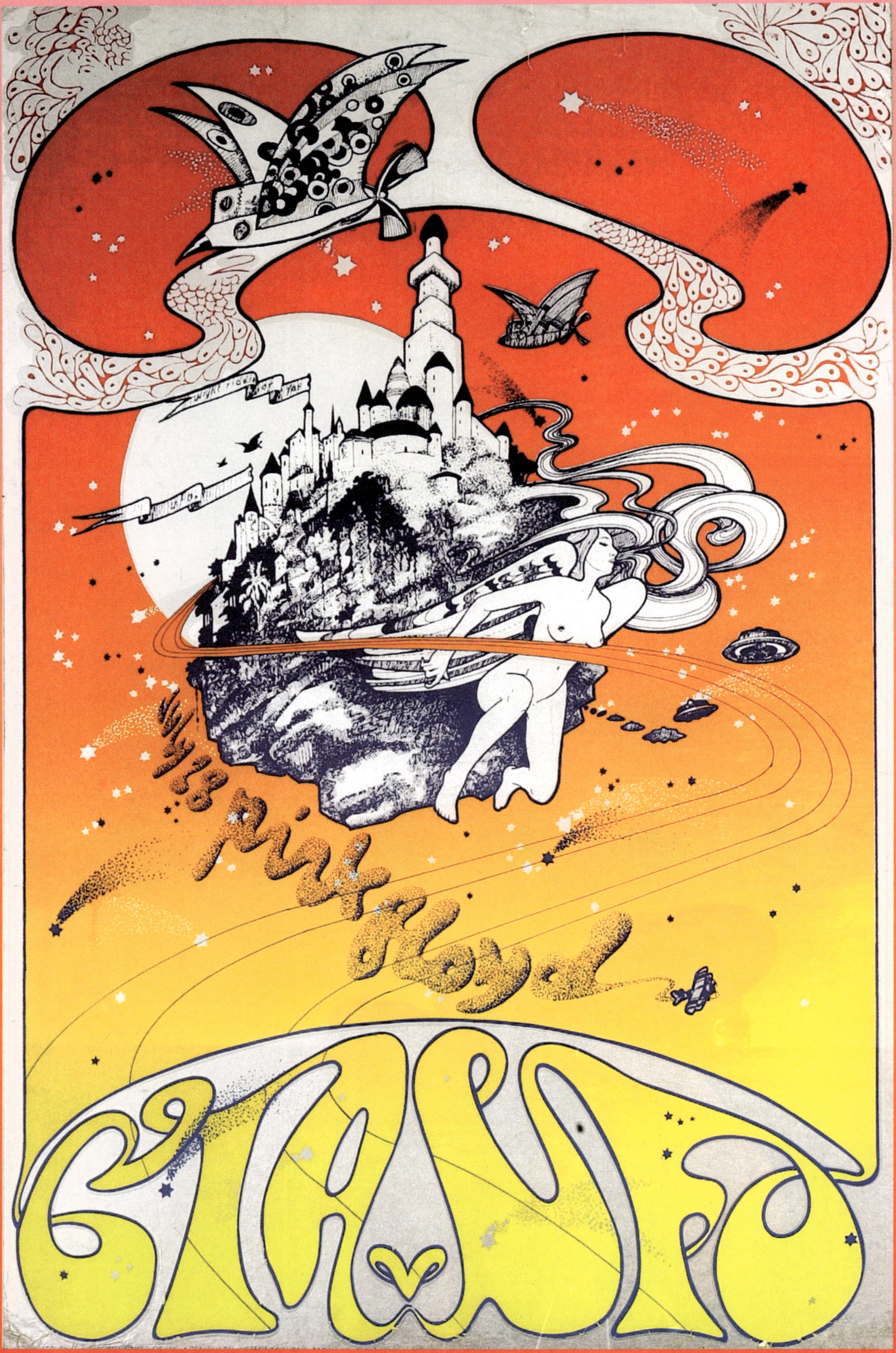

HAPSHASH AND THE COLOURED COAT (MICHAEL ENGLISH, 1941–2009; NIGEL WAYMOUTH, 1941–)

AFTER STUDYING AT EALING SCHOOL OF ART ALONGSIDE THE LIKES OF PETE TOWNSHEND AND BRIAN ENO, ENGLISH WORKED AS A CARNABY ST. WINDOW-DRESSER BEFORE BEING ASKED TO DESIGN THE POSTER FOR A NEW CLUB CALLED NITE TRIPPER (LATER UFO). SOON AFTER THE CLUB OPENED, HE MET WAYMOUTH, A FRIEND OF MUSIC PRODUCER JOE BOYD (WHO RAN UFO WITH JOHN 'HOPPY' HOPKINS). WAYMOUTH WAS PART OWNER OF BOUTIQUE GRANNY TAKES A TRIP, AND WAS RESPONSIBLE FOR DESIGNING THE APPEARANCE OF ITS EYE-CATCHING, CONSTANTLY CHANGING STORE FRONT. THE TWO BEGAN WORKING TOGETHER IN EARLY 1967, ADOPTING THE MONIKER 'HAPSHASH AND THE COLOURED COAT' AFTER AN EVENING LOOKING THROUGH BOOKS ABOUT ANCIENT EGYPT AT AUTHOR BARRY MILES'S APARTMENT. THE NAME COMBINED THAT OF QUEEN HATSHEPSUT WITH 'HASH' AND THE BIBLICAL 'COAT OF MANY COLORS' (THIS WAS WELL BEFORE THE SUCCESS OF THE MUSICAL *JOSEPH AND HIS AMAZING TECHNICOLOR DREAMCOAT*). CONSIDERING MOST CONTEMPORARY POSTERS TO BE UNINSPIRING AND OVER-WORDY, ENGLISH AND WAYMOUTH EVOLVED A DISTINCTIVE STYLE OF VIBRANT SILK-SCREEN PRINTS, USING SQUEEGEES TO MERGE SEVERAL DIFFERENT COLORS (USUALLY FLUORESCENT AND METALLIC) TOGETHER. DRUG CULTURE, OP ART, SYMBOLISM, ALPHONSE MUCHA, AUBREY BEARDSLEY, AND EVEN EXTRATERRESTRIAL SPACECRAFT FED INTO THEIR ARRESTING, FREQUENTLY SEXUAL DESIGNS. SOON THEY WERE CALLED ON TO DESIGN ALBUM COVERS, SHOPS, AND VENUES—INCLUDING BEATLES MANAGER BRIAN EPSTEIN'S SAVILLE THEATRE IN LONDON. THEIR POSTERS WERE ALSO SOLD AS WORKS OF ART IN THEIR OWN RIGHT, MARKETED THROUGH JOE BOYD'S COMPANY OSIRIS VISIONS. HAPSHASH BECAME A BAND AND RELEASED TWO ALBUMS, BUT BY 1968 THEY WERE DRIFTING APART. ENGLISH RETURNED TO PAINTING AND PRINT-MAKING, TAKING ON OCCASIONAL COMMERCIAL COMMISSIONS. WAYMOUTH BECAME A PAINTER AND NOW WORKS AS A SUCCESSFUL PORTRAITIST.

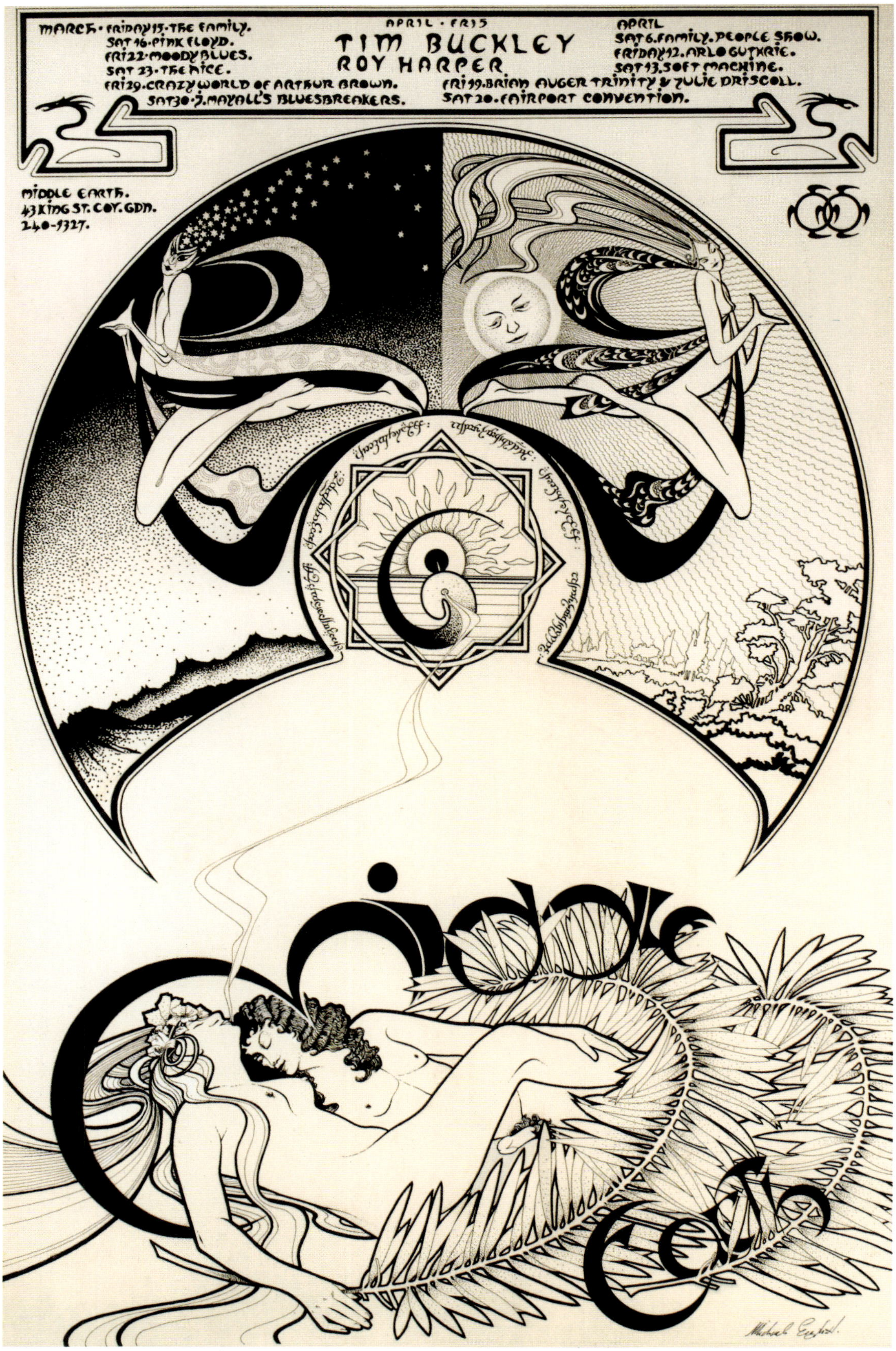

MIDDLE EARTH

Opportunistic businessmen soon realized there was money to be made from hippies, and the Middle Earth venue duly opened in London in competition with the UFO Club. Only one poster (and a calendar) was published to promote it, but it is a classic from Hapshash and the Coloured Coat that utilizes the themes of night and day. The club, however, censored the Beardsley-esque lovers, removing the man's very visible penis (see opposite). English later expressed his frustration with the compromise, as he felt it toned down the passion being depicted.

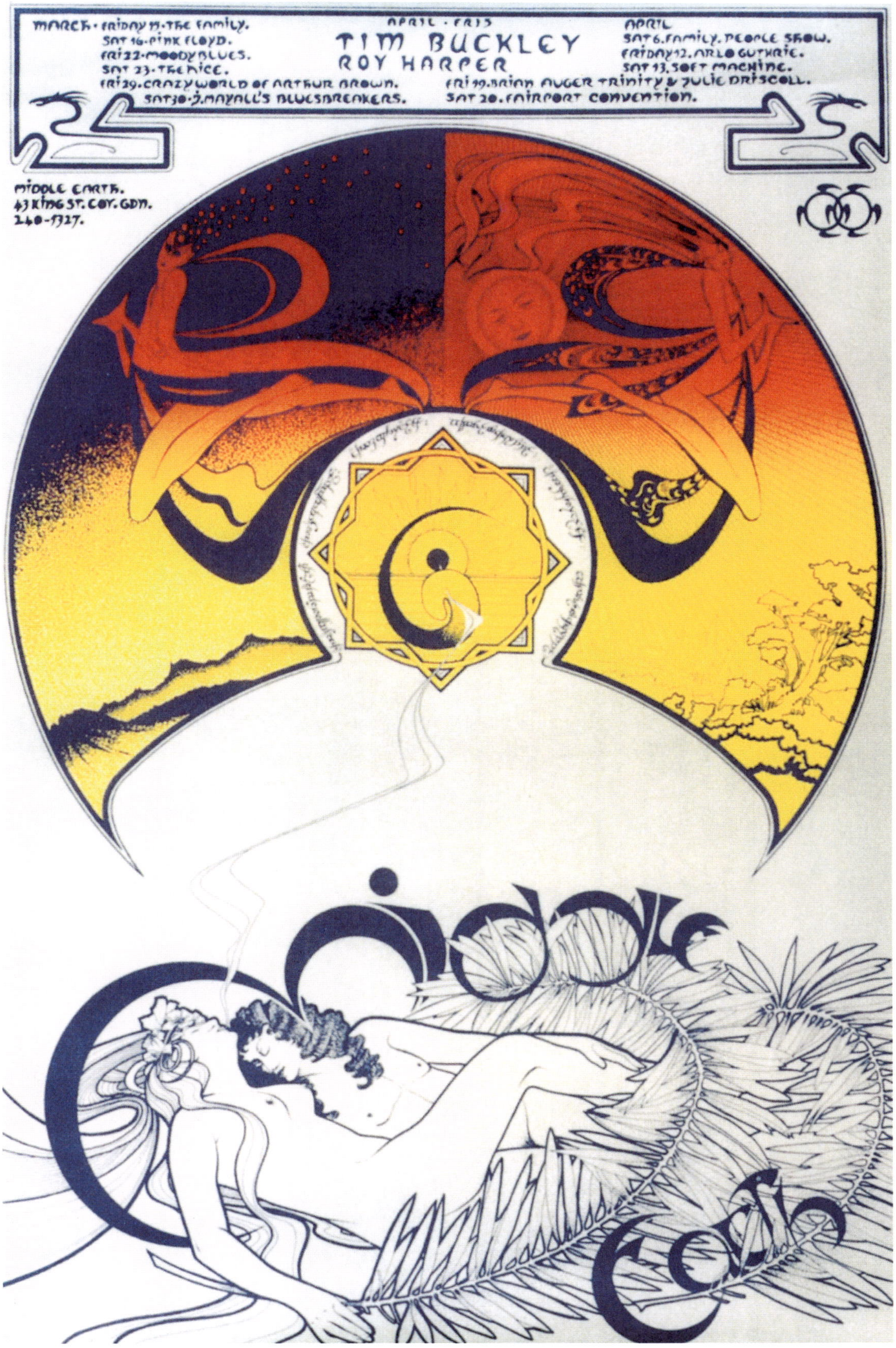

➳ Original artwork and printed poster for Middle Earth, designed by Hapshash and the Coloured Coat, 1968. Offset lithography was chosen as the production method, rather than the silk-screen process that Hapshash usually favored. The image, like the name of the club itself, was inspired by the works of J. R. R. Tolkein. The design is influenced by the eroticism of Aubrey Beardsley and Alphonse Mucha (the latter particularly in the rendering of the female figure).

MIKE McINNERNEY

Mike McInnerney was part of what might be termed the 'London Psychedelic School,' alongside Michael English, Nigel Waymouth, and Martin Sharp. McInnerney, who worked on *IT*, designed the dreamy Art Nouveau-style poster for the 14-Hour Technicolor Dream at Alexandra Palace, using such a wide variety of rainbow inks that no two posters are the same. Along with several other poster designers, McInnerney crossed over into the music scene: perhaps his most famous design is the gatefold sleeve for The Who's rock-opera album *Tommy* (1969), created not long after Martin Sharp's covers for Cream's albums *Disraeli Gears* (1967) and *Wheels of Fire* (1968).

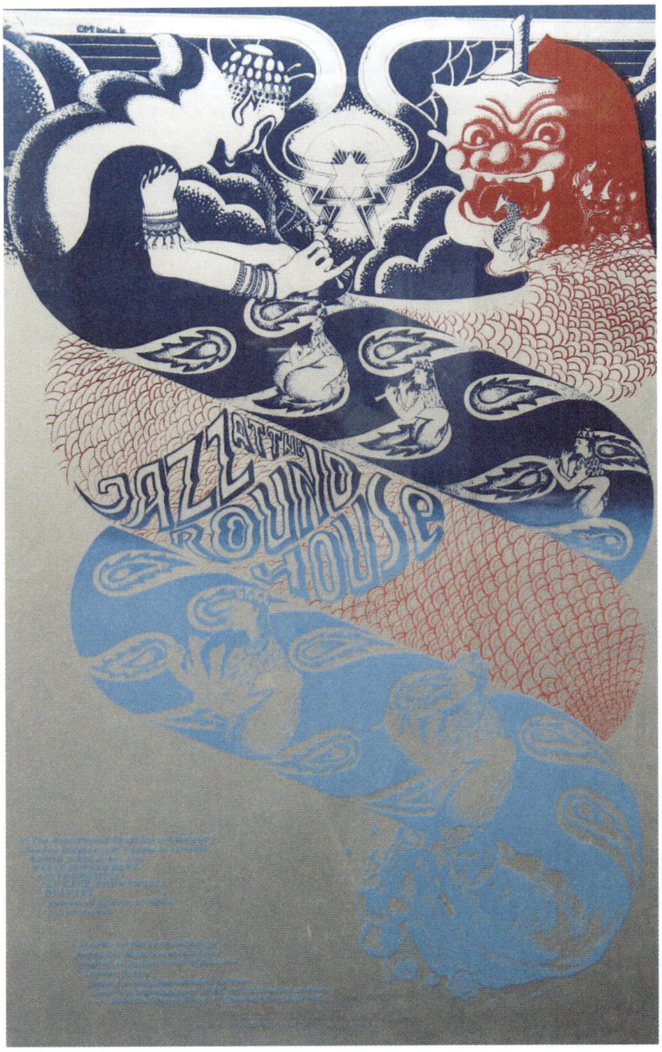

⋙→ Four examples of Mike McInnerney's work. ⋙→ This page, top right: *Jazz at the Roundhouse*, 1967, created with Dudley Edwards as design partnership OM Tentacle. The design features the opposing forces of good (represented by a pipe-playing Pan) and evil (embodied by the red devil). In other words, as McInnerney himself has noted, 'This has very little to do with jazz.' ⋙→ Bottom left and right: two variants of a poster for the 14-Hour Technicolor Dream at London's Alexandra Palace in 1967. ⋙→ Opposite: a poster promoting 'UFO—Dusk to Dawn,' 1967.

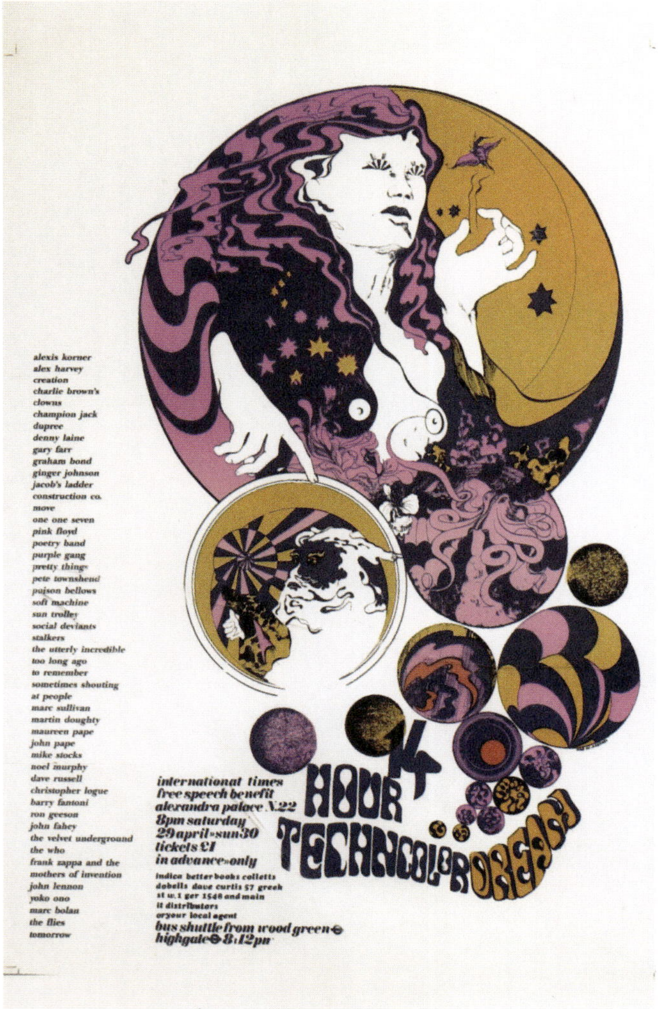

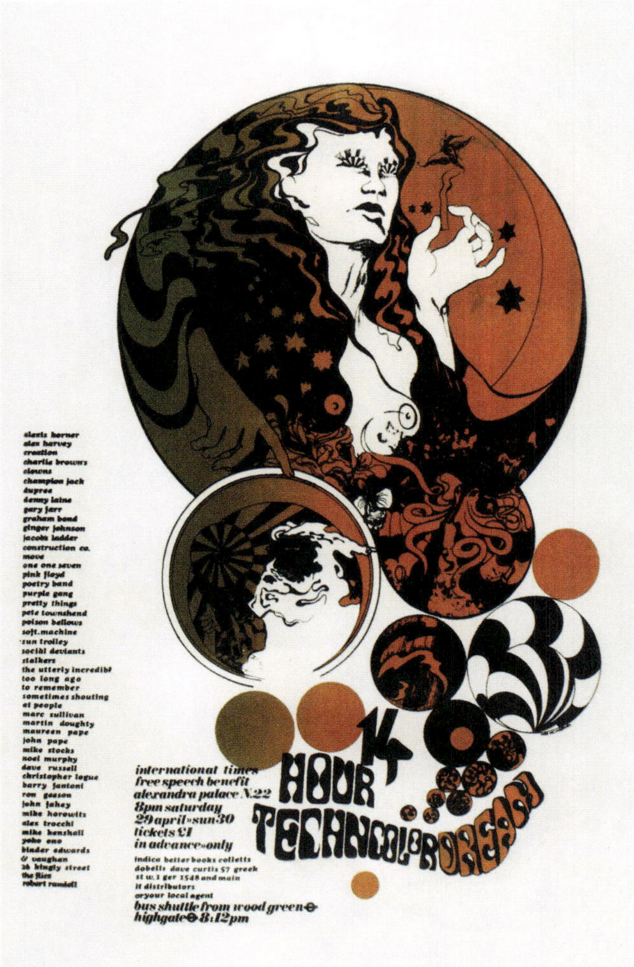

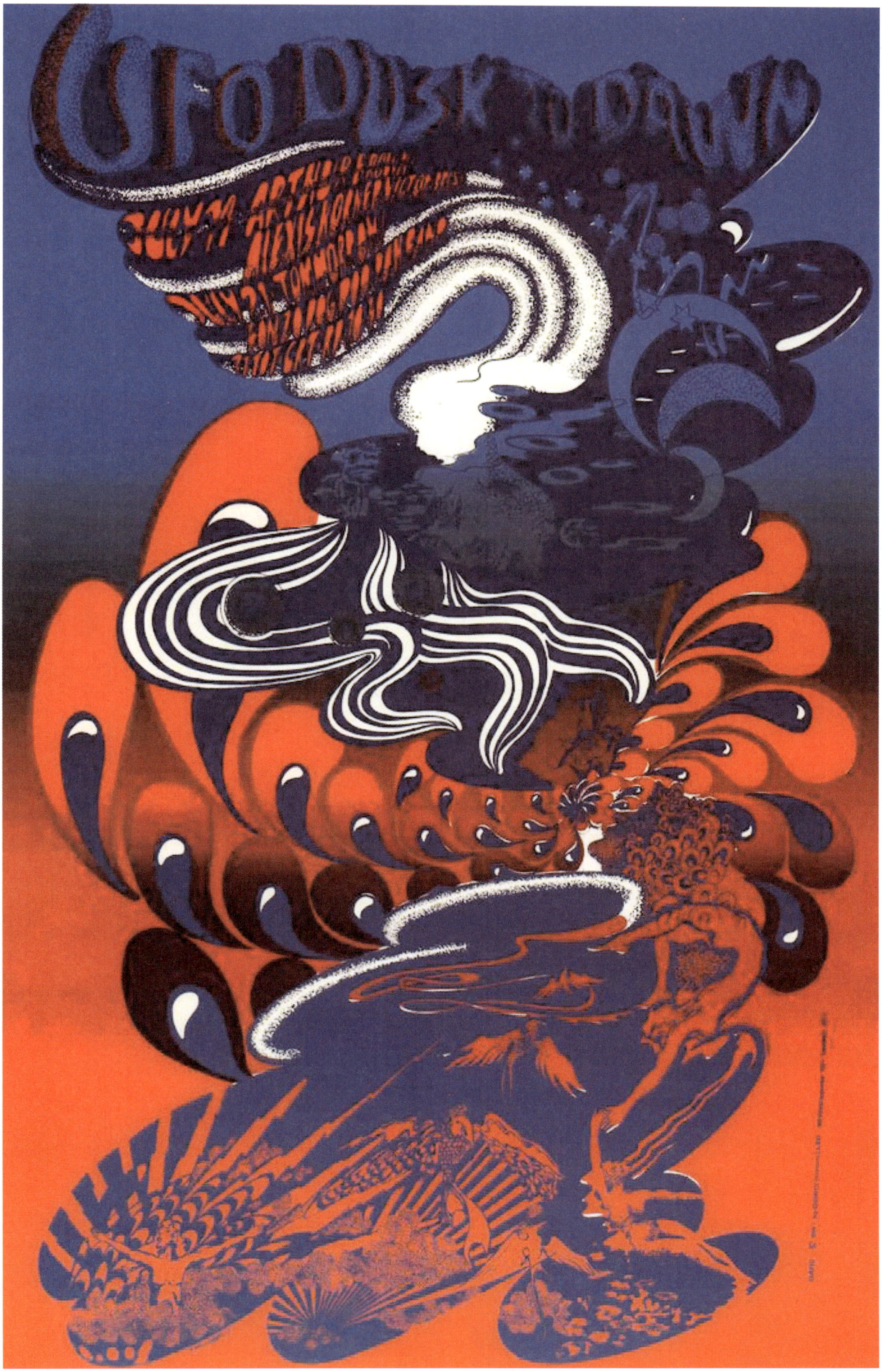

MIKE McINNERNEY

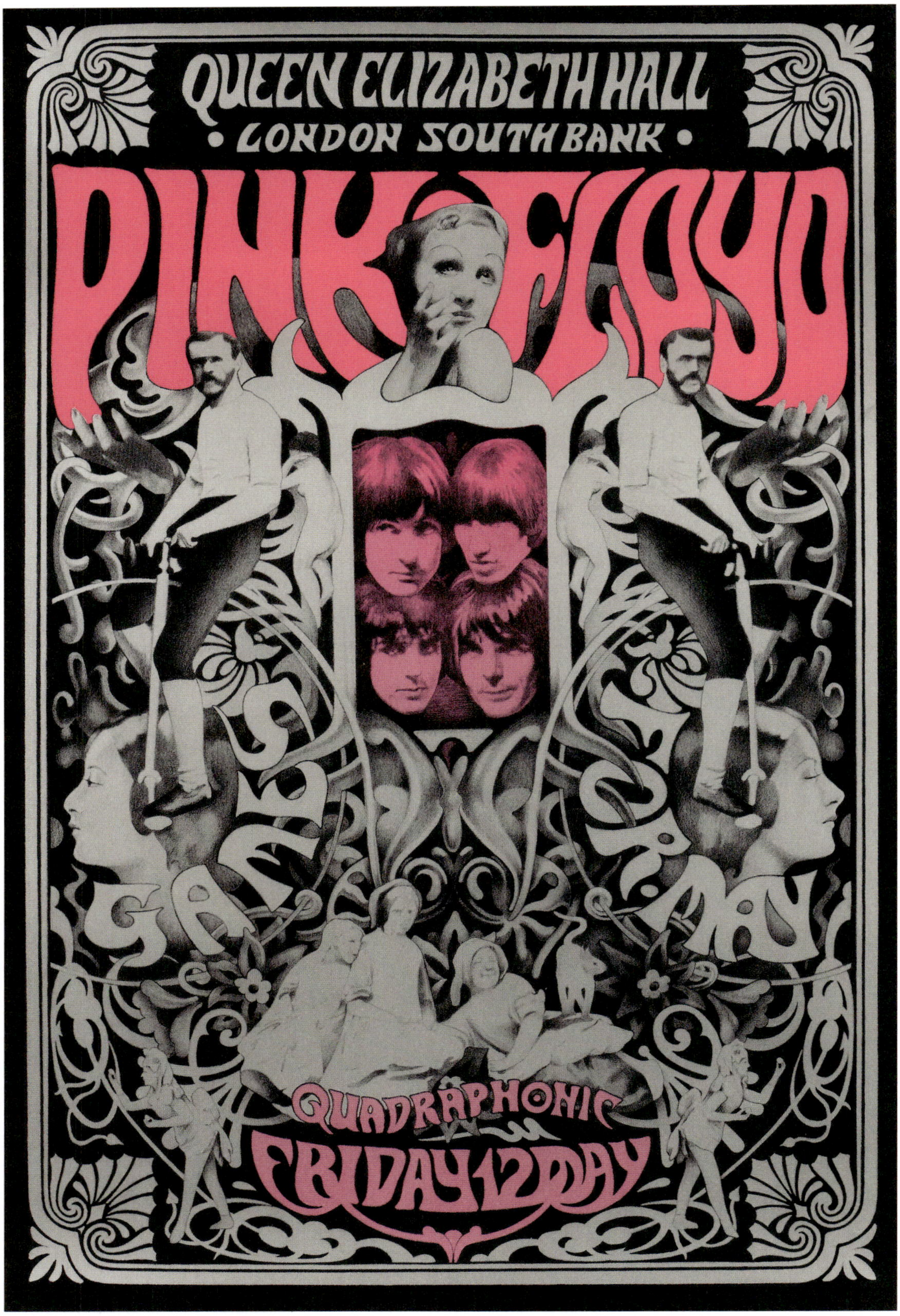

PINK FLOYD

➳ This page: a Victoriana-themed poster for Pink Floyd's gig at the Queen Elizabeth Hall, 1967. The concert is more familiarly known as 'Games for May.' ➳ Opposite: poster for the band's New York debut at Manhattan's Cheetah Club, 1967.

Lyricist and singer Syd Barrett was the only member of Pink Floyd to fully embrace the psychedelic lifestyle, but the band became inextricably associated with the underground because they were essentially the 'house band' at the UFO Club. Their headline gig at Queen Elizabeth Hall marked the first use of quadraphonic surround-sound, pre-figuring the use of advanced stage technology that characterized their act after Barrett left in 1968. *IT* applauded the event as 'a genuine 20th-century chamber music concert.'

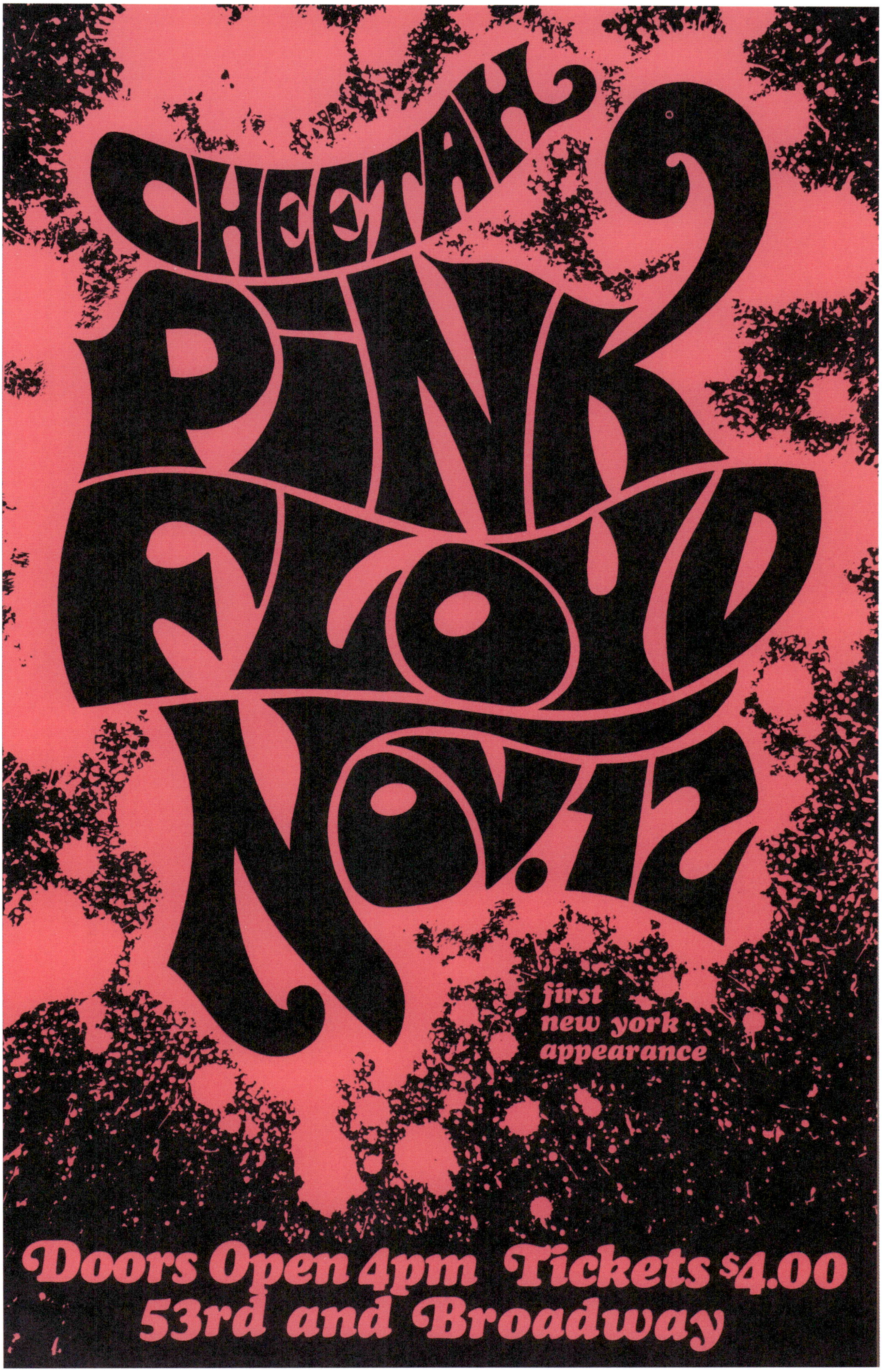
CHEETAH
PINK
FLOYD
NOV.12
first
new york
appearance
Doors Open 4pm Tickets $4.00
53rd and Broadway

LEGALISE POT RALLY

The Legalise Pot Rally in Hyde Park on July 16, 1967 was advertised by superb posters, including *Legalise Pot* by *IT* art director Mike McInnerney (see opposite). Attendees included Yoko Ono and beat poet Allen Ginsberg. Rally organizer Steve Abrams caused debate—and prompted questions in the House of Commons—by running a full-page ad (paid for by the Beatles) in *The Times* advocating a change in the pot laws. Despite the controversy, a second rally took place in 1968.

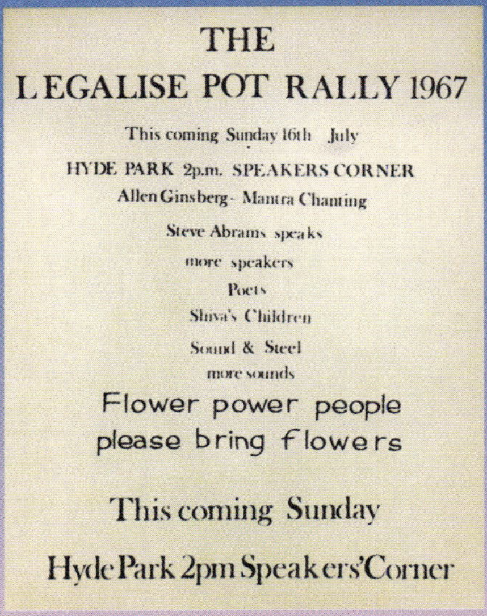

THE
LEGALISE POT RALLY 1967
This coming Sunday 16th July
HYDE PARK 2p.m. SPEAKERS CORNER
Allen Ginsberg- Mantra Chanting
Steve Abrams speaks
more speakers
Poets
Shiva's Children
Sound & Steel
more sounds
Flower power people
please bring flowers
This coming Sunday
Hyde Park 2pm Speakers'Corner

Handbill for the Legalise Pot Rally 1967 ➳ The event was one of a number of gatherings—akin to the US West Coast's 'Be-Ins'—that had recently taken place in London's Primrose Hill and Hampstead Heath.

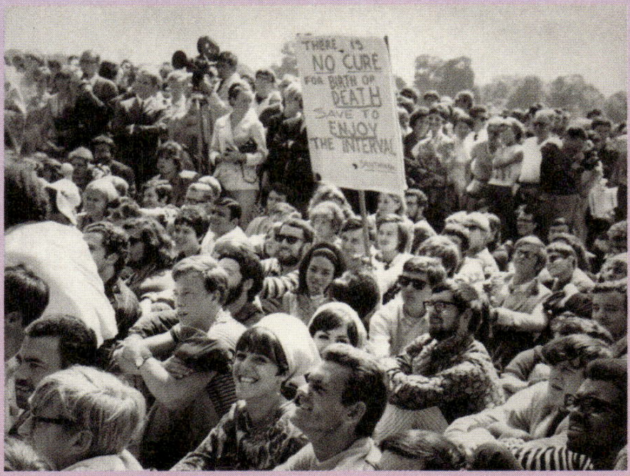

The crowd at the Legalise Pot Rally, 1967 ➳ This snapshot of the day includes a philosophical placard.

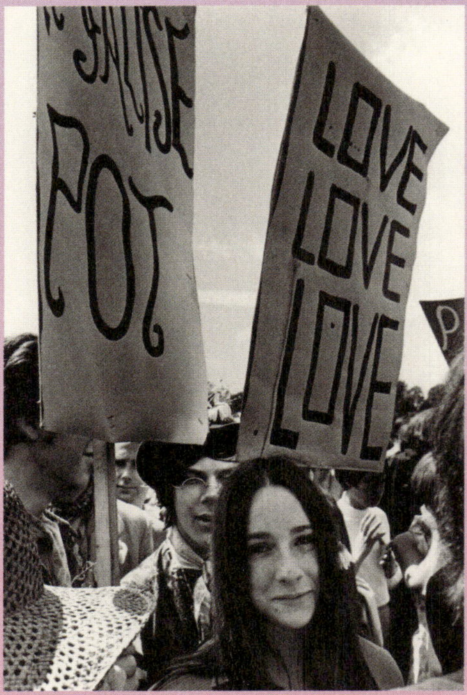

On the march ➳ Placards at the Legalise Pot Rally, 1967.

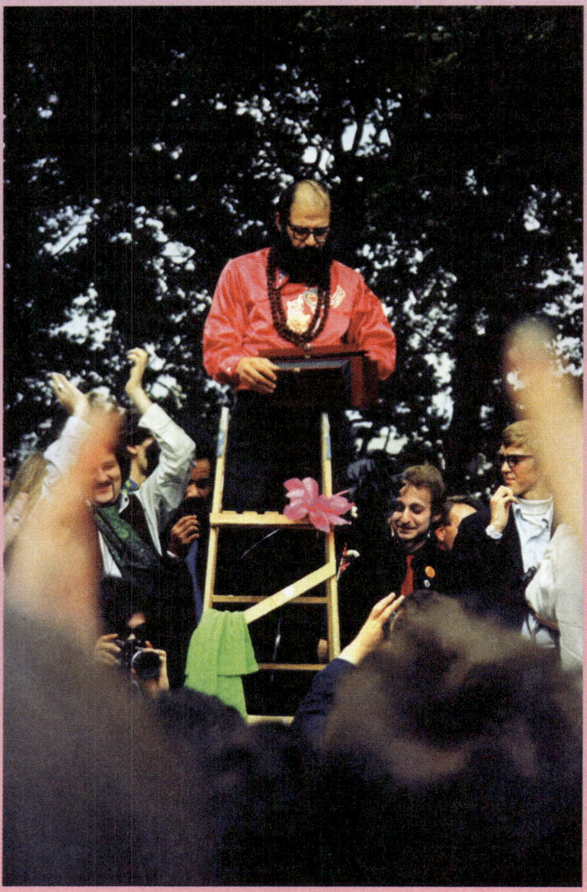

Allen Ginsberg performs at the Legalise Pot Rally, 1967 ➳ The poet gave a speech about Shiva, then chanted and played a small harmonium. Yoko Ono can be seen with a camera in the lower left corner of the photograph.

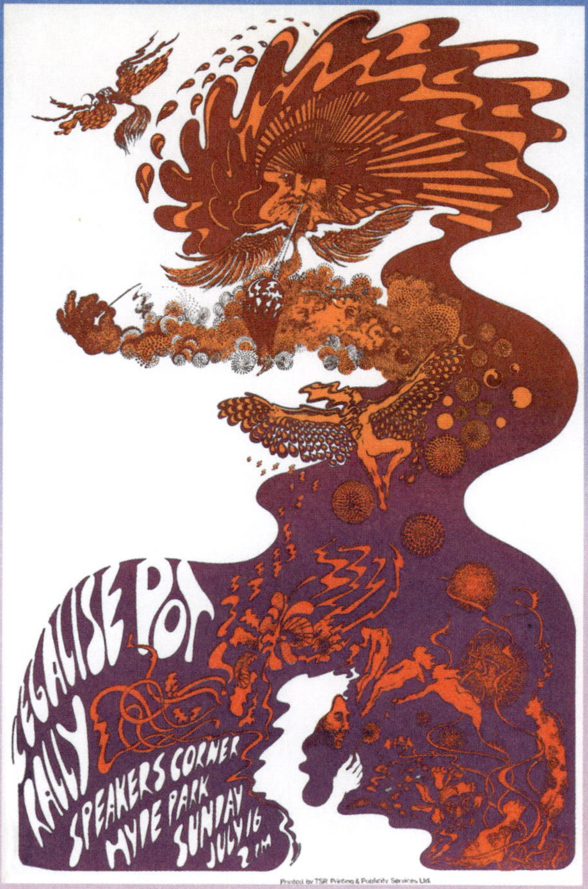

Poster for the Legalise Pot Rally, 1967 ⟿ The designer was Mike McInnerney; the poster was commissioned by agency Osiris. According to McInnerney, 'The poster's poured shape and blobby, melting forms attempt to illustrate the formless, liquid state of being high.'

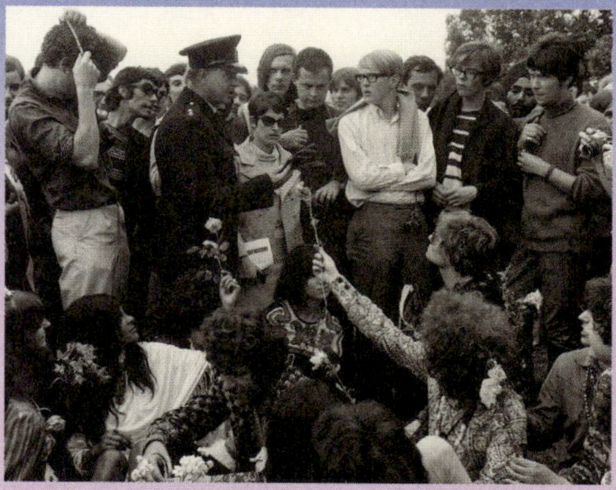

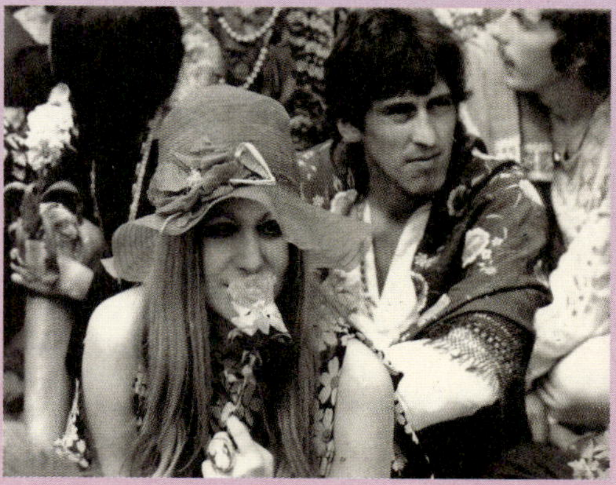

Hippies in Hyde Park ⟿ Flowers were much in evidence at the Hyde Park rally. When a policeman intervened in Allen Ginsberg's performance, informing him that he was breaking the park's by-laws, Ginsberg obligingly desisted, dismounted, and pinned a flower on the PC.

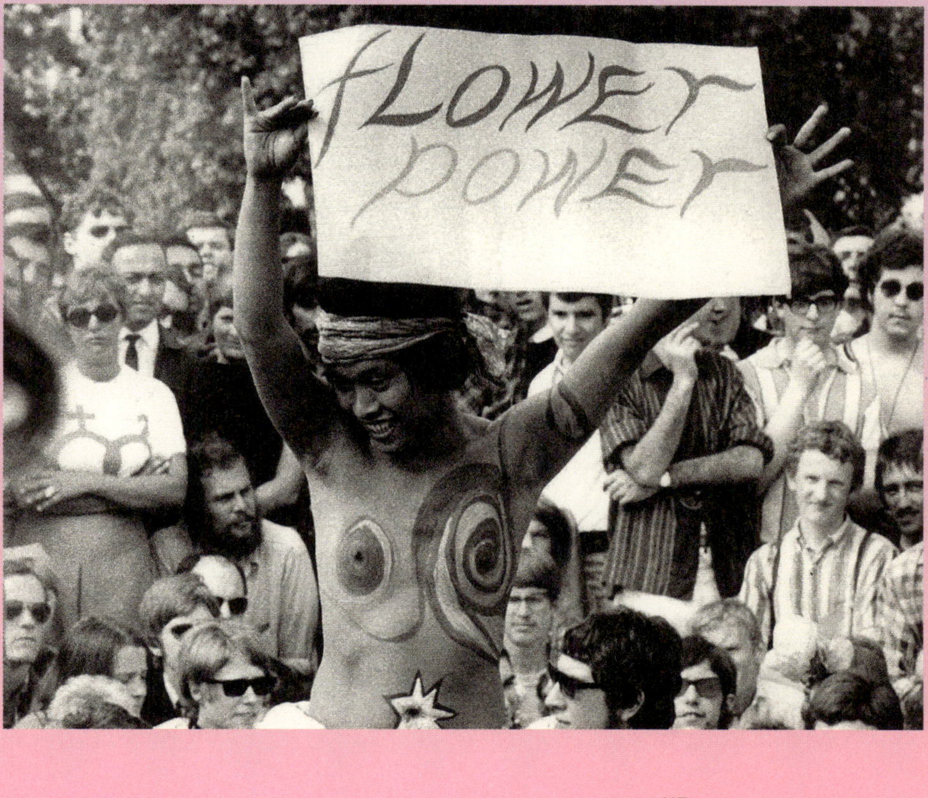

Flower Power ⟿ This photograph demonstrates the non-confrontational stance of the 5,000-odd rally-goers.

THE FOOL

The Fool were a Dutch collective who designed clothes, posters, and murals, and decorated cars and instruments. Simon Posthuma and Marijke Koger came to London from Ibiza in 1966, and were joined by Dutch colleague Josje Leeger and Englishman Barry Finch. Calling themselves 'The Fool' after the tarot card, they moved straight into the fashionable London rock 'n' roll scene, designing album sleeves for The Hollies and The Incredible String Band, and even the clothes worn by the Beatles on the worldwide satellite broadcast of 'All You Need Is Love.' They also designed a three-story mural on the Apple Boutique in central London—set up by the Beatles to feature the Dutch collective's outlandish clothes.

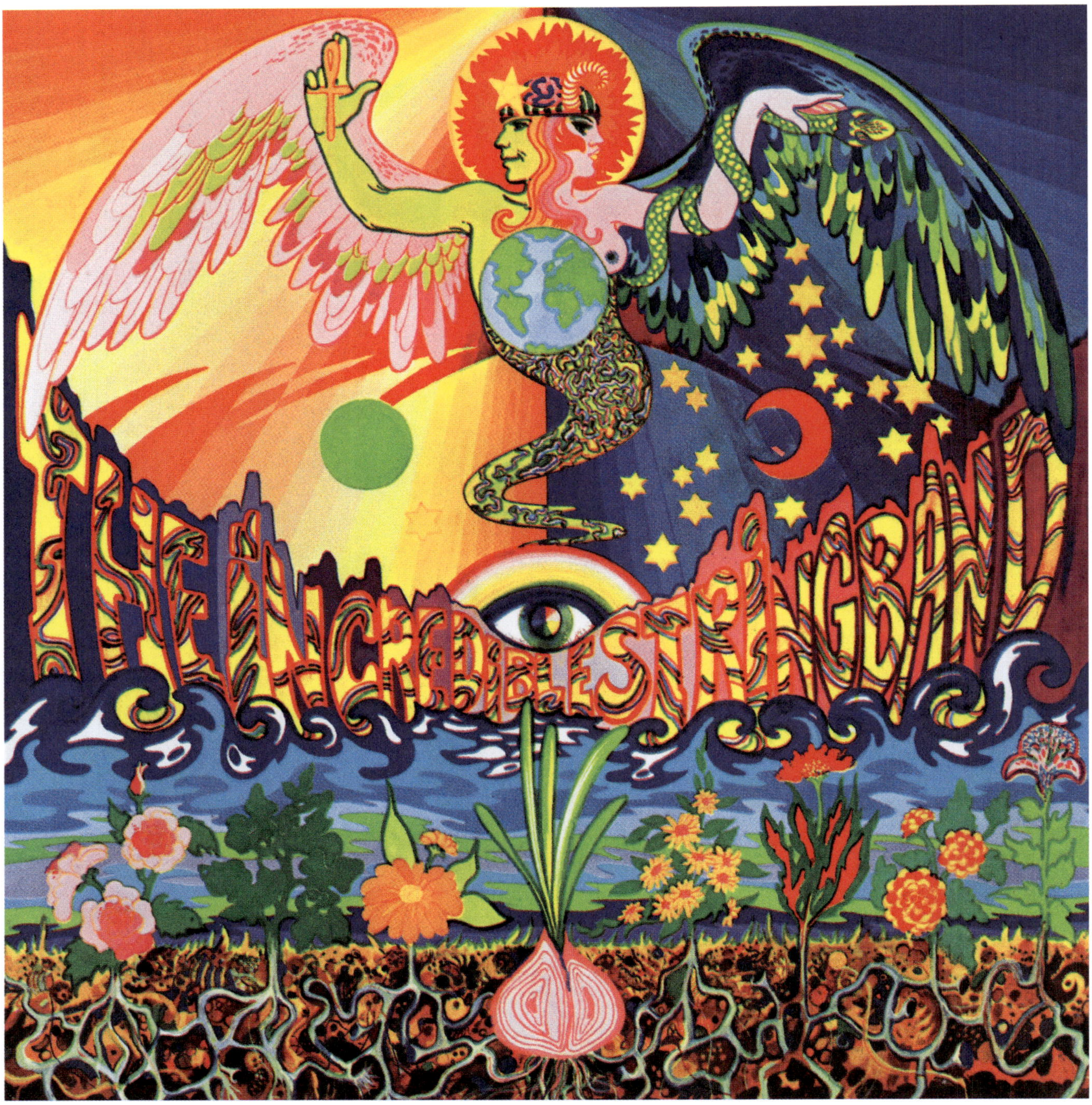

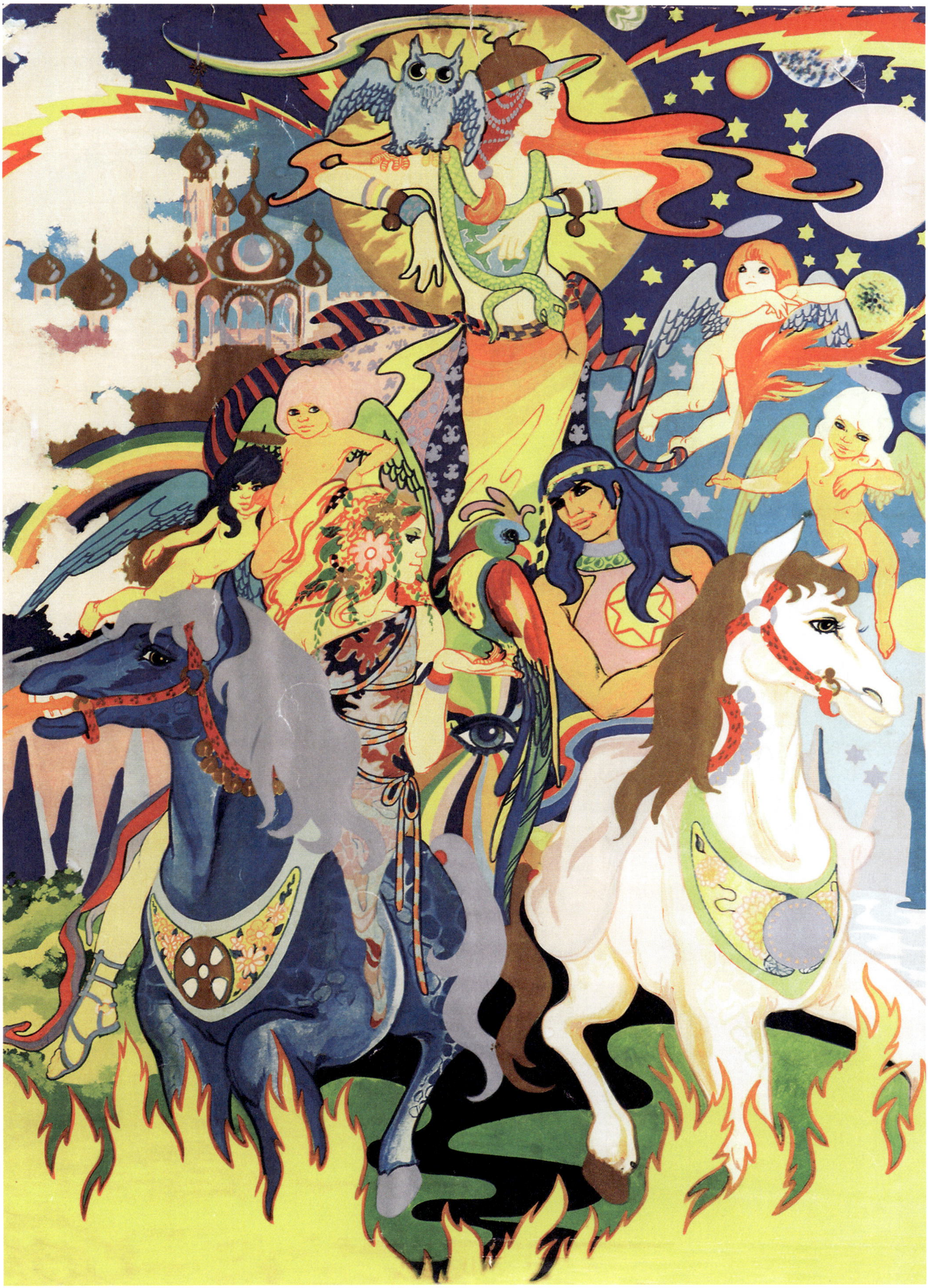

⋙→ Opposite: the cover for The Incredible String Band's album *The 5000 Spirits or the Layers of the Onion*, 1967. ⋙→ This page: *Athena*, a poster created by Marijke Koger, shows the design tropes often employed by the group, including bright colors, mystic folk symbolism, and overlapping psychedelic patterns.

GANDALF'S GARDEN

Gandalf's Garden magazine (the name came from Tolkien) was 'a mystical scene magazine' published and edited by Muz Murray—seen emerging from his egg on the cover of the first issue. It was produced from the World's End on the King's Road, Chelsea, where Murray ran a tea shop of the same name. By day, homeless people slept in the basement, where spiritual meetings were held each evening.

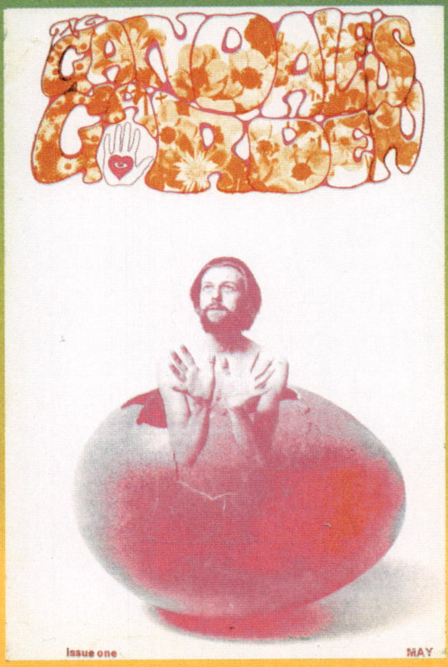

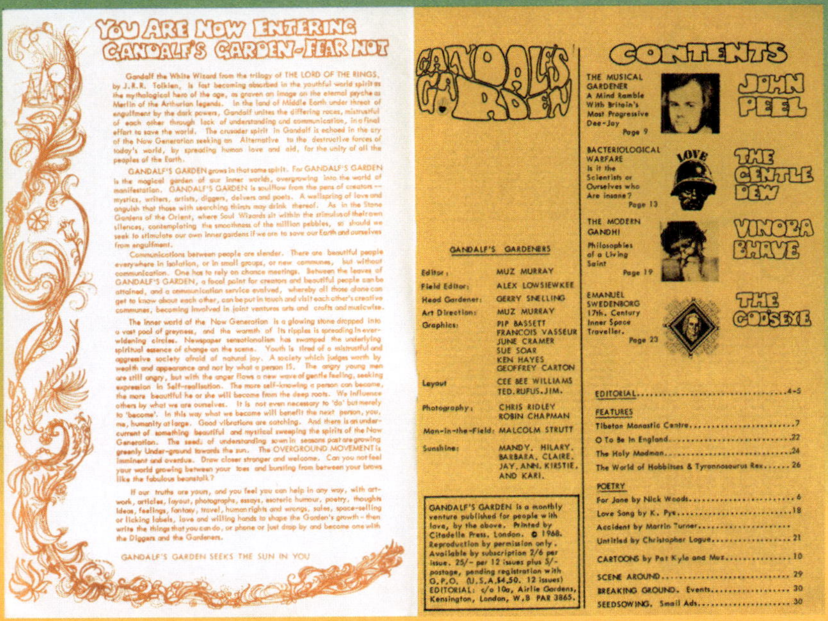

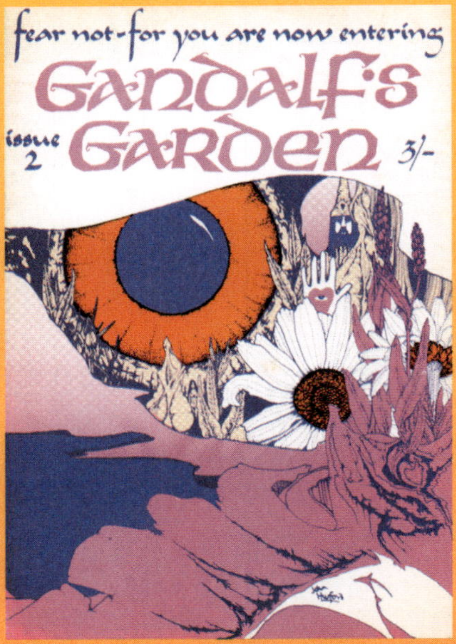

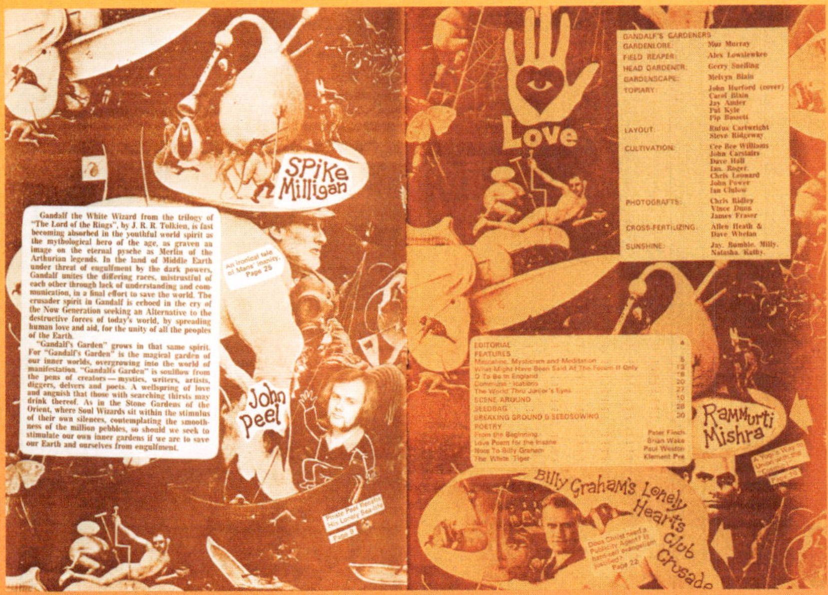

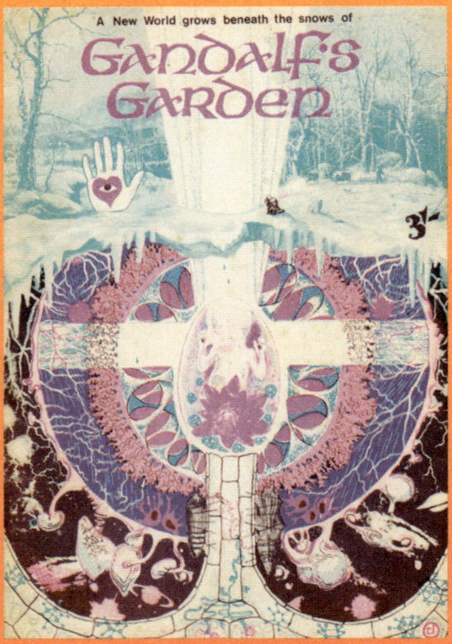

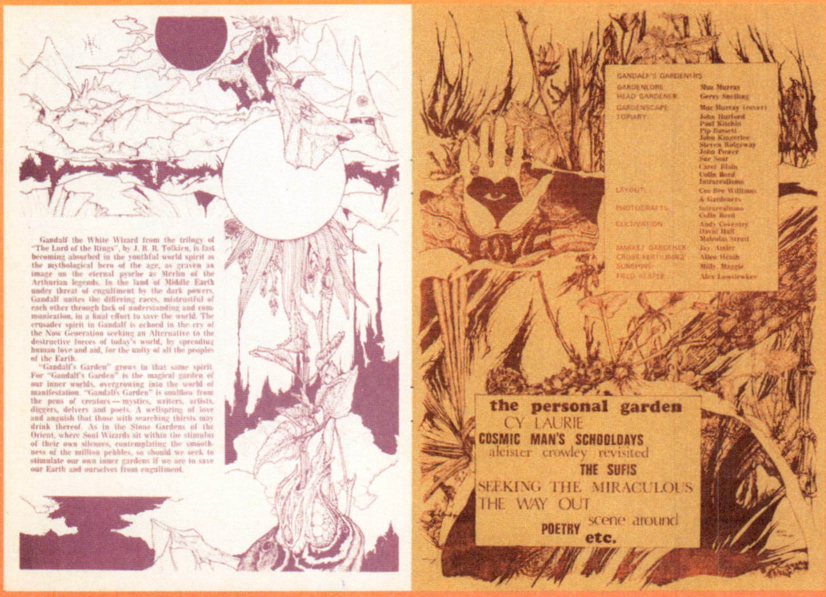

→ *Gandalf's Garden* ran for six issues, starting in 1968, and catered to the mystical end of the underground scene. As well as editing, Muz Murray designed the covers and interior layouts for issues 3, 4, and 5. The magazine's playfully experimental approach to design encompassed collage, hand-drawn illustration, and the use of an eclectic range of typefaces. Its color palette was generally more subtle than that of *OZ*. Content-wise, *Gandalf's Garden* embraced philosophy and eastern belief systems, rather than drug culture, and included contributions from Spike Milligan, Joan Baez, and DJ John Peel among others.

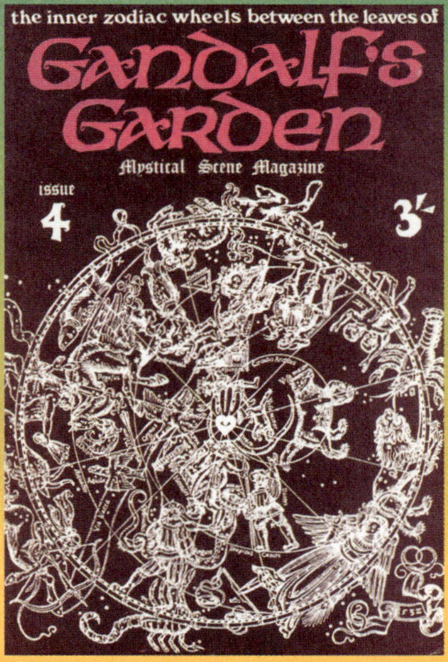

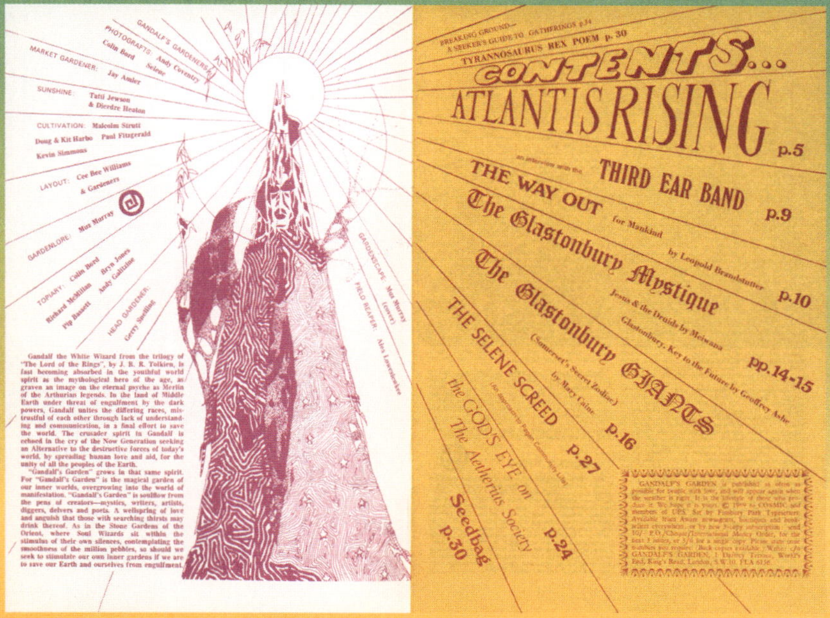

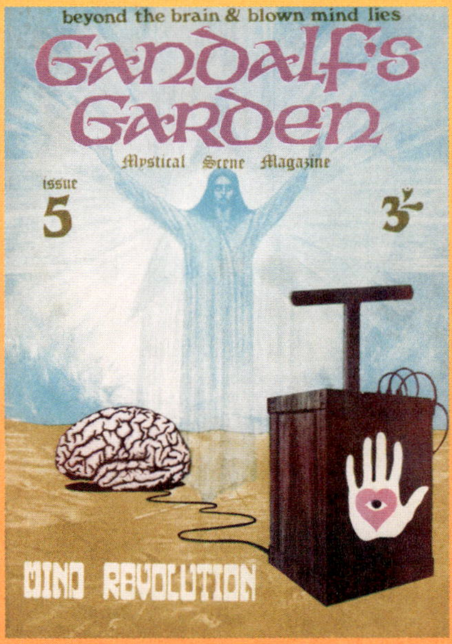

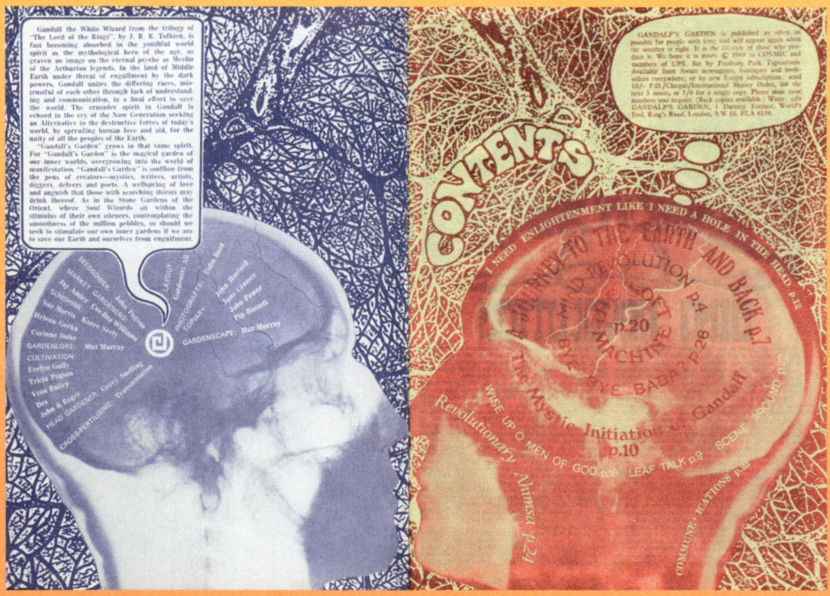

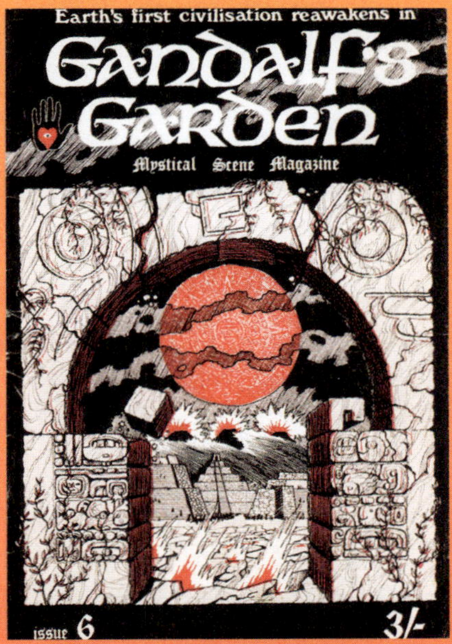

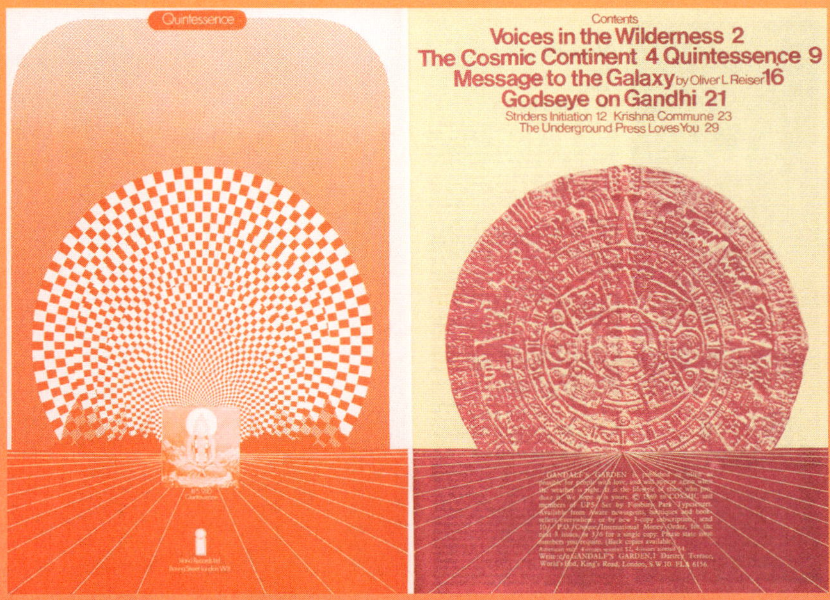

ATELIER POPULAIRE

In 1968, art students at Paris's École des Beaux-Arts occupied the studios and workshops of the college and worked twenty-four hours a day to produce posters in support of the May revolt, a series of student protests that led to general strikes and briefly crippled the French economy. The Atelier Populaire met each afternoon to discuss the choice of designs and slogans, which were posted on the streets within hours, allowing them to respond quickly to the fast-changing political situation. Posters were created by silk-screen printing, lithography, and stencils, according to what best suited the images, which were made as simple (and humorous) as possible—usually just silhouettes and a hand-lettered slogan. 'Lots of people came to the Atelier and took posters home to collect them,' recalled activist Philippe Vermès. 'People took them off the walls and kept them. When we left the Beaux-Arts we gave a collection to the Bibliothèque Nationale.'

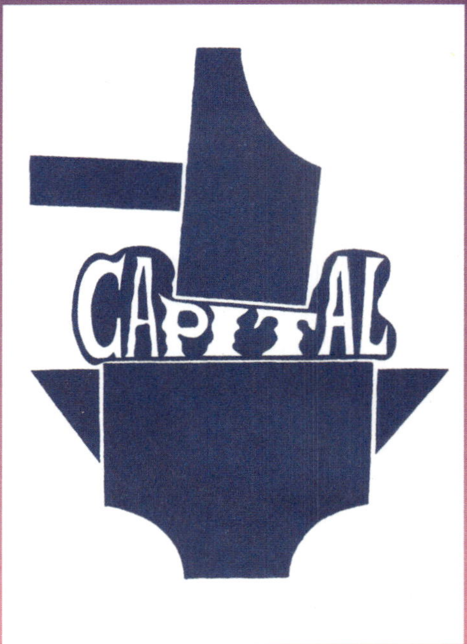

Capital, 1968 ⋙→ The word 'capital' is shown crushed between a hammer and anvil in this poster. The May '68 revolt began as an anti-capitalist student protest.

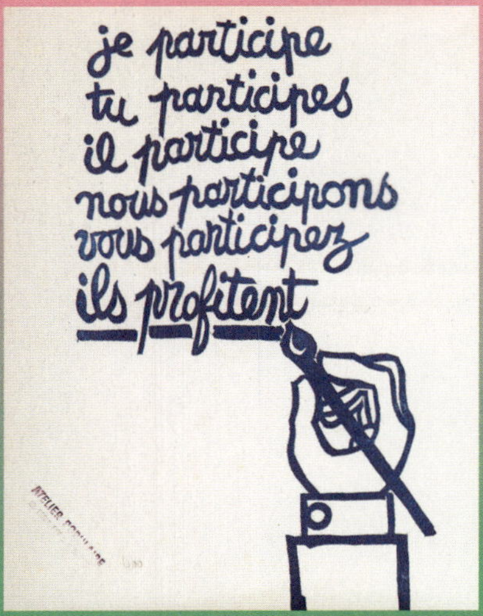

Je Participe ..., 1968 ⋙→ A child's copybook presentation based on President Charles de Gaulle's May 1968 call for citizens' participation, ending with a message of dissent.

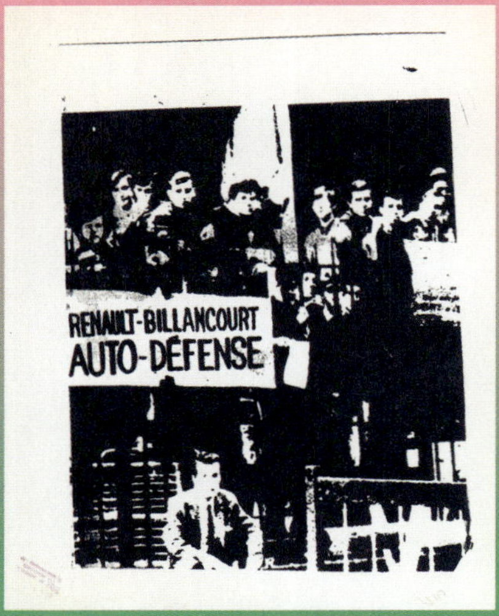

Renault-Billancourt, 1968 ⋙→ Fueled by the student protests, a series of strikes in factories across France saw the occupation of Renault's plant at Boulogne-Billancourt.

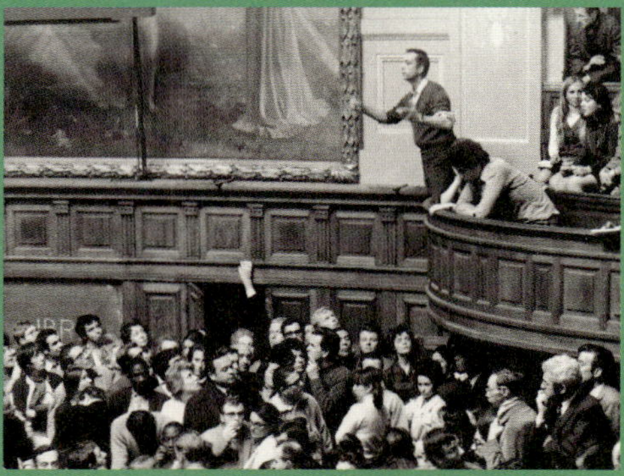

Occupying the Grand Amphitheatre in Paris, June 15, 1968 ⋙→ While the speeches are heard, press photographers shelter in the doorway.

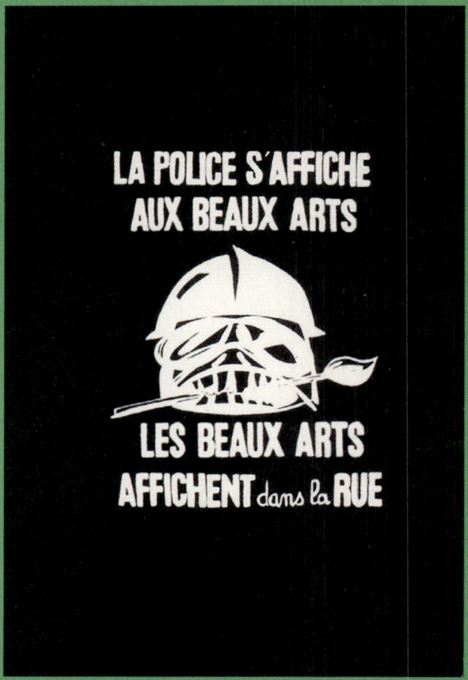

La Police S'Affiche Aux Beaux Arts..., 1968 ⋙→ 'The police post themselves at the Beaux Arts, the Beaux Arts poster the streets.'

Poster, 1968 → 'The posters produced by the Atelier Populaire are weapons in the service of the struggle and are an inseparable part of it,' reads part of the collective's manifesto.

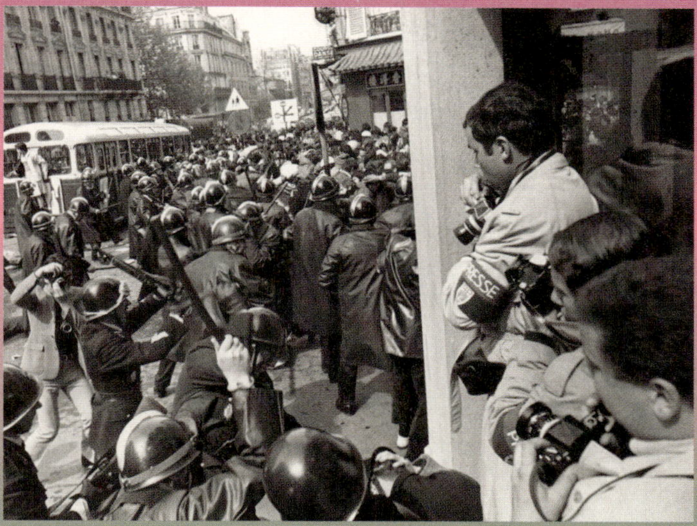

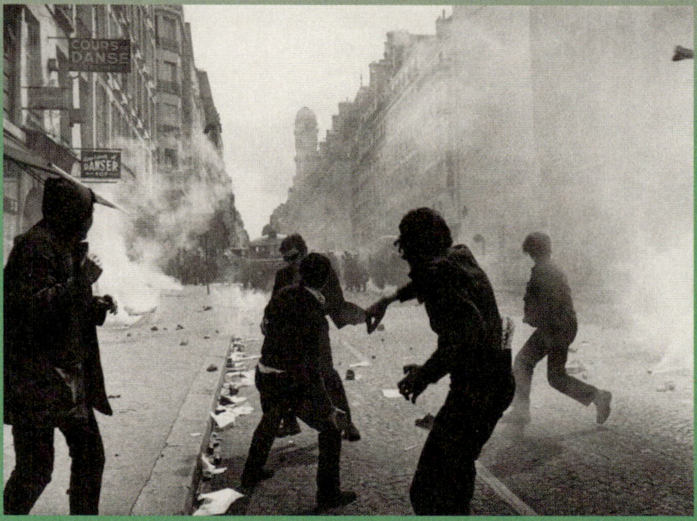

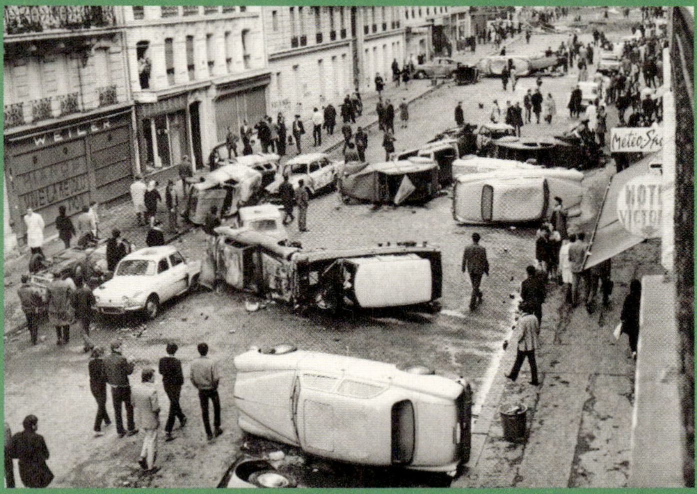

Demonstrations and violence in Paris, May 1968 → Top: police move into action during the student riots; press photographers shelter and look on from a doorway. → Center: students throw stones at police. → Bottom: overturned cars act as road-blocks on Rue Gay-Lussac.

PROTO-PUNK PHOTO PRINTS

These progressive proofs for Paul Kagan's posters promoting Steve Miller Band and Tim Buckley concerts show how he was able to use color overlays successfully to make two separate posters.

At first sight, the amorous naked couple and woodland scene may hardly have seemed suitable for the big-city group Velvet Underground, who dressed in black, wore shades, and hated the hippie scene. However, Kagan's use of jarring colors—recalling the work of Victor Moscoso—and brash juxtaposition of imagery were perhaps more in keeping with the band's ideology.

In the late seventies, graphic designers such as Jamie Reid were to adopt a similar approach by incorporating Day-Glo colors and brutal photomontage into punk-rock record sleeves and posters.

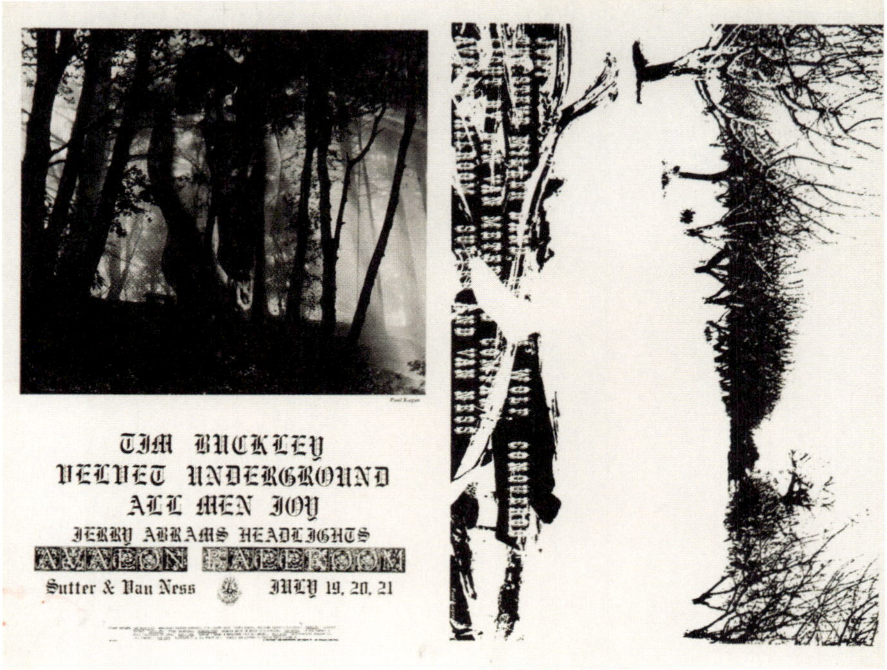

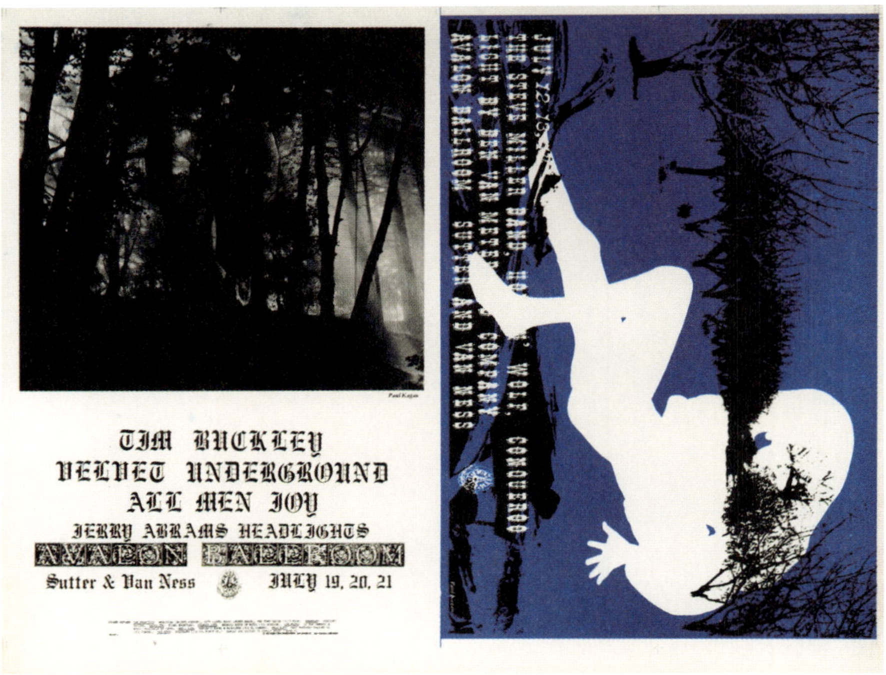

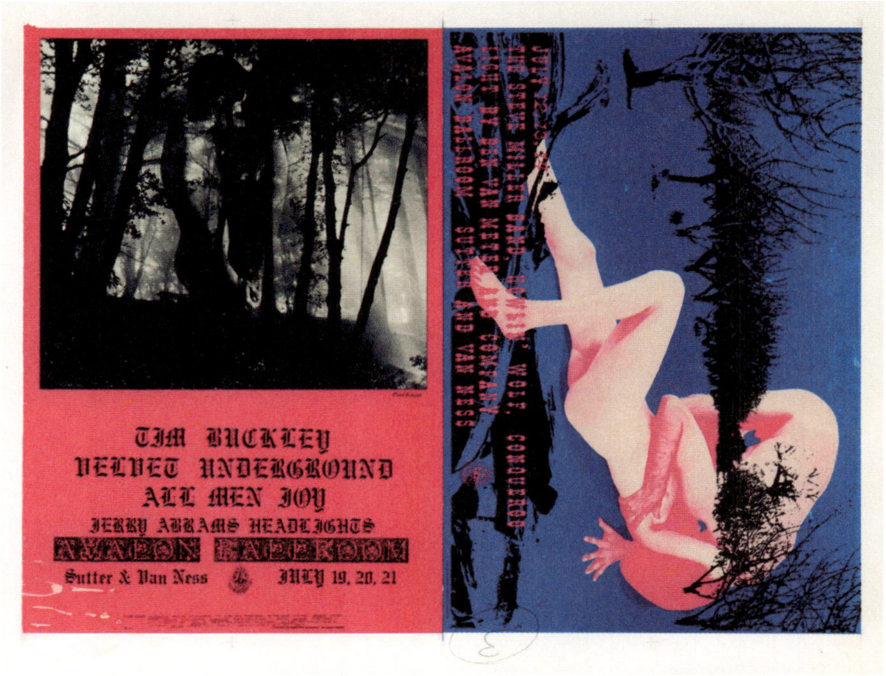

➳ Progressive proofs for posters advertising two gigs at the Avalon Ballroom in July 1968. The montage of a couple against tree trunks on a magenta background for the Tim Buckley/Velvet Underground concert is known as *In a Woodpile*. The image for The Steve Miller Band gig is known as *Forest*.

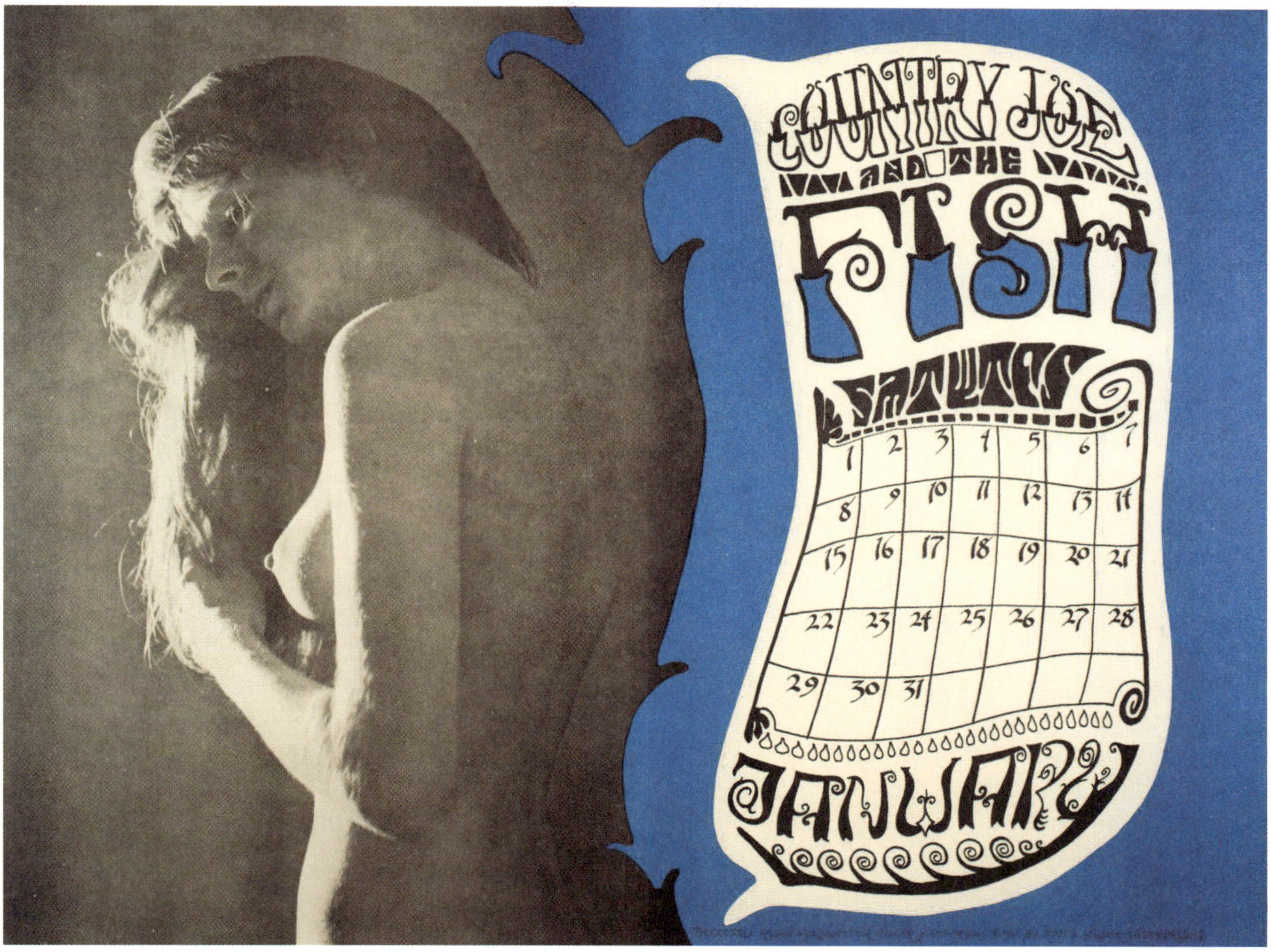

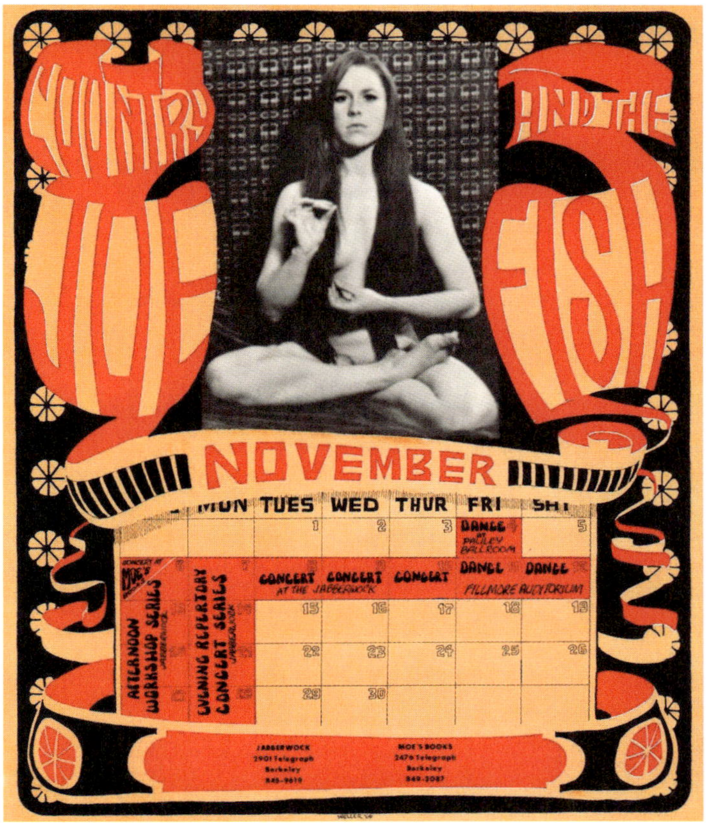

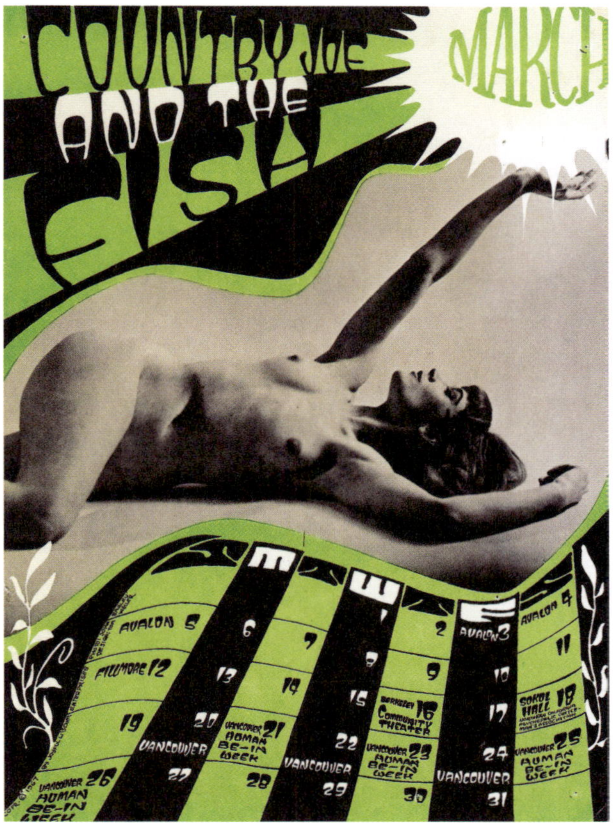

⋙→ Excerpts from a calendar promoting Country Joe and the Fish, dating from 1966. The images here are for November 1966 (a proof) and January and March 1967. They show all the band's concerts for those months. Paul Kagan photographed the nudes, while the artwork was by Tom Weller, the band's go-to artist.

GRIFFIN'S MOTIFS

Rick Griffin's iconic artwork featured several signature symbols and motifs, to which he returned time and time again. Perhaps the best known is his peerless flying eyeball. It originated in ancient Macedonia and Egypt, where it was a symbol for the Eye in the Sky or God's Eye. Griffin's design was also inspired by the work of Kenneth Howard (aka Von Dutch), the 'Godfather of Modern Day Pinstriping' or car customizing. Griffin brought life and artistic substance to the symbol, adding tentacles of flame and placing the eyeball in a wide range of imaginative scenarios, creating perhaps the most iconic of all the sixties psychedelic images.

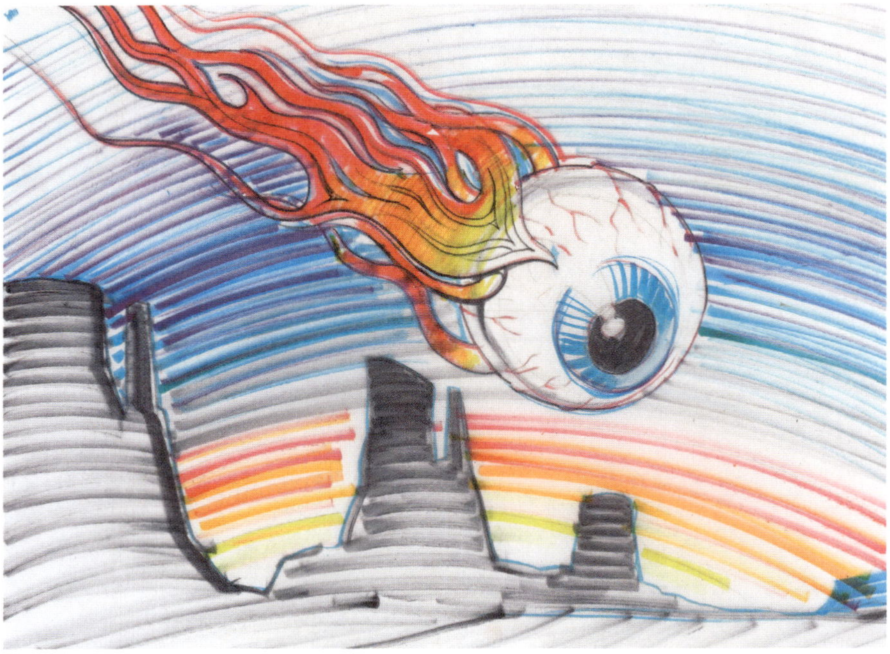

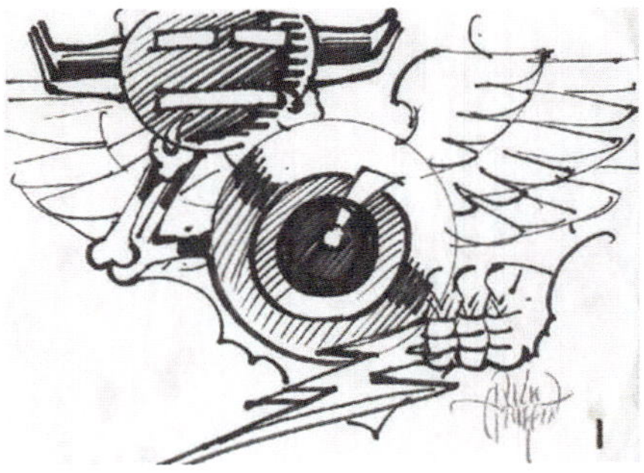

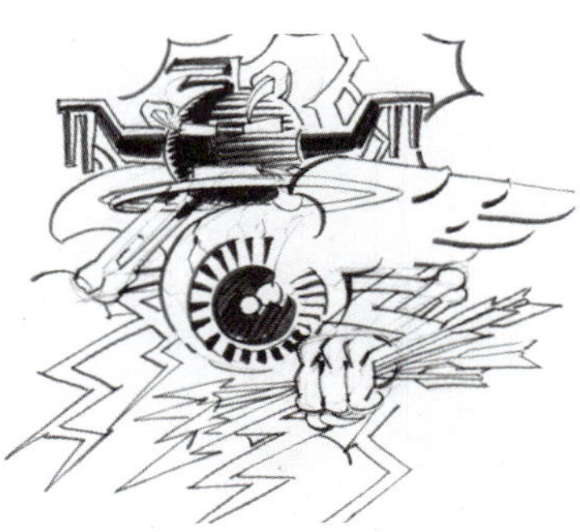

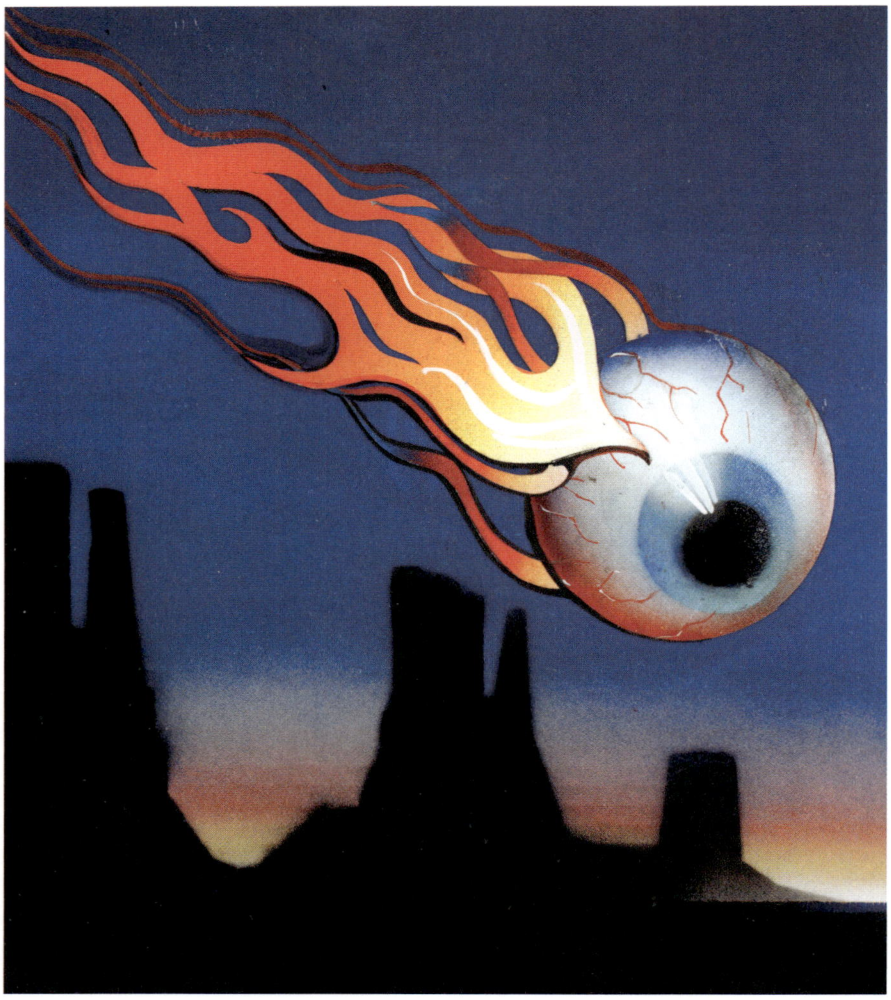

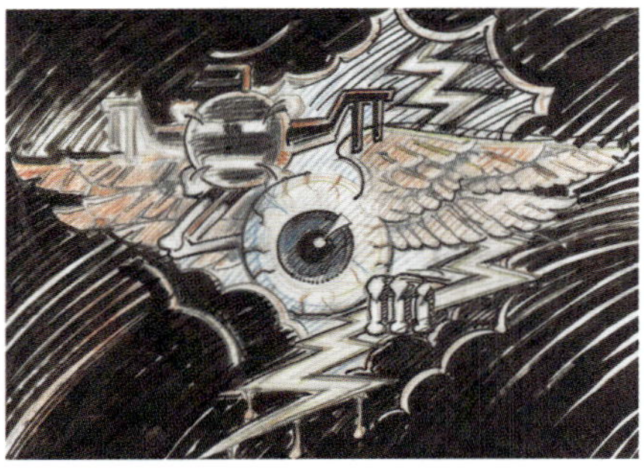

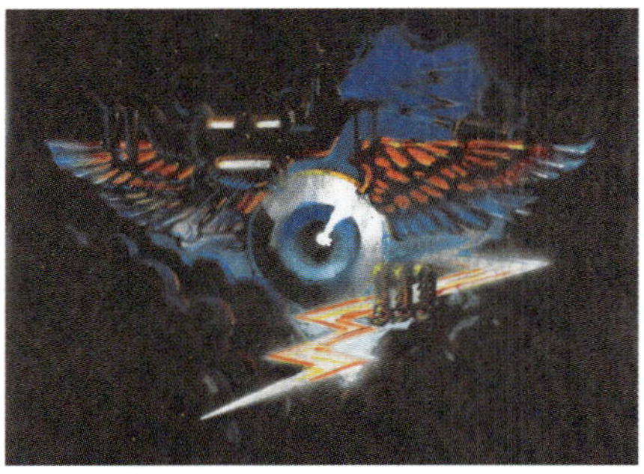

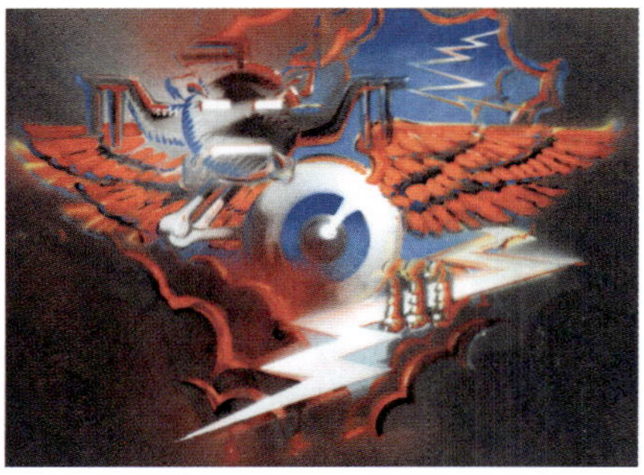

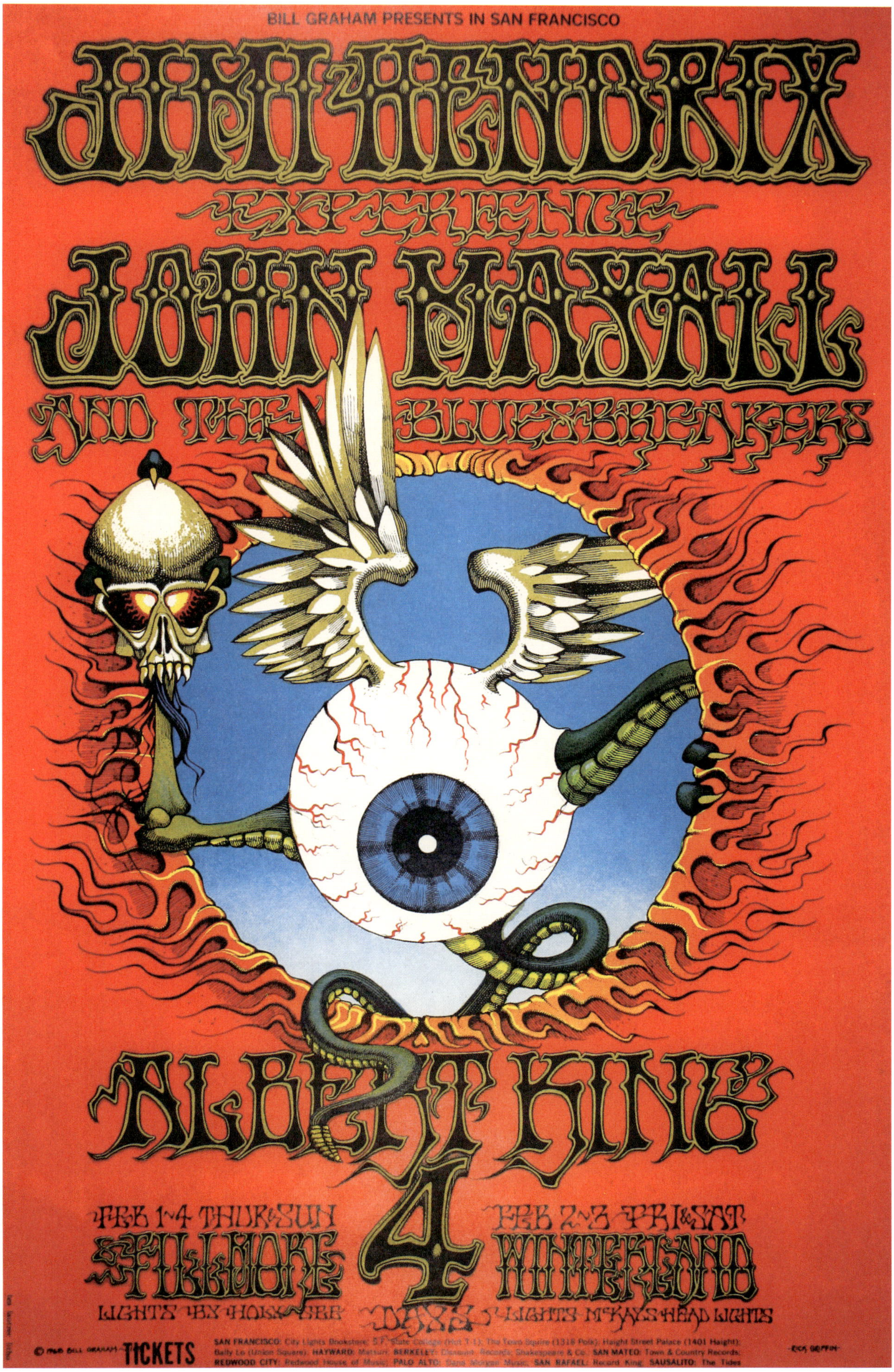

⋙→ Opposite: the development of Rick Griffin's signature flying eyeball across the years. ⋙→ This page: Griffin's iconic poster for a gig headlined by Jimi Hendrix at San Francisco's Fillmore Auditorium in February 1968. He reproduced it as a painting, on a far larger scale, in 1987. Griffin's mature lettering style was very sophisticated. He reduced the spaces between the letters, joining them up to make a block of calligraphy, not unlike classical Arabic, usually with two or three distinct eyelines, embellished with drop serifs. Moreover, rather than appropriating images and photographs, he drew his own.

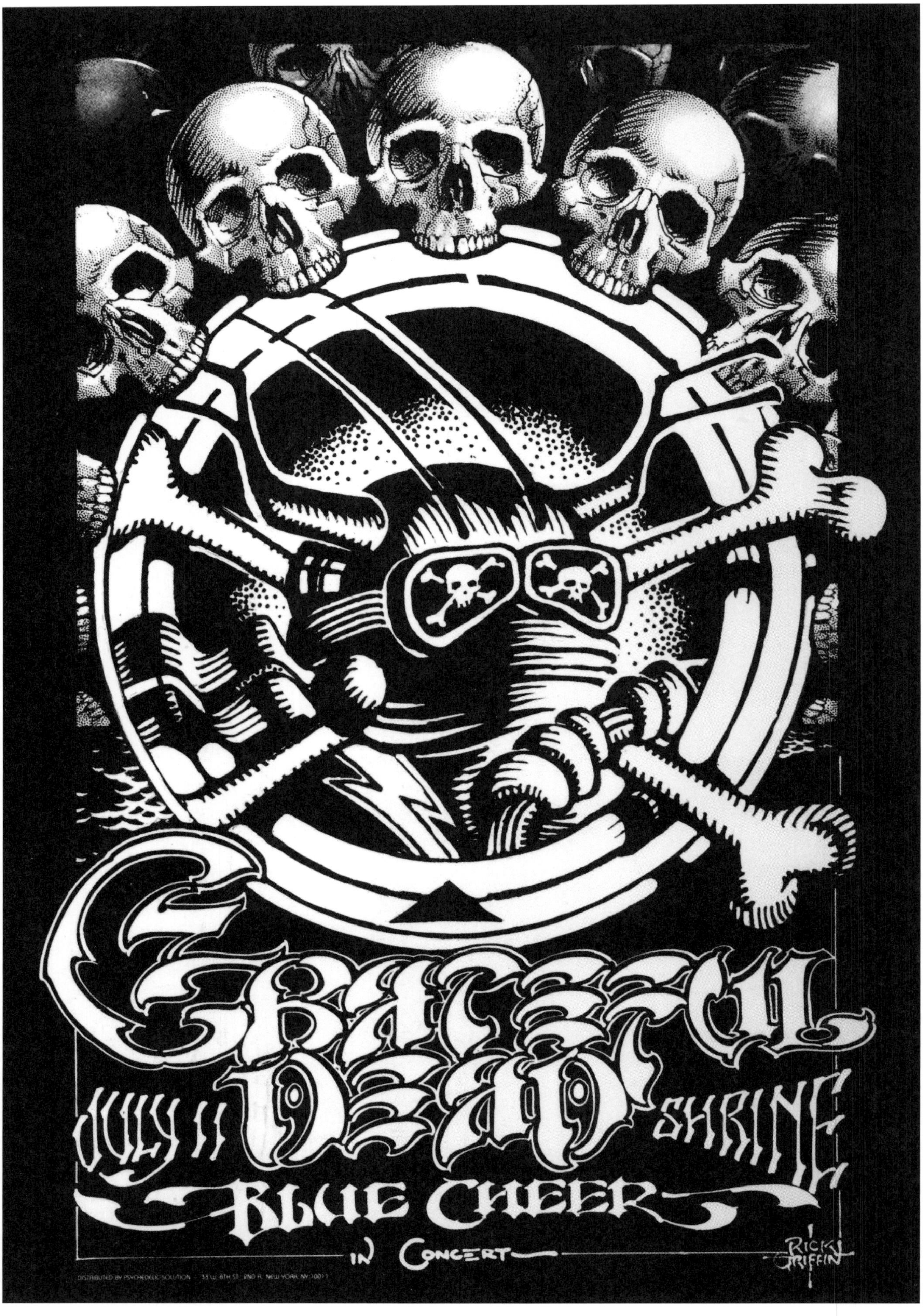

⋙→ Posters from the late sixties were awash with shocking color-clash and psychedelic patterns, but bold black-and-white imagery still packed a graphic punch. ⋙→ This page: a promo for a Grateful Dead/Blue Cheer concert at LA's Shrine Auditorium in 1968. It was printed in several variants, including black with white, pale green, or yellow.

⋙→ Opposite: a pirate girl adorns a poster proof for *Zap Comix*, within the framework of the Grateful Dead poster. Griffin contributed to a handful of *Zap* issues, from #2 to #12. He also drew for a range of other comix from the late sixties to the eighties, including *Man from Utopia* (which he created).

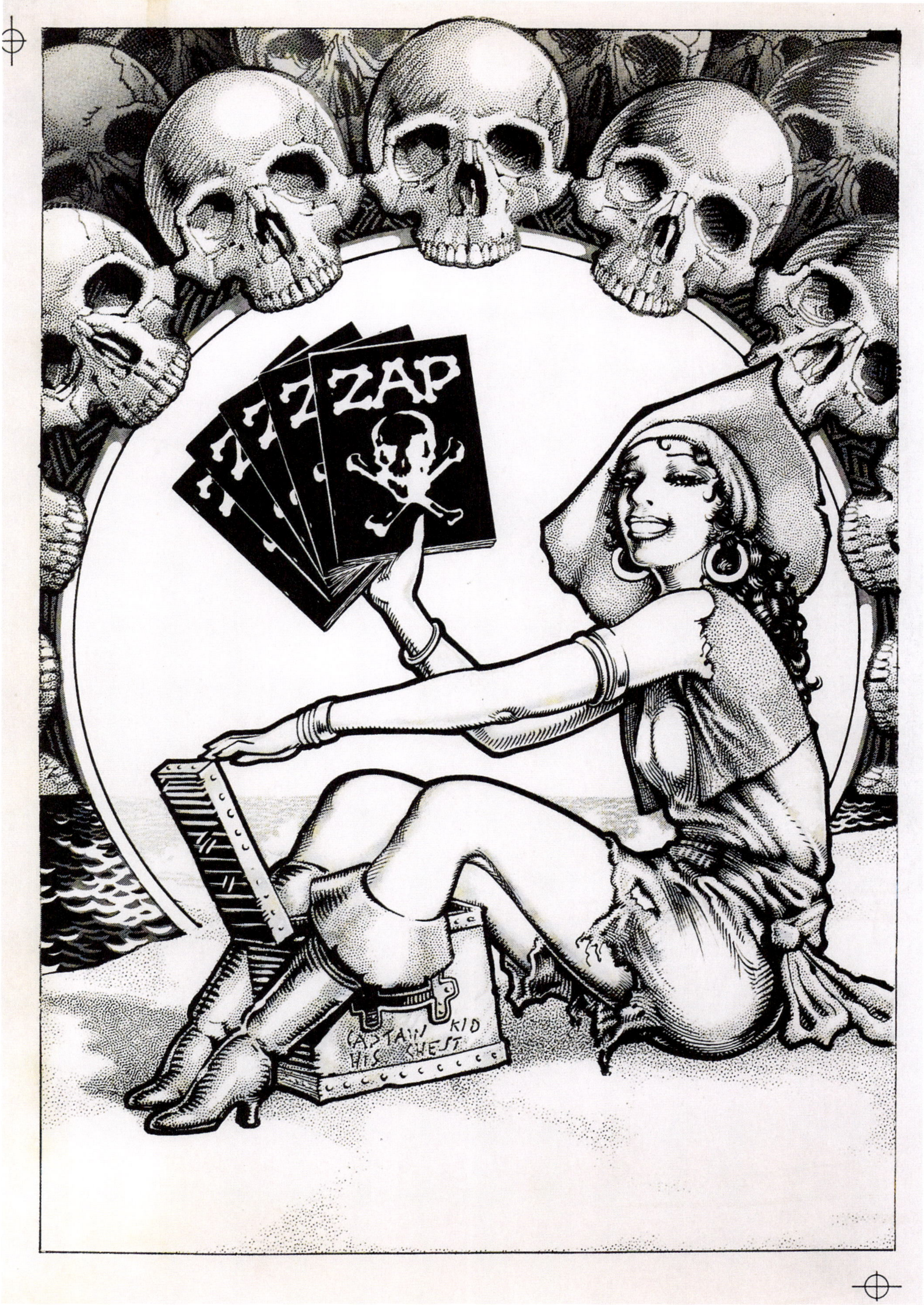
ZAP
CAPTAIN KID
HIS CHEST

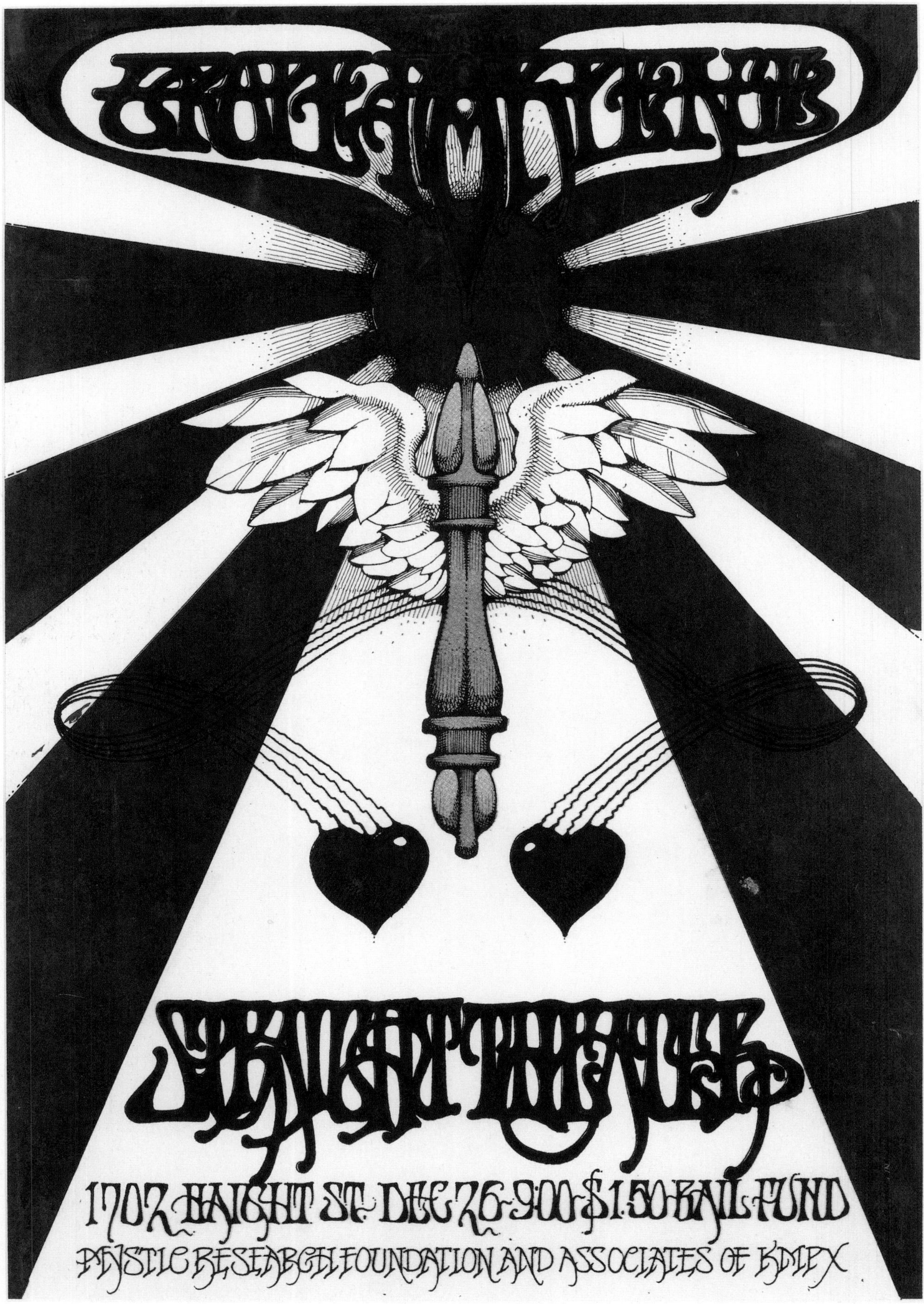
1702 HAIGHT ST. DEC 26 · 9:00 · $1.50 · BAIL · FUND
MYSTIC RESEARCH FOUNDATION AND ASSOCIATES OF KMPX

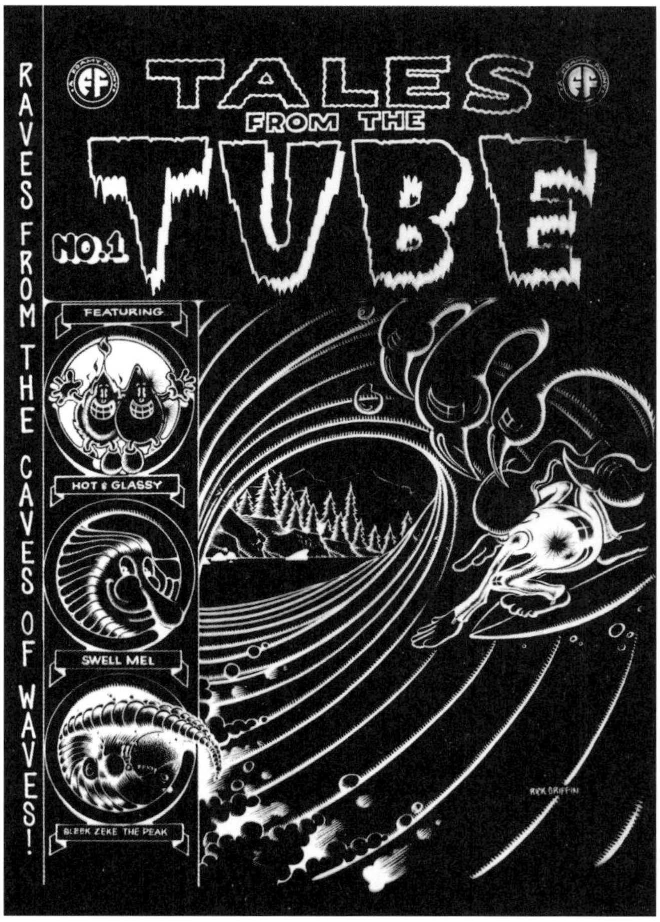

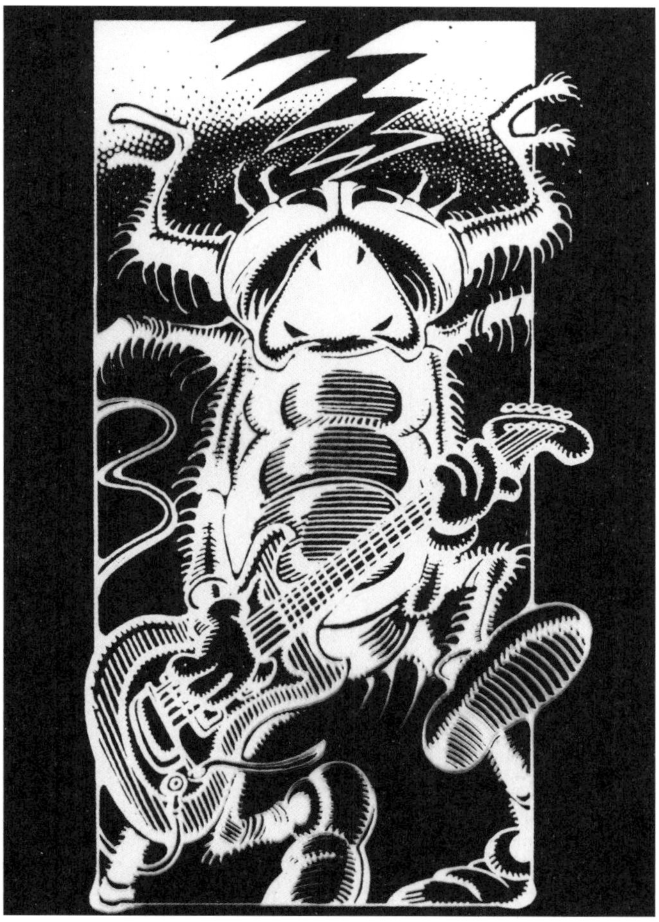

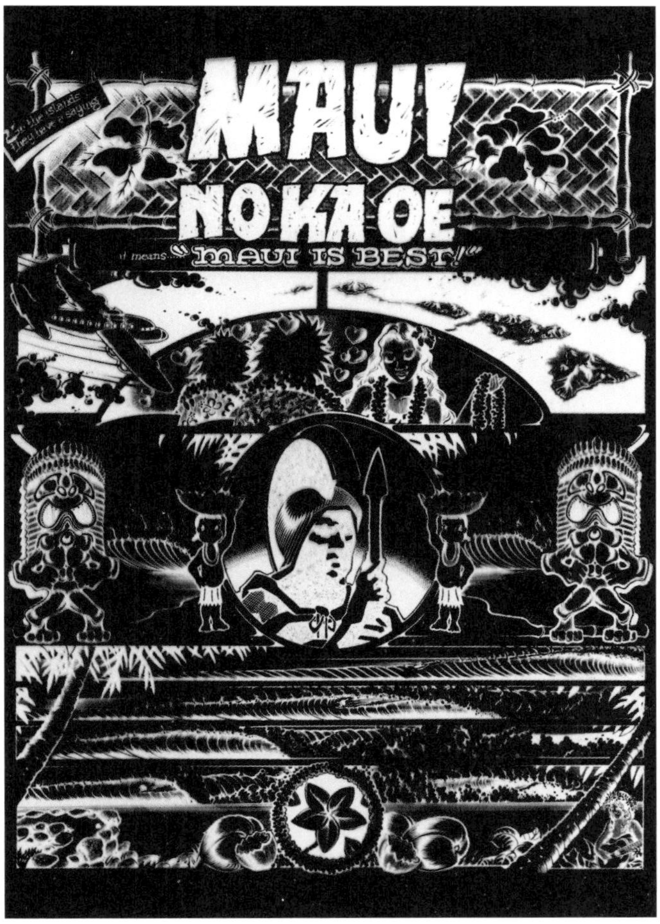

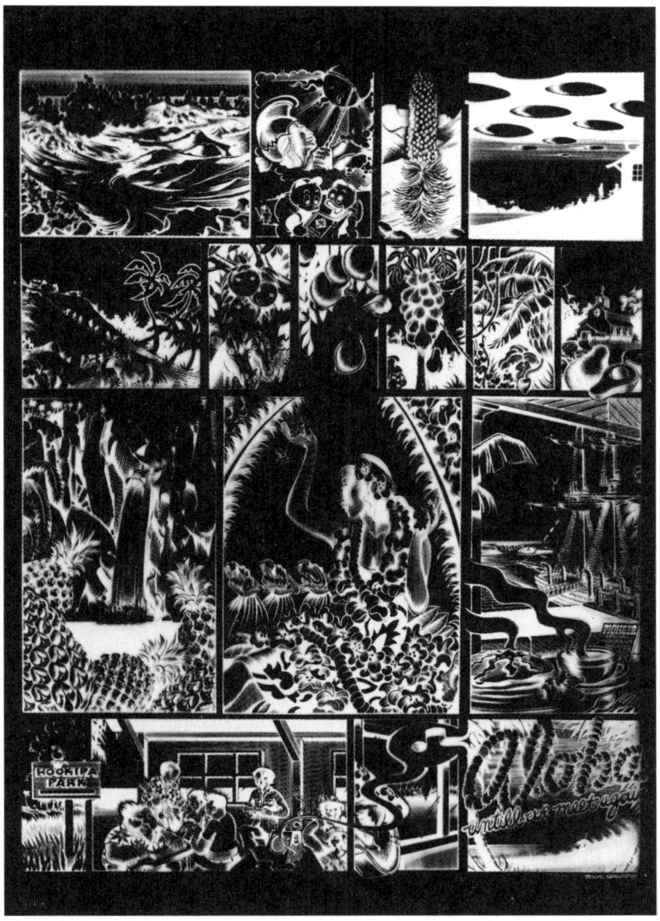

⋙→ Opposite: the film overlay for a Griffin poster for the Straight Theater; the venue was run by hippies rather than businessmen. ⋙→ This page: overlays for other Griffin projects. Top left: the cover for *Tales from the Tube* #1, from 1973. This comix book first appeared as an insert in *Surfer* magazine. As well as his own work, it had contributions from the likes of Robert Crumb, Robert Williams, S. Clay Wilson, and Glenn Chase. ⋙→ Top right: part of Griffin's artwork for 'Why Don't We Do It In The Road?' for Alan Aldridge's *The Beatles Illustrated Lyrics*. ⋙→ Bottom: Griffin's Hawaiian-themed strip 'Maui No Ka Oe,' from *Tales from the Tube*.

LEE CONKLIN

Lee Conklin sold some work to the *Los Angeles Free Press* and worked as a cartoonist there before reading about the San Francisco poster scene in *Time* magazine and relocating. He went to the Fillmore Auditorium office and showed his portfolio to Bill Graham who, much to Conklin's surprise, hired him on the spot. Conklin produced thirty-three posters for Graham alone. His work is characterized by his attention to drawing and, unlike many poster artists, his posters usually have a defined picture plane. His best known work is the pen-and-ink-lion album sleeve for Santana's 1969 debut album.

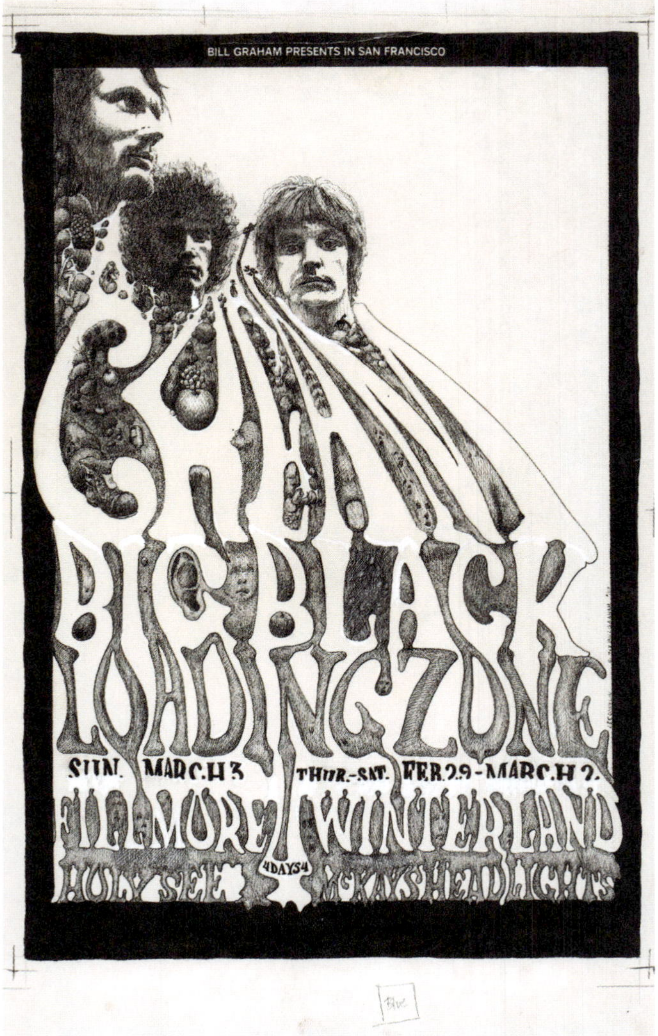

➳ This page, top and bottom right: original artwork and full-color poster for Cream concerts at two of Bill Graham's venues. ➳ Bottom left: a May 1968 poster that recalls the surrealistic Renaissance portraits of Giuseppe Arcimboldo. ➳ Opposite: Conklin based his lion image for this Bill Graham poster on one in a book of animal pictures that he owned. Bill Graham approved—as did Carlos Santana, who asked Conklin to redraw the lion for the cover of his band's 1969 debut album.

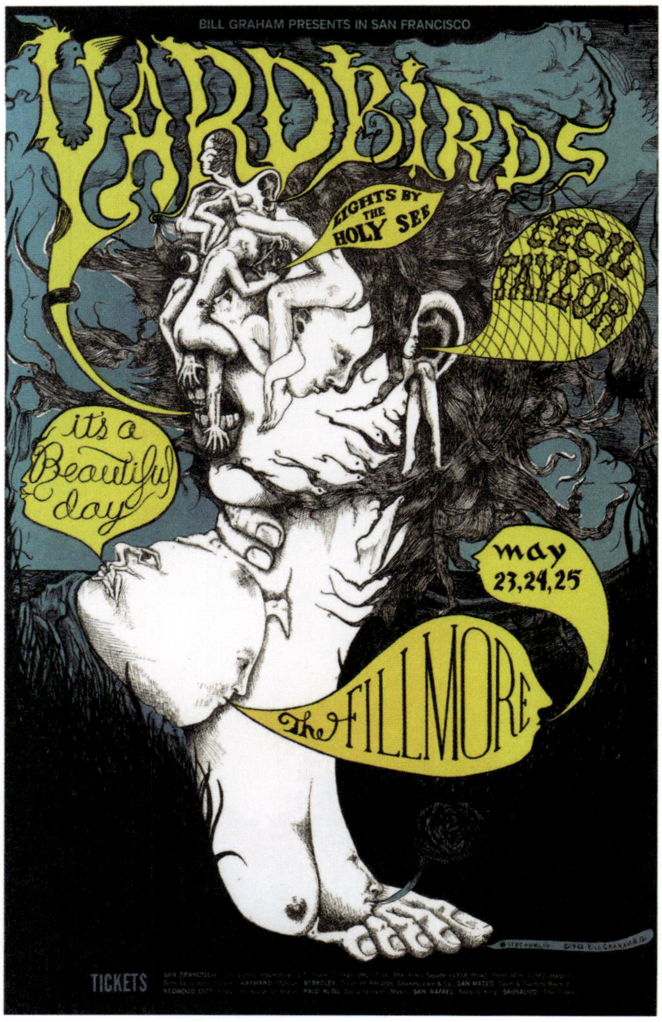

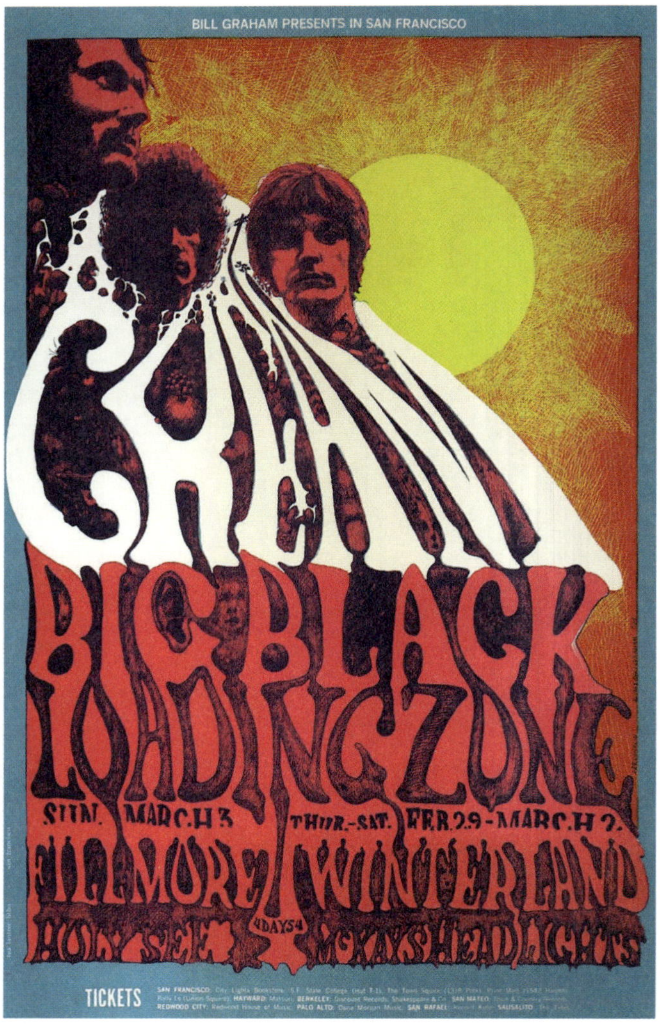

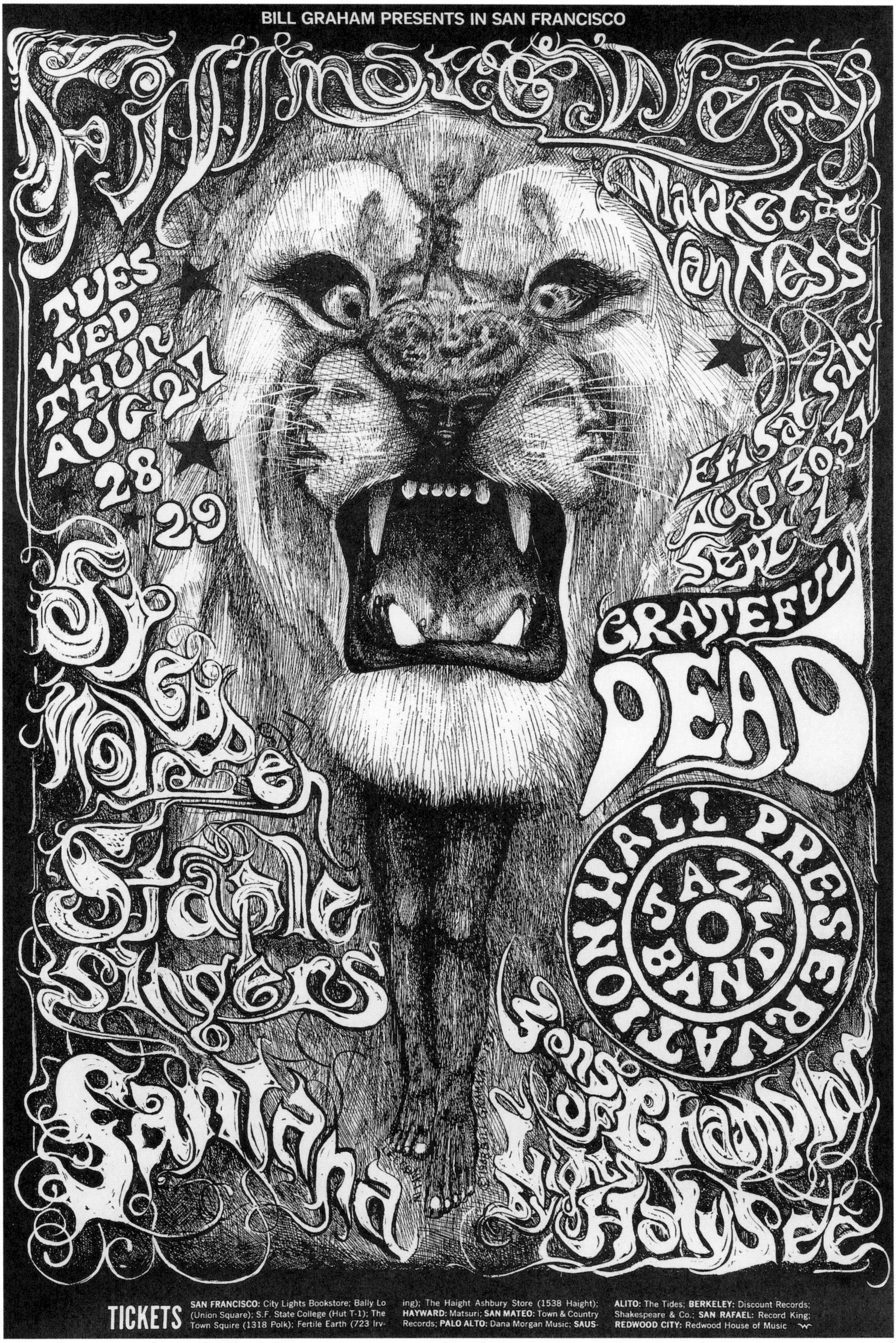
BILL GRAHAM PRESENTS IN SAN FRANCISCO
Fillmore West
Market at Van Ness
TUES WED THUR AUG 27 28 29
Fri Sat Sun Aug 30 31 Sept 1
GRATEFUL DEAD
PRESERVATION HALL JAZZ BAND
Staple Singers
Santana
Sons of Champlin
Lights by Holy See
TICKETS SAN FRANCISCO: City Lights Bookstore; Bally Lo (Union Square); S.F. State College (Hut T-1); The Town Squire (1318 Polk); Fertile Earth (723 Irving); The Haight Ashbury Store (1538 Haight); HAYWARD: Matsuri; SAN MATEO: Town & Country Records; PALO ALTO: Dana Morgan Music; SAUSALITO: The Tides; BERKELEY: Discount Records; Shakespeare & Co.; SAN RAFAEL: Record King; REDWOOD CITY: Redwood House of Music

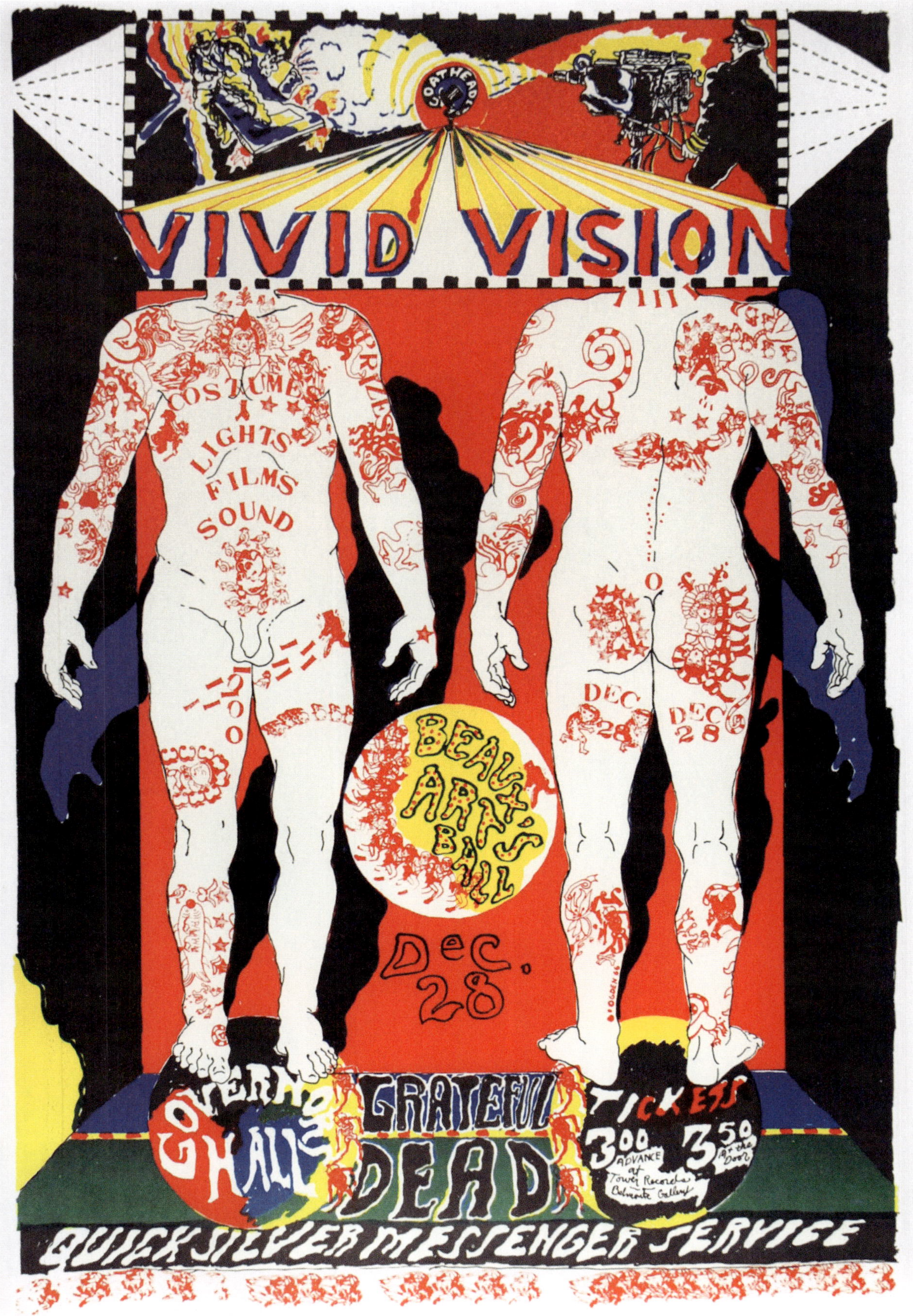

BEYOND THE BAY

In the late sixties, Los Angeles became the hub of the US recording industry, with many labels moving there from New York. Local bands included The Byrds, The Seeds, The Doors, The Mothers of Invention, Love, and Buffalo Springfield. There was an active club scene on Sunset Strip, with the Shrine Auditorium staging bigger shows. Many bands lived in the canyons, and were joined by English musicians such as John Mayall. It was a far bigger scene than that of San Francisco.

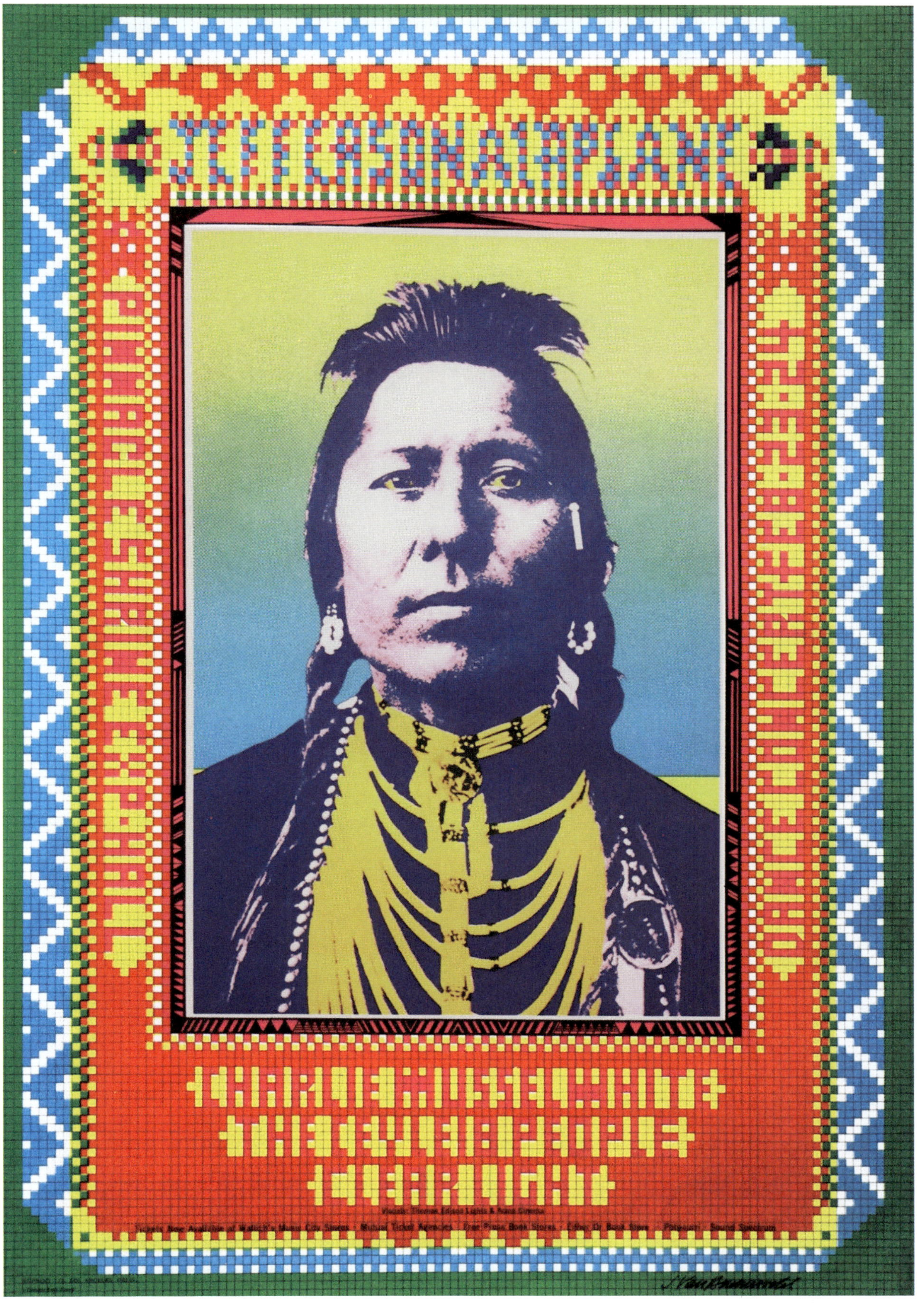

⋙→ The posters on these pages offer a marked contrast to the more familiar high-intensity psychedelic designs. ⋙→ Opposite: a poster by Jack Ogden for a Grateful Dead appearance at the end of 1966 at the Governor's Hall in Sacramento, California. ⋙→ This page: another Native American portrait forms the centerpiece of a poster by John Van Hamersveld. The 'embroidered' frame adds to the illusion of antiquity.

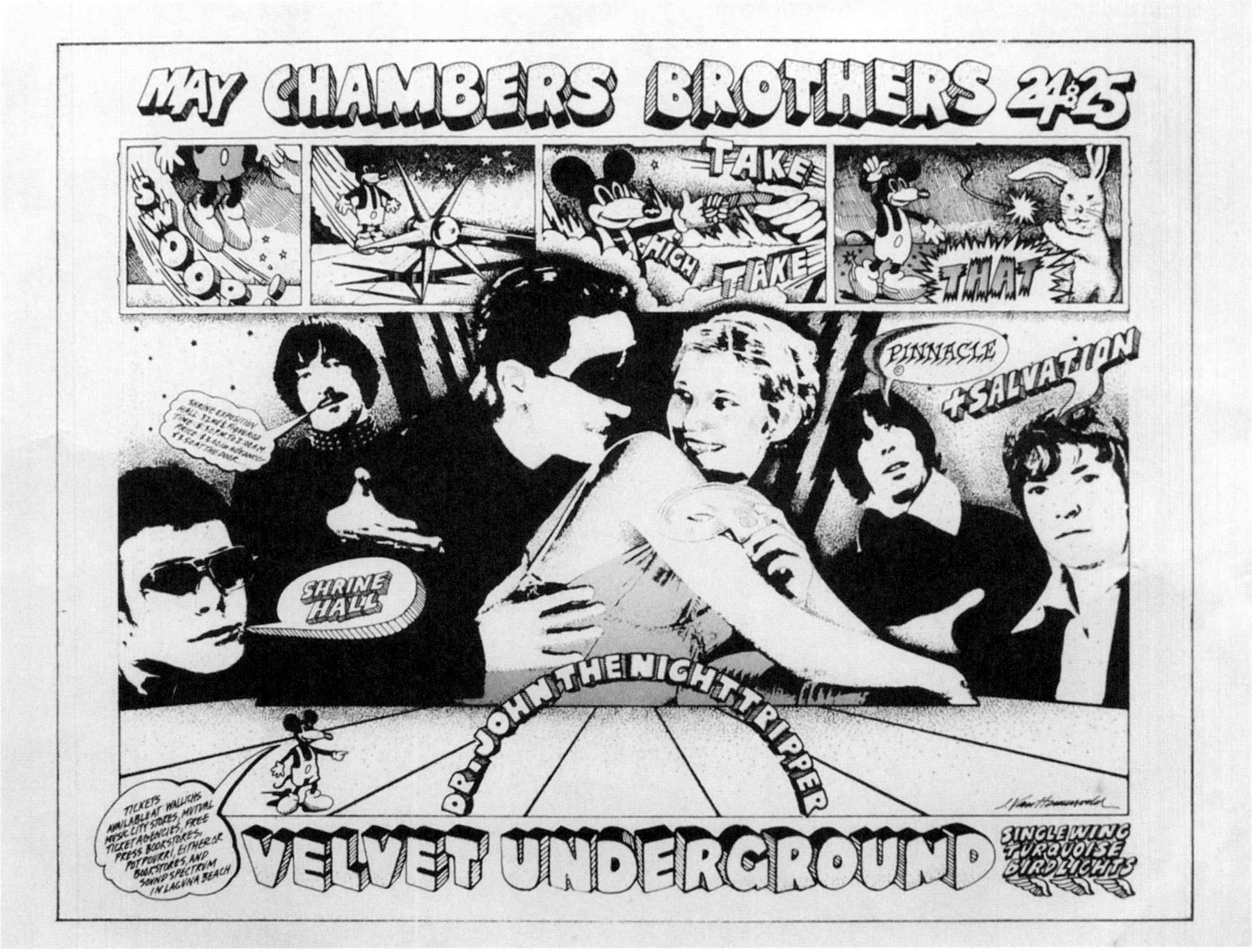
MAY CHAMBERS BROTHERS 24&25
SWOOP
TAKE
HIGH
TAKE
THAT
PINNACLE
+SALVATION
SHRINE HALL
DR. JOHN THE NIGHT TRIPPER
TICKETS AVAILABLE AT WALLICHS MUSIC CITY STORES, MUTUAL TICKET AGENCIES, FREE PRESS BOOKSTORES, POTPOURRI, EITHER OR BOOKSTORES, AND SOUND SPECTRUM IN LAGUNA BEACH
VELVET UNDERGROUND
SINGLE WING TURQUOISE BIRD LIGHTS

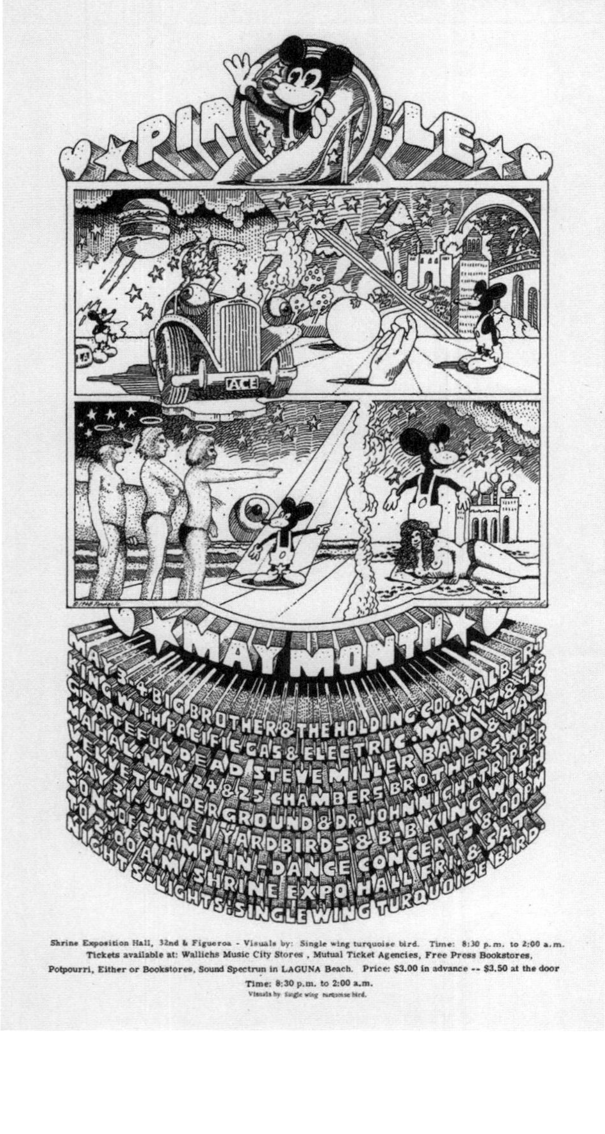
MAY MONTH
MAY 3-4 BIG BROTHER & THE HOLDING CO. & ALBERT KING WITH PACIFIC GAS & ELECTRIC. MAY 17 & 18 GRATEFUL DEAD STEVE MILLER BAND & TAJ MAHAL. MAY 24 & 25 CHAMBERS BROTHERS WITH VELVET UNDERGROUND & DR. JOHN NIGHT TRIPPER MAY 31 - JUNE 1 YARDBIRDS & B. B. KING WITH SONS OF CHAMPLIN - DANCE CONCERTS 8:00 PM TO 2:00 A.M. SHRINE EXPO HALL FRI. & SAT. NIGHTS - LIGHTS: SINGLE WING TURQUOISE BIRD
Shrine Exposition Hall, 32nd & Figueroa - Visuals by: Single wing turquoise bird. Time: 8:30 p.m. to 2:00 a.m.
Tickets available at: Wallichs Music City Stores, Mutual Ticket Agencies, Free Press Bookstores,
Potpourri, Either or Bookstores, Sound Spectrun in LAGUNA Beach. Price: $3.00 in advance -- $3.50 at the door
Time: 8:30 p.m. to 2:00 a.m.
Visuals by Single wing turquoise bird.

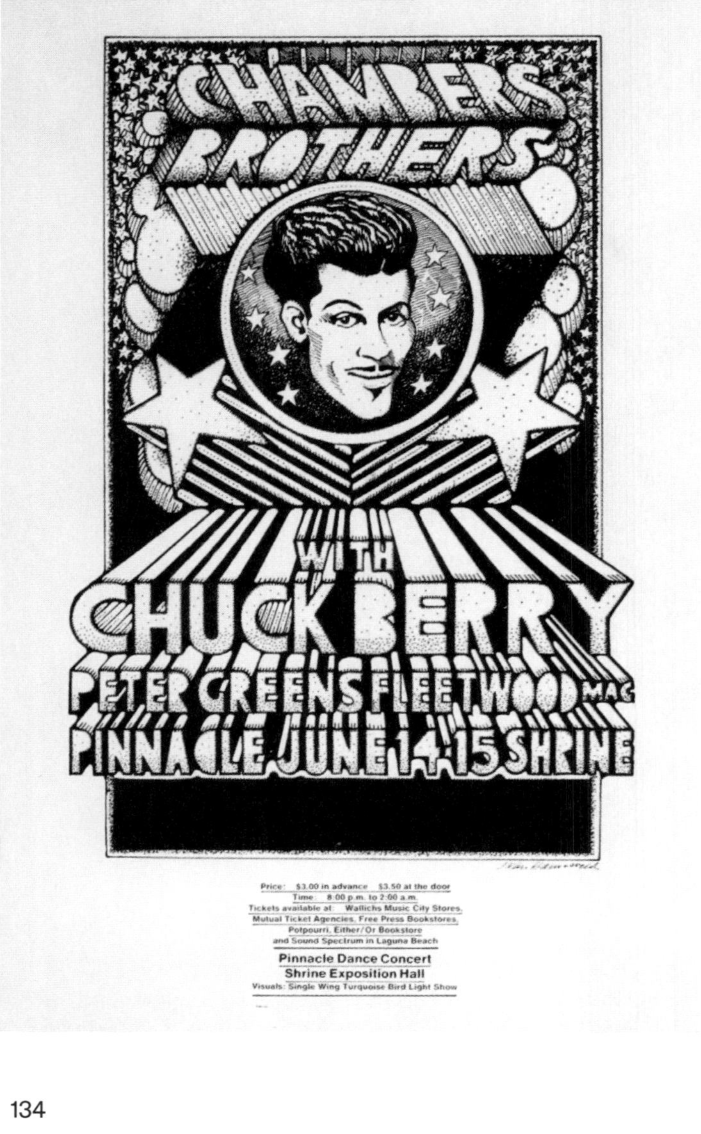
CHAMBERS BROTHERS
WITH
CHUCK BERRY
PETER GREENS FLEETWOOD MAC
PINNACLE JUNE 14-15 SHRINE
Price: $3.00 in advance $3.50 at the door
Time: 8:00 p.m. to 2:00 a.m.
Tickets available at: Wallichs Music City Stores,
Mutual Ticket Agencies, Free Press Bookstores,
Potpourri, Either/Or Bookstore
and Sound Spectrum in Laguna Beach
Pinnacle Dance Concert
Shrine Exposition Hall
Visuals: Single Wing Turquoise Bird Light Show

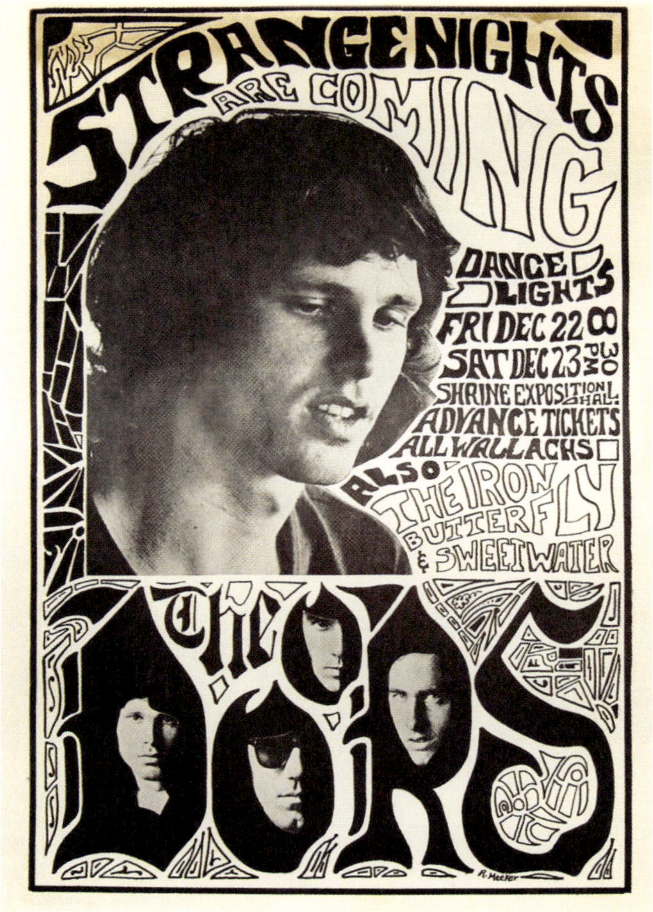

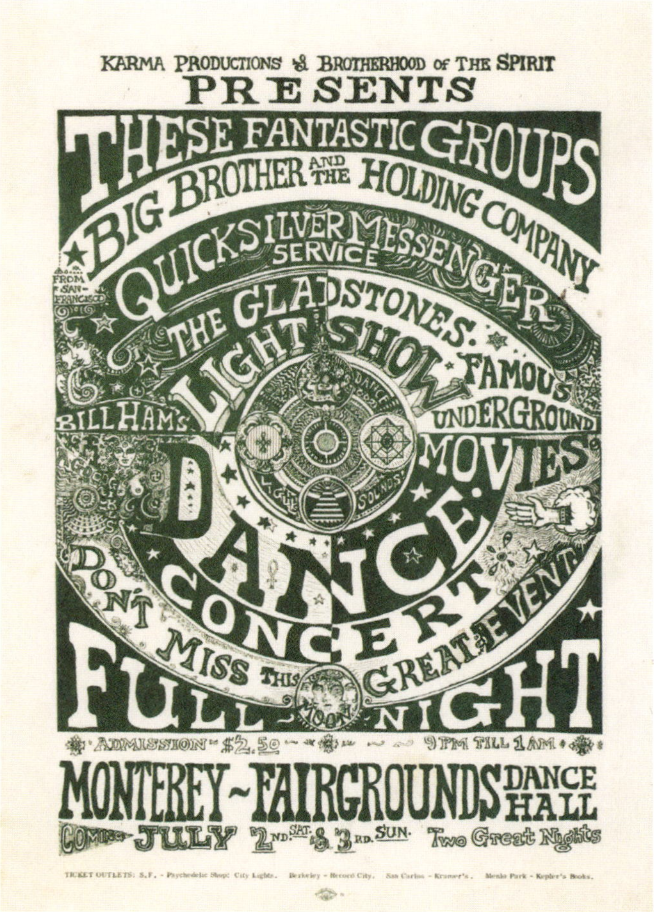

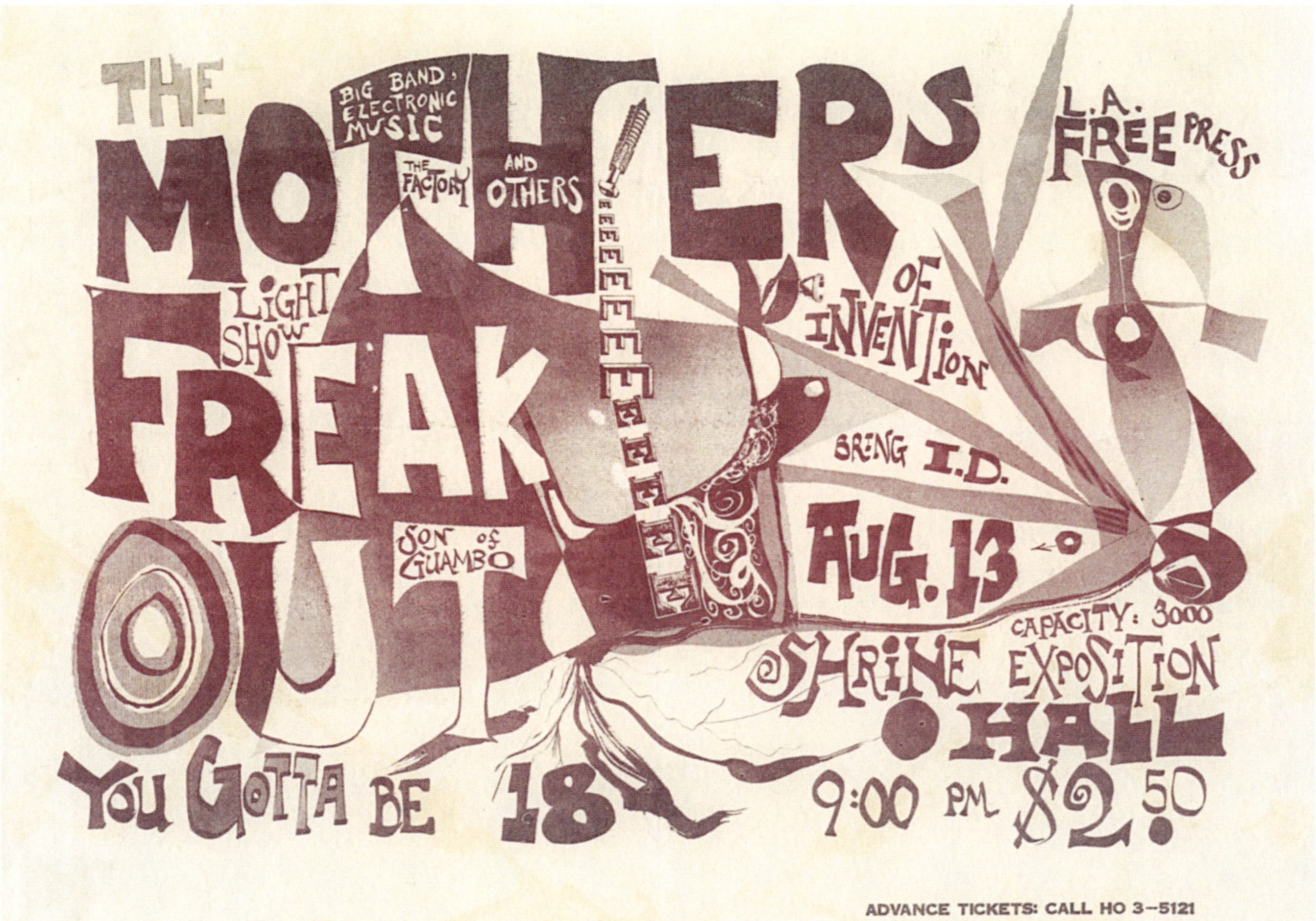

⋙→ Opposite: the influence of underground comix is evident in these examples, all by John Van Hamersveld—not least in the Mickey Mouse character, which Robert Crumb mimicked in *Zap Comix*. ⋙→ This page: lettering dominates image in these three selections, from the relatively straightforward 1967 Doors poster (top left), to the mandala-esque design for a 1966 Big Brother/Quicksilver Messenger Service concert (top right). ⋙→ Bottom: perhaps the most straightforward design seen here, this 1966 poster may have been designed by Frank Zappa himself.

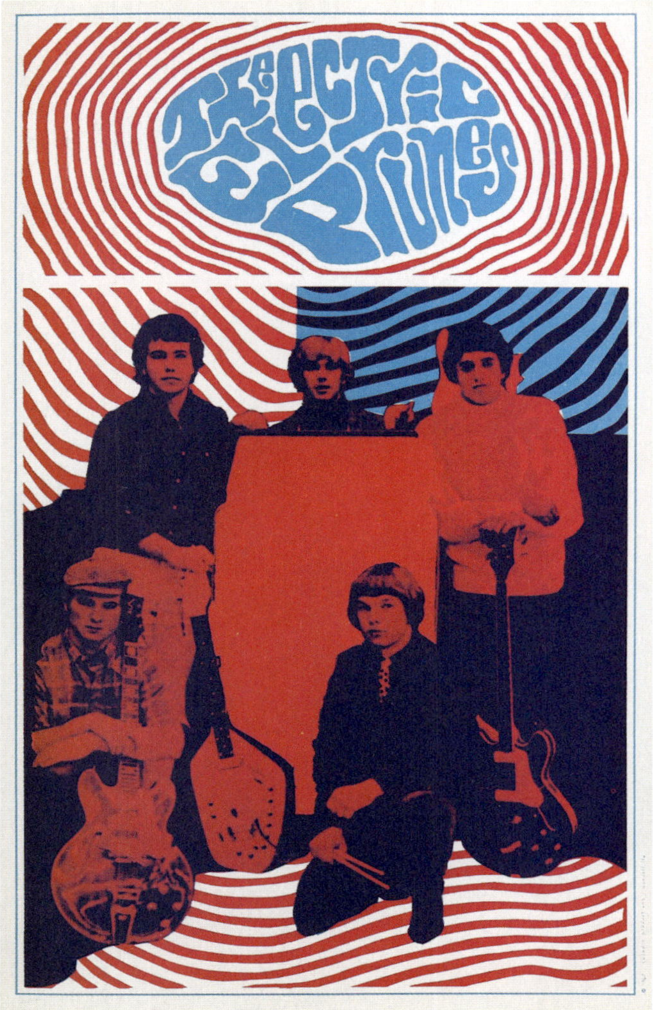

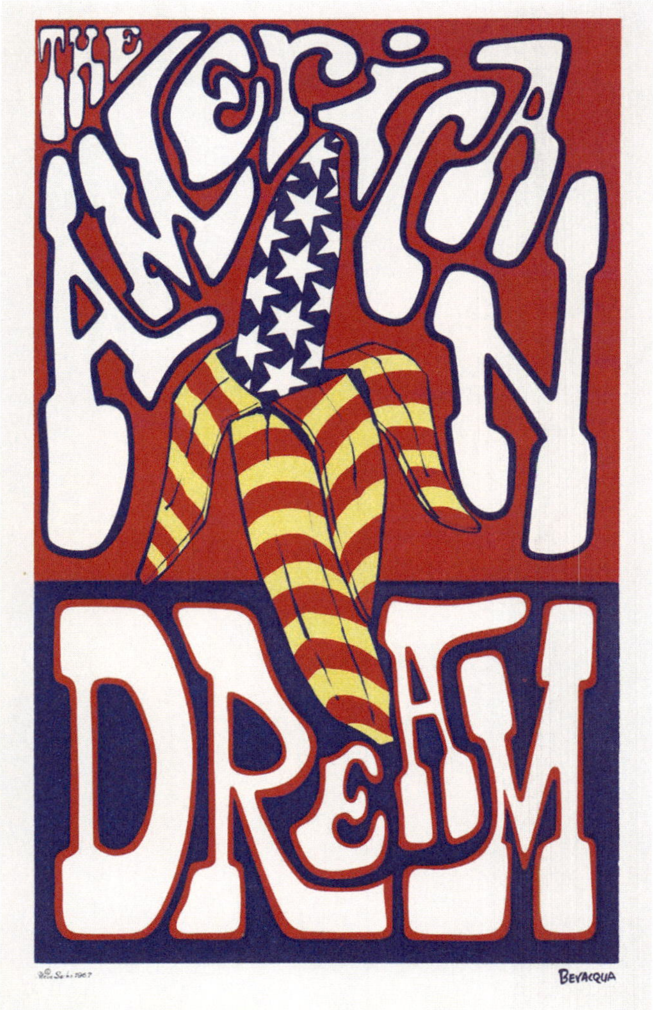

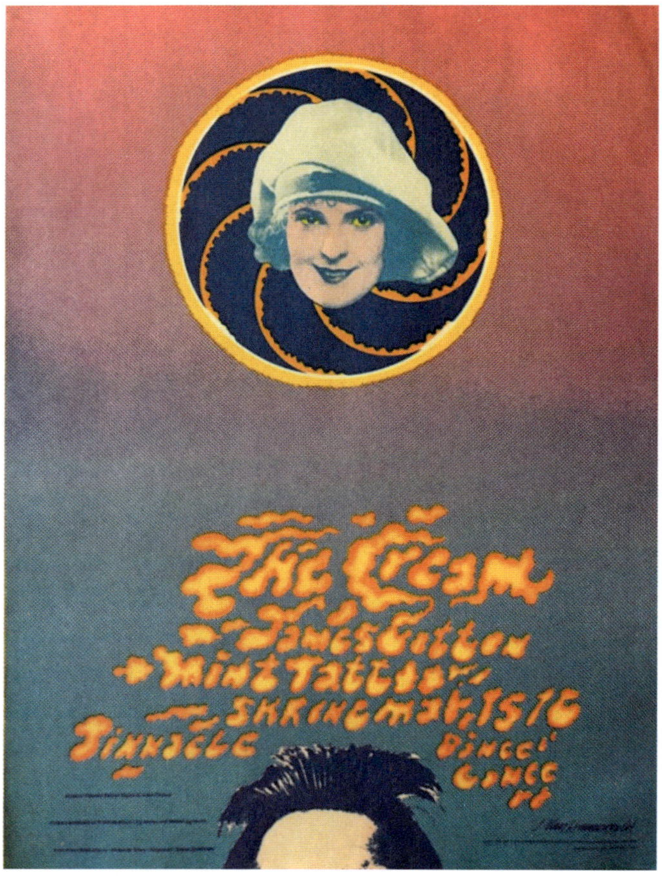

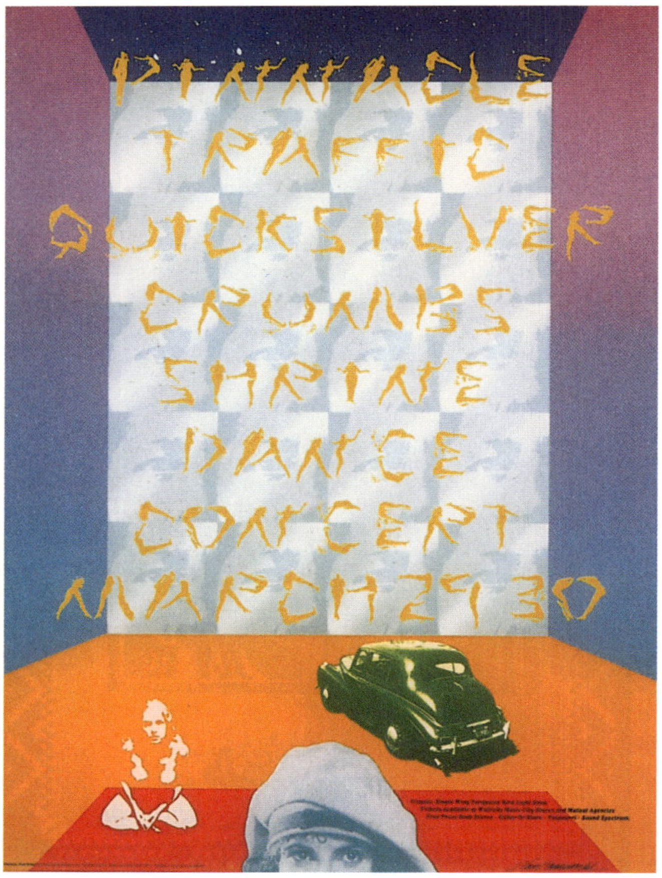

⋙→Top left: a hand-pulled serigraph from 1967 for Los Angeles's Saladin Headshop. The Electric Prunes scored a US No.11 with 'I Had Too Much To Dream Last Night.' ⋙→ Top right: a blacklight poster by Art Bevacqua from 1967. ⋙→ Bottom left: John Van Hamersveld's poster for Cream's appearance at LA's Shrine Auditorium in 1968 re-uses part of the portrait of a Native American seen in full on p. 133. ⋙→ Bottom right: several cross-references pop up in this Van Hamersveld design for another 1968 Shrine concert. The cropped head at the bottom echoes the Cream poster, while repeats of the Native American's eye appear in the background.

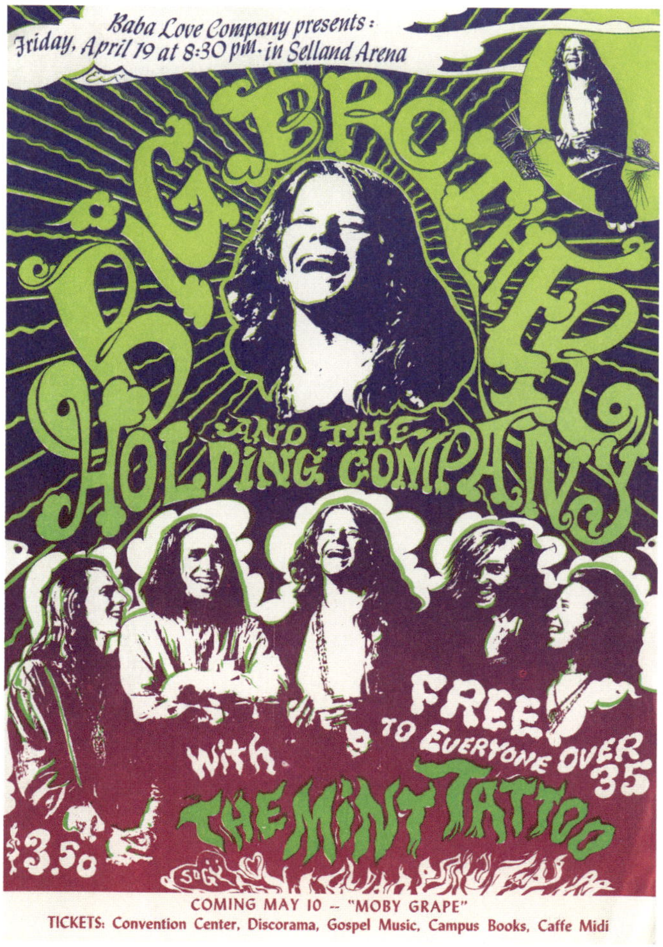

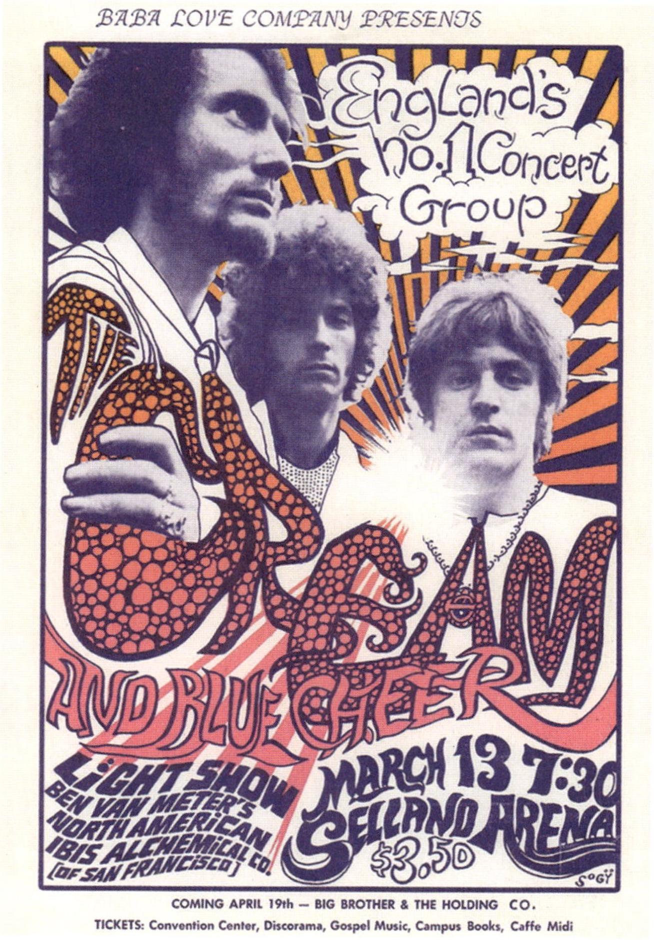

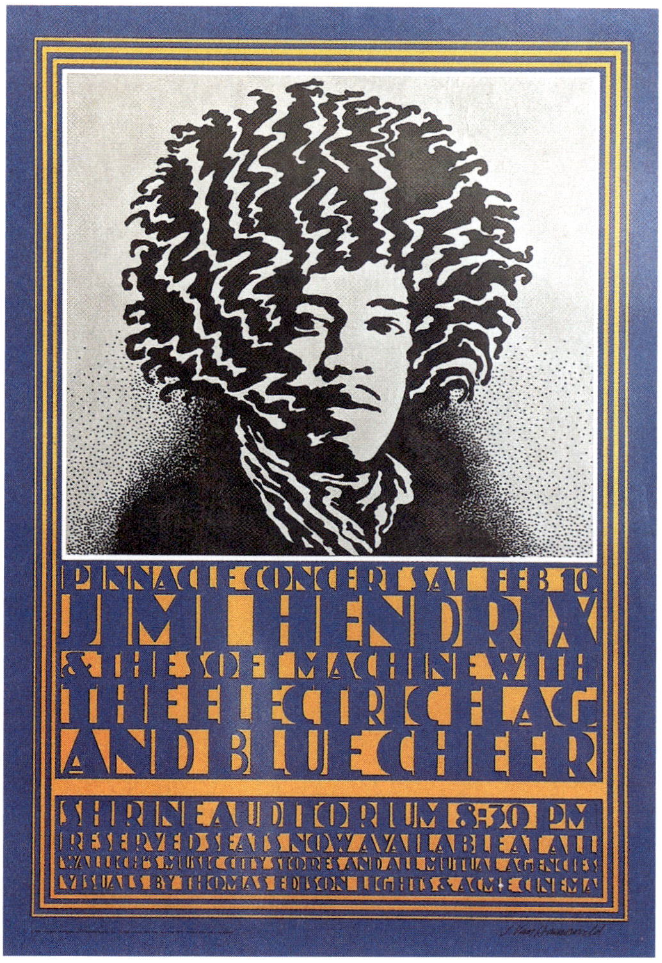

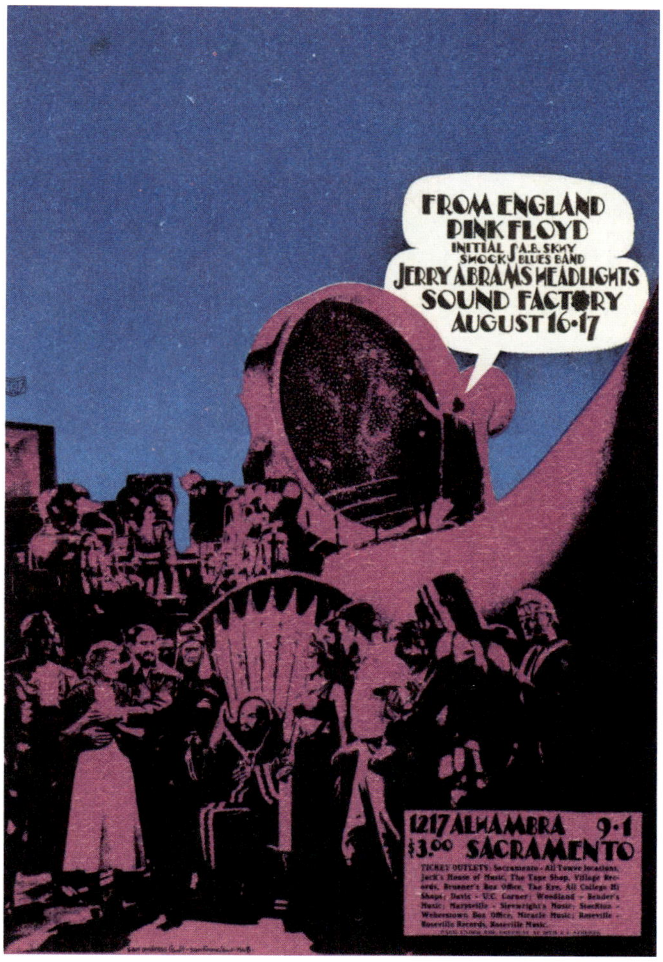

➳ This page: four posters from 1968. The top two designs were produced by the Baba Love company for concerts at the Selland Arena in Fresno, California.

➳ Top left and right: designs by Dale Oftedal (also known as Sogy) for a Big Brother gig (left) and Cream (right), the latter based on a commonly used photograph.

➳ Bottom left: another John Van Hamersveld design from 1968. Hendrix was still touring with his band the Experience at the time, despite the solo credit.

➳ Bottom right: San Andreas Fault (aka Tad Hunter) produced this image for a Pink Floyd gig in Sacramento, which took place toward the end of their US tour.

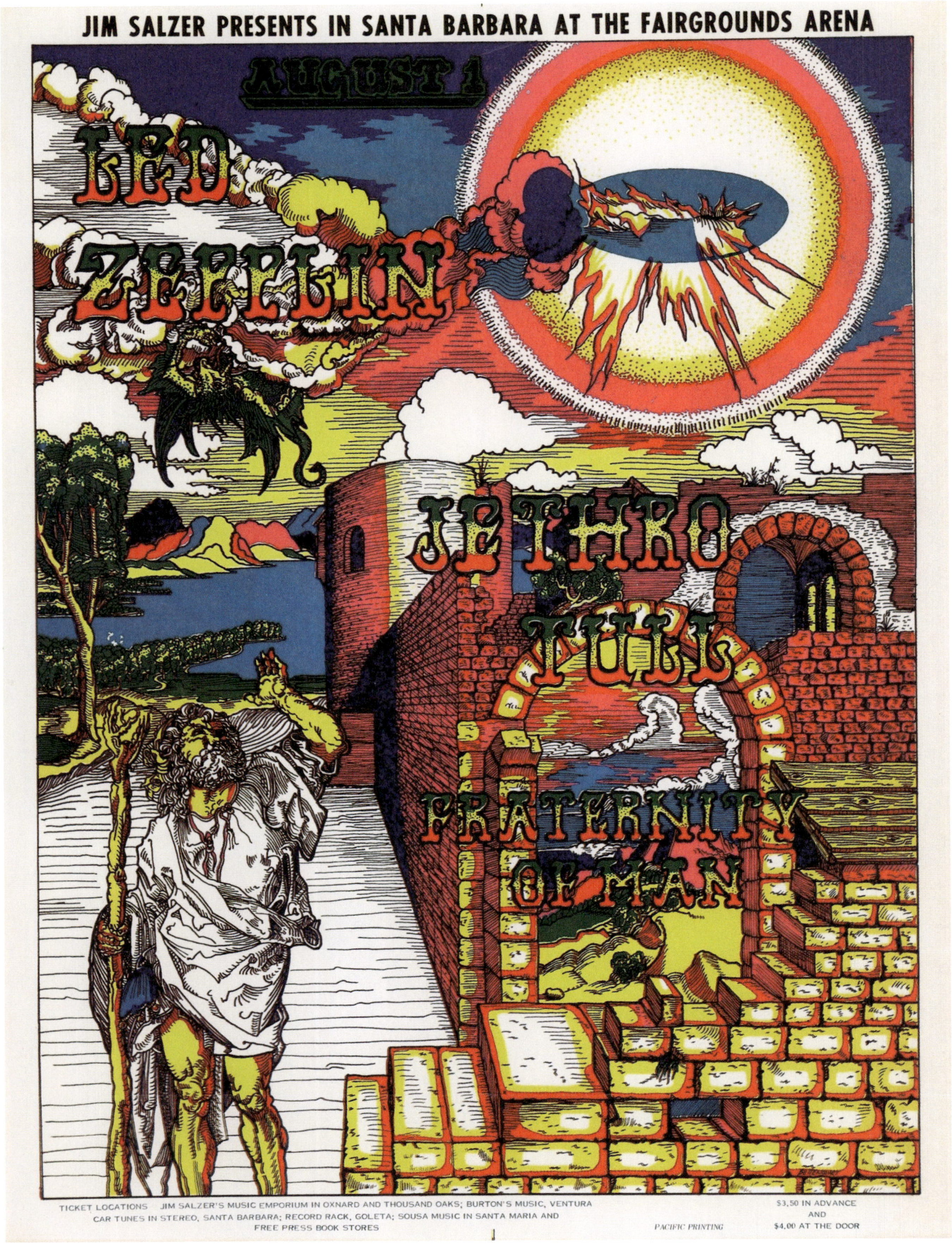

FRANK BETTENCOURT

The psychedelic style developed in many different ways. Frank Bettencourt's designs—created in Santa Barbara, outside Los Angeles—mostly used raw primary colors but were adapted according to needs. While attending high school and Santa Barbara City College during the late sixties, Bettencourt made posters for local venues when big-name acts came to town.

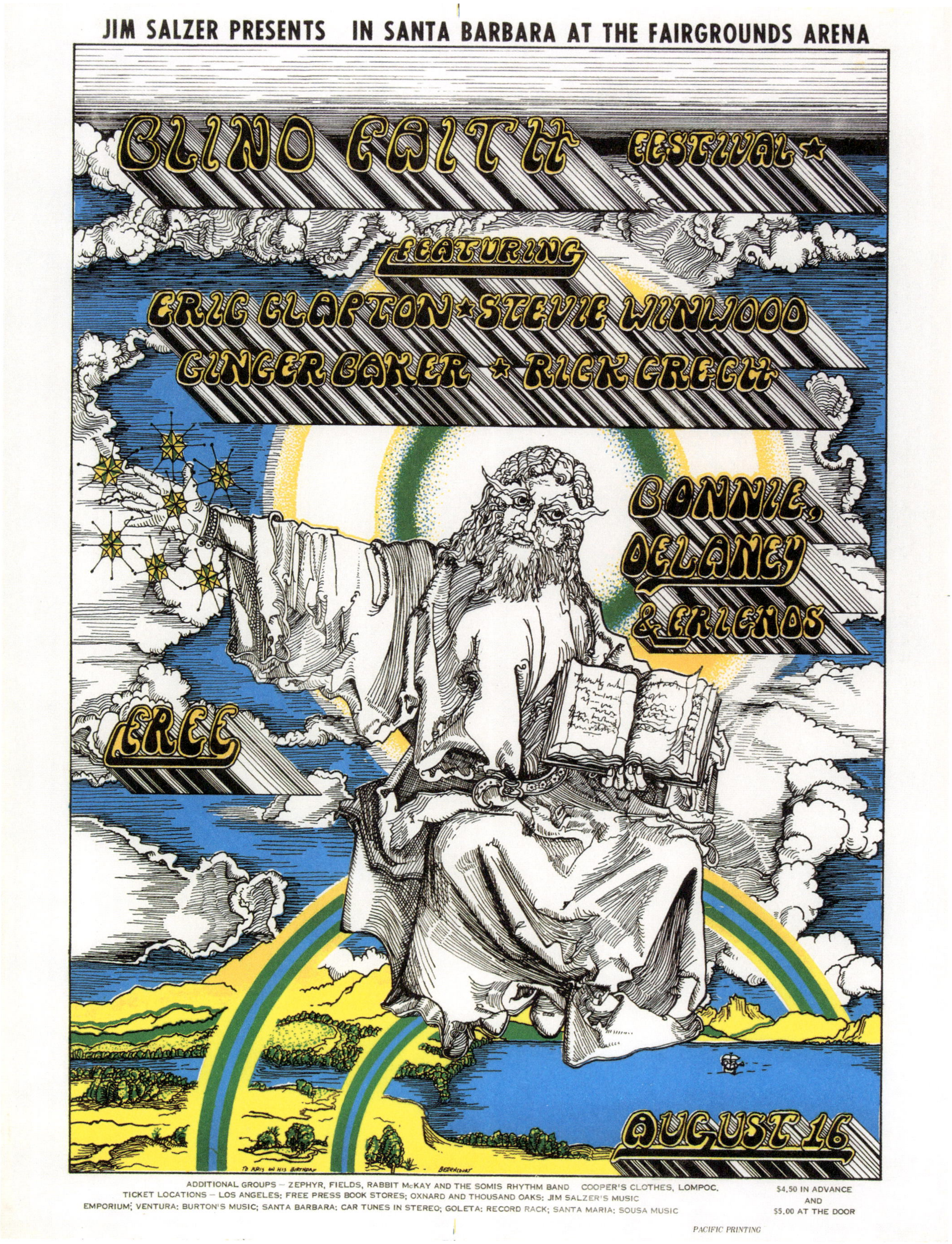

⟫→ Opposite: Bettencourt's poster for a 1969 concert headlined by Led Zeppelin is a riot of clashing and overlapping color, but misspells the headline act's name. The poster made clever use of some pantone primary colors that Bettencourt's printer had left over from another job.

⟫→ This page: Bettencourt's poster for a 1969 Blind Faith concert, also featuring Delaney & Bonnie & Friends, appropriates Renaissance engraving motifs and incorporates them into his psychedelic design.

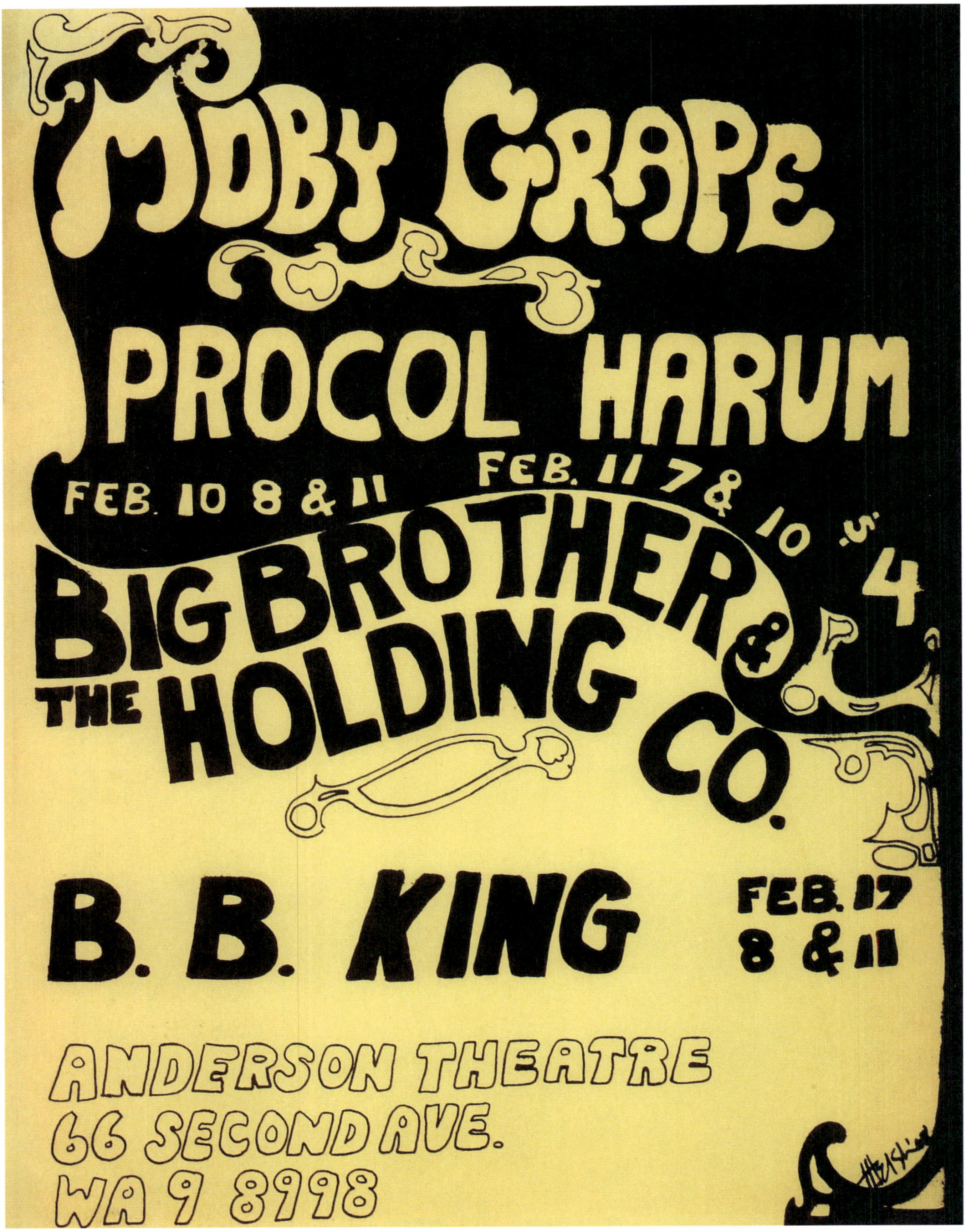

THE NEW YORK SCENE

New York was always much harder and heavier than California. The Velvet Underground dressed somberly, sometimes in leather, and preferred heroin to LSD. Bob Dylan looked more like an English mod. Many of the finest soul singers moved there and the rock bands such as Steely Dan, Blood Sweat and Tears, or Simon & Garfunkel assumed a much higher standard of musical ability than the Bay Area bands. The Greenwich Village folk revival demanded more authenticity, though it also produced commercial-sounding bands such as The Lovin' Spoonful and the Mamas & the Papas. Most played at Bill Graham's Fillmore East (which opened in 1968) when he expanded his business empire to the East Coast.

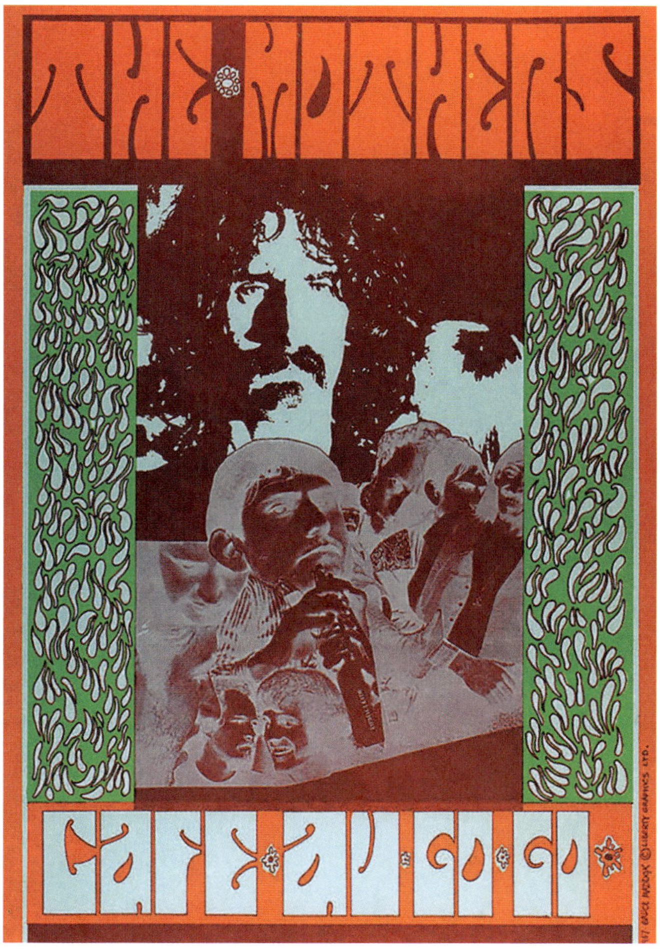

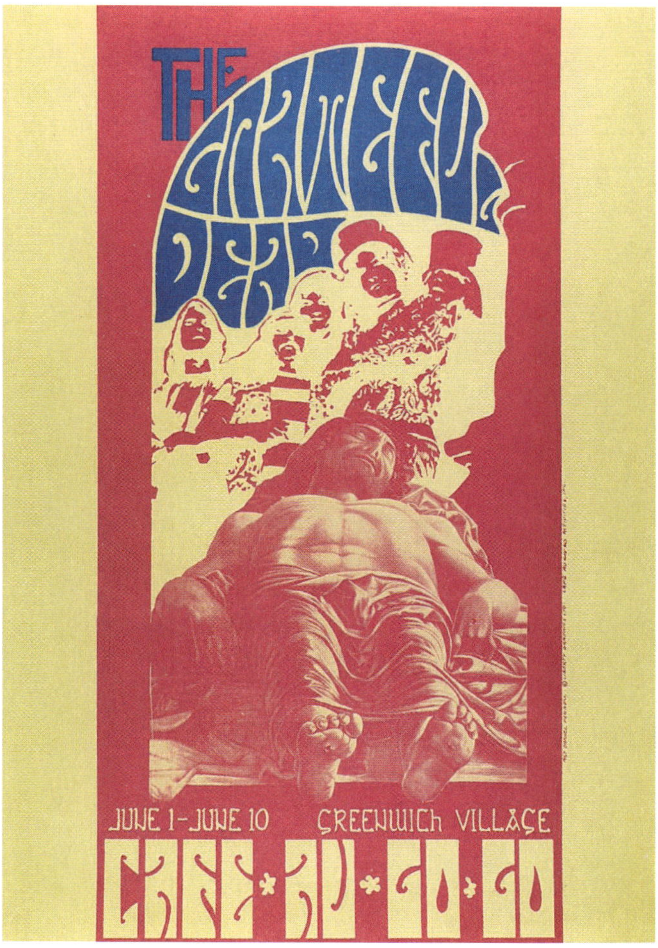

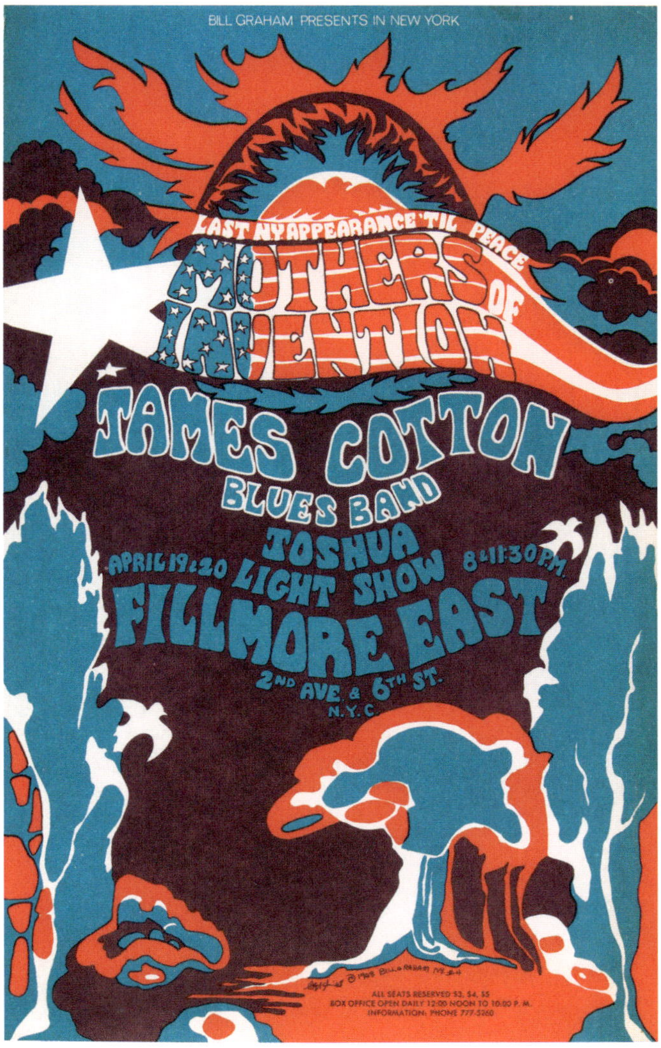

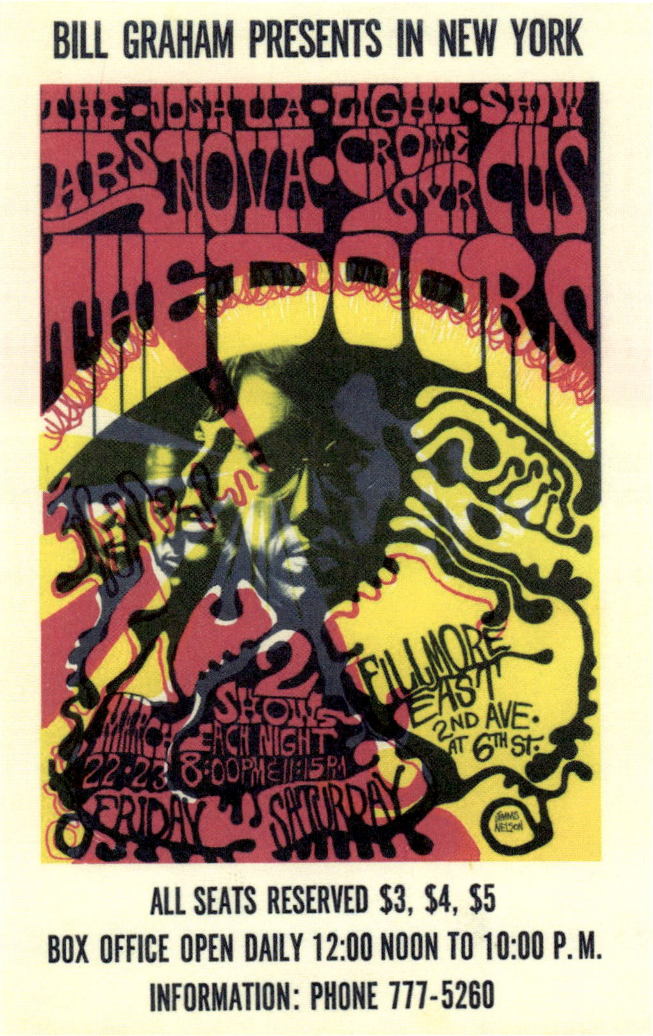

⟶ Opposite: design for a US/UK line-up at the Anderson Theatre.

⟶ This page: posters promoting gigs at the Cafe Au Go Go (top) and the Fillmore East (bottom) by artists including Bruce Maddox for Liberty Graphics (top left) and Helen Hersh (bottom left).

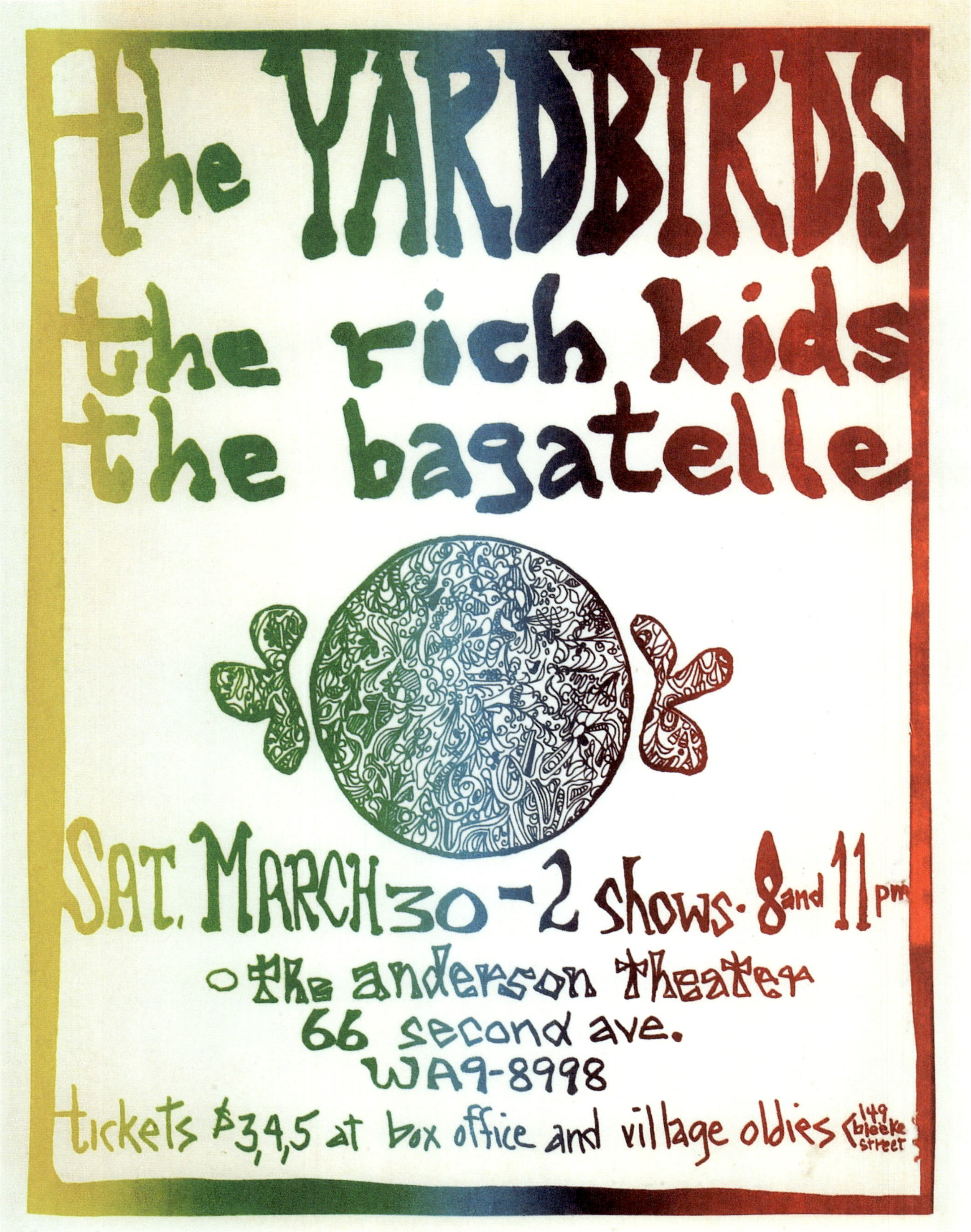

THE SPLIT-FOUNTAIN EFFECT

Split-fountain printing has been around since the mid-19th century. During the psychedelic poster period, it was revived, usually on manual silk-screen prints; the colored inks were placed at the top of the screen and pulled down with a squeegee. As the popularity of the designs increased, it was used to mass-produce posters by loading the ink trays, or fountains, with different colored inks and letting the rollers spread the inks evenly. In both cases, the inks eventually bled into each other, making no two impressions exactly the same.

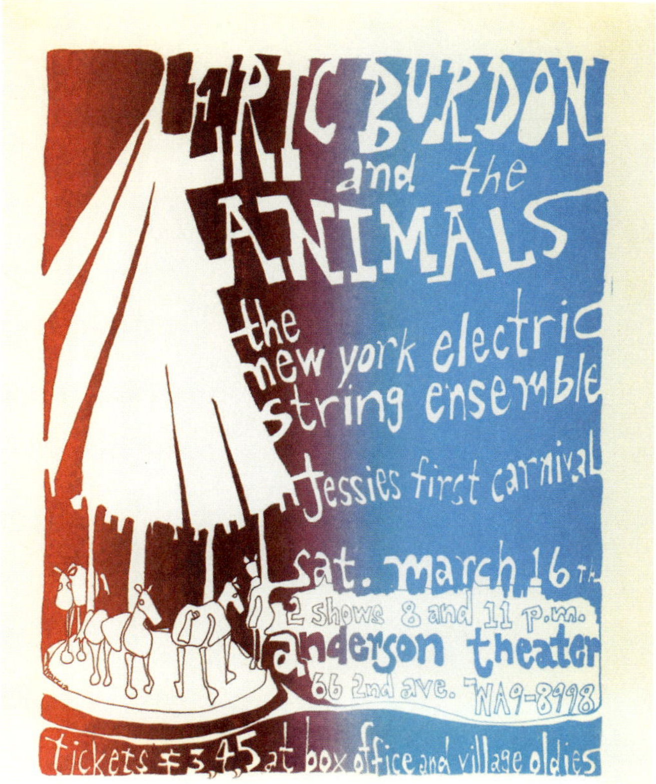

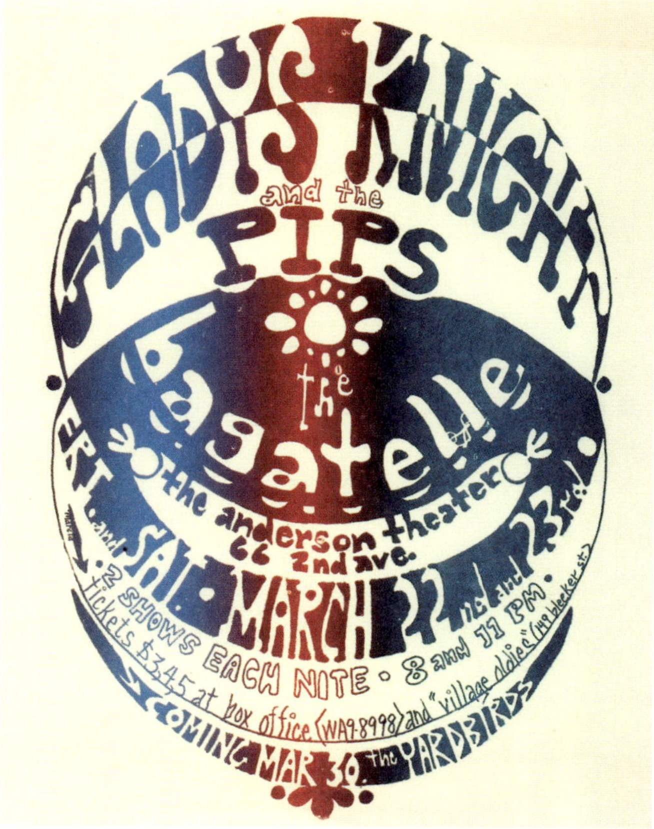

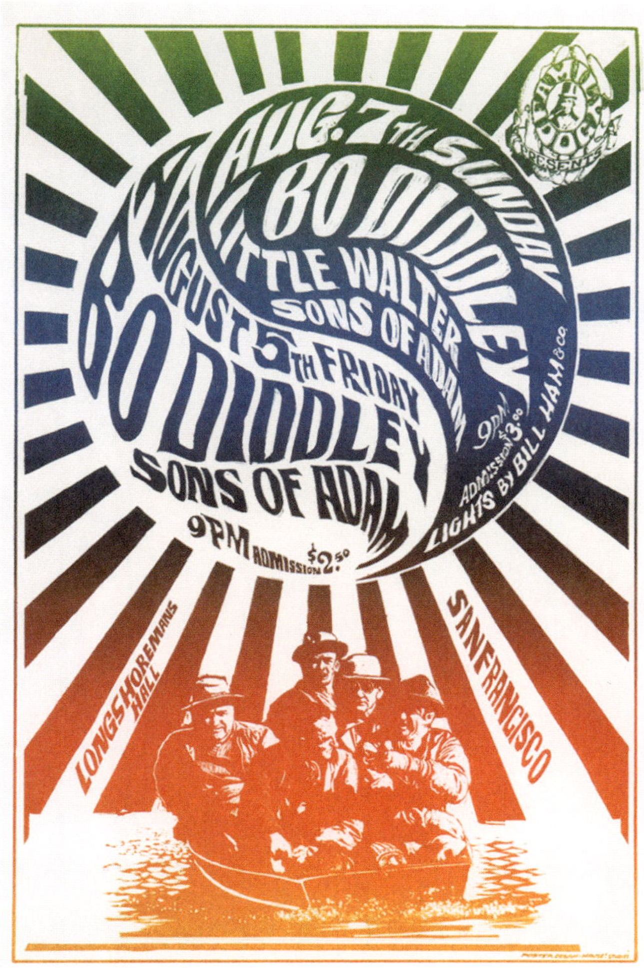

⟫→ Opposite: the Anderson was about a block down the street from Bill Graham's Fillmore East, on the opposite side of the road. This 1968 Yardbirds concert was recorded and initially released by Epic in 1971, but Jimmy Page had it withdrawn, feeling the performance was sub-par. He later produced the songs himself and released them on his own label in 2017.

⟫→ This page: four more examples of split-fountain printing for 1968 concerts. The 1968 poster for Gladys Knight and The Pips advertises the aforementioned Yardbirds concert at the same venue. The Bo Diddley poster, by Mouse and Kelley for Family Dog, dates from 1966 and is known as *Five Men in a Boat*.

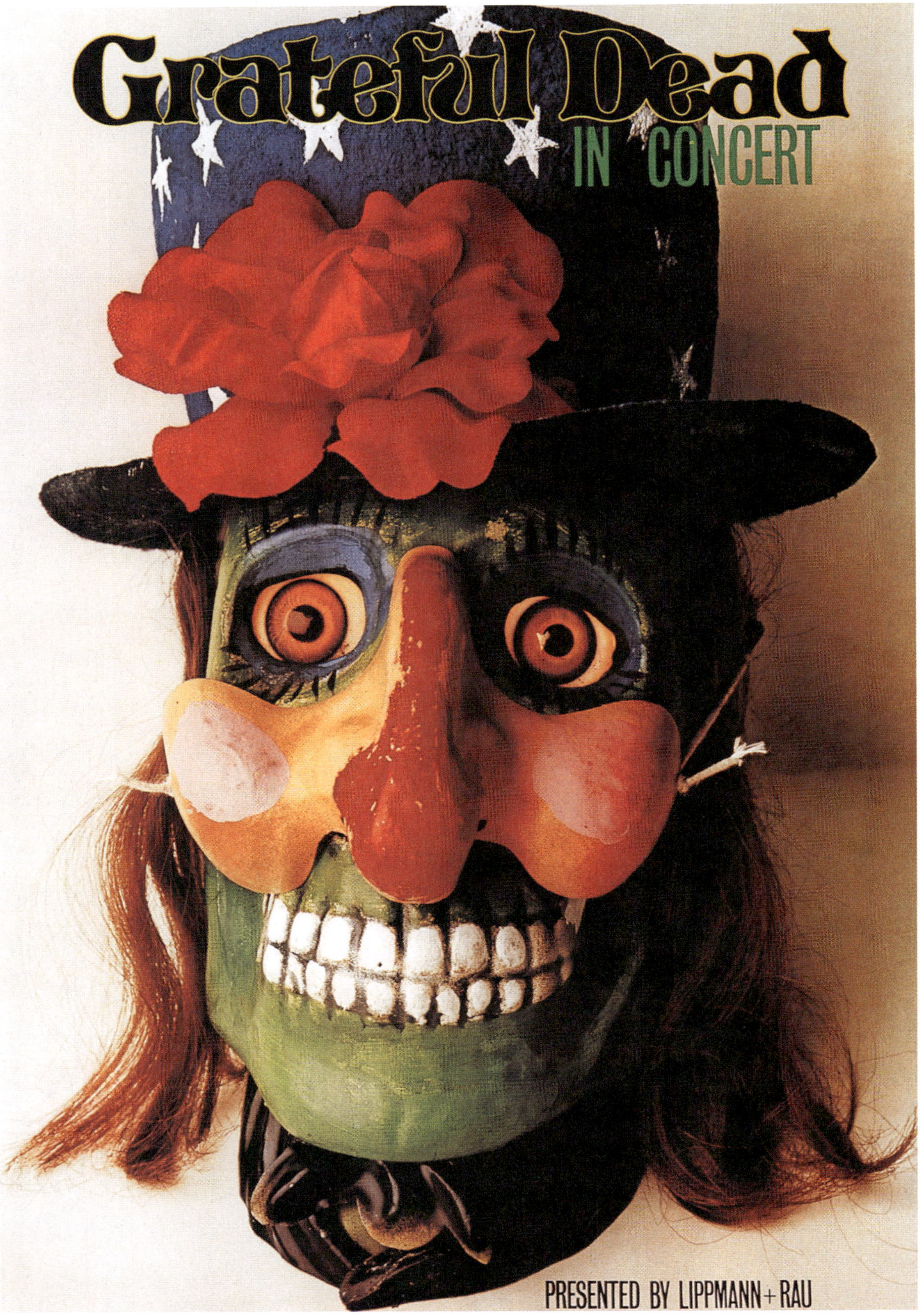

GÜNTHER KIESER

Günther Kieser began his career as a graphic designer in 1949. His work for the concert agency Lippmann + Rau led him to design the famous 1969 Jimi Hendrix poster seen here, made by attaching cables to a portrait of Hendrix and photographing the result. In those pre-digital days everything had to be made by hand: thus, he hand-crafted the decorated Grateful Dead skull for their 1974 German concert tour and photographed it. Berlin curator Tobias Hoffmann has noted of Kieser's style, 'His way of fantasy is his specialty with the picture. Kieser really hates words on his images, so he always puts the typography away from the picture, which is the most important thing.'

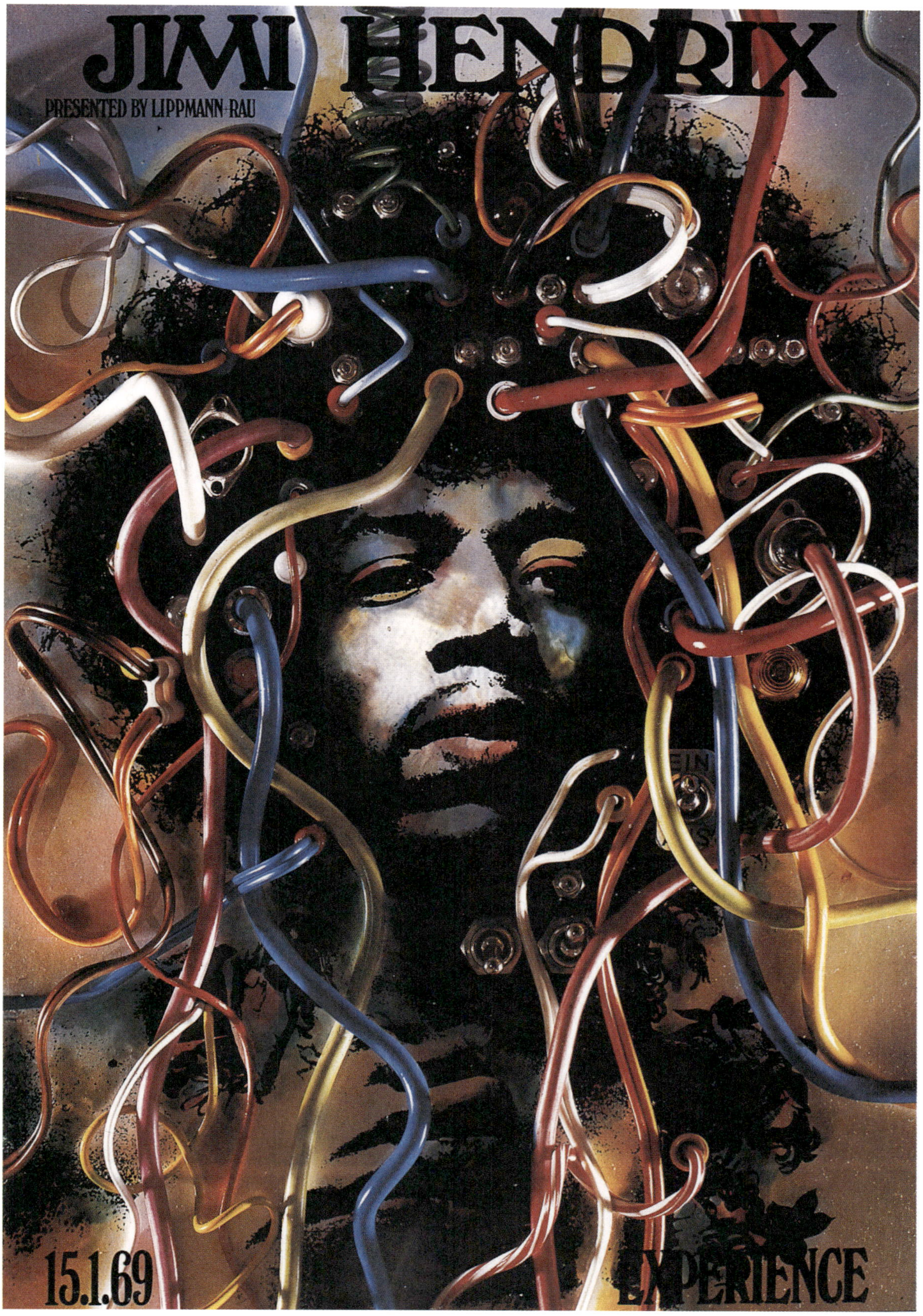

➳ Opposite: Kieser's design reworks the classic Grateful Dead skull and rose in 3D. It was re-used for concerts at various venues on their 1972 European Tour. ➳ This page: a wired-up Hendrix for a poster predictably known as *Medusa*. The concert was actually four days later than the date shown.

ALTAMONT

The end of the hippie scene was heralded by a disastrous free concert staged by the Rolling Stones at Altamont Speedway in California on December 6, 1969. Irked by criticism of high ticket prices for their comeback US concerts that year, the Stones decided to finish the tour with a free event as a goodwill gesture. Bad vibes grew as the day went on, however. Organization was poor and as chaotic scenes escalated there was violence in the crowd —which was 'policed' by Hells Angels. In a grisly climax, fan Meredith Hunter, toting a gun, was stabbed to death by an Angel.

The following year, the era lost two of its major icons. Jimi Hendrix died on September 18, 1970, ignominiously choking on his own vomit. Just over two weeks later, on October 4, Janis Joplin overdosed on heroin.

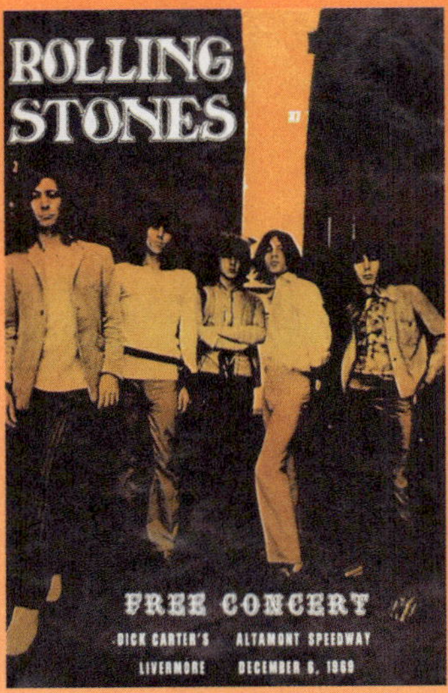

Altamont concert poster, 1969 → The posters for the concert were rush-produced in a couple of days; this image had already been used for the Stones' Oakland Coliseum gig on November 9. The shot of the band in an alley was taken by Ron Rafaelli.

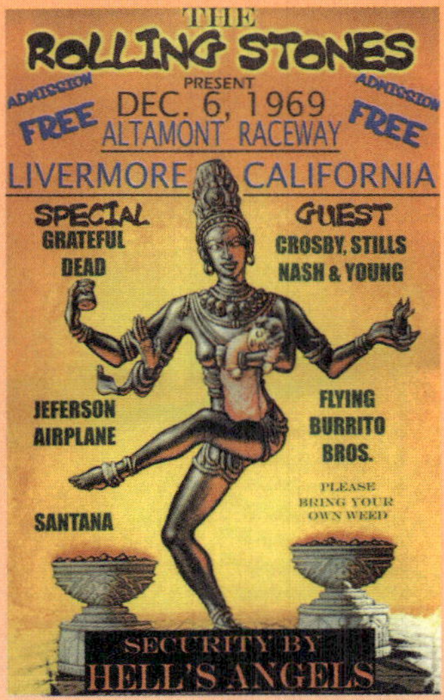

One of the variant Altamont posters, 1969 → West Coast bands dominated the support slots for the Stones at Altamont. In the event, the Grateful Dead—increasingly concerned at the deteriorating situation—left the site before playing a note.

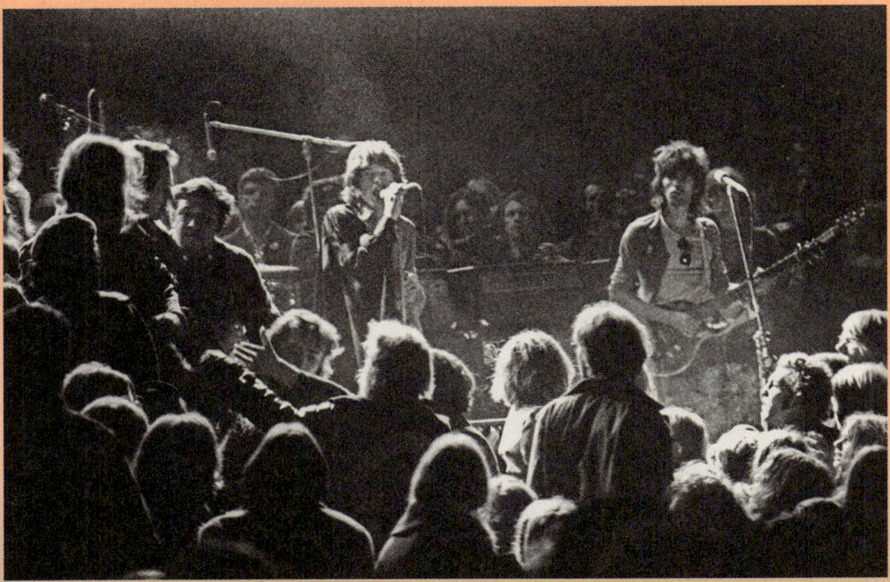

Trouble brewing → A wary Mick Jagger is distracted by off-stage disturbances during the Stones' evening set.

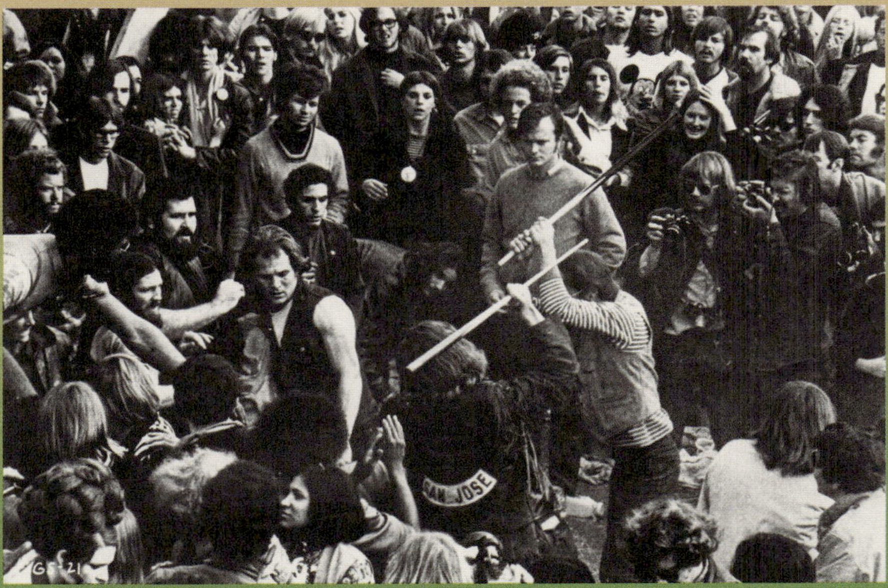

Cue violence → Hells Angels enforce crowd control as a group of aghast concert-goers look on (and take pictures).

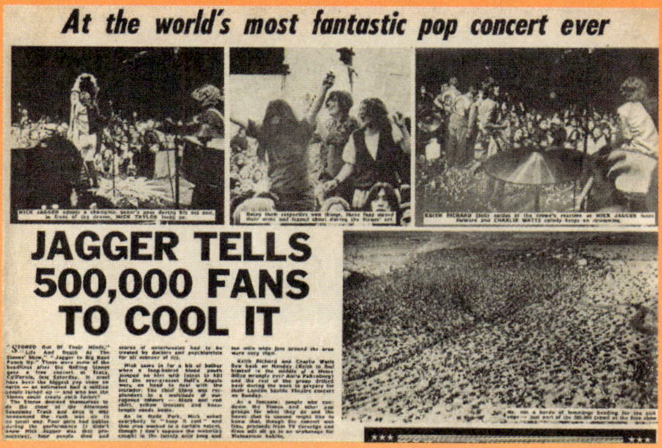

At the world's most fantastic pop concert ever

JAGGER TELLS 500,000 FANS TO COOL IT

Report in *NME*, December 13, 1969 ⟿ A contemporary newspaper report describes the grim scenes at Altamont and Mick Jagger's efforts to play peace-maker. The figure of half a million fans is an overexaggeration.

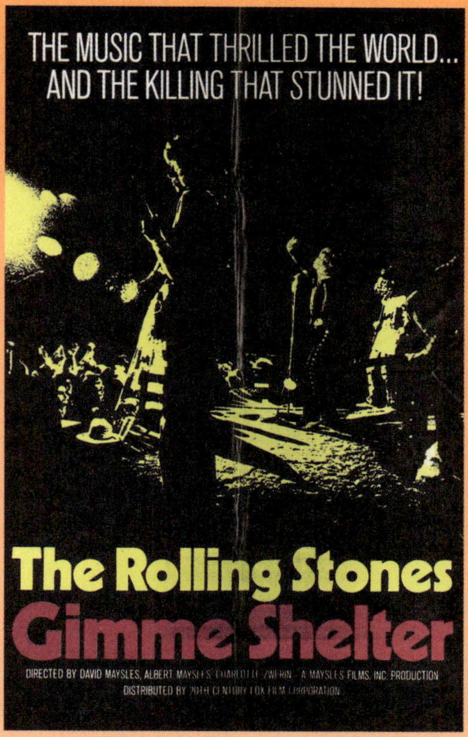

Poster for the movie ⟿ Documentary makers the Maysles brothers had produced a *cinéma vérité*-style film of the Beatles' first US tour. Their account of the Stones' 1969 US jaunt, while featuring some brilliant on-stage performances, wound up capturing the death of the sixties dream.

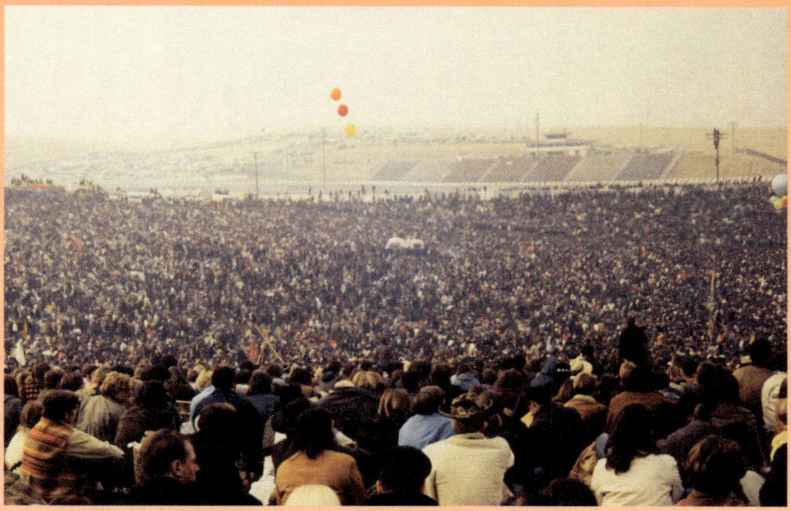

The audience ⟿ Around 300,000 fans turned up for the free concert. The huge gathering contributed to the logistical problems, although the legendary Woodstock Festival, which had taken place just three months earlier and was largely peaceful, had drawn an even larger crowd.

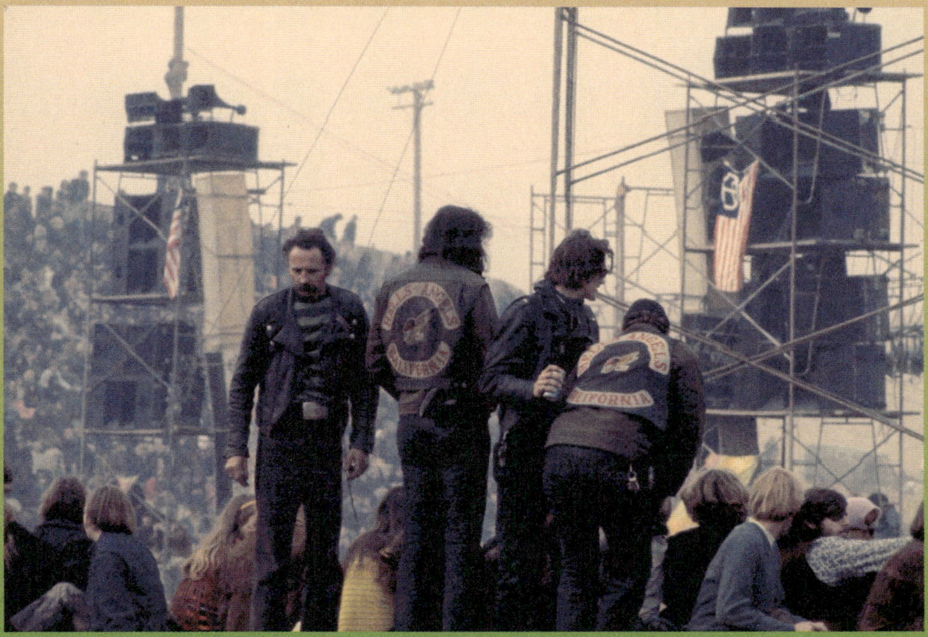

Hells Angels ⟿ Four gang members survey the crowd. 'When you read about a thing this size—like 300,000 people, four people born, four people killed—you don't think of it as a violent thing,' reflected new Stones guitarist Mick Taylor later. 'But that's all I saw: violence all the time.... I've just never seen anything like that before.'

2

COUNTER-CULTURE TAKES CENTER STAGE

’70 ↓ ’77

BY THE SEVENTIES THE
NO LONGER UNDERGROUND.
A MULTI-MILLION-DOLLAR
AND PROMOTERS, BANDS
GREW REMOTE FROM THEIR
WERE EARNING MILLIONS
NEW LINES SUCH AS
LUCRATIVE—AND MORE
RUSHED TO REBRAND THEIR
TO THIS ENORMOUS NEW
PALE REFERENCES TO

COUNTER-CULTURE WAS
ROCK 'N' ROLL HAD BECOME
INDUSTRY. RECORD LABELS
AND THEIR MANAGEMENT
ROOTS. DRUG DEALERS
AND INTRODUCED
COCAINE THAT WERE MORE
ADDICTIVE. BUSINESSMEN
PRODUCTS TO APPEAL
YOUTH MARKET, USING
PSYCHEDELIA TO DO SO.

THE FILLMORE

Bill Graham had never liked the illegibility of psychedelic posters, feeling that it hurt their commercial potential. By 1969, rock had become big business and he could have his own way: he outlined the posters, indicating how big the type should be and where the details should fall, and a designer executed them. This task fell mostly to collagist David Singer, who arrived with a portfolio of thousands of collages and made more posters for Graham than anyone else, beginning with catalog number BG-178 in June 1969 and ending with BG-289 in June 1972. His run included the final Fillmore commemorative poster in June 1972, presented as a gift to Graham after the last show at the venue. Singer's work represents the interim period before rock-poster design went mainstream.

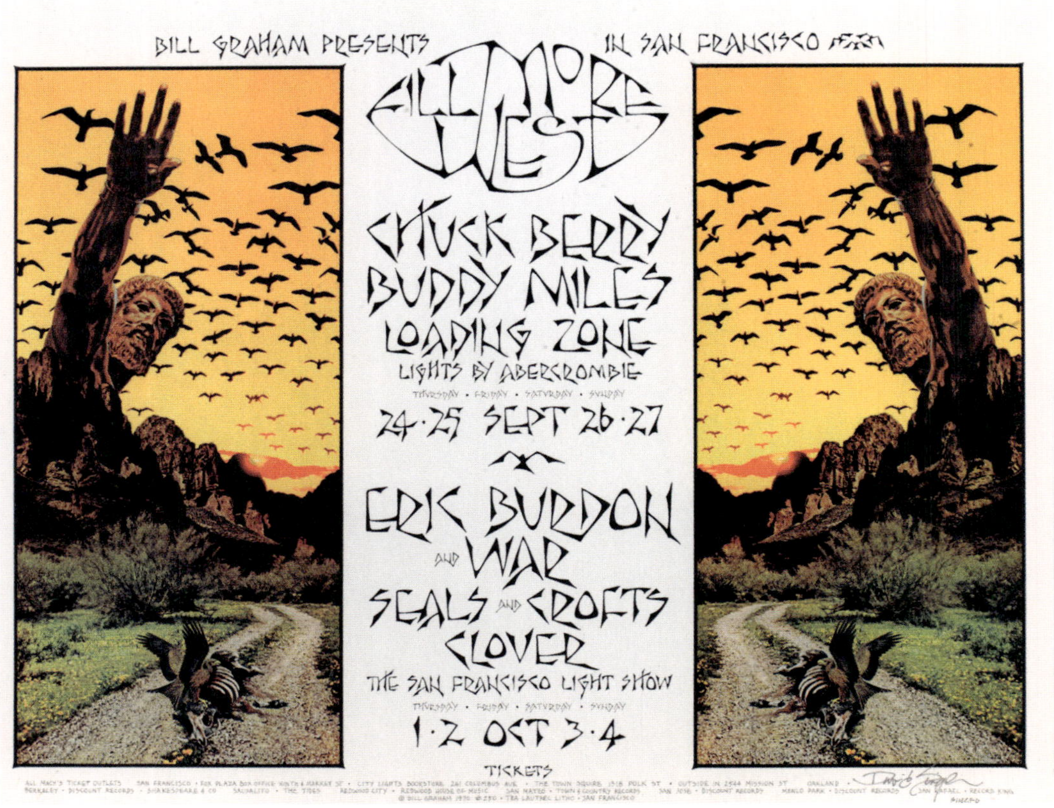

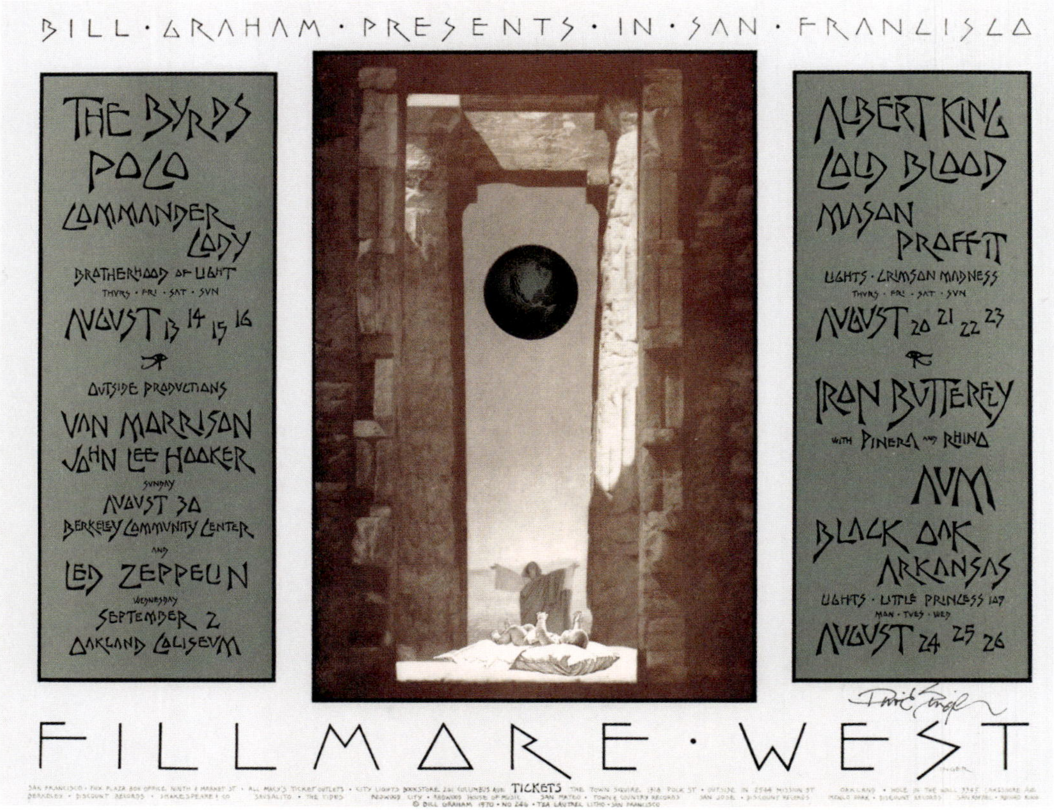

⋙→ This page and opposite: no one was to produce more posters for Bill Graham than David Singer, with his highly distinctive and polished collage work and dream-like designs. The conceptual overtones of the designs, and the sparse but elegant typography, reflect the changing times. The rock market was maturing in the late sixties and early seventies and LPs had replaced singles as the format of choice. ⋙→ Opposite, top: original artwork paste-up (left) and final poster (right) for shows at the Fillmore West and Winterland in April 1970. ⋙→ Opposite, bottom: although fundamentally a collage artist, Singer also created this pair of stylish, Beardsley-esque freehand designs for two May 1971 concerts.

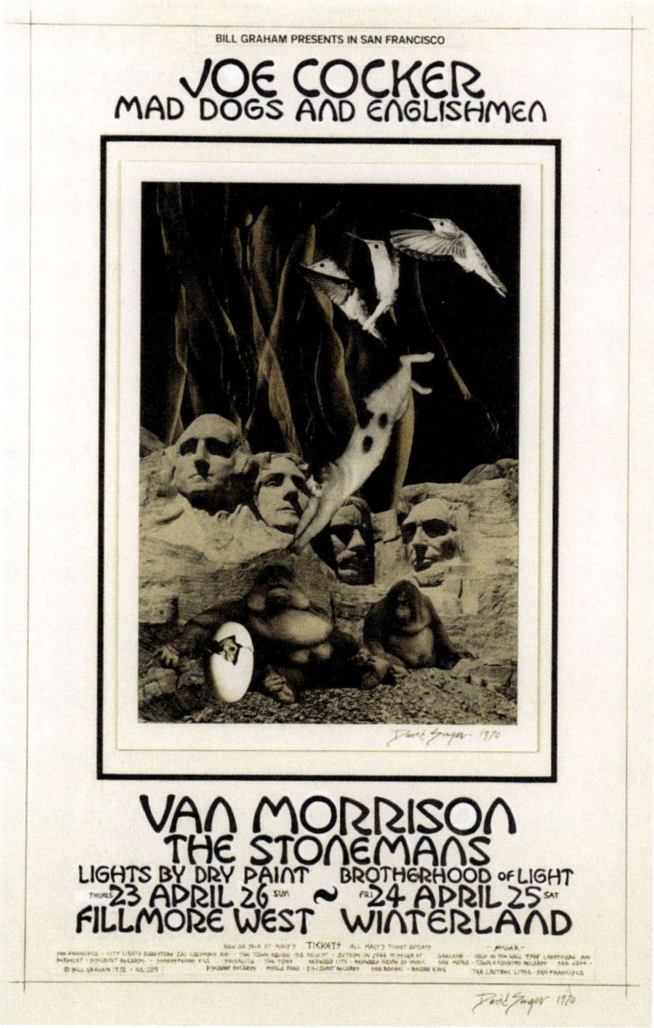
BILL GRAHAM PRESENTS IN SAN FRANCISCO
JOE COCKER
MAD DOGS AND ENGLISHMEN
VAN MORRISON
THE STONEMANS
LIGHTS BY DRY PAINT
BROTHERHOOD OF LIGHT
THURS 23 APRIL 26 SUN
FRI 24 APRIL 25 SAT
FILLMORE WEST
WINTERLAND
TICKETS

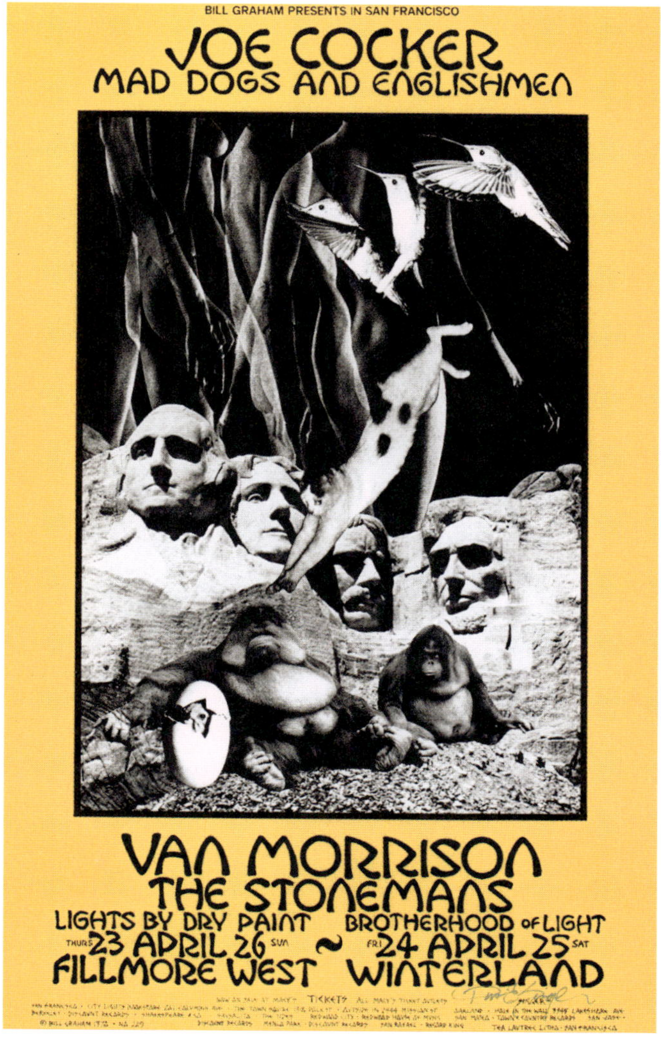
BILL GRAHAM PRESENTS IN SAN FRANCISCO
JOE COCKER
MAD DOGS AND ENGLISHMEN
VAN MORRISON
THE STONEMANS
LIGHTS BY DRY PAINT
BROTHERHOOD OF LIGHT
THURS 23 APRIL 26 SUN
FRI 24 APRIL 25 SAT
FILLMORE WEST
WINTERLAND
TICKETS

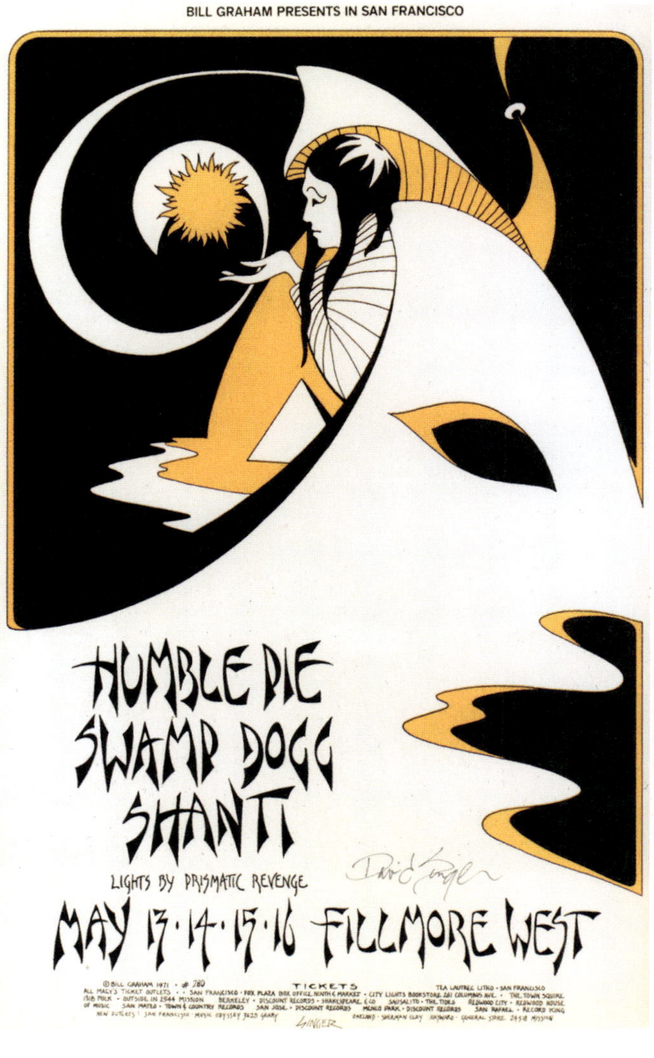
BILL GRAHAM PRESENTS IN SAN FRANCISCO
HUMBLE PIE
SWAMP DOGG
SHANTI
LIGHTS BY PRISMATIC REVENGE
MAY 13·14·15·16 FILLMORE WEST
TICKETS

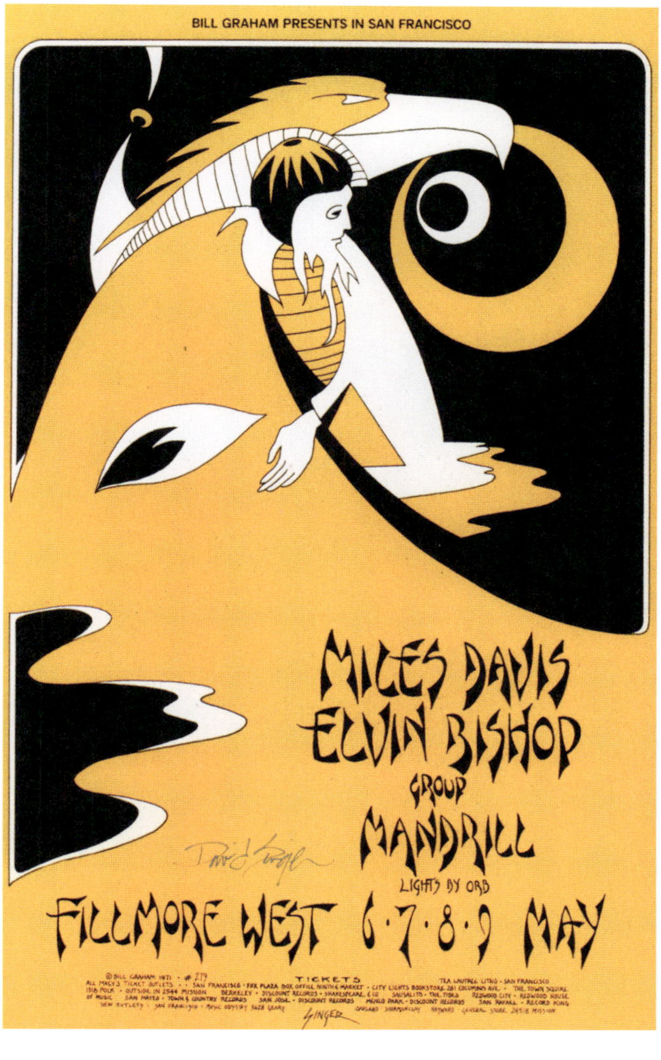
BILL GRAHAM PRESENTS IN SAN FRANCISCO
MILES DAVIS
ELVIN BISHOP
GROUP
MANDRILL
LIGHTS BY ORB
FILLMORE WEST 6·7·8·9 MAY
TICKETS

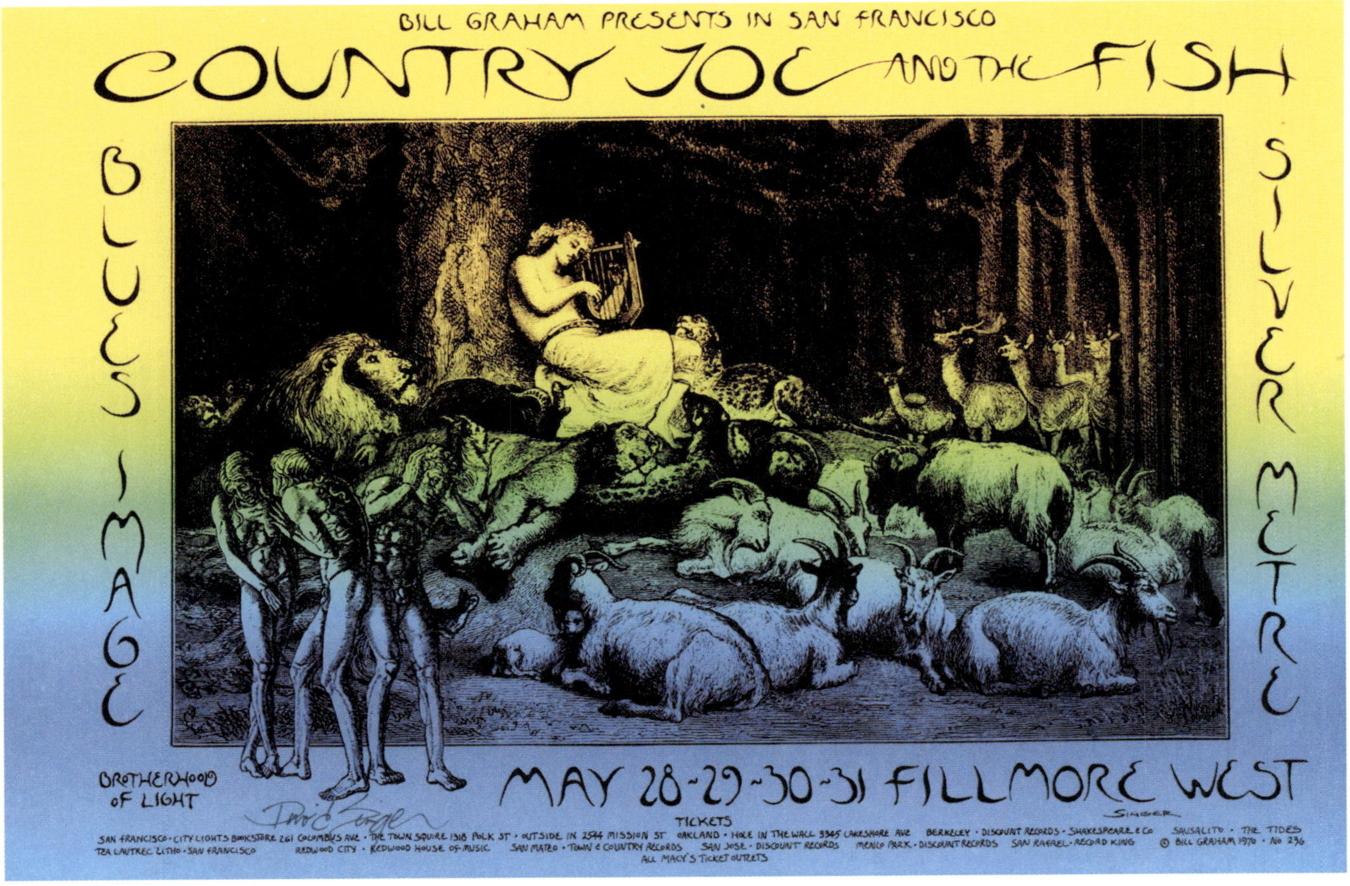

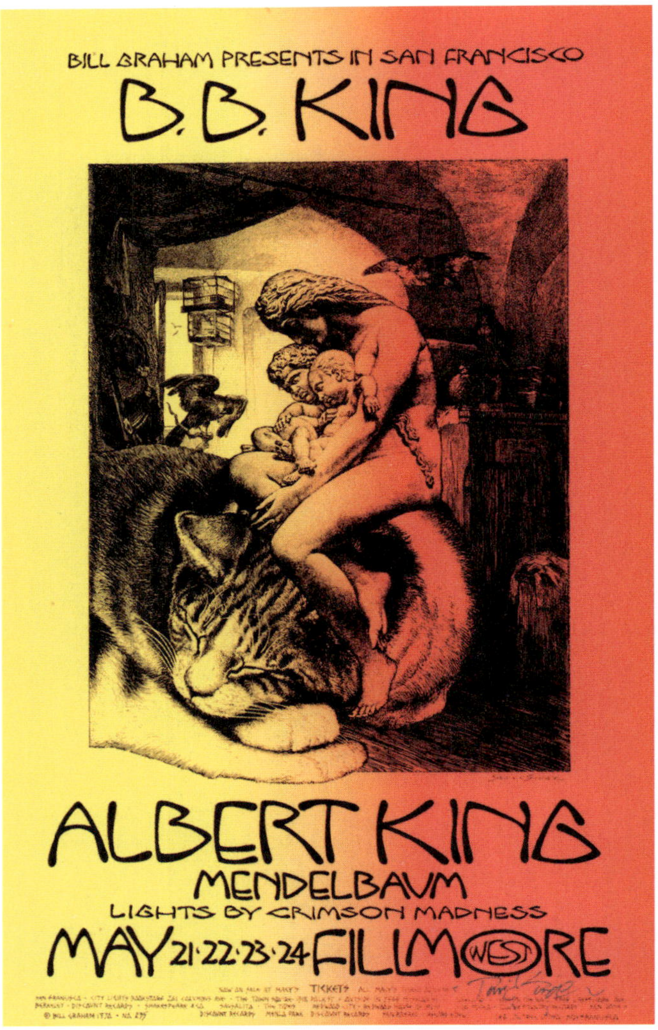

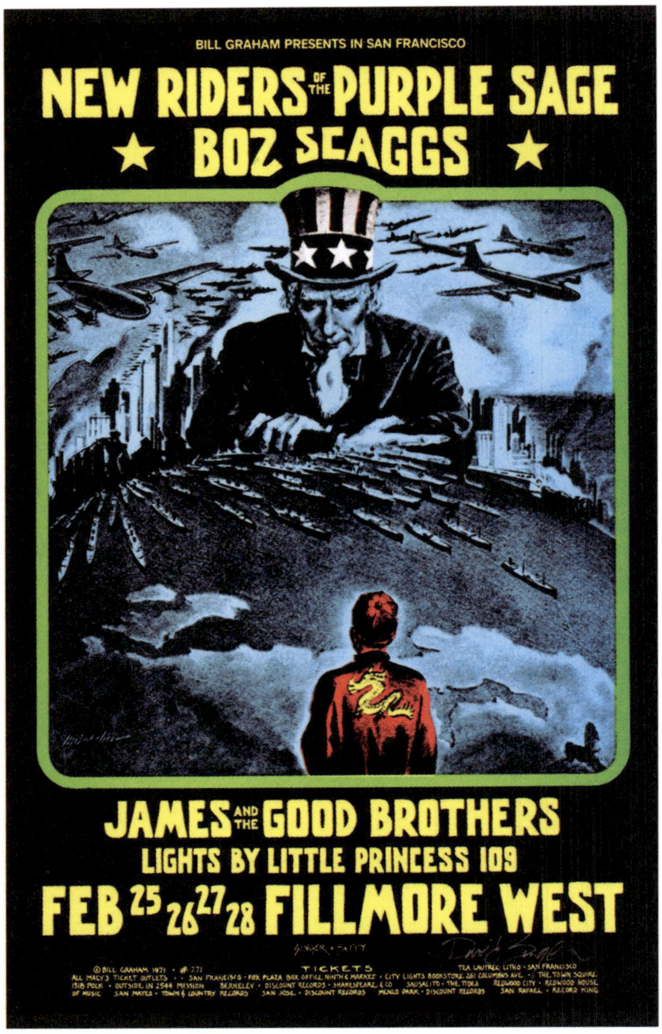

⋙→ This page: all David Singer's posters for Bill Graham were printed at Tea Lautrec Litho. Split-fountain printing enriches two of the designs above, both from 1970. Those in the bottom row were made with Wilfried Sätty; the one on the right (from 1971) is a rare explicit comment on the Vietnam War. ⋙→ Opposite: Singer combines vintage artwork and fluid Art Nouveau lines. The lettering on the Spencer Davis paste-up and poster (center row) reflects the lunar theme of the main image. The cryptic blue design (catalog number BG-287) at the bottom was made for the very last Fillmore show and given to Bill Graham as a gift afterward.

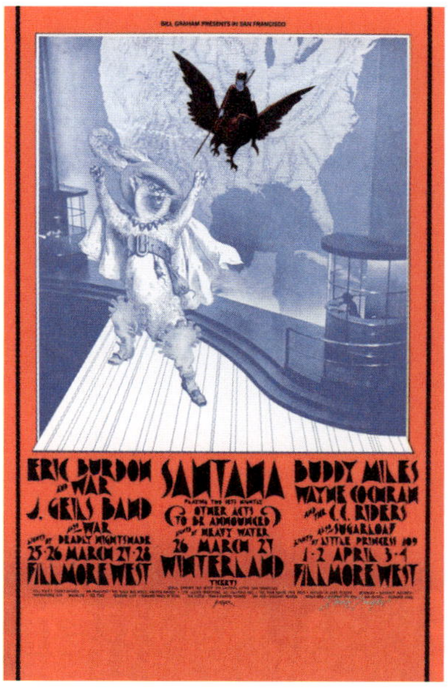
BILL GRAHAM PRESENTS IN SAN FRANCISCO
ERIC BURDON AND WAR
J. GEILS BAND
SANTANA
BUDDY MILES
WAYNE COCHRAN AND THE C.C. RIDERS
25-26 MARCH 27-28 FILLMORE WEST
26 MARCH 27 WINTERLAND
1-2 APRIL 3-4 FILLMORE WEST

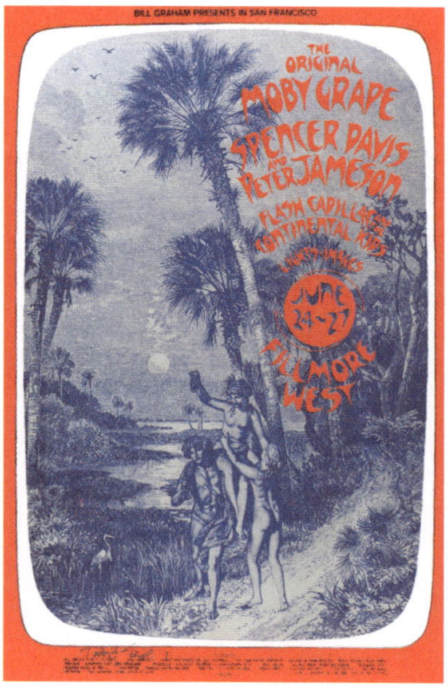
BILL GRAHAM PRESENTS IN SAN FRANCISCO
THE ORIGINAL MOBY GRAPE
SPENCER DAVIS AND PETER JAMESON
FILLMORE WEST

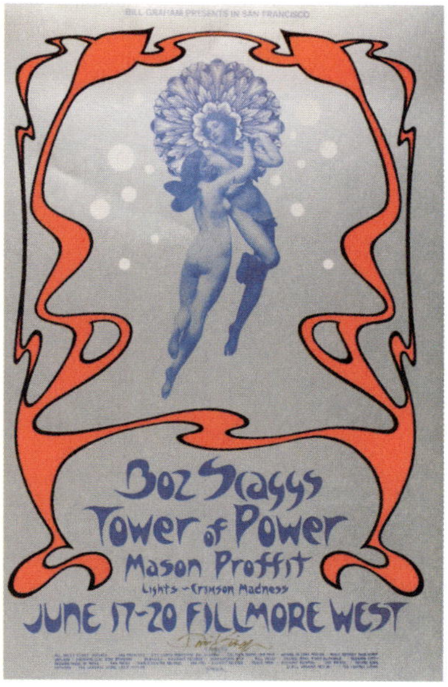
BILL GRAHAM PRESENTS IN SAN FRANCISCO
BOZ SCAGGS
TOWER of POWER
Mason Proffit
Lights - Crimson Madness
JUNE 17-20 FILLMORE WEST

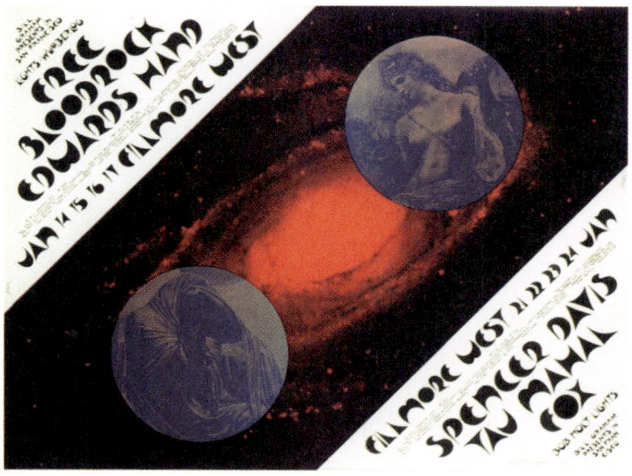
FREE
BLOODROCK
EDWARDS HAND
JAN 14 15 16 17 FILLMORE WEST
FILLMORE WEST 21 22 23 24 JAN
SPENCER DAVIS
TAJ MAHAL
COX

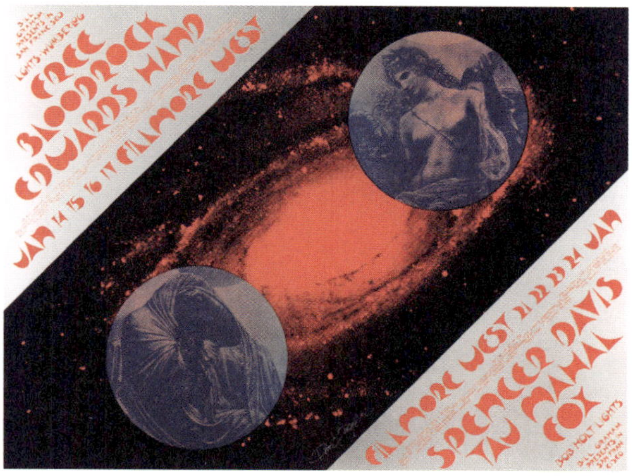
FREE
BLOODROCK
EDWARDS HAND
JAN 14 15 16 17 FILLMORE WEST
FILLMORE WEST 21 22 23 24 JAN
SPENCER DAVIS
TAJ MAHAL
COX

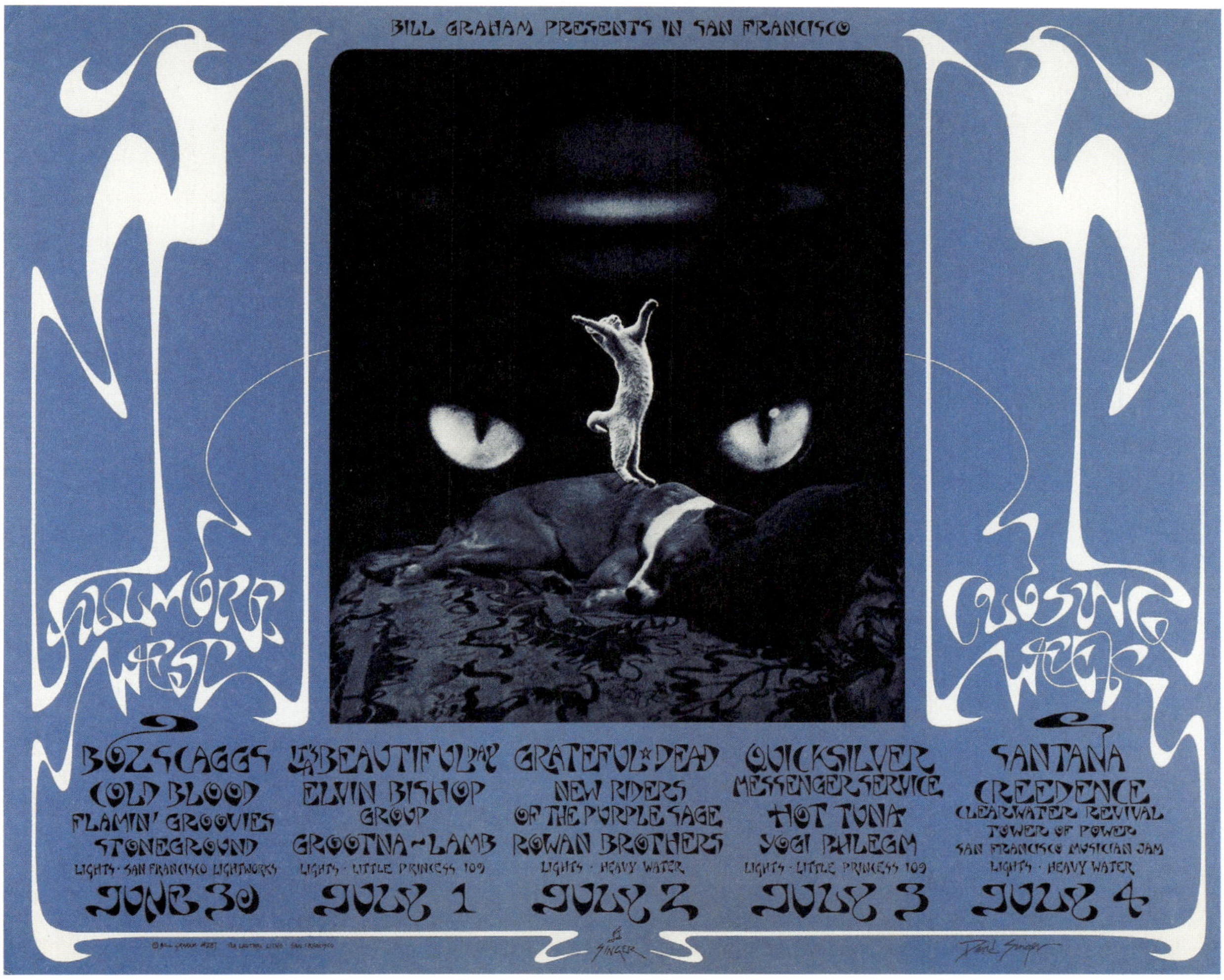
BILL GRAHAM PRESENTS IN SAN FRANCISCO
FILLMORE WEST
CLOSING WEEK
BOZ SCAGGS
COLD BLOOD
FLAMIN' GROOVIES
STONEGROUND
LIGHTS · SAN FRANCISCO LIGHTWORKS
JUNE 30
IT'S A BEAUTIFUL DAY
ELVIN BISHOP GROUP
GROOTNA ~ LAMB
LIGHTS · LITTLE PRINCESS 109
JULY 1
GRATEFUL DEAD
NEW RIDERS OF THE PURPLE SAGE
ROWAN BROTHERS
LIGHTS · HEAVY WATER
JULY 2
QUICKSILVER MESSENGER SERVICE
HOT TUNA
YOGI PHLEGM
LIGHTS · LITTLE PRINCESS 109
JULY 3
SANTANA
CREEDENCE CLEARWATER REVIVAL
TOWER OF POWER
SAN FRANCISCO MUSICIAN JAM
LIGHTS · HEAVY WATER
JULY 4

→ For this Fillmore West/Winterland poster, Singer made a rare departure from the signature picture-frame style he usually used in his work for Bill Graham, although he retained collage as his medium of choice. The central motif of the hand holding the stem with eyes for petals is based on a detail in the painting *Saint Lucy* by Francesco del Cossa (*c.* 1430–1477).

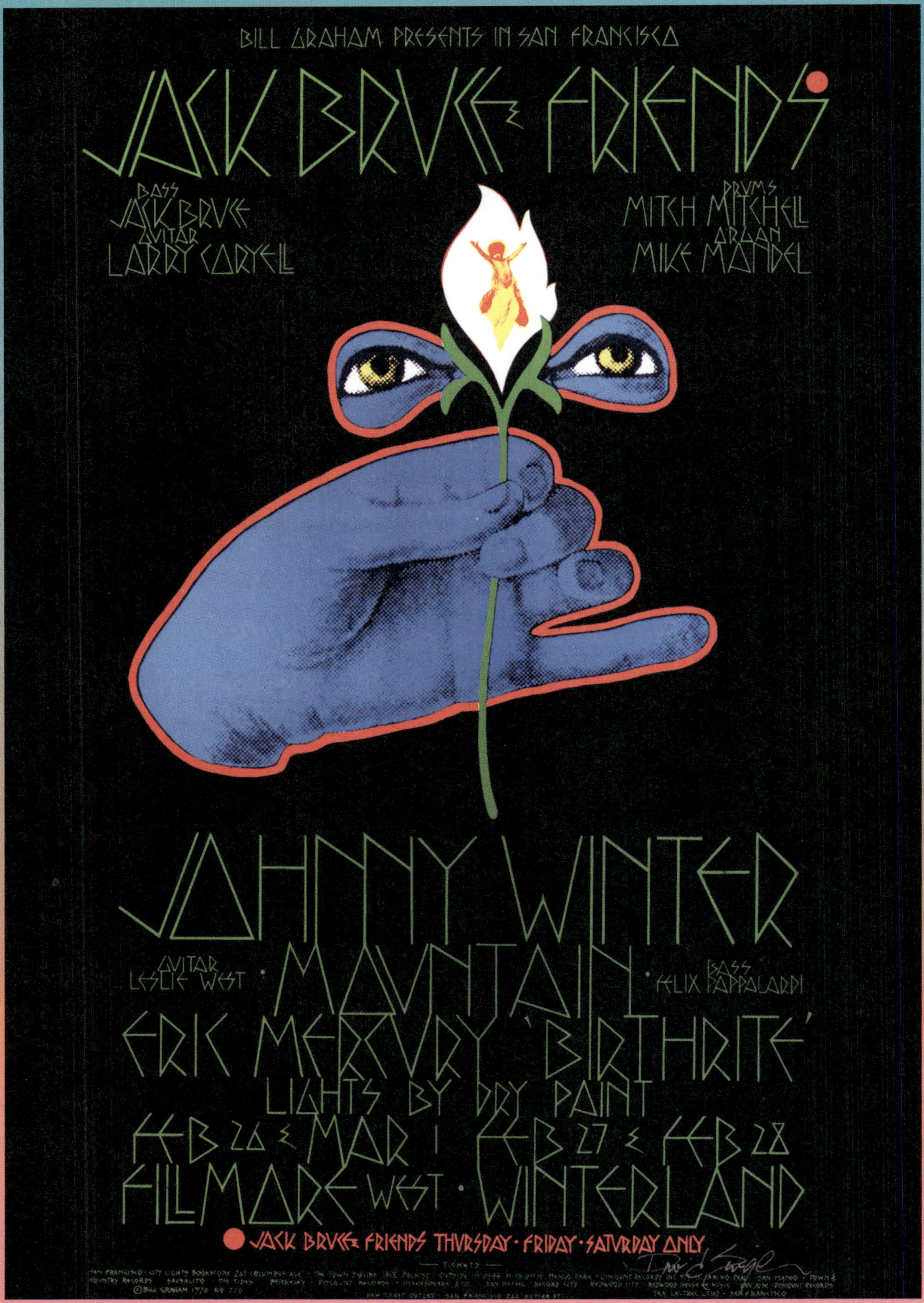

DAVID SINGER (1941–)

THE FILLMORE'S LAST AND MOST PROLIFIC POSTER ARTIST, DAVID SINGER WAS RAISED IN PENNSYLVANIA, AND PENNSYLVANIA DUTCH IMAGERY AND ANTIQUES WERE AN EARLY INFLUENCE ON HIS ART. AFTER A YEAR AT PENN STATE UNIVERSITY HE JOINED THE NAVY AND WAS EVENTUALLY POSTED TO SAN FRANCISCO, WHERE HE RETURNED AFTER HIS DISCHARGE IN 1964. ⟶ HE SETTLED INTO THE HIPPIE SCENE, BEGAN SMOKING POT, AND WENT TO THE AVALON AND FILLMORE AT WEEKENDS. THE POSTERS OF MOSCOSO, MOUSE, KELLEY AND WILSON INSPIRED HIM TO TRY FOR A COMMERCIAL CAREER IN ART. A CHANCE GLIMPSE OF A MOSCOSO POSTER FEATURING A COLLAGE GALVANIZED HIM TO CREATE HIS OWN COLLAGE PORTFOLIO. HE WORKED ON HIS LIVING-ROOM FLOOR, USING PICTURES HE HAD TORN OUT OF MAGAZINES OVER THE YEARS. ⟶ TURNED DOWN BY SEVERAL PUBLISHERS AND UNSURE HOW TO MAKE COMMERCIAL USE OF HIS WORK, SINGER APPROACHED MOSCOSO FOR ADVICE. MOSCOSO WAS IMPRESSED BY HIS PORTFOLIO AND SUGGESTED HE CONTACT BILL GRAHAM. AT THEIR FIRST MEETING, GRAHAM—EQUALLY IMPRESSED—COMMISSIONED TWELVE POSTERS FROM HIM ON THE SPOT. ⟶ FROM 1969 TO 1971, SINGER PRODUCED SIXTY-SEVEN POSTERS FOR BILL GRAHAM, INCLUDING THE SPECIAL DOUBLE-SIZE POSTER FOR THE FINAL FILLMORE WEEKLY CONCERT IN JULY 1971. HIS POSTERS OFTEN BROKE WITH THEIR PSYCHEDELIC PREDECESSORS' HALLMARKS OF LURID COLORS, COMPLEX PATTERNS, AND DELIBERATELY ILLEGIBLE LETTERING. ⟶ AFTER THE FILLMORE CLOSED, SINGER DESIGNED A FURTHER EIGHT POSTERS FOR BILL GRAHAM SPECIAL EVENTS FEATURING ARTISTS SUCH AS THE STONES, THE WHO, SANTANA, AND PAUL MCCARTNEY. HE REMAINS AN ACTIVE ARTIST—MOST NOTABLY, HE HAS CREATED THE LOGO AND SOME ONE HUNDRED POSTER DESIGNS FOR CALIFORNIA BAND MOONALICE.

US UNDERGROUND COMIX

Beginning with Robert Crumb's *Zap* in 1968, many poster artists realized there was more scope for their imagination (and more money if their ideas caught on) in underground comix. Publishers such as Apex Novelties and Print Mint weathered lawsuits to sell them through head shops and other underground outlets. The boom years were 1970–72, but the rapid decline of the counter-culture scene in 1973 led to the 'Great Comix Slump.'

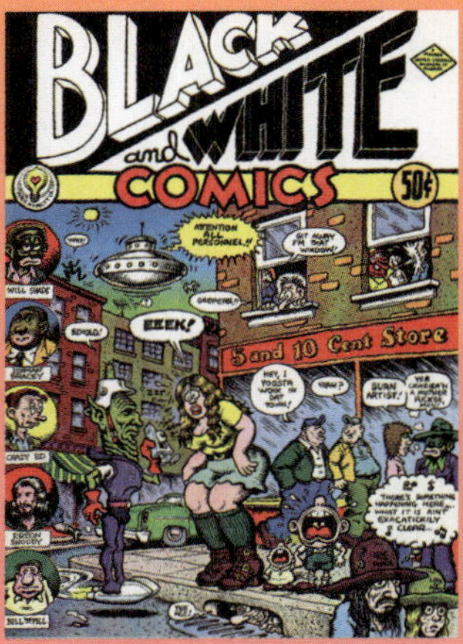

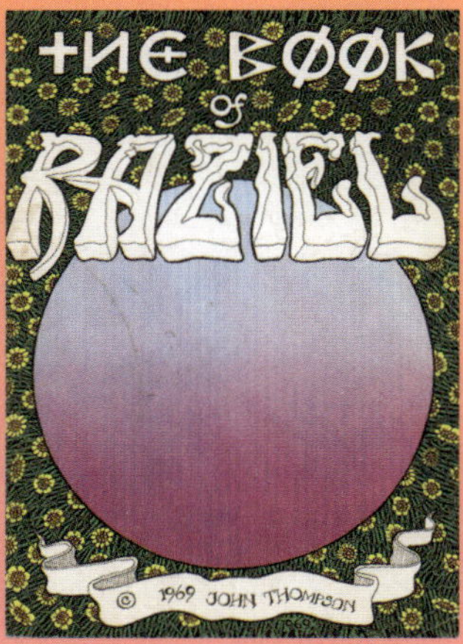

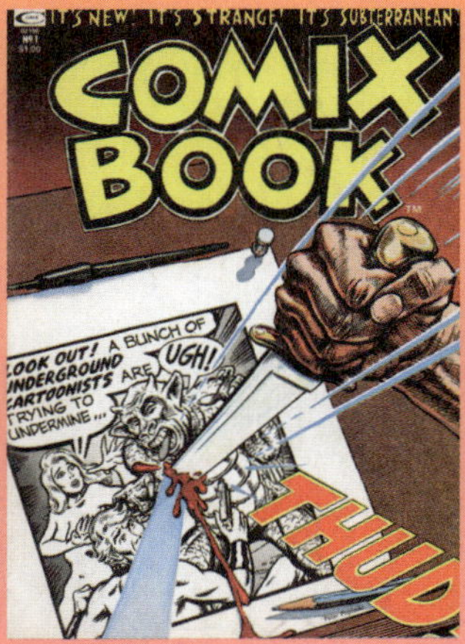

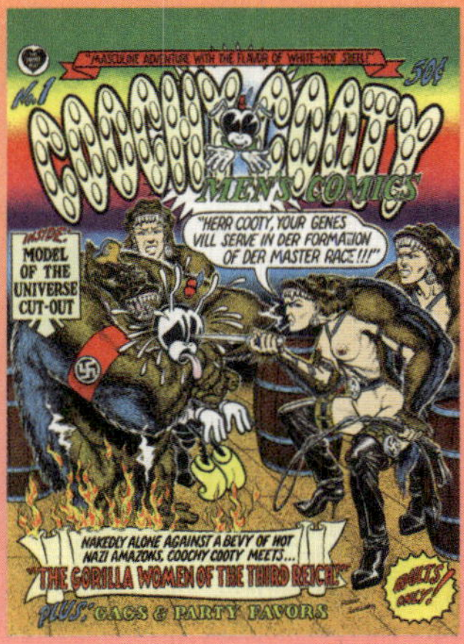

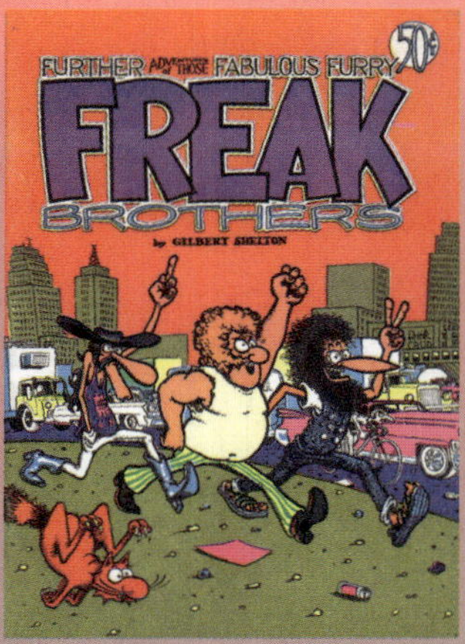

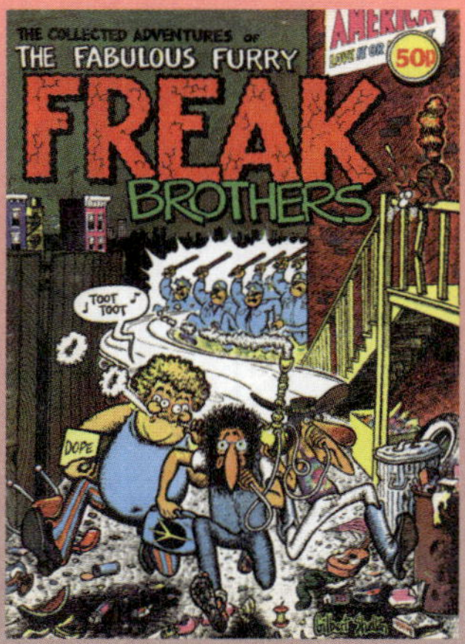

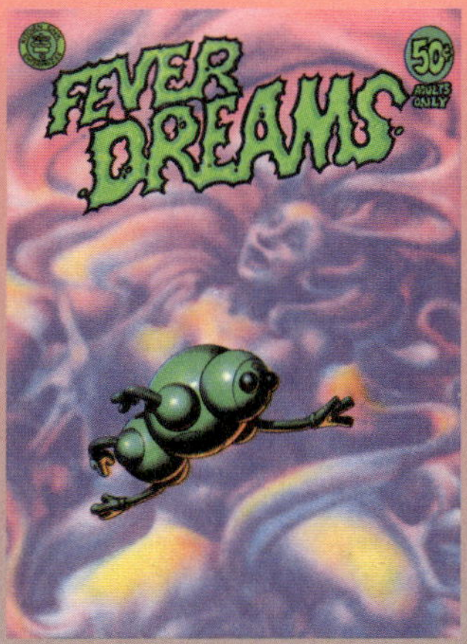

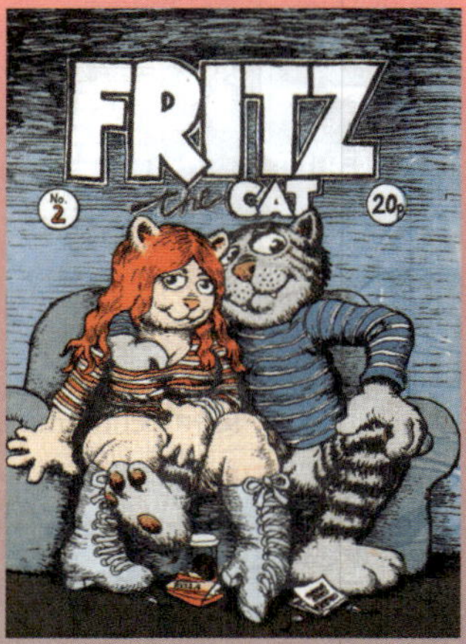

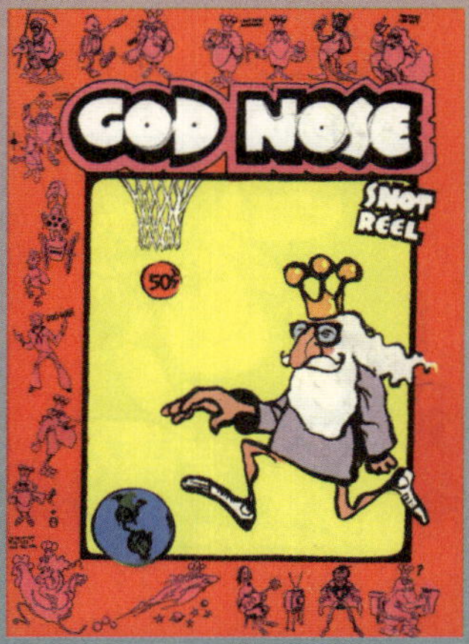

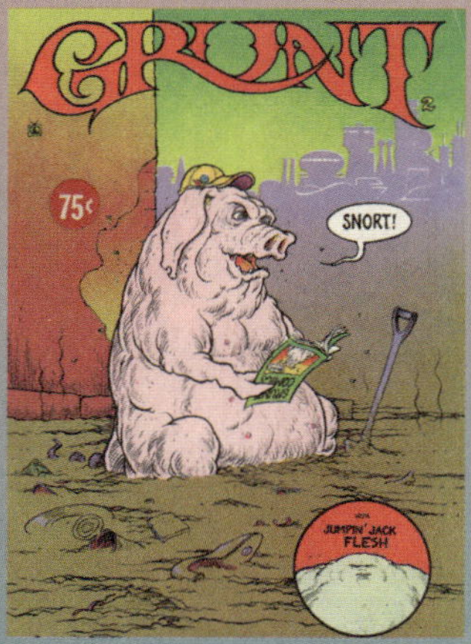

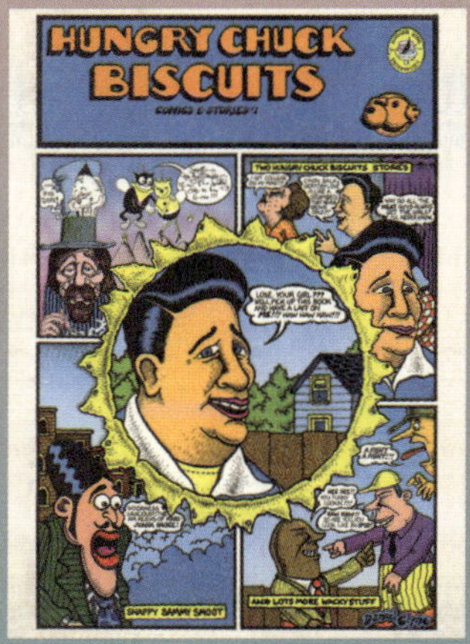

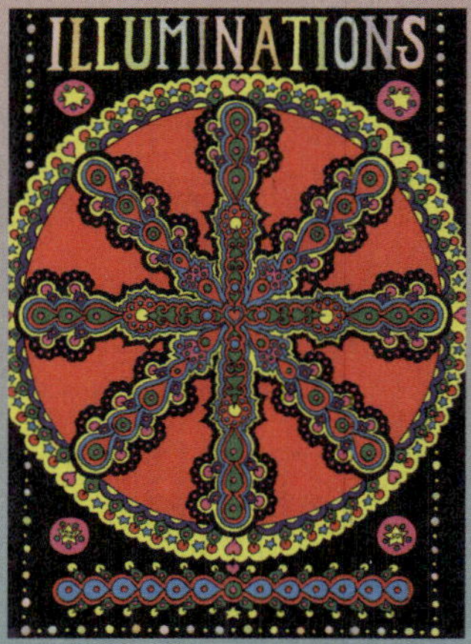

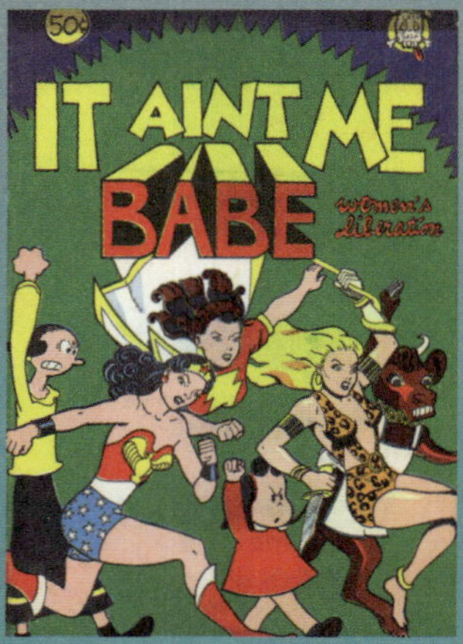

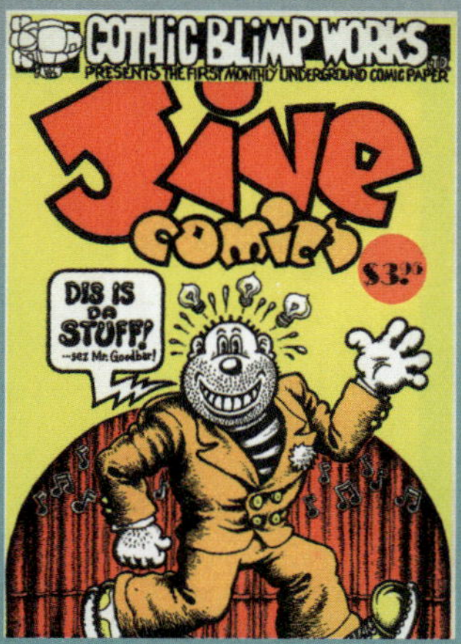

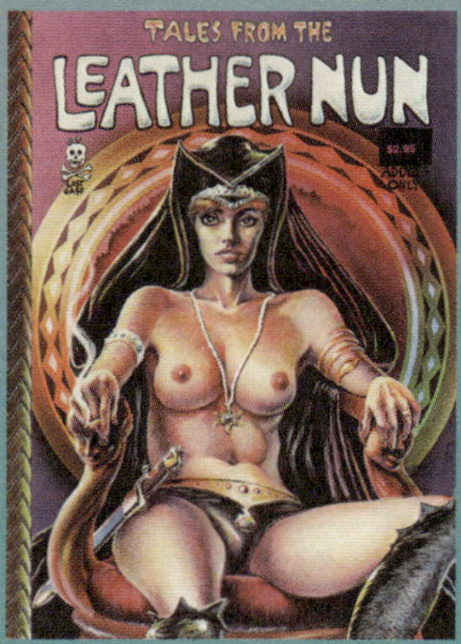

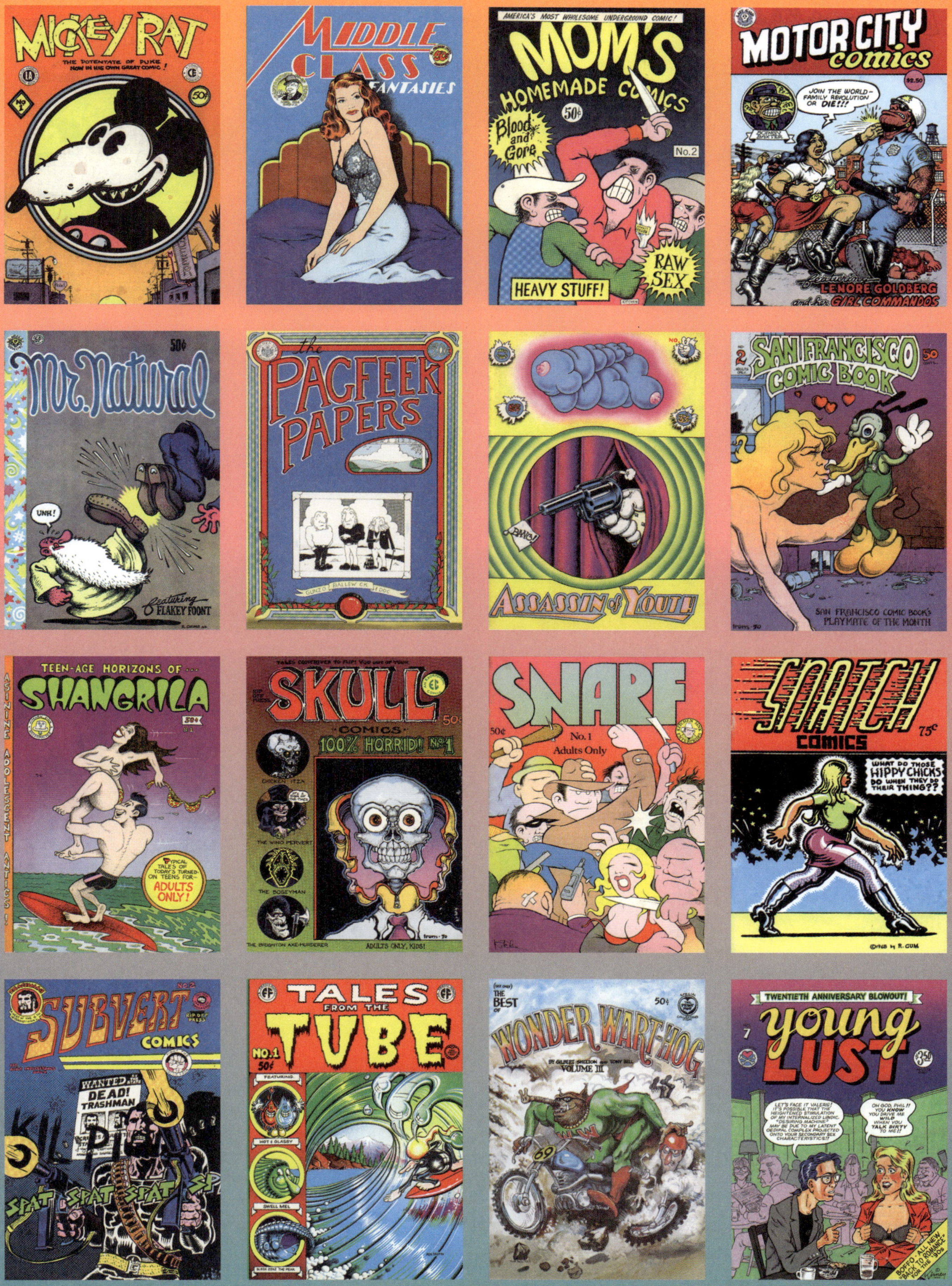

American underground comix were very much parodies of the existing full-color comic books that the cartoonists had grown up with, such as *Superman* and *Detective Comics*, but they stuck very closely to the existing design conventions. Creators used exactly the same size format as conventional comics so that distributors and retailers would take their work, and although their title lettering reflected its sixties counter-cultural origins, it was designed for legibility and sales (unlike the posters).

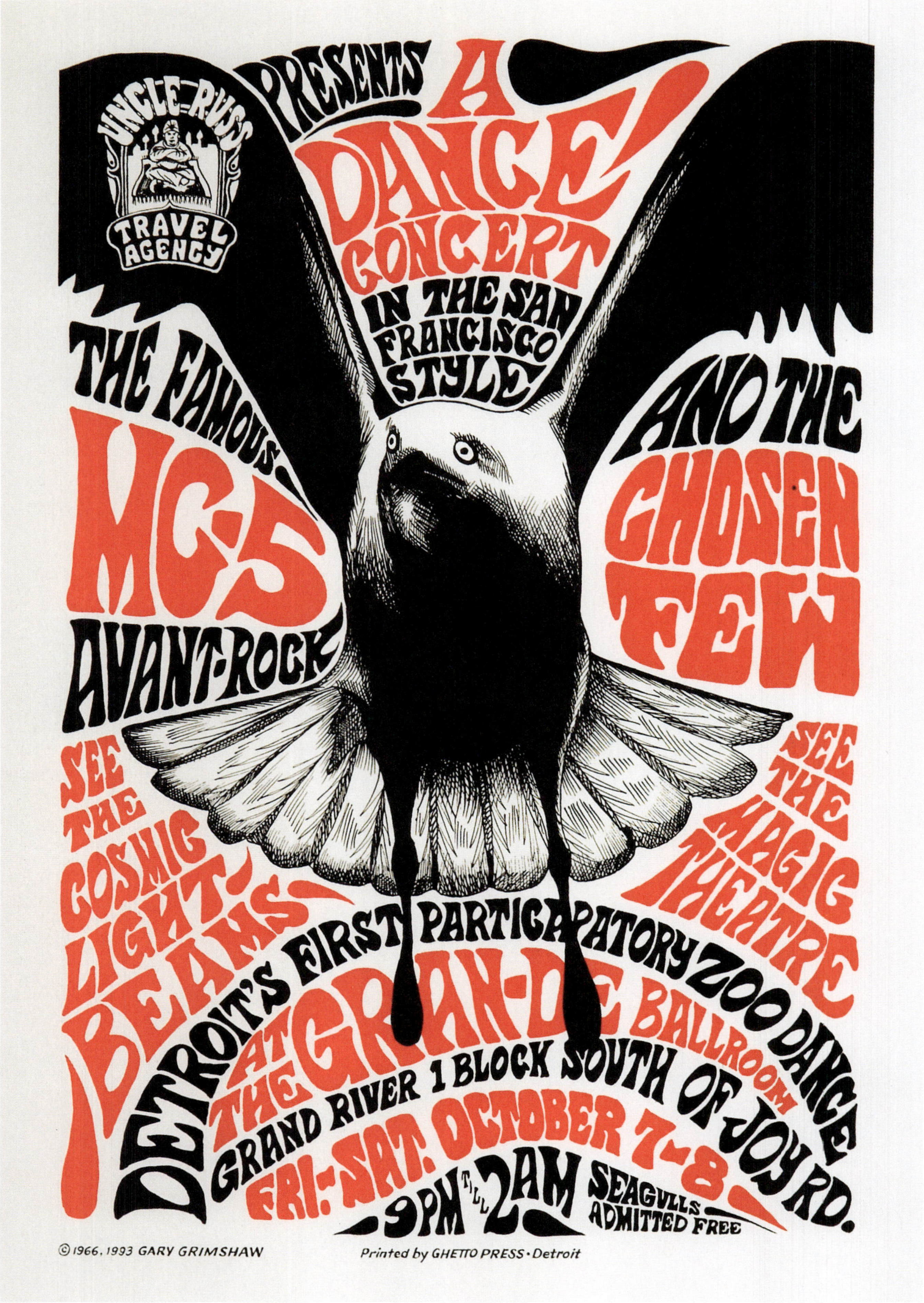

⟫→ This page: *The Seagull,* a dramatic Gary Grimshaw design for an October 1966 concert in Detroit. MC5 were an incendiary rock act from the city with a genuinely revolutionary spirit. They were managed by John Sinclair, who later formed the White Panther Party. ⟫→ Opposite, top: a Grimshaw poster for an arcade named 'Pinball Alley' in Ann Arbor, Michigan. The original black-and-white ink artwork is shown with and without a celluloid overlay. ⟫→ Bottom: a 1971 poster for an Alice Cooper gig at North Baltimore's Park venue, showing the original artwork paste-up with and without the celluloid color overlay.

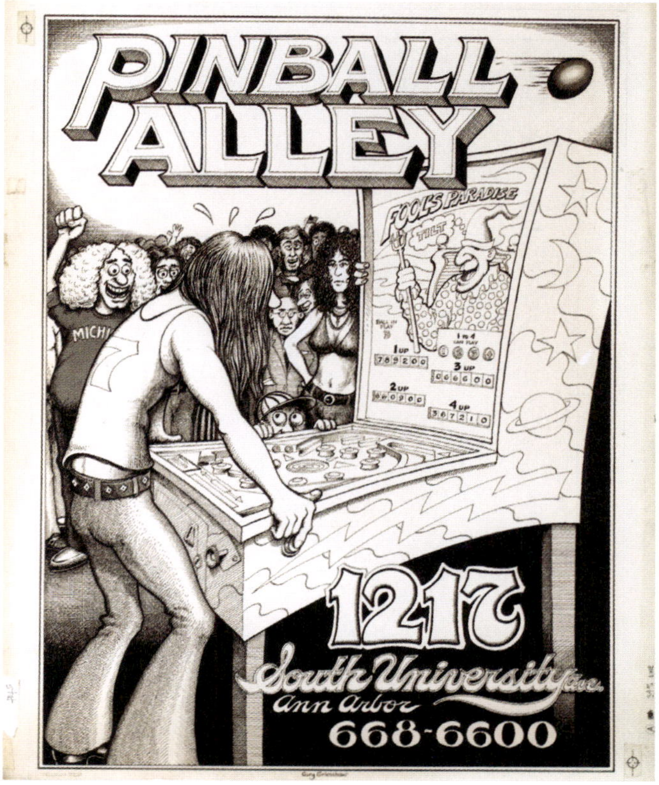

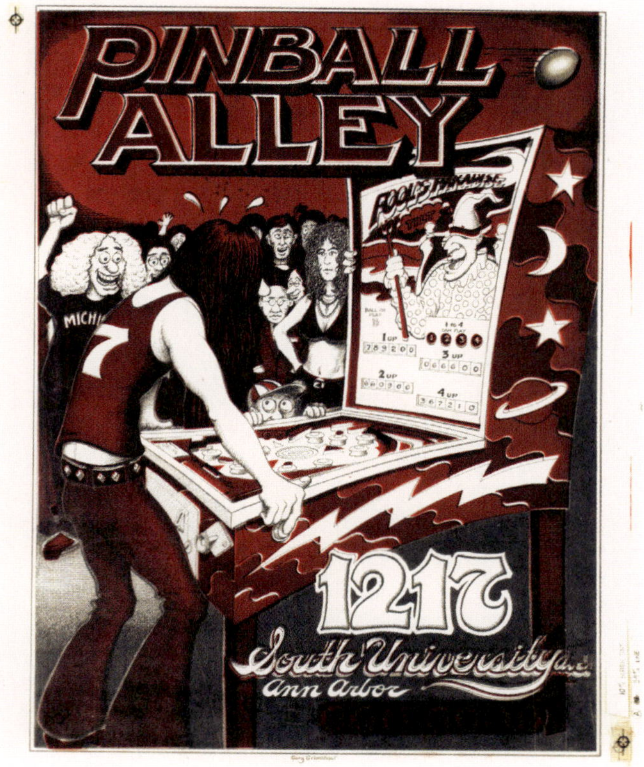

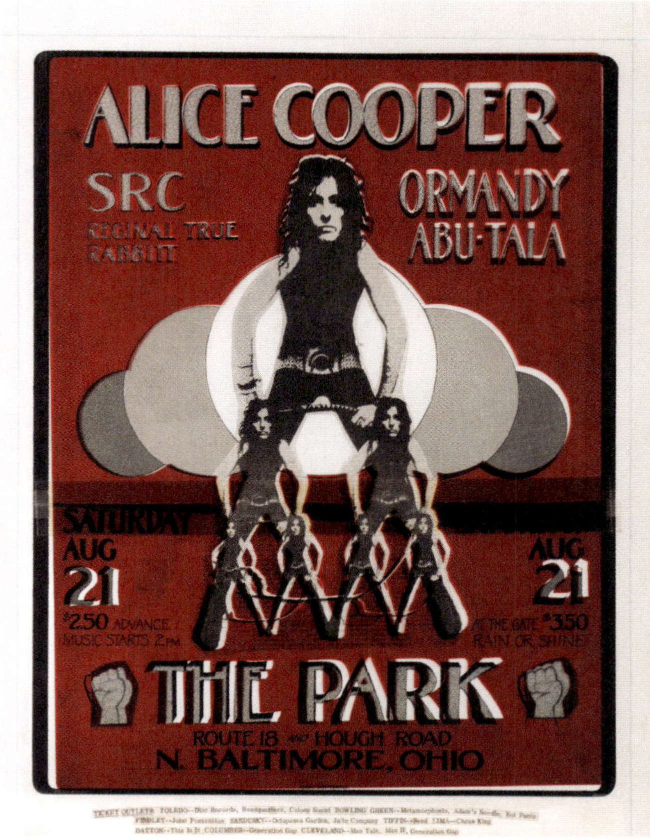

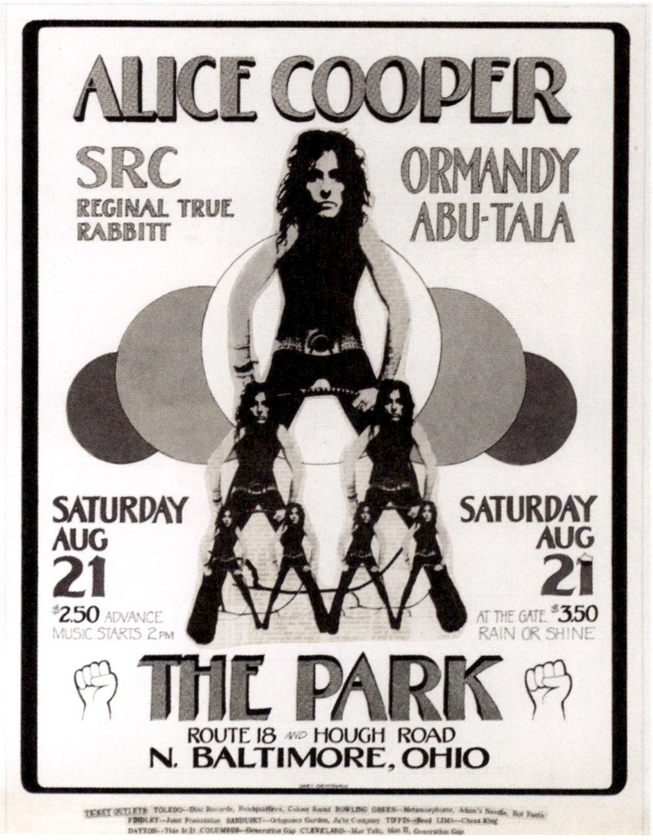

THE DETROIT SCENE

Russ Gibb took over the Grande Ballroom in Detroit in 1966 and strove to do what Bill Graham and The Family Dog were doing. Local artist Gary Grimshaw provided the posters. Graphic design was in his blood: his aunt was an illustrator, his uncle worked as a printer, while his grandfather had been a stylist at General Motors. Grimshaw had spent some time in Haight-Ashbury and quickly mastered the techniques of the genre, using his lettering to make patterns that its target audience would appreciate. He even contributed to the city's underground newspaper *The Oracle*. In high school, Grimshaw befriended Rob Tyner—lead singer with Detroit rock band The MC5—and later became a close friend of John Sinclair (and prominent member of Sinclair's White Panther Party); one of his most interesting designs is the rainbow pagination of Sinclair's book *Guitar Army* (1972).

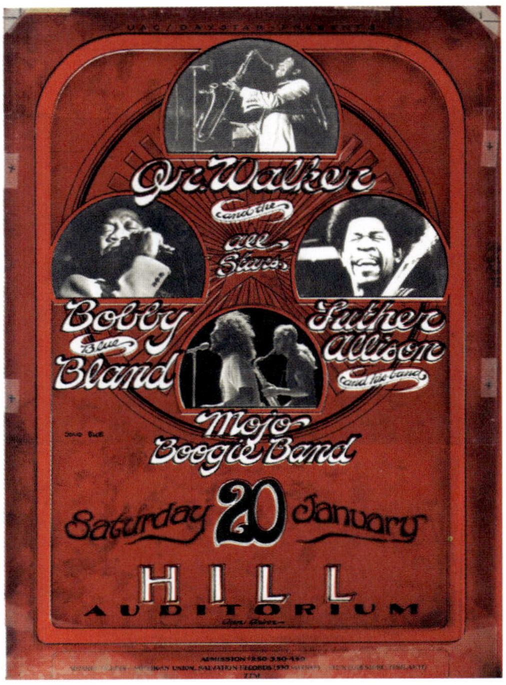
Dr. Walker
and the
all Stars
Bobby Blue Bland
Luther Allison
and his band
Mojo Boogie Band
Saturday 20 January
HILL
AUDITORIUM

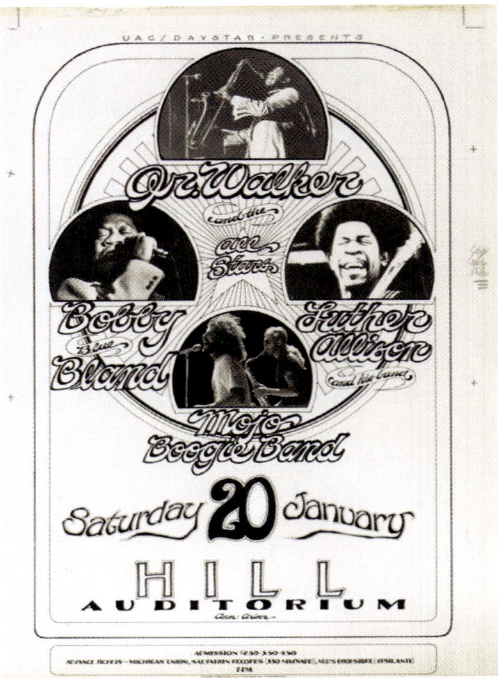
UAC/DAYSTAR · PRESENTS
Dr. Walker
and the
all Stars
Bobby Blue Bland
Luther Allison
and his band
Mojo Boogie Band
Saturday 20 January
HILL
AUDITORIUM

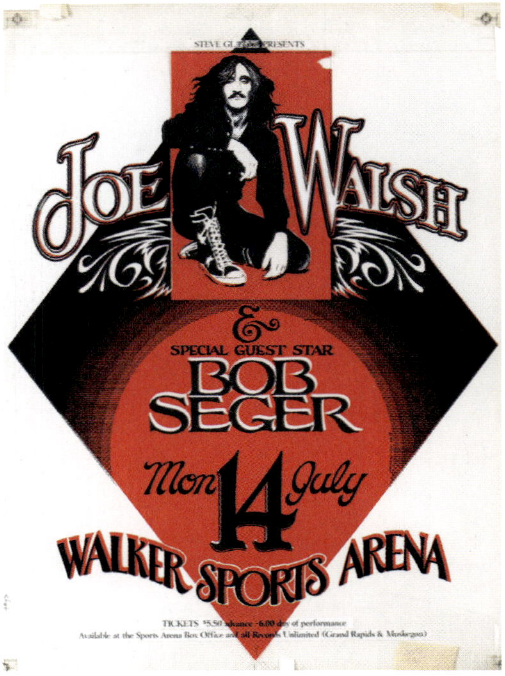
JOE WALSH
&
SPECIAL GUEST STAR
BOB SEGER
Mon 14 July
WALKER SPORTS ARENA
TICKETS $5.50 advance – 6.00 day of performance
Available at the Sports Arena Box Office and all Records Unlimited (Grand Rapids & Muskegon)

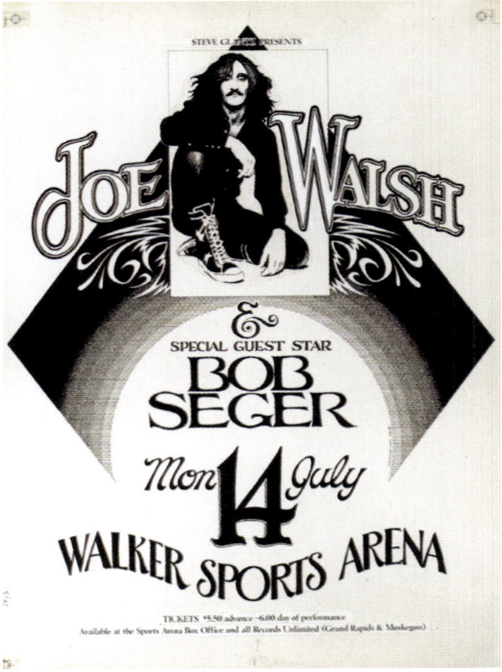
JOE WALSH
&
SPECIAL GUEST STAR
BOB SEGER
Mon 14 July
WALKER SPORTS ARENA
TICKETS $5.50 advance – 6.00 day of performance
Available at the Sports Arena Box Office and all Records Unlimited (Grand Rapids & Muskegon)

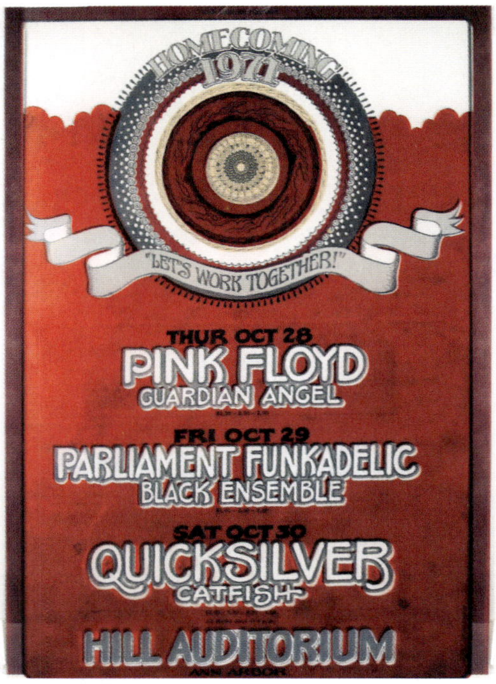
HOMECOMING 1971
"LET'S WORK TOGETHER!"
THUR OCT 28
PINK FLOYD
GUARDIAN ANGEL
FRI OCT 29
PARLIAMENT FUNKADELIC
BLACK ENSEMBLE
SAT OCT 30
QUICKSILVER
CATFISH
HILL AUDITORIUM
ANN ARBOR

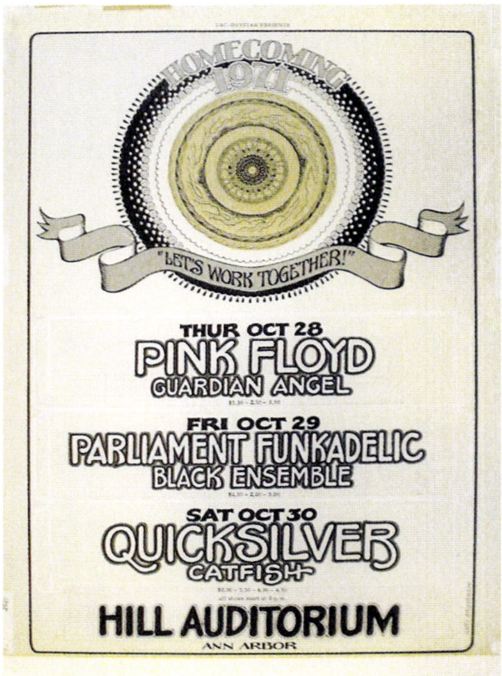
HOMECOMING 1971
"LET'S WORK TOGETHER!"
THUR OCT 28
PINK FLOYD
GUARDIAN ANGEL
FRI OCT 29
PARLIAMENT FUNKADELIC
BLACK ENSEMBLE
SAT OCT 30
QUICKSILVER
CATFISH
HILL AUDITORIUM
ANN ARBOR

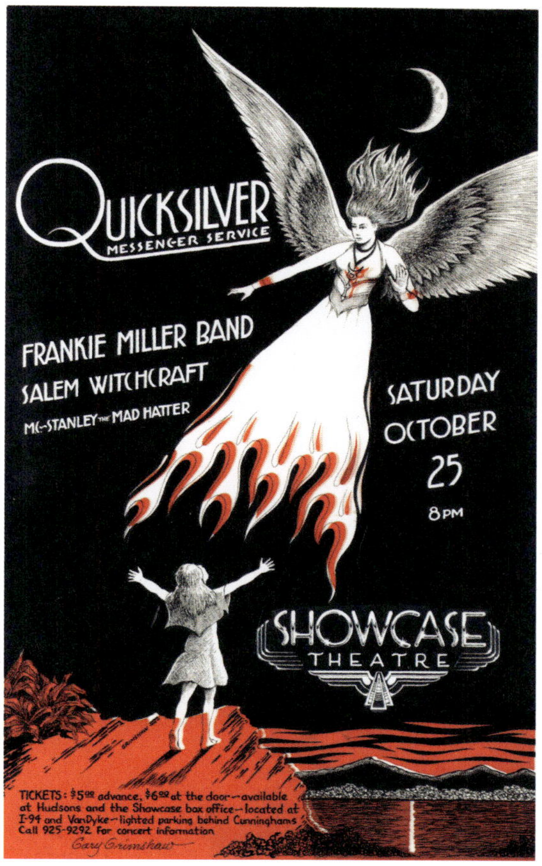

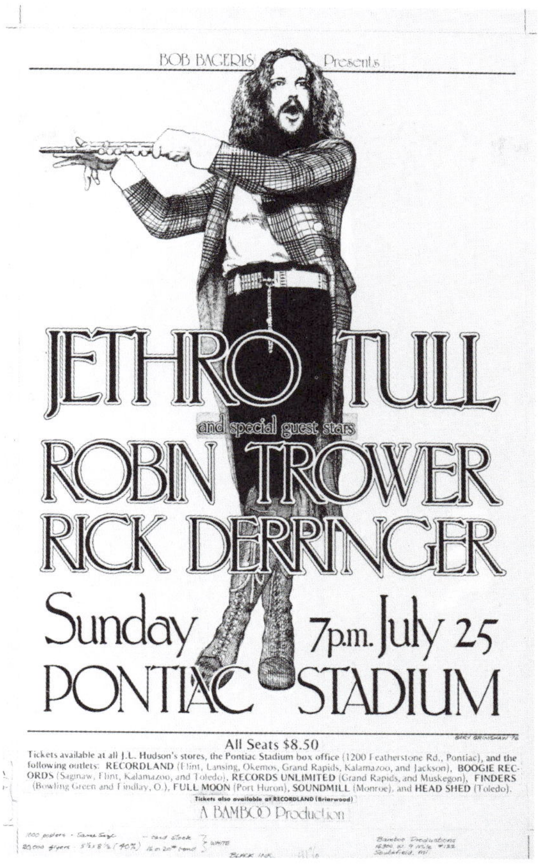

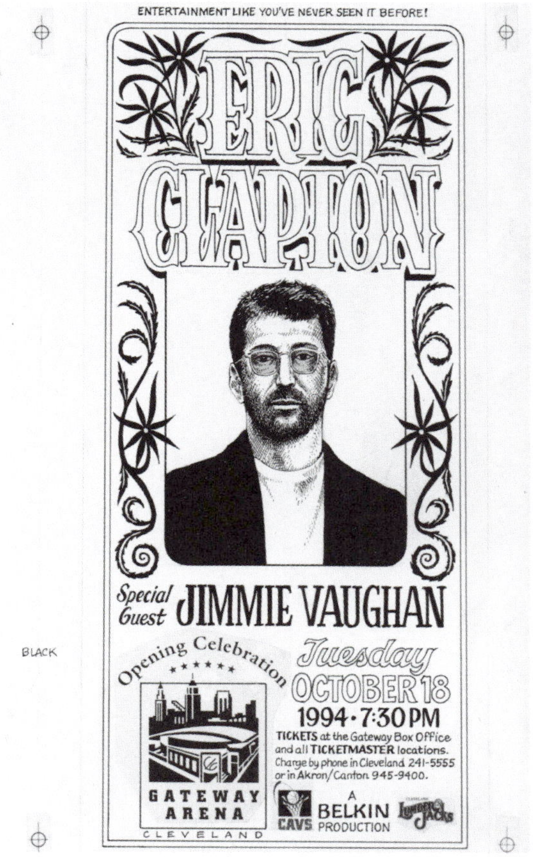

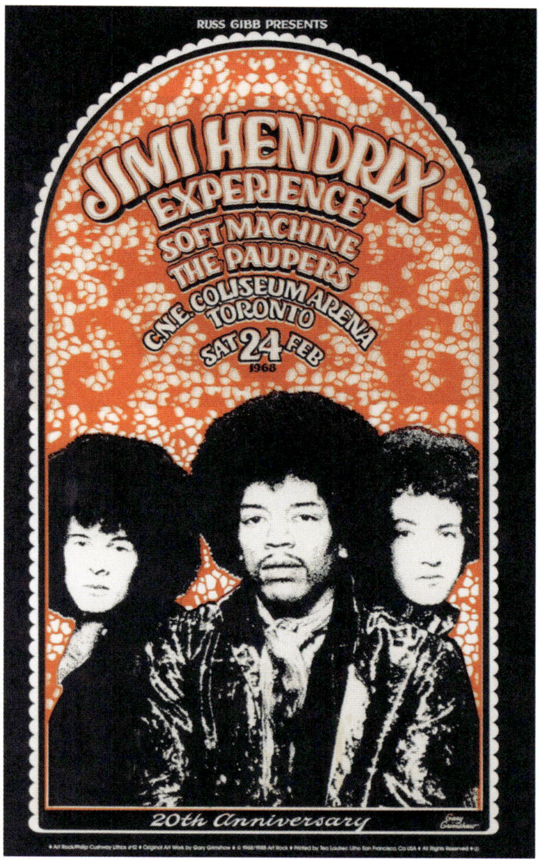

⋙→ Opposite: black-and-white paste-ups and celluloid overlays for three posters by Gary Grimshaw. ⋙→ Top: promoting a blues/R&B night in 1973 at the Hill Auditorium on the University of Michigan's Ann Arbor campus. ⋙→ Center: advertising the mid-seventies legends appearing at a modestly sized Midwest venue in 1975. ⋙→ Bottom: touting a 1971 appearance in Ann Arbor by former psychedelic darlings Pink Floyd. ⋙→ This page: Grimshaw's deft skills are evident in his posters for appearances by Quicksilver Messenger Service (1975), Jethro Tull (1975), and Eric Clapton (1994). The Jimi Hendrix poster is a special anniversary edition produced two decades after the original concert, which took place in 1968. The original monochrome paste-ups here appear with celluloid overlays (top left, bottom right) and without them (top right, bottom left).

Grimshaw transforms lettering into pure—but still legible—design for this poster advertising forthcoming gigs for September 1967 at Detroit's Grande Ballroom.

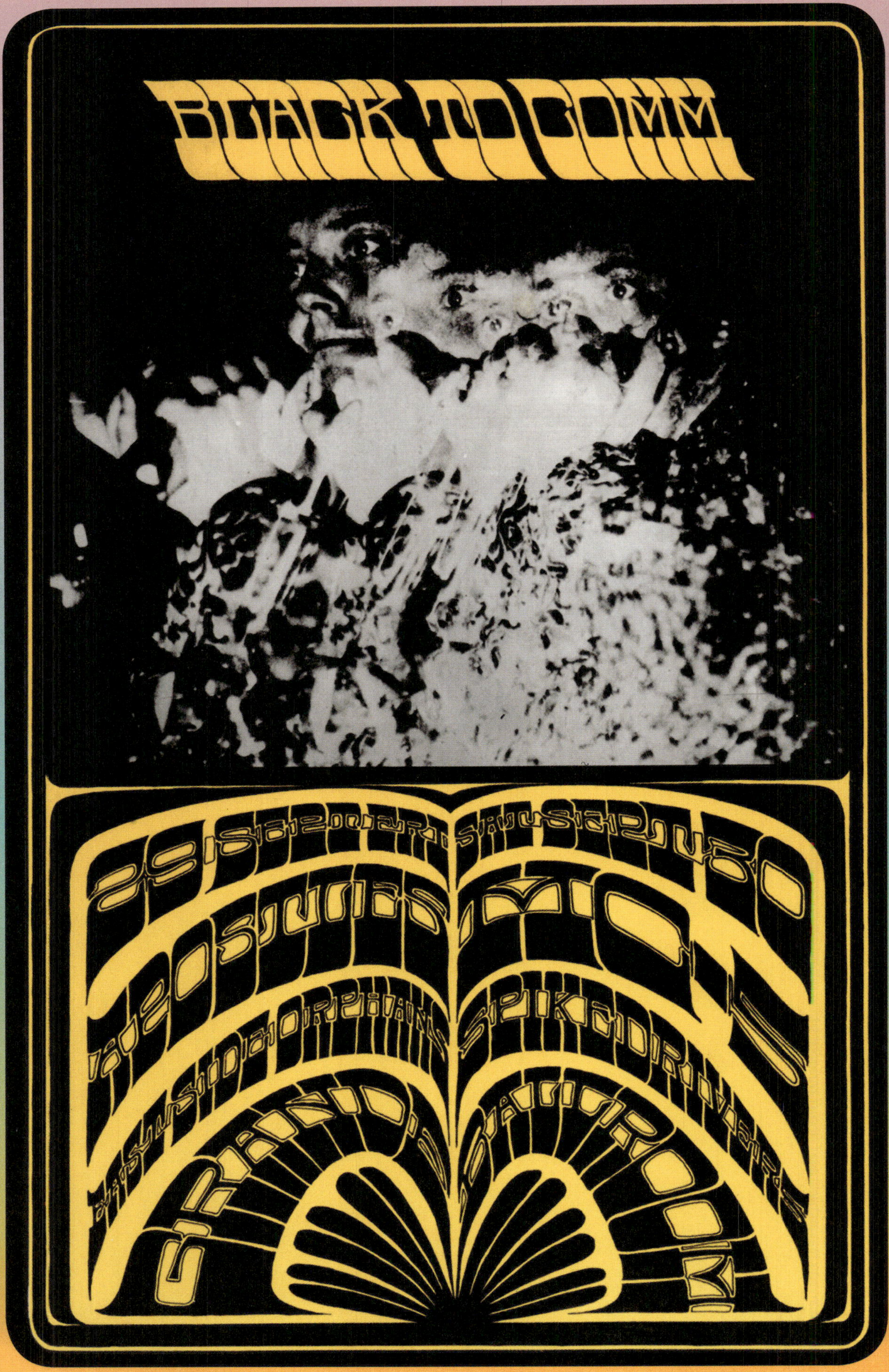

GARY GRIMSHAW (1946—2014)

BY L. E. GRIMSHAW

AT THE END OF THE LAST CENTURY, GARY GRIMSHAW'S HOMETOWN NEWSPAPER, THE *DETROIT FREE PRESS*, PLACED HIM ON THEIR LIST OF 'MICHIGAN'S 100 GREATEST ARTISTS AND ENTERTAINERS OF THE 20TH CENTURY,' ADDING: 'IF HE HADN'T BEEN THE POSTER ARTIST FOR THE COUNTER-CULTURE, HE COULD HAVE BEEN ITS POSTER CHILD.' THEY WERE RIGHT TO HAVE PLACED HIM ON THAT LIST AND RIGHT TO POINT OUT HOW MUCH HE WAS A PRODUCT OF HIS CULTURE. AT THAT POINT, HIS CAREER IN ART HAD BEEN GOING STRONG FOR THIRTY-THREE YEARS. HE WOULD CREATE WORKS FOR MUSIC-RELATED PROJECTS AND COMMUNITY EVENTS UNTIL MONTHS BEFORE HIS DEATH. → FROM THE FIRST GRANDE BALLROOM POSTER DESIGN, WHEN HE WAS FRESH FROM A NAVY DISCHARGE AND HANGING OUT IN SAN FRANCISCO IN THE EARLIEST DAYS OF THE AVALON AND FILLMORE, IT WAS ASSUMED THAT GARY WAS THE ARTIST IN HIS GROUP OF DETROIT PALS AND COULD DELIVER WHAT WAS ASKED OF HIM. HE WAS TOTALLY UP TO THE CHALLENGE OF PRODUCING THE FIRST POSTER 'LIKE THEY DO IN SAN FRANCISCO.' HIS WORK STANDS FIRM NEXT TO THE 'BIG FIVE' OF THE WEST COAST POSTER ARTISTS AND IN THE MIDWEST. HE WAS A TRAILBLAZER OF PSYCHEDELIC LETTERING. HE THOUGHT THE WEST COAST TYPOGRAPHY WAS VERY COOL, BUT FOUND IT EXCLUSIVE (BEING ILLEGIBLE). HE CONSCIOUSLY DEVELOPED A STYLE THAT WOULD BECOME INCLUSIVE—YOU DIDN'T NEED TO BE PART OF AN 'IN' CROWD, OR BE ON DRUGS, TO MAKE OUT WHAT THE POSTER WAS ADVERTISING. GARY'S UNCLE, IVOR DAVIDSON, WAS THE PRINTER—HE TAUGHT GARY THE ART OF CUTTING FILM FOR PRINT (AN OLD-SCHOOL PROCESS). GARY LEARNED ABOUT THE COST OF PRINTING AND THOUGHT TO HIMSELF, 'WHY SPEND MONEY ADVERTISING SOMETHING THAT PEOPLE CAN'T READ?' → HE WAS KNOWN AS AN ARTIST OF THE PEOPLE AND HIS INFLUENCE ON HIS COMMUNITY WAS HUGE. HIS ARTWORK IS STILL AN IMPORTANT INFLUENCE ON ARTISTS WHO FOLLOW THE PATH HE CREATED.

THE JOHN SINCLAIR FREEDOM RALLY

Underground organizer John Sinclair, of the White Panther Party and the Rainbow People's Party, was given a ten-year jail sentence in 1969 for possession of two joints of marijuana, a blatant attempt to stamp out his political activism. It was a sentence so outrageous that it became a rallying cry for the whole movement. Stevie Wonder, Commander Cody, Phil Ochs, John Lennon, and Yoko Ono and many others took part in a protest rally on December 10, 1971 in Detroit, where the speakers included Bobby Seale, Allen Ginsberg, and Rennie Davis. Sinclair was released shortly afterward.

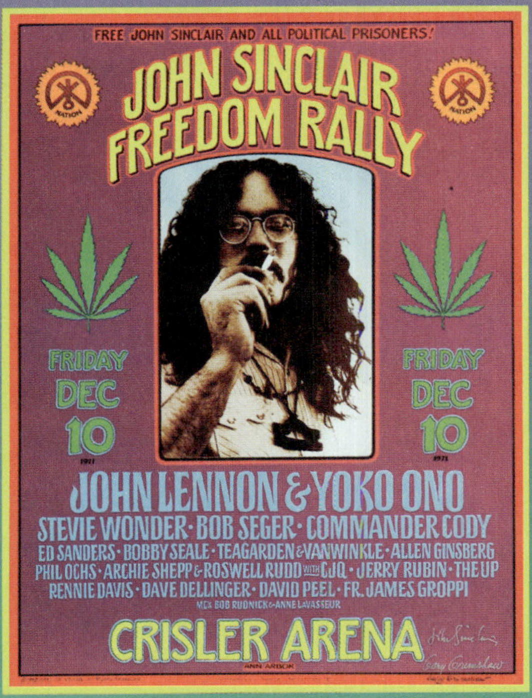

Rally to the cause ⋙→ Stars from the mainstream and counter-culture lined up to support John Sinclair in 1971. The day was filmed and later released as the movie *Ten For Two*. The Gary Grimshaw poster handed out on the day was created in advance, and the list of performers was not final. In this version, also by Gary Grimshaw, the artist updated the lettering to show the true line-up.

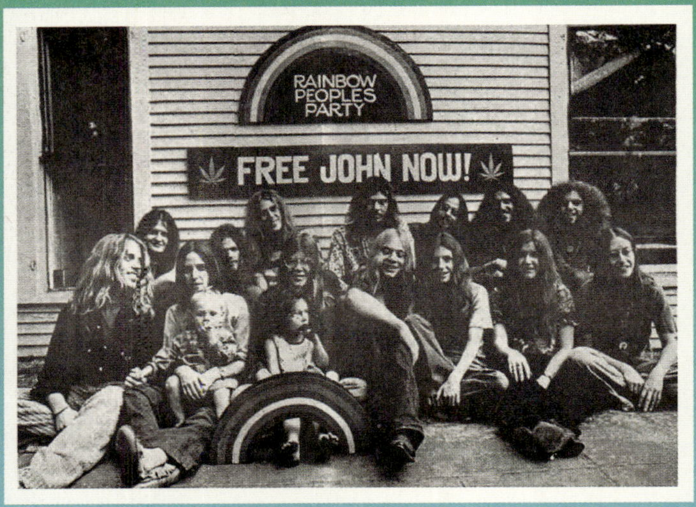

Community spirit ⋙→ While Sinclair was still in prison, his White Panther Party renamed itself as the less provocative Rainbow People's Party. It broke up in 1973. 'Free John Now' was the title of the newspaper the group set up to push the case for Sinclair's release.

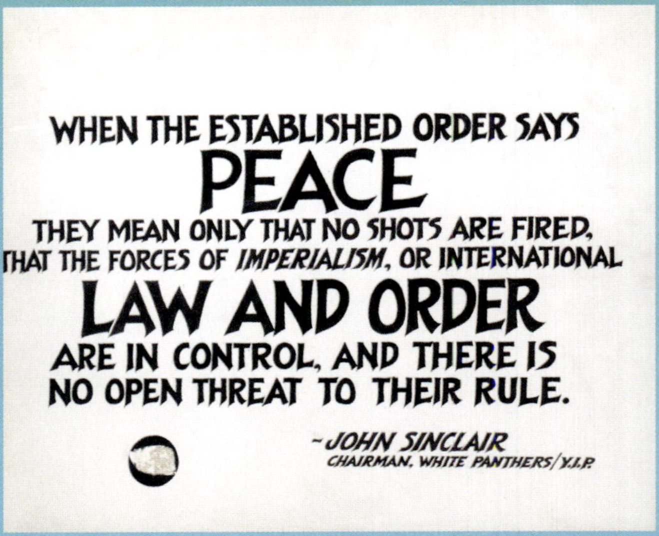

Peace, Law, and Order, 1970 ⋙→ A quote from Sinclair that originally appeared in this form in the pages of the White Panther Party's newspaper *Sun/Dance*. The poster is generally attributed to Gary Grimshaw.

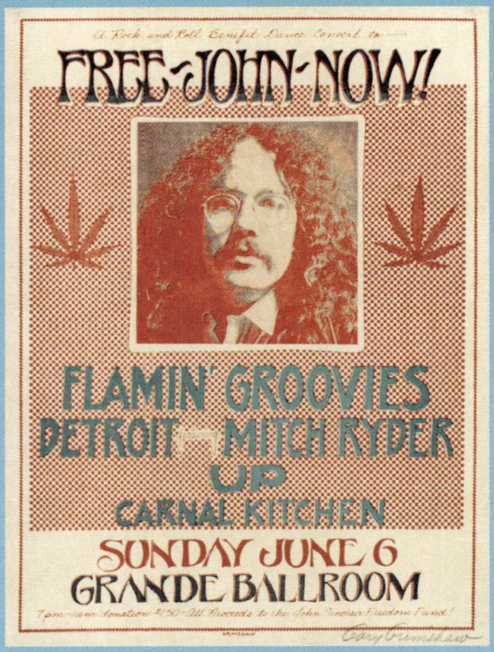

Leave it ⋙→ Marijuana plants decorate this signed Grimshaw poster for a June 1971 benefit gig at the Grande Ballroom.

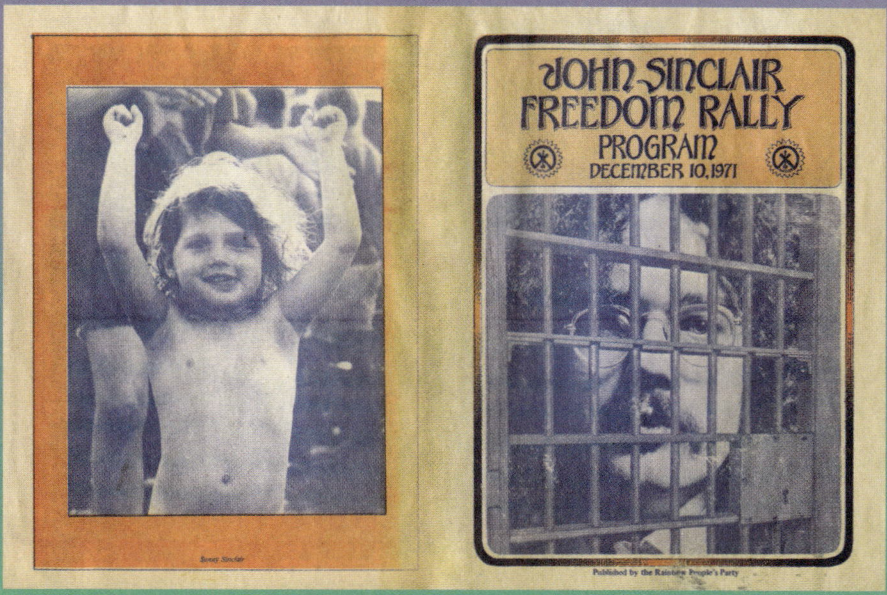

Program for change ⟫→ The Rainbow People's Party published this booklet for the Sinclair benefit rally and concert in December 1971.

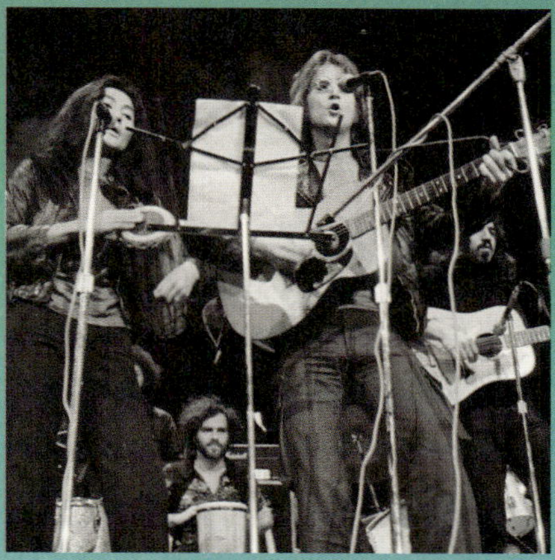

Star support ⟫→ John Lennon and Yoko Ono on stage at the concert. They played four tracks ('John Sinclair,' 'Attica State,' 'Sisters, O Sisters,' and 'Luck Of The Irish'), all to feature on their *Sometime In New York City* album, released in 1972.

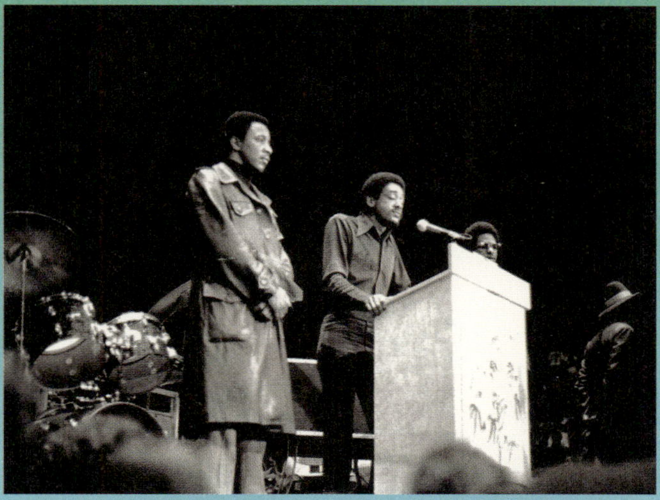

Radical speech ⟫→ Black Panther chairman Bobby Seale takes to the rostrum at the Sinclair rally.

Taking America to task ⟫→ Three pages from the rally program. To the far right are Lennon's lyrics from his song 'John Sinclair.' The recurring marijuana plant motifs serve as a reminder of the reason for Sinclair's incarceration.

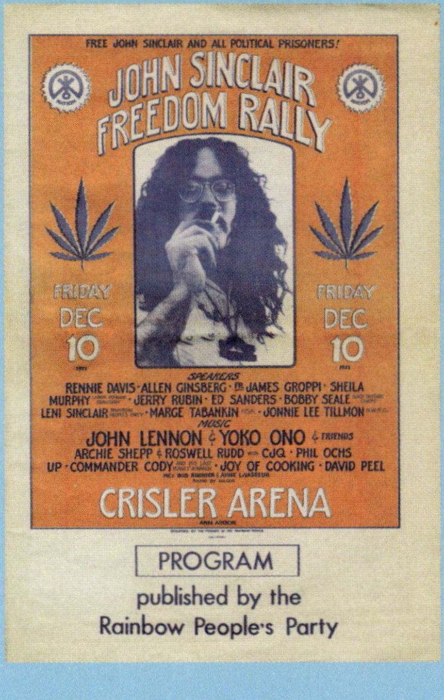

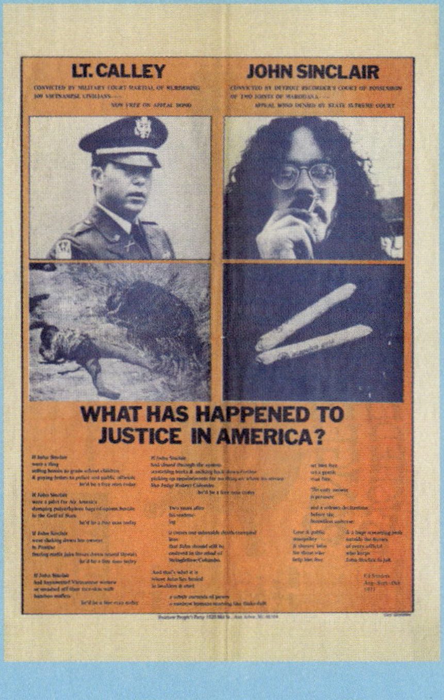

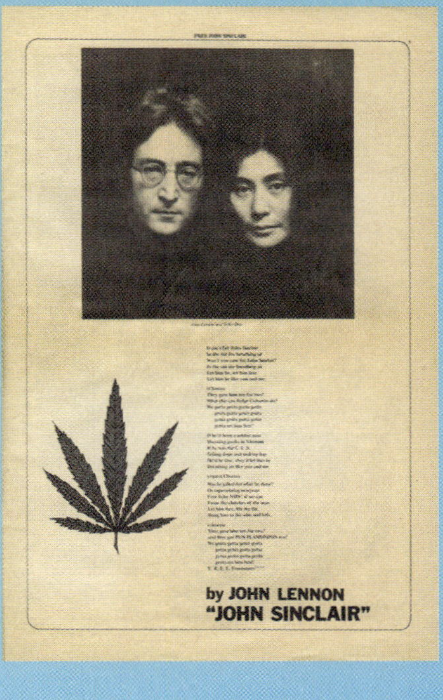

THE 'SKULL AND ROSES' TOUR 1971

The Grateful Dead used the iconic Stanley Mouse and Alton Kelley image of the skeleton with roses from the 1966 Family Dog poster for their tour in 1971. Kelley did the full range of graphics, including the tickets and concert posters, shown here, and the sleeve for the accompanying live double album; Mouse was in London at the time. The official Warner Brothers album title was *Grateful Dead*, but the band had wanted to call it 'Skull Fuck,' which would have meant that a great many record outlets would not have stocked it. Most fans refer to it as 'Skull and Roses' because of the album cover art.

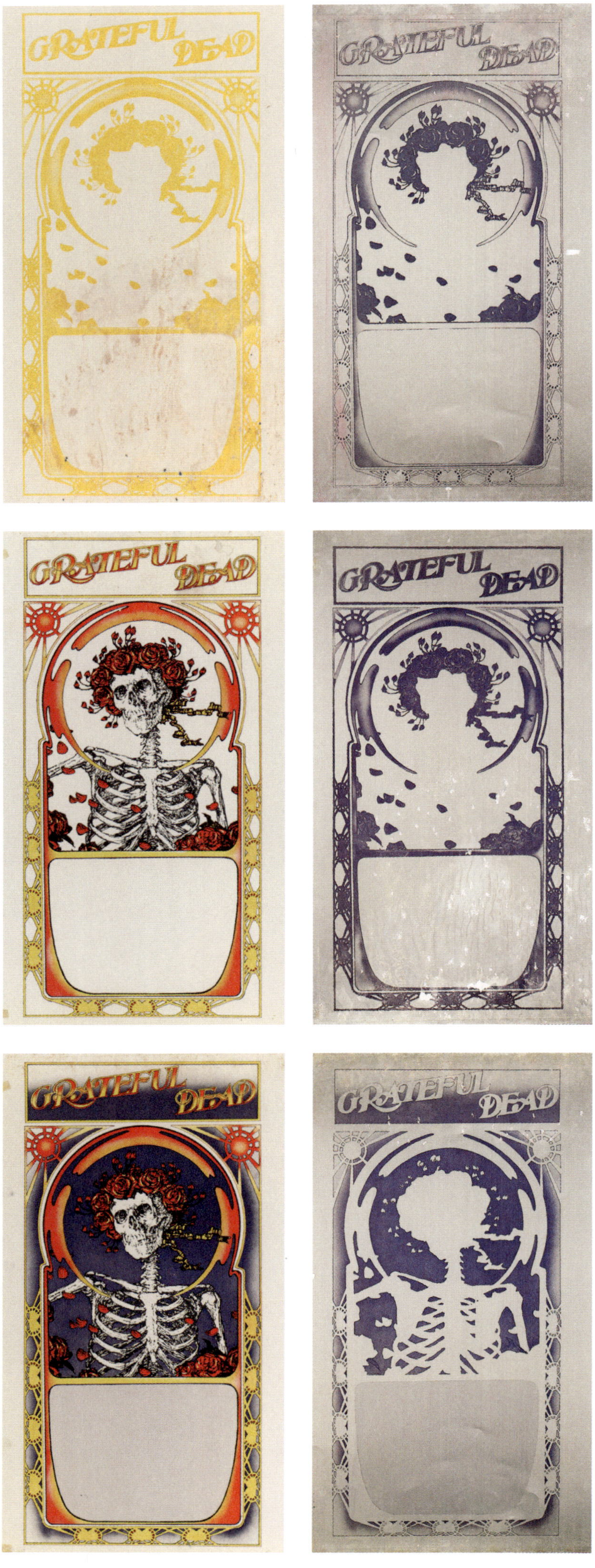

➳→Metal printing plates and color separations for (this page) posters and (opposite) tickets for the 1971 'Skull and Roses' tour. Spaces were left for details of the venues and dates to be added. The smallest images here—seen in double rows at the far right of each of the images on the opposite page—were printed up as name cards for the Grateful Dead's office.

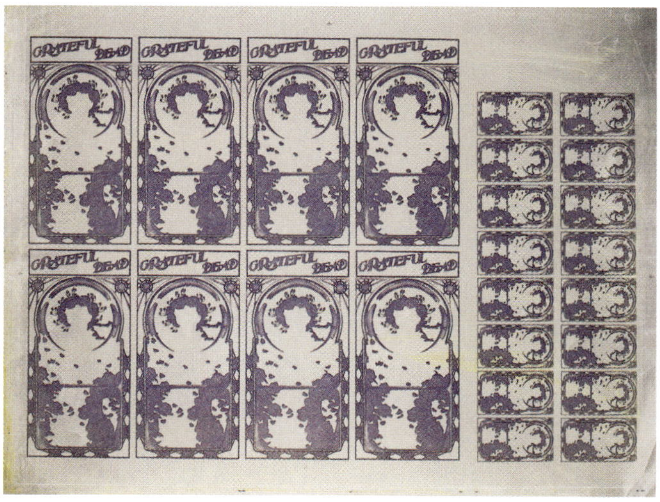
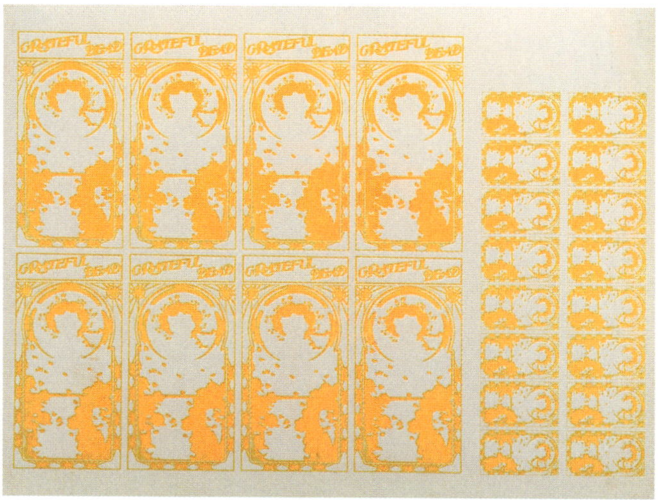
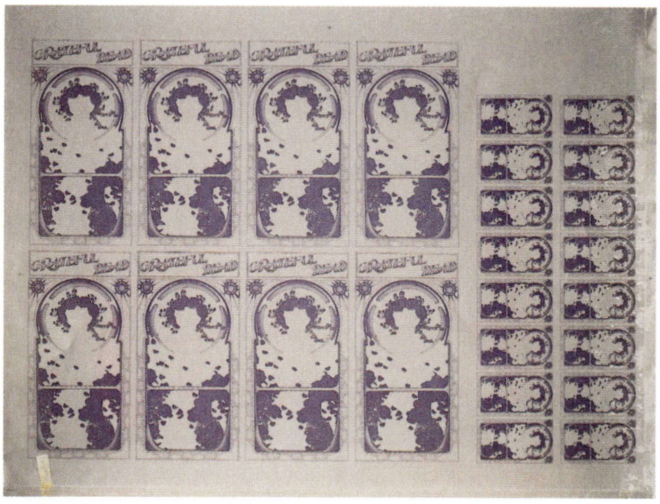
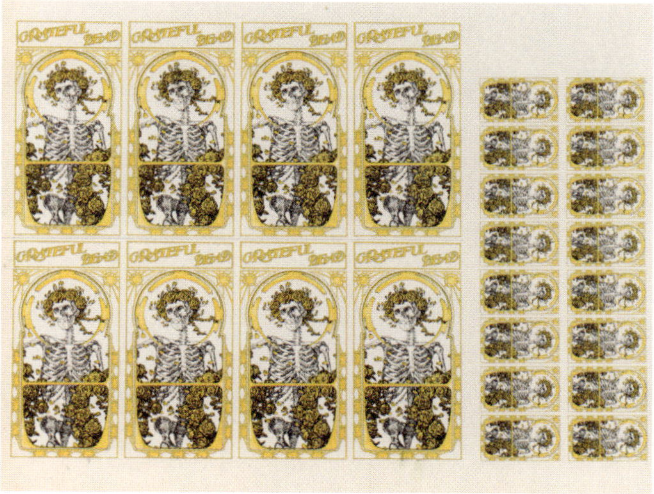
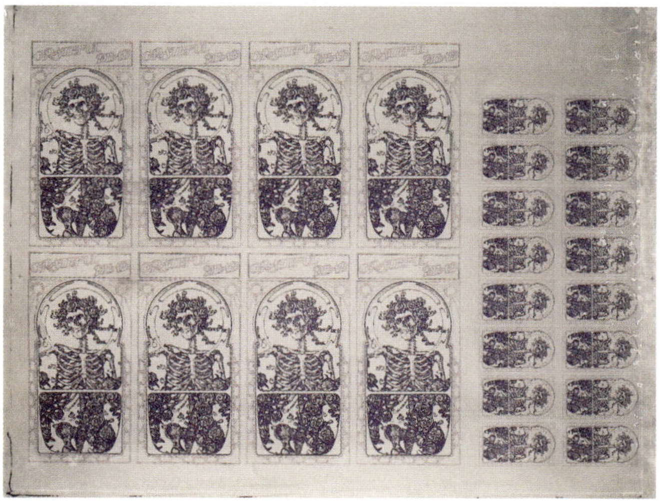
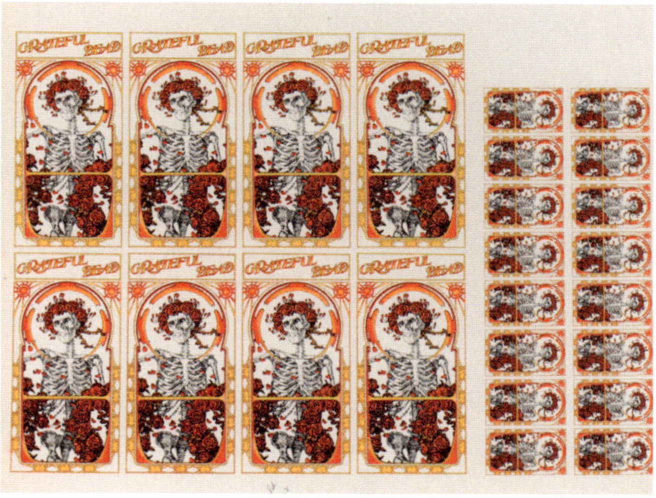
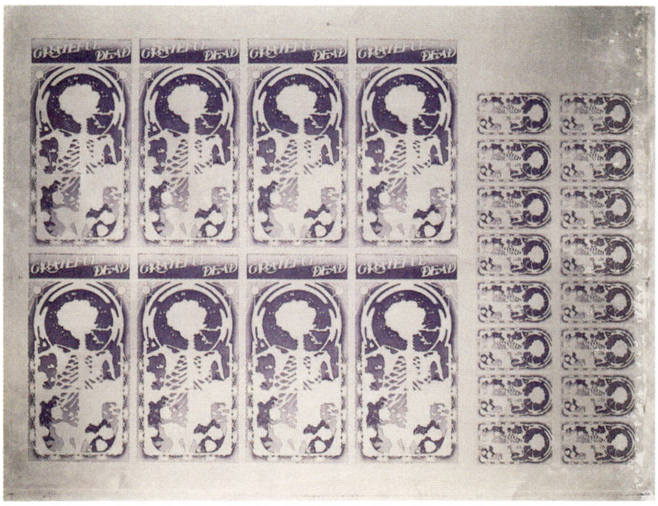
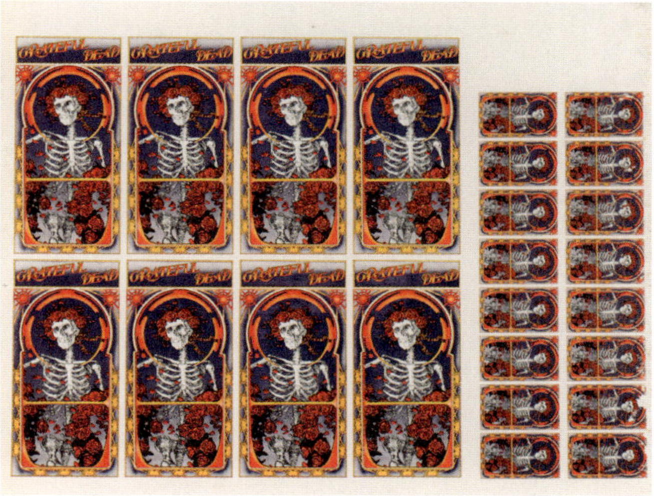

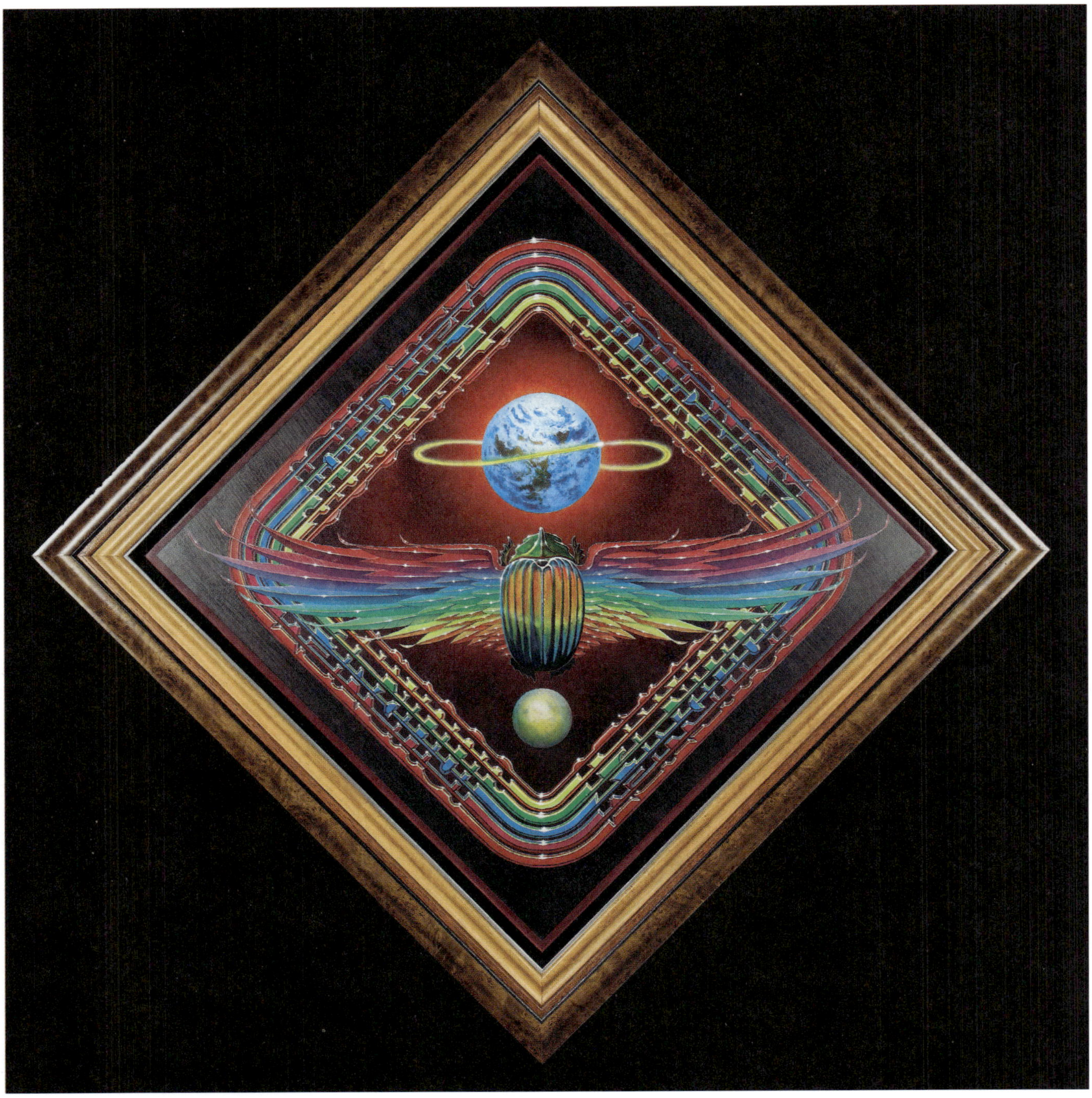

MOUSE AND KELLEY IN THE SEVENTIES

⟿ Rather than work through a series of preliminary sketches, Kelley preferred to present clients with finished artworks—as seen on these pages. ⟿ This page: Kelley's acrylic-and-airbrush design for Journey's 1980 album *Departure* and accompanying world tour has as its centerpiece a winged scarab. ⟿ Opposite: all four Kelley images seen here were airbrushed. The main image was produced for the cover of Grateful Dead drummer Mickey Hart's *Rolling Thunder* album in 1972.

After the collapse of the Haight-Ashbury community, Stanley Mouse had left for London, where (although a commission to flame Eric Clapton's Rolls-Royce fell through) he had met the city's psychedelic poster artists and created work for Blind Faith, the Beatles, *International Times* and *Nova* magazine. Meanwhile, Alton Kelley, now in Boston, had been hired to create signage for Woodstock; Mouse returned to the USA to help. Back together, they worked for Intermedia in Cambridge, Massachusetts. One of their projects was an airbrushed Art Nouveau scarab design for the cover of a Jimi Hendrix album. Hendrix's death came soon after, and the album was never released; later, the duo would transform the scarab into a series of cover artworks for Journey. Back in San Francisco, they produced *The Ice Cream Kid* and *Foot Through the Rainbow* for the Grateful Dead's *Europe '72* album in 1972. In the mid seventies, they formed T-shirt company Monster, and a few years later, they started to create their intricate airbrush covers for Journey's albums, as well as the Pegasus for Steve Miller's *Book of Dreams* and artwork for the Grateful Dead's *From The Mars Hotel*. In 1980, wanting space for self-expression, Mouse and Kelley went their separate ways.

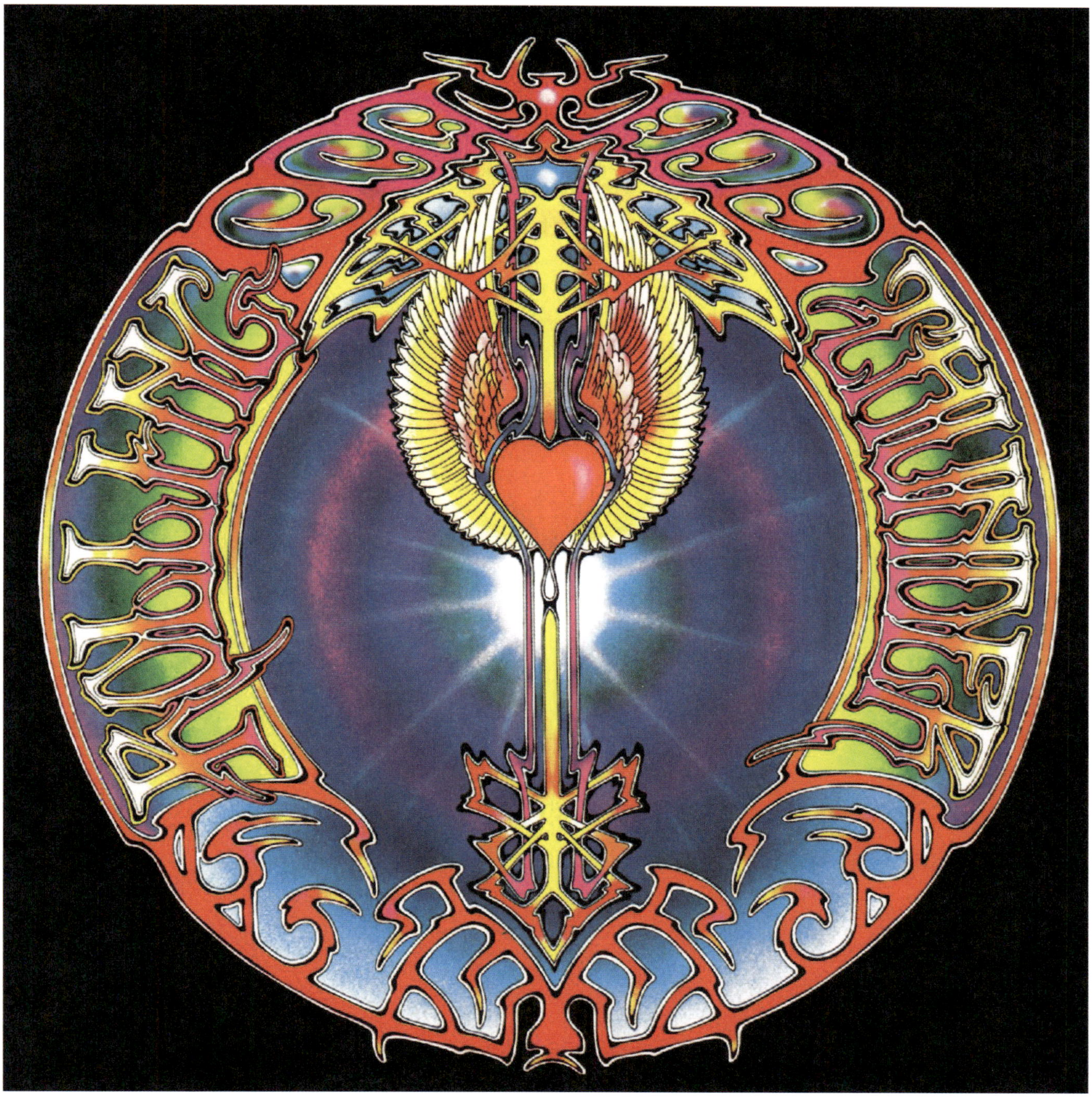

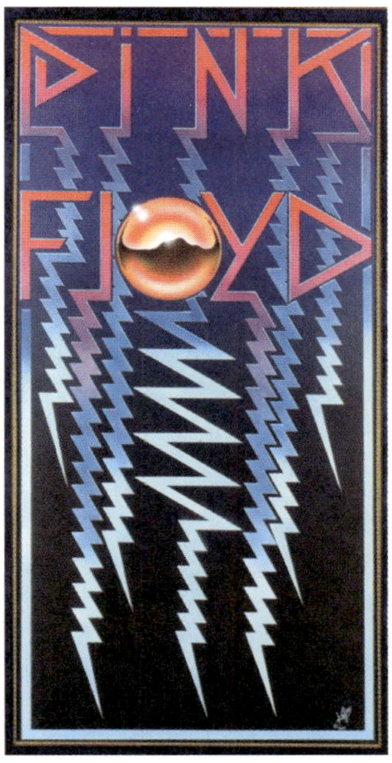
PINK
FLOYD

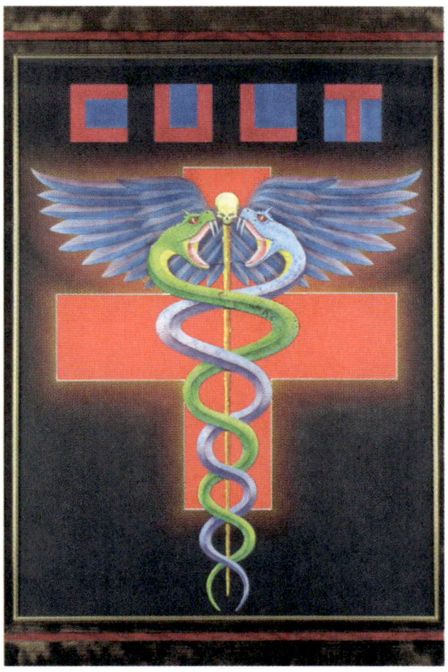
CULT

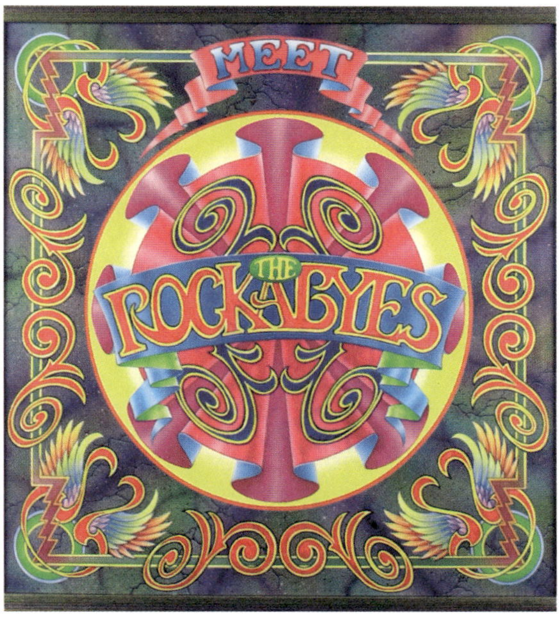
MEET
THE
ROCKABYES

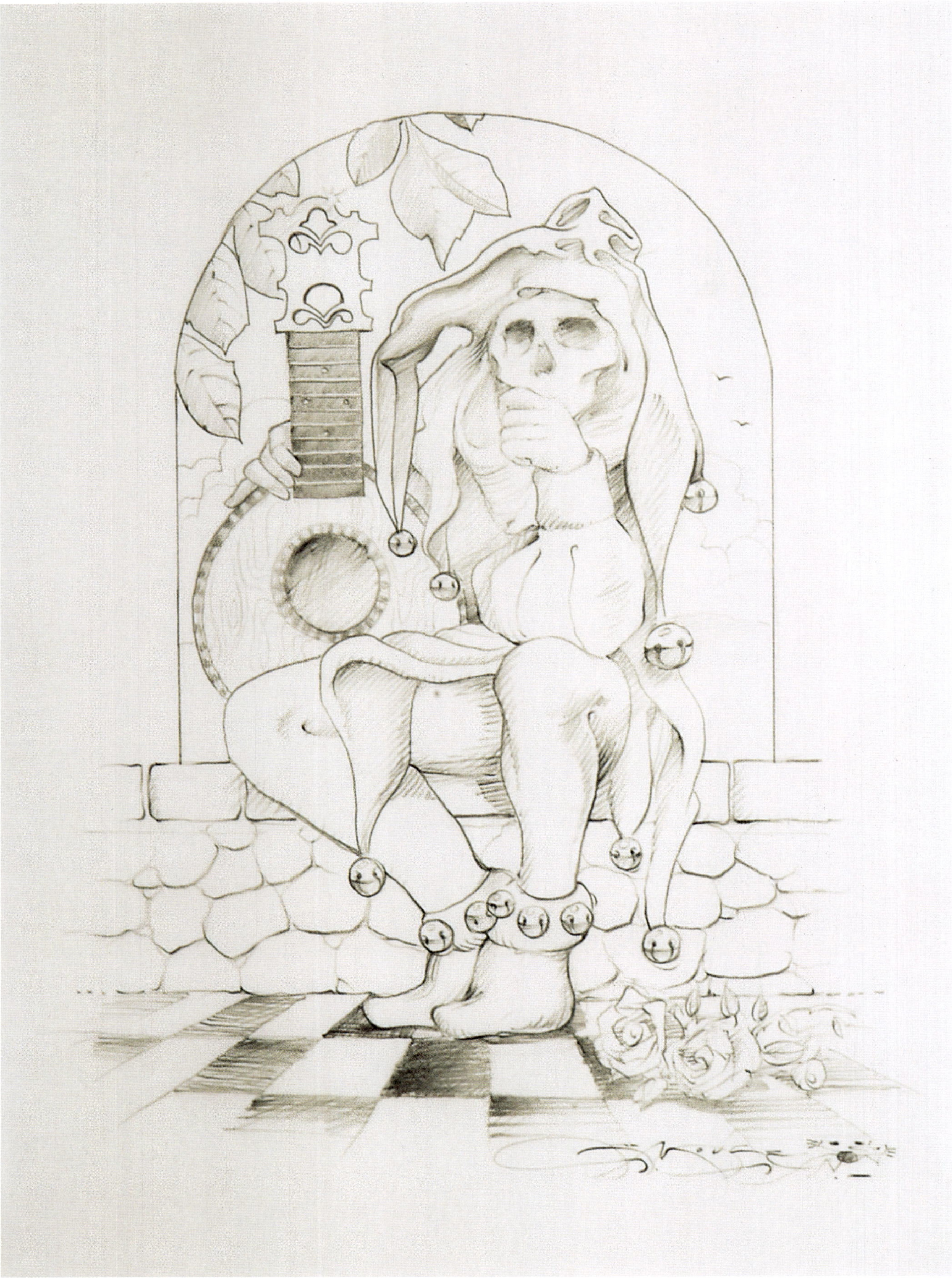

This page: Stanley Mouse's *Jester* drawing for the cover of *The Grateful Dead Songbook*, published in 1973. Opposite: the full-color cover, in pencil and airbrush. The book featured songs from the two classic Dead albums *Workingman's Dead* and *American Beauty* (both 1970), both of which featured Mouse and Kelley covers. The Jester joined the skull and roses as an iconic image for the Grateful Dead and would be used by the band across a range of promotional material.

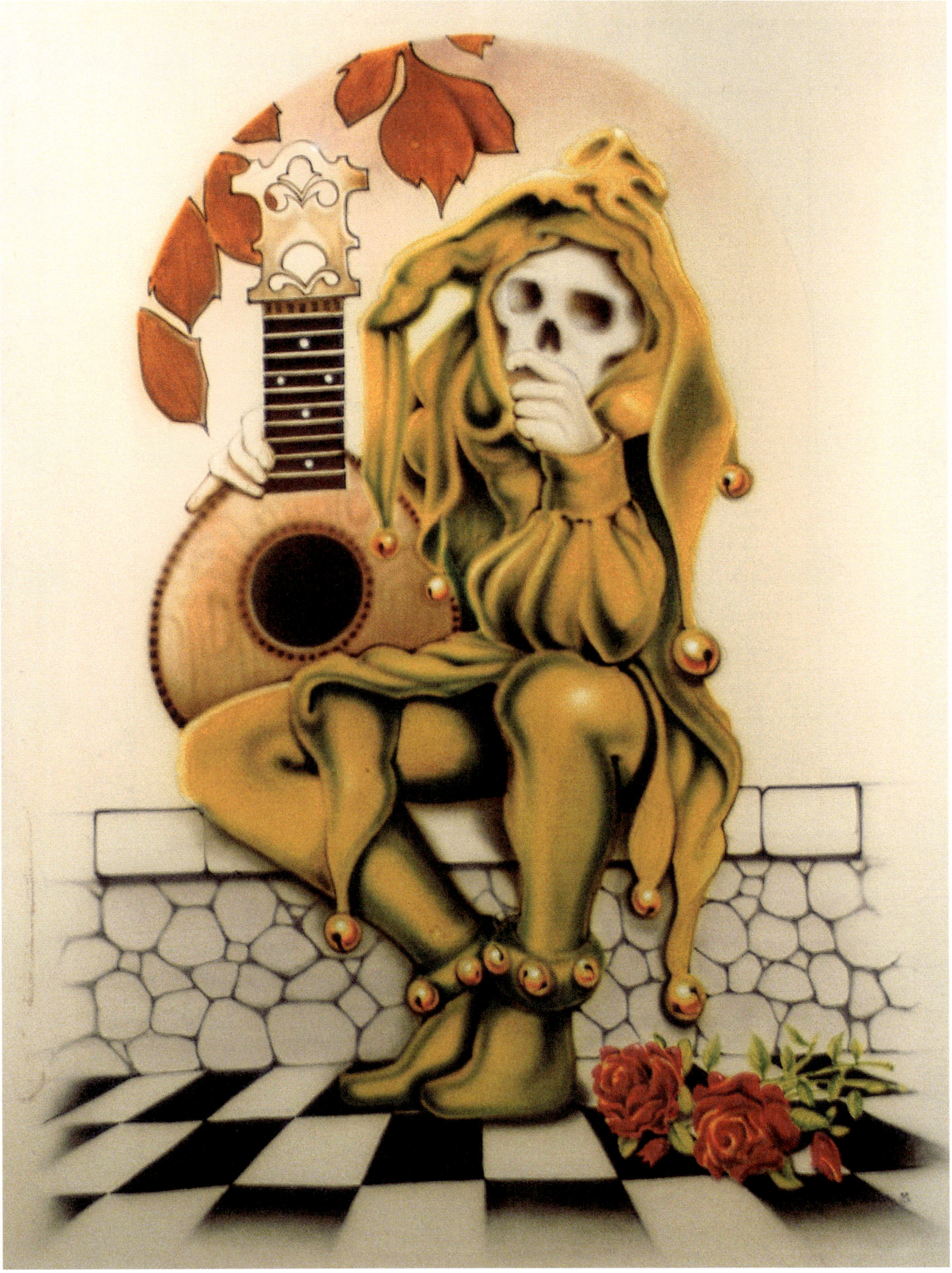

UK UNDERGROUND COMIX

Underground comix artists first began drawing cartoon strips for the American underground press (*East Village Other* in particular) and the British underground papers tried their hand at them as well, hoping to get a second income stream. *International Times* brought out *Nasty Tales*, but neglected to restrict it to 'Adults Only,' resulting in an obscenity trial that put the comic out of business. It ran to seven issues, from 1971 to 1972. Despite facing the famous *Oz* Obscenity Trial in 1971 after inviting a group of schoolchildren to edit its 'Schoolkids Oz' issue, *Oz* magazine tried its hand next. Its *cOZmic Comics* racked up twenty-one titles between 1972 and 1975, some of them American reprints, before also closing.

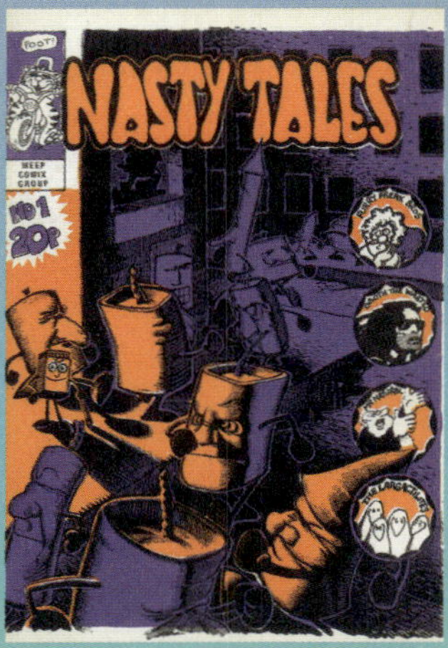

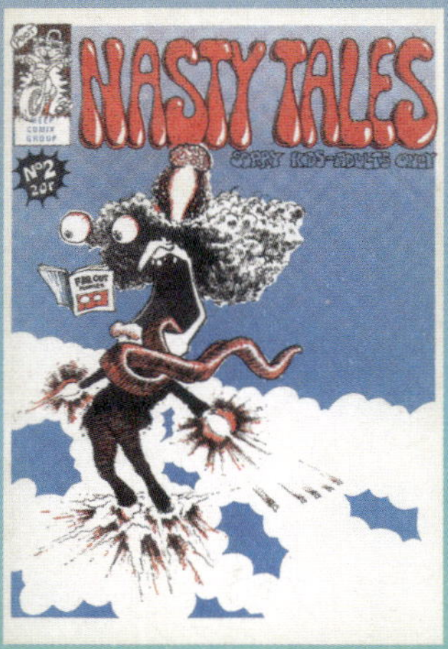

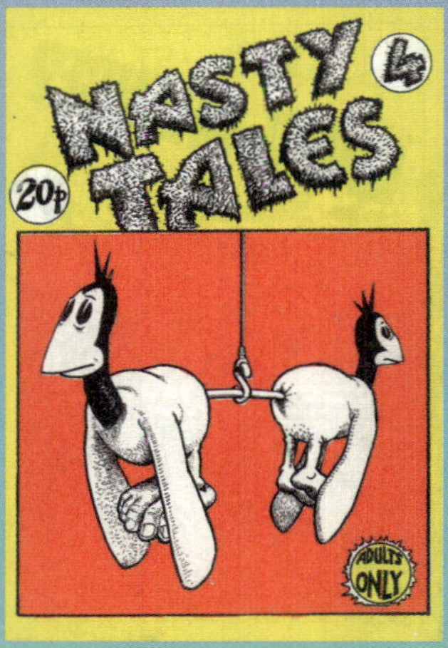

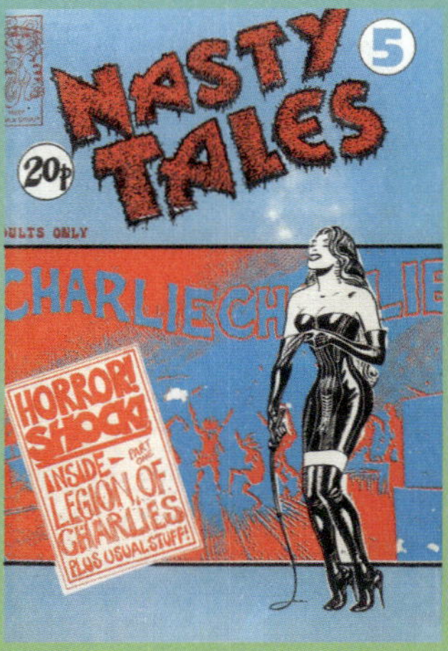

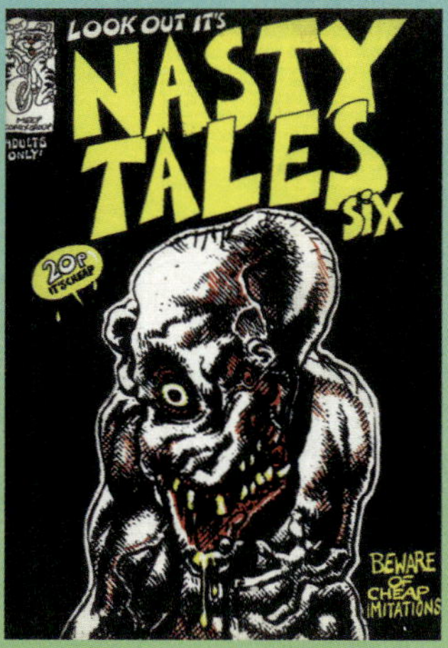

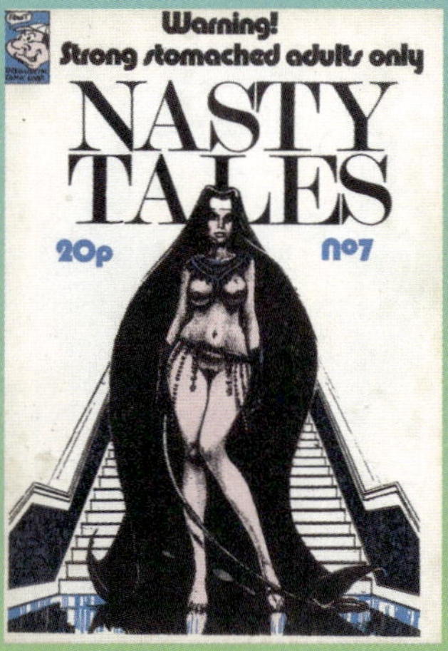

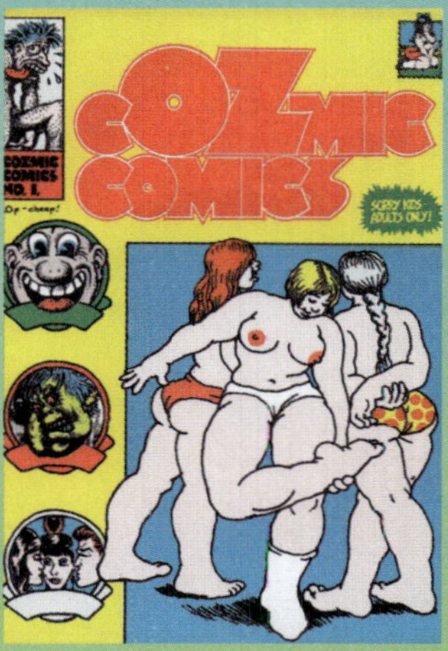

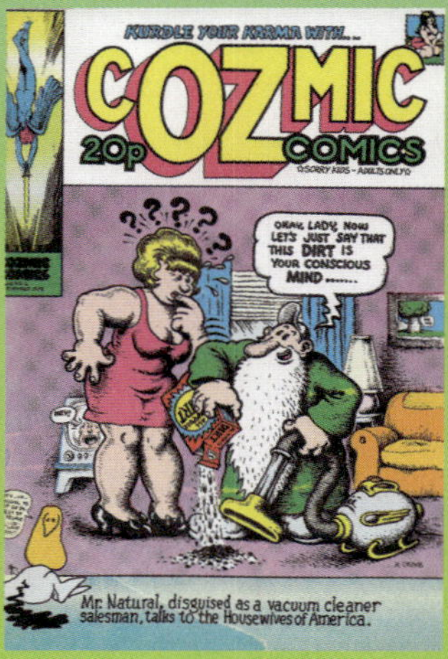

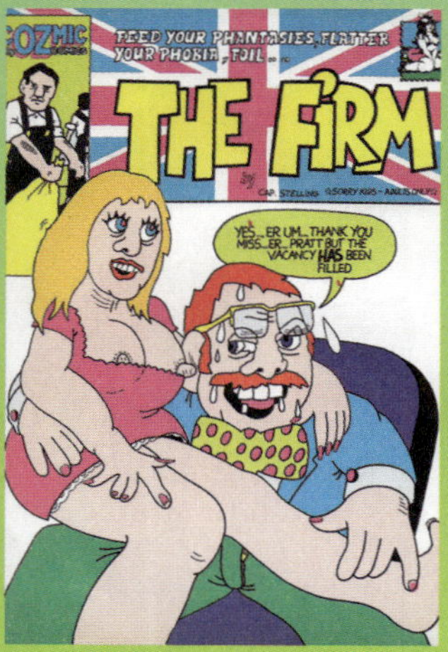

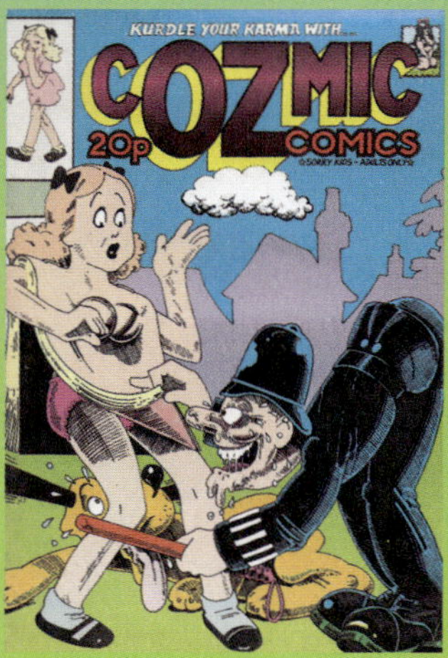

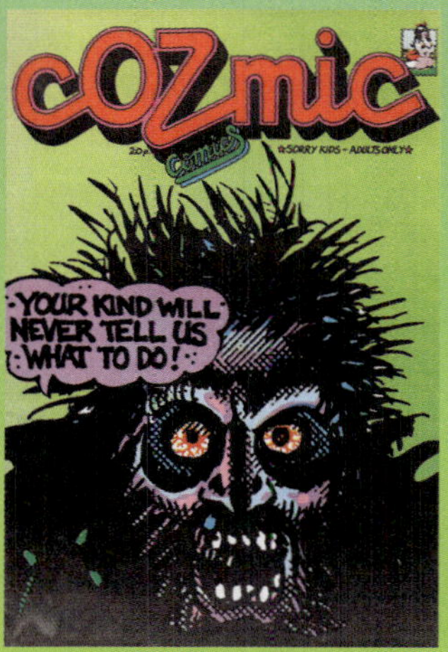

→ *East Village Other* spawned the American underground cartoonist movement, but the comix themselves were independent of the newspapers that initially printed them. In Britain, at least to begin with, there were only two comix publishers, both divisions of underground papers *Oz* and *IT*. *Oz*'s *cOZmic Comics* had the distinction of being the first to devote an entire issue to one comix artist's work: #3, 'The Firm,' was all by Captain Stelling, real name Mike Weller. Their seventh publication, 'Edward's Heave', was entirely the work of Edward Barker, cartoonist for *IT*, whose work was normally very popular. However, the title and the art turned people

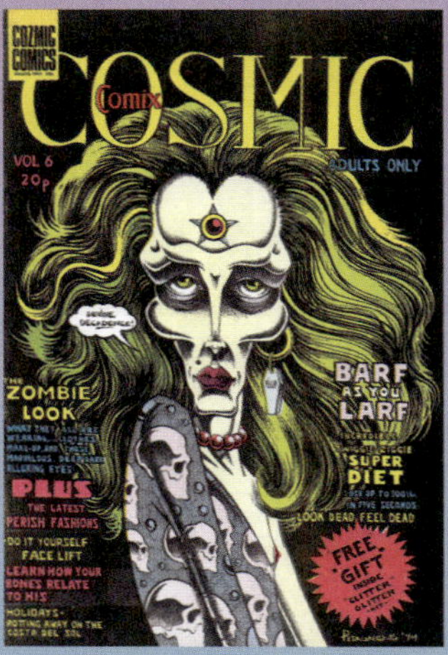

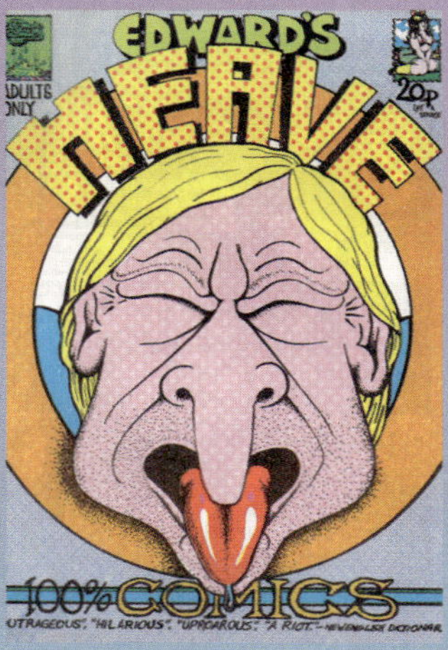

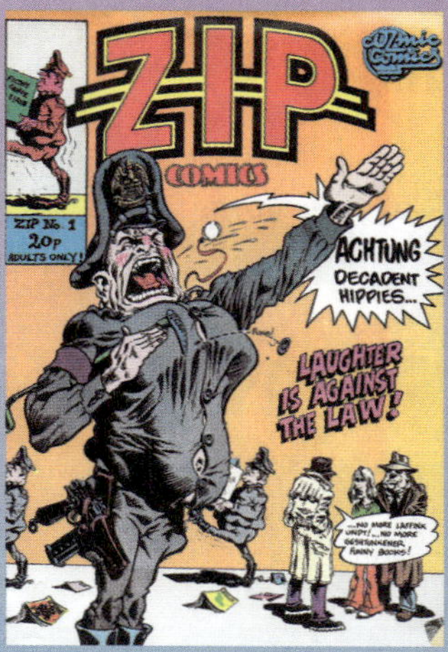

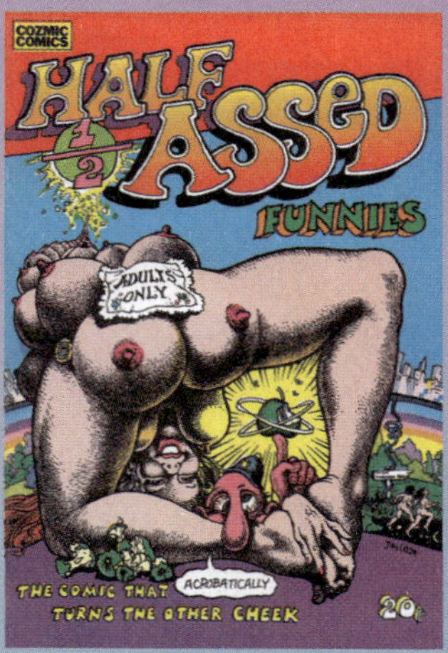

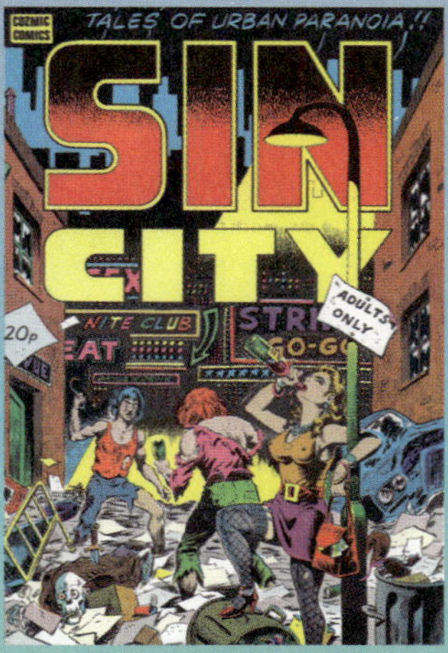

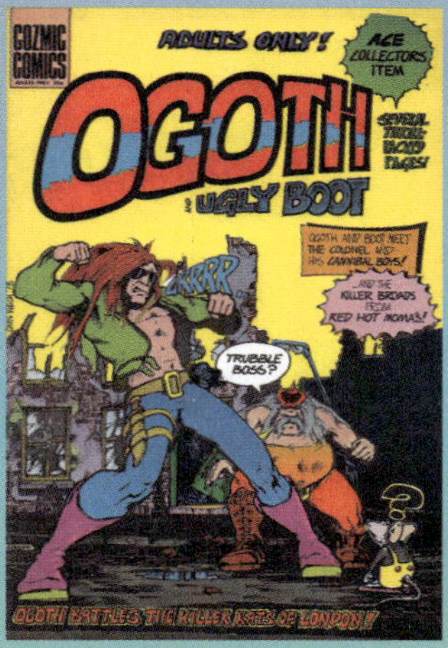

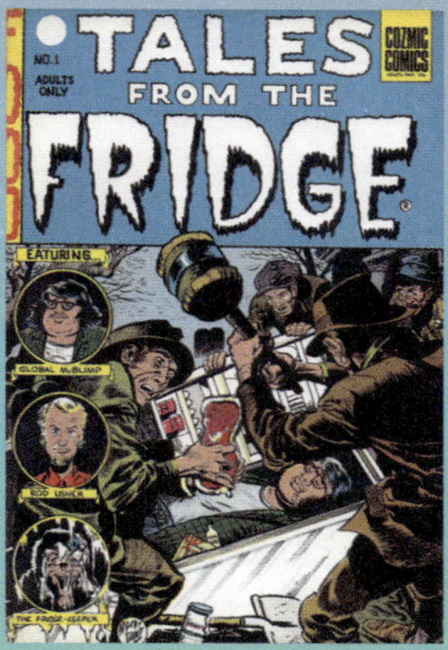

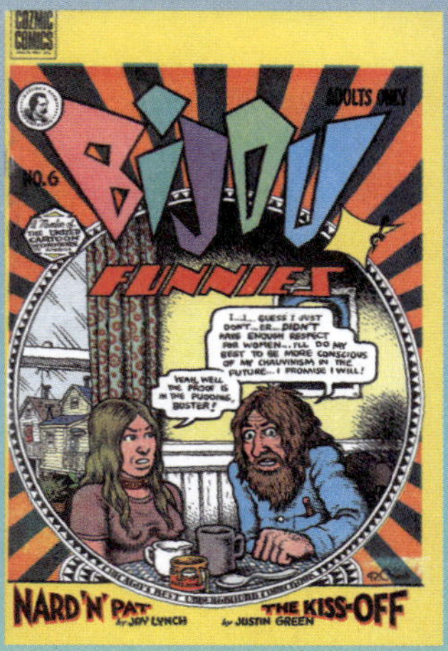

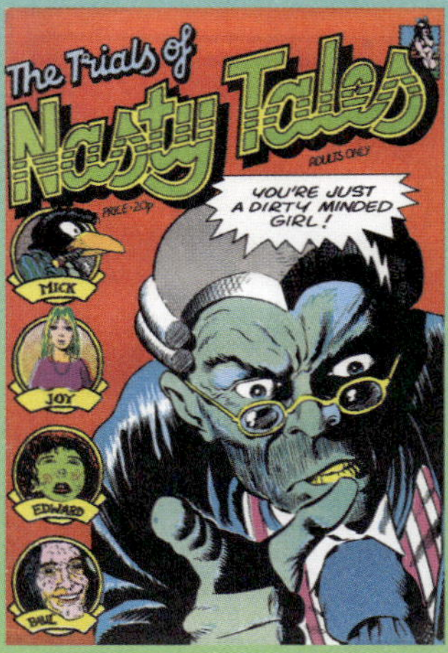

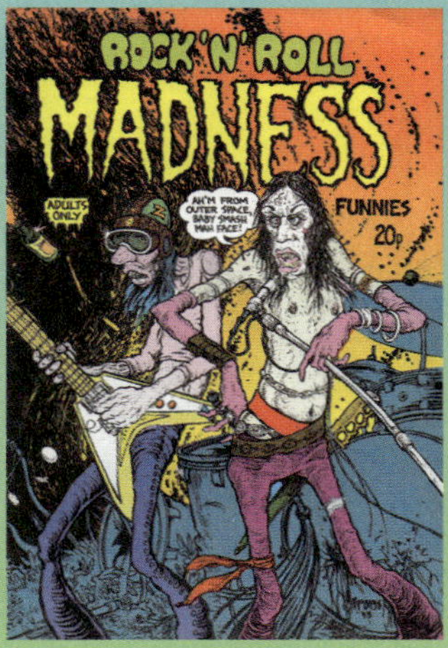

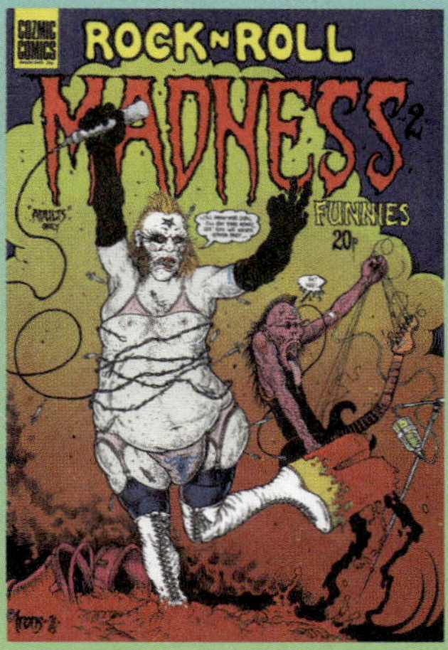

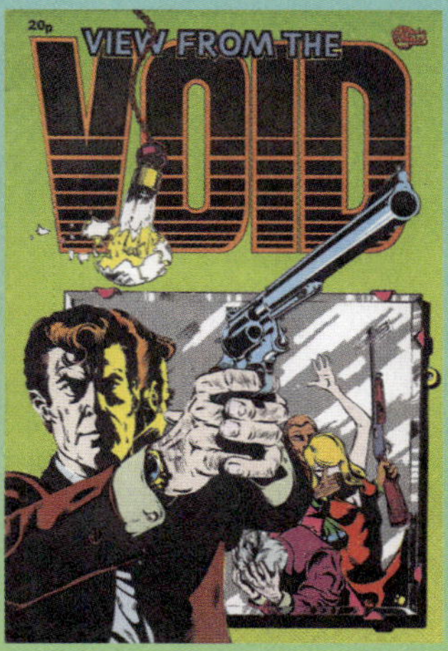

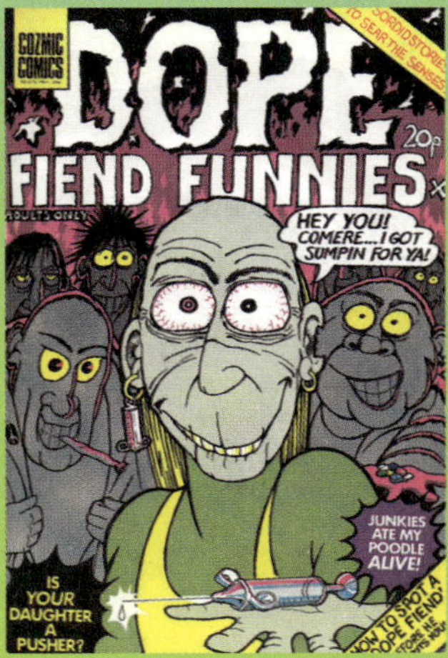

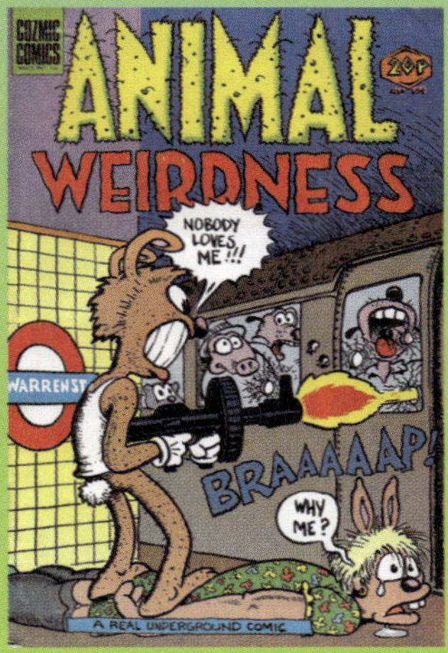

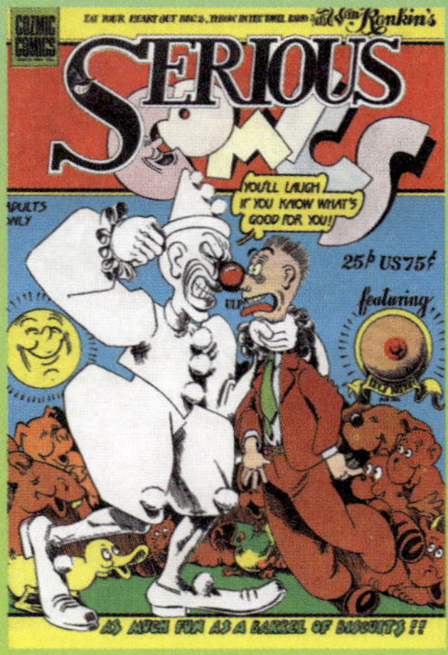

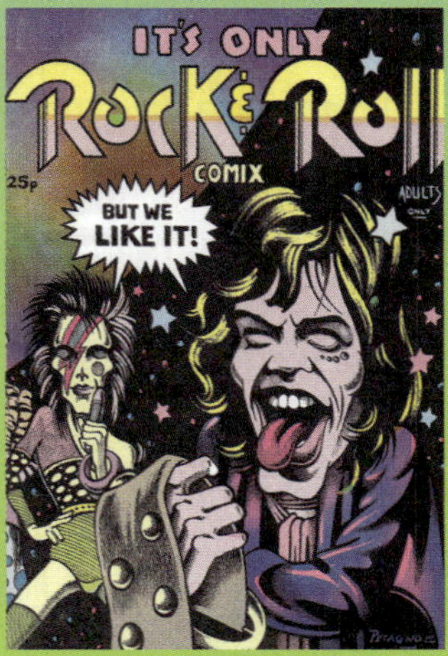

off and it was the worst-selling comic of the twenty-one that *cOZmic* produced. Ogoth and Ugly Boot had been very popular in *Nasty Tales*, so *cOZmic Comics* published them as a one-off. Again, it was entirely drawn by one artist, Chris Welch, with *IT* staffers Chris Rowley and Mick Farren supplying the storyline.

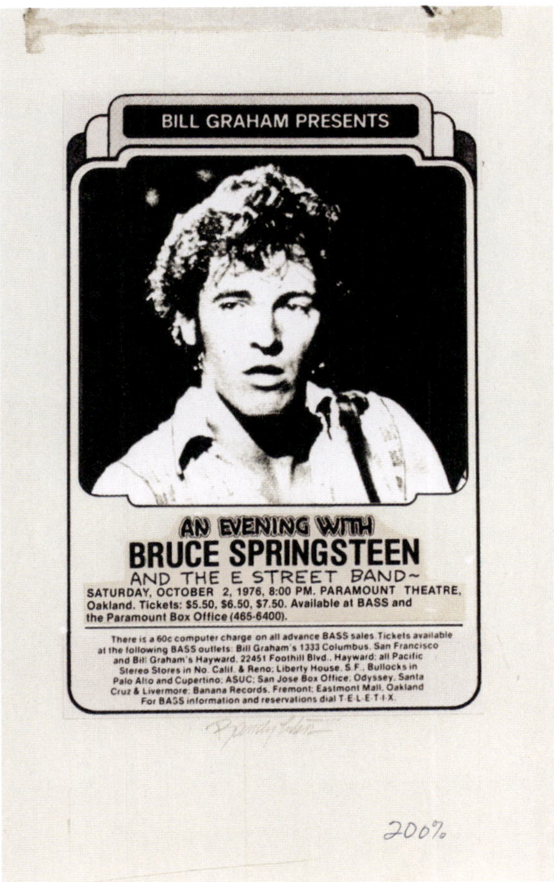

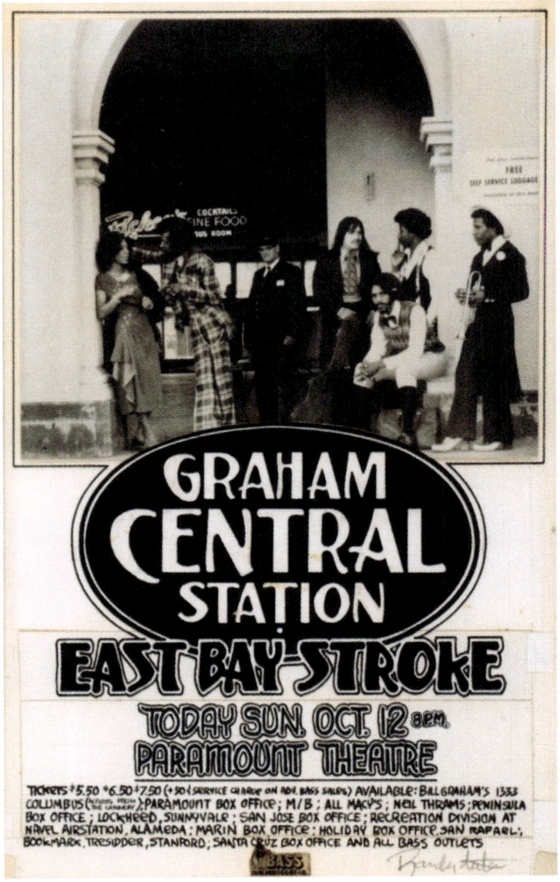

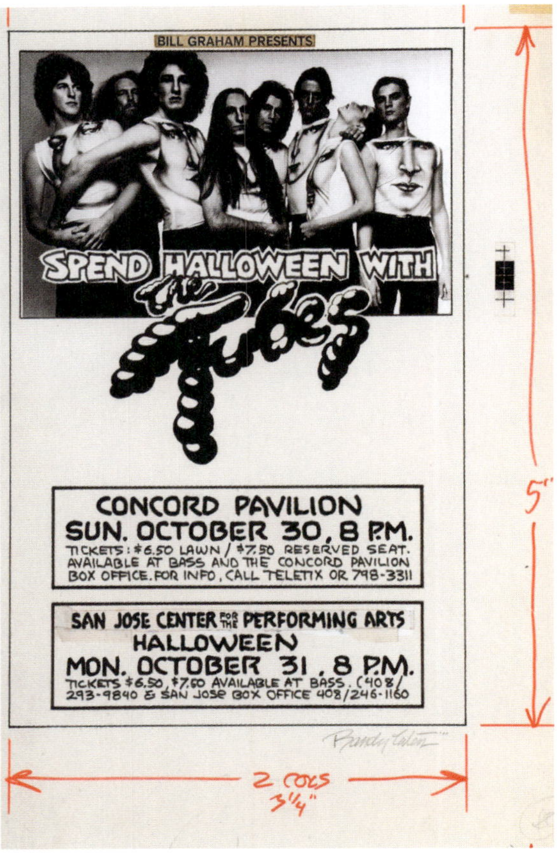

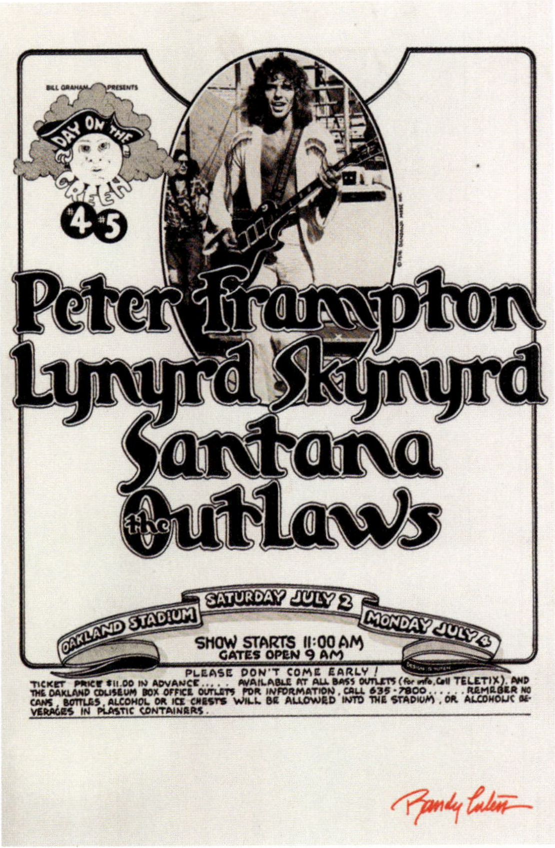

RANDY TUTEN

Randy Tuten did his first poster for Bill Graham in January 1969. He went on to produce dozens more for the promoter, often alternating with David Singer; the last one appeared in May 1971. Tuten produced ads for Graham for years to come, although over time virtually all traces of his original San Francisco design sensibility vanished and the work became purely commercial. As can be seen from the images here, by then most bands had a brand lettering for their name, which was used in all their strip ads. Rock 'n' roll advertising had come full circle and now looked just like it did before anyone dropped their first tab of acid.

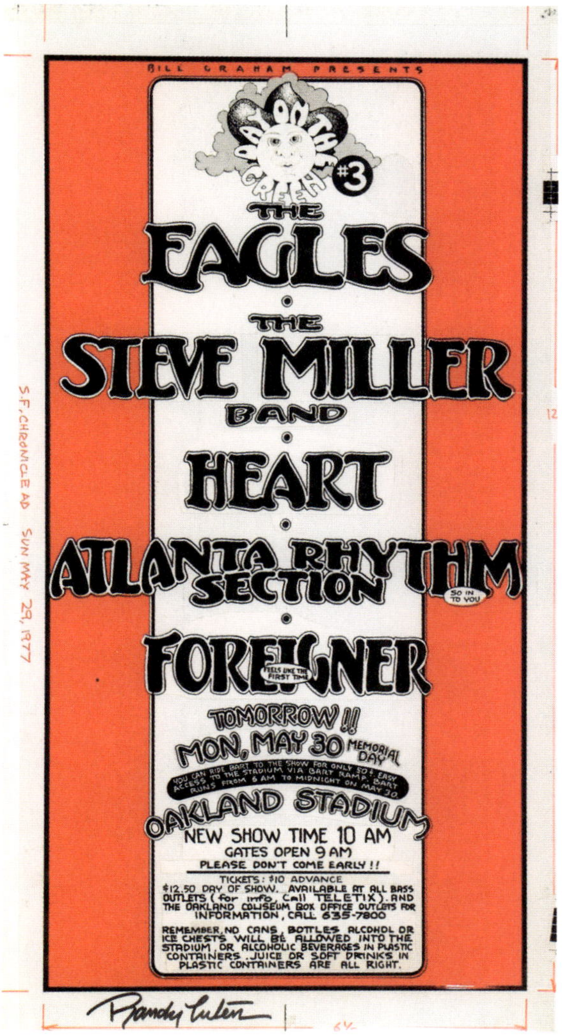

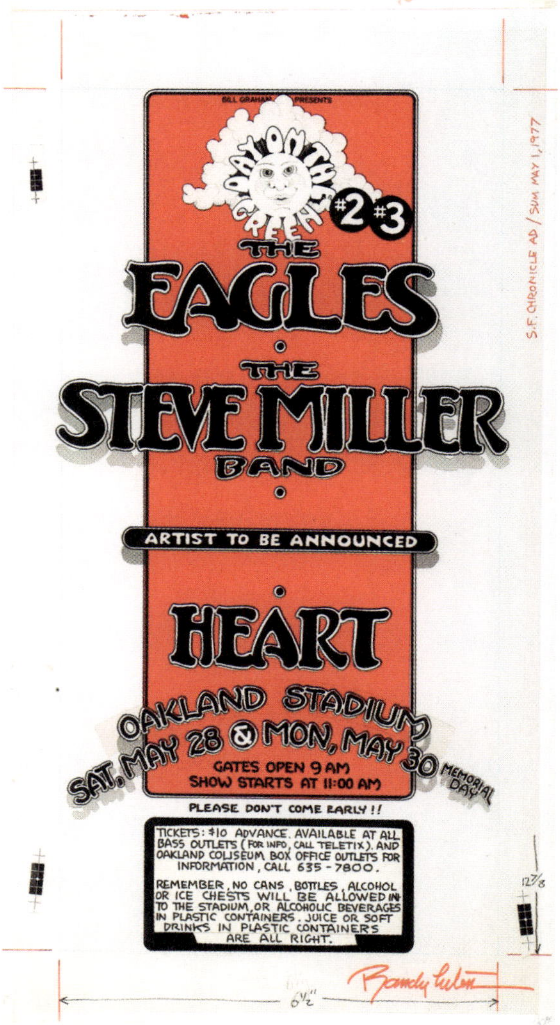

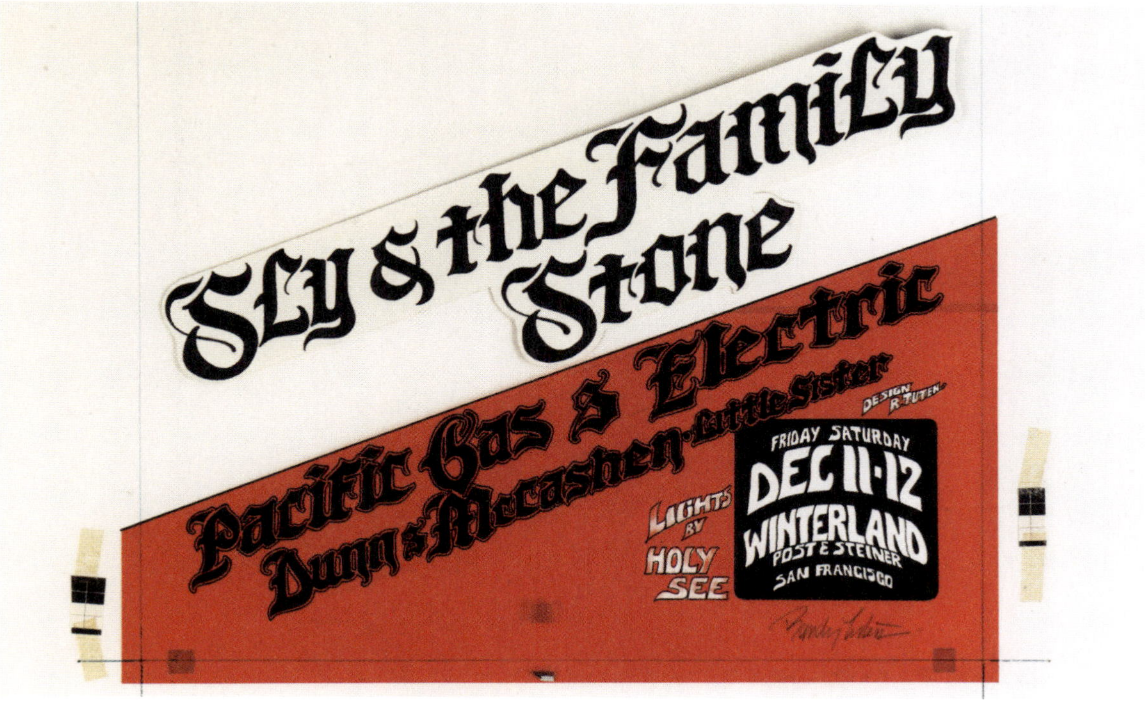

➳ Opposite: Original paste-ups for posters promoting (clockwise from top left): a 1976 Bruce Springsteen and The E Street Band concert; a 1975 Graham Central Station gig (the photo featured on the cover of their debut album); two July 1977 events headlined by Peter Frampton; two Halloween Tubes concerts in 1977. ➳ This page: original paste-ups with celluloid overlay for Bill Graham's 1977 Day On The Green festival (top left and right) and a strapline for a December 1970 gig at Winterland (bottom).

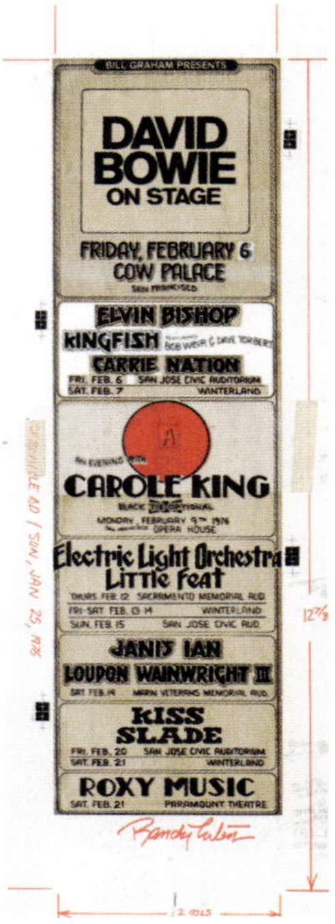
BILL GRAHAM PRESENTS
DAVID BOWIE
ON STAGE
FRIDAY, FEBRUARY 6
COW PALACE
ELVIN BISHOP
KINGFISH
CARRIE NATION
CAROLE KING
Electric Light Orchestra
Little Feat
JANIS IAN
LOUDON WAINWRIGHT III
KISS
SLADE
ROXY MUSIC

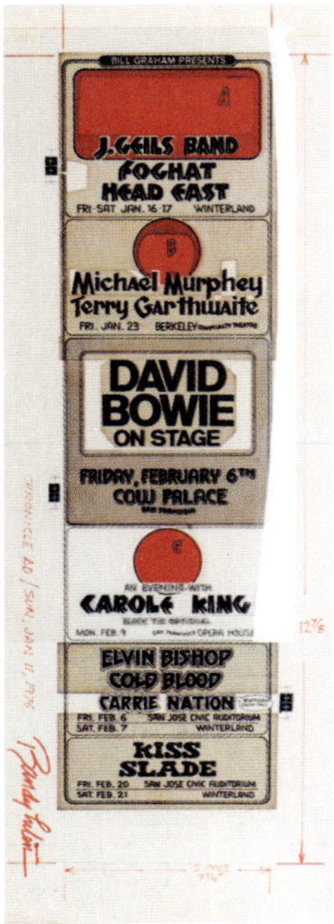
BILL GRAHAM PRESENTS
J. GEILS BAND
FOGHAT
HEAD EAST
Michael Murphey
Terry Garthwaite
DAVID BOWIE
ON STAGE
FRIDAY, FEBRUARY 6TH
COW PALACE
CAROLE KING
ELVIN BISHOP
COLD BLOOD
CARRIE NATION
KISS
SLADE

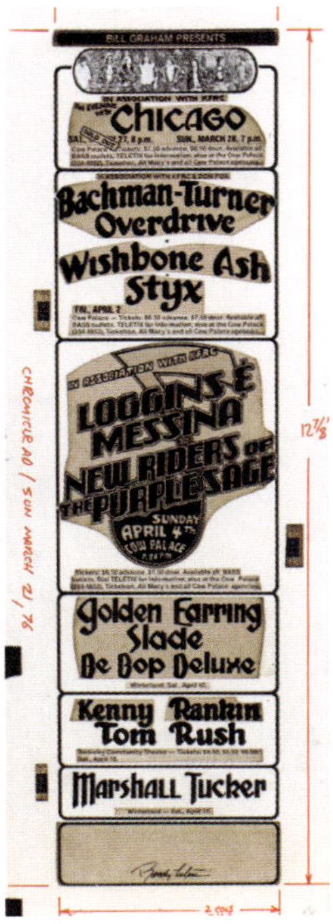
BILL GRAHAM PRESENTS
Chicago
Bachman-Turner Overdrive
Wishbone Ash
Styx
LOGGINS & MESSINA
NEW RIDERS OF THE PURPLE SAGE
Golden Earring
Slade
Be Bop Deluxe
Kenny Rankin
Tom Rush
Marshall Tucker

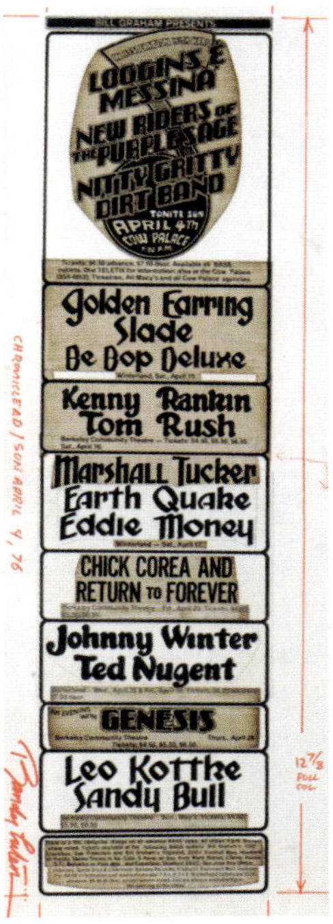
BILL GRAHAM PRESENTS
LOGGINS & MESSINA
NEW RIDERS OF THE PURPLE SAGE
NITTY GRITTY DIRT BAND
Golden Earring
Slade
Be Bop Deluxe
Kenny Rankin
Tom Rush
Marshall Tucker
Earth Quake
Eddie Money
CHICK COREA AND RETURN TO FOREVER
Johnny Winter
Ted Nugent
GENESIS
Leo Kottke
Sandy Bull

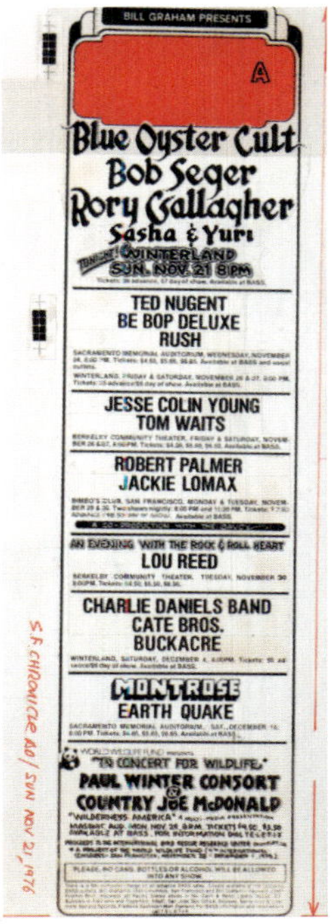
BILL GRAHAM PRESENTS
Blue Oyster Cult
Bob Seger
Rory Gallagher
Sasha & Yuri
WINTERLAND
SUN. NOV. 21 8 PM
TED NUGENT
BE BOP DELUXE
RUSH
JESSE COLIN YOUNG
TOM WAITS
ROBERT PALMER
JACKIE LOMAX
LOU REED
CHARLIE DANIELS BAND
CATE BROS.
BUCKACRE
MONTROSE
EARTH QUAKE
PAUL WINTER CONSORT
COUNTRY JOE McDONALD

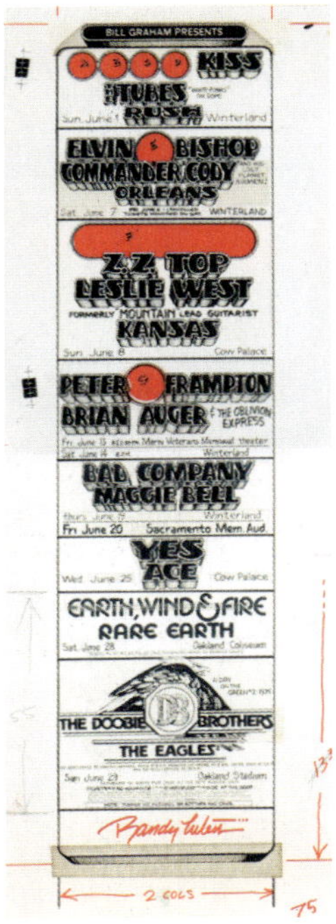
BILL GRAHAM PRESENTS
KISS
TUBES
RUSH
ELVIN BISHOP
COMMANDER CODY
ORLEANS
ZZ TOP
LESLIE WEST
KANSAS
PETER FRAMPTON
BRIAN AUGER
BAD COMPANY
MAGGIE BELL
YES
ACE
EARTH, WIND & FIRE
RARE EARTH
THE DOOBIE BROTHERS
THE EAGLES

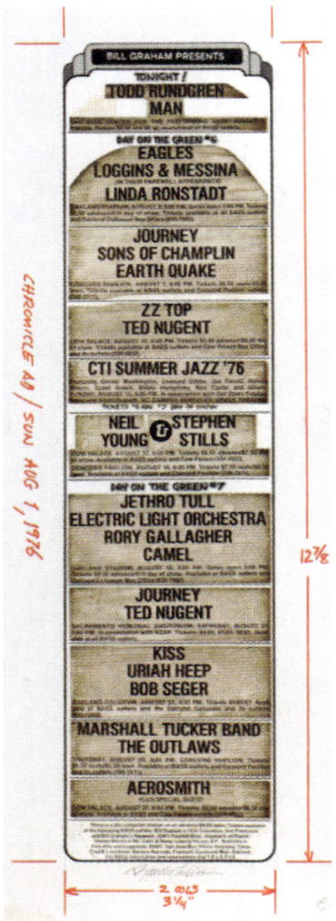
BILL GRAHAM PRESENTS
TODD RUNDGREN
EAGLES
LOGGINS & MESSINA
LINDA RONSTADT
JOURNEY
SONS OF CHAMPLIN
EARTH QUAKE
ZZ TOP
TED NUGENT
CTI SUMMER JAZZ '76
NEIL YOUNG
STEPHEN STILLS
JETHRO TULL
ELECTRIC LIGHT ORCHESTRA
RORY GALLAGHER
CAMEL
JOURNEY
TED NUGENT
KISS
URIAH HEEP
BOB SEGER
MARSHALL TUCKER BAND
THE OUTLAWS
AEROSMITH

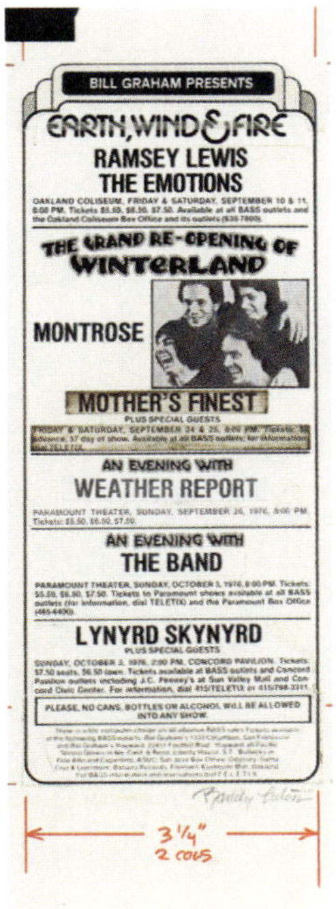
BILL GRAHAM PRESENTS
EARTH, WIND & FIRE
RAMSEY LEWIS
THE EMOTIONS
THE GRAND RE-OPENING OF WINTERLAND
MONTROSE
MOTHER'S FINEST
AN EVENING WITH
WEATHER REPORT
AN EVENING WITH
THE BAND
LYNYRD SKYNYRD
PLEASE, NO CANS, BOTTLES OR ALCOHOL WILL BE ALLOWED INTO ANY SHOW

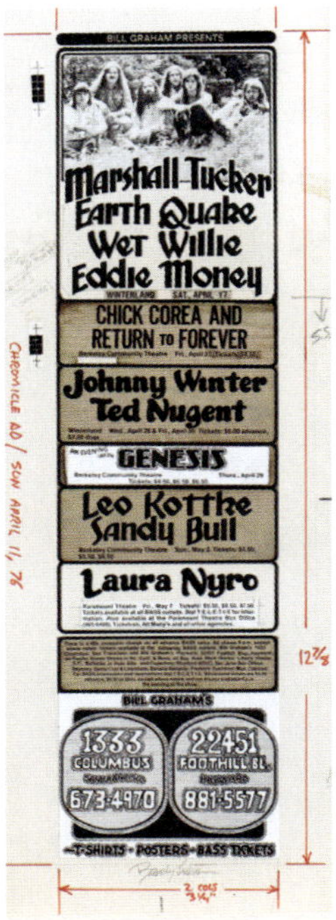
BILL GRAHAM PRESENTS
Marshall Tucker
Earth Quake
Wet Willie
Eddie Money
CHICK COREA AND RETURN TO FOREVER
Johnny Winter
Ted Nugent
GENESIS
Leo Kottke
Sandy Bull
Laura Nyro
BILL GRAHAM'S
1333 COLUMBUS
673-4970
22451 FOOTHILL BL.
881-5577
T-SHIRTS • POSTERS • BASS TICKETS

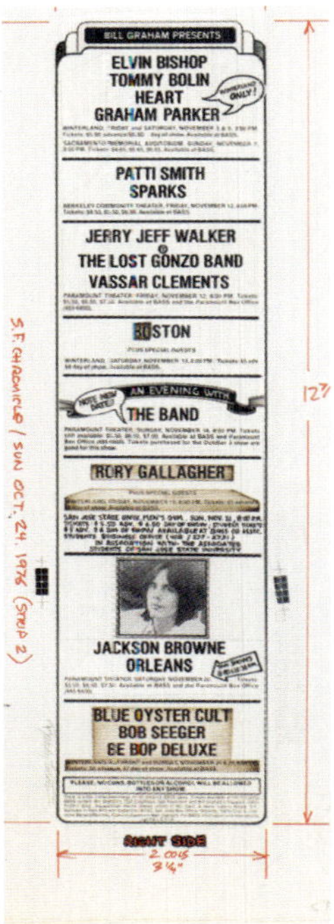
BILL GRAHAM PRESENTS
ELVIN BISHOP
TOMMY BOLIN
HEART
GRAHAM PARKER
PATTI SMITH
SPARKS
JERRY JEFF WALKER
THE LOST GONZO BAND
VASSAR CLEMENTS
BOSTON
AN EVENING WITH
THE BAND
RORY GALLAGHER
JACKSON BROWNE
ORLEANS
BLUE OYSTER CULT
BOB SEGER
BE BOP DELUXE

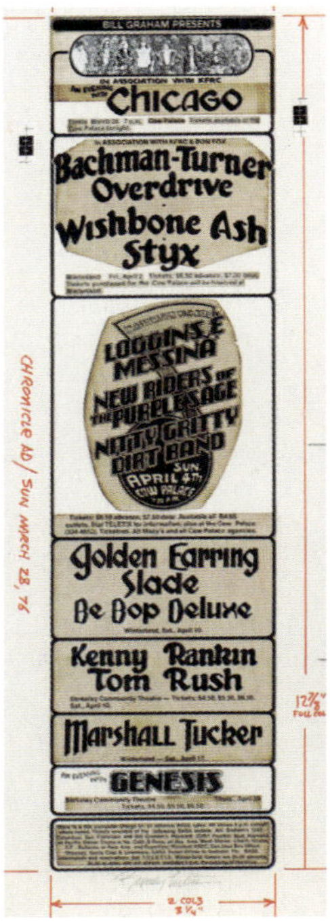
BILL GRAHAM PRESENTS
Chicago
Bachman-Turner Overdrive
Wishbone Ash
Styx
LOGGINS & MESSINA
NEW RIDERS OF THE PURPLE SAGE
NITTY GRITTY DIRT BAND
Golden Earring
Slade
Be Bop Deluxe
Kenny Rankin
Tom Rush
Marshall Tucker
GENESIS

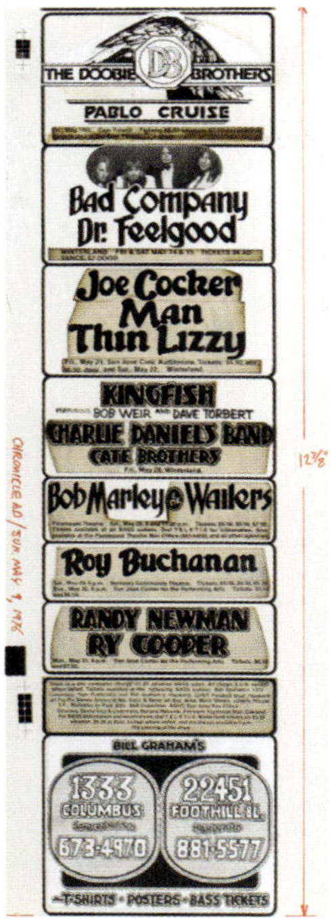
THE DOOBIE BROTHERS
PABLO CRUISE
Bad Company
Dr. Feelgood
Joe Cocker
Man
Thin Lizzy
KINGFISH
BOB WEIR
CHARLIE DANIELS BAND
CATE BROTHERS
Bob Marley & the Wailers
Roy Buchanan
RANDY NEWMAN
RY COODER
BILL GRAHAM'S
1333 COLUMBUS
673-4970
22451 FOOTHILL BL.
881-5577
T-SHIRTS • POSTERS • BASS TICKETS

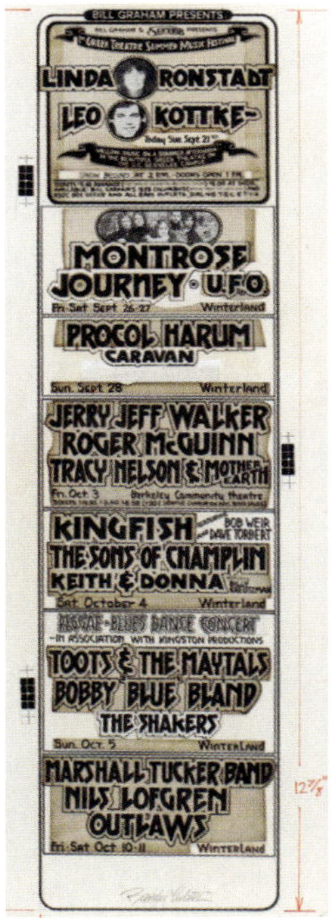
BILL GRAHAM PRESENTS
LINDA RONSTADT
LEO KOTTKE
MONTROSE
JOURNEY
U.F.O.
PROCOL HARUM
CARAVAN
JERRY JEFF WALKER
ROGER McGUINN
TRACY NELSON & MOTHER EARTH
KINGFISH
BOB WEIR
DAVE TORBERT
THE SONS OF CHAMPLIN
KEITH & DONNA
TOOTS & THE MAYTALS
BOBBY BLUE BLAND
THE SHAKERS
MARSHALL TUCKER BAND
NILS LOFGREN
OUTLAWS

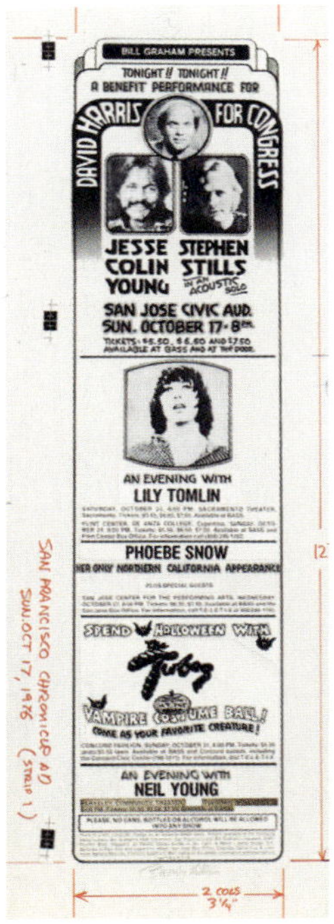
BILL GRAHAM PRESENTS
TONIGHT!! TONIGHT!!
A BENEFIT PERFORMANCE FOR
DAVID HARRIS FOR CONGRESS
JESSE COLIN YOUNG
STEPHEN STILLS
SAN JOSE CIVIC AUD.
SUN. OCTOBER 17
AN EVENING WITH
LILY TOMLIN
PHOEBE SNOW
AN EVENING WITH
NEIL YOUNG

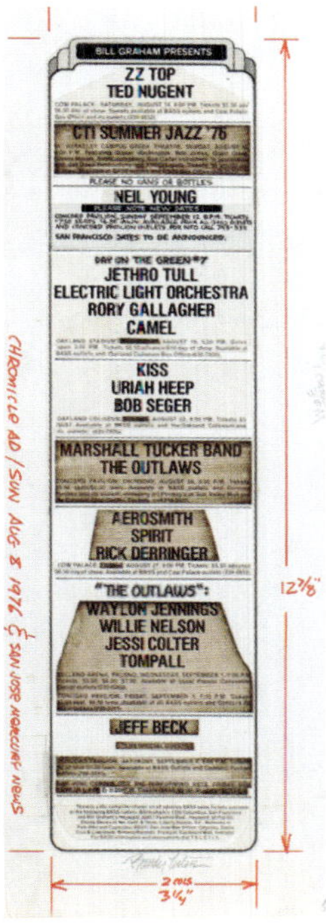
BILL GRAHAM PRESENTS
ZZ TOP
TED NUGENT
CTI SUMMER JAZZ '76
NEIL YOUNG
JETHRO TULL
ELECTRIC LIGHT ORCHESTRA
RORY GALLAGHER
CAMEL
KISS
URIAH HEEP
BOB SEGER
MARSHALL TUCKER BAND
THE OUTLAWS
AEROSMITH
SPIRIT
RICK DERRINGER
"THE OUTLAWS":
WAYLON JENNINGS
WILLIE NELSON
JESSI COLTER
TOMPALL
JEFF BECK

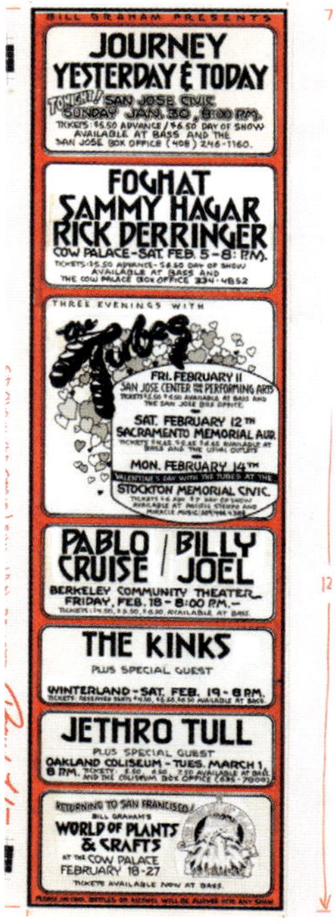

BILL GRAHAM PRESENTS
JOURNEY
YESTERDAY & TODAY
FOGHAT
SAMMY HAGAR
RICK DERRINGER
COW PALACE - SAT. FEB. 5 - 8 P.M.
THREE EVENINGS WITH
The Tubes
PABLO CRUISE
BILLY JOEL
THE KINKS
JETHRO TULL
WORLD OF PLANTS & CRAFTS

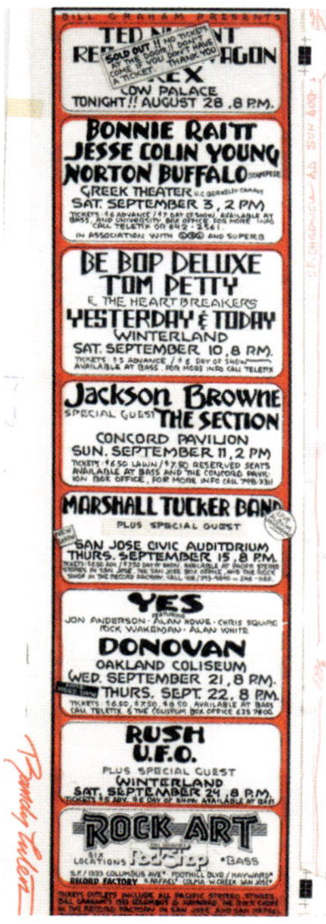

TED NUGENT
REO SPEEDWAGON
REX
COW PALACE
BONNIE RAITT
JESSE COLIN YOUNG
NORTON BUFFALO
BE BOP DELUXE
TOM PETTY & THE HEARTBREAKERS
YESTERDAY & TODAY
Jackson Browne
THE SECTION
MARSHALL TUCKER BAND
YES
DONOVAN
RUSH
U.F.O.
ROCK ART

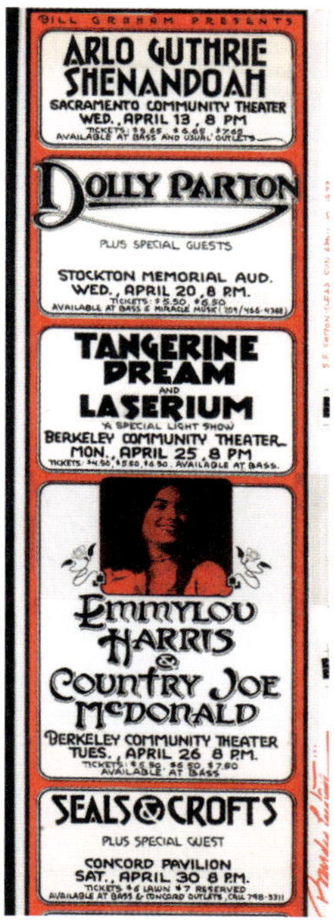

BILL GRAHAM PRESENTS
ARLO GUTHRIE
SHENANDOAH
DOLLY PARTON
TANGERINE DREAM
LASERIUM
Emmylou Harris
Country Joe McDonald
SEALS & CROFTS

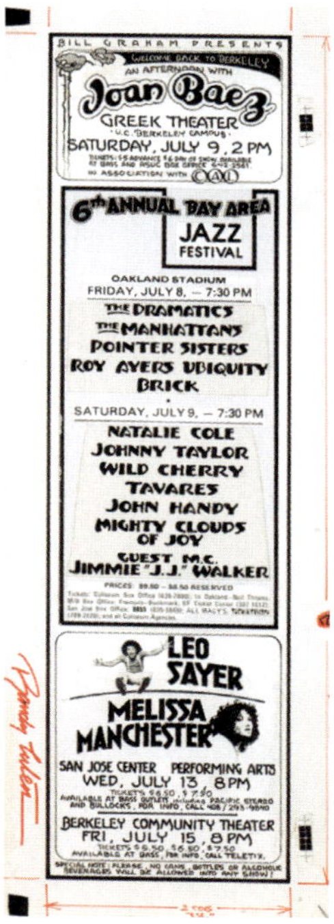

BILL GRAHAM PRESENTS
Joan Baez
6th ANNUAL BAY AREA JAZZ FESTIVAL
THE DRAMATICS
THE MANHATTANS
POINTER SISTERS
ROY AYERS UBIQUITY
BRICK
NATALIE COLE
JOHNNY TAYLOR
WILD CHERRY
TAVARES
JOHN HANDY
MIGHTY CLOUDS OF JOY
JIMMIE "J.J." WALKER
LEO SAYER
MELISSA MANCHESTER

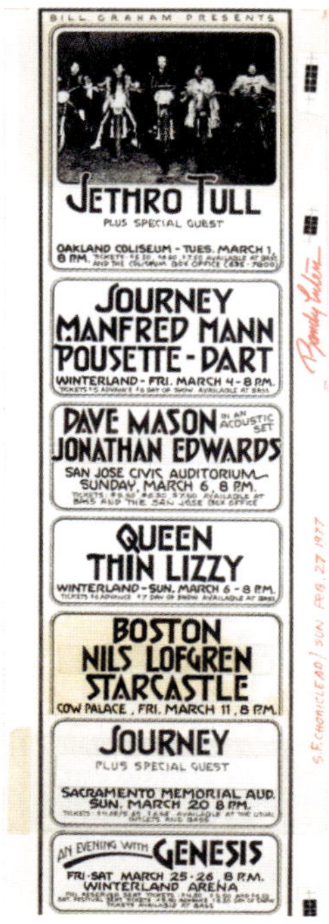

BILL GRAHAM PRESENTS
JETHRO TULL
JOURNEY
MANFRED MANN
POUSETTE-DART
DAVE MASON
JONATHAN EDWARDS
QUEEN
THIN LIZZY
BOSTON
NILS LOFGREN
STARCASTLE
JOURNEY
GENESIS

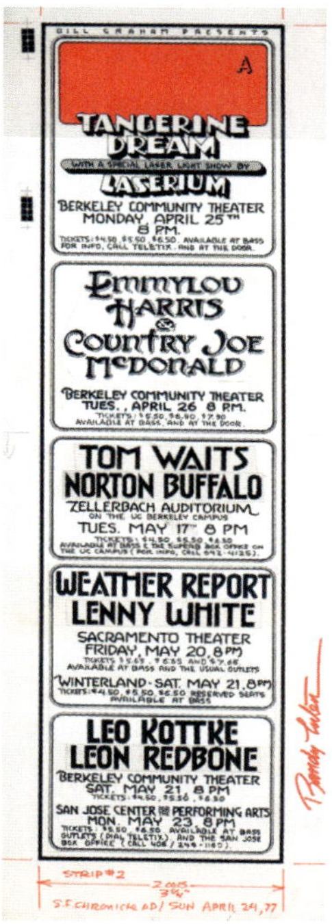

BILL GRAHAM PRESENTS
TANGERINE DREAM
LASERIUM
Emmylou Harris
Country Joe McDonald
TOM WAITS
NORTON BUFFALO
WEATHER REPORT
LENNY WHITE
LEO KOTTKE
LEON REDBONE

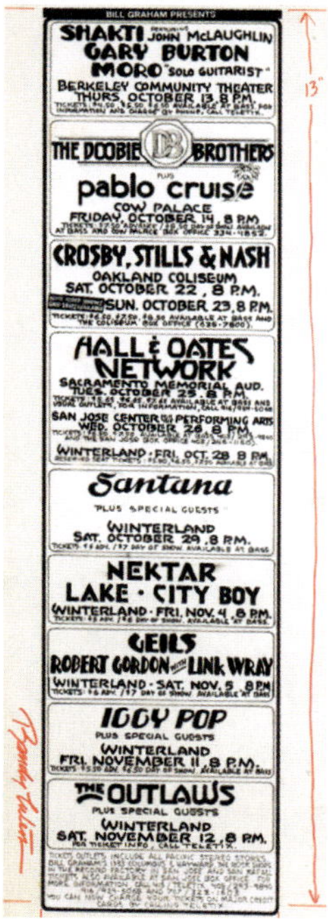

BILL GRAHAM PRESENTS
SHAKTI
GARY BURTON
THE DOOBIE BROTHERS
pablo cruise
CROSBY, STILLS & NASH
HALL & OATES
NETWORK
Santana
NEKTAR
LAKE · CITY BOY
GEILS
ROBERT GORDON LINK WRAY
IGGY POP
THE OUTLAWS

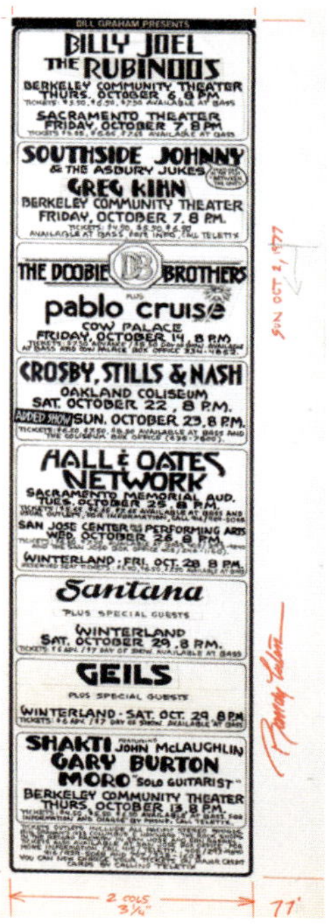

BILL GRAHAM PRESENTS
BILLY JOEL
THE RUBINOOS
SOUTHSIDE JOHNNY & THE ASBURY JUKES
GREG KIHN
THE DOOBIE BROTHERS
pablo cruise
CROSBY, STILLS & NASH
HALL & OATES
NETWORK
Santana
GEILS
SHAKTI
GARY BURTON

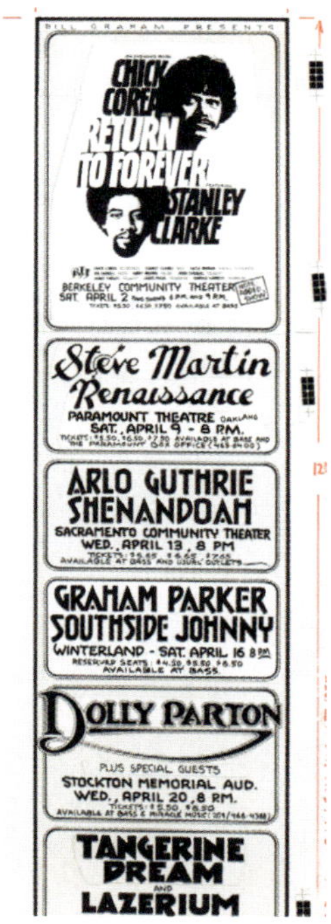

BILL GRAHAM PRESENTS
CHICK COREA
RETURN TO FOREVER
STANLEY CLARKE
Steve Martin
Renaissance
ARLO GUTHRIE
SHENANDOAH
GRAHAM PARKER
SOUTHSIDE JOHNNY
DOLLY PARTON
TANGERINE DREAM
LAZERIUM

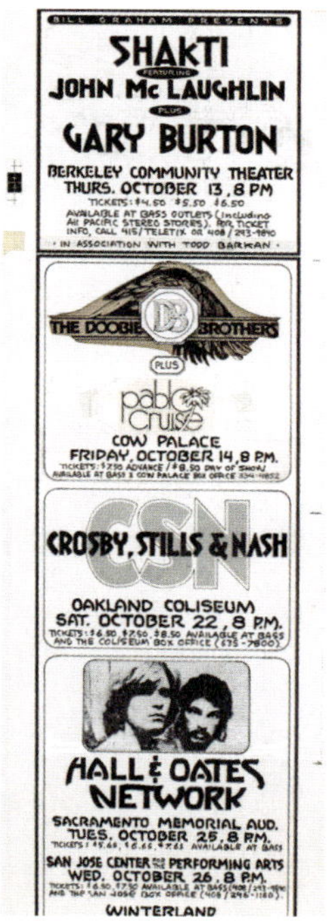

BILL GRAHAM PRESENTS
SHAKTI
JOHN McLAUGHLIN
GARY BURTON
THE DOOBIE BROTHERS
pablo cruise
CROSBY, STILLS & NASH
HALL & OATES
NETWORK

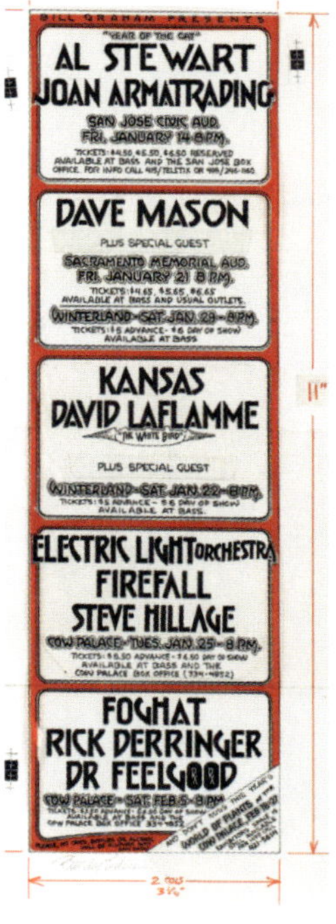

BILL GRAHAM PRESENTS
AL STEWART
JOAN ARMATRADING
DAVE MASON
KANSAS
DAVID LAFLAMME
ELECTRIC LIGHT ORCHESTRA
FIREFALL
STEVE HILLAGE
FOGHAT
RICK DERRINGER
DR FEELGOOD

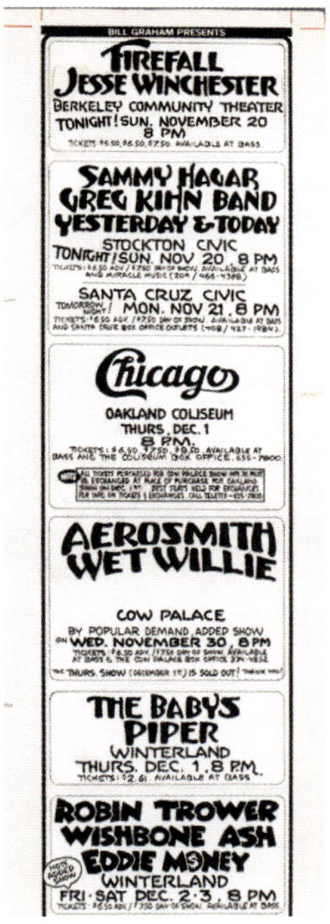

BILL GRAHAM PRESENTS
FIREFALL
JESSE WINCHESTER
SAMMY HAGAR
GREG KIHN BAND
YESTERDAY & TODAY
Chicago
AEROSMITH
WET WILLIE
THE BABYS
PIPER
ROBIN TROWER
WISHBONE ASH
EDDIE MONEY

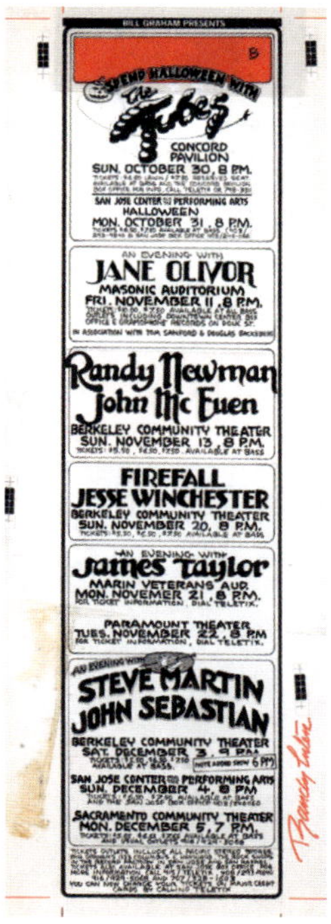

BILL GRAHAM PRESENTS
The Tubes
JANE OLIVOR
Randy Newman
John McEuen
FIREFALL
JESSE WINCHESTER
James Taylor
STEVE MARTIN
JOHN SEBASTIAN

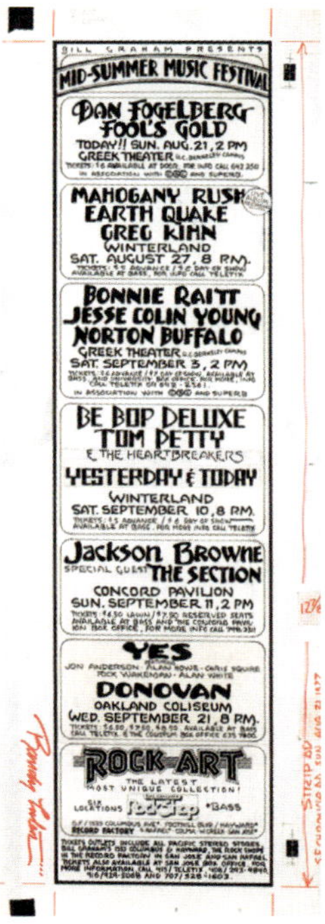

BILL GRAHAM PRESENTS
MID-SUMMER MUSIC FESTIVAL
DAN FOGELBERG
FOOL'S GOLD
MAHOGANY RUSH
EARTH QUAKE
GREG KIHN
BONNIE RAITT
JESSE COLIN YOUNG
NORTON BUFFALO
BE BOP DELUXE
TOM PETTY & THE HEARTBREAKERS
YESTERDAY & TODAY
Jackson Browne
THE SECTION
YES
DONOVAN
ROCK ART

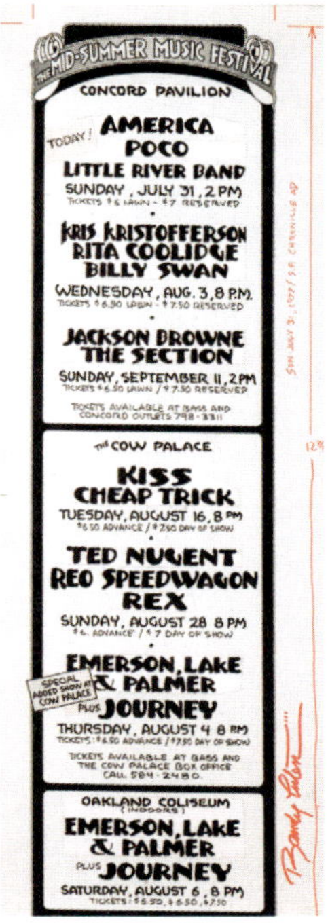

MID-SUMMER MUSIC FESTIVAL
CONCORD PAVILION
AMERICA
POCO
LITTLE RIVER BAND
KRIS KRISTOFFERSON
RITA COOLIDGE
BILLY SWAN
JACKSON BROWNE
THE SECTION
COW PALACE
KISS
CHEAP TRICK
TED NUGENT
REO SPEEDWAGON
REX
EMERSON, LAKE & PALMER
JOURNEY
OAKLAND COLISEUM
EMERSON, LAKE & PALMER
JOURNEY

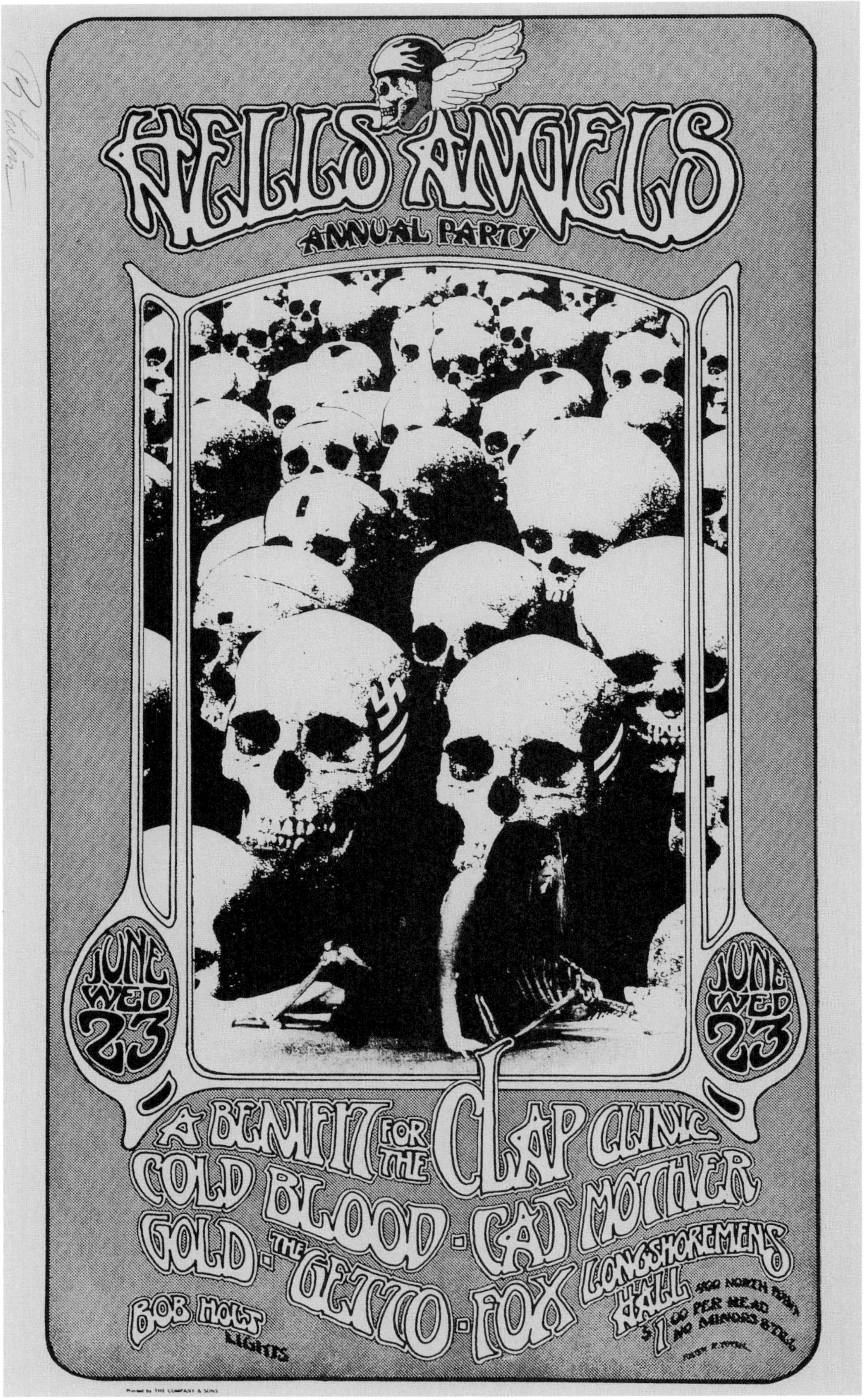

⋙→ Previous pages: a cross-section of bands of the era, seen through artwork paste-ups for press ads. ⋙→ These pages: test proof and (opposite) test proof with overlay for a Hells Angels benefit gig ('for the clap clinic') in 1971 at San Francisco's Longshoremen's Hall. The amorous foreground figures add some macabre humor.

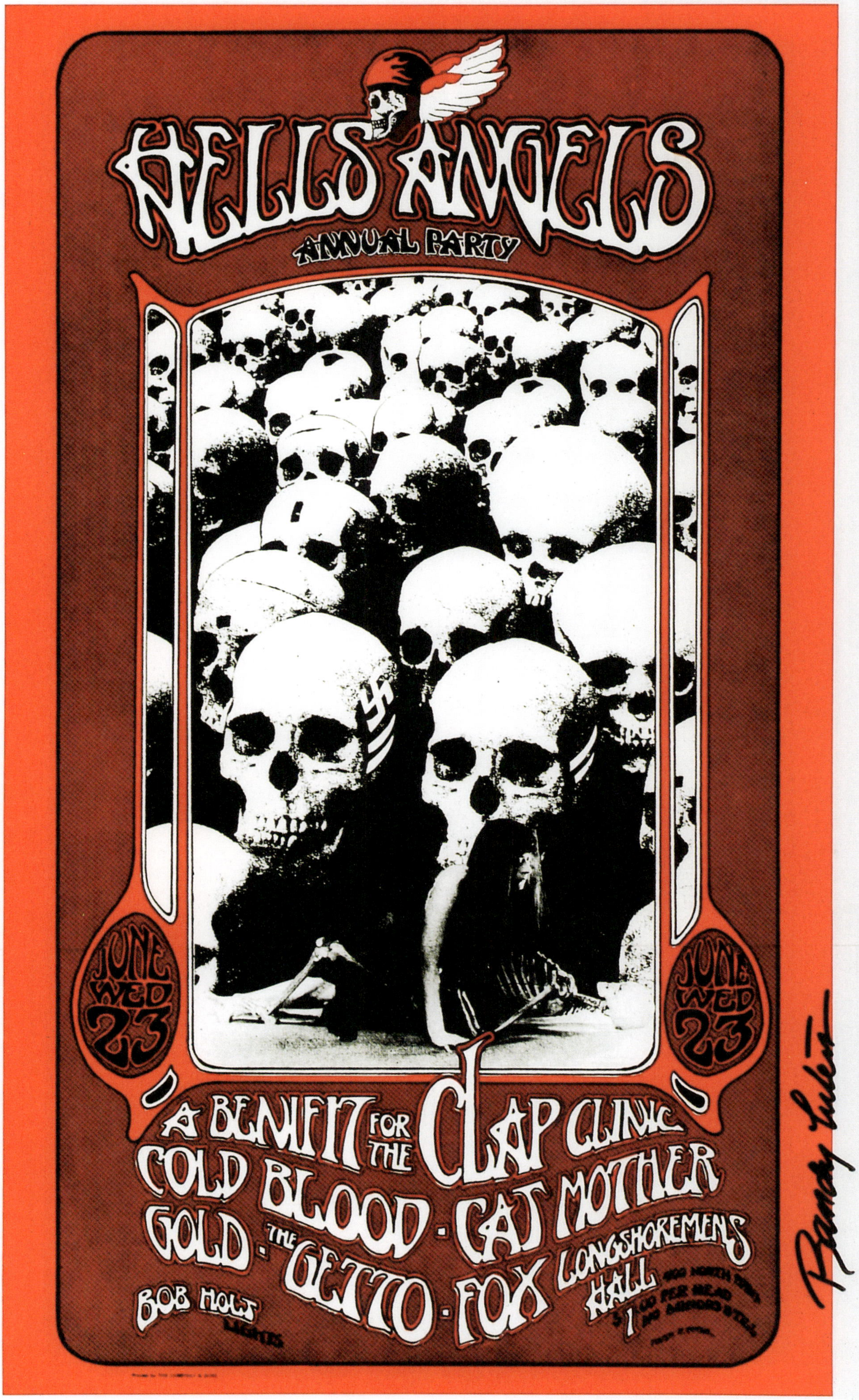
HELLS ANGELS
ANNUAL PARTY
JUNE WED 23
JUNE WED 23
A BENEFIT FOR THE CLAP CLINIC
COLD BLOOD · CAT MOTHER
GOLD · THE GETTO · FOX
LONGSHOREMENS HALL
$1.00 PER HEAD
BOB HOLT LIGHTS
Randy Tuten

RANDY TUTEN

⟿ A commemorative poster by Tuten celebrating The Doors' appearance at Madison Square Garden, New York, on January 24, 1969.

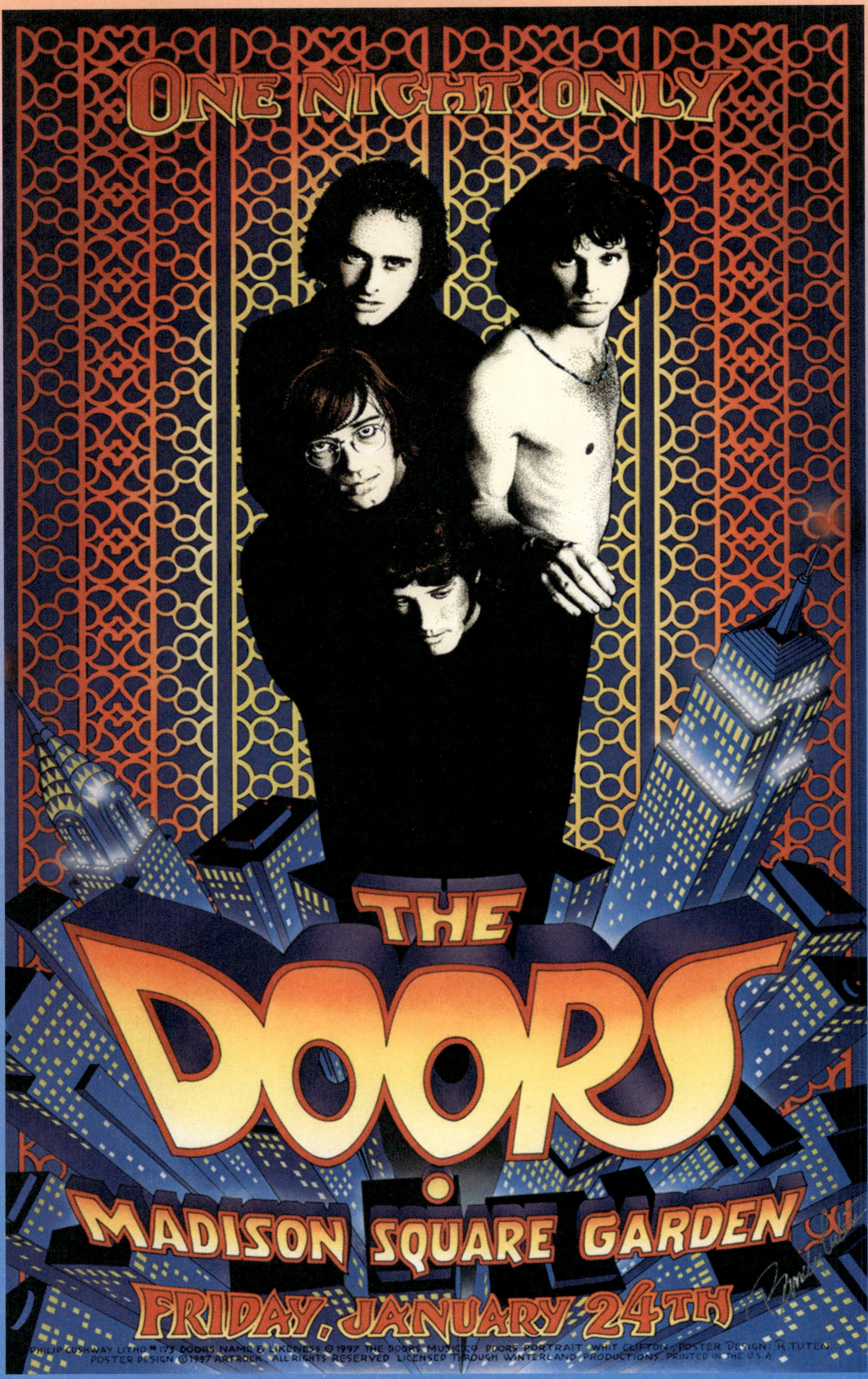

RANDY TUTEN (1946–)

BORN IN SAN FRANCISCO, RANDY TUTEN CAME OF AGE IN LA DURING THE LATE FIFTIES. HE WAS A REBELLIOUS TEENAGER AND SELF-TAUGHT ARTIST WHOSE TALENT WAS EVIDENT EVEN IN JUNIOR HIGH. AT COLLEGE, TUTEN WORKED FOR THE ART DEPARTMENT AND REGULARLY CUT OTHER CLASSES IN FAVOR OF HANGING ART EXHIBITS IN THE COLLEGE GALLERY. ⟶ IN 1966 HE MADE A HABIT OF HITCHHIKING TO SAN FRANCISCO, SOAKING UP EVERYTHING THAT WAS HAPPENING MUSICALLY AT THE AVALON BALLROOM AND THE FILLMORE AUDITORIUM. IT WAS THE POSTERS OF MOUSE, KELLEY, AND GRIFFIN THAT FUELED HIS IMAGINATION AND INFLUENCED HIS ARTISTIC APPROACH. ⟶ TUTEN MOVED TO SAN FRANCISCO IN JANUARY 1967, MAKING ENDS MEET AS A FREELANCE GRAPHIC DESIGNER. IN JANUARY 1969, AFTER A YEAR OF BEING REJECTED AS A POSTER ARTIST BY CHET HELMS AT THE AVALON BALLROOM, THE 23-YEAR-OLD TOOK HIS PORTFOLIO TO THE FILLMORE, WHERE BILL GRAHAM IMMEDIATELY HIRED HIM. IN SAN FRANCISCO, TUTEN ALSO MET GRAPHIC ILLUSTRATOR DADDY BREAD (BILL BOSTEDT). THEY WOULD COLLABORATE ON MANY PROJECTS, INCLUDING SOME OF THE MOST FAMOUS ROCK POSTERS, UNTIL DADDY BREAD'S DEATH IN 1998. ⟶ IN 1980, SUFFERING FROM BURNOUT, TUTEN MOVED UP TO LAKE COUNTY. HE CONTINUED TO PRODUCE POSTERS FOR BILL GRAHAM AND OTHERS UNTIL HE SUFFERED A DEBILITATING STROKE IN EARLY 1984. STRUGGLING TO RECOVER, HE PRODUCED NO WORK IN 1984 OR 1985, BUT RICK GRIFFIN VISITED HIM IN HOSPITAL AND SUGGESTED THEY COLLABORATE IN SANTA ANA ONCE HE HAD SUFFICIENTLY RECOVERED. BEGINNING IN 1986, TUTEN MADE MULTIPLE TRIPS TO SANTA ANA TO WORK WITH GRIFFIN. ⟶ IN 1989 TUTEN RETURNED TO THE BAY AREA, WHERE HE CURRENTLY RESIDES. THE ONLY DESIGNER TO SPAN FIVE DECADES CREATING POSTERS FOR THE FILLMORE, HE IS STILL A PROLIFIC FULL-TIME ARTIST TODAY. HIS WORK HAS LONG BEEN RECOGNIZED FOR ITS SEMINAL INFLUENCE ON THE ART OF MODERN ROCK 'N' ROLL.

3

MONSTERS OF ROCK

'78 ↓ '88

BY THE LATE SEVENTIES,
LIFESTYLE WAS THE
AND PUNK WAS THE COUNTER-
OCCUPIED JUST AS SMALL A
BACK IN THE MID- TO LATE
ROCK'S BIG HITTERS
PROMOTERS, SUCH AS BILL
LONG CONCERTS FEATURING
CALLED FOR FANTASTIC SET
BACKDROPS THAT MADE AN

'ROCK' AND ITS ASSOCIATED
DOMINANT YOUTH CULTURE
CULTURE. IN AMERICA, PUNK
NICHE AS PSYCHEDELIA HAD
SIXTIES—AND MANY OF
CONTINUED TO FLOURISH.
GRAHAM, PUT ON HUGE, DAY-
STADIUM BANDS THAT
DESIGNS AND EYE-CATCHING
IMPACT FROM A DISTANCE.

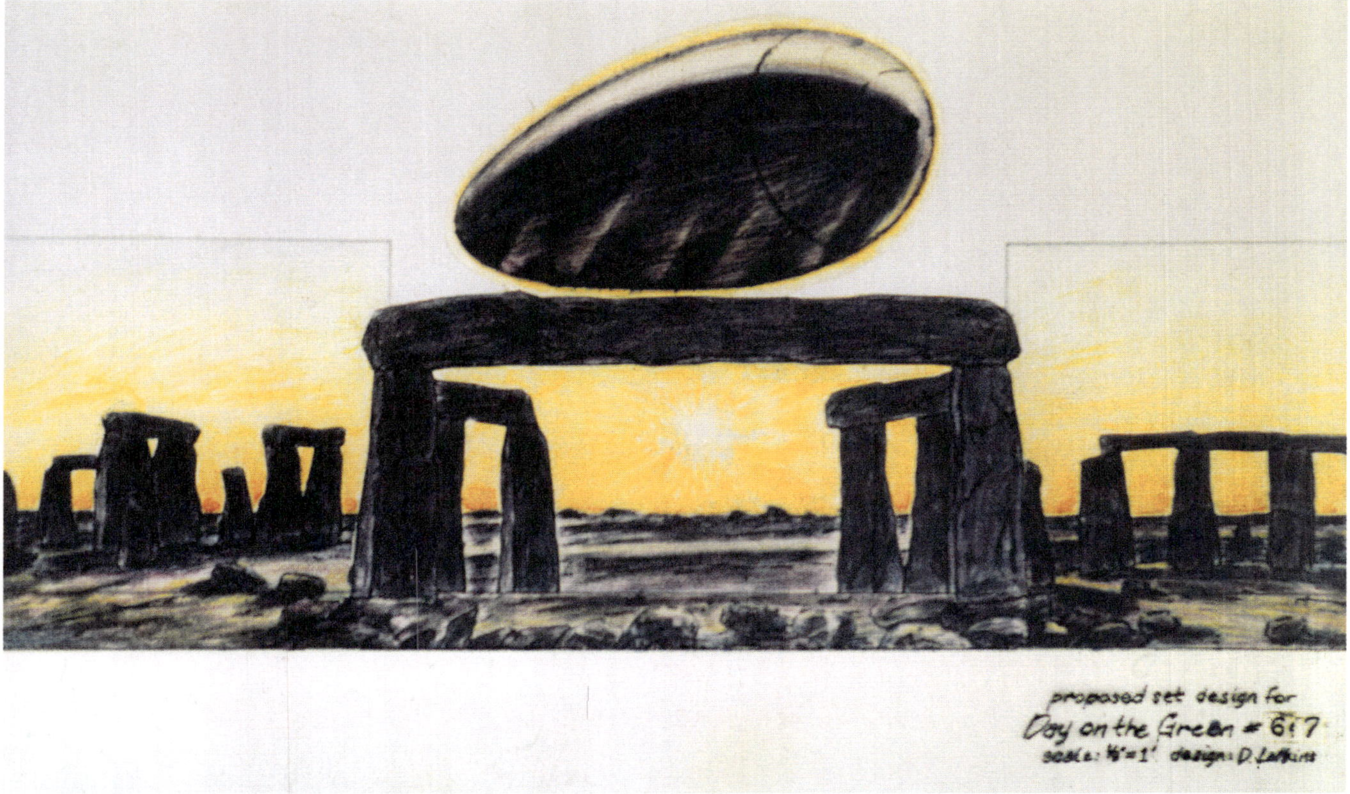

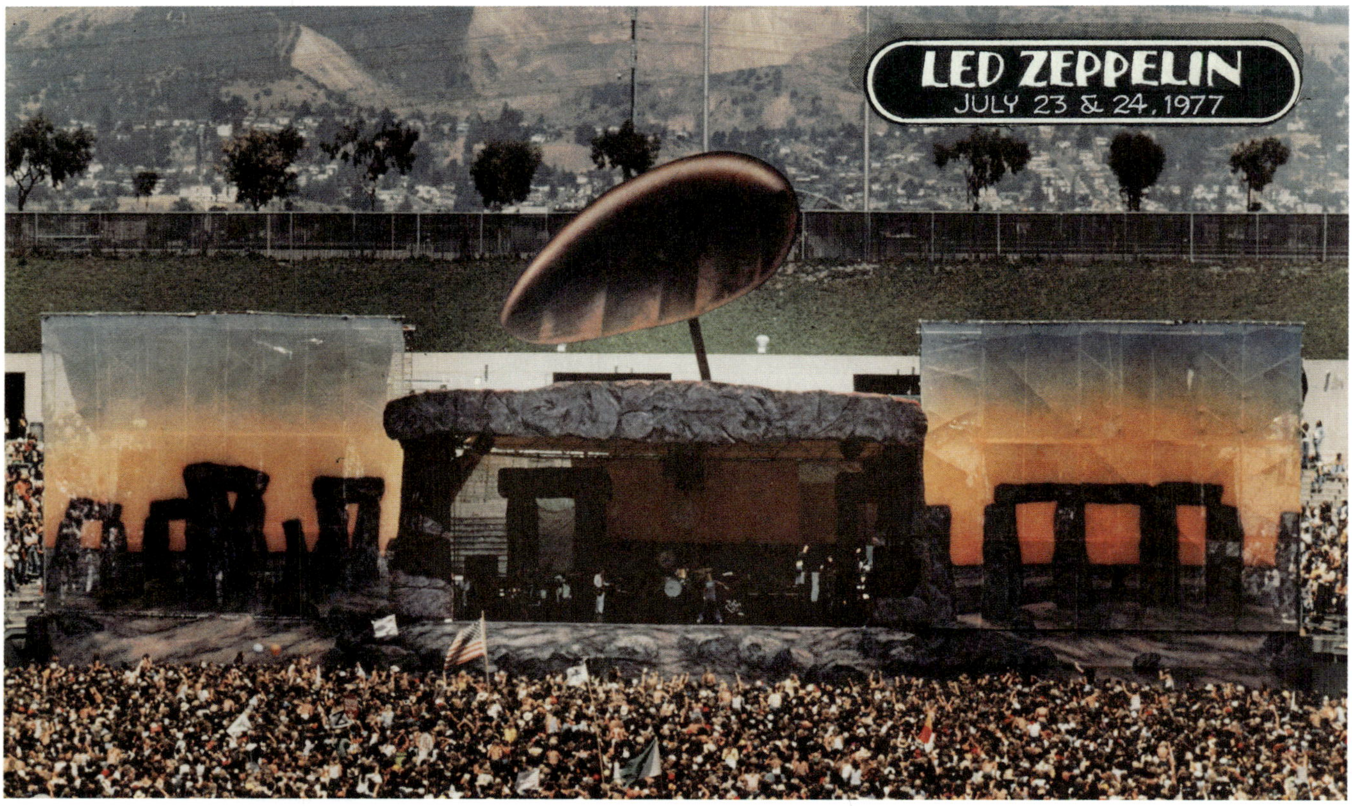

DAY ON THE GREEN

Day on the Green was a series of daytime concerts featuring monster stadium bands such as Led Zeppelin, The Eagles, Foreigner, and AC/DC. They were presented by promoter Bill Graham in Oakland, California, from 1973 until his death in a helicopter crash in 1991 (the last of the events took place the following year).

By now, rock 'n' roll was little more than big business. Concerts had become huge spectacles: the bands (and promoters) made more in one gig than they would have earned from several months' residency in a club. Stage design took premier position and artists such as Dennis Larkins, who created all the sets shown here, provided innovative backdrops to make up for the fact you could barely see the bands themselves.

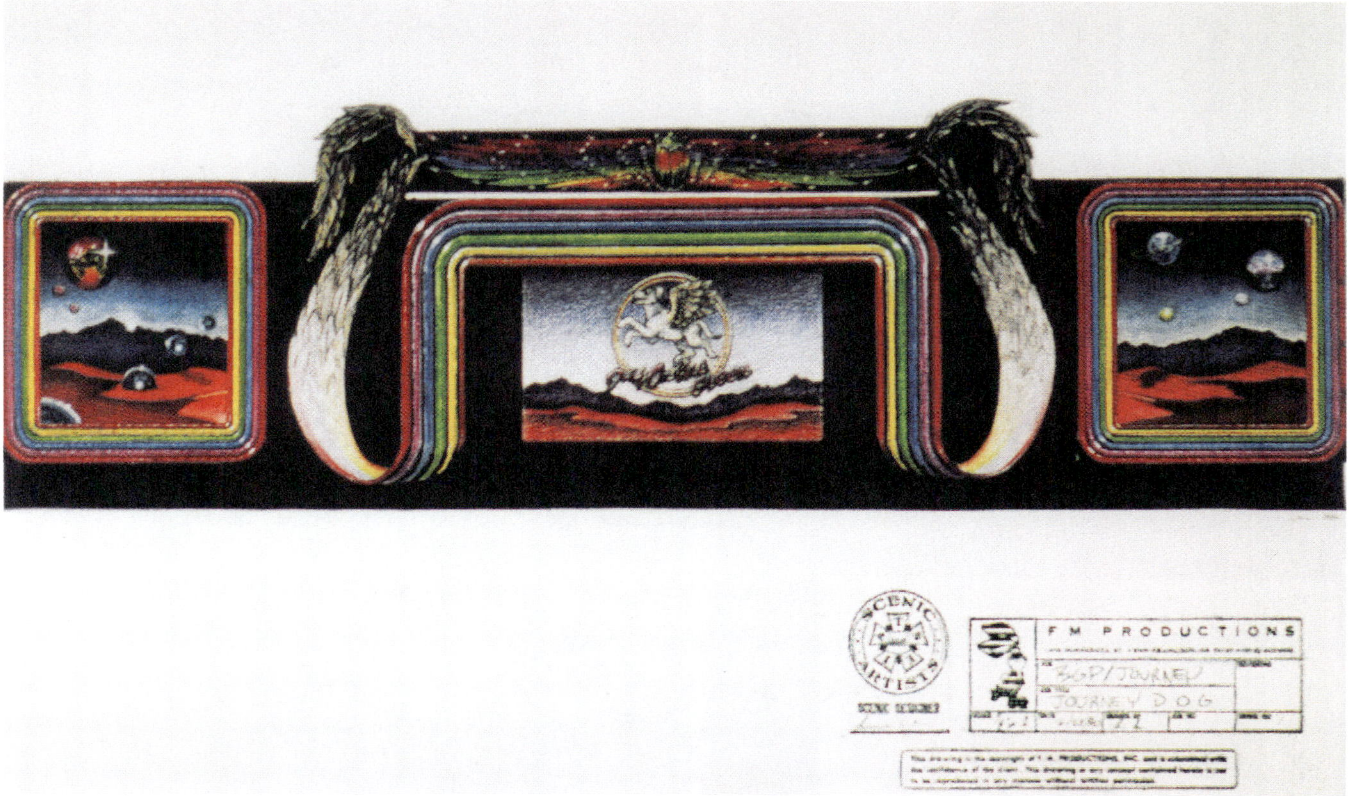

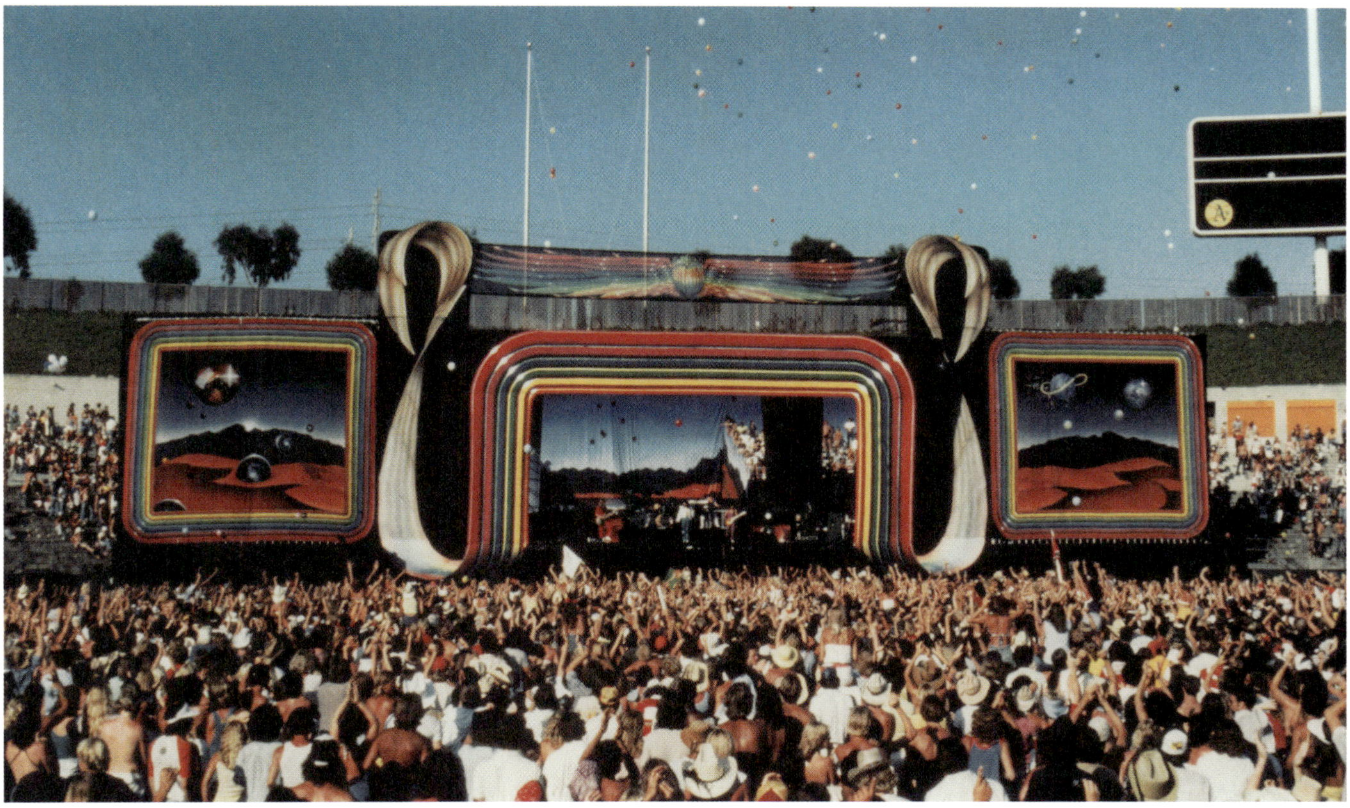

⋙→ Dennis Larkins had once worked as a scenic artist for the San Francisco Opera, and in the early seventies he began painting backdrops for some of the Bill Graham Presents shows. ⋙→ Opposite: preparatory artwork and finished design for a set for Led Zeppelin's two 1977 performances at Day on the Green. ⋙→ This page: a signed-off proof and finished stage-set design for Journey's appearance in 1980.

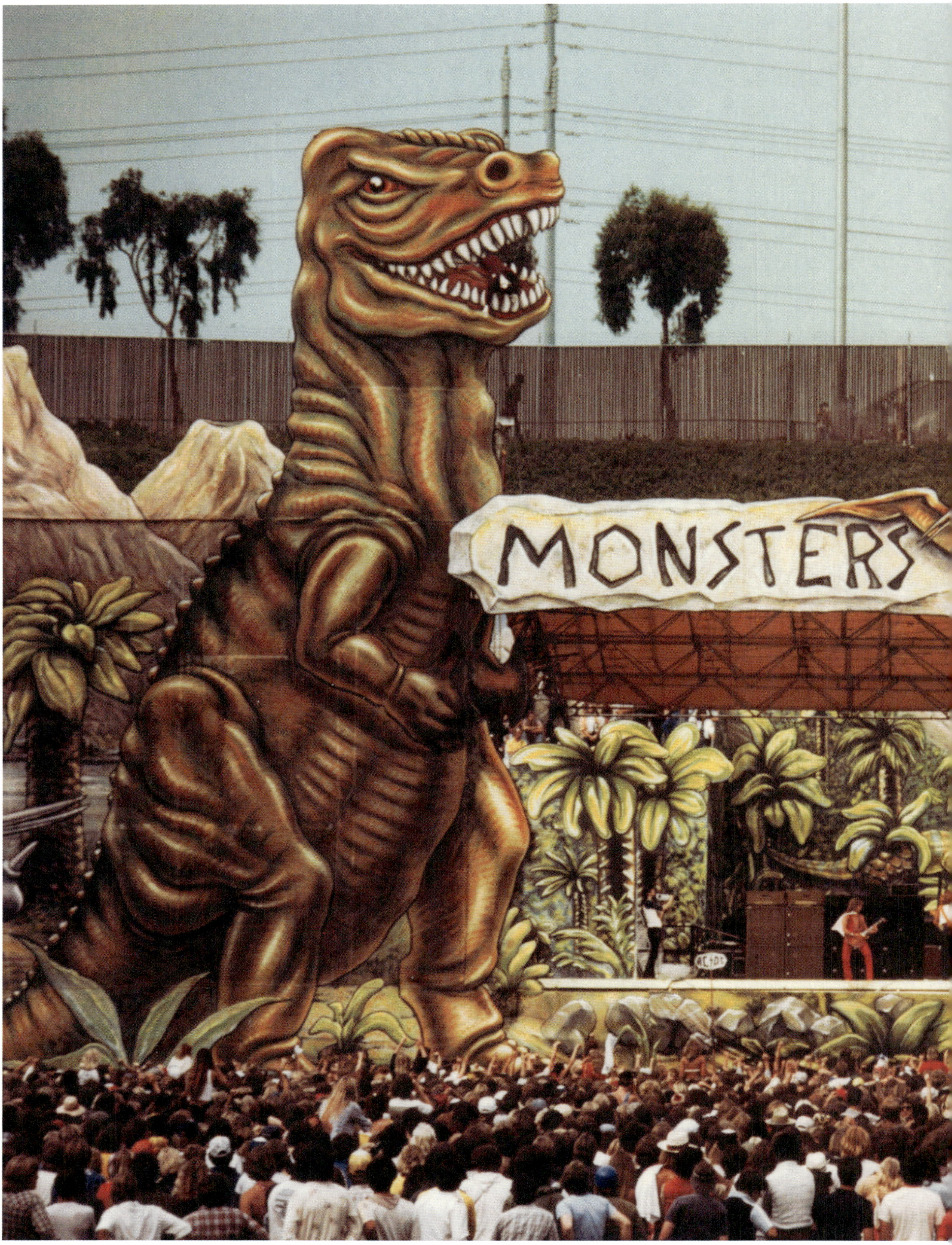

⟿ On July 21, 1979—the third day of that year's festival—there were appearances by AC/DC, Aerosmith, Rush, and (shown here) Ted Nugent. 'As part of the birth and development of rock 'n' roll shows, I was able to design and create some of the largest-scale public art installations of their time,' Larkins reflected later. 'These monumental undertakings were, of course, collaborative projects [...] Nevertheless, I was given great creative leeway to express my personal artistic style, often drawing inspiration from the underground art of the era, notably rock album and poster art, underground comics, etc.' Larkins was justifiably proud of his achievements, admitting, 'Although rock concert production values and technologies have certainly evolved over the years, I look back with fond memories on these huge hand-painted monoliths as the bold and audacious art pioneers they turned out to be.'

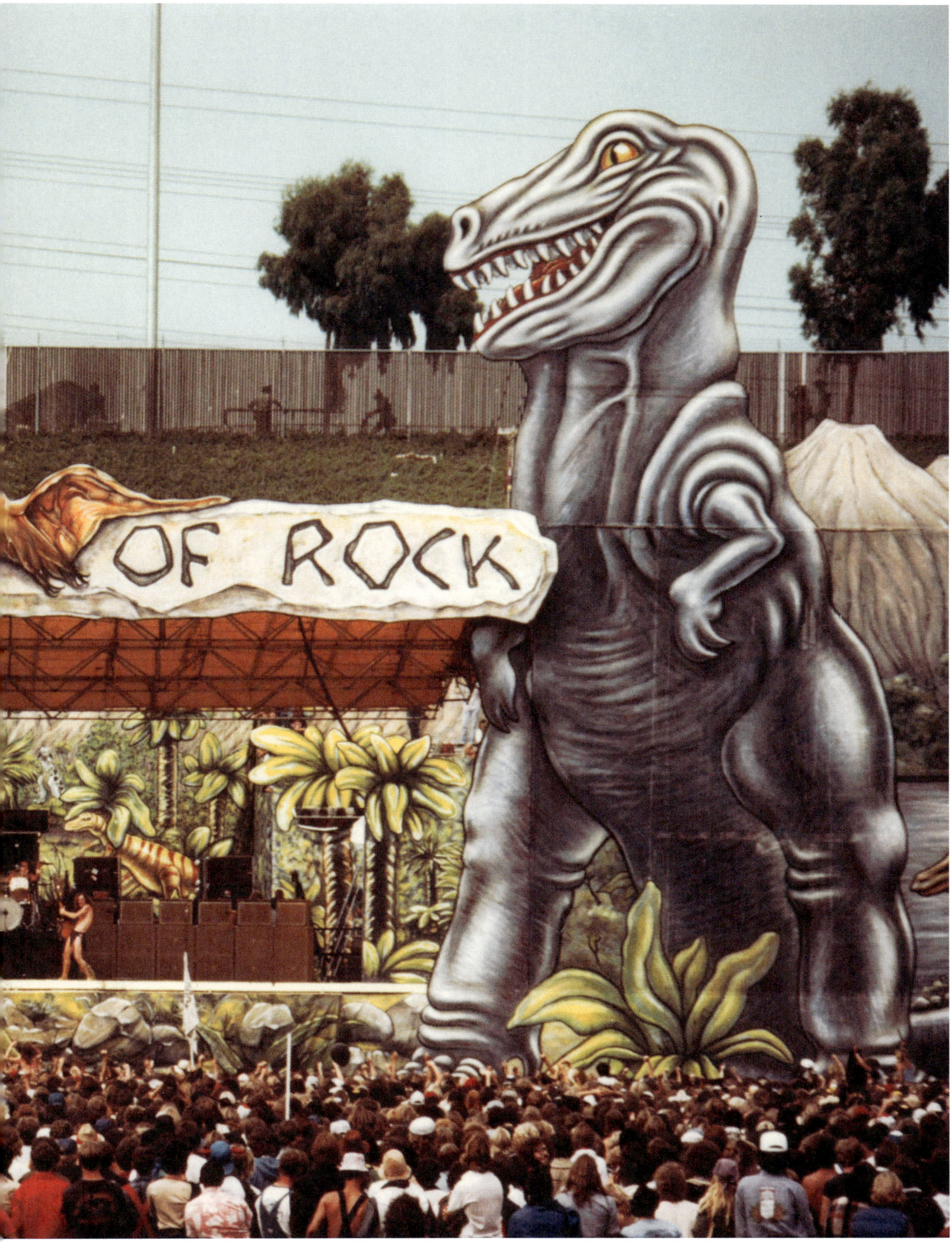
OF ROCK

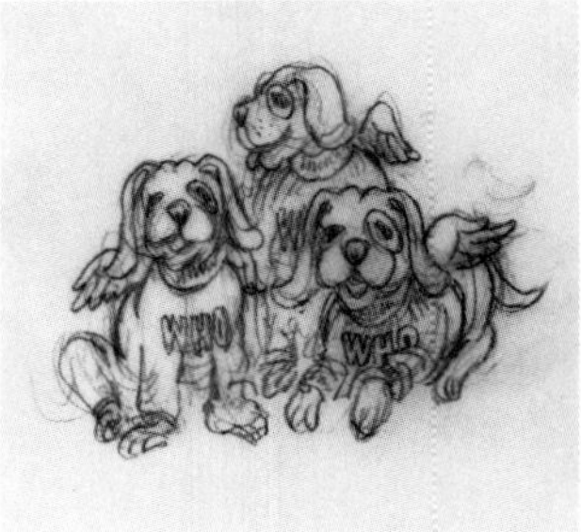
WHO

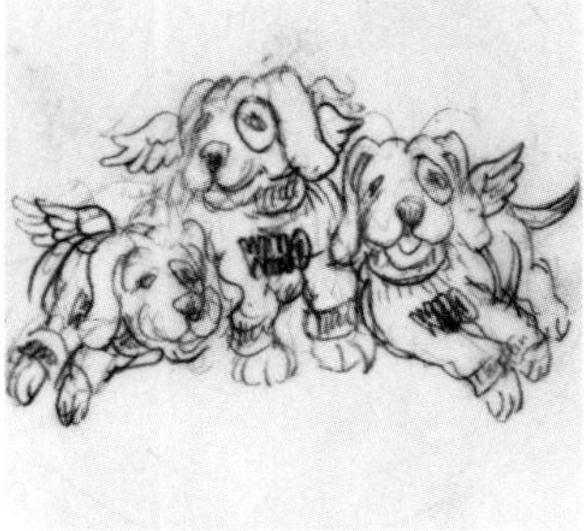
WHO

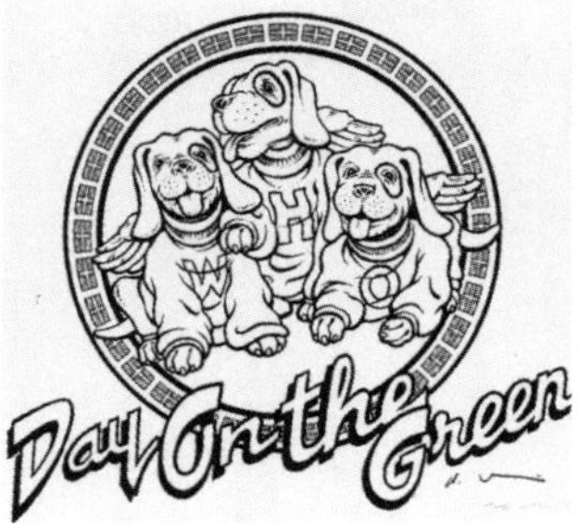
Day On the Green

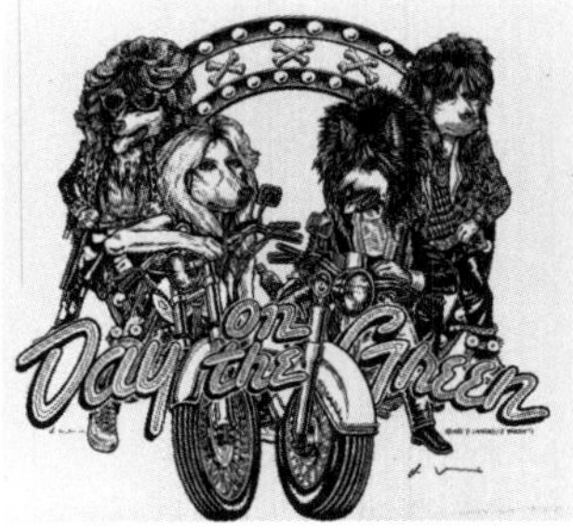
Day on the Green

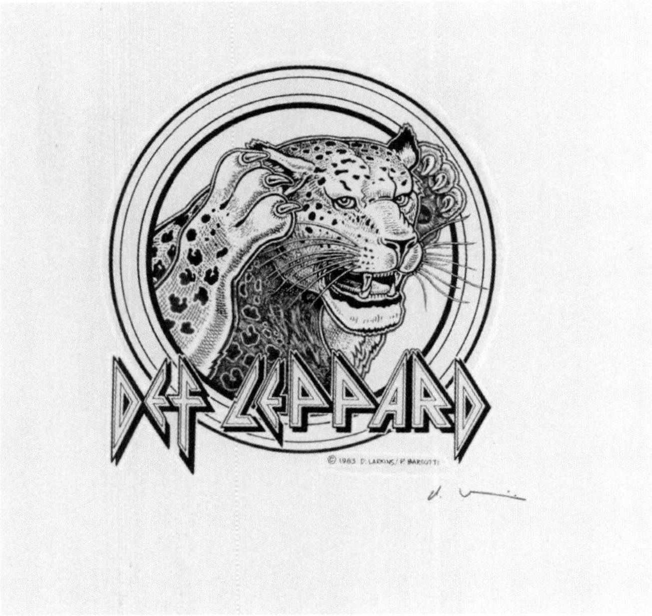
DEF LEPPARD

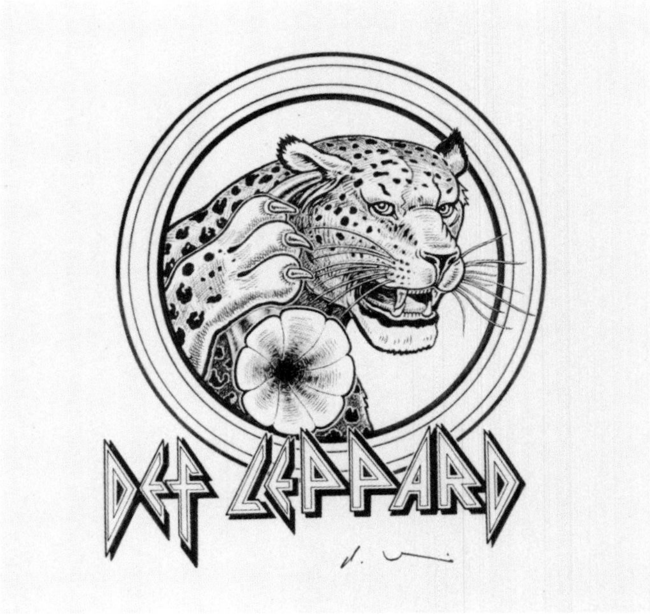
DEF LEPPARD

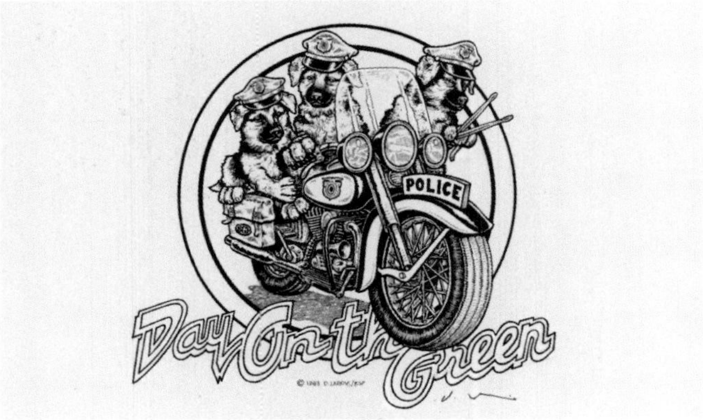
POLICE
Day On the Green

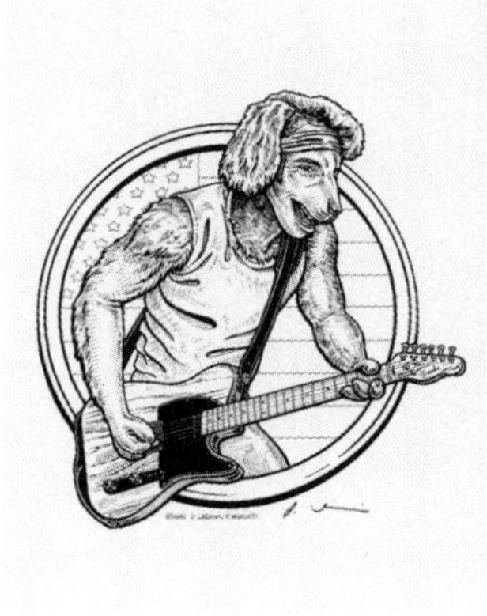

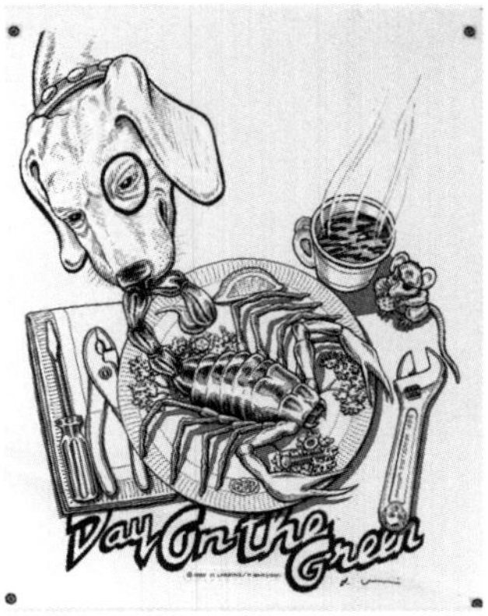
Day On the Green

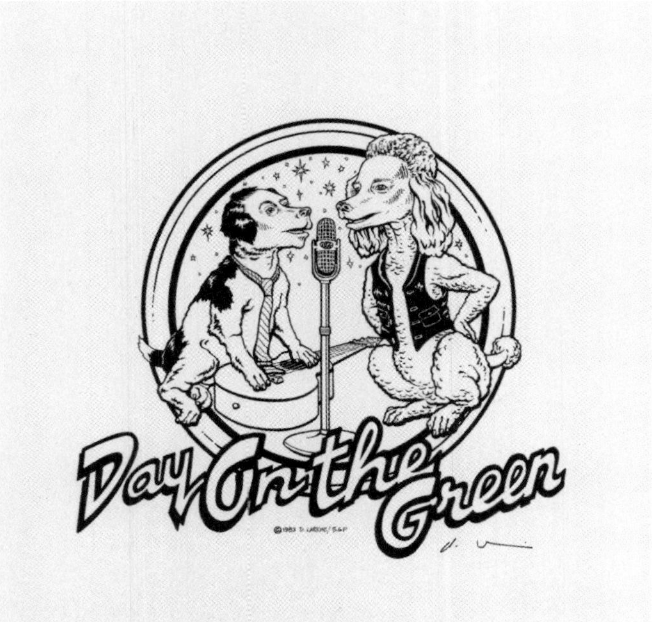
Day On the Green

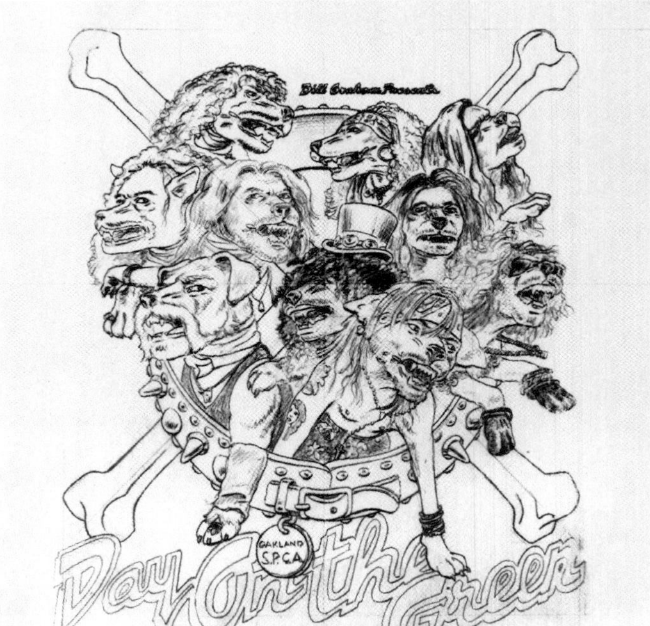
OAKLAND S.P.C.A
Day On the Green

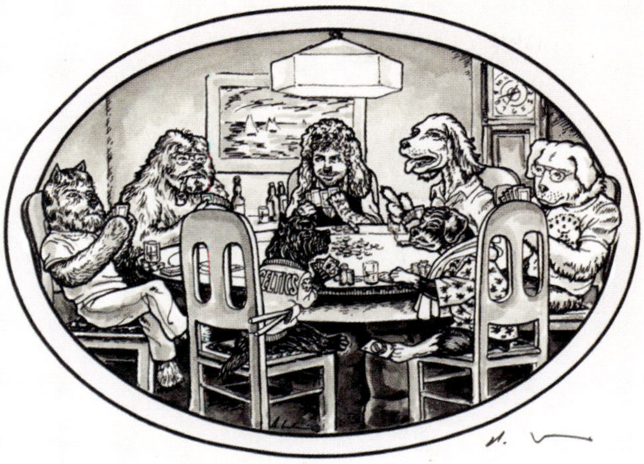

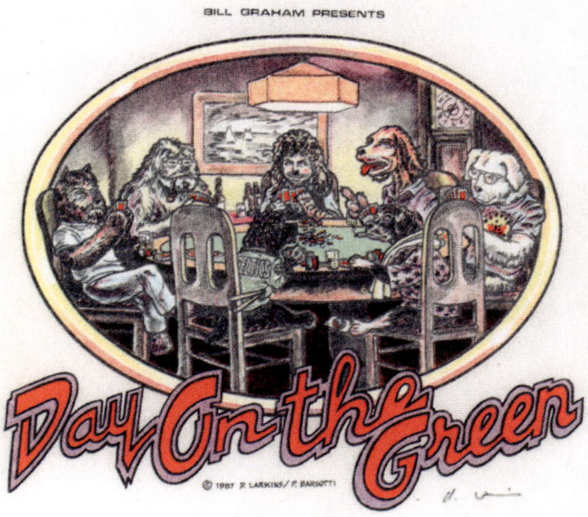

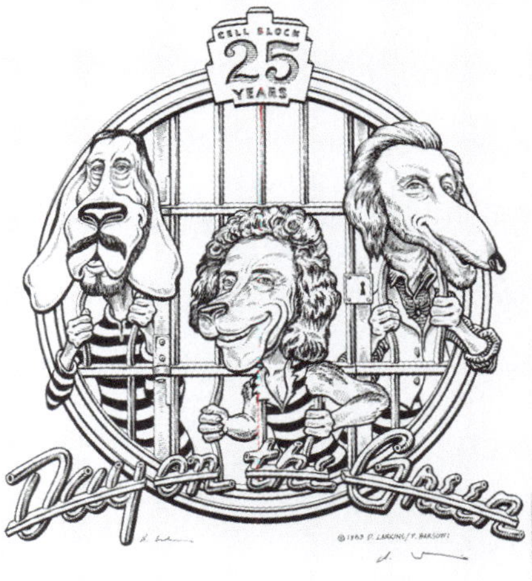

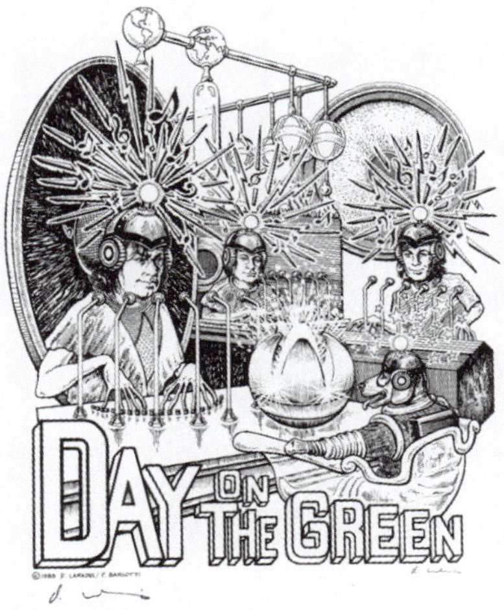

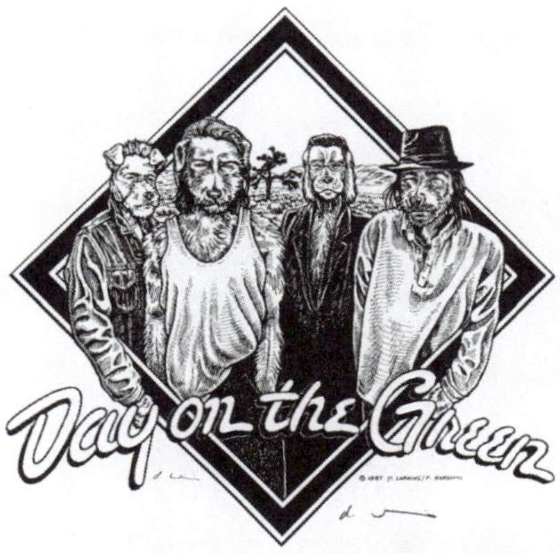

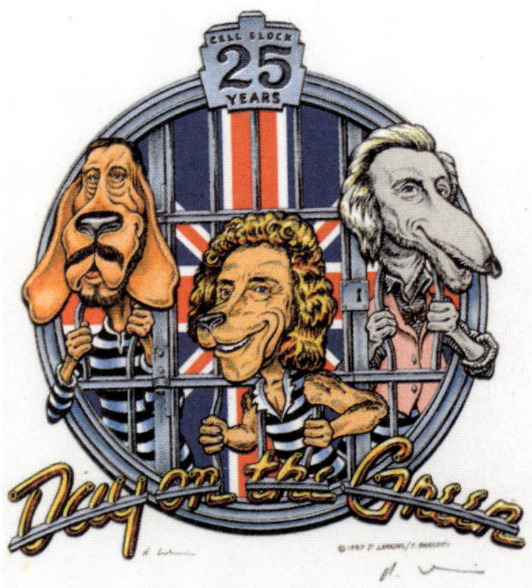

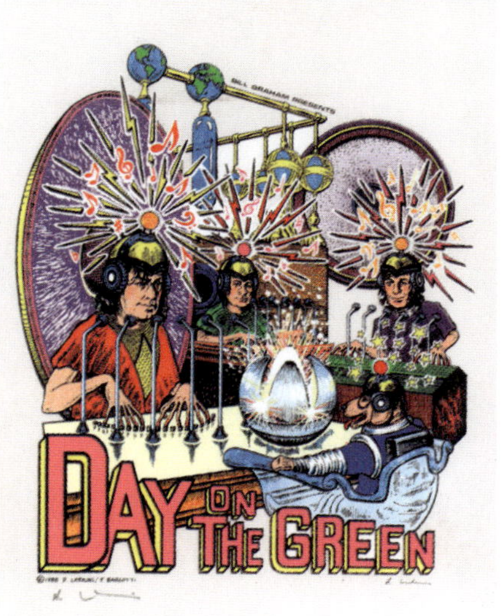

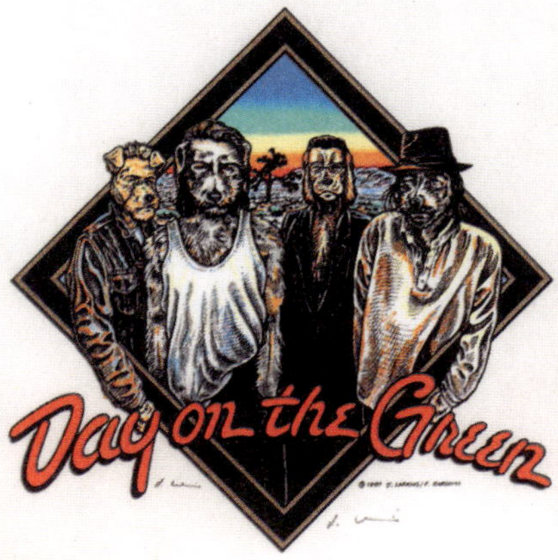

⋙→ Bill Graham commissioned Dennis Larkins to create special T-shirts as gifts for the backstage crews working at Day on the Green. His production company referred to the events as 'D.O.G.' shows, so headline acts were made over as canines. Larkins took inspiration from Petey, the dog in the *Our Gang* movies, who sometimes cropped up in the images too. Seen here is a selection of original artworks—rough and complete—and finished color images. The canine caricatures include The Who, Mötley Crüe, Def Leppard, Simon & Garfunkel, Bruce Springsteen, The Scorpions, Guns N' Roses, the Grateful Dead, and U2.

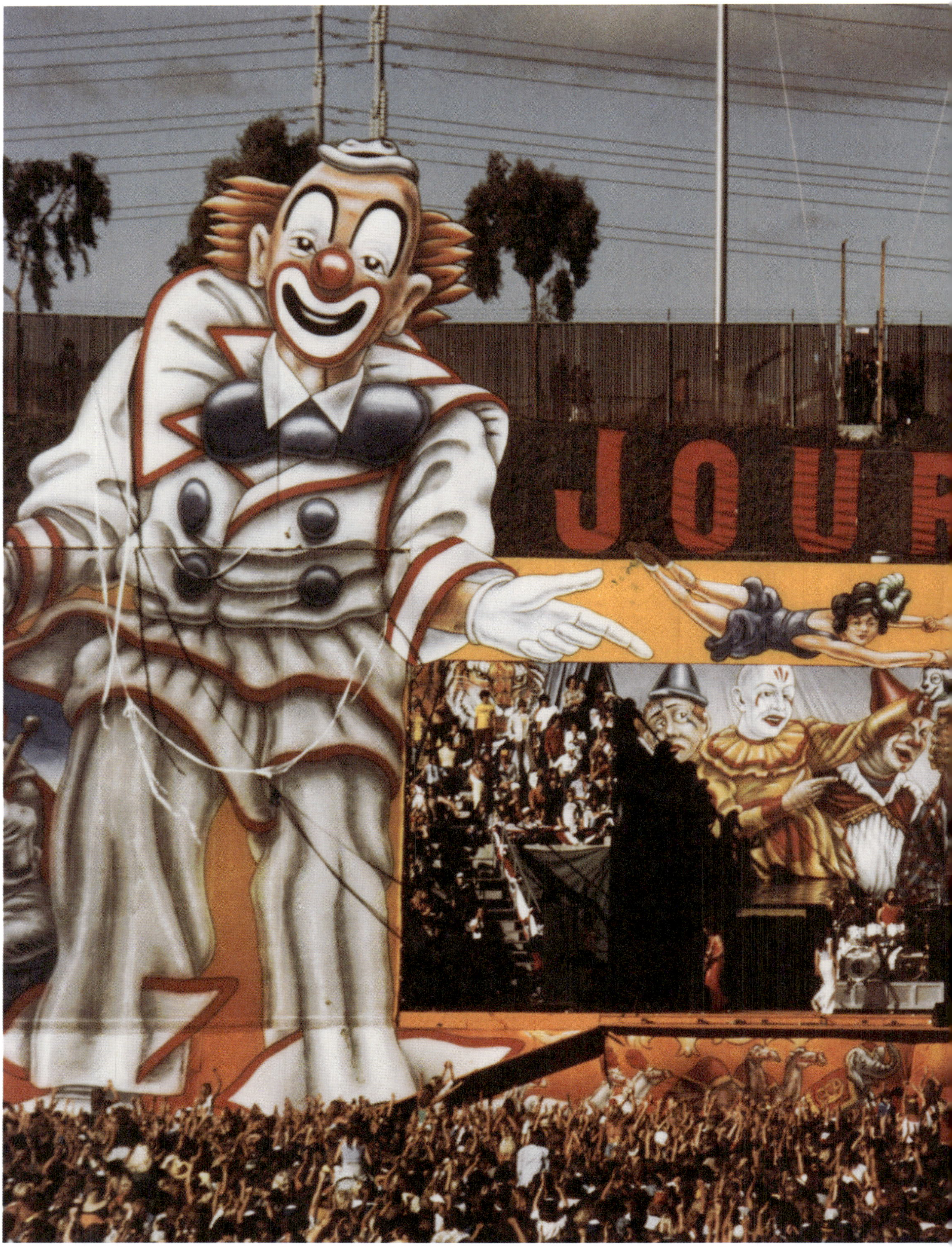

➳→ Journey perform at Day on the Green in Oakland Stadium, California, on July 4, 1979, surrounded by the 'Rock 'n' Roll Circus' stage set designed by Dennis Larkins. According to Larkins, the giant clown to the right of the stage represents Bill Graham. Larkins recalled: 'This set was originally designed and mostly painted in the previous year, intended to headline Ted Nugent. However, when Ted was notified of the set design (three days before the show!), he exclaimed, "If that set has clowns in it, I'm not going on! Change the clowns to attack dogs!" Fulfilling his request was, of course, an impossibility (we created a "Rumble in the Jungle" set over those next three days instead). The nearly completed set was held over to the next season and a very different show.'

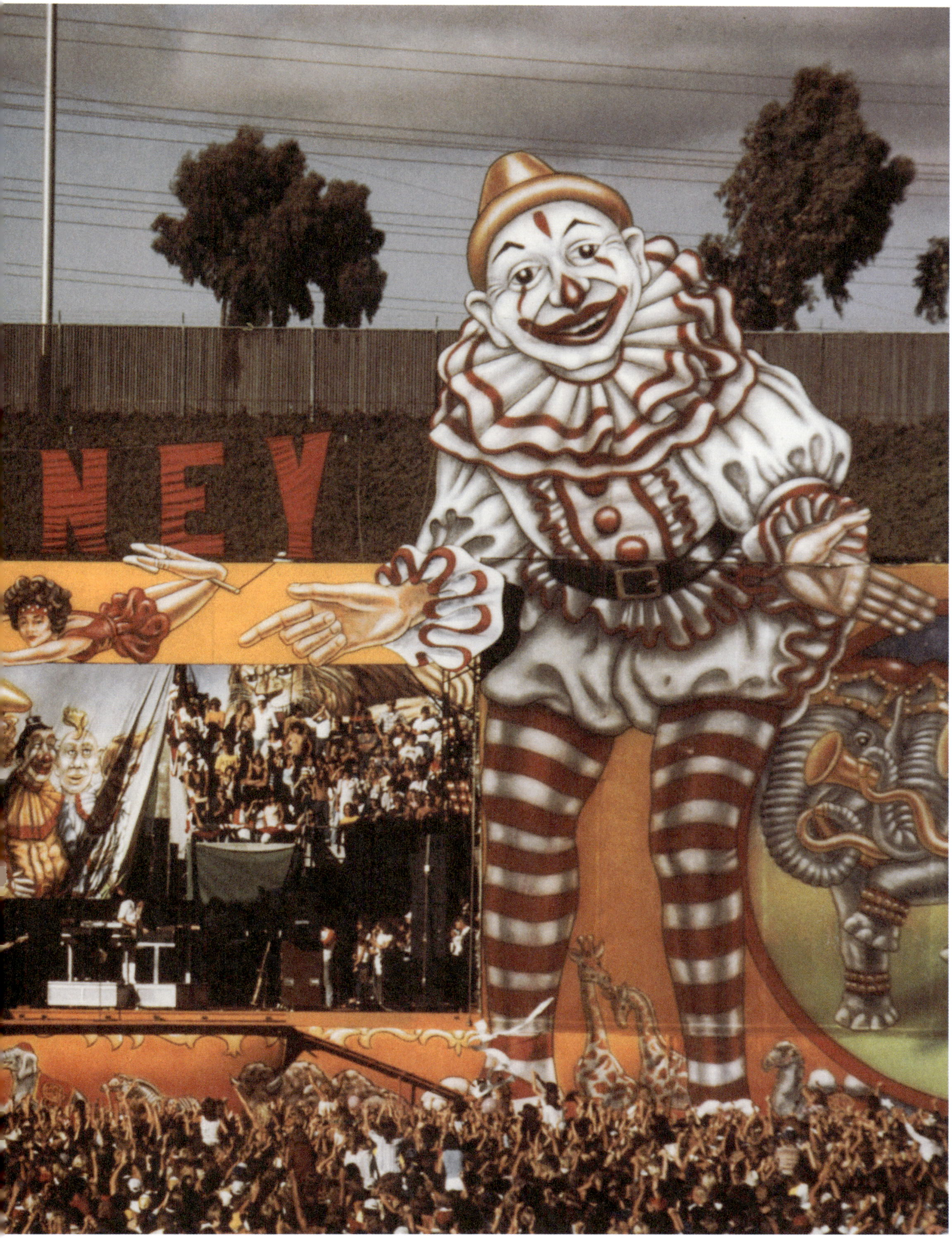
NEY

One of Larkins's best-known Grateful Dead posters, this work promotes their 1980 shows at New York's historic Radio City Music Hall.

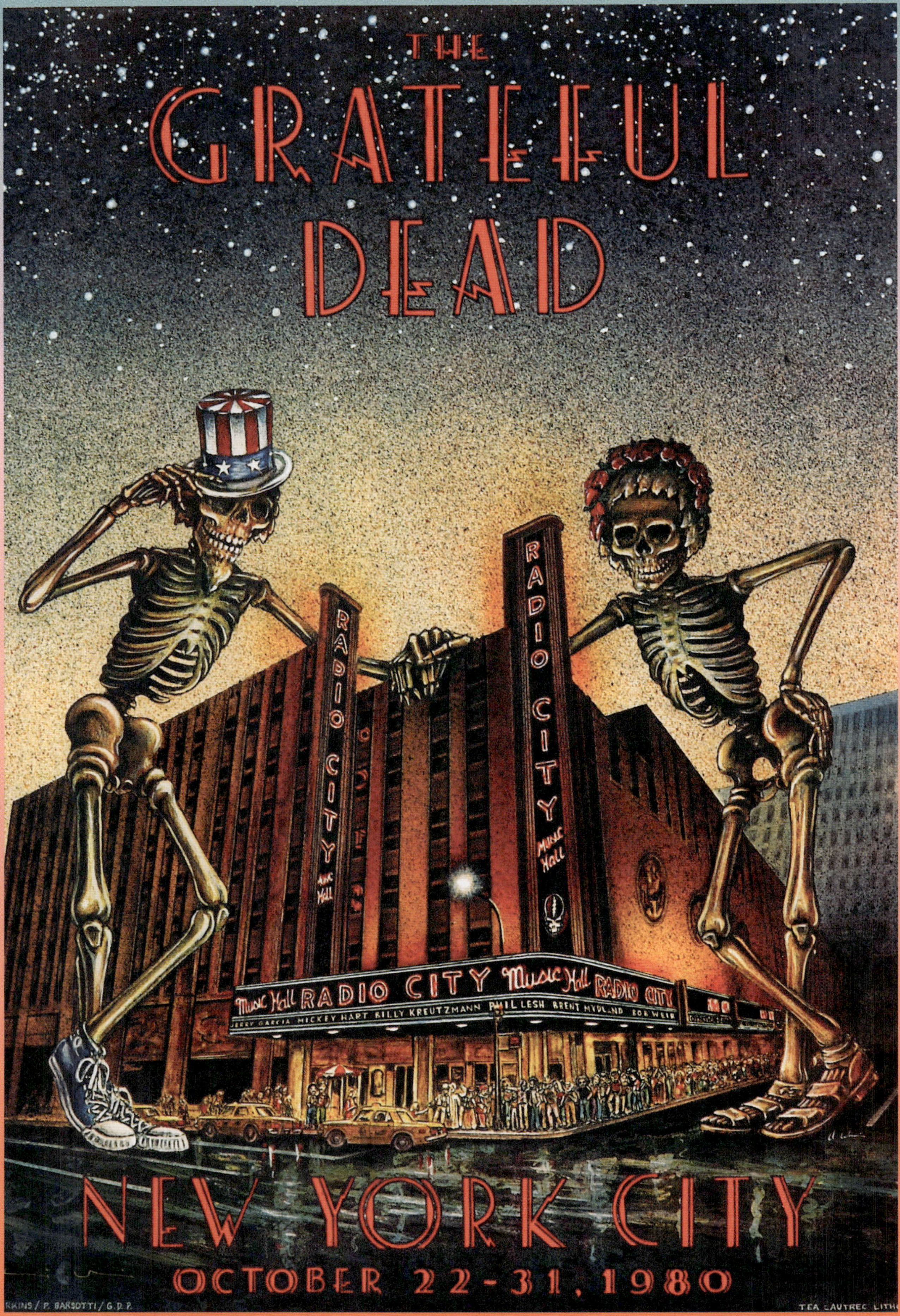

DENNIS LARKINS (1943–)

DENNIS LARKINS WAS BORN AND RAISED IN AMERICA'S HEARTLAND OF THE FORTIES AND FIFTIES, BUT HIS SIGHTS WERE SET ON A MUCH LARGER WORLD. HE WAS ALWAYS AN ARTIST: HIS EARLIEST INFLUENCES WERE FROM COPYING COMIC BOOK COVERS AS A VERY SMALL CHILD. AS A TEEN, RADICAL SHIFTS IN PERSPECTIVE CAME FROM IMMERSION IN *MAD* MAGAZINE AND EARLY ROCK 'N' ROLL. BUT EVEN WITH THE DISCIPLINES OF ART SCHOOL IN KANSAS CITY, IT WAS HIS EARLY INFLUENCES COMBINED WITH THE CREATIVE EXPLOSION OF THE SIXTIES COUNTER-CULTURE WITH ITS UNDERGROUND COMIX, ROCK ALBUM ART AND PSYCHEDELIC POSTERS THAT REALLY GOT HIS ATTENTION AND INSPIRED HIS ARTISTIC DIRECTION. ⟶ HIS PAINTING CAREER HAD FIRST BROUGHT HIM TO SANTA FE, NESTLED IN THE MOUNTAINS OF NORTHERN NEW MEXICO, BUT IT WAS ON A VISIT TO SAN FRANCISCO IN THE EARLY SEVENTIES THAT HIS LIFE WAS CATAPULTED INTO HYPER-DRIVE IN THE FORM OF A CHANCE OPPORTUNITY TO WORK AS A SCENIC ARTIST AND ROCK 'N' ROLL SET DESIGNER FOR PROMOTER BILL GRAHAM. LARKINS'S HUGE STAGE SETS FOR BILL'S LEGENDARY DAY ON THE GREEN CONCERTS BECAME DEFINITIVE STATEMENTS IN THE WORLD OF ARENA ROCK 'N' ROLL, HOSTING SUCH ACTS AS LED ZEPPELIN, THE EAGLES, AND THE ROLLING STONES. HIS ASSOCIATION WITH BILL LED TO A PAIR OF POSTERS FOR THE GRATEFUL DEAD IN 1980. THE BEST KNOWN WAS FOR NEW YORK'S RADIO CITY MUSIC HALL, AND OTHER POSTERS FOLLOWED. ⟶ AFTER YEARS OF WORK IN POPULAR CULTURE, INCLUDING PAINTING BACKDROPS FOR MOVIES, DESIGNING THEME-PARK ATTRACTIONS FOR DISNEY AND EXHIBITING PAINTINGS IN THE LA UNDERGROUND, LARKINS IS BACK IN SANTA FE WHERE IT ALL STARTED, BUT THIS TIME HIS ART SHOWS ALL THE EFFECTS OF HIS MANY CREATIVE PATHS. THE THEATRICAL AND WHIMSICAL QUALITIES OF HIS EARLY POSTERS NOW JUXTAPOSE WITH RETRO-POP IMAGERY TO CREATE HIS UNIQUE LOWBROW/POP-SURREALIST PAINTINGS.

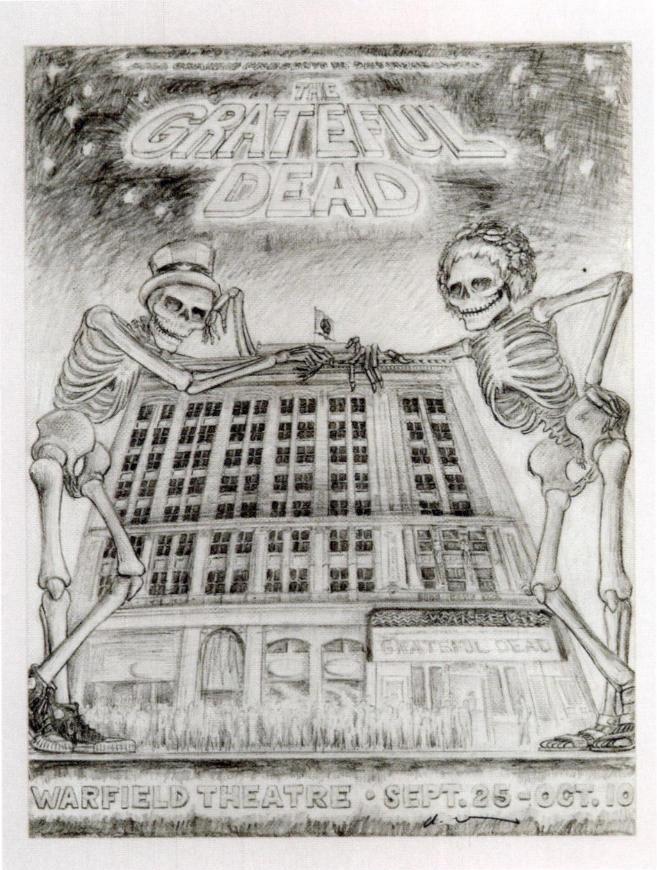

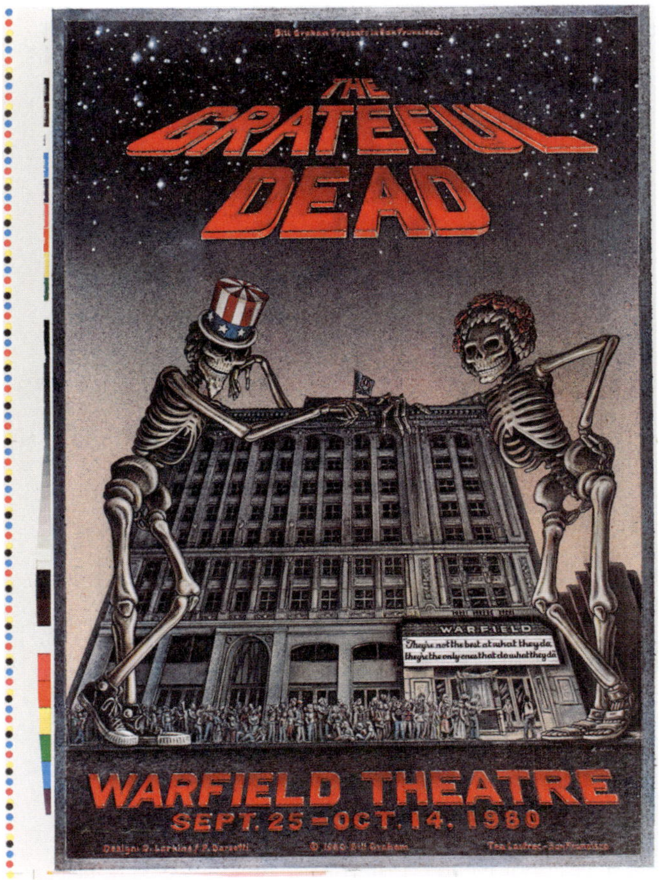

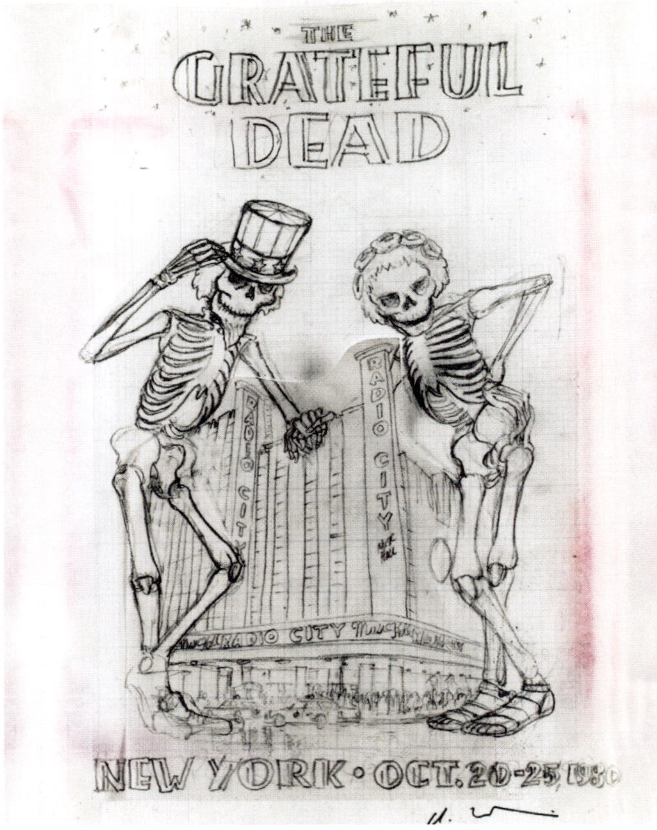

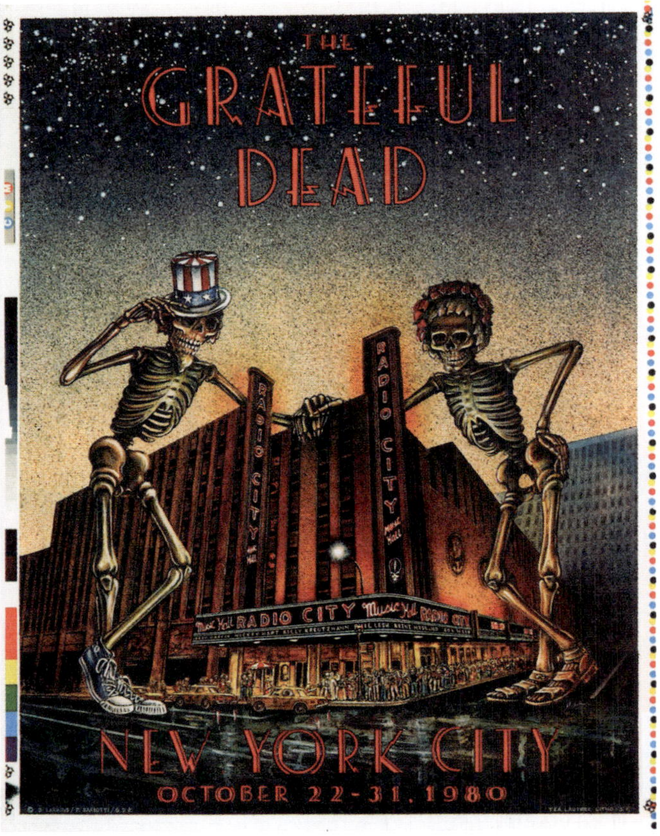

LARKINS AND THE DEAD

The Grateful Dead refused to die; they kept on touring and releasing albums, followed by faithful 'Deadhead' fans. They employed Dennis Larkins to polish and maintain their signature skeleton image, but inevitably any darkness attached to the name had long gone. The new dancing skeletons looked more like Disney than anything else, suggesting a radical new approach to life. The progressive proofs show how complex the imagery had become.

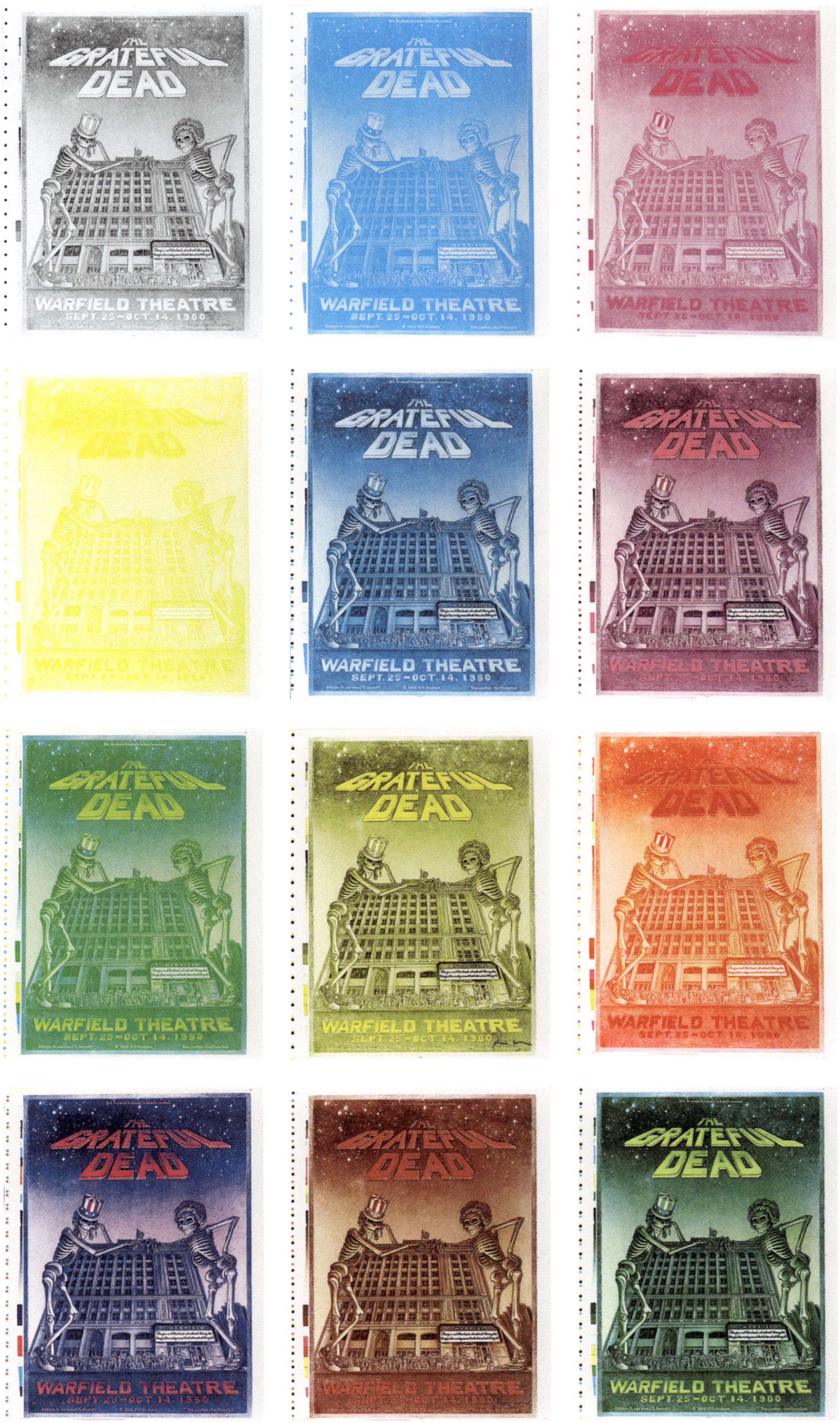

➳ Opposite: artwork and printers' proofs for two sets of Grateful Dead concerts. The Warfield Theatre poster's success led to a commission by the band to create one for their upcoming shows at New York's Radio City Music Hall in 1980. The venue—uncomfortable with the association between the Dead's signature skeletons and the historic building—objected to the poster, and it was pulled. ➳ This page: test color separations for the Warfield Theatre poster.

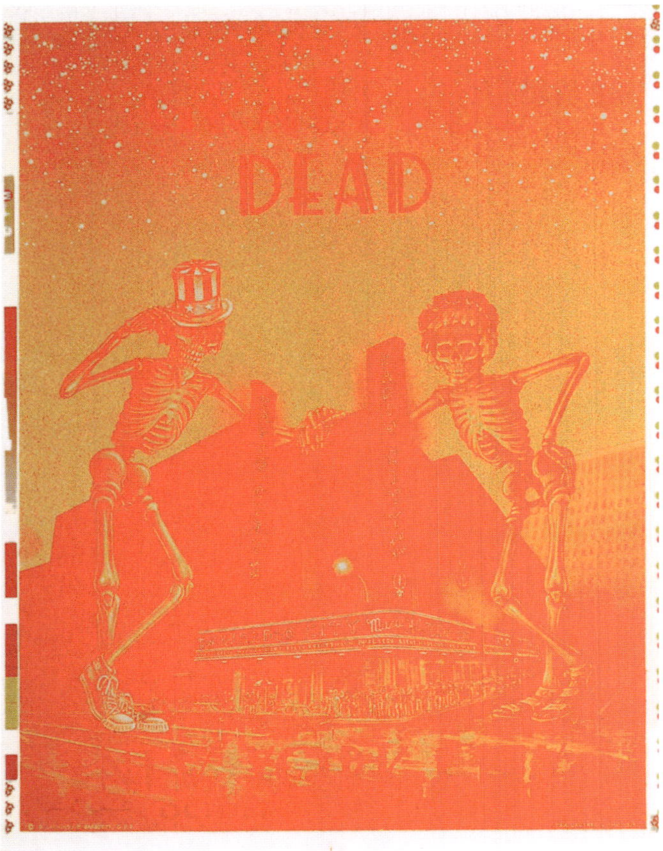

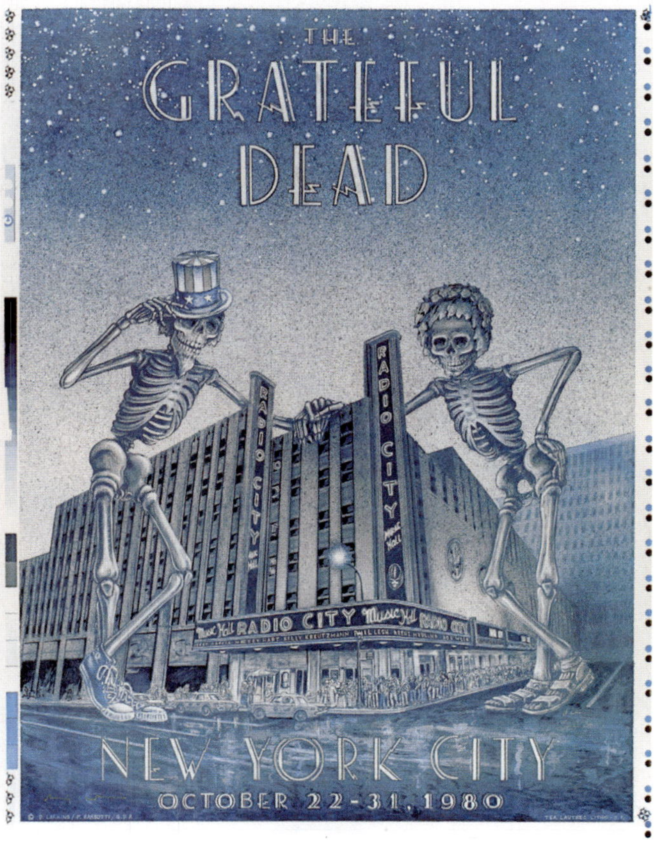

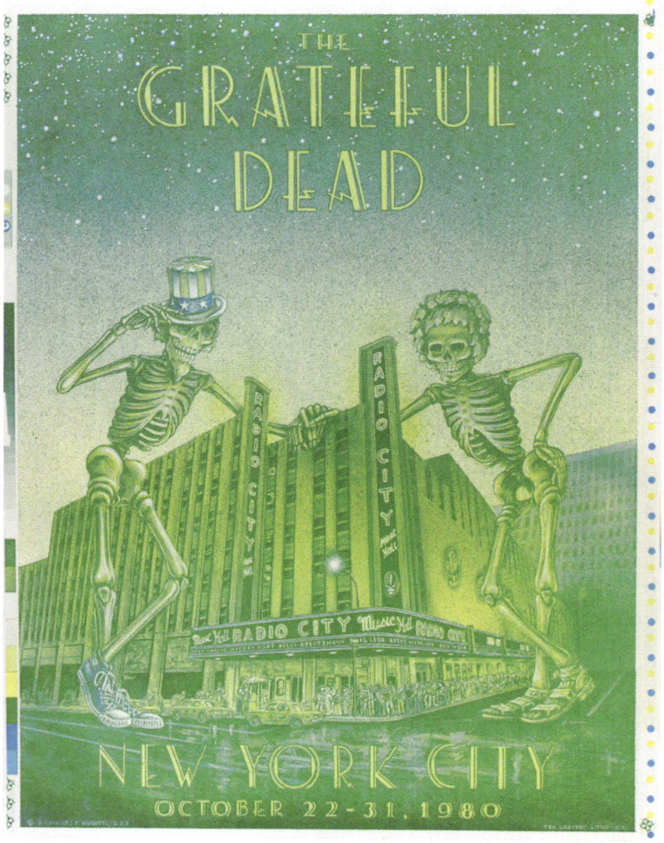

➳ This page: color separations for the never-used Radio City poster.
➳ Opposite: the finished full-color design.

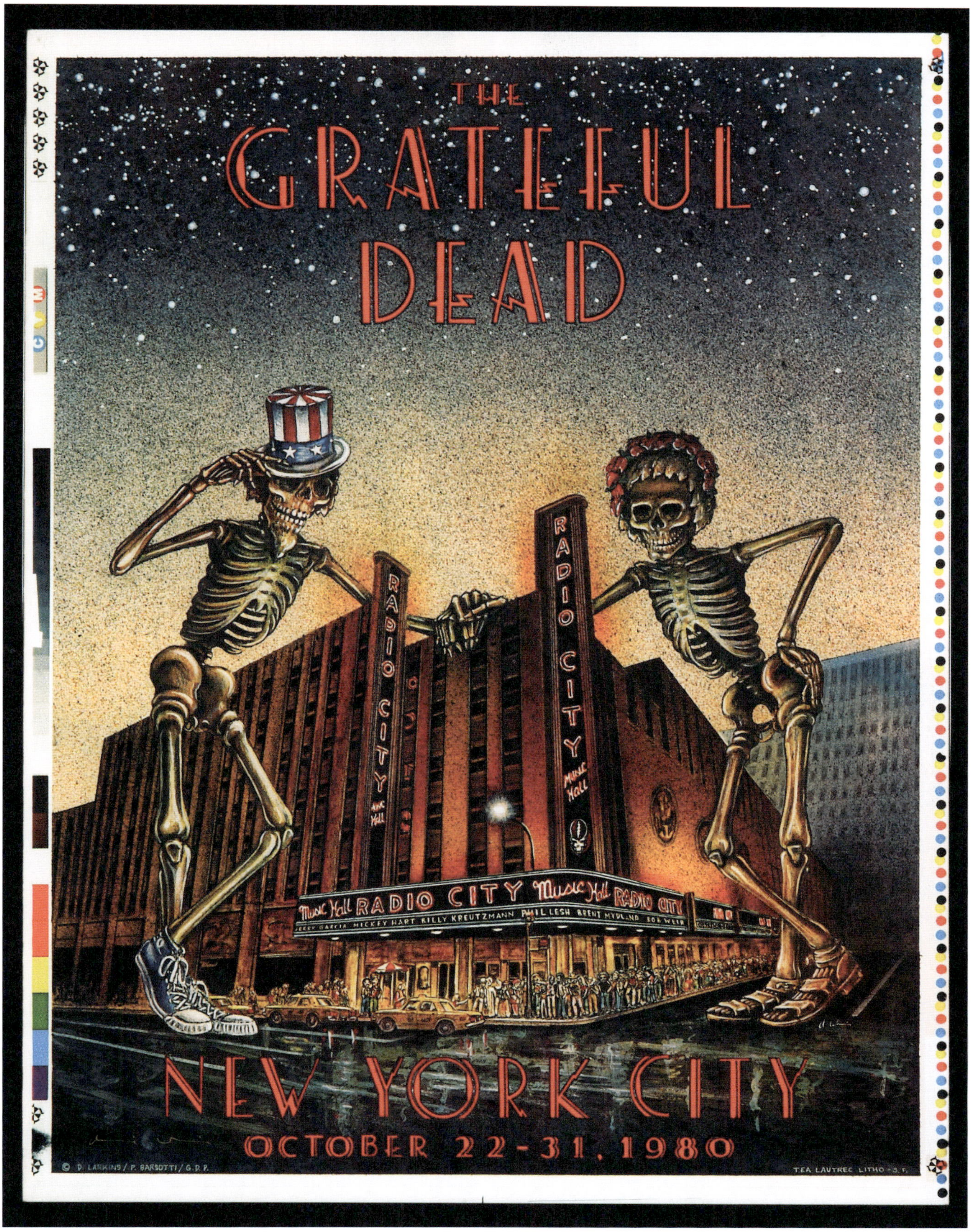
THE
GRATEFUL
DEAD
RADIO CITY
RADIO CITY Music Hall
Music Hall RADIO CITY Music Hall RADIO CITY
MICKEY HART BILLY KREUTZMANN PHIL LESH BRENT MYDLAND BOB WEIR
NEW YORK CITY
OCTOBER 22-31, 1980
© D. LARKINS / P. BARSOTTI / G.D.P.
TEA LAUTREC LITHO - S.F.

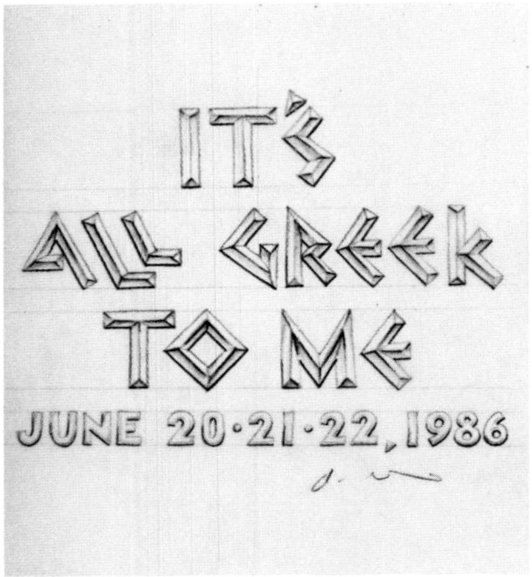

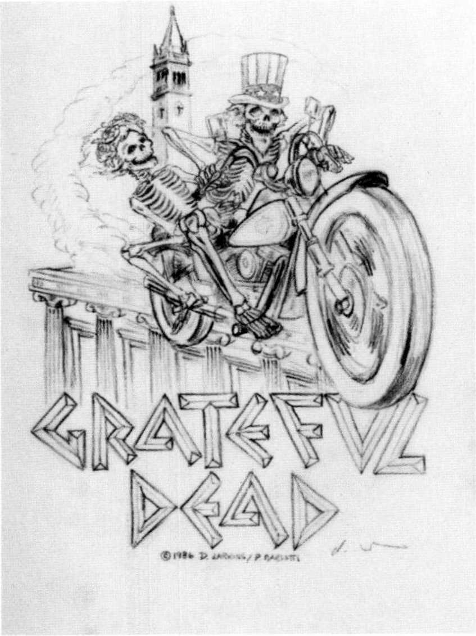

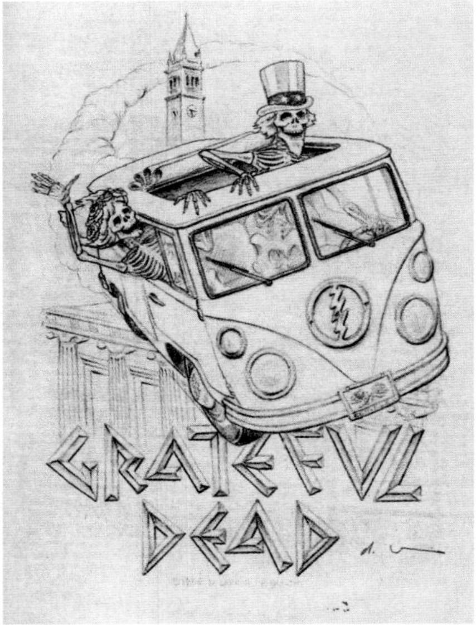

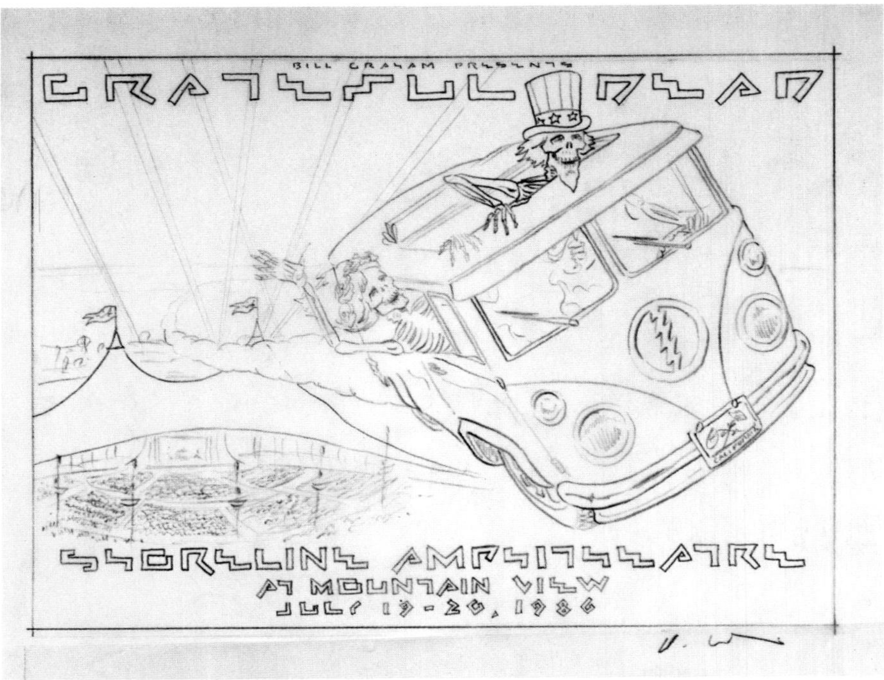

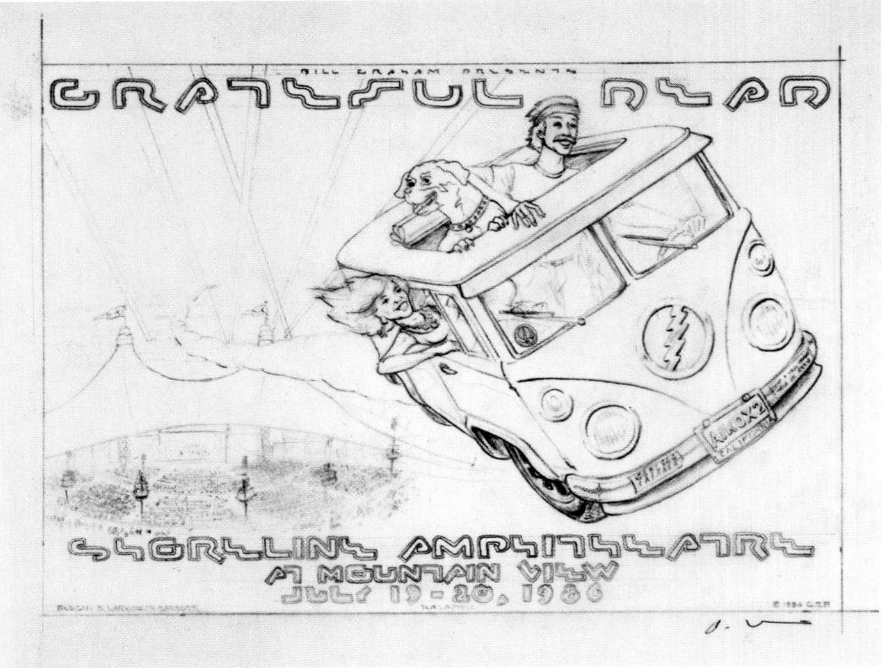

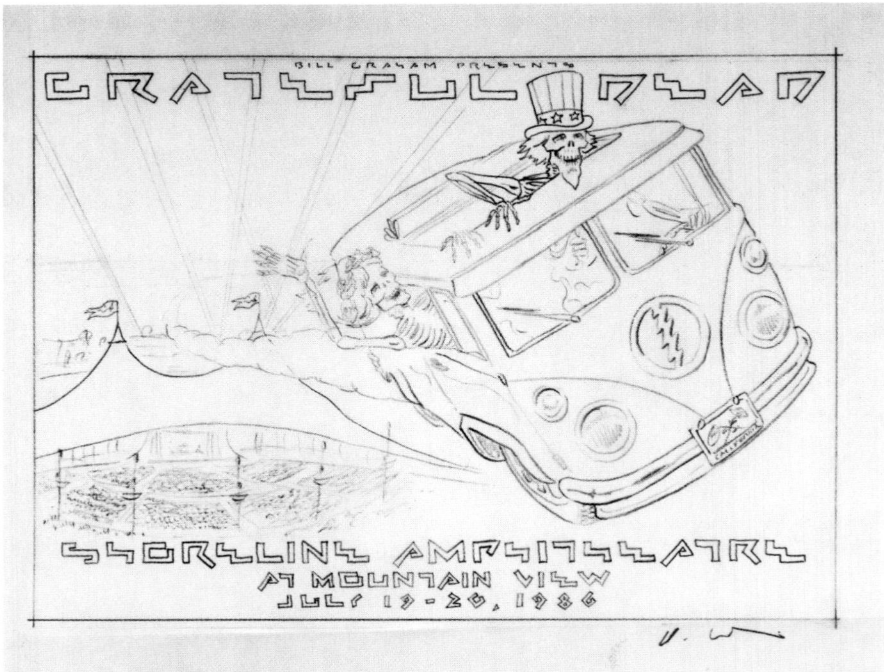

⋙→ This page, left column: preliminary artwork for the Grateful Dead's shows at the Greek Theatre in 1986. ⋙→ Right column: more sketched designs, this time for the Dead's gig at the Shoreline Amphitheatre the same year. ⋙→ Opposite: a range of different scripts for a T-shirt design to mark the Grateful Dead's show in Telluride, Colorado, in 1987.

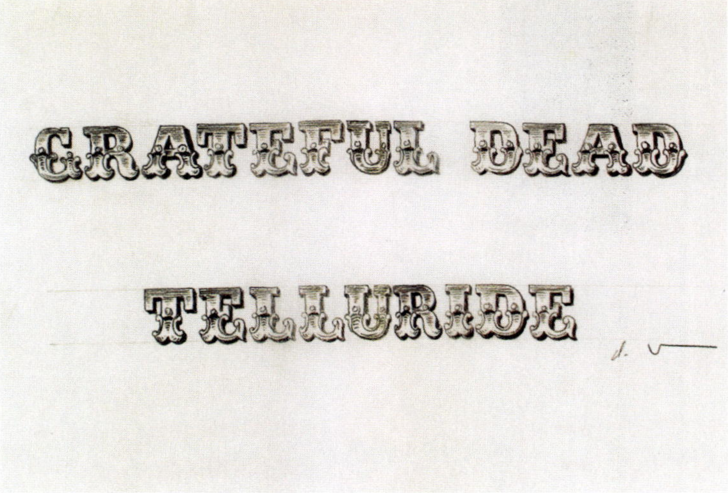
GRATEFUL DEAD
TELLURIDE

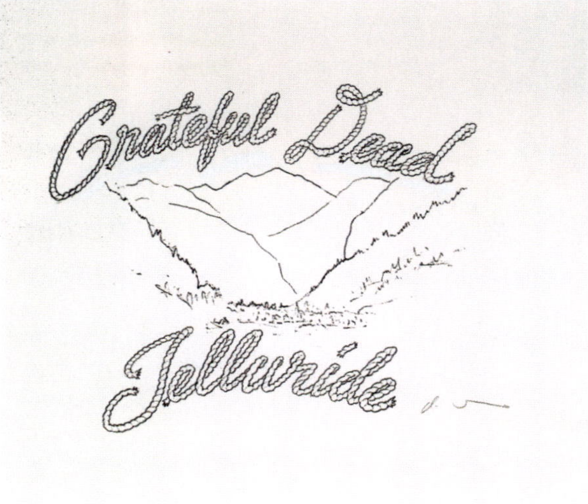
Grateful Dead
Telluride

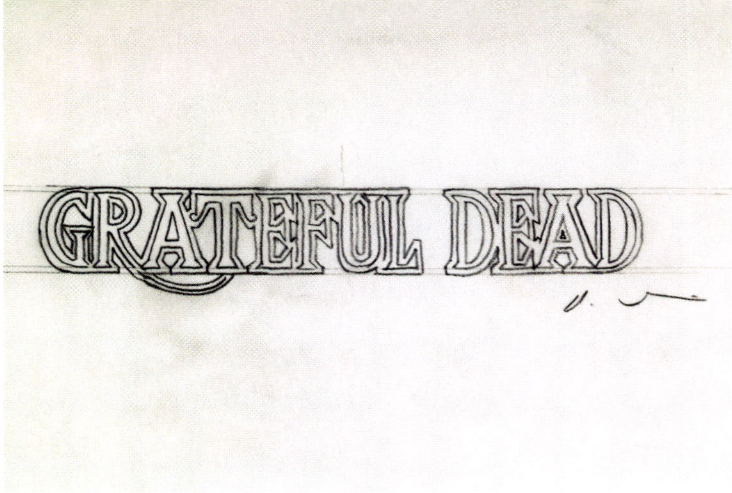
GRATEFUL DEAD

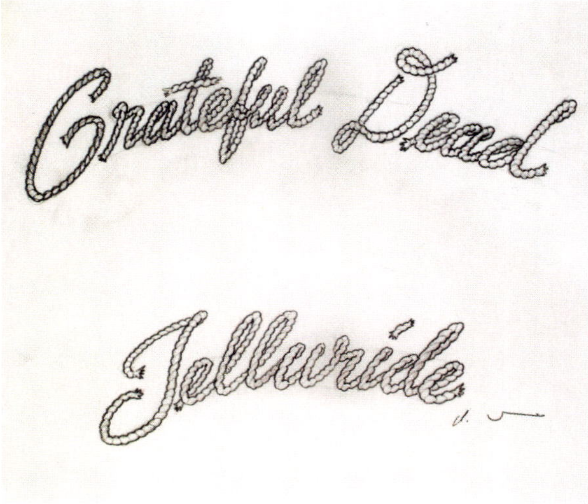
Grateful Dead
Telluride

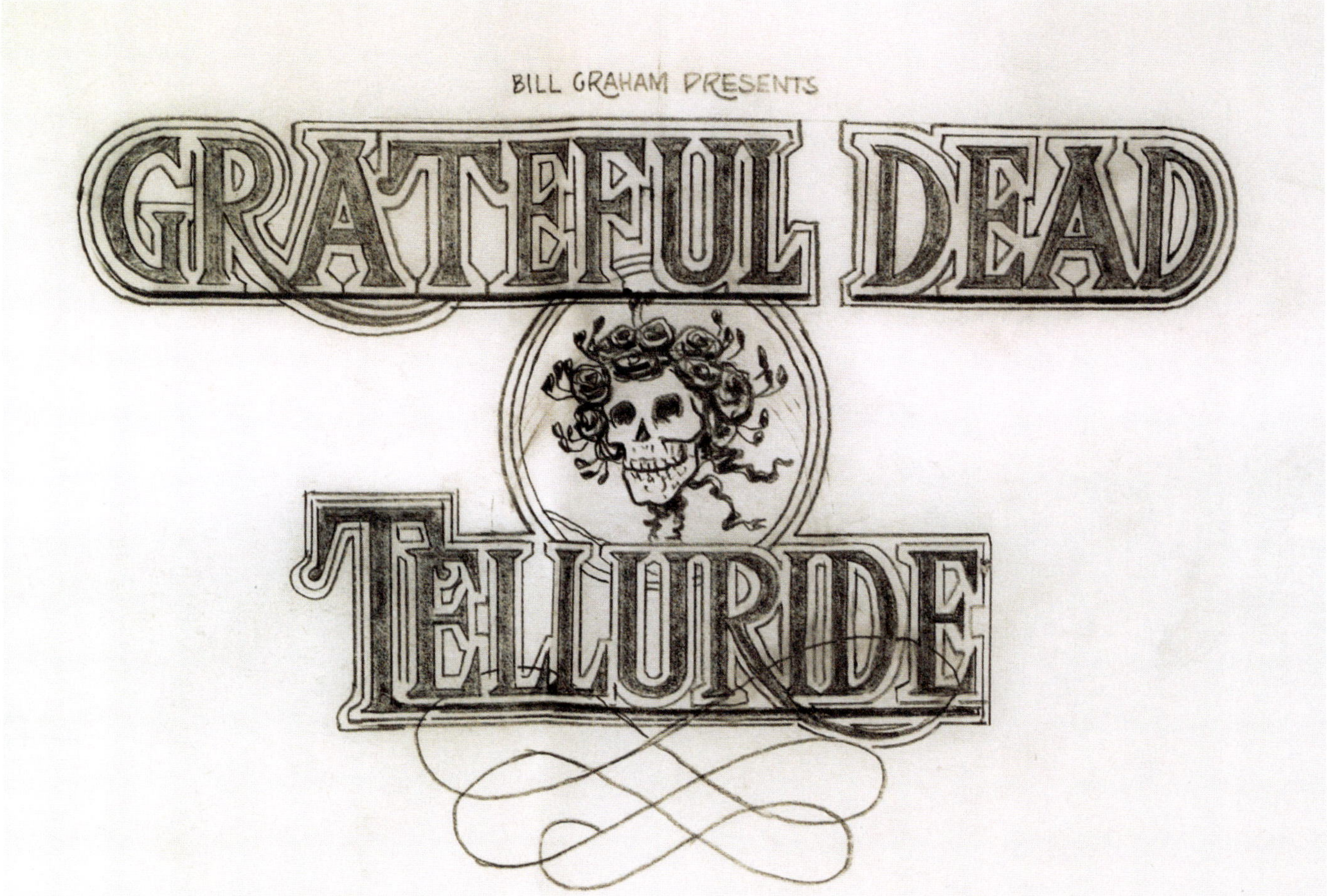
BILL GRAHAM PRESENTS
GRATEFUL DEAD
TELLURIDE

DESIGNING THE DEAD

Rick Griffin continued to work with the Grateful Dead, playing with every possible combination of the skeleton image to try to keep it fresh. Examples of his overlays are presented on p. 209, showing his appropriation of Jan de Bray's *The Regents of the Children's Orphanage in Haarlem* (1663) and his combination skull and sphinx. The Dead's visit to Egypt was a very useful source of new imagery for Griffin. The following pages (pages 206–07) show his working experiments with the lettering of their name, deconstructing it, looking for a new angle.

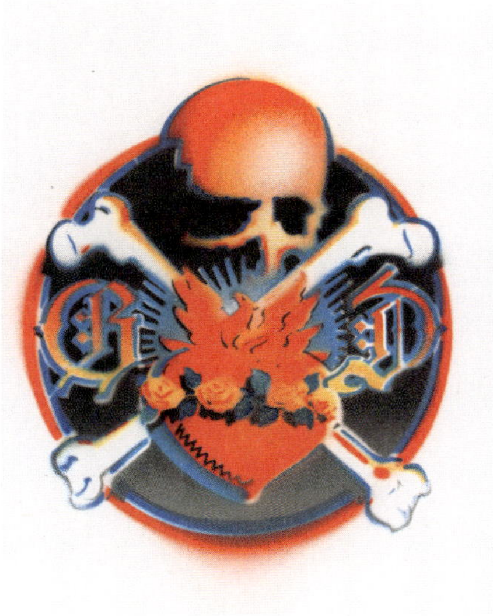

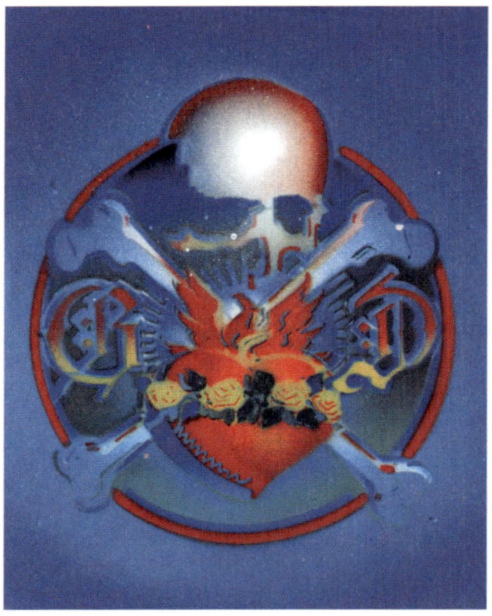

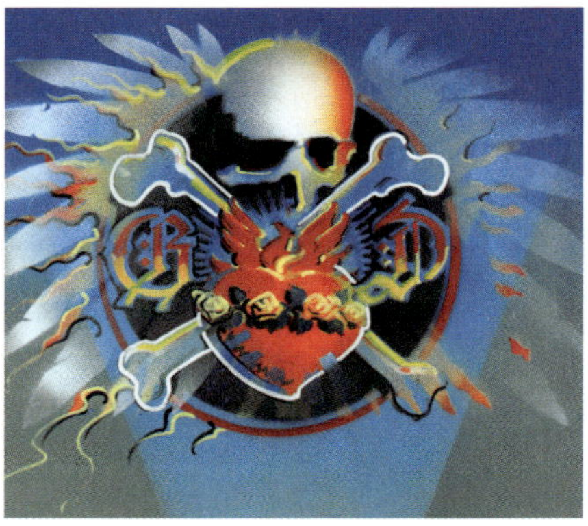

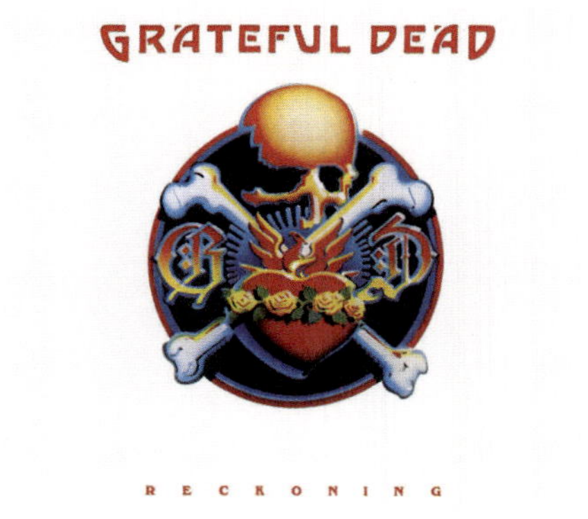

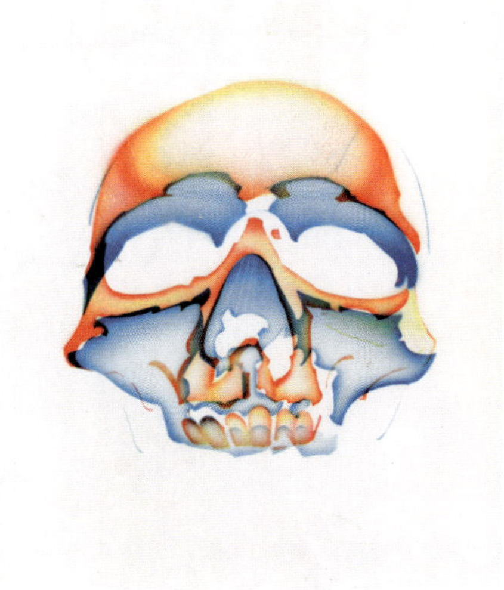

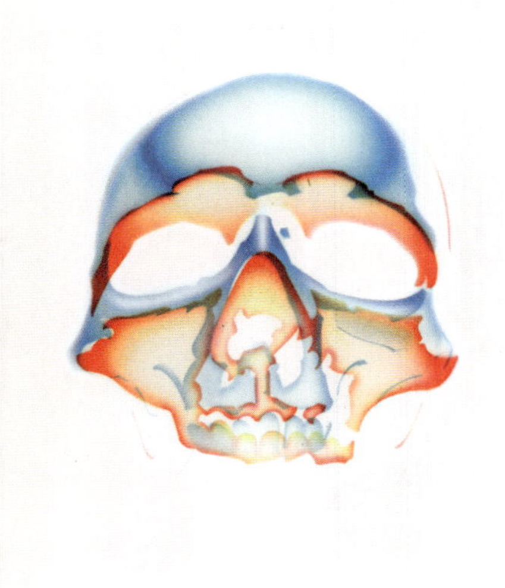

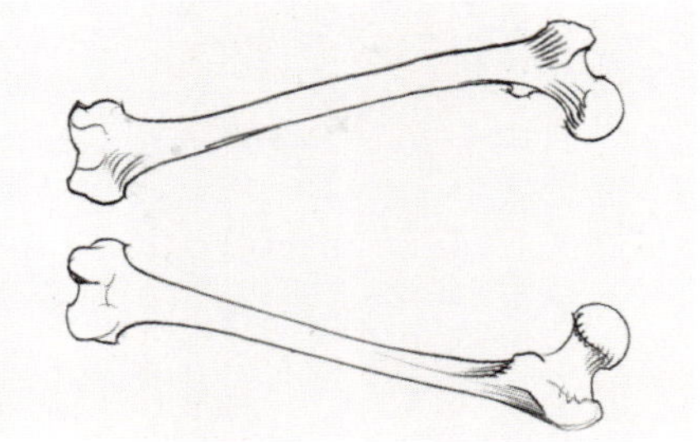

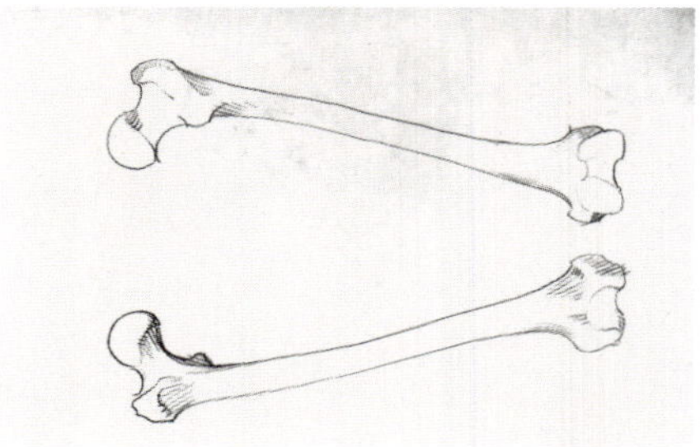

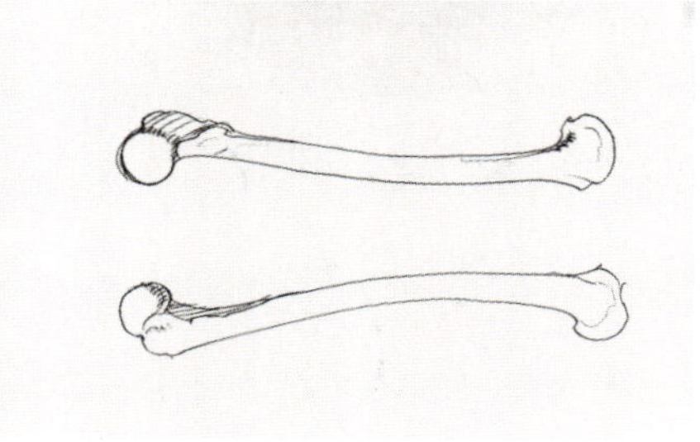

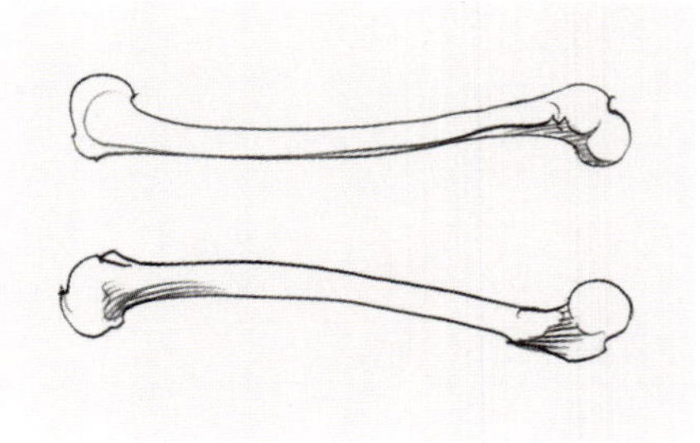

→ This page, top two rows: designs for the Grateful Dead's double live album *Reckoning* (1981). → Bottom three rows: an airbrushed skull and hand-drawn bones for the compilation *What A Long, Strange Trip It's Been: The Best Of The Grateful Dead* (1977). → Opposite: preparatory artwork, color separations, celluloid overlays and finished design for a poster to promote a Dead gig at Berkeley's Community Center in 1984. Unfortunately, the band's management had not officially approved the poster. Griffin had been selling posters featuring this design after the concert, but most of them were confiscated.

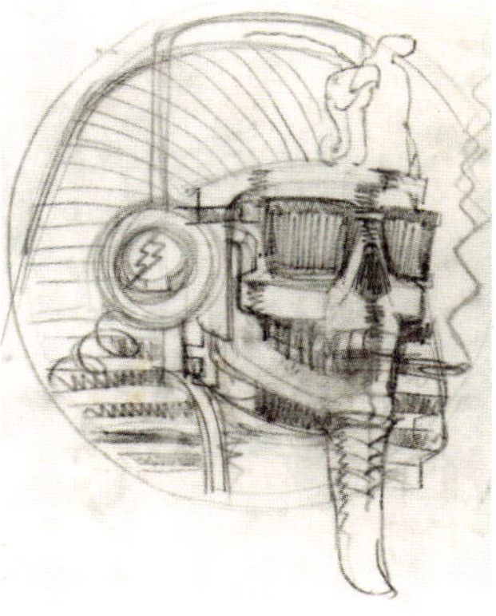
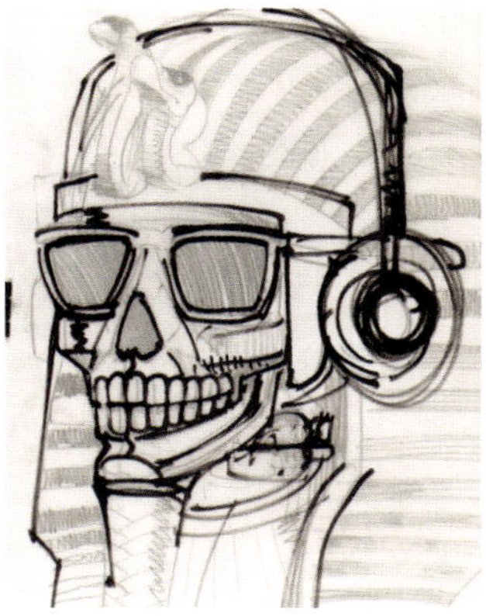
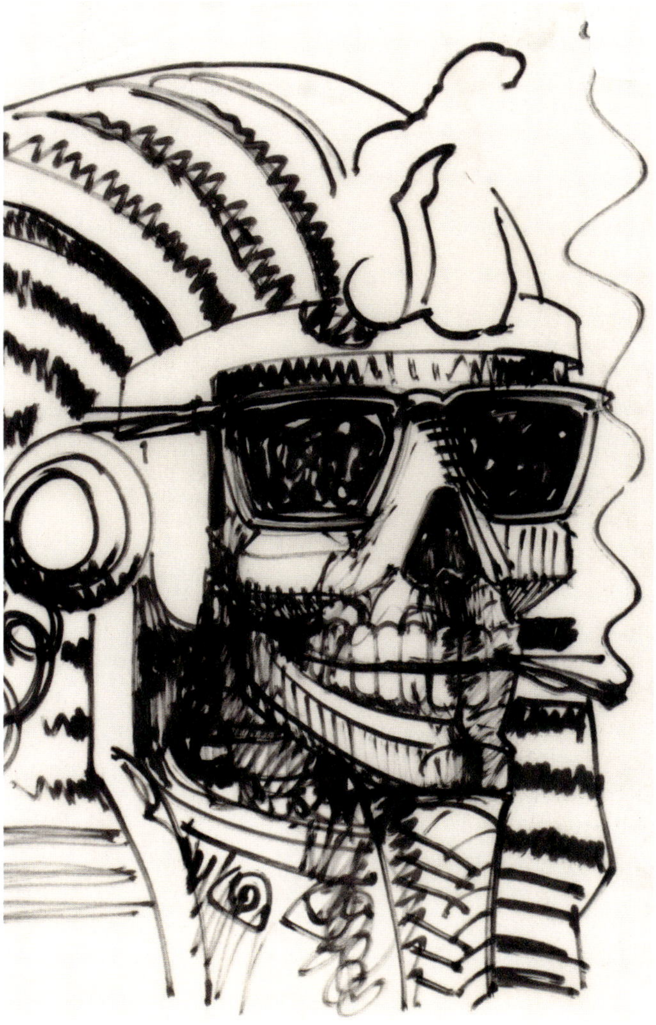
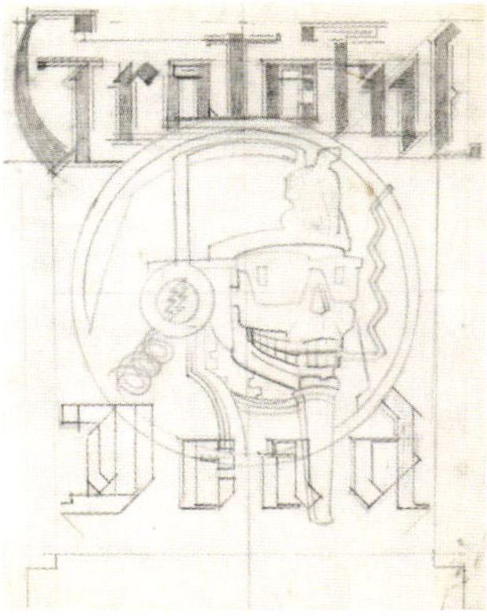
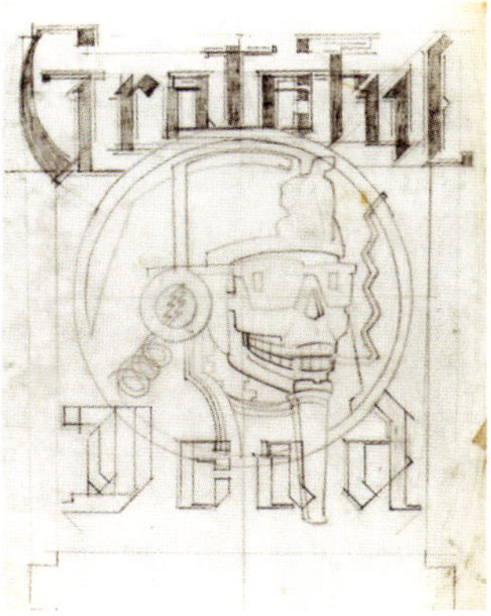
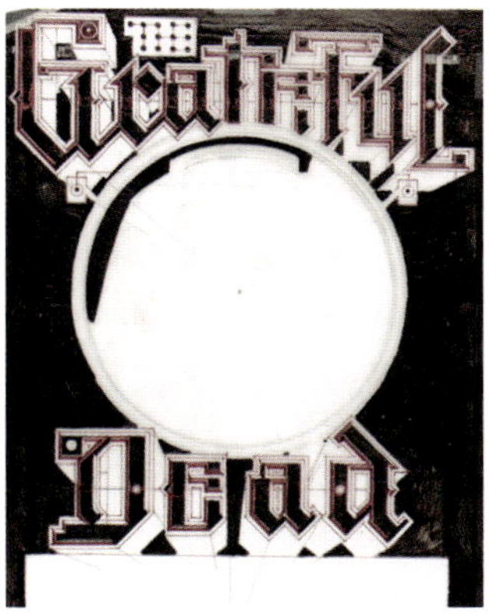
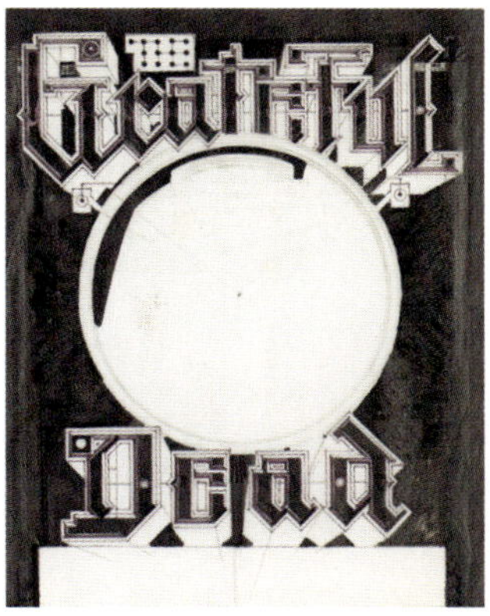
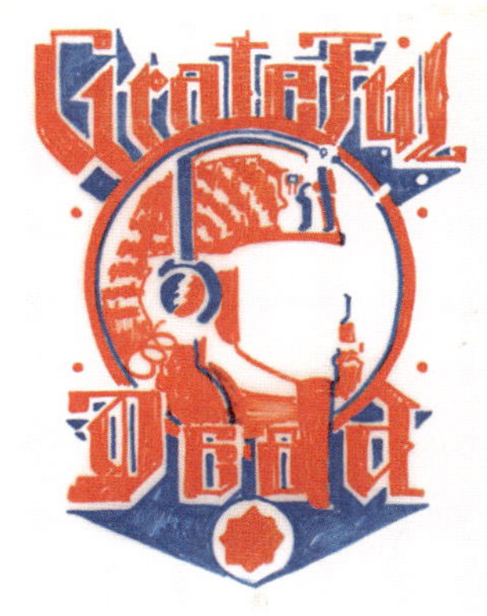
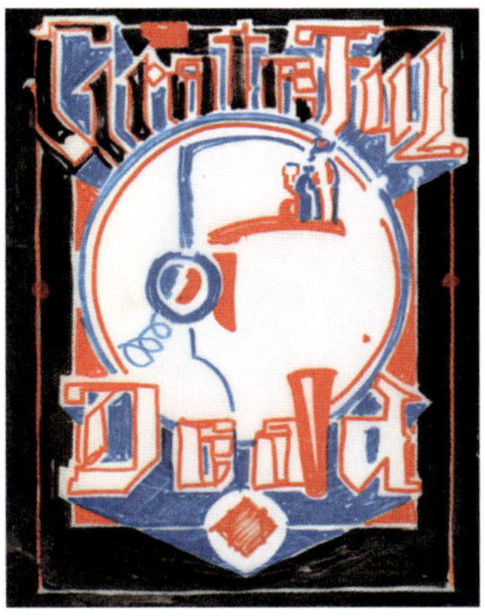
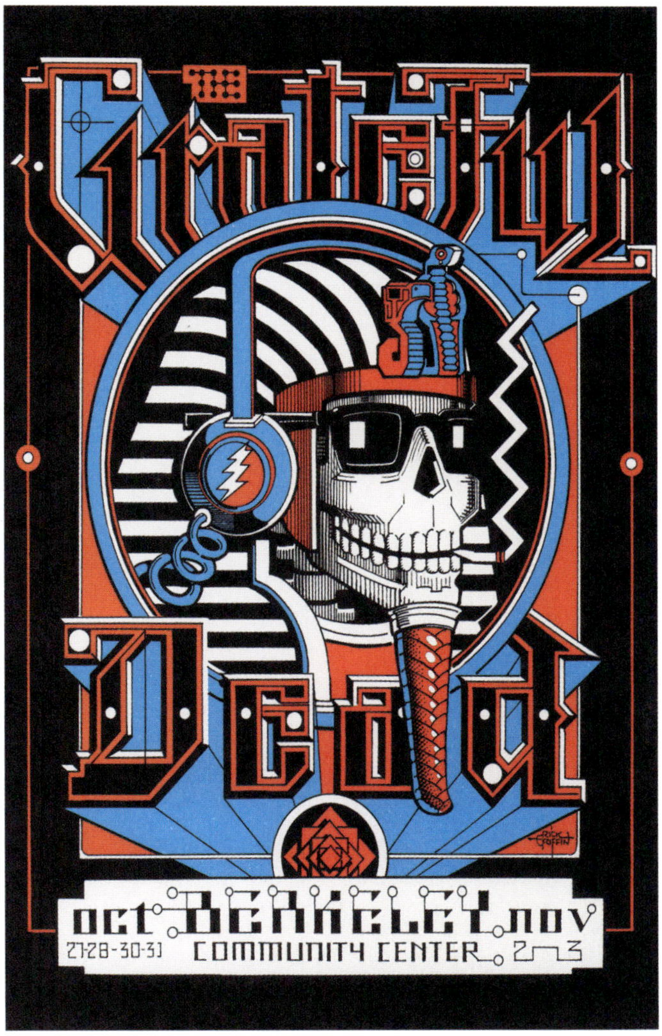
Grateful
Dead
oct BERKELEY nov
27-28-30-31 COMMUNITY CENTER 2-3
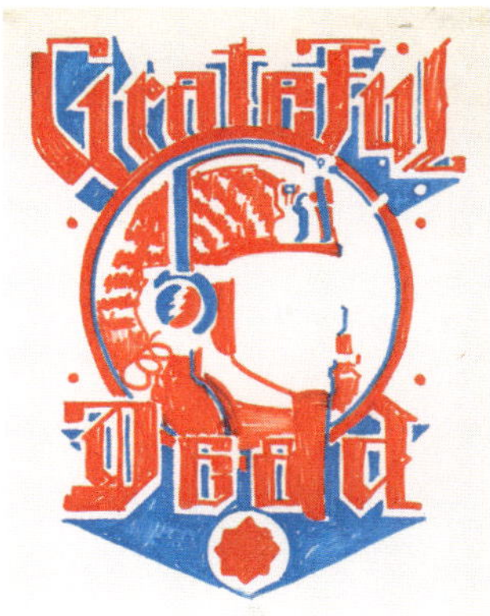
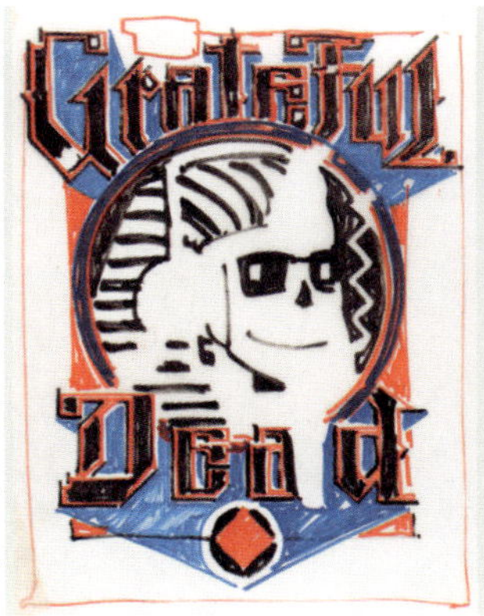

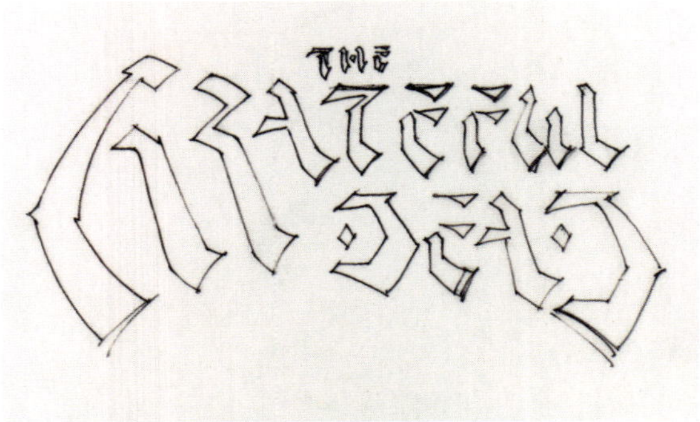
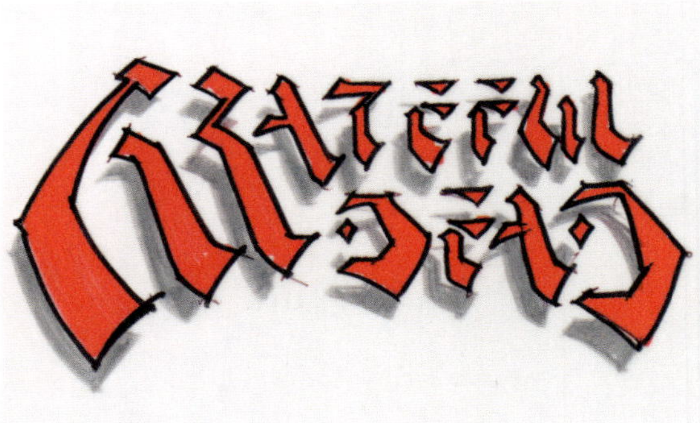
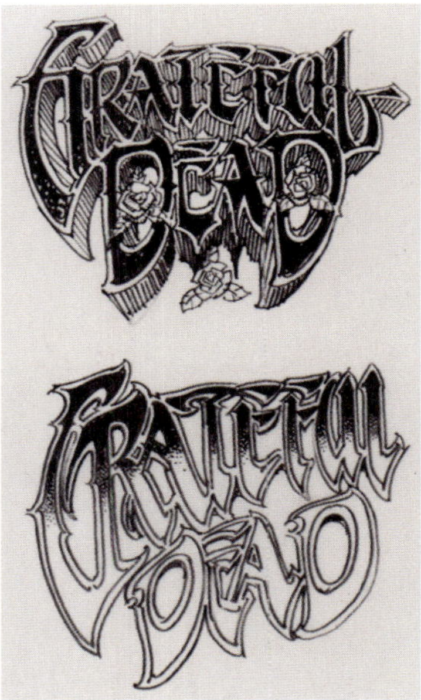
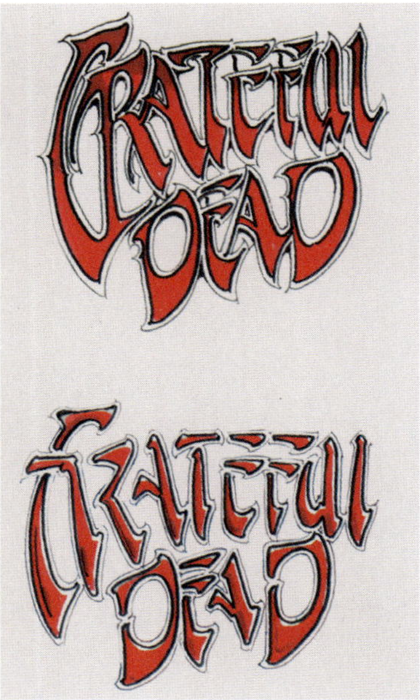
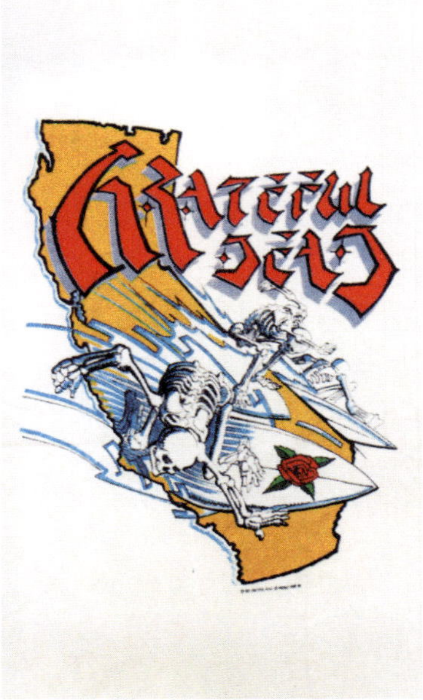
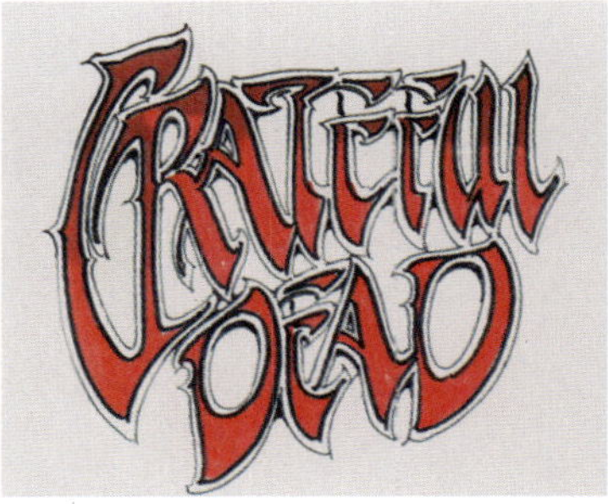

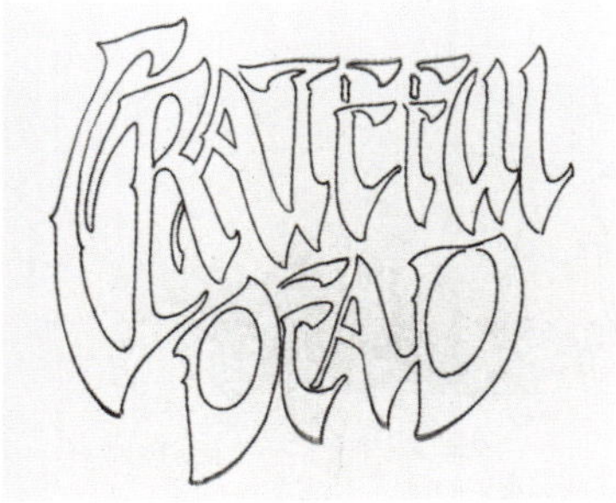
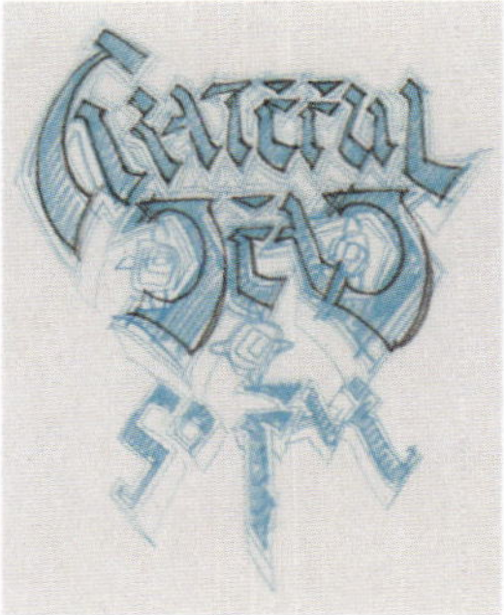
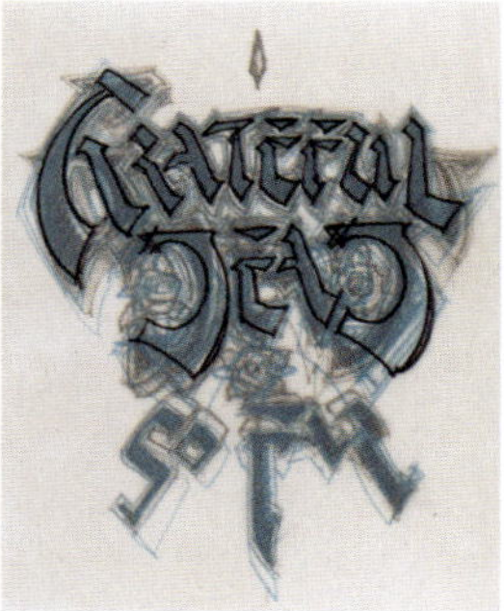
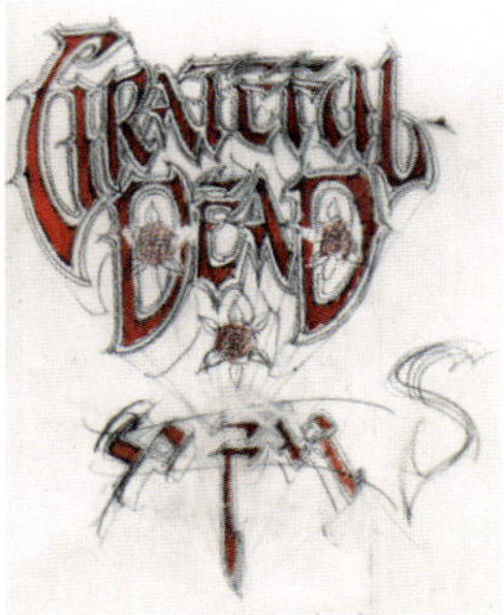
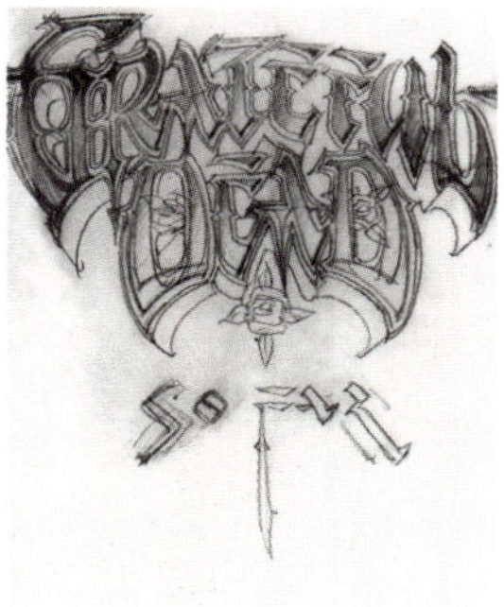

⟿ This page: Griffin's progressive designs for a handbill for the twentieth-anniversary music documentary *The Grateful Dead: 20 Years So Far*. Seen here are initial drawings, worked up pen-and-pencil sketches, pasted-up overlay, and painted artwork board. These artworks are from 1985; the final documentary appeared in September 1987. ⟿ Opposite: a series of Grateful Dead logos designed by Griffin between 1985 and 1990. The images in the left-hand column are all on black film.

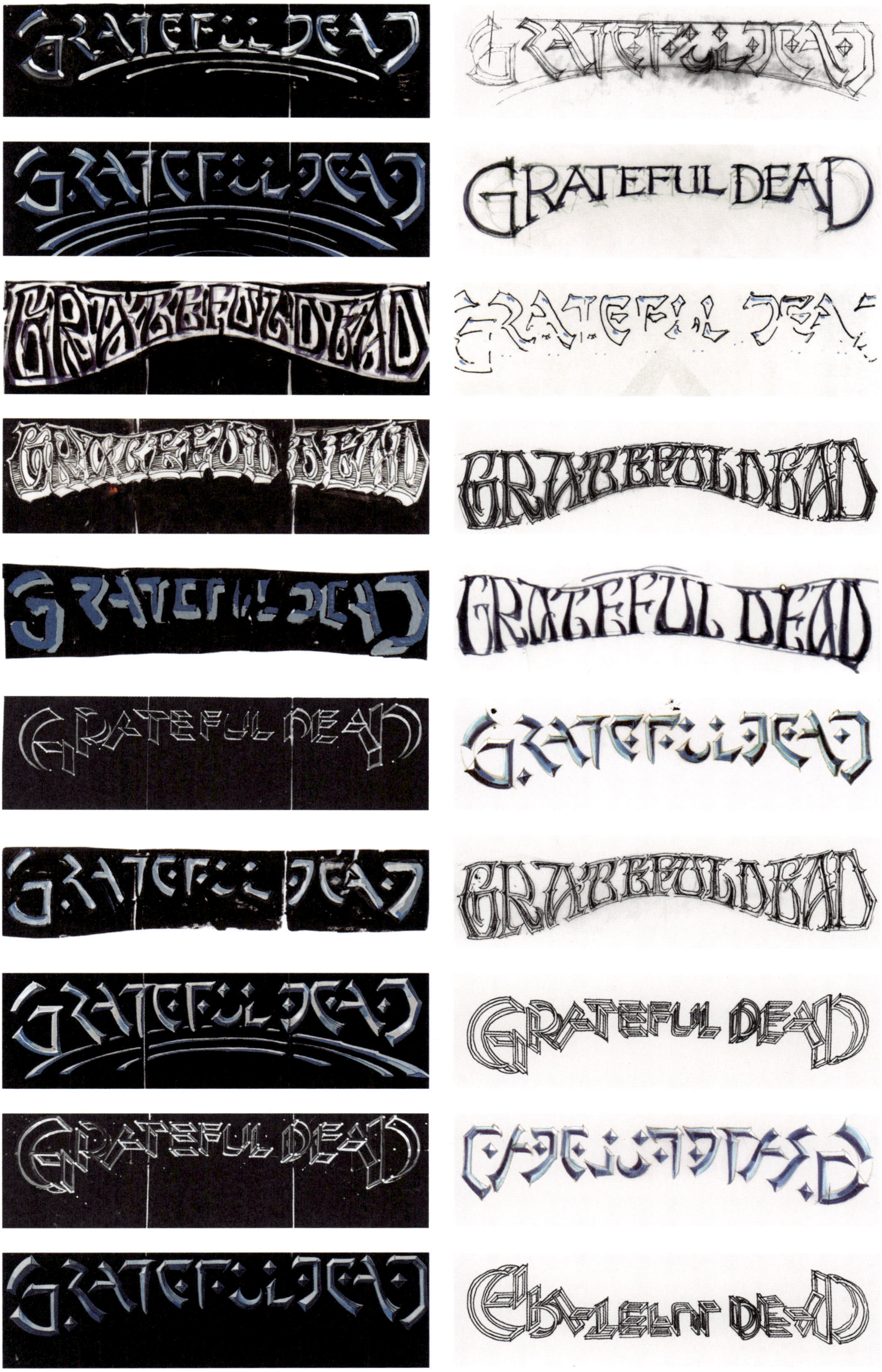

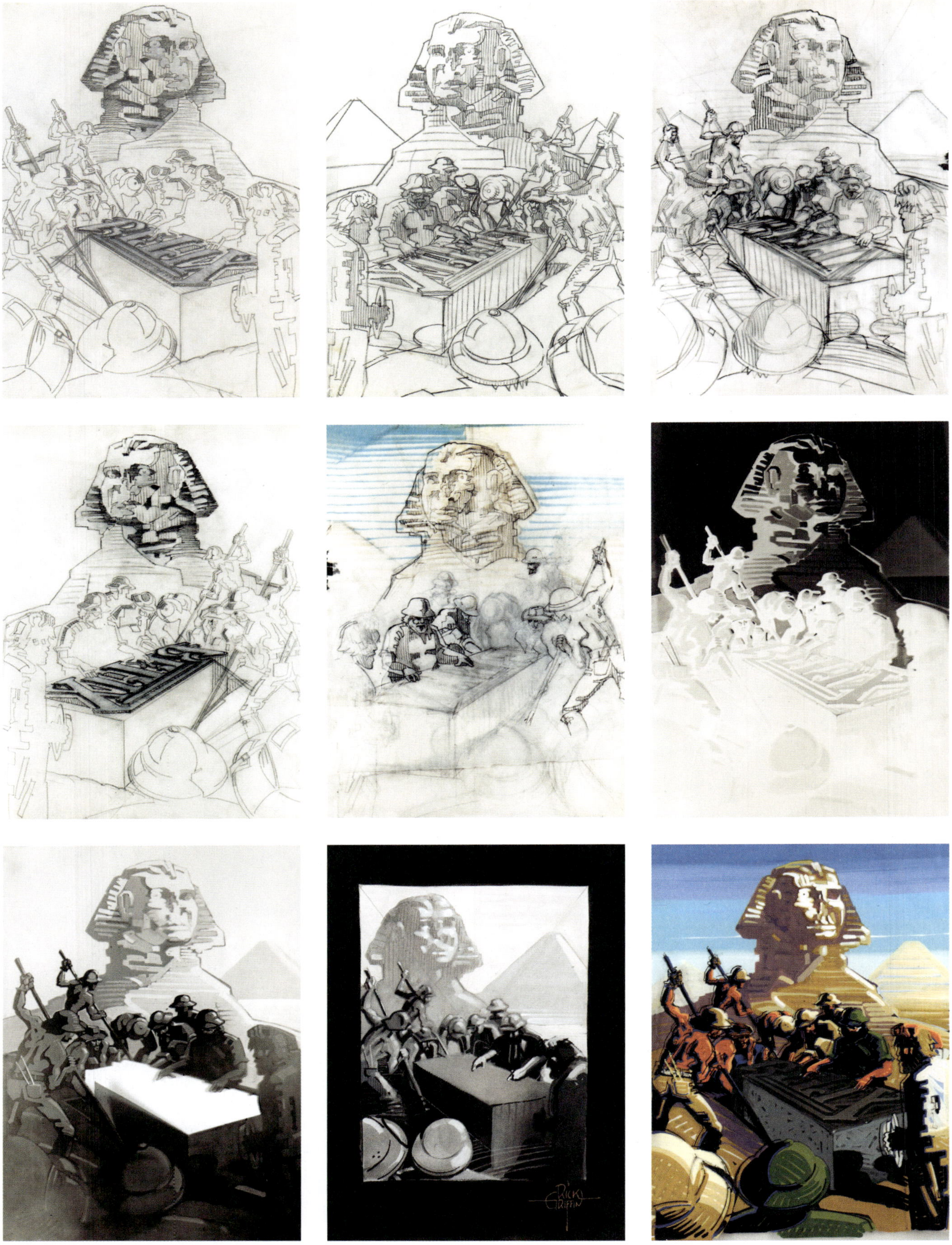

»→ This page: Rick Griffin's detailed sketches and worked-up designs to mark three Grateful Dead concerts at the Sound and Light Theater in Giza, site of the legendary Egyptian pyramids, on September 14–16, 1978. The image was created for the band's magazine *Relix*. The final image (bottom right) comprises gouache on celluloid overlays. »→ Opposite: sketches for the Grateful Dead Christmas card, based on Jan de Bray's *The Regents of the Children's Orphanage in Haarlem* (1663). The image was later used to advertise Griffin's only British exhibition, at the Roundhouse in London's Camden Town in 1976.

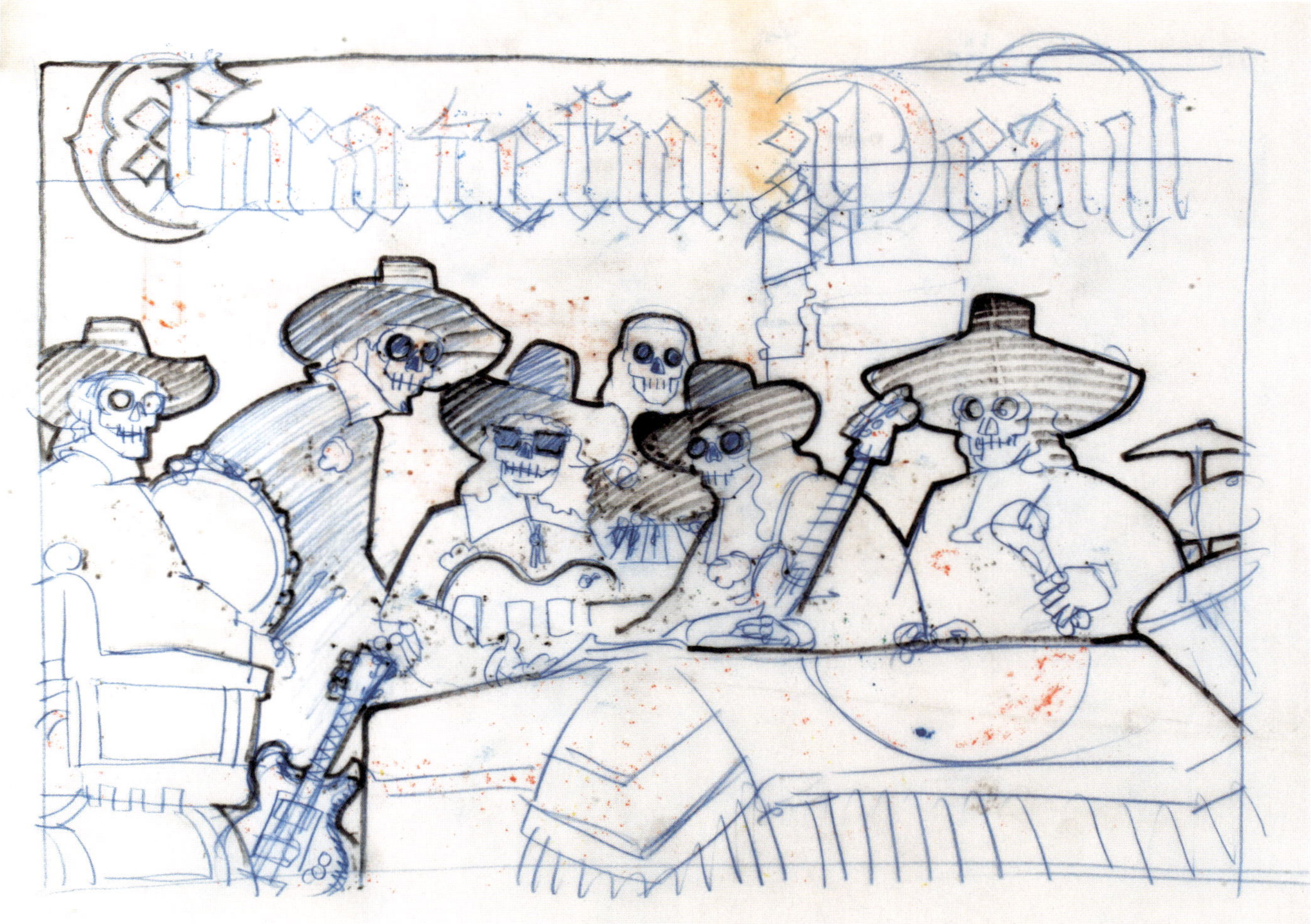
Grateful Dead

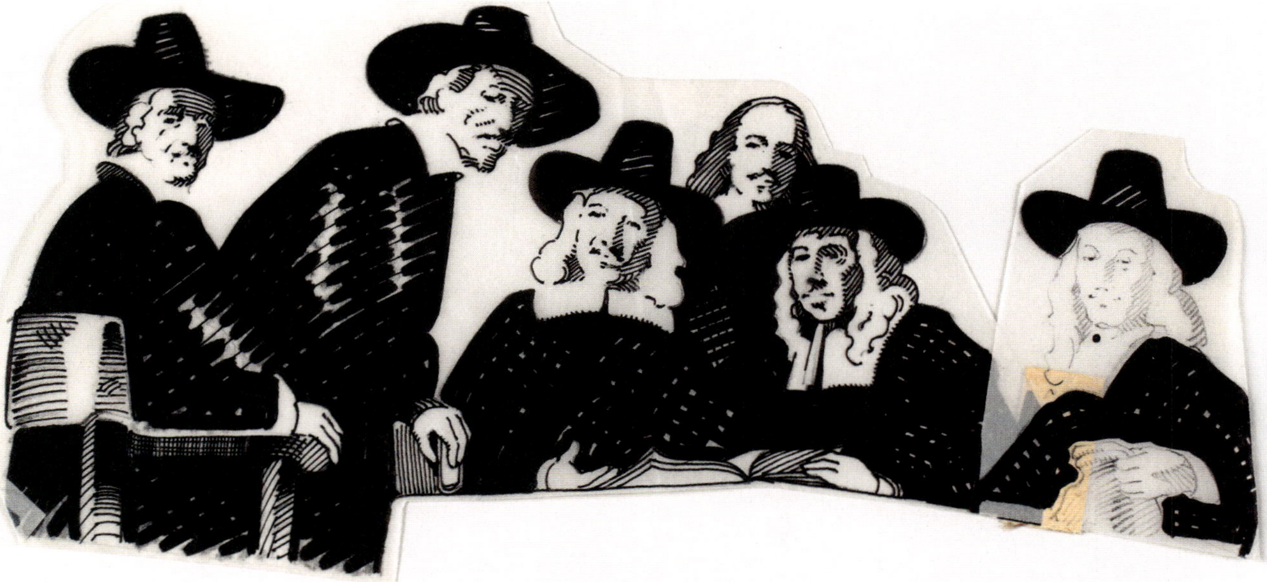

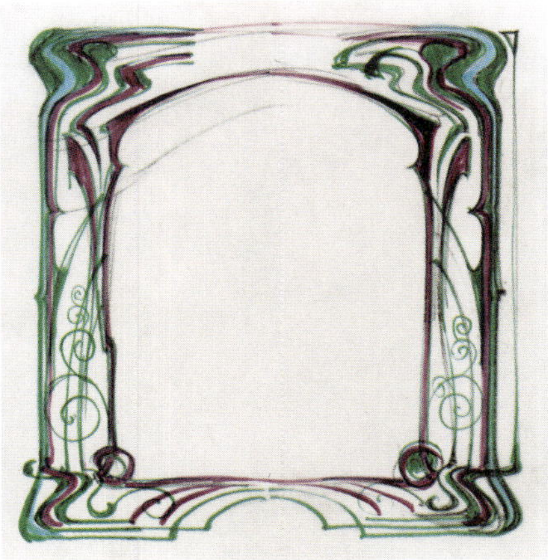

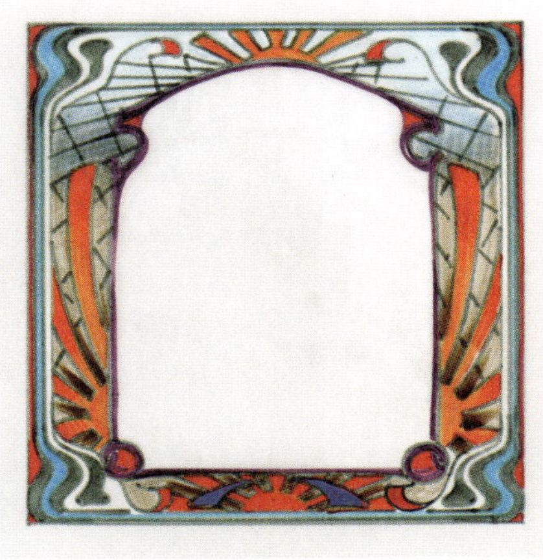

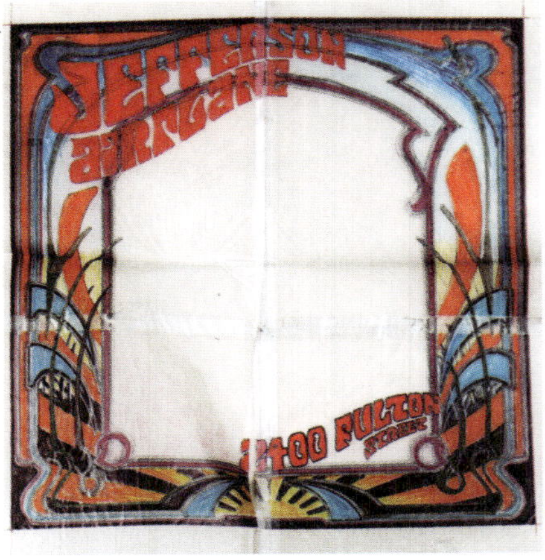

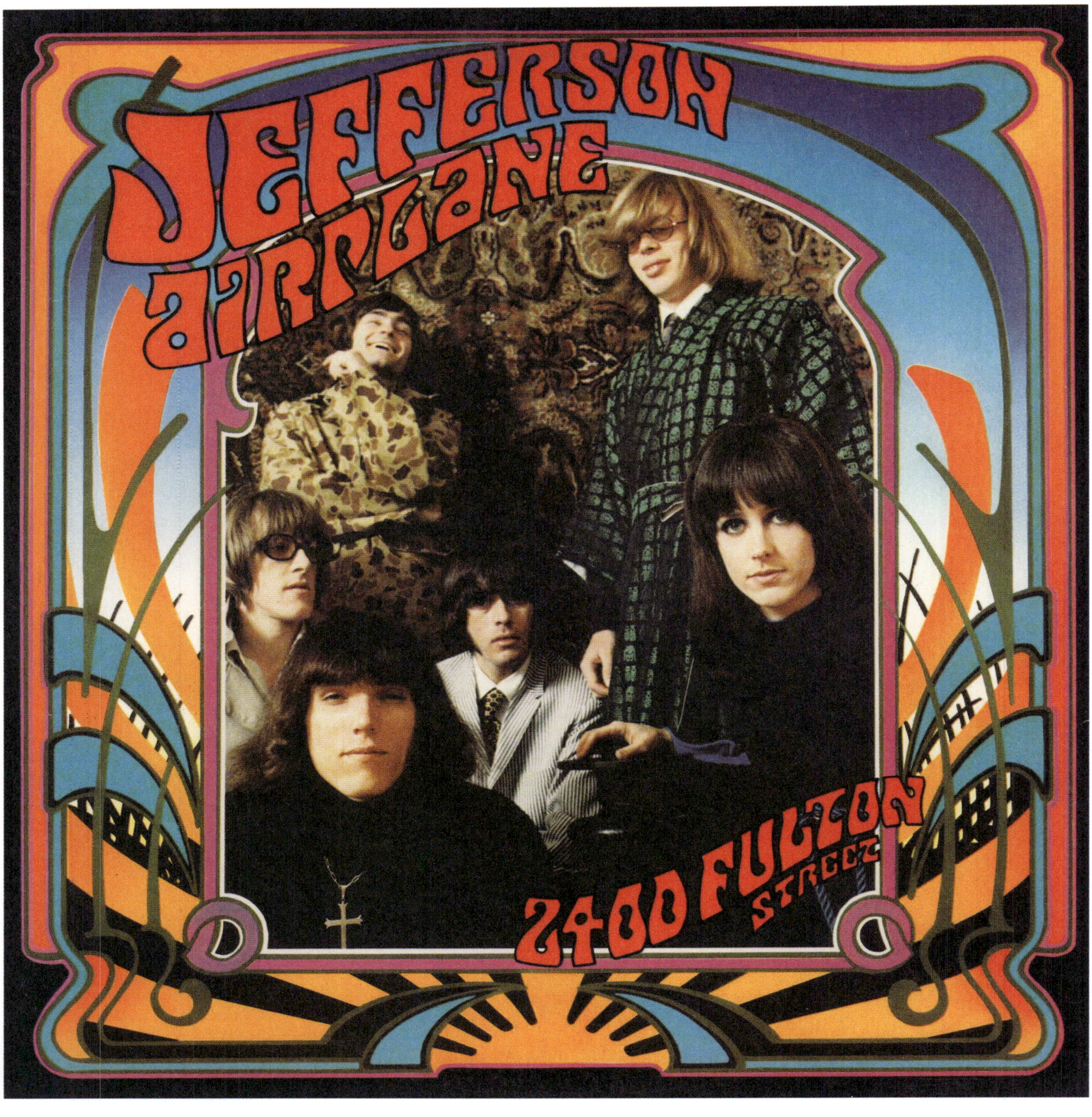

RECORD COVER DESIGN

In time, poster artists were asked to design record covers. They built these in much the same way as their posters—through layers of process, adding color and detail on the way. In classic psychedelic style, the calligraphic text here is integrated into the patterned border, and photographic elements anchor the design in the center.

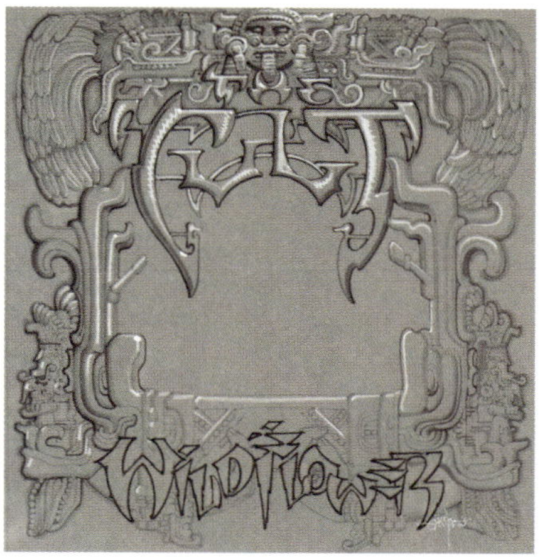

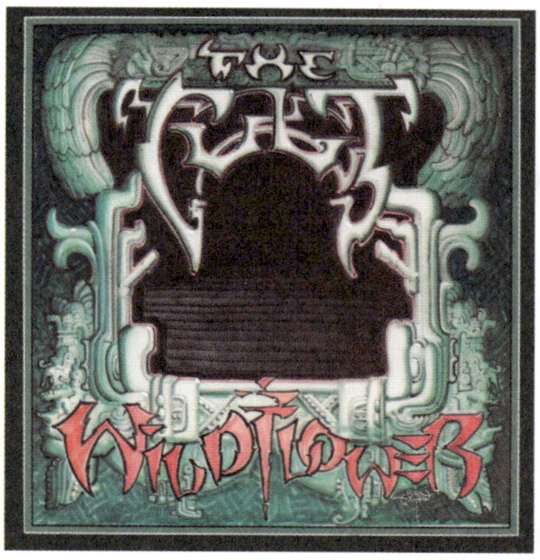

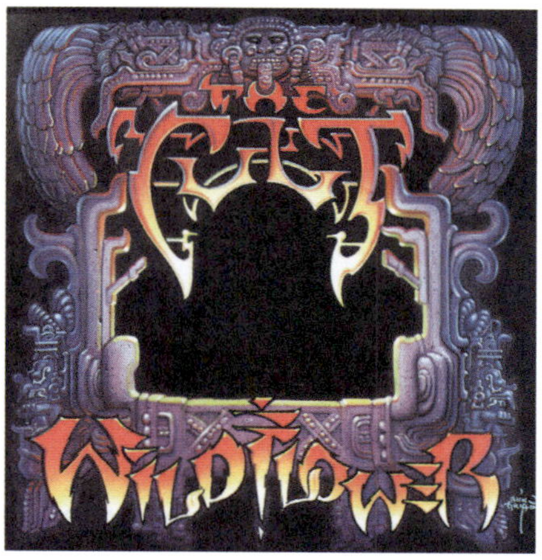

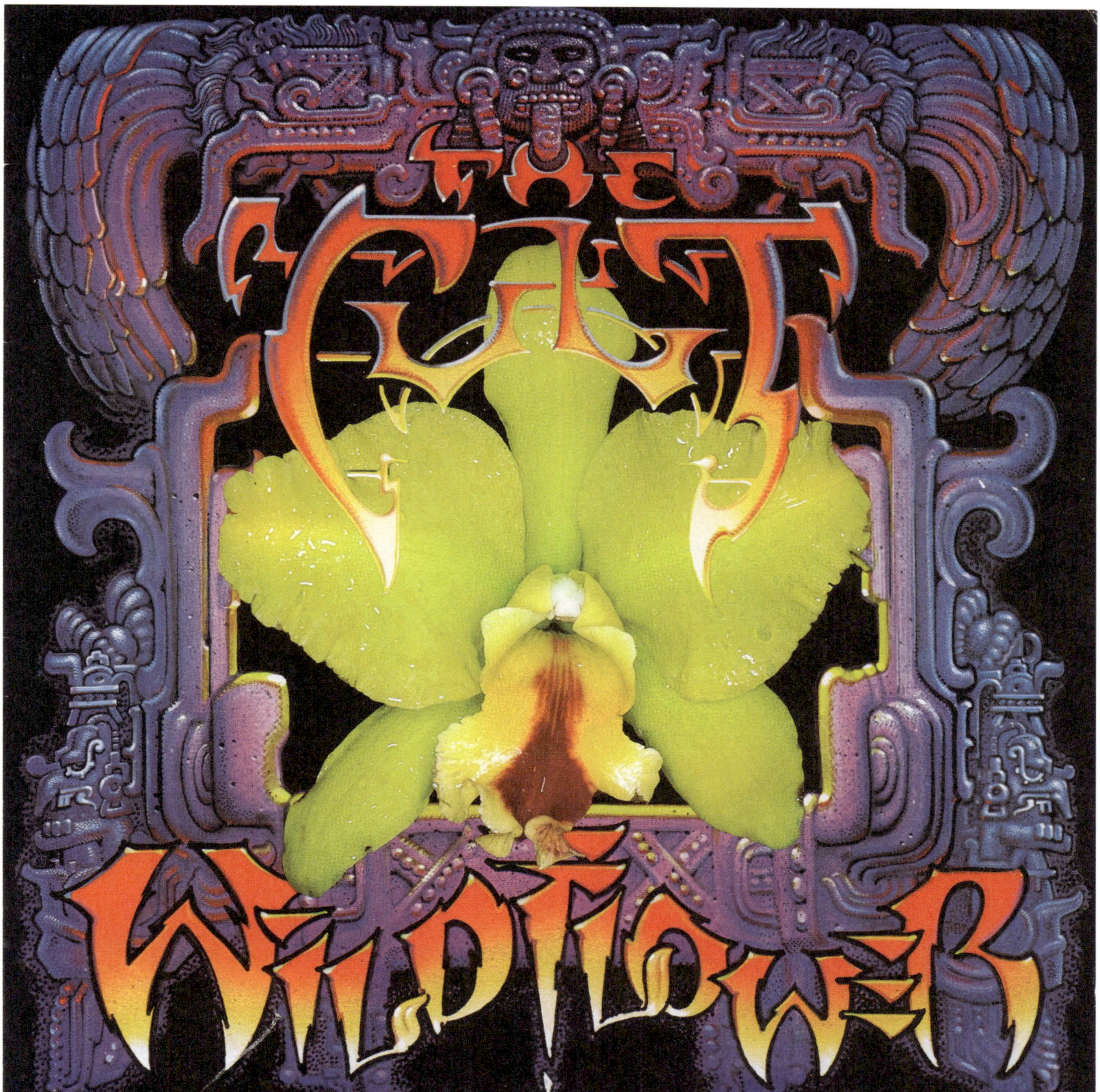

➳ Opposite: in collaboration with Randy Tuten, Griffin revisited his past for this 1987 compilation of highlights from Jefferson Airplane's late-sixties heyday. The sixties lettering combines with an Art Deco-inspired decorative border. ➳ This page: Griffin's ornate lettering for this single by British rock band The Cult successfully reproduces the visual sensibility of his earlier flamboyant work. The image of a yellow orchid, flanked by an ornate frame completes the design for this 1987 release.

DYLAN AND THE DEAD

Bob Dylan's management approached Rick Griffin to provide a cover for the singer's album *Down in the Groove* (1988). Unfortunately, after repeated requests for changes, all were rejected—much to the designer's chagrin. Eventually, Columbia Records chose a straightforward—though markedly less characterful—photograph of Dylan instead. A selection of Griffin's rough sketches are shown here.

In July 1987, Dylan and the Grateful Dead did six poorly received shows together. It came as a surprise when, two years later, Dylan decided to release a live album from the tour. Mickey Hart commented, 'It was not our finest hour, nor his. I don't know why it was even made into a record.' The Dead called upon Rick Griffin to do the album graphics, which combined the Dead's skull and roses with a youthful portrait of Dylan.

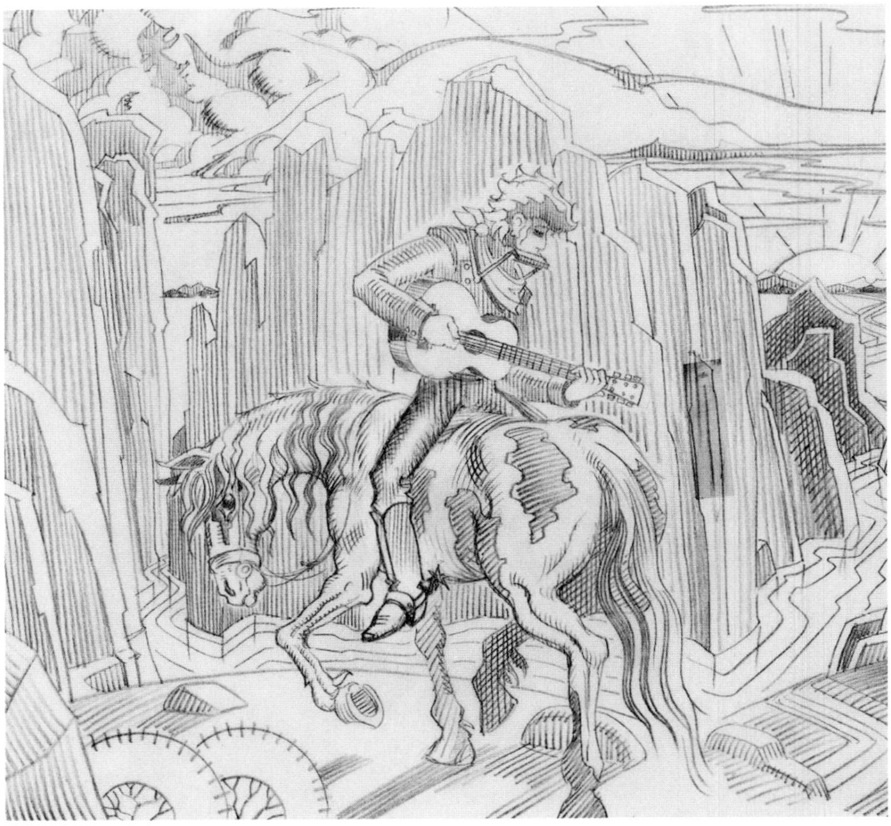

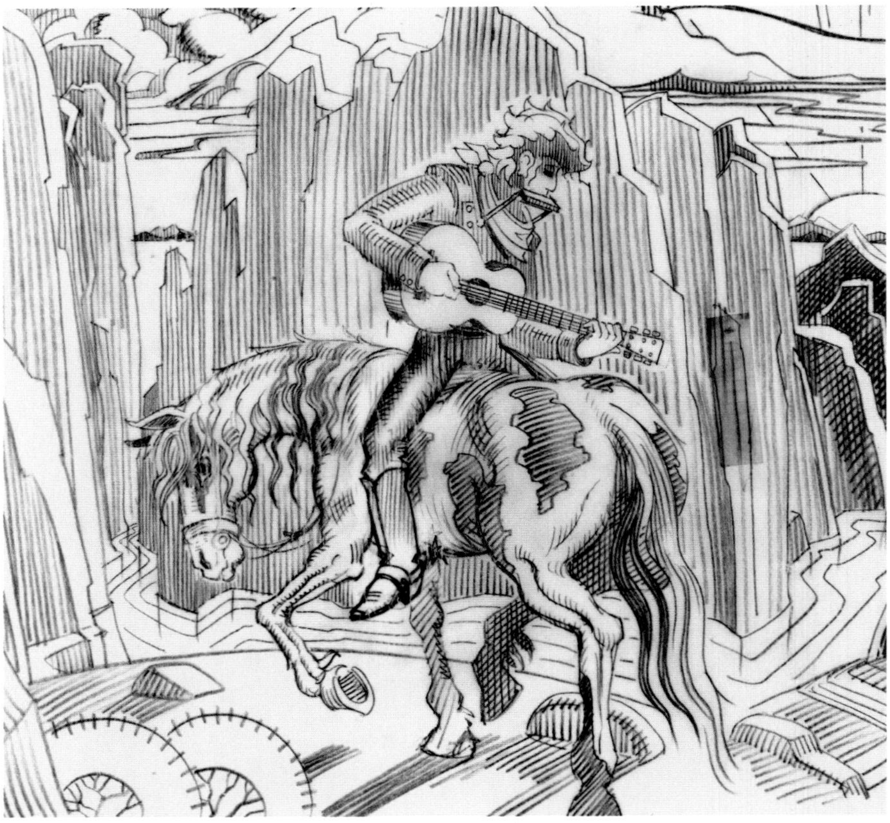

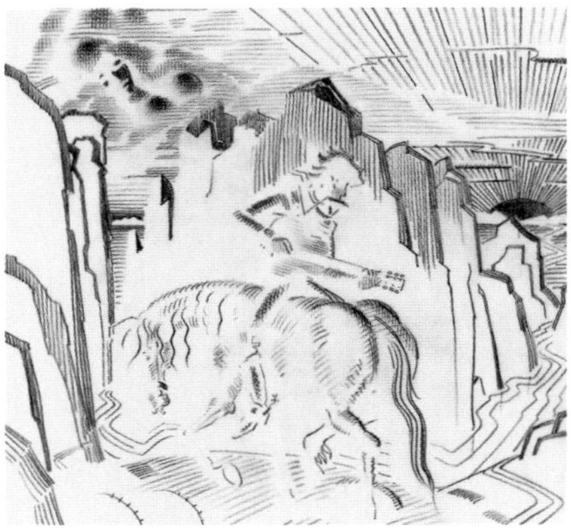

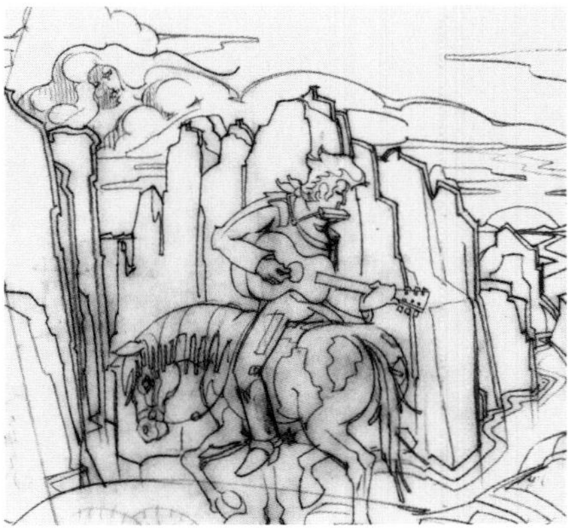

⋙→ This page: pencil and pen drawings for Griffin's aborted *Down in the Groove* cover designs. ⋙→ Opposite: Griffin's design for the less-than-stellar *Dylan & The Dead* LP (1989). The performers' names in the top row were created on tracing paper. The series of four images in the second row are film overlays, painted in reverse colorways.

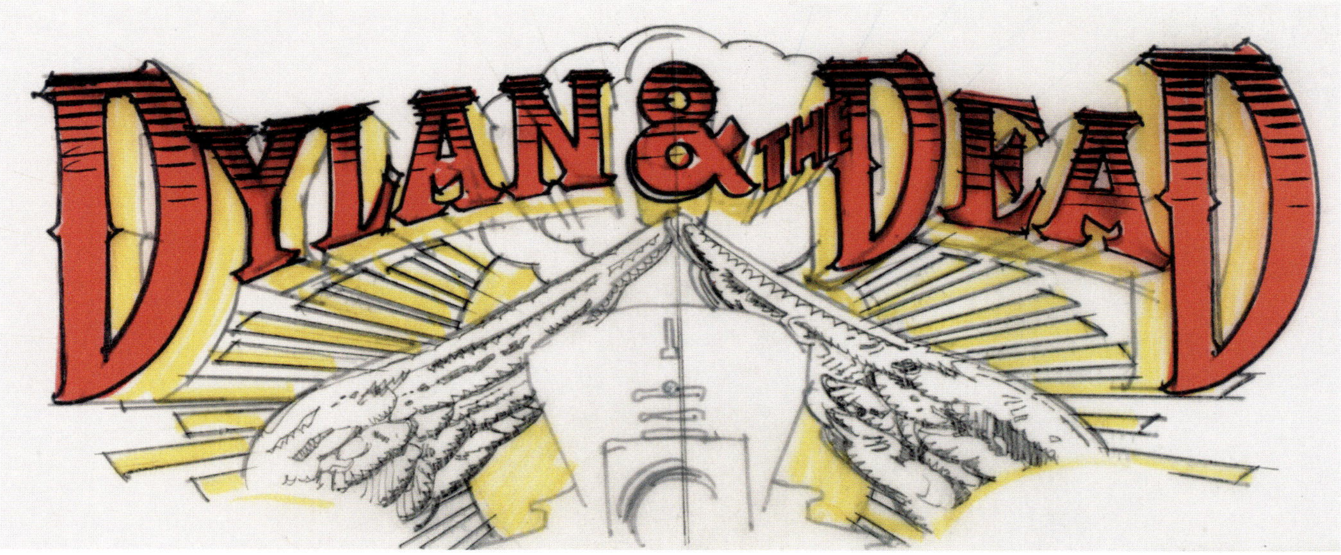
DYLAN & THE DEAD

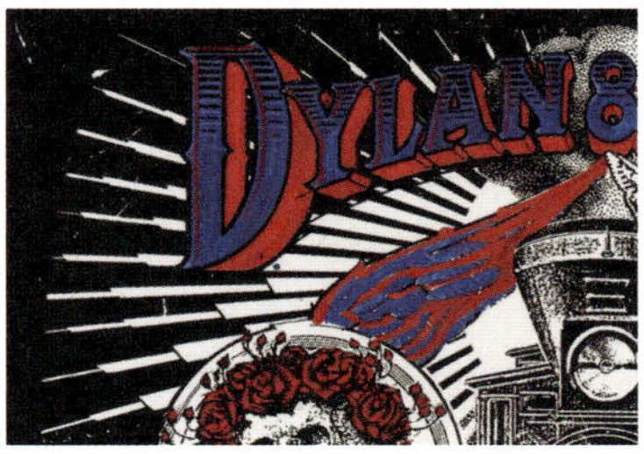

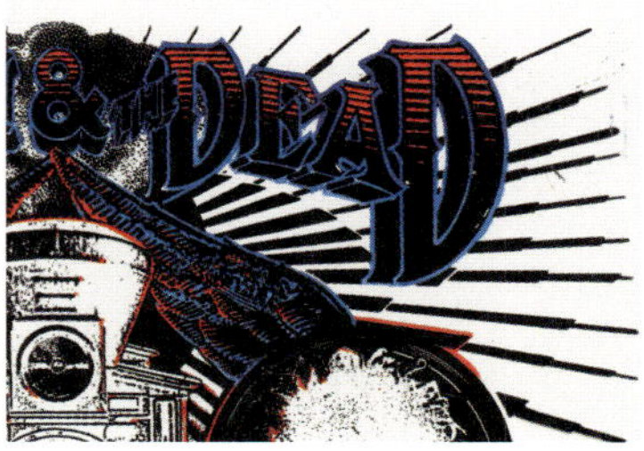

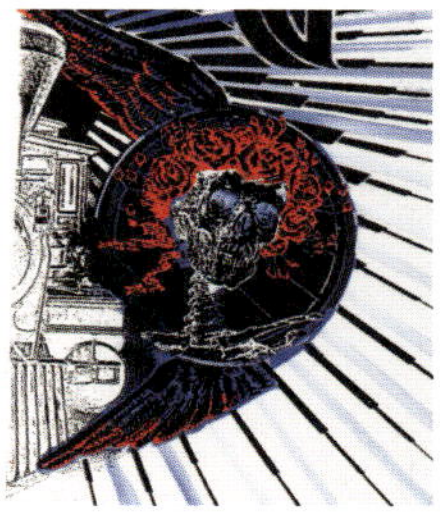

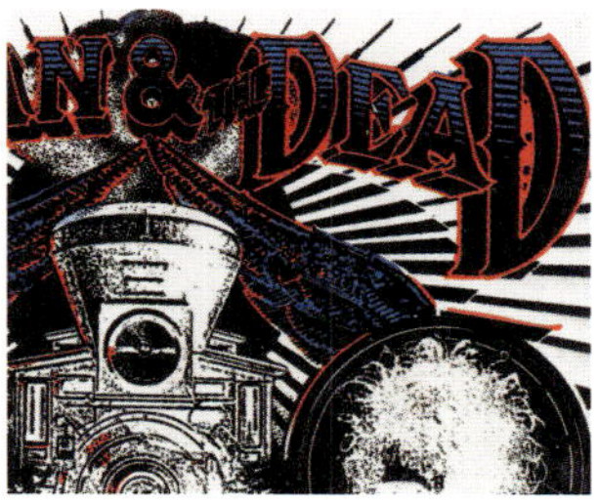

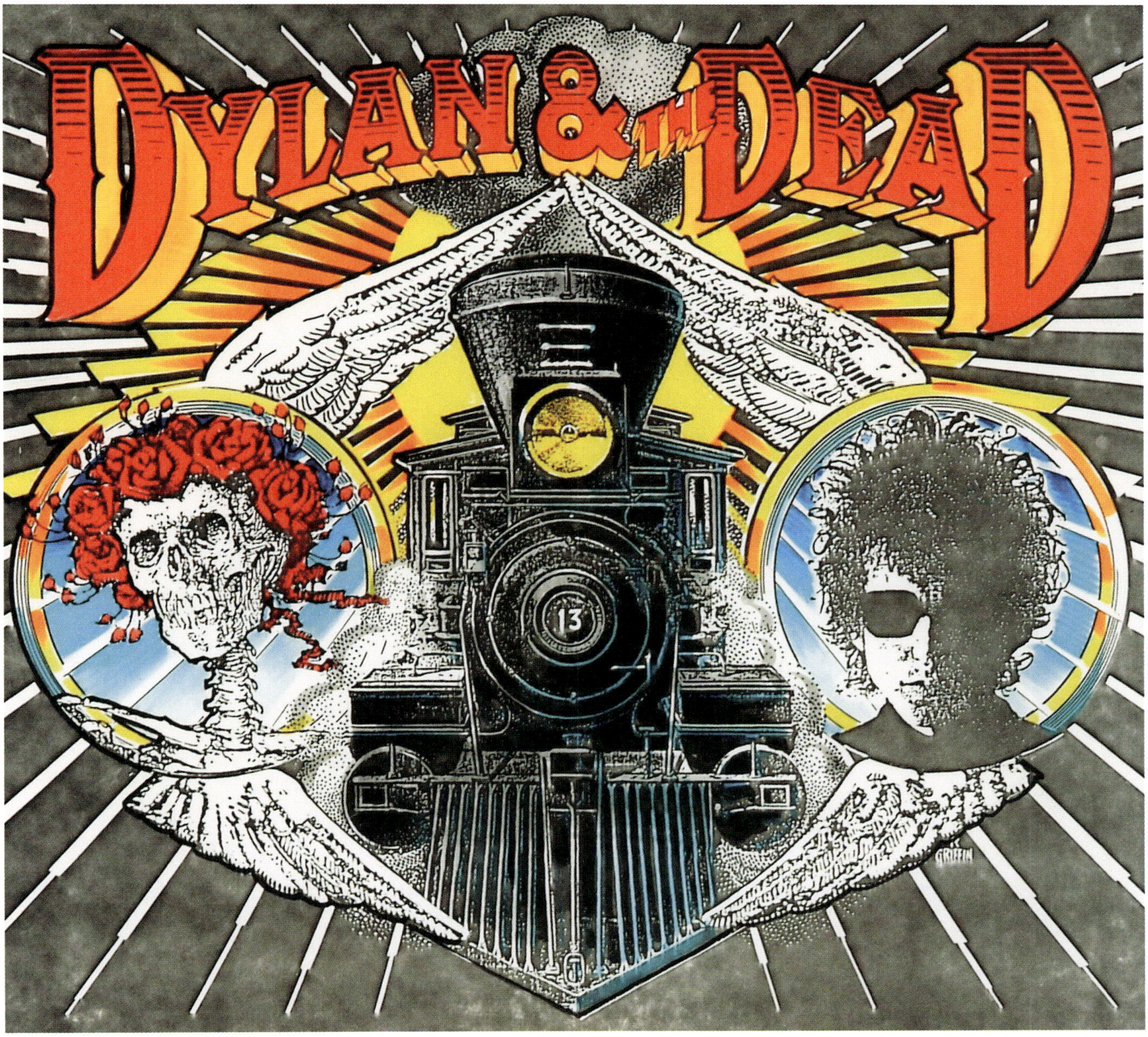
DYLAN & THE DEAD
13
GRIFFIN

BIOS OF THE DUDES

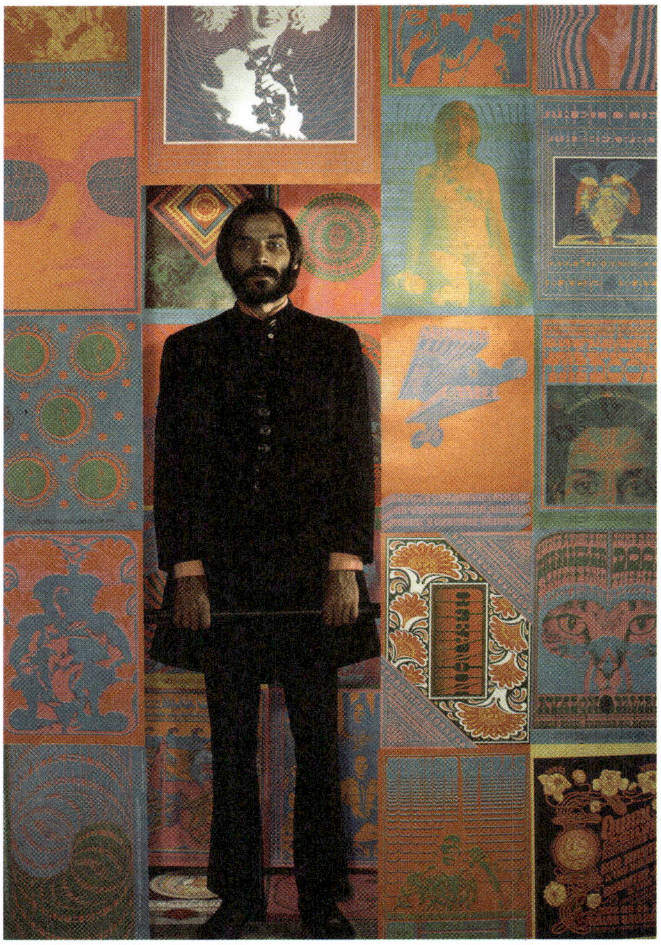

→ Ted Streshinsky's photographs of three great sixties poster artists surrounded by examples of their work, taken in San Francisco during the sixties. → From left to right: Victor Moscoso; Stanley Mouse; Rick Griffin.

ALAN ALDRIDGE

Aldridge was an illustrator for *The Sunday Times Magazine* before becoming editor at Penguin Books. While there, he commissioned several key artists, including Rick Griffin and Stanley Mouse, for *The Beatles Illustrated Lyrics* song book.

FRANK BETTENCOURT

Bettencourt trained in fine, graphic, and technical art. Producing rock posters for big-name groups while still at school, he also worked on several spacecraft, including *Voyager*, with his engineer father. His later career retained a dual focus on art and space.

BERKELEY BONAPARTE

A company formed by the 'Big Five' San Francisco poster artists (Rick Griffin, Wes Wilson, Stanley Mouse, Alton Kelley, and Victor Moscoso), and photographer Bob Seidemann, to create and market contemporary rock and counter-culture posters.

MICHAEL BOWEN, *THE ORACLE*

Emerging out of the fifties beat generation, Bowen became the art director of San Francisco's underground paper *The Oracle*, which operated from his studio. In January 1967, he also helped organize the city's Human Be-In event.

LEE CONKLIN

Conklin produced many West Coast rock posters in the late sixties, notably for Bill Graham's Fillmore West venue. He specialized in complex images built from human bodies or body parts. Famously, he also designed the cover image for Santana's 1969 debut album.

ALLEN COHEN, *THE ORACLE*

Born in Brooklyn, Cohen moved to San Francisco in 1963 and was co-founder of the city's underground paper *The Oracle*. Poetry always remained his passion. He co-edited the award-winning poetry anthology *An Eye For an Eye: Poets on 9/11* in 2002.

ROBERT CRUMB

Crumb became an underground comix legend with his deft but disturbing cartoons for *Zap Comix*, which debuted in 1968 and which he co-founded. His best-known strip is probably Fritz the Cat. He has also illustrated many album covers.

MICHAEL ENGLISH

As half of British design team Hapshash and the Coloured Coat, English was responsible for some of UK psychedelia's most imaginative graphic art, designing posters for the UFO Club and programs for Brian Epstein's Saville Theatre.

THE FAMILY DOG

Initially a loose collective comprising, among others, Alton Kelley, The Family Dog put on early hippie gigs and events, some at the Red Dog Saloon. Chet Helms later took over, promoting gigs at San Francisco's Avalon Ballroom and commissioning all the 'Big Five.'

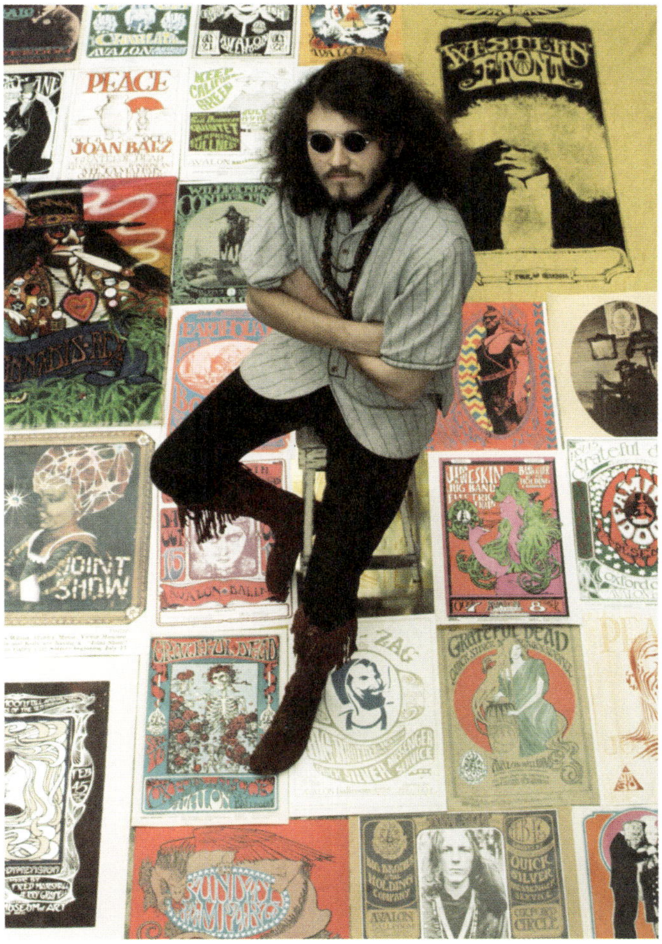

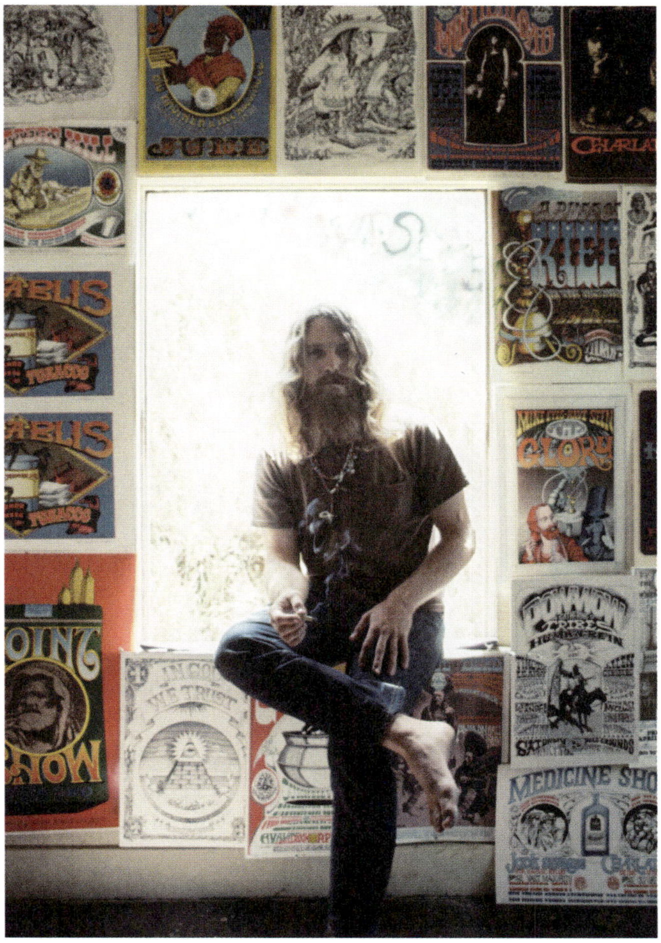

ROBERT FRIED

After studying graphic art in New York, Fried became a commercial artist. His first rock poster, for a Charlatans gig at the Avalon Ballroom, came via Rick Griffin. He went on to work for Chet Helms and Bill Graham before turning to fine-art prints and lecturing.

IDA GRIFFIN

A talented artist, Ida Pfefferle (who was born in London) met future husband Rick while both were students at Chouinard Art School in Los Angeles in 1964. They had four children. She also created concert posters for Berkeley Bonaparte.

JOHN VAN HAMERSVELD

After creating the iconic 'Endless Summer' film poster while still at art school, Van Hamersveld went on to design poster art and album covers for artists including the Stones, the Beatles, and Jimi Hendrix over the course of a fifty-year career.

ALLEN GINSBERG

A pivotal poet of the beat generation, Ginsberg's most famous work is still the extraordinary 'Howl' (1965). He remained an active counter-cultural figure in the sixties and read at key events, including the 'International Poetry Incarnation' in London in 1965.

RICK GRIFFIN

From youthful cartoons for *Surfer* magazine, via sixties psychedelic posters, to his art as a born-again Christian, Griffin proved himself a consummate draftsman with a prolific imagination. Probably the most influential poster artist of his time.

CHET HELMS

Helms was founder and manager of Big Brother and the Holding Company before he took over Family Dog Productions in 1966. Initially working with Bill Graham at the Fillmore Auditorium, he went on to host his own events at the Avalon Ballroom.

BILL GRAHAM

Despite tragic setbacks in early life, Graham went on to become a hugely successful, hard-nosed businessman, who ran the Fillmore venues, started the Day on the Green annual event, and put on many hugely profitable festivals.

GARY GRIMSHAW

A phenomenally talented poster designer, Grimshaw had few peers outside San Francisco in the late sixties. He created a string of memorable posters for events at Detroit's Grande Ballroom and also art-directed thirteen issues of *The Oracle*.

JOHN HOPKINS

'Hoppy' Hopkins was a key figure in sixties London counter-culture. With Barry Miles, he launched the *International Times* underground newspaper in 1966. He was also a co-founder of the short-lived UFO Club, which hosted Pink Floyd.

PAUL KAGAN

Kagan's erotic photographs graced a host of concert posters in the sixties, and were sometimes adapted by other artists (including Stanley Mouse). He also worked as a commercial photographer, writer for television news, and magazine art director.

VICTOR MOSCOSO

Moscoso worked as a lithography teacher and graphic artist, before creating posters for Family Dog and Bill Graham. His best-known works feature eye-dazzling color clashes, as seen in his Neon Rose series for The Matrix. He also drew for *Zap Comix*.

DAVID SINGER

The sophistication of Singer's collage work (he had collected images from newspapers and magazines since his youth) impressed Bill Graham enough to commission him. Singer created seventy-five posters for him—more than any other poster designer.

ALTON KELLEY

Having designed early handbills for Family Dog promotions, Kelley met Stanley 'Mouse' Miller in 1966. The two formed a prolific creative partnership, producing iconic posters and album artwork for various groups, notably the Grateful Dead.

STANLEY MOUSE

Honing his skills pinstriping hot-rod cars in Detroit, Mouse moved to San Francisco in the mid-sixties. Working with Alton Kelley, he produced some of the most enduring posters of the age. Together, they devised the Grateful Dead's iconic 'Skull and Roses'.

THE FOOL

This Anglo-Dutch collective was led by Simon Posthuma and Marijke Koger. They designed clothes (and a short-lived mural) for the Beatles' Apple Boutique, clothes for pop stars, and LP covers for the likes of The Hollies and The Incredible String Band.

GÜNTHER KIESER

One of Germany's most important graphic designers, Kieser was a key producer of the country's rock poster art during the sixties. Often working with concert agency Lippmann + Rau, he designed for Jimi Hendrix, The Who and Miles Davis, among others.

MUZ MURRAY, *GANDALF'S GARDEN*

Murray was editor for this influential British hippie magazine (which only ran to six issues) and also ran a shop under the same name. He embarked on a pilgrimage to Nepal and India, honing interests in yoga and meditation. He now sees himself as a mystic master.

RANDY TUTEN

After quitting Los Angeles for San Francisco, Tuten created designs for The Family Dog, starting in 1968. He worked for Bill Graham throughout the seventies, both in posters (including several for Winterland) and newspaper strip ads.

DENNIS LARKINS

Starting out in the early seventies as a scenic artist with the San Francisco Opera, Larkins went on to become a set designer for rock acts. This culminated in his gigantic sets for the Day on the Green festivals. Latterly, his Moonalice artwork has become much admired.

RICHARD NEVILLE

Having co-founded *Oz* magazine in Australia, Neville came to London (with artist Martin Sharp) in the mid-sixties and re-launched the magazine. A key counter-culture publication, *Oz* foundered after a well-known trial for obscenity.

NIGEL WAYMOUTH

Waymouth co-founded iconic London boutique Granny Takes a Trip before making a major impact on the UK's psychedelic graphic art scene as half of British design team Hapshash and the Coloured Coat. He later became a fine artist, specializing in portraiture.

TIMOTHY LEARY

A former Harvard lecturer, Leary became fascinated by the potential of LSD. He enthusiastically promoted its use and emerged as a key counter-cultural figure in the sixties, coining the phrase 'Turn on, tune in, drop out.' His later interests included cybernetics.

DENNIS NOLAN

A San Francisco native with an MA in painting, Dennis Nolan created two poster designs for Family Dog as part of a varied and wide-ranging artistic career. He went on to become a well-regarded illustrator and eventually taught illustration at degree level.

WES WILSON

Wilson's first poster was an anti-Vietnam War image in 1965. He went on to become a key psychedelic poster artist, developing complex lettering styles and deliberately employing vibrant color clashes. He worked for both Family Dog and Bill Graham.

MIKE McINNERNEY

Art director of *International Times*, McInnerney also designed street murals and posters, including the florid *Legalise Pot* image for a rally in London in 1967. His most famous design is perhaps the gatefold sleeve for The Who's album *Tommy* (1969).

MARTIN SHARP

This highly original and inventive artist was an early contributor to Australia's *Oz* magazine. After moving to London in 1966, he went on to work with Cream, designing the psychedelic covers for their classic LPs *Disraeli Gears* (1967) and *Wheels of Fire* (1968).

→ Opposite: a Haight-Ashbury poster shop in 1967.

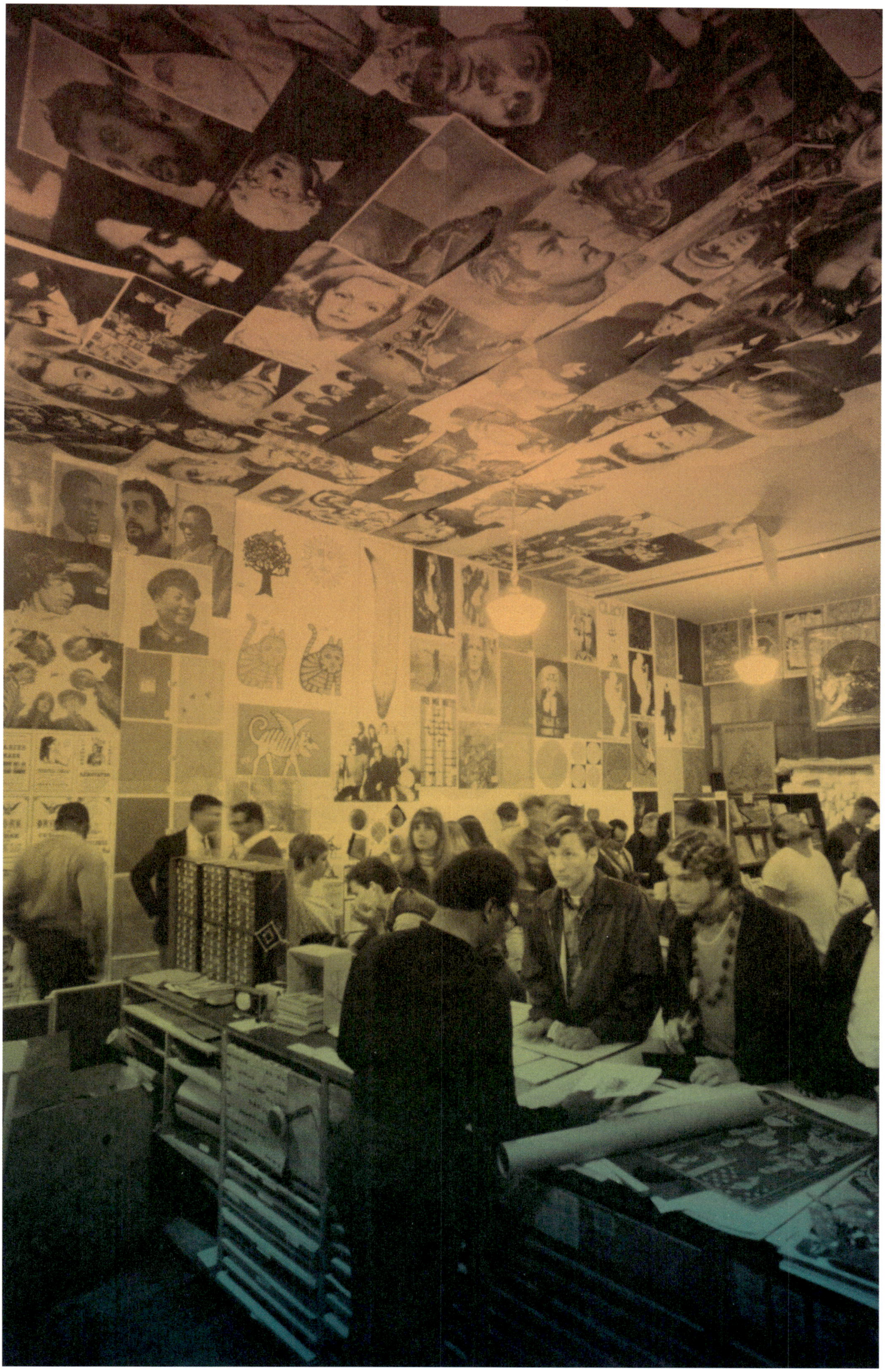

ENDNOTES AND FURTHER READING

1 Gallo, Max, *The Poster In History*, London: Hamlyn, 1974, p. 300.
2 Grushkin, Paul, *The Art of Rock*, New York: Artabras, 1987, p. 69.
3 *Vanity Fair. 'Suddenly That Summer'* by Sheila Weller, June 14, 2012 [accessed February 2017].
4 Grushkin, Paul, *The Art of Rock*, New York: Artabras, 1987, p. 70.
5 'The Fugitive Truth' Moanna Castell interviewed by Greg Healey, *Shindig!*, December 3, 2015 [accessed February 2017].
6 Mouse, Stanley, *Freehand. The Art of Stanley Mouse.* Berkeley, CA: SLG Books, 1993 [unpaginated].
7 Ibid.
8 *Vanity Fair. 'Suddenly That Summer'* by Sheila Weller, June 14, 2012 [accessed February 2017].
9 Ibid.
10 Ibid.
11 English, Michael, *3D Eye*, Limpsfield, Surrey: Dragon's World, 1979, p. 12.
12 Evans, Mike, *The Art of British Rock*, London: Frances Lincoln, 2010, p. 54.
13 Melly, George, 'Poster Power' in *The Observer*, December 3, 1967.

Gruskin, Paul, *The Art of Rock: Posters from Presley to Punk*, New York: Abbeville, 1987.
Harvey, Doug, *Heart and Torch: Rick Griffin's Transcendence*, Laguna Beach, CA: Laguna Art Museum/Ginkgo Press, 2007.
Miles, Barry, *In the Sixties*, London: Jonathan Cape, 2002.
Sandhaus, Louise, *Earthquakes, Mudslides, Fires and Riots: California & Graphic Design 1936–1986*, London: Thames & Hudson, 2014.

SOURCES OF ILLUSTRATIONS

Every effort has been made to locate and credit copyright holders of the material reproduced in this book. The authors and publisher apologize for any omissions or errors, which can be corrected in future editions.

a = above, b = below, c = center, l = left, r = right

1 Courtesy Peter Golding;
2 artwork by Victor Moscoso. © 1966, 1984, 1994 Rhino Entertainment Company. Used with permission. All rights reserved. www.familydog.com;
4–5 artwork by Paul Kagan. © 1968, 1984, 1996 Rhino Entertainment Company. Used with permission. All rights reserved. www.familydog.com;
6–7 courtesy Stanley Mouse and Marguerite Kelley;
8–9 courtesy Ida Griffin;
10–11 courtesy Peter Golding;
12-13 photo by Richard McCaffrey;
18 row 1 photo by Loomis Dean/ The LIFE Picture Collection/ Getty Images;
18 row 2l photo by Michael Stroud/ Express/Getty Images;
18 row 2r Bettmann/Contributor;
18 row 4 photo by NY Daily News Archive via Getty Images;
18 row 5l ASSOCIATED PRESS;
18 row 5r photo by John Olson/ The LIFE Picture Collection/ Getty Images;
18 row 6 photo by Frank Micelotta/ Getty Images;
19 row 1l photo by H. William Tetlow/Fox Photos/ Getty Images;
19 row 1r dpa picture alliance/ Alamy Stock Photo;
19 row 2l Bettmann;
19 row 2r photo by Keystone/ Getty Images;
19 row 3 photo by Jacques Haillot/ Apis/Sygma/Sygma via Getty Images;
19 row 4l photo by Joseph Louw/ The LIFE Images Collection/ Getty Images;
19 row 4r photo by: Sovfoto/UIG via Getty Images;
19 row 5l photo by Les Lee/Daily Express/Getty Images;
19 row 5r photo by Debi Doss/ Redferns;
19 row 6l photo by Justin Sullivan/ Getty Images;
19 row 6r photo by Jon Sievert/ Getty Images;
20l *A Woman and a Cat*, c. 1793–94, Kitagawa Utamaro, Metropolitan Museum of Art, New York;
20r *The Climax*, 1893, Aubrey Beardsley, *A Portfolio of Aubrey Beardsley's drawings illustrating 'Salome' by Oscar Wilde*, John Lane, London, 1907;
21l *Jane Avril*, 1893, Henri de Toulouse-Lautrec, Metropolitan Museum of Art, New York;
21r *Dreaming* or *Rêverie*, 1897, Alphonse Mucha, F. Champenois, Paris;
22–23 private collection;
24l Michael Ferguson & George Hunter;
24r courtesy Marguerite Kelley;
25l Paul Foster;
25r artwork by Wes Wilson. © 1966, 1984, 1994 Rhino Entertainment Company. Used with permission. All rights reserved. www.familydog.com;
26–27 courtesy Ida Griffin;
28–29 artwork by Victor Moscoso. © 1967, 1984, 1995 Rhino Entertainment Company. Used with permission. All rights reserved. www.familydog.com;
30 courtesy Peter Golding;
31al, ar Colin Duffield;
31bl, br courtesy Ali Zayeri;
32l mikemcinnerney.com;
32r Hapshash and the Coloured Coat, Michael English and Nigel Waymouth;
33l Hapshash and the Coloured Coat, Michael English and Nigel Waymouth;
33r artwork by Mike McInnerney, courtesy Barry Miles;
34–35 courtesy Ida Griffin;
36l artwork by Rick Griffin and Alton Kelley, courtesy Peter Golding;
36r courtesy Peter Golding;
37l provided courtesy of Bill Graham archives LLC (www.wolfgangs.com), all rights reserved. © Bill Graham Archives LLC;
37r courtesy Stanley Mouse and Marguerite Kelley;
42–43 courtesy Peter Golding;
44a *The Rubaiyat of Omar Khayyam*, Edward Fitzgerald (trans.), illustrations by Edmund J. Sullivan, Avenel Books, New York, courtesy Peter Golding;
44bl courtesy Stanley Mouse and Marguerite Kelley;
44br, 45 artwork by Stanley Mouse and Alton Kelley. © 1966, 1984, 1999 Rhino Entertainment Company. Used with permission. All rights reserved. www.familydog.com;
46–47 artwork by Stanley Mouse and Alton Kelley. © 1966, 1984, 1994 Rhino Entertainment Company. Used with permission. All rights reserved. www.familydog.com;
48 artwork by Stanley Mouse and Alton Kelley. © 1966, 1984, 1994 Rhino Entertainment Company. Used with permission. All rights reserved. www.familydog.com;
50al, ar courtesy Wes Wilson;
50bl, br provided courtesy of Bill Graham archives LLC (www.wolfgangs.com), all rights reserved. © Bill Graham Archives LLC;
51 provided courtesy of Bill Graham archives LLC (www.wolfgangs.com), all rights reserved. © Bill Graham Archives LLC;
52–53 artwork by Stanley Mouse and Alton Kelley. © 1966, 1984, 1994 Rhino Entertainment Company. Used with permission. All rights reserved. www.familydog.com;
54ar photo by © Ted Streshinsky/ CORBIS/Corbis via Getty Images;
54cr, cl, b, 55 The Digger Archives (www.diggers.org);
56–57 artwork by Rick Griffin. © 1967, 1984, 1995 Rhino Entertainment Company. Used with permission. All rights reserved. www.familydog.com;
58 courtesy Ida Griffin;
60–61 courtesy Ida Griffin;
62–63 artwork by Rick Griffin. © 1967, 1984, 1995 Rhino Entertainment Company. Used with permission. All rights reserved. www.familydog.com;
64 provided courtesy of Bill Graham archives LLC (www.wolfgangs.com), all rights reserved. © Bill Graham Archives LLC;
65 artwork by Rick Griffin. © 1967, 1984, 1995 Rhino Entertainment Company. Used with permission. All rights reserved. www.familydog.com;
66–67 courtesy Ida Griffin;
68a photo © Ted Streshinsky/ CORBIS/Corbis via Getty Images;
68cl photo by Paul Sequeira/ Getty Images;
68cr private collection;
68b Joseph Gomez;
69al Volume 1, Issue 2, *The Haight Ashbury Maverick*, 1967;

69ar private collection;
69bl photo © Ted Streshinsky/CORBIS/Corbis via Getty Images;
69br private collection;
70 artwork by Victor Moscoso. © 1967, 1984, 1995 Rhino Entertainment Company. Used with permission. All rights reserved. www.familydog.com;
72, 73bl–br artwork by Victor Moscoso. © 1966, 1984, 1994 Rhino Entertainment Company. Used with permission. All rights reserved. www.familydog.com;
73al, ar, cl–cr artwork by Victor Moscoso. © 1967, 1984, 1995 Rhino Entertainment Company. Used with permission. All rights reserved. www.familydog.com;
74–75 artwork by Victor Moscoso. © 1967, 1984, 1995 Rhino Entertainment Company. Used with permission. All rights reserved. www.familydog.com;
76–79 © 1967 Neon Rose, www.victormoscoso.com;
80–81 courtesy Peter Golding;
82 private collection;
83al *Love Dylan* by Marikje Koger Dunham of The Fool;
83ar private collection;
83bl artwork by William Henry. © 1967, 1984, 1995 Rhino Entertainment Company. Used with permission. All rights reserved. www.familydog.com;
83br The Digger Archives (www.diggers.org);
84ar photo by Michael Ochs Archives/Getty Images;
84cl, bl courtesy Ida Griffin;
84cr provided courtesy of Bill Graham archives LLC (www.wolfgangs.com), all rights reserved. © Bill Graham Archives LLC;
85al photo by Brian Shuel/Redferns
85acl photo by Estate of Keith Morris/Redferns;
85ar courtesy Peter Golding;
85bl photo by Evening Standard/Getty Images;
85br FIREBIRD VISIONS Ivan Tyrrell & Fred Carver;
86al, ar courtesy Peter Golding;
86 bcl, bl, br courtesy Stanley Mouse and Marguerite Kelley;
87al, ar courtesy Peter Golding;
87bl, br artwork by Mark Kanen, courtesy Peter Golding;
88 courtesy Peter Golding;
89al, ar artwork by Mari Tepper, courtesy Peter Golding;
89bl, br courtesy Peter Golding;
90a artwork by Evelyn Berdel, courtesy Peter Golding;
90b courtesy Reg E Williams/Straight Theater Presents. All rights reserved;
91al artwork by Kaleidoscope Studios, courtesy Peter Golding;
91ar artwork by Allan Terk, courtesy Peter Golding;
91bl, br courtesy Peter Golding;
92–93 artwork by Dennis Nolan. © 1967, 1984, 1995 Rhino Entertainment Company. Used with permission. All rights reserved. www.familydog.com;
94ar artwork by Harvey Cohen;
94al courtesy Ida Griffin;
94br photo by Hulton Archive/Getty Images;
94bl courtesy Peter Golding;
95al Hapshash and the Coloured Coat, Michael English and Nigel Waymouth;
95ar private collection;
95b photo by Robert Altman/Michael Ochs Archives/Getty Images;
96–99 artwork by Robert Fried. © 1967, 1984, 1995 Rhino Entertainment Company. Used with permission. All rights reserved. www.familydog.com;
100–101 courtesy Barry Miles;
102ar private collection;
102bl, br photo by Andrew Whittuck/Redferns;
103al photo by Wolfgang Kunz/ullstein bild via Getty Images;
103ar photo by PYMCA/UIG via Getty Images;
103cr Peter Strausfeld for the Academy Cinema;
103b Hapshash and the Coloured Coat, Michael English and Nigel Waymouth;
104–105 Hapshash and the Coloured Coat, Michael English and Nigel Waymouth;
106 Hapshash and the Coloured Coat, Michael English and Nigel Waymouth;
108–109 Hapshash and the Coloured Coat, Michael English and Nigel Waymouth;
110–111 mikemcinnerney.com;
112 artwork by Steve Harradine, courtesy Peter Golding;
113 courtesy Peter Golding;
114ar private collection;
114cl PA/PA Archive/PA Images;
114cr photo by Wolfgang Kunz/ullstein bild via Getty Images;
114bl © Robert Whitaker;
115al mikemcinnerney.com;
115ar Trinity Mirror/Mirrorpix/Alamy Stock Photo;
115cr Keystone Pictures USA/Alamy Stock Photo;
115bl Trinity Mirror/Mirrorpix/Alamy Stock Photo;
116 Jeff Morgan 08/Alamy Stock Photo;
117 "Athena" by Marikje Koger Dunham of The Fool;
118–119 © Muz Murray, *Gandalf's Garden* creator and founder/editor;
120ar photo by API/Gamma-Rapho via Getty Images;
120cl, c, br courtesy Peter Golding;
120bl photo by Daniele Dailloux/Gamma-Rapho via Getty Images;
121al photo by API/Gamma-Rapho via Getty Images;
121acr photo by Reg Lancaster/Getty Images;
121bcr photo by © Hulton-Deutsch Collection/CORBIS/Corbis via Getty Images;
121br Bettmann;
122 artwork by Paul Kagan. © 1968, 1984, 1996 Rhino Entertainment Company. Used with permission. All rights reserved. www.familydog.com;
123 Tom Weller;
124 courtesy Ida Griffin;
125 provided courtesy of Bill Graham archives LLC (www.wolfgangs.com), all rights reserved. © Bill Graham Archives LLC;
126–127 courtesy Ida Griffin;
128–129 courtesy Ida Griffin;
130–131 provided courtesy of Bill Graham archives LLC (www.wolfgangs.com), all rights reserved. © Bill Graham Archives LLC;
132 Jack Ogden;
133, 134 © John Van Hamersveld + Post-Future;
135 private collection;
136al private collection;
136ar Art Bevacqua;
136bl, br © John Van Hamersveld + Post-Future;
137al, ar Dale 'Sogy' Oftedal, 1968, Fresno, CA
137bl © John Van Hamersveld + Post-Future;
137br San Andreas Fault;
138–139 artist: Frank Bettencourt, venue: Earl Warren Showgrounds, Santa Barbara, California, promoter: Jim Salzer Presents;
140 courtesy Peter Golding;
141al Bruce Maddox, Liberty Graphics;
141ar Daniel Fennell, Liberty Graphics;
141bl, br provided courtesy of Bill Graham archives LLC (www.wolfgangs.com), all rights reserved. © Bill Graham Archives LLC;
142 courtesy Peter Golding;
143al, ar courtesy Peter Golding;
143bl artwork by Stanley Mouse and Alton Kelley. © 1966, 1984, 1994 Rhino Entertainment Company. Used with permission. All rights reserved. www.familydog.com;
143br private collection;
144–145 archive files Günther Kieser © Günther Kieser;
146a, cr private collection;
146cl photo by Robert Altman/Michael Ochs Archives/Getty Images;
146br photo by Bill Owens/20th Century Fox/Hulton Archive/Getty Images;
147al, cr private collection;
147cl, br photos by William L. Rukeyser/Getty Images;
152–156 provided courtesy of Bill Graham archives LLC (www.wolfgangs.com), all rights reserved. © Bill Graham Archives LLC;
158–159 courtesy Barry Miles;
160–164 art by Gary Grimshaw © Gary Grimshaw Legacy Foundation;
166ar art by Gary Grimshaw © 1971/1993/2018 Gary Grimshaw Legacy Foundation;
166cl private collection
166cr, bl art by Gary Grimshaw © Gary Grimshaw Legacy Foundation;
167a Rainbow People's Party, Ann Arbor District Library;
167cr photo by David Fenton/Getty Images;
167cl photo by Leni Sinclair/Getty Images;
167bl, bc, br Rainbow People's Party, Ann Arbor District Library;
168–169 courtesy Stanley Mouse and Marguerite Kelley;
170–171 courtesy Marguerite Kelley;
172–173 courtesy Stanley Mouse;
174–175 courtesy Barry Miles;
176–182 Randy Tuten;
188 courtesy Dennis Larkins;
189a courtesy Dennis Larkins;
189b photo by Ken Friedman, courtesy Dennis Larkins;
190–196 courtesy Dennis Larkins;
198al, ar provided courtesy of Bill Graham archives LLC (www.wolfgangs.com), all rights reserved. © Bill Graham Archives LLC;
198bl, br courtesy Dennis Larkins;
199 provided courtesy of Bill Graham archives LLC (www.wolfgangs.com), all rights reserved. © Bill Graham Archives LLC;
200–203 courtesy Dennis Larkins;
204–209 courtesy Ida Griffin;
210 artwork by Rick Griffin and Randy Tuten, courtesy Peter Golding;
211–213 courtesy Ida Griffin;
214–215 photo © Ted Streshinsky/CORBIS/Corbis via Getty Images;
217 photo © Ted Streshinsky/CORBIS/Corbis via Getty Images

INDEX

Page references to illustrations are in *italic*.

14-Hour Technicolor Dream *110*

A Woman and a Cat (Utamaro) *20*
Abrams, Steve 114
acid 25, 28
Acid Man (Kanen) 86, *87*
Acid Test parties 18, 25, *25*
airbrush work *170–1*
Albers, Josef 71, 76
album sleeves *see* record covers
Aldridge, Alan *129*, 214
Alexandra Palace, London *110*
Altamont 1969 concert 18, *146–7*
Anderson Theatre, Greenwich Village *10–11*, *140*, *142*
Apex Novelties 158
Are You Experienced (Hendrix) *104*
Armadillo World Headquarters 37
Art Deco 24, 28
Art Nouveau 20, 24, *82–3*, *155*
Atelier Populaire *120–1*
Athena (Koger) *117*
Austin, Texas 37
Avalon Ballroom, San Francisco *2*, *4*, 24, 28, *29*, *44–6*, *56–7*, *62–3*, *65*, *70*, *73–5*, *83*, *92–3*, *94*, *98–9*, *122*

Baba Love *137*
Babb, Ken 25
Bachelis, Lisa *76*
badges 36
Bailey, Peter 25
Balin, Marty 76
Barker, Edward *175*
Barrett, Syd *102*, 112
Beardsley, Aubrey *20*, 29, 109
beat generation 20
Beatles 18, 28, 29, 72, *94*, 116, 170
The Beatles Illustrated Lyrics (Aldridge) *129*
Berdel, Evelyn *90*
Berkeley Bonaparte 33, *35*, 62, *66–7*, *84*, 214
Bettencourt, Frank *138–9*, 214
Bevacqua, Art *136*
Big Brother and the Holding Company
  Berkeley performances *94*
  Fresno performances *137*
  New York performances *140*
  San Francisco performances *2*, 24, 25, 28, 36, *43*, *53*, *64*, *76*, *92–3*, *135*
Big O Posters 32
Binder, Edwards and Vaughan 32
Black Panthers 18
Blarney Club, London 29, 102
Blind Faith *138*, 170
Blissful Ignorance Productions *88*
Blue Cheer *126*
Blues Project *79*
Bo Diddley *143*
Bobbsey Twins 74
Book of Dreams (Steve Miller) 170
Bostedt, Bill *37*, 183
Bowen, Michael 80, 214
Bowie, David 19
Boyd, Joe 29, 102, 107
Brand, Stewart 25
Brighton 32, 85
Brown and Company 33
Broxton, Peter 32
Buchwald, Joe 21
Buckley, Tim *4*, *122*
Buddhism 29
Buffalo Springfield *96–7*
Butler, Bill 32, 85

Cafe Au Go Go, New York *141*
California Hall, San Francisco 24
Canned Heat *98–9*
Captain Beefheart and His Magic Band *58*
Captain Stelling *174*
Carousel Ballroom, San Francisco 36
Castell, Luria 21, 24
Charles Lloyd Quartet *89*
Cheetah Club, Manhattan *113*
Chéret, Jules 20
Clapton, Eric *139*, *163*
Cocker, Joe *153*
Cohen, Allen 80, 214
Cohen, Bob 21
Cohen, Harvey W. *94*
collage *152*, 157
comix 37, *134*, *158–9*, *174–5*
Commander Cody 166
Committee Theatre, San Francisco *89*
Conklin, Lee *82*, *88*, *130–1*, 214
Conner, Bruce *81*
Cooper, Alice *161*
Country Joe and the Fish *29*, *123*
cOZmic Comics 174–5
Cream 32, 110, *130*, *136*, *137*
Creedance Clearwater Revival *155*
Crumb, Robert 36, 37, 64, 214
Curtis, Edward S. *48*

Daddy Bread *see* Bostedt, Bill
Davidson, Ivor 165
Davis, Rennie 166
Davis, Spencer *155*
Day on the Green festival *12–13*, 19, 37, *177*, *188–95*
De Bray, Jan 204, *209*
'Death of Hippie' mock funeral procession 36, *69*
Def Leppard *192*
Delaney & Bonnie and Friends *139*
Departure (Journey) *170*
Detroit 37, 161, 166
Detroit Artists Workshop 37
Dexter, Jeff 33
Diddley, Bo *53*

Dog House, San Francisco 21
Donovan 28
Double-H Press *88*, *91*
Dreaming (Mucha) *21*
Dylan, Bob 140, *212*

East Totem West 29
East Village Other 37
Eastern mysticism 29, *94–5*
École des Beaux-Arts, Paris *120–1*
Edwards, Dudley *110*
Electric Prunes *136*
English, Michael 29–32, *95*, 102, 104, *106*, 107, 214
Epstein, Brian 32, *105*, 107
Eric Burdon and the Animals *10*
Essam, John *110*
Europe '72 (Grateful Dead) 170
Evans, Mike 29

Family Dog 21, 24, 36, *45–6*, 49, 50, *52–3*, *70*, 96, *143*, 214
Family Dog Collective 21
Family Dog, Denver 92, *96–7*
Family Dog logo *72*
'Family Dog Presents A Tribute To Ming The Merciless,' Longshoremen's Hall 24, 28
'Family Dog Presents A Tribute To Sparkle Plenty,' Longshoremen's Hall 24
Family Dog Productions *2*, 28, 62
Family Portrait (Nolan) *92–3*
Farren, Mick 175
Ferguson, Mike 21, *24*
Fillmore Auditorium, San Francisco 25, 28, *50–1*, *125*, 130
Fillmore East, New York 36, 140, *141*
Fillmore West, San Francisco 18, 36, *152–6*, 157
Finch, Barry 116
Five Men in a Boat 143
Foreigner *177*
Foster, Paul 25, *25*
Frampton, Peter *176*
France *120–1*
Franklin, Jim 37
Fraternity of Man *138*
Free City 55
Fried, Robert 29, *84*, *96–9*, 215
From The Mars Hotel (Grateful Dead) 170
Front, Charles 72
Funky Features 33

'Games for May' concert *112*
Gandalf's Garden 118–19, 216
Garcia, Carolyn 25
Garcia, Jerry 50, *68*
Gawler-Wright, Susie *33*
George, Adrian 32
George, Lowell *90*
Gibb, Russ 161
Ginsberg, Allen 18, *68*, *114*, 115, 166, 215
Gladys Knight & The Pips *143*
Glaser, Milton 37
Glick, Jeff 33
Glide Foundation *55*
Gomez, Joe *68*
Graham, Bill
  Bill Graham Presents *37*
  biography 215
  Day on the Green festival 19, 37, 188
  Fillmore venues 18, 28, 36
  hires David Singer 152, 157
  hires Dennis Larkins 197
  hires Lee Conklin 130
  hires Randy Tuten 176, 183
  hires Rick Griffins 62
  hires Wes Wilson 50, 51
  MacLean, Bonnie 29
  Trips Festival 25
Graham Central Station *176*
Grande Ballroom, Detroit 161, *164*, 166
Granny Takes a Trip *85*, *105*, 107
Grateful Dead
  1960s performances 21, 25, 36, *47*, *50*, 92, *131*, *132*
  1970s performances 37, *37*, *144*
  1980s performances *8–9*, *196*, *198–203*, *205–6*
  acid use 28
  Bob Dylan performances 212, *213*
  Cafe Au Go Go performance *141*
  Christmas card *209*
  Egypt *208*
  Haight-Ashbury 24, 68
  'Jester' 49, *172–3*
  last Fillmore show *155*
  logos *207*
  record covers 170, *204*
  Shrine Auditorium *126*
  'Skull and Roses' tour *168–9*
  Skulls and Roses *6–7*, *44–5*, 49
Grateful Dead Songbook 172–3
'Great Comix Slump' 158
Greene, Herb 57
Greenwich Village, New York 140
Griffin, Ida 215
Griffin, Rick
  biography 37, 215
  career development 59
  comix *81*
  logos *207*
  motifs 28, *124–9*
  photo *215*
  posters *8–9*, 28, 33, *34–6*, *56–8*, *60–7*, *84*, *205–6*, *208*
  record covers *204*, *210–13*
  Surfer 26–7
  works with Randy Tuten 183
Grimes, Hamish 29
Grimshaw, Gary 37, *160–4*, 165, *166*, 215
Grushkin, Paul 21, 24, 52
Guitar Army (Sinclair) 161
Guns N' Roses *193*
Gurley, James 92
Haight Ashbury Love Street 69
Haight-Ashbury, San Francisco 24, 33, 36, 68–9
Ham, Bill 21
Hapshash and the Coloured Coat 29, *32*, 33, *33*, *95*, 102, *103–6*, 107, *108–9*, 110
Hare Krishna *95*
Harmon, Ellen 21, *24*
Harradine, Steve *36*
Hart, Mickey *171*, 212
Harwayne, R. *90*
head shops 33, *34–5*, *66–7*, *68*, 84, *87*, *136*
Heart *177*
Hells Angels *146–7*, *180–1*
Helms, Chet
  biography 215
  Family Dog 21, 24, 25, *25*, 28, 52, 96
  works with Rick Griffins 62
  works with Wes Wilson *25*, 37, 50, 52
Hendrix, Jimi 28, 102, *104*, *125*, *137*, *145*, 146, *163*, 170
Henry, William *83*
Hersh, Helen *141*
Hill Auditorium, Ann, Arbor, Michigan *162*
Hill, Jennie & Robert *88*
Hinduism 29
Hipgnosis 37
Hodges, Dave *54*
Hoffmann, Tobias 144
Hollywood 33
Hooker, John Lee *152*
Hopkins, John 102, 215
Hughes, Lynne 20
Human Be-In 19, 60, *61*, *68*, *81*
Hung on You *85*, *95*
Hunter, George 21, *24*, 56, 57
Hunter, Meredith 146
Hunter, Tad *137*

I Can See For Miles (The Who) *105*
ice cream LSD 25
Indian religion *94–5*
Intermedia 170
International Situationists 100
International Society for Krishna Consciousness *95*
International Times (*IT*) 32, *33*, *100–1*, 102, 170
Iron Butterfly *74*, *95*, *152*
Irons, Greg 29

Jagger, Mick *146–7*
'Jane Avril' series (Toulouse-Lautrec) 20, *21*
Jazz at the Roundhouse 110
Jeff Beck Group *28*
Jefferson Airplane 21, 25, 28, 36, 76, *133*, *210*
Jester (Mouse) *172–3*

Jethro Tull *138*, *163*
Jim Kweskin Jug Band 24
John Sinclair Freedom Rally *166–7*
Jones, Mike 20
Jook Savages 61
Joplin, Janis 24, 64, 146
Journey 49, *170*, *189*, *194–5*

Kagan, Paul *4–5*, 122, *123*, 216
Kanen, Mark 86, *87*
Kelley, Alton
  biography 37, 216
  Family Dog Collective 21
  handbills & tickets *6–7*
  posters *36*, *37*
  work with Stanley Mouse 24–5, 37, *44–8*, 49, *52–3*, *86*, *143*, *168–9*, 170
Kesey, Ken 18, 25, *25*, 68
Kieser, Günther *144*, 216
King, Albert 28
King, B. B. *140*
King's Road, Chelsea, London 32, *85*, *118*
Kitty (Fried) *96–7*
Klimt, Gustav 20
Koger, Marijke 32, *83*, 116, *117*
Krassner, Paul 55

Larkins, Dennis *12–13*, 37, *188–96*, 197, *198–201*, 216
Leary, Timothy 60, *80*, 216
Led Zeppelin *12–13*, *36*, *37*, *138*, *152*, *188*
Ledeboer, Peter 32
Leeger, Josje 116
Legalise Pot Rally *1*, *114–15*
Lennon, John 166, *167*
Les Chats (Manet) 20
Liberty Graphics *141*
Lippmann + Rau 144
Little, Albert *85*
logos 29, 44, *52–3*, 56, *72*
London 29–33, 37, *85*
'London Psychedelic School' 102, 110
Longshoremen's Hall, San Francisco 21–4, 25, *180–1*
Los Angeles 36, 132
Los Angeles Free Press 130
Loughlin, Chandler 20
Love 28, *87*
Love Conspiracy Commune *88*
Love Dylan (Koger) 32, *83*
LSD 18, 25, 28
Lynyrd Skynyrd *176*

McInnerney, Mike 32, *32*, *33*, *110*, *111*, 114, *115*, 216
McKenzie, Scott 33
McHugh, Joe 29
Mackintosh, Charles Rennie 20
MacLean, Bonnie 29
Maddox, Bruce *141*
Magill, Amy 21–4
Maharishi Mahesh Yogi 29
Manet, Édouard 20
Mantra-Rock Dance *94*
Max, Peter 37
Mayall, John 28
MC5 37, *160*, 161
Melly, George 33
Melody Maker 33
Merry Pranksters 18, 68
Michael Wood/Pyxis Studios *94*
Mickey Mouse *134*
Middle Earth, London 33, *108–9*
Miles, Barry 101
Miller, Steve 170 *see also* The Steve Miller Band
Moby Grape *28*, *74*, *86*, *87*, *140*
Monster 170
Morrison, Van *152*, *153*
Moscoso, Victor
  biography 37, 216
  career development 71
  influence on others 157
  Neon Rose *76–9*
  on other artists 28
  photo *214*
  posters *2*, *28*, *29*, *70*, *72–5*
  typography 72
  work with Rick Griffin 64
Mötley Crüe *193*
Mouse, Stanley
  biography 37, 216
  book covers *172*
  handbills & tickets *6–7*
  in London 170
  photo *215*
  posters *37*
  record covers *170*
  work with Alton Kelley 24, 37, *44–8*, 49, *52–3*, *86*, *143*, *168–9*, 170
Mucha, Alphonse 20, *21*, 24, 29, 83, 109
Murray, Muz *118*, 216
mysticism, Eastern 29, *94–5*

Nasty Tales 19, *174*, *175*
Neon Rose *76–9*
'Neptune's Notions' *74*
Neville, Richard 32, 216
New Musical Express 33
New York 33, 36, 37, *140–1*
Nickolds, Nick 29
Nolan, Dennis *92–3*, 216
Nova 170
Nugent, Ted *190–1*, 194

Ochs, Phil 166
offset lithography printing 32, 42, 109
Oftedal, Dale (Sogy) *137*
Ogden, Jack *132*
OM Tentacle *110*
Ono, Yoko *114*, 166, *167*
Osiris Visions 29, 107, *115*
Oz 19, 32, *174*
Page, Jimmy 143
Pallavicini, D. *91*
Parliament Funkadelic *162*
Peacock Ball *75*
Peel, John 33
Personality Posters 36
Pike, Brian 29
Pinball Alley, Ann Arbor, Michigan *161*
Pink Floyd
  albums 37, *82*
  logos 29, *171*
  Queen Elizabeth Hall performance *112*
  UFO Club performances 32, *102*, *106*, 112
  USA performances *113*, *137*, *162*
Piper at the Gates of Dawn (Pink Floyd) *82*
Pitschel Players *88*
posters
  'boxing-style' 20, *22–3*, 29
  as decorative wall art 32, 33–6
  psychedelic development 21–9
Posthuma, Simon 116
press ads *178–9*
Print Mint 158
printing plates 42
Proby, P.J. *87*
Procul Harum *140*
psychedelic art development 20–9
Psychedelic Shop, San Francisco 33, *60–1*
Psychedelicatessen, New York 33
Ptooff! (The Deviants) 32
punk 18, 186–7

Queen Elizabeth Hall, London *112*
Quicksilver Messenger Service
  last Fillmore show *155*
  Michigan performances *162*, *163*
  Sacramento performances *132*
  San Francisco performances 36, *43*, *48*, *62–3*, *65*, *73*, *75*, *89*, *135*

Rackham, Arthur 29
Radio City Music Hall, New York *196*, 199, *200–1*
Rafaelli, Ron *146*
Rainbow People's Party *166*, *167*
Rainey, Michael 85
Ramparts *86*
Rapid Repro Shop 21
Ratha Yatra ('Chariot Festival') *95*
Reckoning (Grateful Dead) *204*
record covers 37, 170, *170*, *204*
Red Dog Saloon, Virginia City, Nevada 20–1, 56
Reid, Jamie 122
Rifkin, Danny 24
rock music development 28
'Rock 'n' Roll Dance And Concert,' Longshoremen's Hall 21–4, *24*
Rock Revolution tour *87*

Rodriguez, Spain 37
Roller, Alfred 28, 50
Rolling Stones 18, 19, 28, 36, *146–7*
Rolling Thunder (Mickey Hart) *171*
Roundhouse, Camden, London 33, 208
Rowley, Chris 175
Rubber Soul (Beatles) 72
Rush, Otis *78*

Saladin Headshop *136*
San Andreas Fault *137*
San Francisco 20–9, 33, 36, 68–9 *see also specific venues*
San Francisco Five 28, 36, 37, 72 *see also* Griffin, Rick; Kelley, Alton; Moscoso, Victor; Mouse, Stanley; Wilson, Wes
San Francisco Mime Troupe 25
Santana *64*, 130, *131*, *155*, *176*
Sätty 29
Sätty, Wilfried *154*
Saville Theatre, London 32, *105*, 107
Schnepf, Bob 29
Scully, Rock 24, *68*
Seale, Bobby 166, *167*
Seger, Bob *162*
Seibert, D. *90*
Seidemann, Bob 57
Selland Arena, Fresno *137*
Selvin, Joel 46
Sender, Ramon 25
Sgt. Pepper's Lonely Hearts Club Band (The Beatles) 18
Sharp, Martin 32, 110, 216
Shelton, Gilbert 36, 37
Shrine Auditorium, Los Angeles *126*, 132, *136*
silk-screen printing 29–32, 107, 142
Simon & Garfunkel *192*
Sinclair, John 37, 160, 161, 166
Singer, David 36, *152–6*, 157, 216
Slick, Grace 28, 76
slogans 36
Sly & the Family Stone *177*
Soft Machine 32
split-fountain printing *142–3*, *154*
Springsteen, Bruce *176*, *192*
Squiggly Trinity *83*
stage sets *12–13*, *188–91*, *194–5*
Stairway to Heaven (Led Zeppelin) *36*
Stanley, Owsley 25
Straight Theatre *128*
Sullivan, Edmund Joseph *44*
Summer of Love 28, 36, 54
Sun/Dance 166
Super Ball (Fried) *98–9*
Surfer *27*, 61, 62
surfing *26*
Surrealism 33

T-shirts 36, 49, 170, *192–3*, 203
Tales from the Tube #1 *129*
Tea Lautrec Litho *154*
Tepper, Mari *89*
Terk, Allen 'Gut' *91*
The 13th Floor Elevators 28
The 5000 Spirits or the Layers of the Onion (The Incredible String Band) *116*
The Ark, Sausalito *83*, 86
The Artists Liberation Front *55*
The Beach Boys 29
The Byrds 28, *51*, *152*
The Chambers Brothers *74*, *77*
The Charlatans (1960s band) 21, 24, *24*, *56–7*
The Climax (Beardsley) *20*
The Crazy World of Arthur Brown 32
The Cult *211*
The Deviants 32
The Digger Papers *55*
The Diggers 36, 54–5, 69, 83
The Doors 28, *29*, *70*, *135*, *141*, *182*
The Eagles *177*
The Factory *90*
The Fat Hummingbird and His Backup Band *43*
The Fool 32, *83*, *116–17*, 216
The Freudian Slips *86*
The Fugs 28
'The Girl With Green Hair' 24
The Great Society 21, 28, *48*, 76
The Haight Ashbury Maverick *69*
The Incredible String Band *116*
The Invisible Circus *54*, *55*
The Lovin' Spoonful 24
The Marbles 21
The Matrix, San Francisco 28, 76, *79*
The Miller Blues Band *70*, *75*, *77*
The Mothers of Invention 24, *141*
The Move *105*
The Only Alternative and His Other Possibilities *79*
The Oracle 68, *80–1*, *94*, 161, 214
The Purple Gang *85*
The Realist 55
The Scorpions *193*
The Seagull (Grimshaw) *160*
The Seed 21, *24*
The Steve Miller Band *5*, *28*, *122*, *177*
The Steve Miller Blues Band *90*
The Velvet Underground *4*
The Who 29, 32, *105*, *193*
The Yardbirds *11*, 29
Thelin, Ron & Jay 33, 80
timeline 18–19
Tommy (The Who) 32
Tomorrow 102
Tonite Let's All Make Love in London (1967) *103*
Toulouse-Lautrec, Henri de 20, *21*
Towle, Jack 21
Transcendental Meditation 29, *94*
Translove 37
Trips Festival, Longshoremen's Hall 25, 50
Tubes *176*
Tuten, Randy 36, *37*, *176*, *182*, 183, 216
Tyner, Rob 161
typography 28, 51, 56, 57, 72, 165
Tyrrell, Ivan 32, *85*

U2 *192*
UFO Club, London 29, *32*, 33, *102–3*, *105–6*, 107, *110*, 112
UFO—Dusk to Dawn *111*
U.F.O. Gallery, San Francisco *91*
Unicorn Bookshop 32, *85*
Unicorn Posters 32
Unobski, Mark 20–1
Utamaro, Kitagawa *20*

Van Hamersveld, John 36–7, *133–4*, *136*, *137*, 215
Vaughan, David 32
Velvet Undergound *122*, 140
Vermès, Philippe 120
Viennese Secessionists 28, 50
Viginia City, Nevada 20–1
Vulcan Gas Company venue, Austin, Texas 37

Walsh, Joe *162*
Waymouth, Nigel 29–32, 85, *95*, 102, *104*, *106*, 107, 216
Weaver, Ken 28
Webb's, Stockton, California *77*, *79*
Weir, Thomas 29
Welch, Chris *175*
Weller, Mike *174*
Weller, Sheila 25
Weller, Tom *123*
Wheels of Fire (Cream) 32
Whisky A-Go-Go *82*, 86, *88*
White Panther Party 160, 161, 166
Whitehead, Peter *103*
Wilson, S. Clay 37, 64
Wilson, Wes 25, *25*, 28, 37, *50–1*, *52–3*, 216
Winterland, San Francisco 36, *51*, *87*, *156*, *177*
Winwood, Steve *139*
Wolfe, Tom *68*
Wonder, Stevie 166
Woodstock Festival 18, 170
Worden, Jenna 20
Works, Don and Roz 20
World's End, King's Road *118*

Yardbirds *130*, *142*
Ye Olde Psychedelic Shoppe, Hollywood 33
Yellow Dog 37

Zap Comix 37, 71, *127*, 158
Zappa, Frank *135*
Zen Buddhism 29
'Zig-Zag Man' 24–5, 49

ACKNOWLEDGMENTS

Peter Golding would like to thank Alex Golding, Giles Golding, James Golding, Cameron Brown, Lord Harry Dalmeny, Stephen Maycock, Ted Owen, Alan & Debbie Caplan, Ida Griffin, Marguerite Trousdale Kelley, Laura Grimshaw, Shelley Warren, Jacaeber Kastor, Gordon McClelland, Jose Kent, Tom Salter, John 'Hoppy' Hopkins, Masaru Kishino, Andrew Sclanders, Aubrey 'Po' Powell, Slim Jim Phantom, Michael English, Nigel Waymouth, Mike McKinnerney, Stanley Mouse, Dennis Larkins, Shannon Ribbons, and The Chelsea Arts Club.

Thanks also go to Thames & Hudson's amazing team: 'Captain' Tristan de Lancey, 'Lady' Jane Laing and 'Princess' Phoebe Lindsley.

With special thanks to Barry Miles for his unique expertise in writing the text as well as his extensive knowledge of the underground press.

The publisher would like to thank Rob Dimery, Rose Blackett-Ord, Paul Hammond, and Celia Falconer, and to extend special thanks to Bill Sagan at Wolfgang's Vault and Dana Jacques at Rhino Entertainment Company. To buy signed Family Dog lithographs please go to www.familydog.com.

ABOUT THE AUTHORS

Peter Golding, musician and creator of the world's first 'designer jean,' began collecting rock 'n' roll art in 1967, naming his collection 'Inspirational Times.' As part of the sixties and seventies fashion movement, Peter Golding's famous ACE boutique in London's Chelsea brought him into regular contact with the biggest names in rock 'n' roll, and he went on to create one of the most comprehensive collections of rock 'n' roll graphics. He curated the first exhibition for 'Inspirational Times' in London in 2003, was a major lender to the Tate Liverpool exhibition 'Summer of Love' in 2005, and more recently contributed to the V&A's 2016–17 exhibition 'You Say You Want a Revolution.'

Barry Miles is the bestselling author of numerous cultural histories and biographies on the Beat Generation and the counterculture of the sixties and seventies, including *The Beat Hotel*, *In the Sixties*, and *Hippie*, and key figures William Burroughs, Allen Ginsberg, and Frank Zappa. One of the founding members, in 1966, of *International Times*, he also wrote regularly for *Oz* magazine until the mid '70s, contributed to *NME* from 1975 to 1978, and was editor of *Time Out* from 1978 to 1979.

Front cover illustration © 1967 Neon Rose, www.victormoscoso.com

First published in the United Kingdom in 2018 by Thames & Hudson Ltd, 181A High Holborn, London WC1V 7QX

Rock Graphic Originals © 2018 Thames & Hudson Ltd, London

For sources of illustrations see pages 218–219

Design by Daniel Streat at Visual Fields

All Rights Reserved. No part of this publication may be reproduced or transmitted in any form or by any means, electronic or mechanical, including photocopy, recording or any other information storage and retrieval system, without prior permission in writing from the publisher.

British Library Cataloguing-in-Publication Data
A catalogue record for this book is available from the British Library

ISBN 978-0-500-29353-9

Printed and bound in China by C&C Offset Printing Co. Ltd

To find out about all our publications, please visit **www.thamesandhudson.com**. There you can subscribe to our e-newsletter, browse or download our current catalogue, and buy any titles that are in print.